1965	1967	1969	1971	1972	1973	1974	1975	1976	1977	1978	1979
204	207	274	288	317	329	319	326	376	436	478	525
14	12	9	10	9	9	10	11	10	8	7	8
492	575	695	751	850	1,017	1,061	1,065	1,023	1,328	1,496	1,742
47	48	58	53	63	81	92	80	105	115	133	154
6	5	5	4	4	5	6	5	5	5	5	6
59.6	63.4	65.7	69.9	72.2	74.5	73.2	75.8	78.5	79.8	80.7	80.7
3.6	2.2	0.4	4.4	3.3	3.3	−1.7	3.5	3.6	1.6	1.1	0.0
22	23	24	23	24	25	25	23	23	24	26	26
39	42	46	48	50	52	53	54	56	58	61	63
400	475	578	659	725	811	890	949	1,059	1,180	1,336	1,501
38.8	38.0	37.7	36.9	37.0	36.9	36.5	36.1	36.1	36.0	35.8	35.7
2.46	2.68	3.04	3.45	3.70	3.94	4.24	4.53	4.86	5.25	5.68	6.16
95	102	115	127	137	145	155	164	175	189	204	220
4.54	5.61	7.96	5.72	5.25	8.03	10.81	7.86	6.84	6.83	9.06	12.67
4.28	5.07	6.67	6.16	6.21	6.84	7.56	7.99	7.61	7.42	8.41	9.44
12.9	12.3	14.3	15.0	19.5	34.4	27.3	25.5	20.2	19.9	25.2	27.4
—	—	—	—	—	—	—	73	75	73	83	94
—	—	—	—	—	—	—	47	50	53	58	66
33.2	27.8	24.1	25.6	24.5	23.0	23.4	25.9	25.0	24.7	24.5	26.1
17.3	14.2	12.1	12.5	11.9	11.1	11.2	12.3	11.8	11.6	11.4	11.7
26	31	36	43	49	71	98	107	115	121	142	184
22	27	36	46	56	70	104	98	124	152	176	212
5.4	2.6	0.4	−1.4	−5.8	7.1	2.0	18.1	4.3	−14.3	−15.1	−0.3
7	8	10	11	12	13	15	16	18	20	23	26

(Continued in back of book)

MICROECONOMICS

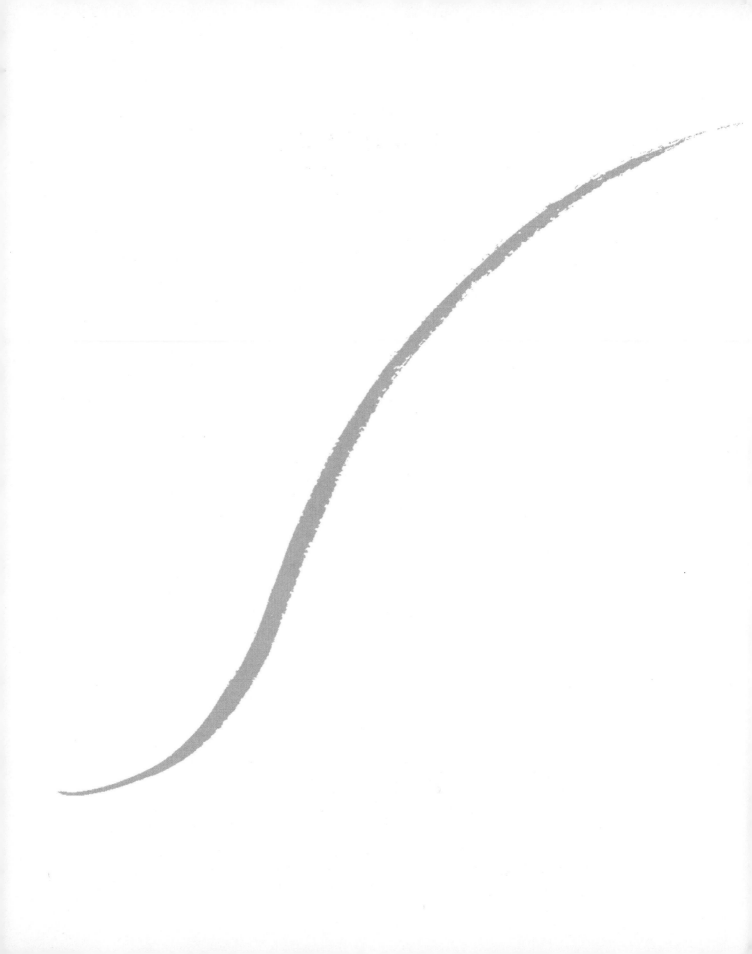

Microeconomics

Principles, Problems, and Policies

Campbell R. McConnell
Professor of Economics, Emeritus
University of Nebraska

Stanley L. Brue
Professor of Economics
Pacific Lutheran University

Boston   Burr Ridge, IL   Dubuque, IA   Madison, WI   New York   San Francisco   St. Louis
Bangkok   Bogotá   Caracas   Kuala Lumpur   Lisbon   London   Madrid   Mexico City
Milan   Montreal   New Delhi   Santiago   Seoul   Singapore   Sydney   Taipei   Toronto

To *Mem* and to *Terri* and *Craig*

McGraw-Hill Higher Education

A Division of The **McGraw-Hill** Companies

MICROECONOMICS: PRINCIPLES, PROBLEMS, AND POLICIES
Published by McGraw-Hill/Irwin, an imprint of The McGraw-Hill Companies, Inc. 1221 Avenue
of the Americas, New York, NY, 10020. Copyright © 2002, 1999, 1996, 1993, 1990, 1987,
1984, 1981, 1978, 1975, 1972, 1969, 1966, 1963, 1960, by The McGraw-Hill Companies, Inc.

Some ancillaries, including electronic and print components, may not be available to customers
outside the United States.

This book is printed on acid-free paper.

4 5 6 7 8 9 0 VNH/VNH 0 9 8 7 6 5 4 3

ISBN 0072340371

Publisher: *Gary Burke*
Sponsoring editor: *Lucille Sutton*
Developmental editor: *Erin Strathmann*
Marketing manager: *Martin Quinn*
Senior project manager: *Jean Lou Hess*
Senior production supervisor: *Lori Koetters*
Coordinator freelance design: *Michael Warrell*
Director of design: *Keith McPherson*
Last Word illustrator: Jacques Cournoyer
Lead supplement coordinator: *Becky Szura*
Senior producer media technology: *Ed Przyzycki*
Compositor: *TechBooks*
Typeface: *10/12 Janson*
Printer: *Von Hoffmann Press, Inc.*

Library of Congress Cataloging-in-Publication Data
McConnell, Campbell R.
    Microeconomics: principles, problems, and policies/Campbell R. McConnell,
Stanley L. Brue.–15th ed.
    p. cm.
    ISBN-0-07-234037-1 (alk. paper)
    1. Microeconomics. I. Brue, Stanley L., 1945-II. Title.
HB172.M3925 2002
338.5–dc21   2001037013

www.mhhe.com

LIST OF KEY GRAPHS

ABOUT THE AUTHORS

Campbell R. McConnell earned his Ph.D. from the University of Iowa after receiving degrees from Cornell College and the University of Illinois. He taught at the University of Nebraska–Lincoln from 1953 until his retirement in 1990. He is also co-author of *Contemporary Labor Economics*, 6th ed. (McGraw-Hill/Irwin) and has edited readers for the principles and labor economics courses. He is a recipient of both the University of Nebraska Distinguished Teaching Award and the James A. Lake Academic Freedom Award and is past president of the Midwest Economics Association. Professor McConnell was awarded an honorary Doctor of Laws degree from Cornell College in 1973 and received its Distinguished Achievement Award in 1994. His primary areas of interest are labor economics and economic education. He has an extensive collection of jazz recordings and enjoys reading jazz history.

Stanley L. Brue did his undergraduate work at Augustana College (SD) and received its Distinguished Achievement Award in 1991. He received his Ph.D. from the University of Nebraska–Lincoln. He is a professor at Pacific Lutheran University, where he has been honored as a recipient of the Burlington Northern Faculty Achievement Award. Professor Brue has also received the national Leavey Award for excellence in economic education. He has served as national president and chair of the Board of Trustees of Omicron Delta Epsilon International Economics Honorary. He is co-author of *Economic Scenes*, *5th edition* (Prentice-Hall) and *Contemporary Labor Economics*, *6th edition* (McGraw-Hill/Irwin) and author of *The Evolution of Economic Thought*, *6th edition* (Harcourt). For relaxation, he enjoys international travel, attending sporting events, and skiing with family and friends.

PREFACE

Welcome to the fifteenth edition of *Microeconomics* (and its companion editions of *Economics* and *Macroeconomics*), the nation's best-selling economics textbook. More than 12 million students worldwide have now used this book. It has been adapted into Canadian, Australian, Italian, and Russian editions, and translated into French, Spanish, and other languages. It continues to be the leading principles book in Russia and several other Russian-speaking countries.

WTO issues, emerging technologies, major mergers, the Microsoft antitrust case, the advent of the euro—what an interesting time to teach and learn microeconomics! Clearly, those who understand microeconomic principles will have a distinct advantage in making sense of the economy and successfully participating in it.

▮ Fundamental Objectives

We have three main goals for *Microeconomics:*

- To help the beginning economics student comprehend the principles essential for understanding the basic economizing problem, specific economic issues, and the policy alternatives.
- To help the student understand and apply the economic perspective and to reason accurately and objectively about economic matters.
- To promote a lasting student interest in economics and the economy.

▮ What's New and Improved?

We thoroughly revised, polished, and updated this edition. The comments and suggestions of more than 100 reviewers and survey correspondents provided encouragement, motivated many improvements, and sparked innovation.

In-Text Web Buttons

We have enhanced the book substantially by linking it directly to newly created pedagogical features found at our website www.mhhe.com/economics/mcconnell15. Three types of icons appear throughout the book, indicating that additional content on a subject can be found online. The Web materials greatly enrich course content for those who wish to use it, but their design and careful placement in the text also allows for instructors to not use the information if they so choose. Therefore the book remains adaptable to many teaching styles and types of courses. Button types include:

- The ▮ symbol directs students to **Analogies, Anecdotes, and Insights** at our website. These short pieces, written by Stan Brue, help students understand and remember the economic ideas by connecting them to other, better-known ideas or easy-to-remember stories and examples.
- The ▮ symbol directs students to **Origins of the Idea.** These brief histories were written by Randy Grant of Linfield College and examine the origins of major ideas identified in the book. Students will find it interesting to learn about the economist who first developed such ideas as opportunity costs, equilibrium price, comparative advantage, and elasticity.
- The ▮ symbol directs students to **Interactive Graphs.** Developed under the supervision of Norris Peterson of Pacific Lutheran University, this interactive feature depicts major graphs and then instructs students to shift the curves, observe the outcomes, and derive relevant generalizations.

Streamlined Presentations

A major revision goal was to streamline presentations where possible without compromising the thoroughness of our explanations. Our efforts resulted not only in a shorter book, but in more efficient organization and greater clarity. An example is Chapter 4, The Market System, which is both shorter and better organized than before. You will find similar kinds of improvements throughout the fifteenth edition. Where needed, of course, the "extra sentence of explanation" remains a distinguishing characteristic of *Microeconomics*. Brevity at the expense of clarity is false economy.

Improved Content

We have made a number of micro discussions less daunting and more interesting by changing abstract, axiomatic examples (such as X and Y) to concrete examples familiar to students. Also, in keeping with our goal of streamlining discussions, we have consolidated and deleted selected content that was either peripheral to the discussion or was covered in further detail in later chapters.

Instructors rarely assign all five micro application chapters (regulation and antitrust; agriculture, income inequality and poverty, labor market issues; and health care economics), but they appreciate the option to select two or three. We gave these chapters particular attention, revising and updating throughout. For example, Chapter 19 on antitrust and regulation is consolidated and now ends with a new Last Word on the Microsoft case. Chapter 20 on agriculture reflects the recent decline in the prices of some farm products and the renewed debate over the Freedom to Farm Act. The discussion of income inequality in Chapter 21 is reorganized for greater clarity and smoother flow. Chapter 23 on health care reflects the latest data and most current issues.

New Last Words

About one-fourth of the Last Words are new and others have been revised and updated. The new topics are: the remarkable organizational ability of markets (Chapter 4); an unusual impact of rent controls (Chapter 7); the economics of criminal behavior (Chapter 8); the positive externalities of antitheft auto tracking devices (Chapter 17); U.S. wealth and its distribution; (Chapter 21); and the struggle for control of capital in Russia (Internet chapter).

Bonus Internet-Only Chapter

A special Internet chapter "Economies in Transition: Russia and China" is available for free use at our website. The chapter contains all the features of regular chapters, is readable in Adobe format, and can be printed if desired. This chapter is fully supported by all the ancillaries to the book.

Internet Math Notes

Although most students in the principles course have only modest math skills, a few have taken advanced mathematics courses in high school or college. For those students, seeing the algebra or calculus behind the economics is highly revealing and useful. Therefore we have included on our website a set of 50 math notes that are keyed to topics in the book. Written by Professor Norris Peterson of Pacific Lutheran University, these notes are keyed to the

book topics and found under the title "Do You Want to See the Math?" They are creative, concise, and undoubtedly will enhance the educational experience of math-minded students.

Other New Topics and Revised Discussions
Along with the improvements just discussed, there are many other revisions. Here are some examples.

- *Part 1. Chapter 1:* Changed terminology from *material wants* to *economic wants;* revised discussion of economic methodology, focusing on the scientific method. *Chapter 2:* Reorganized section on applications of the production possibilities model; greatly consolidated section on economic systems. *Chapter 3:* Several new examples including increased demand for coffee drinks, soy-enhanced hamburger as an inferior good, increased supply of Internet service provision. *Chapter 4:* New chapter title and introduction; revised section on competition to generalize beyond pure competition; consolidation of the Five Fundamental Questions to Four, with discussion explicitly organized around each; shorter chapter. *Chapter 5:* New chapter title; new terminology: "horizontally organized firms," "vertically integrated firms," and "conglomerates"; new Figure 5-7 on government spending. *Chapter 6:* New Figure 6-1 showing the types of international flows (trade flows, resource flows, information and technology flows, and money flows); new discussion of the euro; expanded discussion of the WTO.

- *Part 2. Chapter 7:* Title changed to reflect chapter content; added applications section on cross elasticity of demand; revamped section on government-controlled prices. *Chapter 8:* Updated applications and extension section; changed language from *budget restraint* to *budget constraint.* *Chapter 9:* Improved explanation of explicit and implicit costs; added "learning-by-doing" to the list of sources of economies of scale; new applications of economies of scale (startup firms and newspapers). *Chapter 10:* Deleted the section on "Qualifications" to shorten the chapter and because we discuss each in detail in later chapters. *Chapter 11:* New, updated examples throughout; substantially revised section "Assessment and Policy Options." *Chapter 12:* Greatly shortened the discussion of cartels by focusing on only recent, rather than historical, OPEC actions; changed the identities of firms in the discussion of kinked demand from A, B, C to hypothetically named firms. *Chapter 13:* Edited down some long lists of examples and added new examples.

- *Part 3. Chapter 14:* Added Tables 14-5 and 14-6 on occupational trends in the United States. *Chapter 15:* Transposed the graphs in Figure 15-3; revised discussion of the minimum wage; new Figure 15-9 shows how wage differentials can arise on either the demand or supply side of labor markets. *Chapter 16:* made the discussion of the single-tax proposal an application of the idea of economic rent.

- *Part 4. Chapter 17:* Revised Table 17-2 on cost-benefit analysis; integrated the discussion of specific antipollution policies within the analysis of negative externalities; added a brief section on global warming; New Global Perspective 17-1 on carbon dioxide emissions. *Chapter 18:* Clarified discussion of the payroll tax; inclusion of new CBO (1999) data on average tax rates of all Federal tax sources by income quintile.

- *Part 5. Chapter 19:* Pared the chapter by eliminating the discussion of industrial concentration and industrial policy; updated examples on antitrust, including the Microsoft case; revised section on industrial regulation for clarity and relevance to today's regulatory and deregulatory climate; reorganized the discussion of social regulation. *Chapter 20:* New Figure 20-3 on U.S. farm exports as a percentage of farm output; new Figure 20-4, which shows inflation-adjusted U.S. agricultural prices for selected commodities, 1950–1998; refocused Table 20-1 from farm population to farm employment; revised the discussion of the Freedom to Farm Act and emergency farm payments 1998–2000. *Chapter 21:* Reorganized discussion of income inequality and trends in income inequality; new discussion of the decline in the number of people on welfare; new discussion of the inequality of wealth. *Chapter 22:* Moved this chapter from Chapter 23 in the previous edition. *Chapter 23:* New issues discussed (patients' bill of rights, prescription drug coverage under Medicare).

- *Part 6. Chapter 24:* Shortened this chapter; replaced the discussion of U.S. trade policy with a section on the WTO. *Chapter 25:* Eliminated the balance sheets in explaining the financing of export and import transactions; updated the discussion of the managed floating system in view of significant bailouts by the IMF and currency interventions by major countries; updated discussion of U.S. trade deficits.

■ Distinguishing Features

This text embraces a number of distinguishing features.

- *Comprehensive Explanations at an Appropriate Level.* *Microeconomics* is comprehensive, analytical, and challenging, yet fully accessible to a wide range of students. Its thoroughness and accessibility enable instructors to select topics for special classroom emphasis with confidence that students can read and comprehend independently other assigned material in the book.

- *Fundamentals of the Market System.* Many economies throughout the world are making difficult transitions from planning to markets. Our detailed description of the institutions and operation of the *market system* in Chapter 4 is even more relevant than before. We pay particular attention to property rights, entrepreneurship, freedom of enterprise and choice, competition, and the role of profits because these concepts are poorly understood by beginning students.

- *Early Integration of International Economics.* We give the principles and institutions of the global economy early treatment. Chapter 6 examines the growth of world trade, the major participants in world trade, specialization and comparative advantage, the foreign exchange market, tariffs and subsidies, and various trade agreements. This strong introduction to international economics permits "globalization" of later microeconomics discussions.

- *Early and Extensive Treatment of Government.* Government is an integral component of modern capitalism. This book introduces the economic functions of government early and accords them systematic treatment in Chapter 5. Chapter 17 examines government and market failure in further detail and Chapter 18 looks at salient facets of public choice theory and taxation. The microeconomic-issues Chapters (19–23) all deal with public policy.

- *Stress on the Theory of the Firm and Technological Advance.* We have given much attention to the theory of the firm and technological advance. These concepts are difficult for most beginning students; abbreviated expositions usually compound these difficulties by raising more questions than they answer. We have also coupled analysis of the various market structures with a discussion of the impact of each market arrangement on price, output levels, resource allocations, and the rate of technological advance. And our Chapter 13 on the microeconomics of technology is unique to principles books.

- *Focus on Economic Issues.* For many students, Part 5 (macroeconomic issues) is where the action is. We sought to guide that action along logical lines through the application of appropriate analytical tools. In these parts we favor inclusiveness; instructors can effectively choose two or three chapters from this group.

▌Organization and Content

Microeconomics reflects the challenge that specific topics and concepts will likely pose for average students. For instance, the theory of the firm and macro output and price-level determination are carefully treated. Here, simplicity is correlated with comprehensiveness, not brevity.

Our experience suggests that in treating each basic topic—elasticity of demand and supply, theory of the firm, and international economics—it is desirable to couple analysis with policy. Generally, we use a three-step development of analytical tools: (1) verbal descriptions and illustrations; (2) numerical examples, and (3) graphical presentation based on these numerical illustrations.

All these considerations prompted us to organize the book into nine parts: Part 1: An Introduction to Economics and the Economy; Part 2: Microeconomics of Product Markets; Part 3: Microeconomics of Resource Markets; Part 4: Microeconomics of Government; Part 5: Microeconomic Issues and Policies; and Part 6: International Economics and the World Economy.

▌Organizational Alternatives

Although instructors generally agree as to the content of the principles of microeconomics course, they often differ as to how to arrange the material. *Microeconomics* provides considerable organizational flexibility. Previous users tell us they often substantially rearrange chapters with little sacrifice of continuity.

Some instructors will prefer to intersperse the microeconomics of Parts 2 through 4 with the problems chapters of Part 5. Chapter 20 on agriculture may follow Chapter 10 on pure competition; Chapter 19 on antitrust and regulation may follow Chapters 12 and 13 on imperfect competition models and technological advance. Chapter 22 on labor market issues (unions, discrimination, and immigration) may follow Chapter 15 on wages; and Chapter 21 on income inequality may follow Chapters 15 and 16 on distributive shares of national income.

▌Pedagogical Aids

Microeconomics has always been student oriented. The "To the Student" statement at the beginning of Part 1 details the book's many pedagogical aids. The fifteenth edition is also accompanied by a variety of high-quality supplements.

Supplements for Students

- ***Study Guide*** William Walstad of the University of Nebraska at Lincoln, who is one of the world's foremost experts on economic education, has prepared the fifteenth edition of the *Study Guide*, which many students find indispensable. Each chapter contains an introductory statement, a checklist of behavioral objectives, an outline, a list of important terms, fill-in questions, problems and projects, objective questions, and discussion questions. The answers to *Microeconomics*' end-of-chapter Key Questions appear at the end of the *Study Guide*, along with the text's glossary.

   The *Guide* comprises a superb "portable tutor" for the principles student.

- ***DiscoverEcon*** This software by Jerry Nelson at the University of Illinois–Champaign/Urbana is available in a CD format or on the Website for those who purchase a code. This menu-driven software provides students with a complete tutorial linked to the text. Each chapter features two essay questions, interactive graphs, a multiple-choice test bank, and links to the glossary—all tied cohesively to the textbook.

- ***Website*** As noted, Web-button icons alert students to points in the book where they can springboard to the Website to learn more. There also are weekly news updates, an interactive glossary, and self-grading tests—all specific to *Microeconomics*. For the math-minded student, there is a "Want to See the Math?" area where they can explore the mathematical details of the concepts in the text. There is also a bonus chapter on the Web titled "Transition Economies: Russia and China."

Supplements for Instructors

- ◾ ***Instructor's Resource Manual*** Janet West of the University of Nebraska at Omaha has revised and updated the *Instructor's Resource Manual.* It includes chapter summaries, listings of "what's new" in each chapter, teaching tips and suggestions, learning objectives, chapter outlines, data and visual aid sources with suggestions for classroom use, and questions and problems.

   Available again in this edition is an MS-Word version of the *Manual.* Instructors can print out portions of the *Manual's* contents, complete with their own additions and alterations, for use as student handouts or in whatever ways they wish. This capability includes printing out answers to the end-of-chapter questions.

- ◾ ***Instructor's Presentation CD-ROM*** This CD-ROM contains everything the instructor needs for a multimedia lecture. Video clips, photos, PowerPoint slides, and much more are included and can be customized with personal material. The CD-ROM also contains key supplements for added flexibility and convenience.

- ◾ ***Three Test Banks*** Two test banks of objective, predominately multiple-choice questions and a third test bank of short-answer essay questions and problems supplement this edition of *Microeconomics.*

   Test Bank I. This test bank includes more than 5900 questions, most written by the text authors.

   Test Bank II. Written by William Walstad, this test bank contains more than 5400 questions. All Test Bank II questions are categorized according to level of difficulty: easy, moderate, or difficult.

   Test Bank III. Also prepared by William Walstad, Test Bank III contains "constructive response" testing to evaluate student understanding in a manner different from conventional multiple-choice and true-false questions. Suggested answers to the essay and problem questions are included.

   For all test items in Test Banks I and II, the nature of each question is identified (for example, G = graphical; C = complex, etc.) as are the numbers of the text's pages that are the basis for each. Also, each chapter in Test Banks I and II has an outline or table of contents that groups questions by topics. In all,

more than 11,000 questions give instructors maximum testing flexibility while assuring the fullest possible text correlation.

Test Banks I, II and III are available in computerized Brownstone Diploma versions. These systems produce high-quality graphs and feature the ability to generate multiple tests, with versions "scrambled" to be distinctive. This software meets the needs of the widest spectrum of computer users. Testbank III, the essay bank, is available in printed and MS Word formats.

- ◾ ***Color transparencies*** There are more than 200 new full-color transparencies for the fifteenth edition. They encompass all the figures appearing in *Microeconomics* and are available on request to adopters.

- ◾ ***PageOut*** This software allows instructors to create a course Website via a relatively easy "paint-by-numbers" method. Simply fill in the templates, choose a design, and within minutes your syllabus will be posted on your own Website. Students can then follow your syllabus and be referred to daily assignments and postings.

- ◾ ***PowerWeb.*** This online resource provides high quality, peer-reviewed content including up-to-date articles from leading periodicals and journals, current news, weekly updates with assessment, interactive exercises, Web research guide, study tips and more. PowerWeb is available packaged with the McConnell & Brue text or for online purchase at the website www.duskin.com/powerweb.

◾ Acknowledgments

We give special thanks to Norris Peterson of Pacific Lutheran University and Randy Grant of Linfield College who teamed up with Stan Brue to create the "button" content on our website. We again thank James Reese of the University of South Carolina at Spartanburg, who wrote 80 end-of-chapter Internet exercises for the previous edition. Although we have replaced many of those questions, several remain virtually unchanged in the new edition. We also thank Robert Jensen of Pacific Lutheran University for his meticulous help in proofreading the entire manuscript (twice).

The fifteenth edition has benefited from a number of perceptive reviews. The contributors, listed at the end of the Preface, were a rich source of suggestions for this revision.

We are greatly indebted to the many professionals at McGraw-Hill—in particular Gary Burke, Lucille Sutton, Erin Strathmann, Jean Lou Hess, Keith McPherson, Martin Quinn, Aric Bright, Lori Koetters—for their publishing and marketing expertise.

We thank Ev Sims for his thorough and sensitive editing and Jacques Cournoyer for his vivid Last Word illustrations. Dean Ruggles provided the colorful cover.

We also strongly acknowledge the McGraw-Hill/Irwin sales staff, which greeted this edition with wholehearted enthusiasm.

Campbell R. McConnell
Stanley L. Brue

CONTRIBUTORS

Reviewers

Neil Alper, *Northeastern University*
Carl Bauer, *Oakton Community College*
Bernadette Chachere, *Delgado Community College*
David Chen, *North Carolina A&T State University*
Al Culver, *Chico State University*
Martin Bookbinder, *Passaic County Community College*
Ron Debeaumont, *Black Hills State College*
Mark DeHainaut, *Penn State University*
Bernice Evans, *Morgan State University*
Larry Frateschi, *College of DuPage*
Arthur Friedberg, *Mohawk Valley Community College*
J. Pat Fuller, *Brevard Community College*
Paul Harris, *Camden County College*
Mark Healy, *William Rainey Harper College*
John Ifediora, *University of Wisconsin*
Jonathan Ikoba, *Scott Community College*
Katherine Huger, *Charleston Southern University*
John Kinworthy, *Concordia University–Nebraska*
Shirley Kress, *Skyline Community College*
Peter Kressler, *Rowan University*
Oluseyi Kuforiji, *Albany State University*
Pat Litzinger, *Robert Morris College*
Andrew Lucassen, *Texas A&M University*
Laura Maghoney, *Solano Community College*
Stephen McGary, *Ricks College*
Barbara Moore, *University of Central Florida*
Ron O'Neal, *Camden Community College*
L. Wayne Plumly Jr., *Valdosta State University*
Henry Ryder, *Gloucester Community College*
Ray Schreffler, *Houston Community College–Northwest*
Ron Schuelke, *Santa Rosa Community College*
Virginia Shingleton, *Valparaiso University*
Dave Shorow, *Richland College*
John Sinton, *Finger Lakes Community College*
Lynn Smith, *Clarion University of Pennsylvania*
Joanne Spitz, *University of Massachusetts–Boston*
Arlena Sullivan, *Jones County Junior College*
Bill Sumrall, *Northwest Mississippi Community College*
Ross Thomas, *Albuquerque TVI*
Donna Thompson, *Brookdale Community College*
Lee VanScyoc, *University of Wisconsin–Oshkosh*
Charles Wagoner, *Delta State University*
Dale Wasson, *Southwest Missouri State*
Janet Weaver, *Drake University*
Janet West, *University of Nebraska at Omaha*
Wendy Wood, *Bevill State Community College*

User Survey Respondents

Thomas Burke, *St. Joseph's University*
Christopher Lee, *Saint Ambrose University*
Kristen Monaco, *University of Wisconsin*
Tahnay Naggar, *West Chester University*
Melvin Oliver Jr., *North Carolina Wesleyan College*
Rebecca Rutz, *Mississippi Gulf Coast Community College*
Mark Schopmeyer, *Jackson Community College*
Lavern Timmer, *Alfred State College*
George Giannakouros, *Loras College*
M. Wayne Martin, *Danville Community College*
Harry Richard Call, *The American River College*
Margarita Rose, *King's College*
Marwan El Nasser, *State University of New York College at Fredonia*
Irving Richards, *Cuyahoga Community College*
Nozar Hashemzadeh, *Radford University*
Charles Reichheld, *Cuyahoga Community College*
Robert Kephart, *Corning Community College*
Kevin Schochart, *University of Northern Iowa*
Kwang-Wen Chu, *California State University–Fullerton*
Charles Link, *University of Delaware*
Janet West, *University of Nebraska at Omaha*
Barry Bomboy, *J. Sargeant Reynolds Community College*
Sarah P. Rook, *University of South Carolina at Spartanburg*
Gaminie Meepagala, *Howard University*
Jim Ciminskie, *Bay de Noc Community College*
Michael Twomy, *University of Michigan at Dearborn*
S. Gokturk, *Saint John's University*
Doug Curtis, *Northeast Community College*
Paul J. Hoyt, *Valencia Community College*
Saul Mekies, *Kirkwood Community College*
Joanna Moss, *San Francisco State University*
Timothy J. Bettner, *University of Laverne*
Lawrence B. Morse, *North Carolina A&T State University*
Frank Leroi, *College of San Mateo*
Kahtan Al Yasiri, *University of Wisconsin at Platteville*
Calvin Shipley, *Henderson State University*
Rosemary Walker, *Washburn University*
William Peek, *Niagara University*
Lee Deavours, *Mississippi Gulf Coast Community College*
Carl Bauer, *Oakton Community College*
Wayne Bartholomew, *Indiana University at South Bend*
Donna Thompson, *Brookdale Community College*
Shiv K. Gupta, *University of Findlay*
Arvnee Grow, *Mesa Community College*
Scott Simkins, *North Carolina A&T State University*

Emmanuel Asigbee, *Kirkwood Community College*
Sister Ann Coyle, *Immaculata College*
Michael McCully, *High Point University*
James Phillips, *Cypress College*
Mashid Jalilvand, *University of Wisconsin–Stout*
Marvin Burnett, *St. Louis Community College at Florissant Valley*
Thomas Kemp, *Tarrant County College*
William Walstad, *University of Nebraska at Lincoln*
Gerald Fox, *High Point University*
Julie Granthen, *Oakland University*
Norm Caldwell, *Indiana Central Community College*
Jerry McElroy, *Saint Mary's College*
Fred Hershede, *Indiana University at South Bend*
Paul Joray, *Indiana University at South Bend*
Patricia Humston, *Coastal Bend College*
John Kirk, *College of San Mateo*
Quentin Ciolfi, *Brevard Community College*
Lawrence Fratecschi, *College of DuPage*
Irwin Kellner, *Hofstra University*
Dan Berszez, *College of DuPage*
Ted Woodruff, *Saint Ambrose University*
David Chen, *North Carolina A&T State University*
C. F. Hawkins, *Lamar University*
Nina Shapiro, *Saint Peter's College*
Roy Howsep, *Western Kentucky University*

Anthony Truong, *University of Hawaii LCC*
Robert Gustavson, *Washington University*
Greg Rose, *Sacramento City College*
Wali Mondal, *Henderson State University*
David Shorow, *Richland College*
Henry Kolendzanos, *Danville Community College*
William Swift, *Hofstra University*
John Dorsey, *University of Maryland*
Martin Melkonian, *Hofstra University*
Emmanuel Nnadozie, *Truman State University*
Salim Harik, *Western Michigan University*
Connie Culbreth, *Brevard Community College*
Elizabeth Hill, *Penn State University*
William Harris, *University of Delaware*
Laddie Sula, *Loras College*
Eugene Williams, *McMurray University*
William Tabel, *South Suburban College*
Maria Gamba, *University of Findlay*
Janice Weaver, *Drake University*
Alan Kessler, *Providence College*
Ismail Shariff, *University of Wisconsin at Green Bay*
John P. Connelly, *Corning Community College*
M. B. Biery, *Tarrant County College*
Erick M. Elder, *University of Arkansas at Little Rock*
Della Sampson, *Dalton State College*

BRIEF CONTENTS

CONTENTS

1

An Introduction to Economics and the Economy

▌ To the Student

This book and its ancillaries contain a number of features designed to help you learn economics:

■ **_In-Text Web Buttons_** A glance through the book will reveal many pages that contain small symbols at the ends of paragraphs. The "buttons" are designed to direct you to the text's Internet site: www.mhhe.com/economics/mcconnell15 The ⚠ button stands for "Analogies, Anecdotes, and Insights." These short pieces help you understand and remember the economic ideas by connecting them to other, better-known, ideas or easy to remember stories and examples. The 🔎 button stands for "Origin of the Idea." These pieces trace the particular idea to the person or persons who first developed it. The 📈 button stands for "Interactive Graphs." Brief exercises ask you to interact with the graphs, for example, by clicking onto a specific curve and dragging it to a new location. These exercises will enhance your understanding of the underlying concepts.

After reading a chapter, thumb back through it to note the symbols and the number that follows them. On the home page of our Internet site, click "In-Text Web Buttons" and find your way to the numbered piece. We think you will find this interactivity between the text and the Internet highly engaging and helpful.

■ **_Other Internet aids_** Our Internet site contains many other aids. In the "For the Student" section you will find self-testing multiple-choice quizzes, links to relevant news articles, a student discussion room, answers to frequently asked questions, and much more. For those of you with very strong mathematics backgrounds, be sure to check out the "Want to See the Math?" section on the website. There, you will find nearly 50 notes that develop the algebra and, in some cases, the calculus that underlies the economic concepts.

■ **_Appendix on graphs_** Be assured, however, that you will need only basic math skills to do well in the principles course. In particular, you will need to be comfortable with graphical analysis and a few quantitative concepts. The appendix to Chapter 1 reviews graphing, slopes of curves, and linear equations. Be sure not to skip it.

■ **_Reviews_** Each chapter contains two or three Quick Reviews and an end-of-chapter summary. These reviews will help you focus on essential ideas and study for exams.

■ **_Key Terms and Key Graphs_** Key terms are set in boldface type within the chapters, listed at the end of each chapter, and defined in the Glossary at the end of the book. Graphs with special relevance are labeled Key Graphs, and each includes a multiple-choice Quick Quiz. Your instructor may not emphasize all these figures, but you should pay special attention to those that are discussed in class; you can be certain that there will be exam questions on them.

■ **_Last Words_** Each chapter concludes with a Last Word minireading. While it is tempting to ignore these sections, don't. Some of them are revealing applications of economic concepts; others are short case studies. Most are fun to read, and all will broaden your grasp of economics.

■ **_Questions_** A comprehensive list of questions is located at the end of each chapter. Answering these questions will enhance your understanding. Several of the questions are designated as Key Questions and are answered in the _Study Guide_ and also at our Internet site.

■ **_Study Guide_** We enthusiastically recommend the _Study Guide_ accompanying this text. This "portable tutor" contains not only a broad sampling of various kinds of questions but a host of useful learning aids. An excellent CD-ROM is also available for use with the book. Although it is not as comprehensive as the _Study Guide_, many students will find it to be very helpful.

Our overriding goal is to help you understand and apply economics. With your effort, our effort, and the effort of your instructor, you will be able to comprehend a whole range of economic, social, and political problems that otherwise would have remained puzzling and perplexing.

Good luck with your study of economics. We think it will be well worth your effort.

C H A P T E R

The Nature and Method of Economics

Want is a growing giant whom the coat of Have was never large enough to cover.
Ralph Waldo Emerson, The Conduct of Life, 1860

PEOPLE'S ECONOMIC WANTS are multitudinous and diverse. Biologically, humans need only air, water, food, clothing, and shelter. But in contemporary society we also seek the many goods and services associated with a comfortable or affluent standard of living. Fortunately, society is blessed with productive resources—labor and managerial talent, tools and machinery, land and mineral deposits—that are used to produce goods and services. This production satisfies many of our economic wants and occurs through the organizational mechanism called the *economic system* or, more simply, the *economy*. ■ The blunt reality, however, is that our economic wants far exceed the productive capacity of our limited or scarce resources. So the complete satisfaction of society's economic wants is impossible. This unyielding truth provides our definition of **economics:** *It is the social science concerned with the efficient use of scarce resources to achieve the maximum satisfaction of economic wants.* ■ Numerous problems and issues are rooted in the challenge of using limited resources efficiently. Although it would be tempting to plunge into them, that sort of analysis must wait. In this chapter, we need to discuss some important preliminaries. 🔑 1.1

■ The Economic Perspective

Economists view things through a unique perspective. This **economic perspective** or *economic way of thinking* has several critical and closely interrelated features.

Scarcity and Choice

From our definition of economics, it is easy to see why economists view the world through the lens of scarcity. Since human and property resources are scarce (limited), it follows that the goods and services we produce must also be limited. Scarcity limits our options and necessitates that we make choices. Because we "can't have it all," we must decide what we will have, and what we must forgo.

At the core of economics is the idea that "there is no free lunch." You may get treated to lunch, making it "free" to you, but there is a cost to someone—ultimately to society. Scarce inputs of land, equipment, farm labor, the labor of cooks and waiters, and managerial talent are required. Because these resources could be used in alternative production activities, they and the other goods and services they could have produced are sacrificed in making the lunch available. Economists call these sacrifices *opportunity costs*. To get more of one thing, you forgo the opportunity of getting something else. So the cost of that which you get is the value of that which is sacrificed to obtain it. We will say much more about opportunity costs in Chapter 2. ⚠ 1.1

Rational Behavior

Economics is grounded on the assumption of "rational self-interest." Individuals pursue actions that will enable them to achieve their greatest satisfaction. Rational behavior means that individuals will make different choices under different circumstances. For example, Jones may decide to buy Coca-Cola in bulk at a warehouse store rather than at a convenience store where it is much more expensive. That will leave him with extra money to buy something else that provides satisfaction. Yet, while driving home from work, he may stop at the convenience store to buy a single can of Coca-Cola.

Rational self-interest also means that individuals will make different choices. High school graduate Alvarez may decide to attend college to major in business. Baker may opt to take a job at a warehouse and buy a new car. Chin may accept a signing bonus and join the Navy. All three choices reflect the pursuit of self-interest and are rational, but they are based on differing preferences and circumstances.

Of course, rational decisions may change as costs and benefits change. Jones may switch to Pepsi when it is on sale. And, after taking a few business courses, Alvarez may decide to change her major to social work.

It is clear that rational self-interest is not the same as selfishness. People make personal sacrifices to help family members or friends, and they contribute to charities because they derive pleasure from doing so. Parents help pay for their children's education for the same reason. These self-interested, but unselfish, acts help maximize the givers' satisfaction as much as any personal purchase of goods or services. Self-interest behavior is simply behavior that enables a person to achieve personal satisfaction, however it may be derived.

Marginalism: Benefits and Costs

The economic perspective focuses largely on **marginal analysis**—comparisons of *marginal benefits* and *marginal costs*. (Used this way, "marginal" means "extra," "additional," or "a change in.") Most choices or decisions involve changes in the status quo (the existing state of affairs). Should you attend school for another year or not? Should you study an extra hour for an exam? Should you add fries to your fast-food order? Similarly, should a business expand or reduce its output? Should government increase or decrease its funding for a missile defense system?

Each option involves marginal benefits and, because of scarce resources, marginal costs. In making choices rationally, the decision maker must compare those two amounts. Example: You and your fiancé are shopping for an engagement ring. Should you buy a $\frac{1}{4}$-carat diamond, a $\frac{1}{2}$-carat diamond, a $\frac{3}{4}$-carat diamond, or a larger one? The marginal cost of the larger-size diamond is the added expense beyond the cost of the smaller-size diamond. The marginal benefit is the greater lifetime pleasure (utility) from the larger-size stone. If the marginal benefit of the larger diamond exceeds its marginal cost, you should buy the larger stone. But if the marginal cost is more than the marginal benefit, you should buy the smaller diamond instead.

In a world of scarcity, the decision to obtain the marginal benefit associated with some specific option always includes the marginal cost of forgoing something else. The money spent on the larger-size diamond means forgoing something else. Again, there is no free lunch!

One somewhat surprising implication of decisions based on marginal analysis is that there can be too much of a good thing. Although certain goods and services seem inherently desirable—education, health care, a pristine environment—we can in fact have too much of them. "Too much" occurs when we keep obtaining them beyond the point where their marginal cost (the value of the forgone options) equals their marginal benefit. Then we are sacrificing alternative products that are more valuable *at the margin*—the place where we consider the very last units of each. Society can have too much health care, and you can have too many CDs. **(Key Question 1)** 🔑 1.2

This chapter's Last Word provides an everyday application of the economic perspective.

■ Why Study Economics?

Is studying economics worth your time and effort? More than half a century ago John Maynard Keynes (1883–1946), one of the most influential economists of this century, said:

> The ideas of economists and political philosophers, both when they are right and when they are wrong, are more powerful than is commonly understood. Indeed the world is ruled by little else. Practical men, who believe themselves to be quite exempt from any intellectual influences, are usually the slaves of some defunct economist.

Most of the ideologies of the modern world have been shaped by prominent economists of the past—Adam Smith, David Ricardo, John Stuart Mill, Karl Marx, and John Maynard Keynes. And current world leaders routinely solicit the advice and policy suggestions of today's economists.

For example, the president of the United States benefits from the recommendations of his Council of Economic Advisers. The broad range of economic issues facing political leaders is suggested by the contents of the annual *Economic Report of the President*. Areas covered typically include unemployment, inflation, economic growth, taxation, poverty, international trade, health care, pollution, discrimination, immigration, regulation, and education, among others. And the Federal Reserve (the U.S. central bank) relies heavily on economic analysis in shaping its monetary policies.

Economics for Citizenship

A basic understanding of economics is essential if we are to be well-informed citizens. Most of today's political problems have important economic aspects: Should we use Federal budget surpluses to pay off the public debt, expand various government programs, or reduce income taxes? How can we make the social security retirement program financially secure? Why do we continue to have large international trade deficits? What must we do to keep inflation in check? What can be done to keep income inequality from growing? How should we respond to growing market dominance by a few firms in some high-technology sectors of the economy?

As voters, we can influence the decisions of our elected officials in responding to such questions. But intelligence at the polls requires a basic working knowledge of economics. And a sound grasp of economics is even more helpful to the politicians themselves.

A survey by the National Center for Research in Economic Education suggests that economic illiteracy is widespread in the United States. The public, including high school seniors and college seniors, shows a broad lack of knowledge of the basic economics needed to understand economic events and changes in the national economy.

Professional and Personal Applications

Economics lays great stress on precise, systematic analysis. Thus, studying economics invariably helps students improve their analytical skills, which are in great demand in the workplace. Also, the study of economics helps us make sense of the everyday activity we observe around us. How is it that so many different people, in so many different places, doing so many different things, produce the goods and services we want to buy? Economics provides an answer.

Economics is also vital to business. An understanding of the basics of economic decision making and the operation of the economic system enables business managers and executives to increase profit. The executive who understands when to use new technology, when to merge with another firm, when to expand employment, and so on, will outperform the executive who is less deft at such decision making. The manager who understands the causes and consequences of recessions (downturns in the overall economy) or inflation (rising prices) can make more intelligent business decisions during these periods.

Economics helps consumers and workers make better buying and employment decisions. How can you spend your limited money income to maximize your satisfaction? How can you hedge against the reduction in the dollar's purchasing power that accompanies inflation? Is it more economical to buy or lease a car? Should you use a credit card or pay cash? Which occupations pay well; which are most immune to unemployment?

Similarly, an understanding of economics makes for better financial decisions. Someone who understands the relationship between budget surpluses and interest rates, between foreign exchange rates and exports, between interest rates and bond prices, is in a better position to successfully allocate personal savings. So, too, is someone who understands the business implications of emerging new technologies.

In spite of these practical benefits, however, you should know that economics is *mainly* an academic, not a vocational, subject. Unlike accounting, advertising, corporate finance, and marketing, economics is not primarily a how-to-make-money area of study. Knowledge of economics and mastery of the economic perspective will help you run a business or manage your personal finances, but that is not the subject's primary objective. Instead, economics ultimately examines problems and decisions from the *social*, rather than the *personal*, point of view. The production, exchange, and consumption of goods and services are discussed from the viewpoint of society's best interest, not strictly from the standpoint of one's own pocketbook.

> **QUICK REVIEW 1.1**
>
> ■ Economics is concerned with obtaining maximum satisfaction through the efficient use of scarce resources.
>
> ■ The economic perspective stresses (a) resource scarcity and the necessity of making choices, (b) the assumption of rational behavior, and (c) comparisons of marginal benefit and marginal cost.
>
> ■ Your study of economics will help you as a voting citizen as well as benefit you professionally and personally.

■ Economic Methodology

Like the physical and life sciences, as well as other social sciences, economics relies on the **scientific method.** It consists of a number of elements:

■ The observation of facts (real-world data).

■ Based on those facts, the formulation of a possible explanation of cause and effect (hypothesis).

■ The testing of this explanation by comparing the outcomes of specific events to the outcome predicted by the hypothesis.

■ The acceptance, rejection, or modification of the hypothesis, based on these comparisons.

■ The continued testing of the hypothesis against the facts. As favorable results accumulate, the

hypothesis evolves into a *theory*. A very well tested and widely accepted theory is referred to as a *law* or *principle*. Combinations of such laws or principles are incorporated into *models*—simplified representations of how something works, such as a market or segment of the economy.

Laws, principles, and models enable the economist, like the natural scientist, to understand and explain reality and to predict the various outcomes of particular actions. But as we will soon see, economic laws and principles are usually less certain than the laws of physics or chemistry.

Theoretical Economics

Economists develop models of the behavior of individuals (consumers, workers) and institutions (businesses, governments) engaged in the production, exchange, and consumption of goods and services. They start by gathering facts about economic activities and economic outcomes. Because the world is cluttered with innumerable interrelated facts, economists, like all scientists, must select the useful information. They must determine which facts are relevant to the problem under consideration. But even when this sorting process is complete, the relevant information may at first seem random and unrelated.

The economist draws on the facts to establish cause-effect hypotheses about economic behavior. Then the hypotheses are tested against real-world observation and data. Through this process, the economist tries to discover hypotheses that rise to the level of theories and principles (or laws)—well-tested and widely accepted generalizations about how individuals and institutions behave. The process of deriving theories and principles is called **theoretical economics** (see the lower box in Figure 1.1). *The role of economic theorizing is to systematically arrange facts, interpret them, and generalize from them.* Theories and principles bring order and meaning to facts by arranging them in cause-and-effect order.

Observe that the arrow from "theories" to "facts" in Figure 1.1 moves in both directions. Some understanding of factual, real-world evidence is required to formulate meaningful hypotheses. And hypotheses are tested through gathering and organizing factual data to see if the hypotheses can be verified.

Economic theories and **principles** *are statements about economic behavior or the economy that enable prediction of the probable effects of certain actions.* Good

Figure 1.1

The relationship between facts, theories, and policies in economics. *Theoretical economics* involves establishing economic theories by gathering, systematically arranging, and generalizing from facts. Good economic theories are tested for validity against facts. Economists use these theories—the most reliable of which are called *laws* or *principles*—to explain and analyze the economy. *Policy economics* entails using the economic laws and principles to formulate economic policies.

theories are those that do a good job of explaining and predicting. They are supported by facts concerning how individuals and institutions actually behave in producing, exchanging, and consuming goods and services. But these facts may change in time, so economists must continually check theories against the shifting economic environment.

Theories, laws, and principles are highly useful in analyzing economic behavior and understanding how the economy operates. They are the ingredients of *analytical economics*—the ascertaining of cause and effect, of action and outcome, within the economic system.

Several other points relating to economic principles are important to know.

Terminology   Economists speak of "hypotheses," "theories," "laws," and "principles." Some of these terms overlap, but they usually reflect a gradation of confidence in the generalizations. A hypothesis needs initial testing; a theory has been tested but needs more testing; a law or principle is a theory that has provided strong predictive accuracy, over and over. The terms "economic laws" and "principles" are useful even though they imply a degree of exactness, universal application, and even moral rightness that is rare in any social science. The word "theory" is often used in economics even though many people incorrectly believe theories have nothing to do with real-world applications. Economists often use the term "model," which combines principles into a simplified representation of reality.

In this book, custom or convenience will govern the use of "theory," "law," "principle," and "model." Thus, to describe the relationship between the price of a product and the amount of it purchased, we will use the term *law of demand*, rather than theory or principle of demand, simply because this is the custom. We will refer to the *circular flow model*, not the circular flow law, because the concept combines several ideas into a single representation.

Generalizations   As we have already mentioned, economic theories, principles, and laws are **generalizations** relating to economic behavior or to the economy itself. They are imprecise because economic facts are usually diverse; no two individuals or institutions act in exactly the same way. *Economic principles are expressed as the tendencies of typical or average consumers, workers, or business firms.* For example, when economists say that consumer spending rises when personal income increases, they are well aware that some households may save *all* of an increase in their incomes. But, on average, and for the full economy, spending goes up when income increases. Similarly, economists say that consumers buy more of a particular product when its price falls. Some consumers may increase their purchases by a large amount, others by a small amount, and a few not at all. This "price-quantity" principle, however, holds for the typical consumer and for consumers as a group.

Other-Things-Equal Assumption   Like other scientists, economists use the *ceteris paribus* or **other-things-equal assumption** to construct their generalizations. They assume that all other variables except those under immediate consideration are held constant for a particular analysis. For example, consider the relationship between the price of Pepsi and the amount of it purchased. It helps to assume that, of all the factors that might influence the amount of Pepsi purchased (for example, the price of Pepsi, the price of Coca-Cola, and consumer incomes and preferences), only the price of Pepsi varies. The economist can then focus on the "price of Pepsi–purchases of Pepsi" relationship without being confused by changes in other variables. 🔍 1.3

Natural scientists such as chemists or physicists can usually conduct controlled experiments where "all other things" are in fact held constant (or virtually so). They can test with great precision the assumed relationship between two variables. For example, they might examine the height from which an object is dropped and the length of time it takes to hit the ground. But economics is not a laboratory science. Economists test their theories using real-world data, which are generated by the actual operation of the economy. In this rather bewildering environment, "other things" *do* change. Despite the development of complex statistical techniques designed to hold other things equal, control is less than perfect. As a result, economic principles are less certain and less precise than those of laboratory sciences. That also means they are more open to debate than many scientific theories (for example, the law of gravity).

Abstractions
Economic principles, or theories, are *abstractions*—simplifications that omit irrelevant facts and circumstances. Economic models do *not* mirror the full complexity of the real world. The very process of sorting out and analyzing facts involves simplification and removal of clutter. Unfortunately, this "abstraction" leads some people to consider economic theory impractical and unrealistic. That is simply nonsense! Economic theories are practical precisely because they are abstractions. The full scope of economic reality itself is too complex and bewildering to be understood as a whole. Economists abstract—that is, develop theories and build models—to give meaning to an otherwise overwhelming and confusing maze of facts. Theorizing for this purpose is highly practical. ❗ 1.2

Graphical Expression
Many of the economic models in this book are expressed graphically; the most important are labeled Key Graphs. Be sure to read the appendix to this chapter as a review of graphs.

Policy Economics

Policy economics recognizes that theories and data can be used to formulate *policies*—courses of action based on economic principles and intended to resolve a specific economic problem or further an economic goal. Economic theories are the foundation of economic policy, as shown in the upper part of Figure 1.1. Economic policy normally is applied to problems after they arise. However, if economic analysis can predict some undesirable event such as unemployment, inflation, or an increase in poverty, then it may be possible to avoid or moderate that event through economic policy. For example, you may read in the newspaper that the Federal Reserve has reduced interest rates to increase private spending and prevent a recession.

Economic Policy
The creation of policies to achieve specific goals is no simple matter. Here are the basic steps in policymaking:

- *State the goal.* The first step is to make a clear statement of the economic goal. If we say that we want "full employment," do we mean that everyone between, say, 16 and 65 years of age should have a job? Or do we mean that everyone who *wants* to work should have a job? Should we allow for some unemployment caused by inevitable changes in the structure of industry and workers voluntarily changing jobs? The goal must be specific.

- *Determine the policy options.* The next step is to formulate alternative policies designed to achieve the goal and determine the possible effects of each policy. This requires a detailed assessment of the economic impact, benefits, costs, and political feasibility of the alternative policies. For example, to achieve full employment, should government use fiscal policy (which involves changing government spending and taxes), monetary policy (which entails altering the supply of money), an education and training policy that enhances worker employability, or a policy of wage subsidies to firms that hire disadvantaged workers?

- *Implement and evaluate the policy that was selected.* After implementing the policy, we need to evaluate how well it worked. Only through unbiased evaluation can we improve on economic policy. Did a specific change in taxes or the money supply alter the level of employment to the extent predicted? Did deregulation of a particular industry (for example, banking) yield the predicted beneficial results? If not, why not? What were the harmful side effects, if any? How might the policy be altered to make it work better? **(Key Question 5)**

Economic Goals If economic policies are designed to achieve certain economic goals, then we need to recognize a number of goals that are widely accepted in the United States and many other countries. They include:

- *Economic growth* Produce more and better goods and services, or, more simply, develop a higher standard of living.
- *Full employment* Provide suitable jobs for all citizens who are willing and able to work.
- *Economic efficiency* Achieve the maximum fulfillment of wants using the available productive resources.
- *Price-level stability* Avoid large upswings and downswings in the general price level; that is, avoid inflation and deflation.
- *Economic freedom* Guarantee that businesses, workers, and consumers have a high degree of freedom in their economic activities.
- *Equitable distribution of income* Ensure that no group of citizens faces poverty while most others enjoy abundance.
- *Economic security* Provide for those who are chronically ill, disabled, laid off, aged, or otherwise unable to earn minimal levels of income.
- *Balance of trade* Seek a reasonable overall balance with the rest of the world in international trade and financial transactions.

Although most of us might accept these goals as generally stated, we might also disagree substantially on their specific meanings. What are "large" changes in the price level? What is a "high degree" of economic freedom? What is an "equitable" distribution of income? How can we measure precisely such abstract goals as "economic freedom"? These objectives are often the subject of spirited public debate.

Also, some of these goals are complementary; when one is achieved, some other one will also be realized. For example, achieving full employment means eliminating unemployment, which is a basic cause of inequitable income distribution. But other goals may conflict or even be mutually exclusive. They may entail **tradeoffs,** meaning that to achieve one we must sacrifice another. For example, efforts to equalize the distribution of income may weaken

incentives to work, invest, innovate, and take business risks, all of which promote economic growth. Taxing high-income people heavily and transferring the tax revenues to low-income people is one way to equalize the distribution of income. But then the incentives to high-income individuals may diminish because higher taxes reduce their rewards for working. Similarly, low-income individuals may be less motivated to work when government stands ready to subsidize them.

When goals conflict, society must develop a system to prioritize the objectives it seeks. If more economic freedom is accompanied by less economic security and more economic security allows less economic freedom, society must assess the tradeoffs and decide on the optimal (best) balance between them.

> **QUICK REVIEW 1.2**
>
> ■ Economists use the scientific method to establish theories, laws, and principles. Economic theories (laws, principles, or models) are generalizations relating to the economic behavior of individuals and institutions; good theories are grounded in facts.
>
> ■ Theoretical economics involves formulating theories (or laws and principles) and using them to understand and explain economic behavior and the economy; policy economics involves using the theories to fix economic problems or promote economic goals.
>
> ■ Policymaking requires a clear statement of goals, a thorough assessment of options, and an unbiased evaluation of results.
>
> ■ Some of society's economic goals are complementary, while others conflict; where conflicts exist, tradeoffs arise.

■ Macroeconomics and Microeconomics

Economists derive and apply principles about economic behavior at two levels.

Macroeconomics

Macroeconomics examines either the economy as a whole or its basic subdivisions or aggregates, such as the government, household, and business sectors. An **aggregate** is a collection of specific economic units treated as if they were one unit. Therefore, we might lump together the millions of consumers in the U.S. economy and treat them as if they were one huge unit called "consumers."

In using aggregates, macroeconomics seeks to obtain an overview, or general outline, of the structure of the economy and the relationships of its major aggregates. Macroeconomics speaks of such economic measures as *total* output, *total* employment, *total* income, *aggregate* expenditures, and the *general* level of prices in analyzing various economic problems. No or very little attention is given to specific units making up the various aggregates. Macroeconomics examines the beach, not the sand, rocks, and shells.

Microeconomics

Microeconomics looks at specific economic units. At this level of analysis, the economist observes the details of an economic unit, or very small segment of the economy, under a figurative microscope. In microeconomics we talk of an individual industry, firm, or household. We measure the price of a *specific* product, the number of workers employed by a *single* firm, the revenue or income of a *particular* firm or household, or the expenditures of a *specific* firm, government entity, or family. In microeconomics, we examine the sand, rocks, and shells, not the beach.

The macro-micro distinction does not mean that economics is so highly compartmentalized that every topic can be readily labeled as either macro or micro; many topics and subdivisions of economics are rooted in both. Example: While the problem of unemployment is usually treated as a macroeconomic topic (because unemployment relates to *aggregate* spending), economists recognize that the decisions made by *individual* workers in searching for jobs and the way *specific* product and labor markets operate are also critical in determining the unemployment rate. **(Key Question 7)**

Positive and Normative Economics

Both macroeconomics and microeconomics involve facts, theories, and policies. Each contains elements of *positive* economics and *normative* economics. **Positive economics** focuses on facts and cause-and-effect relationships. It includes description, theory development, and theory testing (theoretical economics). Positive economics avoids value judgments, tries to establish scientific statements about economic behavior, and deals with what the economy is

actually like. Such scientific-based analysis is critical to good policy analysis.

Policy economics, on the other hand, involves **normative economics,** which incorporates value judgments about what the economy should be like or what particular policy actions should be recommended to achieve a desirable goal. Normative economics looks at the desirability of certain aspects of the economy. It underlies expressions of support for particular economic policies.

Positive economics concerns *what is*, while normative economics embodies subjective feelings about *what ought to be*. Examples: Positive statement: "The unemployment rate in several European nations is higher than that in the United States." Normative statement: "European nations ought to undertake policies to reduce their unemployment rates." A second positive statement: "Other things equal, if tuition is substantially increased, college enrollment will fall." Normative statement: "College tuition should be lowered so that more students can obtain an education." Whenever words such as "ought" or "should" appear in a sentence, there is a strong chance you are encountering a normative statement.

Most of the disagreement among economists involves normative, value-based policy questions. Of course, there is often some disagreement about which theories or models best represent the economy and its parts. But economists agree on a full range of economic principles. Most economic controversy thus reflects differing opinions or value judgments about what society should be like. **(Key Question 8)**

> **QUICK REVIEW   1.3**
>
> Macroeconomics examines the economy as a whole; microeconomics focuses on specific units of the economy.
>
> Positive economics deals with factual statements ("what is"); normative economics involves value judgments ("what ought to be"). Theoretical economics is "positive"; policy economics is "normative."

■ Pitfalls to Objective Thinking

Because they affect us so personally, we often have difficulty thinking objectively about economic issues. Here are some common pitfalls to avoid in successfully applying the economic perspective.

Biases

Most people bring a bundle of biases and preconceptions to the field of economics. For example, some might think that corporate profits are excessive or that lending money is always superior to borrowing money. Others might believe that government is necessarily less efficient than businesses or that more government regulation is always better than less. Biases cloud thinking and interfere with objective analysis. All of us must be willing to shed biases and preconceptions that are not supported by facts.

Loaded Terminology

The economic terminology used in newspapers and popular magazines is sometimes emotionally biased, or loaded. The writer or the interest group he or she represents may have a cause to promote or an ax to grind and may slant an article accordingly. High profits may be labeled "obscene," low wages may be called "exploitive," or self-interested behavior may be "greed." Government workers may be referred to as "mindless bureaucrats," and those favoring stronger government regulations may be called "socialists." To objectively analyze economic issues, you must be prepared to reject or discount such terminology.

Definitions

Some of the terms used in economics have precise technical definitions that are quite different from those implied by their common usage. This is generally not a problem if everyone understands these definitions and uses them consistently. For example, "investment" to the average citizen means the purchase of stocks and bonds in security markets, as when someone "invests" in Microsoft stock or government bonds. But to the economist, "investment" means the purchase of newly created real capital assets such as machinery and equipment or the construction of a new factory building. It does not mean the purely financial transaction of swapping cash for securities. ⚠ 1.3

Fallacy of Composition

Another pitfall in economic thinking is the assumption that what is true for one individual or part of a whole is necessarily true for a group of individuals or the whole. This is a logical fallacy called the **fallacy of composition;** the assumption is *not* correct. A statement that is valid for an individual or part is *not* necessarily valid for the larger group or whole.

Consider the following example from outside of economics: You are at a football game and the home team makes an outstanding play. In the excitement, you leap to your feet to get a better view. A valid statement: "If you, *an individual,* stand, your view of the game is improved." But is this also true for the group—for everyone watching the play? Not necessarily. If *everyone* stands to watch the play, probably nobody—including you—will have a better view than when all remain seated.

A second example comes from economics: An *individual* farmer who reaps a particularly large crop is likely to realize a sharp gain in income. But this statement cannot be generalized to farmers as a *group.* The individual farmer's large or "bumper" crop will not noticeably influence (reduce) crop prices because each farmer produces a negligible fraction of the total farm output. But for *all* farmers as a group, prices decline when total output increases. Thus, if all farmers reap bumper crops, the total output of farm products will rise, depressing crop prices. If the price declines are relatively large, total farm income might actually *fall.*

Recall our earlier distinction between macroeconomics and microeconomics: *The fallacy of composition reminds us that generalizations valid at one of these levels of analysis may or may not be valid at the other.*

Causation Fallacies

Causation is sometimes difficult to identify in economics. Two important fallacies often interfere with economic thinking.

Post Hoc Fallacy
You must think very carefully before concluding that because event A precedes event B, A is the cause of B. This kind of faulty reasoning is known as the *post hoc, ergo propter hoc,* or **"after this, therefore because of this," fallacy.**

Example: Suppose that early each spring the medicine man of a tribe performs a special dance. A week or so later the trees and grass turn green. Can we safely conclude that event A, the medicine man's dance, has caused event B, the landscape's turning green? Obviously not. The rooster crows before dawn, but that does not mean the rooster is responsible for the sunrise!

Fast-Food Lines: An Economic Perspective

How can the economic perspective help us understand the behavior of fast-food consumers?

You enter a fast-food restaurant. Do you immediately look to see which line is the shortest? What do you do when you are in the middle of a long line and a new serving station opens? Have you ever gone to a fast-food restaurant, seen very long lines, and then left? Have you ever become annoyed when someone in front of you in line placed an order that took a long time to fill?

The economic perspective is useful in analyzing the behavior of fast-food customers. These consumers are at the restaurant because they expect the marginal benefit from the food they buy to match or exceed its marginal cost. When customers enter the restaurant, they go to the shortest line, believing that that line will minimize their time cost of obtaining food. They are acting purposefully; time is limited, and people prefer using it in some way other than standing in line.

If one fast-food line is temporarily shorter than other lines, some people will move to that line. These movers apparently view the time saving associated with the shorter line to exceed the cost of moving from their present line. The line switching tends to equalize line lengths. No further movement of customers between lines occurs once all lines are about equal.

Fast-food customers face another cost-benefit decision when a clerk opens a new station at the counter. Should they move to the new station or stay put? Those who shift to the new line decide that the time saving from the move exceeds the extra cost of physically moving. In so deciding, customers must also consider just how quickly they can get to the new station compared with others who may be contemplating the same move. (Those who hesitate in this situation are lost!)

Customers at the fast-food establishment do not have perfect information when they select lines. For example, they do not first survey those in the lines to determine what they are ordering before deciding which line to enter. There are two reasons for this. First, most customers would tell them "It's none of your business," and therefore no information would be forthcoming. Second, even

---

A professional football team hires a new coach and the team's record improves. Is the new coach the cause? Maybe. But perhaps the presence of more experienced and talented players or an easier schedule is the true cause.

Correlation versus Causation Do not confuse correlation, or connection, with causation. Correlation between two events or two sets of data indicates only that they are associated in some systematic and dependable way. For example, we may find that when variable X increases, Y also increases. But this correlation does not necessarily mean that there is causation—that an increase in X is the cause of an increase in Y. The relationship could be purely coincidental or dependent on some other factor, Z, not included in the analysis.

Here is an economic example: Economists have found a positive correlation between education and income. In general, people with more education earn higher incomes than those with less education. Common sense suggests education is the cause and higher incomes are the effect; more education implies a more knowledgeable and productive worker, and such workers receive larger salaries.

But causation could also partly run the other way. People with higher incomes could buy more education, just as they buy more furniture and steaks. Or is part of the relationship explainable in still other ways? Are education and income correlated because the characteristics required to succeed in education—ability and motivation—are the same ones required to be a productive and highly paid worker? If so, then people with those traits will probably obtain more education *and* earn higher incomes. But greater education will not be the sole cause of the higher income. **(Key Question 9)**

▌A Look Ahead

The ideas in this chapter will come into much sharper focus as you advance through Part 1, where we develop specific economic principles and models. Specifically, in Chapter 2 we build a model of the production choices facing an economy. In Chapter 3 we develop laws of demand and supply that will help you understand how prices and quantities of goods and services are established in markets. In Chapter 4 we combine all markets in the economy to see how the *market system* works. And in Chapters 5 and 6 we examine important sectors (components) of the economy, specifically, the private sector, the government sector, and the international sector.

if they could obtain the information, the amount of time necessary to get it (a cost) would most certainly exceed any time saving associated with finding the best line (the benefit). Because information is costly to obtain, fast-food patrons select lines without perfect information. Thus, not all decisions turn out as expected. For example, you might enter a short line and find someone in front of you is ordering hamburgers and fries for 40 people in the Greyhound bus parked out back (and the employee is a trainee)! Nevertheless, at the time you made your decision, you thought it was optimal.

Imperfect information also explains why some people who arrive at a fast-food restaurant and observe long lines decide to leave. These people conclude that the marginal cost (monetary plus time costs) of obtaining the fast food is too large relative to the marginal benefit. They would not have come to the restaurant in the first place had they known the lines would be so long. But getting that information by, say, employing an advance scout with a cellular phone would cost more than the perceived benefit.

Finally, customers must decide what food to order when they arrive at the counter. In making their choices, they again compare marginal costs and marginal benefits in attempting to obtain the greatest personal satisfaction or well-being for their expenditure.

Economists believe that what is true for the behavior of customers at fast-food restaurants is true for economic behavior in general. Faced with an array of choices, consumers, workers, and businesses rationally compare marginal costs and marginal benefits in making decisions.

SUMMARY

1. Economics is the study of the efficient use of scarce resources in the production of goods and services to achieve the maximum satisfaction of economic wants.

2. The economic perspective includes three elements: scarcity and choice, rational behavior, and marginalism. It sees individuals and institutions making rational decisions based on comparisons of marginal costs and marginal benefits.

3. Knowledge of economics contributes to effective citizenship and provides useful insights for politicians, consumers, and workers.

4. Economists employ the scientific method, in which they form and test hypotheses of cause-and-effect relationships to generate theories, laws, and principles. Economists often combine theories into representations called models.

5. Generalizations stated by economists are called principles, theories, laws, or models. The derivation of these principles is the object of theoretical economics. Good theories explain real-world relationships and predict real-world outcomes.

6. Because economic principles are valuable predictors, they are the bases for economic policy, which is designed to identify and solve problems to the greatest extent possible and at the least possible cost. This type of application of economics is called policy economics.

7. Our society accepts certain shared economic goals, including economic growth, full employment, economic efficiency, price-level stability, economic freedom, equity in the distribution of income, economic security, and a reasonable balance in international trade and finance. Some of these goals are complementary; others entail tradeoffs.

8. Macroeconomics looks at the economy as a whole or its major aggregates; microeconomics examines specific economic units or institutions.

9. Positive statements state facts ("what is"); normative statements express value judgments ("what ought to be").

10. In studying economics, we encounter such pitfalls as biases and preconceptions, unfamiliar or confusing terminology, the fallacy of composition, and the difficulty of establishing clear cause-effect relationships.

TERMS AND CONCEPTS

economics
economic perspective
marginal analysis
scientific method
theoretical economics

principles
generalizations
other-things-equal
    assumption
policy economics

tradeoffs
macroeconomics
aggregate
microeconomics
positive economics

normative economics
fallacy of composition
"after this, therefore
    because of this," fallacy

STUDY QUESTIONS

1. **Key Question** Use the economic perspective to explain why someone who is normally a light eater at a standard restaurant may become a bit of a glutton at a buffet-style restaurant that charges a single price for all you can eat.

2. What is the scientific method, and how does it relate to theoretical economics? What is the difference between a hypothesis and an economic law or principle?

3. Why is it significant that economics is not a laboratory science? What problems may be involved in deriving and applying economic principles?

4. Explain the following statements:
   a. Good economic policy requires good economic theory.
   b. Generalization and abstraction are nearly synonymous.
   c. Facts serve to sort out good and bad hypotheses.
   d. The *other-things-equal assumption* helps isolate key economic relationships.

5. **Key Question** Explain in detail the interrelationships between economic facts, theory, and policy. Critically evaluate this statement: "The trouble with economic theory is that it is not practical. It is detached from the real world."

6. To what extent do you accept the eight economic goals stated and described in this chapter? What priorities do you assign to them?

7. **Key Question** Indicate whether each of the following statements applies to microeconomics or macroeconomics:
   a. The unemployment rate in the United States was 4.2 percent in January 2001.
   b. The Alpo dog-food plant in Bowser, Iowa, laid off 15 workers last month.
   c. An unexpected freeze in central Florida reduced the citrus crop and caused the price of oranges to rise.
   d. U.S. output, adjusted for inflation, grew by 5 percent in 2000.
   e. Last week Wells Fargo Bank lowered its interest rate on business loans by one-half of 1 percentage point.
   f. The consumer price index rose by 3.4 percent in 2000.

8. **Key Question** Identify each of the following as either a positive or a normative statement:

   a. The high temperature today was 89 degrees.
   b. It was too hot today.
   c. Other things equal, higher interest rates reduce the total amount of borrowing.
   d. Interest rates are too high.

9. **Key Question** Explain and give an example of (*a*) the fallacy of composition, and (*b*) the "after this, therefore because of this," fallacy. Why are cause-and-effect relationships difficult to isolate in economics?

10. Suppose studies show that students who study more hours receive higher grades. Does this relationship guarantee that any particular student who studies longer will get higher grades?

11. Studies indicate that married men on average earn more income than unmarried men of the same age. Why must we be cautious in concluding that marriage is the *cause* and higher income is the *effect*?

12. **(Last Word)** Use the economic perspective to explain the behavior of the *workers* (rather than the customers) observed at a fast-food restaurant. Why are these workers there, rather than, say, cruising around in their cars? Why do they work so diligently? Why do so many of them quit these jobs once they have graduated high school?

13. **Web-Based Question:** *Three economic goals—are they being achieved?* Three major economic goals are economic growth (rises in real GDP), full employment (less than 5 percent unemployment), and price-level stability (less than 2 percent inflation as measured by the consumer price index, or CPI). The White House statistical website, www.whitehouse.gov/fsbr/esbr.html, provides links to economic information produced by a number of federal agencies. Visit the separate links for Employment, Output, and Prices to assess whether the United States is currently meeting each of these three goals.

14. **Web-Based Question:** *Normative economics—Republicans versus Democrats* Visit both the Republicans' www.rnc.org/ and the Democrats' www.democrats.org/ websites. Identify an economic issue that both parties address, and compare and contrast their views on that issue. Generally speaking, how much of the disagreement is based on normative economics compared to positive economics? Give an example of loaded terminology from each site.

Graphs and Their Meaning

If you glance quickly through this text, you will find many graphs. Some seem simple, while others seem more formidable. All are included to help you visualize and understand economic relationships. Physicists and chemists sometimes illustrate their theories by building arrangements of multicolored wooden balls, representing protons, neutrons, and electrons, which are held in proper relation to one another by wires or sticks. Economists most often use graphs to illustrate their models. By understanding these "pictures," you can more readily comprehend economic relationships. Most of our principles or models explain relationships between just two sets of economic facts, which can be conveniently represented with two-dimensional graphs.

Construction of a Graph

A *graph* is a visual representation of the relationship between two variables. Table 1 is a hypothetical illustration showing the relationship between income and consumption for the economy as a whole. Without even studying economics, we would expect intuitively that people would buy more goods and services when their incomes go up. Thus we are not surprised to find in Table 1 that total consumption in the economy increases as total income increases.

The information in Table 1 is expressed graphically in Figure 1. Here is how it is done: We want to show visually or graphically how consumption

changes as income changes. Since income is the determining factor, we represent it on the **horizontal axis** of the graph, as is customary. And because consumption depends on income, we represent it on the **vertical axis** of the graph, as is also customary. Actually, what we are doing is representing the *independent variable* on the horizontal axis and the *dependent variable* on the vertical axis.

Now we arrange the vertical and horizontal scales of the graph to reflect the ranges of values of consumption and income, and we mark the scales in convenient increments. As you can see, the values marked on the scales cover all the values in Table 1. The increments on both scales are $100 for approximately each $\frac{1}{2}$ inch.

Because the graph has two dimensions, each point within it represents an income value and its associated consumption value. To find a point that represents one of the five income-consumption combinations in Table 1, we draw perpendiculars from the appropriate values on the vertical and horizontal

Table 1
The Relationship between Income and Consumption

Income per Week	Consumption per Week	Point
$ 0	$ 50	a
100	100	b
200	150	c
300	200	d
400	250	e

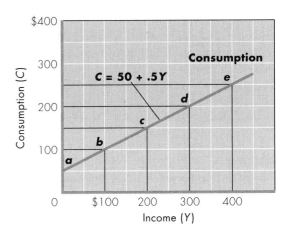

Figure 1

Graphing the direct relationship between consumption and income. Two sets of data that are positively or directly related, such as consumption and income, graph as an upsloping line.

15

axes. For example, to plot point *c* (the $200 income–$150 consumption point), we draw perpendiculars up from the horizontal (income) axis at $200 and across from the vertical (consumption) axis at $150. These perpendiculars intersect at point *c*, which represents this particular income-consumption combination. You should verify that the other income-consumption combinations shown in Table 1 are properly located in Figure 1. Finally, by assuming that the same general relationship between income and consumption prevails for all other incomes, we draw a line or smooth curve to connect these points. That line or curve represents the income-consumption relationship.

If the graph is a straight line, as in Figure 1, we say the relationship is *linear*.

Direct and Inverse Relationships

The line in Figure 1 slopes upward to the right, so it depicts a direct relationship between income and consumption. By a **direct relationship** (or positive relationship) we mean that two variables—in this case, consumption and income—change in the *same* direction. An increase in consumption is associated with an increase in income; a decrease in consumption accompanies a decrease in income. When two sets of data are positively or directly related, they always graph as an *upsloping* line, as in Figure 1.

In contrast, two sets of data may be inversely related. Consider Table 2, which shows the relationship between the price of basketball tickets and game attendance at Gigantic State University (GSU). Here we have an **inverse relationship** (or negative relationship) because the two variables change in *opposite* directions. When ticket prices decrease, attendance increases. When ticket prices increase, attendance decreases. The six data points in Table 2 are plotted

in Figure 2. Observe that an inverse relationship always graphs as a *downsloping* line.

Dependent and Independent Variables

Although it is not always easy, economists seek to determine which variable is the "cause" and which is the "effect." Or, more formally, they seek the independent variable and the dependent variable. The **independent variable** is the cause or source; it is the variable that changes first. The **dependent variable** is the effect or outcome; it is the variable that changes because of the change in the independent variable. As noted in our income-consumption example, income generally is the independent variable and consumption the dependent variable. Income causes consumption to be what it is rather than the other way around. Similarly, ticket prices (set in advance of the season) determine attendance at GSU basketball games; attendance at games does not determine the ticket prices for those games. Ticket price is the independent variable, and the quantity of tickets purchased is the dependent variable.

You may recall from your high school courses that mathematicians always put the independent variable (cause) on the horizontal axis and the depen-

Table 2

The Relationship between Ticket Prices and Attendance

Ticket Price	Attendance, Thousands	Point
$50	0	a
40	4	b
30	8	c
20	12	d
10	16	e
0	20	f

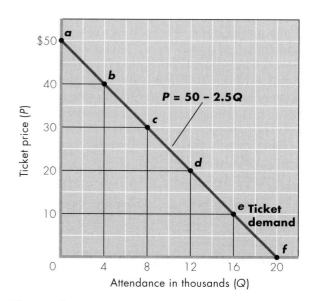

Figure 2

Graphing the inverse relationship between ticket prices and game attendance. Two sets of data that are negatively or inversely related, such as ticket price and the attendance at basketball games, graph as a downsloping line.

dent variable (effect) on the vertical axis. Economists are less tidy; their graphing of independent and dependent variables is more arbitrary. Their conventional graphing of the income-consumption relationship is consistent with mathematical presentation, but economists put price and cost data on the vertical axis. Hence, economists' graphing of GSU's ticket price–attendance data conflicts with normal mathematical procedure.

Other Things Equal

Our simple two-variable graphs purposely ignore many other factors that might affect the amount of consumption occurring at each income level or the number of people who attend GSU basketball games at each possible ticket price. When economists plot the relationship between any two variables, they employ the *ceteris paribus* (other-things-equal) assumption. Thus, in Figure 1 all factors other than income that might affect the amount of consumption are presumed to be constant or unchanged. Similarly, in Figure 2 all factors other than ticket price that might influence attendance at GSU basketball games are assumed constant. In reality, "other things" are not equal; they often change, and when they do, the relationship represented in our two tables and graphs will change. Specifically, the lines we have plotted would shift to new locations.

Consider a stock market "crash." The dramatic drop in the value of stocks might cause people to feel less wealthy and therefore less willing to consume at each level of income. The result might be a downward shift of the consumption line. To see this, you should plot a new consumption line in Figure 1, assuming that consumption is, say, $20 less at each income level. Note that the relationship remains direct; the line merely shifts downward to reflect less consumption spending at each income level.

Similarly, factors other than ticket prices might affect GSU game attendance. If GSU loses most of its games, attendance at GSU games might be less at each ticket price. To see this, redraw Figure 2, assuming that 2000 fewer fans attend GSU games at each ticket price. **(Key Appendix Question 2)**

Slope of a Line

Lines can be described in terms of their slopes. The **slope of a straight line** is the ratio of the vertical change (the rise or drop) to the horizontal change (the run) between any two points of the line.

Positive Slope   Between point *b* and point *c* in Figure 1 the rise or vertical change (the change in consumption) is +$50 and the run or horizontal change (the change in income) is +$100. Therefore:

$$\text{Slope} = \frac{\text{vertical change}}{\text{horizontal change}} = \frac{+50}{+100} = \frac{1}{2} = .5$$

Note that our slope of $\frac{1}{2}$ or .5 is positive because consumption and income change in the same direction; that is, consumption and income are directly or positively related.

The slope of .5 tells us there will be a $1 increase in consumption for every $2 increase in income. Similarly, it indicates that for every $2 decrease in income there will be a $1 decrease in consumption.

Negative Slope   Between any two of the identified points in Figure 2, say, point *c* and point *d*, the vertical change is −10 (the drop) and the horizontal change is +4 (the run). Therefore:

$$\text{Slope} = \frac{\text{vertical change}}{\text{horizontal change}} = \frac{-10}{+4}$$

$$= -2\frac{1}{2} = -2.5$$

This slope is negative because ticket price and attendance have an inverse relationship.

Note that on the horizontal axis attendance is stated in thousands of people. So the slope of −10/+4 or −2.5 means that lowering the price by $10 will increase attendance by 4000 people. This is the same as saying that a $2.50 price reduction will increase attendance by 1000 persons.

Slopes and Measurement Units   The slope of a line will be affected by the choice of units for either variable. If, in our ticket price illustration, we had chosen to measure attendance in individual people, our horizontal change would have been 4000 and the slope would have been

$$\text{Slope} = \frac{-10}{+4000} = \frac{-1}{+400} = -.0025$$

The slope depends on the way the relevant variables are measured.

Slopes and Marginal Analysis   Recall that economics is largely concerned with changes from the status quo. The concept of slope is important in economics because it reflects marginal changes—

those involving 1 more (or 1 less) unit. For example, in Figure 1 the .5 slope shows that $.50 of extra or marginal consumption is associated with each $1 change in income. In this example, people collectively will consume $.50 of any $1 increase in their incomes and reduce their consumption by $.50 for each $1 decline in income.

Infinite and Zero Slopes

Many variables are unrelated or independent of one another. For example, the quantity of wristwatches purchased is not related to the price of bananas. In Figure 3a we represent the price of bananas on the vertical axis and the quantity of watches demanded on the horizontal axis. The graph of their relationship is the line parallel to the vertical axis, indicating that the same quantity of watches is purchased no matter what the price of bananas. The slope of such a line is *infinite*.

Similarly, aggregate consumption is completely unrelated to the nation's divorce rate. In Figure 3b we put consumption on the vertical axis and the divorce rate on the horizontal axis. The line parallel to the horizontal axis represents this lack of relatedness. This line has a slope of *zero*.

Vertical Intercept

A line can be located on a graph (without plotting points) if we know its slope and its vertical intercept. The **vertical intercept** of a line is the point where the line meets the vertical axis. In Figure 1 the intercept is $50. This intercept means that if current income were zero, consumers would still spend $50. They might do this through borrowing or by selling some of their assets. Similarly, the $50 vertical intercept in Figure 2 shows that at a $50 ticket price, GSU's basketball team would be playing in an empty arena.

Equation of a Linear Relationship

If we know the vertical intercept and slope, we can describe a line succinctly in equation form. In its general form, the equation of a straight line is

$$y = a + bx$$

where y = dependent variable
a = vertical intercept
b = slope of line
x = independent variable

For our income-consumption example, if C represents consumption (the dependent variable) and Y represents income (the independent variable), we can write $C = a + bY$. By substituting the known values of the intercept and the slope, we get

$$C = 50 + .5Y$$

This equation also allows us to determine the amount of consumption C at any specific level of income. You should use it to confirm that at the $250 income level, consumption is $175.

When economists reverse mathematical convention by putting the independent variable on the vertical axis and the dependent variable on the horizontal axis, then y stands for the independent variable, rather than the dependent variable in the general form. We noted previously that this case is relevant for our GSU ticket price–attendance data. If P represents the ticket price (independent variable) and Q represents attendance (dependent variable), their relationship is given by

$$P = 50 - 2.5Q$$

where the vertical intercept is 50 and the negative slope is $-2\frac{1}{2}$ or -2.5. Knowing the value of P lets us solve for Q, our dependent variable. You should use

Figure 3

Infinite and zero slopes. (a) A line parallel to the vertical axis has an infinite slope. Here, purchases of watches remain the same no matter what happens to the price of bananas. (b) A line parallel to the horizontal axis has a slope of zero. Here, consumption remains the same no matter what happens to the divorce rate. In both (a) and (b), the two variables are totally unrelated to one another.

this equation to predict GSU ticket sales when the ticket price is $15. **(Key Appendix Question 3)**

Slope of a Nonlinear Curve

We now move from the simple world of linear relationships (straight lines) to the more complex world of nonlinear relationships. The slope of a straight line is the same at all its points. The slope of a line representing a nonlinear relationship changes from one point to another. Such lines are referred to as *curves*. (It is also permissible to refer to a straight line as a "curve.")

Consider the downsloping curve in Figure 4. Its slope is negative throughout, but the curve flattens as we move down along it. Thus, its slope constantly changes; the curve has a different slope at each point.

To measure the slope at a specific point, we draw a straight line tangent to the curve at that point. A line is *tangent* at a point if it touches, but does not intersect, the curve at that point. Thus line *aa* is tangent to the curve in Figure 4 at point *A*. The slope of the curve at that point is equal to the slope of the tangent line. Specifically, the total vertical change (drop) in the tangent line *aa* is −20 and the total horizontal change (run) is +5. Because the slope of the tangent line *aa* is −20/+5, or −4, the slope of the curve at point *A* is also −4.

Line *bb* in Figure 4 is tangent to the curve at point *B*. Following the same procedure, we find the slope at *B* to be −5/+15, or −$\frac{1}{3}$. Thus, in this flatter part of the curve, the slope is less negative. **(Key Appendix Question 6)**

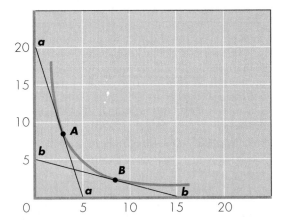

Figure 4

Determining the slopes of curves. The slope of a nonlinear curve changes from point to point on the curve. The slope at any point (say, *B*) can be determined by drawing a straight line that is tangent to that point (line *bb*) and calculating the slope of that line.

APPENDIX SUMMARY

1. Graphs are a convenient and revealing way to represent economic relationships.

2. Two variables are positively or directly related when their values change in the same direction. The line (curve) representing two directly related variables slopes upward.

3. Two variables are negatively or inversely related when their values change in opposite directions. The curve representing two inversely related variables slopes downward.

4. The value of the dependent variable (the "effect") is determined by the value of the independent variable (the "cause").

5. When the "other factors" that might affect a two-variable relationship are allowed to change, the graph of the relationship will likely shift to a new location.

6. The slope of a straight line is the ratio of the vertical change to the horizontal change between any two points. The slope of an upsloping line is positive; the slope of a downsloping line is negative.

7. The slope of a line or curve depends on the units used in measuring the variables. It is especially relevant for economics because it measures marginal changes.

8. The slope of a horizontal line is zero; the slope of a vertical line is infinite.

9. The vertical intercept and slope of a line determine its location; they are used in expressing the line—and the relationship between the two variables—as an equation.

10. The slope of a curve at any point is determined by calculating the slope of a straight line tangent to the curve at that point.

APPENDIX TERMS AND CONCEPTS

horizontal axis

vertical axis

direct relationship

inverse relationship

independent variable

dependent variable

slope of a straight line

vertical intercept

APPENDIX STUDY QUESTIONS

1. Briefly explain the use of graphs as a way to represent economic relationships. What is an inverse relationship? How does it graph? What is a direct relationship? How does it graph? Graph and explain the relationships you would expect to find between (*a*) the number of inches of rainfall per month and the sale of umbrellas, (*b*) the amount of tuition and the level of enrollment at a university, and (*c*) the popularity of an entertainer and the price of her concert tickets.

   In each case cite and explain how variables other than those specifically mentioned might upset the expected relationship. Is your graph in part *b*, above, consistent with the fact that, historically, enrollments and tuition have both increased? If not, explain any difference.

2. **Key Appendix Question** Indicate how each of the following might affect the data shown in Table 2 and Figure 2 of this appendix:
   a. GSU's athletic director schedules higher-quality opponents.
   b. An NBA team locates in the city where GSU plays.
   c. GSU contracts to have all its home games televised.

3. **Key Appendix Question** The following table contains data on the relationship between saving and income. Rearrange these data into a meaningful order and graph them on the accompanying grid. What is the slope of the line? The vertical intercept? Interpret the meaning of both the slope and the intercept. Write the equation that represents this line. What would you predict saving to be at the $12,500 level of income?

Income per Year	Saving per Year
$15,000	$1,000
0	−500
10,000	500
5,000	0
20,000	1,500

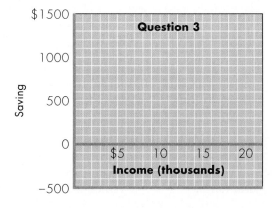

4. Construct a table from the data shown on the graph below. Which is the dependent variable and which the independent variable? Summarize the data in equation form.

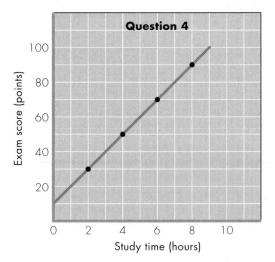

5. Suppose that when the interest rate on loans is 16 percent, businesses find it unprofitable to invest in machinery and equipment. However, when the interest rate is 14 percent, $5 billion worth of investment is profitable. At 12 percent interest, a total of $10 billion of investment is profitable. Similarly, total investment increases by $5 billion for each successive 2-percentage-point decline in the interest rate. Describe the relevant relationship between the interest rate and investment in words, in a table, on a graph, and as an equation. Put the interest rate on the vertical axis and investment on the horizontal axis. In your equation use the form $i = a + bI$, where i is the interest rate, a is the vertical intercept, b is the slope of the line (which is negative), and I is the level of investment. Comment on the advantages and disadvantages of the verbal, tabular, graphical, and equation forms of description.

6. **Key Appendix Question** The accompanying graph shows curve *XX'* and tangents at points *A*, *B*, and *C*. Calculate the slope of the curve at these three points.

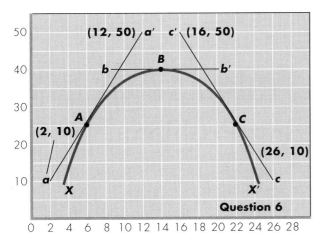

Question 6

7. In the accompanying graph, is the slope of curve *AA'* positive or negative? Does the slope increase or decrease as we move along the curve from *A* to *A'*? Answer the same two questions for curve *BB'*.

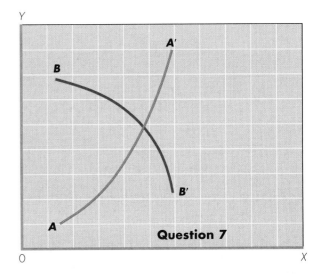

Question 7

2

The Economizing Problem

YOU MAKE DECISIONS every day that capture the essence of economics. Suppose you have $40 and are deciding how to spend it. Should you buy a new pair of jeans? Two or three compact discs? A ticket for a concert? ■ Should you forgo work while you are attending college and concentrate solely on your coursework and grades? Is that an option for you, given the high cost of college? If you decide to work, should it be full-time or part-time? Should you work on campus at lower pay or off campus at higher pay? What are the implications of your employment for your course grades? ■ Money and time are both scarce, and making decisions in the context of scarcity always means there are costs. If you choose the jeans, the cost is the forgone CDs or concert. If you work full-time, the cost might be greater stress, poorer performance in your classes, or an extra year or two in college. ■ This chapter examines the fundamentals of economics—scarcity, choices, and costs. We first examine the *economizing problem*, focusing closely on *wants* and *resources*. Next, we develop two economic models: (1) a *production possibilities model* that incorporates and illustrates several key ideas, and (2) a simple *circular flow model* that identifies the major groups of decision makers and major markets in the economy.

■ The Foundation of Economics

Two fundamental facts together constitute the **economizing problem** and provide a foundation for economics:

■ Society's economic wants—that is, the economic wants of its citizens and institutions—are virtually unlimited and insatiable.

■ Economic resources—the means of producing goods and services—are limited or scarce.

All that follows depends directly on these two facts.

Unlimited Wants

What do we mean by "economic wants"? We mean, first, the desires of consumers to obtain and use various goods and services that provide **utility**—that is, pleasure or satisfaction. These wants extend over a wide range of products, from *necessities* (food, shelter, clothing) to *luxuries* (perfumes, yachts, race cars).

Some wants—basic food, clothing, and shelter—have biological roots. Other wants—for example, the specific kinds of food, clothing, and shelter we seek—are rooted in the conventions and customs of society.

Over time, wants change and tend to multiply, fueled by new products. Not long ago, we did not want personal computers, Internet service, digital recorders, lattes, or pagers because they simply did not exist. Also, the satisfaction of certain wants tends to trigger others: the acquisition of a Neon or Civic has been known to whet the appetite for a Porsche or a Mercedes.

Services, as well as products, satisfy our wants. Car repair work, the removal of an inflamed appendix, legal and accounting advice, and haircuts all satisfy human wants. Actually, we buy many goods, such as automobiles and washing machines, for the services they render. The differences between goods and services are often smaller than they appear to be.

Businesses and units of government also strive to satisfy economic goals. Businesses want factories, machinery, trucks, warehouses, and phone systems to help them achieve their production goals. Government, reflecting the collective wants of its citizens or goals of its own, seeks highways, schools, and military equipment.

All these wants are *insatiable*, or *unlimited*, meaning that our desires for goods and services cannot be completely satisfied. Our desires for a *particular* good or service can be satisfied; over a short period of time we can surely get enough toothpaste or pasta. And one appendectomy is plenty. But goods *in general* are another story. We do not, and presumably cannot, get enough. Suppose all members of society were asked to list the goods and services they would buy if they had unlimited income. That list would probably never end.

In short, individuals and institutions have innumerable unfilled wants. *The objective of all economic activity is to fulfill wants.* 🔎 2.1

Scarce Resources

The second fundamental fact is that *economic resources are limited or scarce.* By **economic resources** we mean all natural, human, and manufactured resources that go into the production of goods and services. That includes all the factory and farm buildings and all the equipment, tools, and machinery used to produce manufactured goods and agricultural products; all transportation and communication facilities; all types of labor; and land and min-

eral resources. Economists classify all these resources as either *property* resources—land, raw materials, and capital—or *human* resources—labor and entrepreneurial ability.

Resource Categories   Let's look at four specific categories of economic resources.

Land   **Land** means much more to the economist than it does to most people. To the economist land includes all natural resources—all "gifts of nature"—that are used in the production process, such as arable land, forests, mineral and oil deposits, and water resources.

Capital   **Capital** (or *capital goods* or *investment goods*) includes all manufactured aids used in producing consumer goods and services—that is, all tools, machinery, equipment, factory, storage, transportation, and distribution facilities. The process of producing and purchasing capital goods is known as **investment.**

Capital goods differ from *consumer goods* in that consumer goods satisfy wants directly, while capital goods do so indirectly by aiding the production of consumer goods. Note that the term "capital" as used by economists refers *not* to money but to *real capital*—tools, machinery, and other productive equipment. Money produces nothing; it is *not* an economic resource. So-called money capital or financial capital is simply a means for purchasing real capital.

Labor   **Labor** is a broad term for all the physical and mental talents of individuals available and usable in producing goods and services. The services of a logger, retail clerk, machinist, teacher, professional football player, and nuclear physicist all fall under the general heading "labor."

Entrepreneurial Ability   Finally, there is the special human resource, distinct from labor, that we label **entrepreneurial ability.** The entrepreneur performs several functions:

- The entrepreneur *takes the initiative* in combining the resources of land, capital, and labor to produce a good or a service. Both a sparkplug and a catalyst, the entrepreneur is the driving force behind production and the agent who combines the other resources in what is hoped will be a successful business venture.

- The entrepreneur *makes basic business-policy decisions*—that is, the nonroutine decisions that set the course of a business enterprise.

■ The entrepreneur is an *innovator*—the one who commercializes new products, new production techniques, or even new forms of business organization.

■ The entrepreneur is a *risk bearer.* The entrepreneur in a market system has no guarantee of profit. The reward for the entrepreneur's time, efforts, and abilities may be profits *or* losses. The entrepreneur risks not only his or her invested funds but those of associates and stockholders as well.

Because these four resources—land, labor, capital, and entrepreneurial ability—are combined to *produce* goods and services, they are called the **factors of production.**

Resource Payments   The income received from supplying raw materials and capital equipment (the property resources) is called *rental income* and *interest income*, respectively. The income accruing to those who supply labor is called *wages*, which include salaries and all wage and salary supplements such as bonuses, commissions, and royalties. Entrepreneurial income is called *profits*, which may be negative—that is, losses.

Relative Scarcity   The four types of economic resources, or factors of production, or *inputs*, have one significant characteristic in common: *They are scarce or limited in supply.* Our planet contains only finite, and therefore limited, amounts of arable land, mineral deposits, capital equipment, and labor. Their scarcity constrains productive activity and output. In the United States, one of the most affluent nations, output per person was limited to roughly $34,000 in 2000. In the poorest nations, annual output per person may be as low as $300 or $400.

▌ Economics: Employment and Efficiency

The economizing problem is at the heart of the definition of economics stated in Chapter 1: *Economics is the social science concerned with the problem of using scarce resources to attain the maximum fulfillment of society's unlimited wants.* Economics is concerned with "doing the best with what we have."

Economics is thus the social science that examines efficiency—the best use of scarce resources. Society wants to use its limited resources efficiently; it desires to produce as many goods and services as possible from its available resources, thereby maximizing total satisfaction.

Full Employment: Using Available Resources

To realize the best use of scarce resources, a society must achieve both full employment and full production. By **full employment** we mean the use of all available resources. No workers should be out of work if they are willing and able to work. Nor should capital equipment or arable land sit idle. But note that we say all *available* resources should be employed. Each society has certain customs and practices that determine what resources are available for employment and what resources are not. For example, in most countries legislation and custom provide that children and the very aged should not be employed. Similarly, to maintain productivity, farmland should be allowed to lie fallow periodically. And we should conserve some resources—fishing stocks and forest, for instance—for use by future generations.

Full Production: Using Resources Efficiently

The employment of all available resources is not enough to achieve efficiency, however. Full production must also be realized. By **full production** we mean that all employed resources should be used so that they provide the maximum possible satisfaction of our material wants. If we fail to realize full production, economists say our resources are *underemployed.*

Full production implies two kinds of efficiency—productive and allocative efficiency. **Productive efficiency** is the production of *any particular mix of goods and services in the least costly way.* When we produce, say, compact discs at the lowest achievable unit cost, we are expending the smallest amount of resources to produce CDs and are therefore making available the largest amount of resources to produce other desired products. Suppose society has only $100 worth of resources available. If we can produce a CD for only $5 of those resources, then $95 will be available to produce other goods. This is clearly better than producing the CD for $10 and having only $90 of resources available for alternative uses.

In contrast, **allocative efficiency** is the production of *that particular mix of goods and services most wanted by society.* For example, society wants resources allocated to compact discs, not to 45-rpm records. We want personal computers (PCs), not manual typewriters. Furthermore, we do not want to devote *all* our resources to producing CDs and PCs; we want to assign some of them to producing automobiles and office buildings. Allocative efficiency requires that an economy produce the "right" mix of goods and services, with each item being produced at the lowest-possible unit cost. This means apportioning limited resources among firms and industries in such a way that society obtains the combination of goods and services it wants the most. **(Key Question 5)**

QUICK REVIEW 2.1

■ People's economic wants are virtually unlimited.

■ Economic resources—land, capital, labor, and entrepreneurial ability—are scarce.

■ Economics is concerned with the efficient allocation of scarce resources to achieve the maximum fulfillment of society's economic wants.

■ Economic efficiency embodies full employment and full production.

■ Full production requires both productive and allocative efficiency.

Production Possibilities Table

Because resources are scarce, a full-employment, full-production economy cannot have an unlimited output of goods and services. Consequently, people must choose which goods and services to produce and which to forgo. The necessity and consequences of those choices can best be understood through a *production possibilities model*. We examine the model first as a table and then as a graph.

Assumptions   We begin our discussion of the production possibilities model with simplifying assumptions:

■ *Full employment and productive efficiency*   The economy is employing all its available resources (full employment) and is producing goods and services at least cost (productive efficiency).

■ *Fixed resources*   The available supplies of the factors of production are fixed in both quantity and quality. Nevertheless, they can be reallocated, within limits, among different uses; for example, land can be used either for factory sites or for food production.

■ *Fixed technology*   The state of technology—the methods used to produce output—does not change during our analysis. This assumption and the previous one imply that we are looking at an economy at a certain point in time or over a very short period of time.

■ *Two goods*   The economy is producing only two goods: pizzas and industrial robots. Pizzas symbolize **consumer goods,** products that satisfy our wants *directly;* industrial robots symbolize **capital goods,** products that satisfy our wants *indirectly* by making possible more efficient production of consumer goods.

The Need for Choice   Given our assumptions, we see that society must choose among alternatives. Fixed resources mean limited outputs of pizza and robots. And since all available resources are fully employed, to increase the production of robots we must shift resources away from the production of pizzas. The reverse is also true: To increase the production of pizzas, we must shift resources away from the production of robots. There is no such thing as a free pizza. This, recall, is the essence of the economizing problem.

A **production possibilities table** lists the different combinations of two products that can be produced with a specific set of resources (and with full employment *and* productive efficiency). Table 2.1 is such a table for a pizza-robot economy; the data are, of course, hypothetical. At alternative A, this economy would be devoting all its available resources to the production of robots (capital goods); at alternative E, all resources would go to pizza production (consumer goods). Those alternatives are unrealistic extremes; an economy typically produces both capital goods and consumer goods, as in B, C, and D. As we move from alternative A to E, we increase the production of pizza at the expense of robot production.

Because consumer goods satisfy our wants directly, any movement toward E looks tempting. In producing more pizzas, society increases the current satisfaction of its wants. But there is a cost: more pizzas mean fewer robots. This shift of resources to consumer goods catches up with society over time as the stock of capital goods dwindles—or at least

Table 2.1

Production Possibilities of Pizzas and Robots with Full Employment and Productive Efficiency

Type of Product	Production Alternatives				
	A	B	C	D	E
Pizzas (in hundred thousands)	0	1	2	3	4
Robots (in thousands)	10	9	7	4	0

K E Y   G R A P H

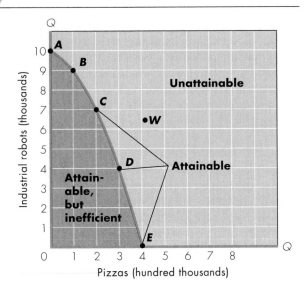

Figure 2.1

The production possibilities curve. Each point on the production possibilities curve represents some maximum combination of two products that can be produced if full employment and full production are achieved. When operating on the curve, more robots means fewer pizzas, and vice versa. Limited resources and a fixed technology make any combination of robots and pizzas lying outside the curve (such as at *W*) unattainable. Points inside the curve are attainable, but they indicate that full employment and productive efficiency are not being realized.

---

ceases to expand at the current rate—with the result that some potential for greater future production is lost. By moving toward alternative E, society chooses "more now" at the expense of "much more later."

By moving toward A, society chooses to forgo current consumption, thereby freeing up resources that can be used to increase the production of capital goods. By building up its stock of capital this way, society will have greater future production and, therefore, greater future consumption. By moving toward A, society is choosing "more later" at the cost of "less now."

Generalization: *At any point in time, an economy achieving full employment and productive efficiency must* *sacrifice some of one good to obtain more of another good. Scarce resources prohibit such an economy from having more of both goods.*

Production Possibilities Curve

The data presented in a production possibilities table can also be shown graphically. We use a simple two-dimensional graph, arbitrarily representing the output of capital goods (here, robots) on the vertical axis and the output of consumer goods (here, pizzas) on the horizontal axis, as shown in **Figure 2.1 (Key Graph).** Following the procedure given in the appendix to Chapter 1, we can graph a **production possibilities curve.** ⌐ 2.1

Each point on the production possibilities curve represents some maximum output of the two products. The curve is a production *frontier* because it shows the limit of attainable outputs. To obtain the various combinations of pizza and robots that fall *on* the production possibilities curve, society must achieve both full employment and productive efficiency. Points lying *inside* (to the left of) the curve are also attainable, but they reflect inefficiency and therefore are not as desirable as points on the curve. Points inside the curve imply that the economy could have more of both robots and pizzas if it achieved full employment and productive efficiency. Points lying *outside* (to the right of) the production possibilities curve, like point *W*, would represent a greater output than the output at any point on the curve. Such points, however, are unattainable with the current supplies of resources and technology.

Law of Increasing Opportunity Cost

Because resources are scarce relative to the virtually unlimited wants they can be used to satisfy, people must choose among alternatives. More pizzas mean fewer robots. The amount of other products that must be forgone or sacrificed to obtain 1 unit of a specific good is called the **opportunity cost** of that good. In our case, the number of robots that must be given up to get another unit of pizza is the *opportunity cost*, or simply the *cost*, of that unit of pizza. 🔑 2.2 ❗ 2.1

In moving from alternative A to alternative B in Table 2.1, we find that the cost of 1 additional unit of pizza is 1 less unit of robots. But as we pursue the concept of cost through the additional production possibilities—B to C, C to D, and D to E—an important economic principle is revealed: The opportunity cost of each additional unit of pizza is greater than the opportunity cost of the preceding one. When we move from A to B, just 1 unit of robots is sacrificed for 1 more unit of pizza; but in going from B to C we sacrifice 2 additional units of robots for 1 more unit of pizza; then 3 more of robots for 1 more of pizza; and finally 4 for 1. Conversely, confirm that as we move from E to A, the cost of an additional robot is $\frac{1}{4}$, $\frac{1}{3}$, $\frac{1}{2}$, and 1 unit of pizza, respectively, for the four successive moves.

Note these points about these opportunity costs:

■ Here opportunity costs are being measured in *real* terms, that is, in actual goods rather than in money terms.

■ We are discussing *marginal* (meaning "extra") opportunity costs, rather than cumulative or total opportunity costs. For example, the marginal opportunity cost of the third unit of pizza in Table 2.1 is 3 units of robots (=7 − 4). But the *total* opportunity cost of 3 units of pizza is 6 units of robots (=1 unit of robots for the first unit of pizza *plus* 2 units of robots for the second unit of pizza *plus* 3 units of robots for the third unit of pizza).

Our example illustrates the **law of increasing opportunity costs:** The more of a product that is produced, the greater is its opportunity cost ("marginal" being implied).

Shape of the Curve   The law of increasing opportunity costs is reflected in the shape of the production possibilities curve: The curve is bowed out from the origin of the graph. Figure 2.1 shows that when the economy moves from *A* to *E*, it must give up successively larger amounts of robots (1, 2, 3, and 4) to acquire equal increments of pizza (1, 1, 1, and 1). This is shown in the slope of the production possibilities curve, which becomes steeper as we move from *A* to *E*. A curve that gets steeper as we move down it is "concave to the origin."

Economic Rationale   What is the economic rationale for the law of increasing opportunity costs? Why does the sacrifice of robots increase as we produce more pizzas? The answer is that *economic resources are not completely adaptable to alternative uses.* Many resources are better at producing one good than at producing others. Fertile farmland is highly suited to producing the ingredients needed to make pizzas, while land rich in mineral deposits is highly suited to producing the materials needed to make robots. As we step up pizza production, resources that are less and less adaptable to making pizzas must be "pushed" into pizza production. If we start at *A* and move to *B*, we can shift the resources whose productivity of pizzas is greatest in relation to their productivity of robots. But as we move from *B* to *C*, *C* to *D*, and so on, resources highly productive of pizzas become increasingly scarce. To get more pizzas, resources whose productivity of robots is great in relation to their productivity of pizzas will be needed. It will take more and more of such resources, and hence greater sacrifices of robots, to achieve each increase of 1 unit in the production of pizzas. This lack of perfect flexibility, or interchangeability, on the part of resources is the cause of increasing opportunity costs. **(Key Question 6)**

Allocative Efficiency Revisited

So far, we have assumed full employment and productive efficiency, both of which are necessary to realize *any point* on an economy's production possibilities curve. We now turn to allocative efficiency, which requires that the economy produce at the most valued, or *optimal*, point on the production possibilities curve. Of all the attainable combinations of pizzas and robots on the curve in Figure 2.1, which is best? That is, what specific quantities of resources should be allocated to pizzas and what specific quantities to robots in order to maximize satisfaction?

Our discussion of the *economic perspective* in Chapter 1 puts us on the right track. Recall that economic decisions center on comparisons of marginal benefits and marginal costs. Any economic activity—for example, production or consumption—should be expanded as long as marginal benefit exceeds marginal cost and should be reduced if marginal cost exceeds marginal benefit. The optimal amount of the activity occurs where MB = MC.

Consider pizzas. We already know from the law of increasing opportunity costs that the marginal cost (MC) of additional units of pizzas will rise as more units are produced. This can be shown by an upsloping MC curve, as in Figure 2.2. We also know

that we obtain extra or marginal benefits (MB) from additional units of pizzas. However, although material wants in the aggregate are insatiable, studies reveal that the second unit of a particular product yields less additional utility or benefit to a person than the first. And a third provides even less MB than the second. So it is for society as a whole. We therefore can portray the marginal benefits from pizzas with a downsloping MB curve, as in Figure 2.2. Although total benefits rise when society consumes more pizza, marginal benefits decline.

The optimal quantity of pizza production is indicated by the intersection of the MB and MC curves: 200,000 units in Figure 2.2. Why is this the optimal quantity? If only 100,000 pizzas were produced, the marginal benefit of pizza would exceed its marginal cost. In money terms, MB might be $15, while MC is only $5. This suggests that society would be *underallocating* resources to pizza production and that more of it should be produced.

How do we know? Because society values an additional pizza as being worth $15, while the alternative products that those resources could produce are worth only $5. Society benefits—it is better off in the sense of having a higher-valued output to enjoy—whenever it can gain something worth $15 by forgoing something worth only $5. Society would use its resources more efficiently by allocating more resources to pizza. Each additional pizza up to 200,000 would provide such a gain, indicating that allocative efficiency would be improved by that production. But when MB = MC, the benefits of producing pizzas or alternative products with the available resources are equal. Allocative efficiency is achieved where MB = MC.

The production of 300,000 pizzas would represent an *overallocation* of resources to pizza production. Here the MC of pizza is $15 and its MB is only $5. This means that 1 unit of pizza is worth only $5 to society, while the alternative products that those resources could otherwise produce are valued at $15. By producing 1 less unit, society loses a pizza worth $5. But by reallocating the freed resources, it gains other products worth $15. When society gains something worth $15 by forgoing something worth only $5, it is better off. In Figure 2.2, such net gains can be realized until pizza production has been reduced to 200,000.

Generalization: *Resources are being efficiently allocated to any product when the marginal benefit and marginal cost of its output are equal (MB = MC).* Suppose that by applying the above analysis to robots, we find

Figure 2.2

Allocative efficiency: MB = MC. Allocative efficiency requires the expansion of a good's output until its marginal benefit (MB) and marginal cost (MC) are equal. No resources beyond that point should get allocated to the product. Here, allocative efficiency occurs when 200,000 pizzas are produced.

their optimal (MB = MC) output is 7000. This would mean that alternative *C* on our production possibilities curve—200,000 pizzas and 7000 robots—would result in allocative efficiency for our hypothetical economy. **(Key Question 9)**

QUICK REVIEW 2.2

■ The production possibilities curve illustrates four concepts: (a) *scarcity* of resources is implied by the area of unattainable combinations of output lying outside the production possibilities curve; (b) *choice* among outputs is reflected in the variety of attainable combinations of goods lying along the curve; (c) *opportunity cost* is illustrated by the downward slope of the curve; (d) the law of *increasing opportunity costs* is implied by the concavity of the curve.

■ Full employment and productive efficiency must be realized in order for the economy to operate on its production possibilities curve.

■ A comparison of marginal benefits and marginal costs is needed to determine allocative efficiency—the best or optimal output mix on the curve.

■ Unemployment, Growth, and the Future

Let's now discard the first three assumptions underlying the production possibilities curve and see what happens.

Unemployment and Productive Inefficiency

The first assumption was that our economy was achieving full employment and productive efficiency. Our analysis and conclusions change if some resources are idle (unemployment) or if least-cost production is not realized. The five alternatives in Table 2.1 represent maximum outputs; they illustrate the combinations of robots and pizzas that can be produced when the economy is operating at full capacity—with full employment and productive efficiency. With unemployment or inefficient production, the economy would produce less than each alternative shown in the table.

Graphically, we represent situations of unemployment or productive inefficiency by points *inside* the original production possibilities curve (reproduced in Figure 2.3). Point *U* is one such point.

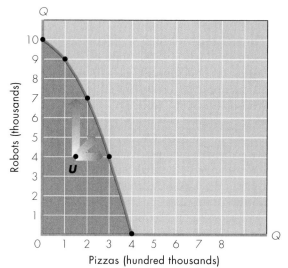

Figure 2.3

Unemployment, productive inefficiency, and the production possibilities curve. Any point inside the production possibilities curve, such as *U*, represents unemployment or a failure to achieve productive efficiency. The arrows indicate that, by realizing full employment and productive efficiency, the economy could operate on the curve. This means it could produce more of one or both products than it is producing at point *U*.

Here the economy is falling short of the various maximum combinations of pizzas and robots represented by the points *on* the production possibilities curve. The arrows in Figure 2.3 indicate three possible paths back to full-employment and least-cost production. A move toward full employment and productive efficiency would yield a greater output of one or both products.

A Growing Economy

When we drop the assumption that the quantity and quality of resources and technology are fixed, the production possibilities curve shifts positions—that is, the potential maximum output of the economy changes.

Increases in Resource Supplies Although resource supplies are fixed at any specific moment, they can and do change over time. For example, a nation's growing population will bring about increases in the supplies of labor and entrepreneurial ability. Also, labor quality usually improves over time. Historically, the economy's stock of capital has increased at a significant, though unsteady, rate. And although we are depleting some of our energy and mineral resources, new sources are being discovered.

The development of irrigation programs, for example, adds to the supply of arable land.

The net result of these increased supplies of the factors of production is the ability to produce more of both pizzas and robots. Thus 20 years from now, the production possibilities in Table 2.2 may supersede those shown in Table 2.1. The greater abundance of resources will result in a greater potential output of one or both products at each alternative. Society will have achieved economic growth in the form of expanded potential output.

But such a favorable change in the production possibilities data does not *guarantee* that the economy will actually operate at a point on its new production possibilities curve. Some 135 million jobs will give the United States full employment now, but 10 or 20 years from now its labor force will be larger, and 135 million jobs will not be sufficient for full employment. The production possibilities curve may shift, but at the future date the economy may fail to produce at a point on that new curve.

Advances in Technology
Our second assumption is that we have constant, unchanging technology. In reality, though, technology has progressed dramatically over time. An advancing technology brings both new and better goods *and* improved ways of producing them. For now, let's think of technological advances as being only improvements in capital facilities—more efficient machinery and equipment. These advances alter our previous discussion of the economizing problem by improving productive efficiency, thereby allowing society to produce more goods with fixed resources. As with increases in resource supplies, technological advances make possible the production of more robots *and* more pizzas.

Thus, when either supplies of resources increase or an improvement in technology occurs, the pro-

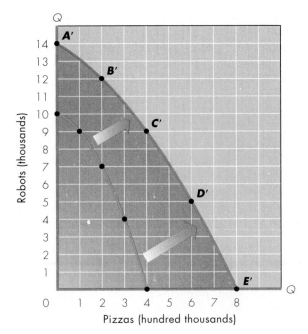

Figure 2.4

Economic growth and the production possibilities curve. The increase in supplies of resources, the improvements in resource quality, and the technological advances that occur in a dynamic economy move the production possibilities curve outward and to the right, allowing the economy to have larger quantities of both types of goods.

duction possibilities curve in Figure 2.3 shifts outward and to the right, as illustrated by curve *A'*, *B'*, *C'*, *D'*, *E'* in Figure 2.4. Such an outward shift of the production possibilities curve represents growth of economic capacity or, simply, **economic growth:** *the ability to produce a larger total output*. This growth is the result of (1) increases in supplies of resources, (2) improvements in resource quality, and (3) technological advances.

The consequence of growth is that our full-employment economy can enjoy a greater output of both robots and pizzas. *While a static, no-growth economy must sacrifice some of one product in order to get more of another, a dynamic, growing economy can have larger quantities of both products.*

Economic growth does not ordinarily mean proportionate increases in a nation's capacity to produce all its products. Note in Figure 2.4 that, at the maximums, the economy can produce twice as many pizzas as before but only 40 percent more robots. To reinforce your understanding of this concept, sketch in two new production possibilities curves: one show-

Table 2.2

Production Possibilities of Pizza and Robots with Full Employment and Productive Efficiency

Type of Product	Production Alternatives				
	A'	B'	C'	D'	E'
Pizzas (in hundred thousands)	0	2	4	6	8
Robots (in thousands)	14	12	9	5	0

ing the situation where a better technique for producing robots has been developed while the technology for producing pizzas is unchanged, and the other illustrating an improved technology for pizzas while the technology for producing robots remains constant.

Present Choices and Future Possibilities

An economy's current choice of positions on its production possibilities curve is a basic determinant of the future location of that curve. Let's designate the two axes of the production possibilities curve as *goods for the future* and *goods for the present*, as in Figure 2.5. Goods for the future are such things as capital goods, research and education, and preventive medicine. They increase the quantity and quality of property resources, enlarge the stock of technological information, and improve the quality of human resources. As we have already seen, goods for the future, like industrial robots, are the ingredients of economic growth. Goods for the present are pure consumer goods, such as pizza, clothing, and soft drinks.

Now suppose there are two economies, Alta and Zorn, which are initially identical in every respect except one: Alta's current choice of positions on its production possibilities curve strongly favors present goods over future goods. Point *A* in Figure 2.5a indicates that choice. It is located quite far down the curve to the right, indicating a high priority for goods for the present, at the expense of fewer goods for the future. Zorn, in contrast, makes a current choice that stresses larger amounts of future goods and smaller amounts of present goods, as shown by point *Z* in Figure 2.5b.

Now, other things equal, we can expect the future production possibilities curve of Zorn to be farther to the right than Alta's curve. By currently choosing an output more favorable to technological advances and to increases in the quantity and quality of resources, Zorn will achieve greater economic growth than Alta. In terms of capital goods, Zorn is choosing to make larger current additions to its "national factory"—to invest more of its current output—than Alta. The payoff from this choice for Zorn is more rapid growth—greater future production capacity. The opportunity cost is fewer consumer goods in the present for Zorn to enjoy.

Is Zorn's choice thus "better" than Alta's? That, we cannot say. The different outcomes simply reflect different preferences and priorities in the two countries. **(Key Questions 10 and 11)** ⤾ 2.2

(a)
Alta

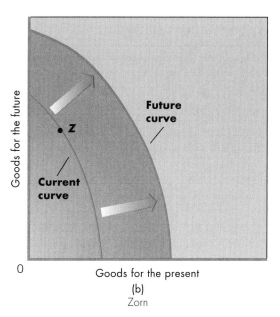

(b)
Zorn

Figure 2.5

An economy's present choice of positions on its production possibilities curve helps determine the curve's future location. A nation's current choice favoring "present goods," as made by Alta in (a), will cause a modest outward shift of the curve in the future. A nation's current choice favoring "future goods," as made by Zorn in (b), will result in a greater outward shift of the curve in the future.

A Qualification: International Trade

Production possibilities analysis implies that an individual nation is limited to the combinations of output indicated by its production possibilities curve. *But we must modify this principle when international specialization and trade exist.*

You will see in later chapters that an economy can avoid, through international specialization and trade, the output limits imposed by its domestic production possibilities curve. *International specialization* means directing domestic resources to output that a nation is highly efficient at producing. *International trade* involves the exchange of these goods for goods produced abroad. Specialization and trade enable a nation to get more of a desired good at less sacrifice of some other good. Rather than sacrifice 3 robots to get a third unit of pizza, as in Table 2.1, a nation might be able to obtain the third unit of pizza by trading only 2 units of robots for it. Specialization and trade have the same effect as having more and better resources or discovering improved production techniques; both increase the quantities of capital and consumer goods available to society. The output gains from greater international specialization and trade are the equivalent of economic growth.

QUICK REVIEW 2.3

■ Unemployment and the failure to achieve productive efficiency cause an economy to operate at a point inside its production possibilities curve.

■ Increases in resource supplies, improvements in resource quality, and technological advance cause economic growth, which are depicted as an outward shift of the production possibilities curve.

■ An economy's present choice of capital and consumer goods helps determine the future location of its production possibilities curve. (See Global Perspective 2.1.)

■ International specialization and trade enable a nation to obtain more goods than its production possibilities curve indicates.

Examples and Applications

There are many possible applications and examples relating to the production possibilities model. We will discuss just a few of them.

Unemployment and Productive Inefficiency   Almost all nations have at one point or another experienced widespread unemployment of resources. That is, they have operated inside of their production possibilities curves. In the depths of the Great Depression of the 1930s, one-quarter of U.S. workers were unemployed and one-third of U.S. production capacity was idle. In the last half of the 1990s, several countries (for example, Argentina, Japan, Mexico, and South Korea) operated inside their production possibilities curves, at least temporarily, because of substantial declines in economic activity.

Economies that experience substantial discrimination based on race, ethnicity, and gender do not achieve productive efficiency, and thus they operate inside their production possibilities curves. Because discrimination prevents those discriminated against from obtaining jobs that best use their skills, society has less output than otherwise. Eliminating discrimination would move such an economy from a point inside its production possibilities curve toward a point on its curve. Similarly, economies in which labor usage and production methods are based on custom, heredity, and caste, rather than on efficiency, operate well inside their production possibilities curves.

Tradeoffs and Opportunity Costs   Many current controversies illustrate the tradeoffs and opportunity costs indicated by movements along a particular production possibilities curve. (Any two categories of "output" can be placed on the axes of production possibilities curves.) Should scenic land be used for logging and mining or be preserved as wilderness? If the land is used for logging and mining, the opportunity cost is the forgone benefits of wilderness. If the land is used for wilderness, the opportunity cost is the lost value of the wood and minerals that society forgoes.

Should society devote more resources to the criminal justice system (police, courts, and prisons) or to education (teachers, books, and schools)? If society devotes more resources to the criminal justice system, other things equal, the opportunity cost is forgone improvements in education. If more resources are allocated to education, the opportunity cost is the forgone benefits from an improved criminal justice system. If we decide to devote more resources to both, what other goods and services do we forgo? ▮ 2.2

Shifts in Production Possibilities Curves   The United States has recently experienced a spurt of new technologies relating to computers, communications, and biotechnology. Technological advances have dropped the prices of computers and greatly enhanced their speed. Cellular phones and the Internet have increased communications capacity, enhancing production and improving the efficiency of markets. Advances in biotechnology, specifically genetic engineering, have resulted in important agricultural and medical discoveries. Many economists believe these new technologies are so significant that they are contributing to faster-than-normal U.S. economic growth (faster rightward shifts of the nation's production possibilities curve).

In some circumstances a nation's production possibilities curve can collapse inward. For example, in the late 1990s Yugoslavian forces began to "ethnically cleanse" Kosovo by driving out its Muslim residents. A decisive military response by the United States and its allies eventually pushed Yugoslavia out of Kosovo. The military action also devastated Yugoslavia's economy. Allied bombing inflicted great physical damage on Yugoslavia's production facilities and its system of roads, bridges, and communications. Consequently, Yugoslavia's production possibilities curve shifted inward.

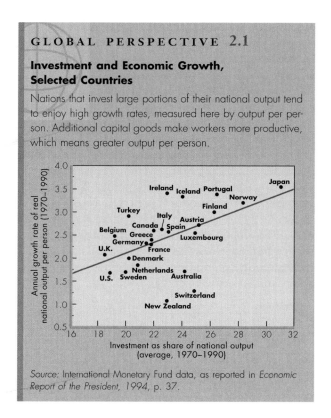

GLOBAL PERSPECTIVE 2.1

Investment and Economic Growth, Selected Countries

Nations that invest large portions of their national output tend to enjoy high growth rates, measured here by output per person. Additional capital goods make workers more productive, which means greater output per person.

Source: International Monetary Fund data, as reported in *Economic Report of the President,* 1994, p. 37.

▌Economic Systems

Every society needs to develop an **economic system**—*a particular set of institutional arrangements and a coordinating mechanism*—to respond to the economizing problem. Economic systems differ as to (1) who owns the factors of production and (2) the method used to coordinate and direct economic activity. There are two general types of economic systems: the market system and the command system.

The Market System

The private ownership of resources and the use of markets and prices to coordinate and direct economic activity characterize the **market system,** or **capitalism.** In that system each participant acts in his or her own self-interest; each individual or business seeks to maximize its satisfaction or profit through its own decisions regarding consumption or production. The system allows for the private ownership of capital, communicates through prices, and coordinates economic activity through *markets*—places where buyers and sellers come together. Goods and services are produced and resources are supplied by whoever is willing and able to do so. The result is competition among independently acting buyers and sellers of each product and resource. Thus, economic decision making is widely dispersed.

In *pure* capitalism—or *laissez-faire* capitalism—government's role would be limited to protecting private property and establishing an environment appropriate to the operation of the market system. The term "laissez-faire" means "let it be," that is, keep government from interfering with the economy. The idea is that such interference will disturb the efficient working of the market system. 🔑 2.3

But in the capitalism practiced in the United States and most other countries, government plays a substantial role in the economy. It not only provides the rules for economic activity but also promotes economic stability and growth, provides certain goods and services that would otherwise be underproduced or not produced at all, and modifies the distribution of income. The government, however, is not the dominant economic force in deciding what to produce, how to produce it, and who will get it. That force is the market.

The Command System

The alternative to the market system is the **command system,** also known as *socialism* or *communism*. In that system, government owns most property resources and economic decision making occurs through a central economic plan. A central planning board appointed by the government makes nearly all the major decisions concerning the use of resources, the composition and distribution of output, and the organization of production. The government owns most of the business firms, which produce according to government directives. A central planning board determines production goals for each enterprise and specifies the amount of resources to be allocated to each enterprise so that it can reach its production goals. The division of output between capital and consumer goods is centrally decided, and capital goods are allocated among industries on the basis of the central planning board's long-term priorities.

A *pure* command economy would rely exclusively on a central plan to allocate the government-owned property resources. But, in reality, even the preeminent command economy—the Soviet Union—tolerated some private ownership and incorporated some markets before its demise in 1992. Recent reforms in Russia and most of the eastern European nations have to one degree or another transformed their command economies to capitalistic, market-oriented systems. China's reforms have not gone as far, but they have reduced the reliance on central planning. Although there is still extensive government ownership of resources and capital in China, the nation has increasingly relied on free markets to organize and coordinate its economy. North Korea and Cuba are the last remaining examples of largely centrally planned economies.

▋ The Circular Flow Model

Because nearly all the major nations now use the market system, we need to gain a good understanding of how this system operates. Our goal in the remainder of this chapter is to identify the market economy's decision makers and major markets. In Chapter 3 we will explain how prices are established in individual markets. Then in Chapter 4 we will detail the characteristics of the market system and explain how the system addresses the economizing problem.

As shown in **Figure 2.6 (Key Graph),** the market economy has two groups of decision makers: *households* and *businesses*. (We will add government as a third decision maker in Chapter 5.) It also has two broad markets: the *resource market* and the *product market*.

The upper half of the diagram represents the **resource market:** *the place where resources or the services of resource suppliers are bought and sold.* In the resource market, households sell resources and businesses demand them. Households (that is, people) own all economic resources either directly as workers or entrepreneurs or indirectly through their ownership of business corporations. They sell their resources to businesses, which buy them because they are necessary for producing goods and services. The funds that businesses pay for resources are costs to businesses but are flows of wage, rent, interest, and profit income to the households. Resources therefore flow from households to businesses, and money flows from businesses to households.

Next consider the lower part of the diagram, which represents the **product market:** *the place where goods and services produced by businesses are bought and sold.* In the product market, businesses combine the resources they have obtained to produce and sell goods and services. Households use the income they have received from the sale of resources to buy goods and services. The monetary flow of consumer spending on goods and services yields sales revenues for businesses.

The **circular flow model** suggests a complex, interrelated web of decision making and economic activity involving businesses and households. Businesses and households are both buyers and sellers. Businesses buy resources and sell products. Households buy products and sell resources. As shown in Figure 2.6, there is a counterclockwise *real flow* of economic resources and finished goods and services, and a clockwise *money flow* of income and consumption expenditures. These flows are simultaneous and repetitive. 🔑 2.4

KEY GRAPH

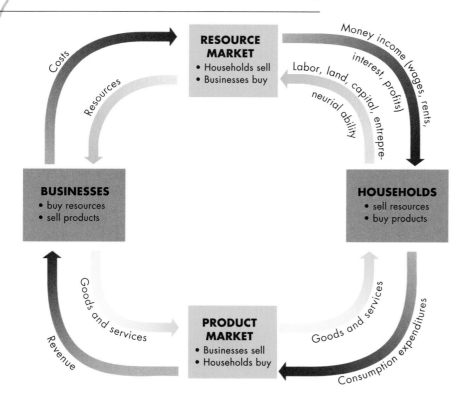

Figure 2.6
The circular flow diagram.
Resources flow from households to businesses through the resource market, and products flow from businesses to households through the product market. Opposite these real flows are monetary flows. Households receive income from businesses (their costs) through the resource market, and businesses receive revenue from households (their expenditures) through the product market.

Women and Expanded Production Possibilities

A Large Increase in the Number of Employed Women Has Shifted the U.S. Production Possibilities Curve Outward.

One of the more remarkable trends of the past half-century in the United States has been the substantial rise in the number of women working in the paid workforce. Today, 60 percent of women work full-time or part-time in paid jobs, compared to only 40 percent in 1965. There are many reasons for this increase.

Women's Rising Wage Rates Over recent years, women have greatly increased their productivity in the workplace, mostly by becoming better educated and professionally trained. As a result, they can earn higher wages. Because those higher wages have increased the opportunity costs—the forgone wage earnings—of staying at home, women have substituted employment in the labor market for more "expensive" traditional home activities. This substitution has been particularly pronounced among married women.

Women's higher wages and longer hours away from home have produced creative reallocations of time and purchasing patterns. Day care services have partly replaced personal child care. Restaurants, take-home meals, and pizza delivery often substitute for traditional home cooking. Convenience stores and catalog and Internet sales have proliferated, as have lawn-care and in-home cleaning services. Microwave ovens, dishwashers, automatic washers and dryers, and other household "capital goods" enhance domestic productivity.

Expanded Job Access Greater access to jobs is a second factor increasing the employment of women. Service industries—teaching, nursing, and clerical work, for instance—that traditionally have employed mainly women have expanded in the past several decades. Also, the population in general has shifted from farms and rural regions to urban areas, where jobs for women are more abundant and more geographically accessible. The decline in the average length of the workweek and the increased availability of part-time jobs have also made it easier for women to combine labor market employment with child-rearing and household activities.

Changing Preferences and Attitudes Women collectively have changed their preferences from household activities to employment in the labor market. Many find personal fulfillment in jobs, careers, and earnings, as evidenced by the huge influx of women into law, medicine, business, and other professions. More broadly, most industrial societies now widely accept and encourage labor-force participation by women, including those with very young children. Today about 65 percent of American mothers with preschool children participate in the labor force, compared to only 30 percent in 1970. More than half return to work before their youngest child has reached the age of 2.

Declining Birthrates There were 3.8 lifetime births per woman in 1957 at the peak of the baby boom. Today the number is less than 2. This marked decline in the size of the typical family, the result of changing lifestyles and the widespread availability of birth control, has freed up time for greater labor-force participation by women. Not only do women now have fewer children; their children are spaced closer together in age. Thus women who leave their jobs during their children's early years can return to the labor force sooner. Higher wage rates have also been at work. On average, women with relatively high wage earnings have fewer children than women with lower earnings. The opportunity cost of children—the income sacrificed by not being employed—rises as wage earnings rise. In the language of economics, the higher "price" associated with children has reduced the "quantity" of children demanded.

Rising Divorce Rates Marital instability, as evidenced by high divorce rates, may have motivated many women to enter and remain in the labor market. Because alimony and child-support payments are often erratic or nonexistent, the economic impact of divorce on nonworking women may be disastrous. Most nonworking women enter the labor force for the first time following divorce. And many married women—perhaps even women contemplating marriage—may have joined the labor force to protect themselves against the financial difficulties of potential divorce.

Slower Growth of Male Wages The earnings of many low-wage and middle-wage male workers grew slowly or even fell in the United States over the past three decades. Many wives may have entered the labor force to ensure the rise of household living standards. The median income of couples with children grew 25 percent between 1969 and 1996. Without the mothers' incomes, that growth would have been only 2 percent. A related issue is that couples of all income levels may be concerned about their family incomes compared to those of other families. So the entry of some women into the labor force may have encouraged still other women to enter in order to maintain their families' *relative* standard of living.

Taken together, these factors have produced a rapid rise in the presence of women workers in the United States. This increase in the *quantity of resources* has helped push the U.S. production possibilities curve outward. In other words, it has contributed greatly to U.S. economic growth.

SUMMARY

1. Economics is grounded on two basic facts: (a) economic wants are virtually unlimited; (b) economic resources are scarce.

2. Economic resources may be classified as property resources—raw materials and capital—or as human resources—labor and entrepreneurial ability. These resources constitute the factors of production.

3. Economics is concerned with the problem of using or managing scarce resources to produce the goods and services that satisfy the material wants of society. Both full employment and the efficient use of available resources are essential to maximize want satisfaction.

4. Efficient use of resources consists of productive efficiency (producing all output combinations in the least costly way) and allocative efficiency (producing the specific output mix most desired by society).

5. An economy that is achieving full employment and productive efficiency—one that is operating on its production possibilities curve—must sacrifice the output of some types of goods and services in order to increase the production of others. Because resources are not equally productive in all possible uses, shifting resources from one use to another brings the law of increasing opportunity costs into play. The production of additional units of one product requires the sacrifice of *increasing* amounts of the other product.

6. Allocative efficiency means operating at the optimal point on the production possibilities curve. That point represents the highest-valued mix of goods and is determined by expanding the production of each good until its marginal benefit (MB) equals its marginal cost (MC).

7. Over time, technological advances and increases in the quantity and quality of resources enable the economy to produce more of all goods and services—that is, to experience economic growth. Society's choice as to the mix of consumer goods and capital goods in current output is a major determinant of the future location of the production possibilities curve and thus of economic growth.

8. The market system and the command system are the two broad types of economic systems used to address the economizing problem. In the market system (or capitalism) private individuals own most resources and markets coordinate most economic activity. In the command system (or socialism or communism), government owns most resources and central planners coordinate most economic activity.

9. The circular flow model locates the product and resource markets and shows the major real and money flows between businesses and households. Businesses are on the buying side of the resource market and the selling side of the product market. Households are on the selling side of the resource market and the buying side of the product market.

TERMS AND CONCEPTS

economizing problem	factors of production	production possibilities table	economic system
utility	full employment	production possibilities curve	market system
economic resources	full production	opportunity cost	capitalism
land	productive efficiency	law of increasing opportunity costs	command system
capital	allocative efficiency	economic growth	resource market
investment	consumer goods		product market
labor	capital goods		circular flow model
entrepreneurial ability			

STUDY QUESTIONS

1. Explain this statement: "If resources were unlimited and were freely available, there would be no subject called *economics*."

2. Comment on the following statement from a newspaper article: "Our junior high school serves a splendid hot meal for $1 without costing the taxpayers anything, thanks in part to a government subsidy."

3. Critically analyze: "Wants aren't insatiable. I can prove it. I get all the coffee I want to drink every morning at breakfast." Explain: "Goods and services

are scarce because resources are scarce." Analyze: "It is the nature of all economic problems that absolute solutions are denied to us."

4. What are economic resources? What are the major functions of the entrepreneur?

5. **Key Question** Why is the problem of unemployment part of the subject matter of economics? Distinguish between productive efficiency and allocative efficiency. Give an illustration of achieving productive, but not allocative, efficiency.

6. **Key Question** Here is a production possibilities table for war goods and civilian goods:

Type of Production	Production Alternatives				
	A	B	C	D	E
Automobiles	0	2	4	6	8
Rockets	30	27	21	12	0

   a. Show these data graphically. Upon what specific assumptions is this production possibilities curve based?
   b. If the economy is at point *C*, what is the cost of one more automobile? One more rocket? Explain how the production possibilities curve reflects the law of increasing opportunity costs.
   c. What must the economy do to operate at some point on the production possibilities curve?

7. What is the opportunity cost of attending college? In 2000 nearly 80 percent of college-educated Americans held jobs, whereas only about 40 percent of those who did not finish high school held jobs. How might this difference relate to opportunity costs?

8. Suppose you arrive at a store expecting to pay $100 for an item but learn that a store 2 miles away is charging $50 for it. Would you drive there and buy it? How does your decision benefit you? What is the opportunity cost of your decision? Now suppose you arrive at a store expecting to pay $6000 for an item but discover that it costs $5950 at the other store. Do you make the same decision as before? Perhaps surprisingly, you should! Explain why.

9. **Key Question** Specify and explain the shapes of the marginal-benefit and marginal-cost curves. How are these curves used to determine the optimal allocation of resources to a particular product? If current output is such that marginal cost exceeds marginal benefit, should more or fewer resources be allocated to this product? Explain.

10. **Key Question** Label point *G inside* the production possibilities curve you drew in question 6. What does it indicate? Label point *H outside* the curve. What does that point indicate? What must occur before the economy can attain the level of production shown by point *H*?

11. **Key Question** Referring again to question 6, suppose improvement occurs in the technology of producing rockets but not in the technology of producing automobiles. Draw the new production possibilities curve. Now assume that a technological advance occurs in producing automobiles but not in producing rockets. Draw the new production possibilities curve. Now draw a production possibilities curve that reflects technological improvement in the production of both products.

12. Explain how, if at all, each of the following events affects the location of the production possibilities curve:
   a. Standardized examination scores of high school and college students decline.
   b. The unemployment rate falls from 9 to 6 percent of the labor force.
   c. Defense spending is reduced to allow government to spend more on health care.
   d. A new technique improves the efficiency of extracting copper from ore.

13. Explain: "Affluence tomorrow requires sacrifice today."

14. Suppose that, on the basis of a nation's production possibilities curve, an economy must sacrifice 10,000 pizzas domestically to get the 1 additional industrial robot it desires but that it can get the robot from another country in exchange for 9000 pizzas. Relate this information to the following statement: "Through international specialization and trade, a nation can reduce its opportunity cost of obtaining goods and thus 'move outside its production possibilities curve.'"

15. Contrast how a market system and a command economy try to cope with economic scarcity.

16. Distinguish between the resource market and the product market in the circular flow model. In what way are businesses and households both *sellers and buyers* in this model? What are the flows in the circular flow model?

17. **(Last Word)** Which two of the six reasons listed in the Last Word do you think are the *most important* in explaining the rise in participation of women in the workplace? Explain your reasoning.

18. **Web-Based Question: *More labor resources— What is the evidence for the United States and France?*** Go to the Bureau of Labor Statistics' website at www.bls.gov/ and click Data and then Most Requested Data. Retrieve U.S. employment data (CPS) for the period of the last 10 years. How many more workers were there at the end of the 10-year period than at the beginning? Next, return to Most Requested Data and click Foreign Labor Statistics. Find the total employment growth of France over the

last 10 years. In which of the two countries did "more labor resources" have the greatest impact on the nation's production possibilities curve over the 10 years?

19. **Web-Based Question:** *Relative size of the military—who's incurring the largest opportunity cost?* To obtain military goods, a nation must sacrifice civilian goods. Of course, that sacrifice may be worthwhile in terms of national defense and protection of national interests. Go to the Central Intelligence Agency's website, www.odci.gov/cia/publications/factbook/index.html, to determine the amount of military expenditures and military expenditures as a percentage of GDP for each of the following five nations: Brazil, Japan, North Korea, Russia, and the United States. Which one is bearing the greatest opportunity cost?

3 CHAPTER

Individual Markets
Demand and Supply

ACCORDING TO AN old joke, if you teach a parrot to say "demand and supply," you have an economist. There is an element of truth in this quip. The tools of demand and supply can take us far in understanding both specific economic issues and how the entire economy works. 🔑 **3.1** ■ With our circular flow model in Chapter 2, we identified the participants in the product market and resource market. We asserted that prices are determined by the "interaction" between buyers and sellers in those markets. In this chapter we examine that interaction in detail and explain how prices and output quantities are determined.

■ Markets

Recall from Chapter 2 that a **market** is *an institution or mechanism that brings together buyers ("demanders") and sellers ("suppliers") of particular goods, services, or resources.* Markets exist in many forms. The corner gas station, e-commerce sites, the local music store, a farmer's roadside stand—all are familiar markets. The New York Stock Exchange and the Chicago Board of Trade are markets where buyers and sellers of stocks and bonds and farm commodities from all over the world communicate with one another to buy and sell. Auctioneers bring together potential buyers and sellers of art, livestock, used farm equipment, and, sometimes, real estate. In labor markets, the quarterback and his agent bargain with the owner of an NFL team. A graduating finance major interviews with Citicorp or Wells Fargo at the university placement office.

All situations that link potential buyers with potential sellers are markets. Some markets are local, while others are national or international. Some are highly personal, involving face-to-face contact between demander and supplier; others are impersonal, with buyer and seller never seeing or knowing each other.

To keep things simple, we will focus in this chapter on markets consisting of large numbers of independently acting buyers and sellers of standardized products. These are the highly competitive markets such as a central grain exchange, a stock market, or a market for foreign currencies in which the price is "discovered" through the interacting decisions of buyers and sellers. They are *not* the markets in which one or a handful of producers "set" prices, such as the markets for commercial airplanes or operating software for personal computers.

▮ Demand

Demand is *a schedule or a curve that shows the various amounts of a product that consumers are willing and able to purchase at each of a series of possible prices during a specified period of time.*[1] Demand shows the quantities of a product that will be purchased at various possible prices, *other things equal.* Demand can easily be shown in table form. Table 3.1 is a hypothetical **demand schedule** for a *single consumer* purchasing bushels of corn.

Table 3.1 reveals the relationship between the various prices of corn and the quantity of corn a particular consumer would be willing and able to purchase at each of these prices. We say "willing and able" because willingness alone is not effective in the market. You may be willing to buy a digital camera, but if that willingness is not backed by the necessary dollars, it will not be effective and, therefore, will not be reflected in the market. In Table 3.1, if the price of corn were $5 per bushel, our consumer would be willing and able to buy 10 bushels per week; if it were $4, the consumer would be willing and able to buy 20 bushels per week; and so forth.

Table 3.1 does not tell us which of the five possible prices will actually exist in the corn market. That depends on demand and supply. Demand is simply a statement of a buyer's plans, or intentions, with respect to the purchase of a product.

To be meaningful, the quantities demanded at each price must relate to a specific period—a day, a week, a month. Saying "A consumer will buy 10 bushels of corn at $5 per bushel" is meaningless. Saying "A consumer will buy 10 bushels of corn per week at $5 per bushel" is meaningful. Unless a specific time period is stated, we do not know whether the demand for a product is large or small.

Table 3.1
An Individual Buyer's Demand for Corn

Price per Bushel	Quantity Demanded per Week
$5	10
4	20
3	35
2	55
1	80

---

[1]This definition obviously is worded to apply to product markets. To adjust it to apply to resource markets, substitute the word "resource" for "product" and the word "businesses" for "consumers."

Law of Demand

A fundamental characteristic of demand is this: *All else equal, as price falls, the quantity demanded rises, and as price rises, the quantity demanded falls.* In short, there is a negative or *inverse* relationship between price and quantity demanded. Economists call this inverse relationship the **law of demand.** 🔑 3.2

The other-things-equal assumption is critical here. Many factors other than the price of the product being considered affect the amount purchased. The quantity of Nikes purchased will depend not only on the price of Nikes but also on the prices of such substitutes as Reeboks, Adidas, and Filas. The law of demand in this case says that fewer Nikes will be purchased if the price of Nikes rises *and if the prices of Reeboks, Adidas, and Filas all remain constant.* In short, if the *relative price* of Nikes rises, fewer Nikes will be bought. However, if the price of Nikes and the prices of all other competing shoes increase by some amount—say, $5—consumers might buy more, less, or the same amount of Nikes.

Why the inverse relationship between price and quantity demanded? Let's look at three explanations, beginning with the simplest one:

■ The law of demand is consistent with common sense. People ordinarily *do* buy more of a product at a low price than at a high price. Price is an obstacle that deters consumers from buying. The higher that obstacle, the less of a product they will buy; the lower the price obstacle, the more they will buy. The fact that businesses have "sales" is evidence of their belief in the law of demand.

■ In any specific time period, each buyer of a product will derive less satisfaction (or benefit, or utility) from each successive unit of the product consumed. The second Big Mac will yield less satisfaction to the consumer than the first, and the third still less than the second. That is, consumption is subject to **diminishing marginal utility.** And because successive units of a particular product yield less and less marginal utility, consumers will buy additional units only if the price of those units is progressively reduced. 🔑 3.3

■ We can also explain the law of demand in terms of income and substitution effects. The **income effect** indicates that a lower price increases the purchasing power of a buyer's money income, enabling the buyer to purchase more of the product than she or he could buy before. A higher price has the opposite effect. The **substitution effect** suggests that at a lower price buyers have the incentive to substitute what is now a less expensive product for similar products that are now *relatively* more expensive. The product whose price has fallen is now "a better deal" relative to the other products.

For example, a decline in the price of chicken will increase the purchasing power of consumer incomes, enabling people to buy more chicken (the income effect). At a lower price, chicken is relatively more attractive and consumers tend to substitute it for pork, mutton, beef, and fish (the substitution effect). The income and substitution effects combine to make consumers able and willing to buy more of a product at a low price than at a high price. 🔎 **3.4**

The Demand Curve

The inverse relationship between price and quantity demanded for any product can be represented on a simple graph, in which, by convention, we measure *quantity demanded* on the horizontal axis and *price* on the vertical axis. In Figure 3.1 we have plotted the five price-quantity data points listed in Table 3.1 and connected the points with a smooth curve, labeled *D*. Such a curve is called a **demand curve.** Its downward slope reflects the law of demand—people buy more of a product, service, or resource as its price falls. The relationship between price and quantity demanded is inverse.

Table 3.1 and Figure 3.1 contain exactly the same data and reflect the same relationship between price and quantity demanded. But the graph shows that relationship more simply and clearly than a table or a description in words.

Market Demand

So far, we have concentrated on just one consumer. But competition requires that more than one buyer be present in each market. By adding the quantities demanded by all consumers at each of the various possible prices, we can get from *individual* demand to *market* demand. If there are just three buyers in the market, as represented in Table 3.2, it is relatively easy to determine the total quantity demanded at each price. Figure 3.2 shows the graphical summing procedure: At each price we add the individual quantities demanded to obtain the total quantity demanded at that price; we then plot the price and the total quantity demanded as one point of the market demand curve.

Competition, of course, ordinarily entails many more than three buyers of a product. To avoid hundreds or thousands or millions of additions, we suppose that all the buyers in a market are willing and able to buy the same amounts at each of the possible prices. Then we just multiply those amounts by the number of buyers to obtain the market demand. This is the way we arrived at curve D_1 in Figure 3.3, for a market with 200 corn buyers whose demand is

Figure 3.1

An individual buyer's demand for corn. Because price and quantity demanded are inversely related, an individual's demand schedule graphs as a downsloping curve such as *D*. Specifically, the law of demand says that, other things equal, consumers will buy more of a product as its price declines. Here and in later figures, *P* stands for price, and *Q* stands for quantity (either demanded or supplied).

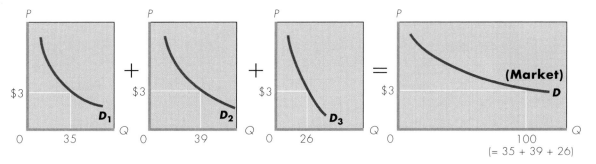

Figure 3.2

Market demand for corn, three buyers. We establish the market demand curve *D* by adding horizontally the individual demand curves (*D₁, D₂,* and *D₃*) of all the consumers in the market. At the price of $3, for example, the three individual curves yield a total quantity demanded of 100 bushels.

that shown in Table 3.1. Table 3.3 shows the calculations.

In constructing a demand curve such as *D₁* in Figure 3.3, economists assume that price is the most important influence on the amount of any product purchased. But economists know that other factors can and do affect purchases. These factors, called **determinants of demand,** are assumed to be constant when a demand curve like *D₁* is drawn. They are the "other things equal" in the relationship between price and quantity demanded. When any of these determinants changes, the demand curve will shift to the right or left. For this reason, determinants of demand are sometimes referred to as *demand shifters.*

The basic determinants of demand are (1) consumers' tastes (preferences), (2) the number of consumers in the market, (3) consumers' incomes, (4) the prices of related goods, and (5) consumer expectations about future prices and incomes.

Change in Demand

A change in one or more of the determinants of demand will change the demand data (the demand schedule) in Table 3.3 and therefore the location of the demand curve in Figure 3.3. A change in the demand schedule or, graphically, a shift in the demand curve is called a *change in demand.*

If consumers desire to buy more corn at each possible price than is reflected in column 4 in Table 3.3, that *increase in demand* is shown as a shift of the demand curve to the right, say, from *D₁* to *D₂.* Conversely, a *decrease in demand* occurs when consumers buy less corn at each possible price than is indicated in column 4, Table 3.3. The leftward shift of the demand curve from *D₁* to *D₃* in Figure 3.3 shows that situation.

Now let's see how changes in each determinant affect demand.

Table 3.2

Market Demand for Corn, Three Buyers

Price per Bushel	First Buyer		Second Buyer		Third Buyer		Total Quantity Demanded per Week
	Quantity Demanded						
$5	10	+	12	+	8	=	30
4	20	+	23	+	17	=	60
3	35	+	39	+	26	=	100
2	55	+	60	+	39	=	154
1	80	+	87	+	54	=	221

Table 3.3

Market Demand for Corn, 200 Buyers

(1) Price per Bushel	(2) Quantity Demanded per Week, Single Buyer		(3) Number of Buyers in the Market		(4) Total Quantity Demanded per Week
$5	10	×	200	=	2,000
4	20	×	200	=	4,000
3	35	×	200	=	7,000
2	55	×	200	=	11,000
1	80	×	200	=	16,000

Figure 3.3

Changes in the demand for corn.   A change in one or more of the determinants of demand causes a change in demand. An increase in demand is shown as a shift of the demand curve to the right, as from D_1 to D_2. A decrease in demand is shown as a shift of the demand curve to the left, as from D_1 to D_3. These changes in demand are to be distinguished from a change in quantity demanded, which is caused by a change in the price of the product, as shown by a movement from, say, point a to point b on fixed demand curve D_1.

Tastes   A favorable change in consumer tastes (preferences) for a product—a change that makes the product more desirable—means that more of it will be demanded at each price. Demand will increase; the demand curve will shift rightward. An unfavorable change in consumer preferences will decrease demand, shifting the demand curve to the left.

New products may affect consumer tastes; for example, the introduction of compact discs greatly decreased the demand for cassette tapes. Consumers' concern over the health hazards of cholesterol and obesity have increased the demand for broccoli, low-calorie sweeteners, and fresh fruit while decreasing the demand for beef, veal, eggs, and whole milk. Over the past several years, the demand for coffee drinks, bottled water, and sports utility vehicles has greatly increased, driven by a change in tastes. So, too, has the demand for leather jackets and fleece outerwear.

Number of Buyers   An increase in the number of buyers in a market increases demand. A decrease in the number of buyers in a market decreases demand. For example, improvements in communications have given financial markets international range

and have thus increased the demand for stocks and bonds. And the baby boom after the Second World War increased demand for diapers, baby lotion, and the services of obstetricians. When the baby boomers reached their twenties in the 1970s, the demand for housing increased. Conversely, the aging of the baby boomers in the 1980s and 1990s was a factor in the relative slump in the demand for housing in those decades. Also, an increase in life expectancy has increased the demand for medical care, retirement communities, and nursing homes. And international trade agreements have reduced foreign trade barriers to American farm commodities, thus increasing the demand for those products.

Income   How changes in income affect demand is a more complex matter. For most products, a rise in income causes an increase in demand. Consumers typically buy more steaks, furniture, and computers as their incomes increase. Conversely, the demand for such products declines as their incomes fall. Products whose demand varies *directly* with money income are called *superior goods*, or **normal goods.**

Although most products are normal goods, there are some exceptions. As incomes increase beyond some point, the demand for used clothing, retread tires, and third-hand automobiles may decrease, because the higher incomes enable consumers to buy new versions of those products. Rising incomes may also decrease the demand for soy-enhanced hamburger. Similarly, rising incomes may cause the demand for charcoal grills to decline as wealthier consumers switch to gas grills. Goods whose demand varies *inversely* with money income are called **inferior goods.**

Prices of Related Goods

A change in the price of a related good may either increase or decrease the demand for a product, depending on whether the related good is a substitute or a complement:

- A **substitute good** is one that can be used in place of another good.
- A **complementary good** is one that is used together with another good.

Substitutes   Beef and chicken are examples of substitute goods or, simply, *substitutes.* When the price of beef rises, consumers buy less beef, increasing the demand for chicken. Conversely, as the price of beef falls, consumers buy more beef, decreasing the demand for chicken. *When two products are substitutes, the price of one and the demand for the other move in the same direction.* So it is with pairs such as Nikes and Reeboks, Colgate and Crest, Toyotas and Hondas, and Coke and Pepsi. So-called *substitution in consumption* occurs when the price of one good rises relative to the price of a similar good.

Complements   Complementary goods (or, simply, *complements*) are goods that are used together and are usually demanded together. If the price of gasoline falls and, as a result, you drive your car more often, the extra driving increases your demand for motor oil. Thus, gas and motor oil are jointly demanded; they are complements. So it is with ham and eggs, tuition and textbooks, movies and popcorn, cameras and film. *When two products are complements, the price of one good and the demand for the other good move in opposite directions.*

Unrelated Goods   The vast majority of goods that are not related to one another are called *independent goods.* Examples are butter and golf balls, potatoes and automobiles, and bananas and wristwatches. A change in the price of one does not affect the demand for the other.

Expectations

Changes in consumer expectations may shift demand. A newly formed expectation of higher future prices may cause consumers to buy now in order to "beat" the anticipated price rises, thus increasing current demand. For example, when freezing weather destroys much of Florida's citrus crop, consumers may reason that the price of orange juice will rise. They may stock up on orange juice by purchasing large quantities now. In contrast, a newly formed expectation of falling prices or falling income may decrease current demand for products.

Similarly, a change in expectations relating to future product availability may affect current demand. In late December 1999 there was a substantial increase in the demand for gasoline. Reason? Motorists became concerned that the Y2K computer problem might disrupt fuel pumps or credit card systems.

Finally, a change in expectations concerning future income may prompt consumers to change their current spending. For example, first-round NFL draft choices may splurge on new luxury cars in anticipation of a lucrative professional football contract. Or workers who become fearful of losing their jobs may reduce their demand for, say, vacation travel.

In summary, an *increase* in demand—the decision by consumers to buy larger quantities of a product at each possible price—may be caused by:

- A favorable change in consumer tastes.
- An increase in the number of buyers.
- Rising incomes if the product is a normal good.
- Falling incomes if the product is an inferior good.
- An increase in the price of a substitute good.
- A decrease in the price of a complementary good.
- A new consumer expectation that either prices or income will be higher in the future.

You should "reverse" these generalizations to explain a *decrease* in demand. Table 3.4 provides additional illustrations of the determinants of demand. **(Key Question 2)**

Changes in Quantity Demanded

A *change in demand* must not be confused with a *change in quantity demanded.* A **change in demand** is a shift of the entire demand curve to the right (an increase in demand) or to the left (a decrease in

Table 3.4

Determinants of Demand: Factors That Shift the Demand Curve

Determinant	Examples
Change in buyer tastes	Physical fitness rises in popularity, increasing the demand for jogging shoes and bicycles; Latin American music becomes more popular, increasing the demand for Latin CDs.
Change in number of buyers	A decline in the birthrate reduces the demand for childrens' toys.
Change in income	A rise in incomes increases the demand for such normal goods as butter, lobster, and filet mignon while reducing the demand for such inferior goods as cabbage, turnips, and inexpensive wine.
Change in the prices of related goods	A reduction in airfares reduces the demand for bus transportation (substitute goods); a decline in the price of compact disc players increases the demand for compact discs (complementary goods).
Change in expectations	Inclement weather in South America creates an expectation of higher future prices of coffee beans, thereby increasing today's demand for coffee beans.

demand). It occurs because the consumer's state of mind about purchasing the product has been altered in response to a change in one or more of the determinants of demand. Recall that "demand" is a schedule or a curve; therefore, a "change in demand" means a change in the entire schedule and a shift of the entire curve.

In contrast, a **change in quantity demanded** is a movement from one point to another point—from one price-quantity combination to another—on a fixed demand schedule or demand curve. The cause of such a change is an increase or decrease in the price of the product under consideration. In Table 3.3, for example, a decline in the price of corn from $5 to $4 will increase the quantity of corn demanded from 2000 to 4000 bushels.

In Figure 3.3 the shift of the demand curve D_1 to either D_2 or D_3 is a change in demand. But the movement from point a to point b on curve D_1 rep-

resents a change in quantity demanded: *demand has not changed; it is the entire curve, and it remains fixed in place.*

QUICK REVIEW 3.1

■ A market is any arrangement that facilitates the purchase and sale of goods, services, or resources.

■ Demand is a schedule or a curve showing the amount of a product that buyers are willing and able to purchase, in a particular time period, at each possible price in a series of prices.

■ The law of demand states that, other things equal, the quantity of a good purchased varies inversely with its price.

■ The demand curve shifts because of changes in (a) consumer tastes, (b) the number of buyers in the market, (c) consumer income, (d) the prices of substitute or complementary goods, and (e) consumer expectations.

■ A change in demand is a shift of the entire demand curve; a change in quantity demanded is a movement from one point to another on a demand curve.

■ Supply

Supply is *a schedule or curve showing the amounts of a product that producers are willing and able to make available for sale at each of a series of possible prices during a specific period.*[2] Table 3.5 is a hypothetical **supply schedule** for a single producer of corn. It shows the quantities of corn that will be supplied at various prices, other things equal.

Table 3.5

An Individual Producer's Supply of Corn

Price per Bushel	Quantity Supplied per Week
$5	60
4	50
3	35
2	20
1	5

---

[2]This definition is worded to apply to product markets. To adjust it to apply to resource markets, substitute "resource" for "product" and "owners" for "producers."

Law of Supply

Table 3.5 shows a positive or direct relationship that prevails between price and quantity supplied. *As price rises, the quantity supplied rises; as price falls, the quantity supplied falls.* This relationship is called the **law of supply.** A supply schedule tells us that firms will produce and offer for sale more of their product at a high price than at a low price. This, again, is basically common sense.

Price is an obstacle from the standpoint of the consumer, who is on the paying end. The higher the price, the less the consumer will buy. But the supplier is on the receiving end of the product's price. To a supplier, price represents *revenue,* which serves as an incentive to produce and sell a product. The higher the price, the greater this incentive and the greater the quantity supplied.

Consider a farmer who can shift resources among alternative products. As price moves up, as shown in Table 3.5, the farmer finds it profitable to take land out of wheat, oats, and soybean production and put it into corn. And the higher corn prices enable the farmer to cover the increased costs associated with more intensive cultivation and the use of more seed, fertilizer, and pesticides. The overall result is more corn.

Now consider a manufacturer. Beyond some quantity of production, manufacturers usually encounter increasing costs per added unit of output. Certain productive resources—in particular, the firm's plant and machinery—cannot be expanded quickly, so the firm uses more of other resources, such as labor, to produce more output. But as time passes, the existing plant becomes increasingly crowded and congested. As a result, each added worker produces less added output, and the cost of successive units of output rises accordingly. The firm will not produce the more costly units unless it receives a higher price for them. Again, price and quantity supplied are directly related.

The Supply Curve

As with demand, it is convenient to represent supply graphically. In Figure 3.4, curve S_1 is a graph of the market supply data given in Table 3.6. Those data assume there are 200 suppliers in the market,

Table 3.6

Market Supply of Corn, 200 Producers

(1) Price per Bushel	(2) Quantity Supplied per Week, Single Producer		(3) Number of Sellers in the Market		(4) Total Quantity Supplied per Week
$5	60	×	200	=	12,000
4	50	×	200	=	10,000
3	35	×	200	=	7,000
2	20	×	200	=	4,000
1	5	×	200	=	1,000

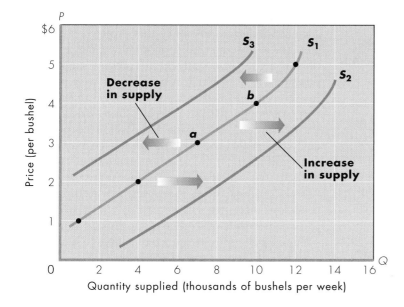

Figure 3.4

Changes in the supply of corn. A change in one or more of the determinants of supply causes a change in supply. An increase in supply is shown as a rightward shift of the supply curve, as from S_1 to S_2. A decrease in supply is depicted as a leftward shift of the curve, as from S_1 to S_3. In contrast, a change in the *quantity supplied* is caused by a change in the product's price and is shown by a movement from one point to another, as from *a* to *b*, on a fixed supply curve.

each willing and able to supply corn according to Table 3.5. We obtain the market **supply curve** by horizontally adding the supply curves of the individual producers. Note that the axes in Figure 3.4 are the same as those used in our graph of market demand (Figure 3.3), except for the change from "quantity demanded" to "quantity supplied" on the horizontal axis.

Determinants of Supply

In constructing a supply curve, we assume that price is the most significant influence on the quantity supplied of any product. But other factors (the "other things equal") can and do affect supply. The supply curve is drawn on the assumption that these other things are fixed and do not change. If one of them does change, a *change in supply* will occur, meaning that the entire supply curve will shift.

The basic **determinants of supply** are (1) resource prices, (2) technology, (3) taxes and subsidies, (4) prices of other goods, (5) price expectations, and (6) the number of sellers in the market. A change in any one or more of these determinants of supply, or *supply shifters*, will move the supply curve for a product either right or left. A shift to the *right*, as from S_1 to S_2 in Figure 3.4, signifies an *increase* in supply: Producers supply larger quantities of the product at each possible price. A shift to the *left*, as from S_1 to S_3, indicates a *decrease* in supply: Producers offer less output at each price.

Changes in Supply

Let's consider how changes in each of the determinants affect supply. The key idea is that costs are a major factor underlying supply curves; anything that affects costs (other than changes in output itself) usually shifts the supply curve.

Resource Prices
The prices of the resources used in the production process help determine the costs of production incurred by firms. Higher *resource* prices raise production costs and, assuming a particular *product* price, squeeze profits. That reduction in profits reduces the incentive for firms to supply output at each product price. For example, an increase in the prices of iron ore and coke will increase the cost of producing steel and reduce its supply.

In contrast, lower *resource* prices reduce production costs and increase profits. So when resource prices fall, firms supply greater output at each product price. For example, a decrease in the prices of seed and fertilizer will increase the supply of corn.

Technology
Improvements in technology (techniques of production) enable firms to produce units of output with fewer resources. Because resources are costly, using fewer of them lowers production costs and increases supply. Example: Recent improvements in the fuel efficiency of aircraft engines have reduced the cost of providing passenger air service. Thus, airlines now offer more flights than previously at each ticket price; the supply of air service has increased.

Taxes and Subsidies
Businesses treat most taxes as costs. An increase in sales or property taxes will increase production costs and reduce supply. In contrast, subsidies are "taxes in reverse." If the government subsidizes the production of a good, it in effect lowers the producers' costs and increases supply.

Prices of Other Goods
Firms that produce a particular product, say, soccer balls, can sometimes use their plant and equipment to produce alternative goods, say, basketballs and volleyballs. The higher prices of these "other goods" may entice soccer ball producers to switch production to those other goods in order to increase profits. This *substitution in production* results in a decline in the supply of soccer balls. Alternatively, when the prices of basketballs and volleyballs decline relative to the price of soccer balls, producers of those goods may decide to produce more soccer balls instead, increasing their supply.

Price Expectations
Changes in expectations about the future price of a product may affect the producer's current willingness to supply that product. It is difficult, however, to generalize about how a new expectation of higher prices affects the present supply of a product. Farmers anticipating a higher corn price in the future might withhold some of their current corn harvest from the market, thereby causing a decrease in the current supply of corn. Similarly, if people suddenly expect that the price of Amazon.com stock will rise significantly in the near future, the supply offered for sale today might decrease. In contrast, in many types of manufacturing industries, newly formed expectations that price will increase may induce firms to add another shift of workers or to expand their production facilities, causing current supply to increase.

Number of Sellers
Other things equal, the larger the number of suppliers, the greater the mar-

ket supply. As more firms enter an industry, the supply curve shifts to the right. Conversely, the smaller the number of firms in the industry, the less the market supply. This means that as firms leave an industry, the supply curve shifts to the left. Example: The United States and Canada have imposed restrictions on haddock fishing to replenish dwindling stocks. As part of that policy, the Federal government has bought the boats of some of the haddock fishers as a way of putting them out of business and decreasing the catch. The result has been a decline in the market supply of haddock.

Table 3.7 is a checklist of the determinants of supply, along with further illustrations. **(Key Question 5)**

Table 3.7

Determinants of Supply: Factors That Shift the Supply Curve

Determinant	Examples
Change in resource prices	A decrease in the price of microchips increases the supply of computers; an increase in the price of crude oil reduces the supply of gasoline.
Change in technology	The development of more effective wireless technology increases the supply of cell phones.
Changes in taxes and subsidies	An increase in the excise tax on cigarettes reduces the supply of cigarettes; a decline in subsidies to state universities reduces the supply of higher education.
Change in prices of other goods	An increase in the price of cucumbers decreases the supply of watermelons.
Change in expectations	An expectation of a substantial rise in future log prices decreases the supply of logs today.
Change in number of suppliers	An increase in the number of Internet service providers increases the supply of such services; the formation of women's professional basketball leagues increases the supply of women's professional basketball games.

Changes in Quantity Supplied

The distinction between a *change in supply* and a *change in quantity supplied* parallels the distinction between a change in demand and a change in quantity demanded. Because supply is a schedule or curve, a **change in supply** means a change in the entire schedule and a shift of the entire curve. An increase in supply shifts the curve to the right; a decrease in supply shifts it to the left. The cause of a change in supply is a change in one or more of the determinants of supply.

In contrast, a **change in quantity supplied** is a movement from one point to another on a fixed supply curve. The cause of such a movement is a change in the price of the specific product being considered. In Table 3.6, a decline in the price of corn from $5 to $4 decreases the quantity of corn supplied per week from 12,000 to 10,000 bushels. This is a change in quantity supplied, not a change in supply. *Supply is the full schedule of prices and quantities shown, and this schedule does not change when price changes.*

QUICK REVIEW 3.2

A supply schedule or curve shows that, other things equal, the quantity of a good supplied varies directly with its price.

The supply curve shifts because of changes in (a) resource prices, (b) technology, (c) taxes or subsidies, (d) prices of other goods, (e) expectations of future prices, and (f) the number of suppliers.

A change in supply is a shift of the supply curve; a change in quantity supplied is a movement from one point to another on a fixed supply curve.

▌ Supply and Demand: Market Equilibrium

We can now bring together supply and demand to see how the buying decisions of households and the selling decisions of businesses interact to determine the price of a product and the quantity actually bought and sold. In Table 3.8, columns 1 and 2 repeat the market supply of corn (from Table 3.6), and columns 2 and 3 repeat the market demand for corn (from Table 3.3). We assume that this is a competitive market—neither buyers nor sellers can set the price.

Table 3.8

Market Supply of and Demand for Corn

(1) Total Quantity Supplied per Week	(2) Price per Bushel	(3) Total Quantity Demanded per Week	(4) Surplus (+) or Shortage (−)*
12,000	$5	2,000	+10,000 ↓
10,000	4	4,000	+6,000 ↓
7,000	**3**	**7,000**	**0**
4,000	2	11,000	−7,000 ↑
1,000	1	16,000	−15,000 ↑

*Arrows indicate the effect on price.

Surpluses

We have limited our example to only five possible prices. Of these, which will actually prevail as the market price for corn? We can find an answer through trial and error. For no particular reason, let's start with $5. We see immediately that this cannot be the prevailing market price. At the $5 price, producers are willing to produce and offer for sale 12,000 bushels of corn, but buyers are willing to buy only 2000 bushels. The $5 price encourages farmers to produce lots of corn but discourages most consumers from buying it. The result is a 10,000-bushel **surplus** or *excess supply* of corn. This surplus, shown in column 4 of Table 3.8, is the excess of quantity supplied over quantity demanded at $5. Corn farmers would find themselves with 10,000 unsold bushels of output.

A price of $5, even if it existed temporarily in the corn market, could not persist over a period of time. The very large surplus of corn would prompt competing sellers to lower the price to encourage buyers to take the surplus off their hands. Suppose the price goes down to $4. The lower price encourages consumers to buy more corn and, at the same time, induces farmers to offer less of it for sale. The surplus diminishes to 6000 bushels. Nevertheless, since there is still a surplus, competition among sellers will once again reduce the price. Clearly, then, the prices of $5 and $4 will not survive because they are "too high." The market price of corn must be less than $4.

Shortages

Let's jump now to $1 as the possible market price of corn. Observe in column 4 of Table 3.8 that at this price, quantity demanded exceeds quantity supplied by 15,000 units. The $1 price discourages farmers from devoting resources to corn production and encourages consumers to attempt to buy more than is available. The result is a 15,000-bushel **shortage** of, or *excess demand* for, corn. The $1 price cannot persist as the market price. Many consumers who want to buy at this price will not get corn. They will express a willingness to pay more than $1 to get some of the available output. Competition among these buyers will drive up the price to something greater than $1.

Suppose the competition among buyers boosts the price to $2. This higher price will reduce, but will not eliminate, the shortage of corn. For $2, farmers devote more resources to corn production, and some buyers who were willing to pay $1 per bushel will not want to buy corn at $2. But a shortage of 7000 bushels still exists at $2. This shortage will push the market price above $2.

Equilibrium Price and Quantity

By trial and error we have eliminated every price but $3. At $3, *and only at this price*, the quantity of corn that farmers are willing to produce and supply is identical with the quantity consumers are willing and able to buy. There is neither a shortage nor a surplus of corn at that price.

With no shortage or surplus at $3, there is no reason for the price of corn to change. Economists call this price the *market-clearing* or **equilibrium price**, "equilibrium" meaning "in balance" or "at rest." At $3, quantity supplied and quantity demanded are in balance at the **equilibrium quantity** of 7000 bushels. So $3 is the only stable price of corn under the supply and demand conditions shown in Table 3.8.

The price of corn, or of any other product bought and sold in competitive markets, will be established where the supply decisions of producers and the demand decisions of buyers are mutually consistent. Such decisions are consistent only at the equilibrium price (here, $3) and equilibrium quantity (here, 7000 bushels). At any higher price, suppliers want to sell more than consumers want to buy and a surplus results; at any lower price, consumers want to buy more than producers make available for sale and a shortage results. Such discrepancies between the supply and demand intentions of sellers and buyers then prompt price changes that bring the two sets of intentions into accord.

A graphical analysis of supply and demand should yield the same conclusions. **Figure 3.5 (Key**

KEY GRAPH

Figure 3.5

Equilibrium price and quantity.

The intersection of the downsloping demand curve *D* and the upsloping supply curve *S* indicates the equilibrium price and quantity, here $3 and 7000 bushels of corn. The shortages of corn at below-equilibrium prices (for example, 7000 bushels at $2) drive up price. The higher prices increase the quantity supplied and reduce the quantity demanded until equilibrium is achieved. The surpluses caused by above-equilibrium prices (for example, 6000 bushels at $4) push price down. As price drops, the quantity demanded rises and the quantity supplied falls until equilibrium is established. At the equilibrium price and quantity, there are neither shortages nor surpluses of corn.

Graph) shows the market supply and demand curves for corn on the same graph. (The horizontal axis now measures both quantity demanded and quantity supplied.)

Graphically, the intersection of the supply curve and the demand curve for a product indicates the market equilibrium. Here, equilibrium price and quantity are $3 per bushel and 7000 bushels. At any above-equilibrium price, quantity supplied exceeds quantity demanded. This surplus of corn causes price re-

ductions by sellers who are eager to rid themselves of their surplus. The falling price causes less corn to be offered and simultaneously encourages consumers to buy more. The market moves to its equilibrium.

Any price below the equilibrium price creates a shortage; quantity demanded then exceeds quantity supplied. Buyers try to obtain the product by offering to pay more for it; this drives the price upward toward its equilibrium level. The rising price simultaneously causes producers to increase the quantity

51

supplied and prompts many buyers to leave the market, thus eliminating the shortage. Again the market moves to its equilibrium. ◢ 3.1 ❗ 3.1

Rationing Function of Prices

The ability of the competitive forces of supply and demand to establish a price at which selling and buying decisions are consistent is called the **rationing function of prices.** In our case, the equilibrium price of $3 clears the market, leaving no burdensome surplus for sellers and no inconvenient shortage for potential buyers. And it is the combination of freely made individual decisions that sets this market-clearing price. In effect, the market outcome says that all buyers who are willing and able to pay $3 for a bushel of corn will obtain it; all buyers who cannot or will not pay $3 will go without corn. Similarly, all producers who are willing and able to offer corn for sale at $3 a bushel will sell it; all producers who cannot or will not sell for $3 per bushel will not sell their product. **(Key Question 7)**

Changes in Supply, Demand, and Equilibrium

We know that demand might change because of fluctuations in consumer tastes or incomes, changes in consumer expectations, or variations in the prices of related goods. Supply might change in response to changes in resource prices, technology, or taxes. What effects will such changes in supply and demand have on equilibrium price and quantity?

Changes in Demand   Suppose that supply is constant and demand increases, as shown in Figure 3.6a. As a result, the new intersection of the supply and demand curves is at higher values on both the price and the quantity axes. Clearly, an increase in demand raises both equilibrium price and equilibrium quantity. Conversely, a decrease in demand, such as that shown in Figure 3.6b, reduces both equilibrium price and equilibrium quantity. (The value of graphical analysis is now apparent: We need not fumble with columns of figures to determine the outcomes; we need only compare the new and the old points of intersection on the graph.)

Changes in Supply   Now suppose that demand is constant but supply increases, as in Figure 3.6c. The new intersection of supply and demand is located at a lower equilibrium price but at a higher

equilibrium quantity. An increase in supply reduces equilibrium price but increases equilibrium quantity. In contrast, if supply decreases, as in Figure 3.6d, the equilibrium price rises while the equilibrium quantity declines.

Complex Cases   When both supply and demand change, the effect is a combination of the individual effects.

Supply Increase; Demand Decrease   What effect will a supply increase and a demand decrease have on equilibrium price? Both changes decrease price, so the net result is a price drop greater than that resulting from either change alone.

What about equilibrium quantity? Here the effects of the changes in supply and demand are opposed: the increase in supply increases equilibrium quantity, but the decrease in demand reduces it. The direction of the change in quantity depends on the relative sizes of the changes in supply and demand. If the increase in supply is larger than the decrease in demand, the equilibrium quantity will increase. But if the decrease in demand is greater than the increase in supply, the equilibrium quantity will decrease.

Supply Decrease; Demand Increase   A decrease in supply and an increase in demand both increase price. Their combined effect is an increase in equilibrium price greater than that caused by either change separately. But their effect on equilibrium quantity is again indeterminate, depending on the relative sizes of the changes in supply and demand. If the decrease in supply is larger than the increase in demand, the equilibrium quantity will decrease. In contrast, if the increase in demand is greater than the decrease in supply, the equilibrium quantity will increase.

Supply Increase; Demand Increase   What if supply and demand both increase? A supply increase drops equilibrium price, while a demand increase boosts it. If the increase in supply is greater than the increase in demand, the equilibrium price will fall. If the opposite holds, the equilibrium price will rise.

The effect on equilibrium quantity is certain: The increases in supply and in demand each raise equilibrium quantity. Therefore, the equilibrium quantity will increase by an amount greater than that caused by either change alone.

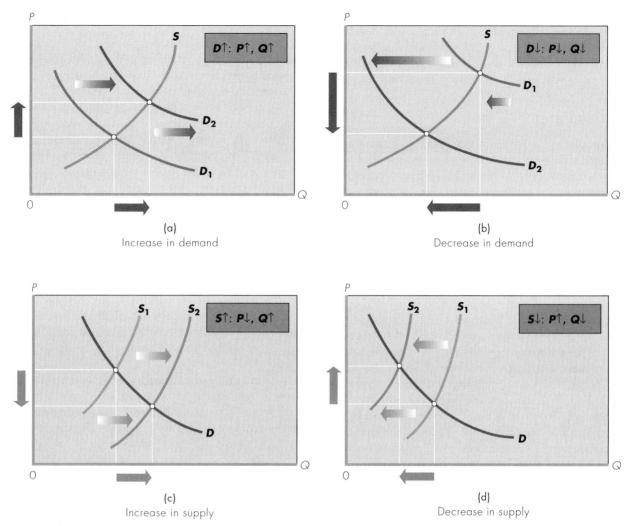

Figure 3.6

Changes in demand and supply and the effects on price and quantity. The increase in demand from D_1 to D_2 in (a) increases both equilibrium price and equilibrium quantity. The decrease in demand from D_1 to D_2 in (b) decreases both equilibrium price and equilibrium quantity. The increase in supply from S_1 to S_2 in (c) decreases equilibrium price and increases equilibrium quantity. The decline in supply from S_1 to S_2 in (d) increases equilibrium price and decreases equilibrium quantity. The boxes in the top right corners summarize the respective changes and outcomes. The upward arrows in the boxes signify increases in demand (D), supply (S), equilibrium price (P), and equilibrium quantity (Q); the downward arrows signify decreases in these items.

Supply Decrease; Demand Decrease What about decreases in both supply and demand? If the decrease in supply is greater than the decrease in demand, equilibrium price will rise. If the reverse is true, equilibrium price will fall. Because decreases in supply and in demand each reduce equilibrium quantity, we can be sure that equilibrium quantity will fall.

Table 3.9 summarizes these four cases. To understand them fully, you should draw supply and demand diagrams for each case to confirm the effects listed in Table 3.9.

Table 3.9

Effects of Changes in Both Supply and Demand

Change in Supply	Change in Demand	Effect on Equilibrium Price	Effect on Equilibrium Quantity
1. Increase	Decrease	Decrease	Indeterminate
2. Decrease	Increase	Increase	Indeterminate
3. Increase	Increase	Indeterminate	Increase
4. Decrease	Decrease	Indeterminate	Decrease

Special cases arise when a decrease in demand and a decrease in supply, or an increase in demand and an increase in supply, exactly cancel out. In both cases, the net effect on equilibrium price will be zero; price will not change. **(Key Question 8)**

A Reminder: "Other Things Equal"

We must stress once again that specific demand and supply curves (such as those in Figure 3.6) show relationships between prices and quantities demanded and supplied, *other things equal*. The downsloping demand curves tell us that price and quantity demanded are inversely related, other things equal. The upsloping supply curves imply that price and quantity supplied are directly related, other things equal.

If you forget the other-things-equal assumption, you can encounter situations that *seem* to be in conflict with these basic principles. For example, suppose salsa manufacturers sell 1 million bottles of salsa at $4 a bottle in 1 year; 2 million bottles at $5 in the next year; and 3 million at $6 in the year thereafter. Price and quantity purchased vary directly, and these data seem to be at odds with the law of demand. But there is no conflict here; the data do not refute the law of demand. The catch is that the law of demand's other-things-equal assumption has been violated over the 3 years in the example. Specifically, because of changing tastes and rising incomes, the demand for salsa has increased sharply, as in Figure 3.6a. The result is higher prices *and* larger quantities purchased.

Another example: The price of coffee occasionally has shot upward at the same time that the quantity of coffee produced has declined. These events seemingly contradict the direct relationship between price and quantity denoted by supply. The catch again is that the other-things-equal assumption underlying the upsloping supply curve was violated. Poor coffee harvests decreased supply, as in Figure 3.6d, increasing the equilibrium price of coffee and reducing the equilibrium quantity.

These examples emphasize the importance of our earlier distinction between a change in quantity demanded (or supplied) and a change in demand (supply). In Figure 3.6a a change in demand causes a change in the quantity supplied. In Figure 3.6d a change in supply causes a change in quantity demanded.

Application: Pink Salmon

To reinforce these ideas, let's briefly examine a real-world market: the market for pink salmon. This market has a standardized product, for which price has substantially declined in recent years.

A decade or two ago, fishers earned a relatively high price for each pound of pink salmon brought to the dock. In Figure 3.7 that price is represented as P_1, at the intersection of supply curve S_1 and demand curve D_1. The corresponding quantity of pink salmon—the type used mainly for canning—is represented as Q_1 pounds.

Over the past few decades, supply and demand shifted in the market for pink salmon. On the supply side, improved technology in the form of larger, more efficient fishing boats greatly increased the catch and lowered the cost of obtaining it. Also, high profits at price P_1 encouraged many new fishers to enter the industry. As a result of these changes, the supply of pink salmon greatly increased and the supply curve shifted to the right, as from S_1 to S_2 in Figure 3.7.

Over the same years, the demand for pink salmon decreased, as represented by the leftward shift from D_1 to D_2 in Figure 3.7. That decrease resulted from increases in consumer income and re-

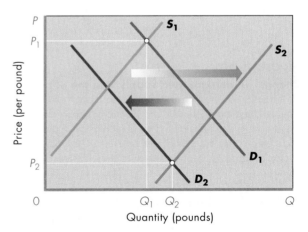

Figure 3.7

The market for pink salmon.   In the last two decades, the supply of pink salmon has increased and the demand for pink salmon has decreased. As a result, the price of pink salmon has declined, here from P_1 to P_2 a pound. Since supply has increased more than demand has declined, the equilibrium quantity of pink salmon has increased, here from Q_1 to Q_2.

LAST WORD

Ticket Scalping: A Bum Rap?

Some Market Transactions Get a Bad Name That Is Not Warranted.

Tickets to athletic and artistic events are sometimes resold at higher-than-original prices—a market transaction known by the term "scalping." For example, the original buyer may resell a $50 ticket to a college bowl game for $200, $250, or more. The media often denounce scalpers for "ripping off" buyers by charging "exorbitant" prices. Scalping and extortion are synonymous in some people's minds.

But is scalping really sinful? We must first recognize that such ticket resales are voluntary transactions. Both buyer and seller expect to gain from the exchange. Otherwise, it would not occur! The seller must value the $200 more than seeing the event, and the buyer must value seeing the event more than the $200.

So there are no losers or victims here: Both buyer and seller benefit from the transaction. The "scalping" market simply redistributes assets (game or concert tickets) from those who value them less to those who value them more.

Does scalping impose losses or injury on other parties, in particular the sponsors of the event? If the sponsors are injured, it is because they initially priced tickets below the equilibrium level. In so doing, they suffer an economic loss in the form of less revenue and profit than they might have otherwise received. But the loss is self-inflicted because of their pricing error. That mistake is quite separate and distinct from the fact that some tickets are later resold at a higher price.

What about spectators? Does scalping deteriorate the enthusiasm of the audience? Usually not! People who have the greatest interest in the event will pay the scalper's high prices. Ticket scalping also benefits the teams and performing artists, because they will appear before more dedicated audiences—ones that are more likely to buy souvenir items or CDs.

So is ticket scalping undesirable? Not on economic grounds. Both seller and buyer of a "scalped" ticket benefit, and a more interested audience results. Event sponsors may sacrifice revenue and profits, but that stems from their own misjudgment of the equilibrium price.

---

ductions in the price of substitute products. As buyers' incomes increased, consumers shifted demand away from canned fish and toward higher-quality fresh or frozen fish, including higher-quality species of salmon such as Atlantic, Chinook, and Coho salmon. Moreover, the emergence of fish farming, in which salmon are raised in net pens, lowered the prices of these substitute species. That, too, reduced the demand for pink salmon.

The increased supply of, and decreased demand for, pink salmon greatly reduced the price, as represented by the drop from P_1 to P_2 in Figure 3.7. Both the supply increase and the demand decrease helped reduce the equilibrium price. However, the equilibrium *quantity* of pink salmon increased, as represented by the move from Q_1 to Q_2. Both shifts of the curves reduced the equilibrium price, but equilibrium quantity increased because the increase in supply exceeded the decrease in demand.

QUICK REVIEW 3.3

■ In competitive markets, prices adjust to the equilibrium level at which quantity demanded equals quantity supplied.

■ The equilibrium price and quantity are those indicated by the intersection of the supply and demand curves for any product or resource.

■ An increase in demand increases equilibrium price and quantity; a decrease in demand decreases equilibrium price and quantity.

■ An increase in supply reduces equilibrium price but increases equilibrium quantity; a decrease in supply increases equilibrium price but reduces equilibrium quantity.

■ Over time, equilibrium price and quantity may change in directions that seem at odds with the laws of demand and supply because the other-things-equal assumption is violated.

SUMMARY

1. A market is any institution or arrangement that brings together buyers and sellers of a product, service, or resource.

2. Demand is a schedule or curve representing the willingness of buyers in a specific period to purchase a particular product at each of various prices. The law of demand implies that consumers will buy more of a product at a low price than at a high price. Therefore, other things equal, the relationship between price and quantity demanded is negative or inverse and is graphed as a downsloping curve. Market demand curves are found by adding horizontally the demand curves of the many individual consumers in the market.

3. Changes in one or more of the determinants of demand (consumer tastes, the number of buyers in the market, the money incomes of consumers, the prices of related goods, and price expectations) shift the market demand curve. A shift to the right is an increase in demand; a shift to the left is a decrease in demand. A change in demand is different from a change in the quantity demanded, the latter being a movement from one point to another point on a fixed demand curve because of a change in the product's price.

4. Supply is a schedule or curve showing the amounts of a product that producers are willing to offer in the market at each possible price during a specific period. The law of supply states that, other things equal, producers will offer more of a product at a high price than at a low price. Thus, the relationship between price and quantity supplied is positive or direct, and supply is graphed as an upsloping curve. The market supply curve is the horizontal summation of the supply curves of the individual producers of the product.

5. Changes in one or more of the determinants of supply (resource prices, production techniques, taxes or subsidies, the prices of other goods, price expectations, or the number of sellers in the market) shift the supply curve of a product. A shift to the right is an increase in supply; a shift to the left is a decrease in supply. In contrast, a change in the price of the product being considered causes a change in the quantity supplied, which is shown as a movement from one point to another point on a fixed supply curve.

6. The equilibrium price and quantity are established at the intersection of the supply and demand curves. The interaction of market demand and market supply adjusts the price to the point at which the quantities demanded and supplied are equal. This is the equilibrium price. The corresponding quantity is the equilibrium quantity.

7. The ability of market forces to synchronize selling and buying decisions to eliminate potential surpluses and shortages is known as the rationing function of prices.

8. A change in either demand or supply changes the equilibrium price and quantity. Increases in demand raise both equilibrium price and equilibrium quantity; decreases in demand lower both equilibrium price and equilibrium quantity. Increases in supply lower equilibrium price and raise equilibrium quantity; decreases in supply raise equilibrium price and lower equilibrium quantity.

9. Simultaneous changes in demand and supply affect equilibrium price and quantity in various ways, depending on their direction and relative magnitudes.

TERMS AND CONCEPTS

market	determinants of demand	supply	surplus
demand	normal goods	supply schedule	shortage
demand schedule	inferior goods	law of supply	equilibrium price
law of demand	substitute good	supply curve	equilibrium quantity
diminishing marginal utility	complementary good	determinants of supply	rationing function of prices
income effect	change in demand	change in supply	
substitution effect	change in quantity demanded	change in quantity supplied	
demand curve			

STUDY QUESTIONS

1. Explain the law of demand. Why does a demand curve slope downward? What are the determinants of demand? What happens to the demand curve when each of these determinants changes? Distinguish between a change in demand and a change in the quantity demanded, noting the cause(s) of each.

2. **Key Question** What effect will each of the following have on the demand for product B?

a. Product B becomes more fashionable.

b. The price of substitute product C falls.

c. Income declines and product B is an inferior good.

d. Consumers anticipate that the price of B will be lower in the near future.

e. The price of complementary product D falls.

f. Foreign tariff barriers on product B are eliminated.

3. Explain the following news dispatch from Hull, England: "The fish market here slumped today to what local commentators called 'a disastrous level'—all because of a shortage of potatoes. The potatoes are one of the main ingredients in a dish that figures on almost every café-menu—fish and chips [French fries]."

4. Explain the law of supply. Why does the supply curve slope upward? What are the determinants of supply? What happens to the supply curve when each of these determinants changes? Distinguish between a change in supply and a change in the quantity supplied, noting the cause(s) of each.

5. **Key Question** What effect will each of the following have on the supply of product B?

a. A technological advance in the methods of producing product B.

b. A decline in the number of firms in industry B.

c. An increase in the prices of resources required in the production of B.

d. The expectation that the equilibrium price of B will be lower in the future than it is currently.

e. A decline in the price of product A, a good whose production requires substantially the same techniques and resources as does the production of B.

f. The levying of a specific sales tax on B.

g. The granting of a 50-cent-per-unit subsidy for each unit of B produced.

6. "In the corn market, demand often exceeds supply and supply sometimes exceeds demand." "The price of corn rises and falls in response to changes in supply and demand." In which of these two statements are the terms "supply" and "demand" used correctly? Explain.

7. **Key Question** Suppose the total demand for wheat and the total supply of wheat per month in the Kansas City grain market are as follows:

Thousands of Bushels Demanded	Price per Bushel	Thousands of Bushels Supplied	Surplus (+) or Shortage (−)
85	$3.40	72	_____
80	$3.70	73	_____
75	$4.00	75	_____
70	$4.30	77	_____
65	$4.60	79	_____
60	$4.90	81	_____

a. What is the equilibrium price? What is the equilibrium quantity? Fill in the surplus-shortage column and use it to explain why your answers are correct.

b. Graph the demand for wheat and the supply of wheat. Be sure to label the axes of your graph correctly. Label equilibrium price *P* and equilibrium quantity *Q*.

c. Why will $3.40 not be the equilibrium price in this market? Why not $4.90? "Surpluses drive prices up; shortages drive them down." Do you agree?

d. Now suppose that the government establishes a ceiling (maximum legal) price of, say, $3.70 for wheat. Explain carefully the effects of this ceiling price. Demonstrate your answer graphically. What might prompt the government to establish a ceiling price?

8. **Key Question** How will each of the following changes in demand and/or supply affect equilibrium price and equilibrium quantity in a competitive market; that is, do price and quantity rise, fall, or remain unchanged, or are the answers indeterminate because they depend on the magnitudes of the shifts? Use supply and demand diagrams to verify your answers.

a. Supply decreases and demand is constant.

b. Demand decreases and supply is constant.

c. Supply increases and demand is constant.

d. Demand increases and supply increases.

e. Demand increases and supply is constant.

f. Supply increases and demand decreases.

g. Demand increases and supply decreases.

h. Demand decreases and supply decreases.

9. "Prices are the automatic regulator that tends to keep production and consumption in line with each other." Explain.

10. Explain: "Even though parking meters may yield little or no net revenue, they should nevertheless be retained because of the rationing function they perform."

11. Use two market diagrams to explain how an increase in state subsidies to public colleges might affect tuition and enrollments in both public and private colleges.

12. Critically evaluate: "In comparing the two equilibrium positions in Figure 3.6a, I note that a larger amount is actually purchased at a higher price. This refutes the law of demand."

13. Suppose you go to a recycling center and are paid $.25 per pound for your aluminum cans. However, the recycling firm charges you $.20 per bundle to accept your old newspapers. Use demand and supply diagrams to portray both markets. Explain how different government policies with respect to the recycling of aluminum and paper might account for these different market outcomes.

14. **Advanced Analysis** Assume that demand for a commodity is represented by the equation $P = 10 - .2Q_d$ and supply by the equation $P = 2 + .2Q_s$, where Q_d and Q_s are quantity demanded and quantity supplied, respectively, and P is price. Using the equilibrium condition $Q_s = Q_d$, solve the equations to determine equilibrium price. Now determine equilibrium quantity. Graph the two equations to substantiate your answers.

15. **(Last Word)** Discuss the economic aspects of ticket scalping, specifying gainers and losers.

16. **Web-Based Question: *Farm commodity prices— supply and demand in action*** The U.S. Department of Agriculture, www.usda.gov/nass, publishes charts on the prices of farm products. Go to the USDA home page and select Graphics. Choose three farm products of your choice and determine whether their prices (as measured by "prices received by farmers") have generally increased, decreased, or stayed the same over the past three years. In which of the three cases, if any, do you think that supply has increased more rapidly than demand? In which of the three cases, if any, do you think that demand has increased more rapidly than supply? Explain your reasoning.

17. **Web-Based Question: *Changes in demand—baby diapers and retirement villages*** Other things equal, an increase in the number of buyers for a product or service will increase demand. Baby diapers and retirement villages are two products designed for different population groups. The U.S. Census Bureau website, www.census.gov/ipc/www/idbpyr.html, provides population pyramids (graphs that show the distribution of population by age and sex) for countries for the current year, 2025, and 2050. View the population pyramids for Mexico, Japan, and the United States. Which country do you think will have the greatest percentage increase in demand for baby diapers in the year 2050? For retirement villages? Which country do you think will have the greatest absolute increase in demand for baby diapers? For retirement villages?

4

The Market System

S UPPOSE THAT YOU were assigned to compile a list of all the individual goods and services available at a large regional shopping mall, including the different brands and variations of each type of product. We think you would agree that this task would be daunting and the list would be long! Although a single shopping mall contains a remarkable quantity and variety of goods, it is only a minuscule part of the national economy. ■ Who decided that the particular goods and services available at the mall and in the broader economy should be produced? How did the producers determine which technology and types of resources to use in producing these particular goods? Who will obtain these products? What accounts for the new and improved products among these goods? ■ In Chapter 3 we saw how equilibrium prices and quantities are established in *individual* product and resource markets. We now widen our focus to take in *all* product markets and resource markets—*capitalism*, also called the *private-enterprise system* or simply the *market system*. In this chapter we examine the characteristics of the market system and how that system answers questions such as those posed above.

■ Characteristics of the Market System

The market system, as practiced in industrially advanced economies, has several notable characteristics. Let's look at them in some detail.

Private Property

In a market system, private individuals and firms, not the government, own most of the property resources (land and capital). In fact, it is this extensive private ownership of capital that gives capitalism its name. This right of **private property**, coupled with the freedom to negotiate binding legal contracts, enables individuals and businesses to obtain, use, and dispose of property resources as they see fit. The right to bequeath—the right of property owners to designate who will receive their property when they die—sustains the institution of private property.

Property rights encourage investment, innovation, exchange, maintenance of property, and economic growth. Why would anyone stock a store, build a factory, or clear land for farming if someone else, or the government itself, could take that property for his or her own benefit?

Property rights also extend to intellectual property through patents, copyrights, and trademarks. Such long-term protection encourages people to write books, music, and computer programs and to invent new products and production processes without fear that others will steal them and the rewards they may bring.

Property rights also facilitate exchange. The title to an automobile or the deed to a cattle ranch assures the buyer that the seller is the legitimate owner. Moreover, property rights encourage owners to maintain or improve their property so as to preserve or increase its value. Finally, property rights enable people to use their time and resources to produce more goods and services, rather than using them to protect and retain the property they have already produced or acquired. ▮ 4.1

Freedom of Enterprise and Choice

Closely related to private ownership of property is freedom of enterprise and choice. The market system requires that various economic units make certain choices, which are expressed and implemented in the economy's markets:

■ **Freedom of enterprise** ensures that entrepreneurs and private businesses are free to obtain and use economic resources to produce their choice of goods and services and to sell them in their chosen markets.

■ **Freedom of choice** enables owners to employ or dispose of their property and money as they see fit. It also allows workers to enter any line of work for which they are qualified. Finally, it ensures that consumers are free to buy the goods and services that best satisfy their wants.

These choices are free only within broad legal limitations, of course. Illegal choices such as selling human organs or buying illicit drugs are punished through fines and imprisonment. (Global Perspective 4.1 reveals that the degree of economic freedom varies greatly from nation to nation.)

Self-Interest

In the market system, **self-interest** is the motivating force of all the various economic units as they express their free choices. Self-interest means that each economic unit tries to do what is best for itself. Entrepreneurs try to maximize profit or minimize

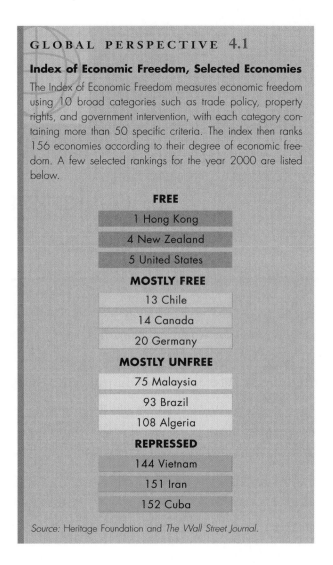

GLOBAL PERSPECTIVE 4.1

Index of Economic Freedom, Selected Economies

The Index of Economic Freedom measures economic freedom using 10 broad categories such as trade policy, property rights, and government intervention, with each category containing more than 50 specific criteria. The index then ranks 156 economies according to their degree of economic freedom. A few selected rankings for the year 2000 are listed below.

FREE
- 1 Hong Kong
- 4 New Zealand
- 5 United States

MOSTLY FREE
- 13 Chile
- 14 Canada
- 20 Germany

MOSTLY UNFREE
- 75 Malaysia
- 93 Brazil
- 108 Algeria

REPRESSED
- 144 Vietnam
- 151 Iran
- 152 Cuba

Source: Heritage Foundation and *The Wall Street Journal.*

loss. Property owners try to get the highest price for the sale or rent of their resources. Workers try to maximize their utility (satisfaction) by finding jobs that offer the best combination of wages, hours, fringe benefits, and working conditions. Consumers try to obtain the products they want at the lowest possible price and apportion their expenditures to maximize their utility. The motive of self-interest gives direction and consistency to what might otherwise be a chaotic economy.

Recall that the pursuit of self-interest is not the same as selfishness. Self-interest involves maximizing some benefit, and it does not preclude helping others. A stockholder may invest to receive maximum corporate dividends and then donate a portion of them to the United Way or give them to grandchildren. A worker may take a second job to help pay college tuition for her or his children. An entrepreneur may make a fortune and donate much of it to a charitable foundation. 🔑 4.1

Competition

The market system depends on **competition** among economic units. The basis of this competition is freedom of choice exercised in pursuit of a monetary return. Very broadly defined, *competition* requires:

- Independently acting sellers and buyers operating in a particular product or resource market.
- Freedom of sellers and buyers to enter or leave markets, on the basis of their economic self-interest.

Competition diffuses economic power within the businesses and households that make up the economy. When there are independently acting sellers and buyers in a market, no one buyer or seller is able to dictate the price of the product.

Consider the supply side of the product market. When a product becomes scarce, its price rises. An unseasonable frost in Florida may seriously reduce the supply of citrus crops and sharply increase the price of oranges. Similarly, if a single producer can somehow restrict the total output of a product, it can raise the product's price. By controlling market supply, a firm can "rig the market" to its own advantage. But that is not possible in markets where suppliers compete. A firm that raises its price will lose part or all of its business to competitors.

The same reasoning applies to the demand side of the market. Because there are multiple buyers, single buyers cannot manipulate the market to their own advantage by refusing to pay the market price.

Competition also implies that producers can enter or leave an industry; there are no insurmountable barriers to an industry's expanding or contracting. This freedom of an industry to expand or contract provides the economy with the flexibility needed to remain efficient over time. Freedom of entry and exit enables the economy to adjust to changes in consumer tastes, technology, and resource availability.

The diffusion of economic power inherent in competition limits the potential abuse of that power. A producer that charges more than the competitive market price will lose sales to other producers. An employer who pays less than the competitive market wage rate will lose workers to other employers. A firm that fails to exploit new technology will lose profits to firms that do. Competition is the basic regulatory force in the market system.

Markets and Prices

Markets and prices are key characteristics of the market system. They give the system its ability to coordinate millions of daily economic decisions. We know from Chapters 2 and 3 that a market is a mechanism that brings buyers (demanders) and sellers (suppliers) into contact. A market system is necessary to convey the decisions made by buyers and sellers of products and resources. The decisions made on each side of the market determine a set of product and resource prices that guide resource owners, entrepreneurs, and consumers as they make and revise their free choices and pursue their self-interest.

Just as competition is the regulatory mechanism of the market system, the market system itself is the organizing mechanism. It serves as an elaborate communication network through which innumerable individual free choices are recorded, summarized, and balanced. Those who respond to market signals and obey market dictates are rewarded with greater profit and income; those who do not respond to these signals and choose to ignore market dictates are penalized. Through this mechanism society decides what the economy should produce, how production can be organized efficiently, and how the fruits of production are to be distributed among the various units that make up the economy.

> **QUICK REVIEW 4.1**
>
> ▪ The market system rests on the private ownership of property and on freedom of enterprise and freedom of choice.
> ▪ The market system permits economic entities—businesses, resource suppliers, and consumers—to pursue and further their self-interest. It prevents any single economic entity from dictating the prices of products or resources.
> ▪ The coordinating mechanism of the market system is a system of markets and prices.

Reliance on Technology and Capital Goods

Another characteristic of the market system is the extensive use of capital goods. In the market system, competition, freedom of choice, self-interest, and personal reward provide the opportunity and motivation for technological advance. The monetary rewards for new products or production techniques accrue directly to the innovator. The market system therefore encourages extensive use and rapid development of complex capital goods: tools, machinery, large-scale factories, and facilities for storage, communication, transportation, and marketing.

Advanced technology and capital goods are important because the most direct methods of production are often the least efficient. The only way to avoid that inefficiency is to rely on **roundabout production.** It would be ridiculous for a farmer to go at production with bare hands. There are huge benefits—in the form of more efficient production and, therefore, more abundant output—to be derived from creating and using such tools of production (capital equipment) as plows, tractors, storage bins, and so on.

Specialization

The extent to which market economies rely on **specialization** is extraordinary. The majority of consumers produce virtually none of the goods and services they consume, and they consume little or nothing of what they produce. The worker who devotes 8 hours a day to installing windows in Fords may own a Honda. Many farmers sell their milk to the local dairy and then buy margarine at the local grocery store. Society learned long ago that self-sufficiency breeds inefficiency. The jack-of-all-trades may be a very colorful individual but is certainly not an efficient producer.

Division of Labor   Human specialization—called the **division of labor**—contributes to a society's output in several ways:

- *Specialization makes use of differences in ability.*   Specialization enables individuals to take advantage of existing differences in their abilities and skills. If caveman A is strong and swift and good at tracking animals, and caveman B is weak and slow but patient, their distribution of talents can be most efficiently used if A hunts and B fishes.
- *Specialization fosters learning by doing.*   Even if the abilities of A and B are identical, specialization may still be advantageous. By devoting all your time to a single task, you are more likely to develop the skills it requires and to devise improved techniques than you would by working at a number of different tasks. You

learn to be a good hunter by going hunting every day.
- *Specialization saves time.*   By devoting all your time to a single task, you avoid the loss of time incurred in shifting from one job to another.

For all these reasons, specialization increases the total output society derives from limited resources.

Geographic Specialization   Specialization also works on a regional and international basis. It is conceivable that oranges could be grown in Nebraska, but because of the unsuitability of the land, rainfall, and temperature, the costs would be very high. And it is conceivable that wheat could be grown in Florida. But for similar reasons such production would be costly. So Nebraskans produce products—wheat in particular—for which their resources are best suited, and Floridians do the same, producing oranges and other citrus fruits. By specializing, both economies produce more than is needed locally. Then, very sensibly, Nebraskans and Floridians swap some of their surpluses—wheat for oranges, oranges for wheat.

Similarly, on an international scale, the United States specializes in producing such items as commercial aircraft and computers, which it sells abroad in exchange for video recorders from Japan, bananas from Honduras, and woven baskets from Thailand. Both human specialization and geographical specialization are needed to achieve efficiency in the use of limited resources. 🔑 4.2

Use of Money

A rather obvious characteristic of the market system is the extensive use of money. Money performs several functions, but first and foremost it is a **medium of exchange.** It makes trade easier.

A convenient means of exchanging goods is required for specialization. Exchange can, and sometimes does, occur through **barter**—swapping goods for goods, say, wheat for oranges. But barter poses serious problems for the economy because it requires a *coincidence of wants* between the buyer and the seller. In our example, we assumed that Nebraskans had excess wheat to trade and wanted oranges. And we assumed that Floridians had excess oranges to trade and wanted wheat. So an exchange occurred. But if such a coincidence of wants is missing, trade is stymied.

Suppose that Nebraska has no interest in Florida's oranges but wants potatoes from Idaho.

And suppose that Idaho wants Florida's oranges but not Nebraska's wheat. And, to complicate matters, suppose that Florida wants some of Nebraska's wheat but none of Idaho's potatoes. We summarize the situation in Figure 4.1.

In none of the cases shown in the figure is there a coincidence of wants. Trade by barter clearly would be difficult. Instead, people in each state use **money**, which is simply a convenient social invention to facilitate exchanges of goods and services. Historically, people have used cattle, cigarettes, shells, stones, pieces of metal, and many other commodities, with varying degrees of success, as a medium of exchange. But to serve as money, an item needs to pass only one test: *It must be generally acceptable to sellers in exchange for their goods and services.* Money is socially defined; whatever society accepts as a medium of exchange *is* money.

Most economies use pieces of paper as money. The use of paper dollars (currency) as a medium of exchange is what enables Nebraska, Florida, and Idaho to overcome their trade stalemate, as demonstrated in Figure 4.1.

On a global basis the fact that different nations have different currencies complicates specialization and exchange. However, markets in which currencies are bought and sold make it possible for U.S. residents, Japanese, Germans, Britons, and Mexicans, through the swapping of dollars, yen, euros, pounds, and pesos, one for another, to exchange goods and services. ▮ 4.2

Active, but Limited, Government

The final characteristic of the market system, as evidenced in modern economies, is an active, but limited, government. Although a market system promotes a high degree of efficiency in the use of its resources, it has certain shortcomings. We will discover in Chapter 5 that government can increase the overall effectiveness of the economic system in several ways.

QUICK REVIEW 4.2

▪ The market systems of modern industrial economies are characterized by extensive use of technologically advanced capital goods. Such goods help these economies achieve greater efficiency in production.

▪ Specialization is extensive in market systems; it enhances efficiency and output by enabling individuals, regions, and nations to produce the goods and services for which their resources are best suited.

▪ The use of money in market systems facilitates the exchange of goods and services that specialization requires.

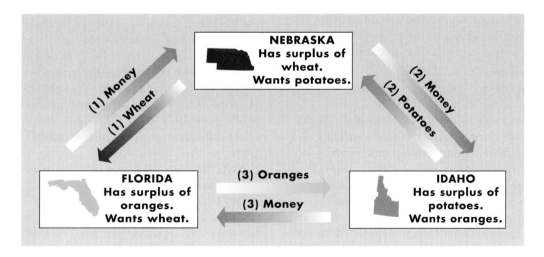

Figure 4.1
Money facilitates trade when wants do not coincide. The use of money as a medium of exchange permits trade to be accomplished despite a noncoincidence of wants. (1) Nebraska trades the wheat that Florida wants for money from Floridians; (2) Nebraska trades the money it receives from Florida for the potatoes it wants from Idaho; (3) Idaho trades the money it receives from Nebraska for the oranges it wants from Florida.

■ The Market System at Work

We have noted that a market system is characterized by competition, freedom of enterprise, and choice. Consumers are free to buy what they choose; entrepreneurs and firms are free to produce and sell what they choose; and resource suppliers are free to make their property and human resources available in whatever use or occupation they choose. We may wonder why such an economy does not collapse in chaos. If consumers want breakfast cereal but businesses choose to produce aerobic shoes and resource suppliers decide to manufacture computer software, production would seem to be deadlocked by the apparent inconsistency of these free choices.

In reality, the millions of decisions made by households and businesses are highly consistent with one another. Firms *do* produce the goods and services that consumers want, and households *do* provide the kinds of labor that businesses want.

To understand the operation of the market system, you must first recognize that every economy must respond to Four Fundamental Questions:

■ What goods and services will be produced?
■ How will the goods and services be produced?
■ Who will get the goods and services?
■ How will the system accommodate change?

The **Four Fundamental Questions** highlight the economic choices underlying the production possibilities curve discussed in Chapter 2. These questions are relevant because of scarce resources in a world of unlimited wants. Let's examine how the market system answers each of these questions and thus addresses the economizing problem.

What Will Be Produced?

With product and resource prices in place, established through competition in both the product and the resource markets, how will a market system decide on the specific types and quantities of goods to be produced? *Because businesses seek profits and avoid losses, the goods and services produced at a continuing profit* will *be produced and those produced at a continuing loss* will not. Profits and losses depend on the difference between the total revenue a firm receives from selling its product and the total cost of producing the product:

Economic profit = total revenue − total cost

Total revenue (TR) is found by multiplying the product price by the quantity of the product sold. Total cost (TC) is found by multiplying the price of each resource used by the amount employed and summing the results.

Economic Costs and Profits   Saying that the products that can be produced profitably *will* be produced and those that cannot *will not* is an accurate generalization only if the meaning of **economic costs** is clearly understood.

Let's think of businesses as simply organizational charts—that is, businesses "on paper," as distinct from the capital, raw materials, labor, and entrepreneurial ability that make them function. To become actual producing firms, these "on-paper" businesses must secure all four types of resources. *Economic costs are the payments that must be made to secure and retain the needed amounts of those resources.* The per-unit size of those costs—the resource prices—are determined by supply and demand in the resource market. As with land, labor, and capital, entrepreneurial ability is a scarce resource that carries a price tag. Consequently, costs must include not only wage and salary payments to labor, and interest and rental payments for capital and land, but also payments to the entrepreneur for organizing and combining the other resources to produce a commodity. The payment for (cost of) the entrepreneur's contributions is called **normal profit.**

A product is produced only if total revenue is large enough to pay wages, interest, rent, and a normal profit (a cost) to the entrepreneur. That way all the economic costs are covered, including the opportunity cost of the entrepreneur's time and talent. If the total revenue from the sale of a product exceeds all these economic costs, the remainder goes to the entrepreneur as an added reward. That return is called *pure profit* or **economic profit.** Economic profit is an above-normal profit, and it *is* what lures other producers to a particular industry.

Profits and Expanding Industries   An example will help explain how the market system determines what goods will be produced. With current technology, suppose the most favorable relationship between total revenue and total cost in producing product X occurs when a firm's output is 15 units. Assume, too, that the least-cost combination of resources in producing 15 units of X is 2 units of labor, 3 units of land, 1 unit of capital, and 1 unit of entrepreneurial ability, selling at prices of $2, $1, $3, and $3, respectively. Finally, suppose that the 15 units of X that these resources produce can be sold for $1 per unit, or $15 total. Will firms produce X? Yes, because each firm will be able to pay wages, rent, interest, and normal profit (a cost) of $13 [= (2 × $2) + (3 × $1) + (1 × $3) + (1 × $3)]. The difference between total revenue of $15 and total cost of $13 is an economic profit of $2.

This economic profit is evidence that industry X is prosperous. It will become an **expanding industry** as new firms, attracted by the above-normal profits, are formed or shift from less profitable industries.

But the entry of new firms will be self-limiting. As new firms enter industry X, the market supply of product X will increase relative to the market demand. This will lower the market price of X, as in Figure 3.6c, and economic profit will gradually diminish and finally disappear. The market supply and demand conditions prevailing when economic profit reaches zero will determine the total amount of X produced. At this point the industry will be at its "equilibrium size," at least until a further change in market demand or supply upsets that equilibrium.

Losses and Declining Industries

But what if the initial market situation for product X were less favorable? Suppose that demand conditions in the product market were such that a firm could sell the 15 units of X at a price of just $.75 per unit. Total revenue would then be $11.25 (= 15 × $.75). After paying wage, rental, and interest costs of $10, and figuring in the normal profit (a cost) of $3, the firm's total cost would again be $13. But because its total revenue is only $11.25, it would incur a loss of $1.75 (= $11.25 − $13).

Certainly, firms would not be attracted to this unprofitable **declining industry.** In fact, if these losses persisted, some of the firms in industry X would go out of business or migrate to more prosperous industries where normal or even economic profits prevailed. However, as that happened, the market supply of X would fall relative to the market demand. Product price would rise (as in Figure 3.6d), and the losses in industry X would eventually disappear. The industry would then stop shrinking. The supply and demand situation that prevailed when economic profit became zero would determine the total output of product X. Again, the industry would for the moment reach its equilibrium size.

Consumer Sovereignty and Dollar Votes

In the market system, consumers are sovereign (in command). **Consumer sovereignty** works through consumer demand, and consumer demand is crucial in determining the types and quantities of goods produced. Consumers spend the income they earn from the sale of their resources on the goods they are most willing and able to buy. Through these **"dollar votes"** consumers register their wants via the demand side of the product market. If the dollar votes for a certain product are great enough to provide a normal profit, businesses will produce that product. If there is an increase in consumer demand, so that enough dollar votes are cast to provide an economic profit, the industry will expand, as will the output of the product.

Conversely, a decrease in consumer demand—meaning fewer dollar votes cast for the product—will result in losses, and, in time, the industry will contract. As firms leave the industry, the output of the product will decline. Indeed, the industry may even cease to exist. Again, the consumers are sovereign; they collectively direct resources away from industries that are not meeting consumer wants.

The dollar votes of consumers determine not only which industries will continue to exist but also which products will survive or fail. Example: In 1991, responding to doctors and nutritionists, McDonald's introduced its low-fat McLean burger. Good idea? Not really. Most consumers found the new product "too dry" and "not tasty," so sales were meager. In 1996 McDonald's quietly dropped the McLean burger from its menu at the same time that it introduced its higher-fat Arch Deluxe burger. In effect, consumers had collectively "voted out" the McLean burger. **!** 4.3

Market Restraints on Freedom

In short, firms are not really free to produce whatever they wish. Consumers' buying decisions make the production of some products profitable and the production of other products unprofitable, thus restricting the choice of businesses in deciding what to produce. Businesses must match their production choices with consumer choices or else face losses and eventual bankruptcy.

The same holds true for resource suppliers. The demand for resources is a **derived demand**—derived, that is, from the demand for the goods and services that the resources help produce. There is a demand for autoworkers because there is a demand for automobiles. There is no demand for buggy-whip braiders because there is no demand for buggy whips. Resource suppliers are not free to allocate their resources to the production of goods that consumers do not value highly. Consumers register their preferences on the demand side of the product market; producers and resource suppliers, prompted by their own self-interest, respond appropriately.

How Will the Goods and Services Be Produced?

The market system steers resources to the industries whose products consumers want—simply because those industries survive, are profitable, and pay for resources. Within each industry, the firms that survive to do the producing also are the ones that are profitable. Because competition weeds out high-cost producers, continued profitability requires that firms produce their output at minimum cost. Achieving least-cost production necessitates, for example, that firms locate their production facilities optimally, considering such factors as resource prices, resource productivity, and transportation costs.

Least-cost production also means that firms must employ the most economically efficient technique of production in producing their output. The most efficient production technique depends on:

■ The available technology, that is, the various combinations of resources that will produce the desired results.
■ The prices of the needed resources.

A technique that requires just a few inputs of resources to produce a specific output may be highly *in*efficient economically *if* those resources are valued very highly in the market. *Economic efficiency means obtaining a particular output of product with the least input of scarce resources, when both output and resource inputs are measured in dollars and cents.* The combination of resources that will produce, say, $15 worth of product X at the lowest possible cost is the most efficient.

Suppose there are three possible techniques for producing the desired $15 worth of product X.

Suppose also that the quantity of each resource required by each production technique and the prices of the required resources are as shown in Table 4.1. By multiplying the required quantities of each resource by its price in each of the three techniques, we can determine the total cost of producing $15 worth of X by means of each technique.

Technique 2 is economically the most efficient, because it is the least costly. It enables society to obtain $15 worth of output by using a smaller amount of resources—$13 worth—than the $15 worth required by the two other techniques. Competition will dictate that producers use technique 2. Thus, the question of how goods will be produced is answered. They will be produced in a least-cost way.

A change in either technology *or* resource prices, however, may cause a firm to shift from the technology it is using. If the price of labor falls to $.50, technique 1 becomes more desirable than technique 2. Firms will find they can lower their costs by shifting to a technology that uses more of the resource whose price has fallen. Exercise: Would a new technique involving 1 unit of labor, 4 of land, 1 of capital, and 1 of entrepreneurial ability be preferable to the techniques listed in Table 4.1, assuming the resource prices shown there? **(Key Question 7)**

Who Will Get the Goods and Services?

The market system enters the picture in two ways when solving the problem of distributing total output. Generally, any product will be distributed to consumers on the basis of their ability and willingness to pay its existing market price. If the price of some product, say, a pocket calculator, is $15, then buyers who are able and willing to pay that price will

Table 4.1

Three Techniques for Producing $15 Worth of Product X

Resource	Price per Unit of Resource	Units of Resource					
		Technique 1		Technique 2		Technique 3	
		Units	Cost	Units	Cost	Units	Cost
Labor	$2	4	$ 8	2	$ 4	1	$ 2
Land	1	1	1	3	3	4	4
Capital	3	1	3	1	3	2	6
Entrepreneurial ability	3	1	3	1	3	1	3
Total cost of $15 worth of X			$15		$13		$15

get a pocket calculator; those who are not, will not. This is the rationing function of equilibrium prices.

The ability to pay the equilibrium prices for pocket calculators and other products depends on the amount of income that consumers have along with their preferences for various goods. If they have sufficient income and want to spend their money on a particular good, they can have it. And the amount of income they have depends on (1) the quantities of the property and human resources they supply and (2) the prices those resources command in the resource market. Resource prices (wages, interest, rent, profit) are key in determining the size of each household's income and therefore each household's ability to buy part of the economy's output.

How Will the System Accommodate Change?

Market systems are dynamic: Consumer preferences, technology, and supplies of resources all change. This means that the particular allocation of resources that is now the most efficient for a *specific* pattern of consumer tastes, range of technological alternatives, and amount of available resources will become obsolete and inefficient as consumer preferences change, new techniques of production are discovered, and resource supplies change over time. Can the market economy adjust to such changes and still use resources efficiently?

Guiding Function of Prices
Suppose consumer tastes change. For instance, assume that consumers decide they want more fruit juice and less milk than the economy currently provides. Those changes in consumer tastes will be communicated to producers through an increase in demand for fruit and a decline in demand for milk. Fruit prices will rise and milk prices will fall.

Now, assuming that firms in both industries were enjoying precisely normal profits before these changes in consumer demand set in, the higher fruit prices will mean economic profit for the fruit industry and the lower milk prices will mean losses for the milk industry. Self-interest will induce new competitors to enter the prosperous fruit industry and will in time force firms to leave the depressed milk industry.

The economic profit that initially follows the increase in demand for fruit will not only induce that industry to expand but will also give it the revenue needed to obtain the resources essential to its growth. Higher fruit prices will permit fruit producers to pay

higher prices for resources, thereby increasing resource demand and drawing resources from less urgent alternative employment. The reverse occurs in the milk industry, where resource demand declines and fewer workers and other resources are employed. These adjustments in the economy are appropriate responses to the changes in consumer tastes. This is consumer sovereignty at work.

The market system is a gigantic communications system. Through changes in prices it communicates changes in such basic matters as consumer tastes and elicits appropriate responses from businesses and resource suppliers. By affecting product prices and profits, changes in consumer tastes direct the expansion of some industries and the contraction of others. Those adjustments are conveyed to the resource market as expanding industries demand more resources and contracting industries demand fewer; the resulting changes in resource prices guide resources from the contracting industries to the expanding industries.

This *directing* or **guiding function of prices** is a core element of the market system. Without such a system, some administrative agency such as a government planning board would have to direct businesses and resources into the appropriate industries. A similar analysis shows that the system can and does adjust to other fundamental changes—for example, to changes in technology and in the availability of various resources.

Role in Promoting Progress
Adjusting to changes is one thing; initiating desirable changes is another. How does the market system promote technological improvements and capital accumulation—two changes that lead to greater productivity and a higher level of material well-being for society?

Technological Advance
The market system provides a strong incentive for technological advance and enables better products and processes to brush aside inferior ones. An entrepreneur or firm that introduces a popular new product will gain revenue and economic profit. Technological advance also includes new and improved methods that reduce production or distribution costs. By passing part of its cost reduction on to the consumer through a lower product price, the firm can increase sales and obtain economic profit at the expense of rival firms. Moreover, the market system is conducive to the *rapid spread* of technological advance throughout an industry. Rival firms must follow the lead of the most innovative firm or else suffer immediate losses and

eventual failure. In some cases, the result is **creative destruction:** The creation of new products and production methods completely destroys the market positions of firms that are wedded to existing products and older ways of doing business. Example: The advent of personal computers and word processing software demolished the market for electric typewriters.

Capital Accumulation   Most technological advances require additional capital goods. The market system provides the resources necessary to produce those goods by adjusting the product market and the resource market through increased dollar votes for capital goods. In other words, the market system acknowledges dollar voting for capital goods as well as for consumer goods.

But who will register votes for capital goods? Entrepreneurs and owners of businesses, as receivers of profit income, often use part of that income to purchase capital goods. Doing so yields even greater profit income in the future if the technological innovation is successful. Also, by paying interest or selling ownership shares, the entrepreneur and firm can attract some of the income of households to cast dollar votes for the production of more capital goods. **(Key Question 9)**

■ Competition and the "Invisible Hand"

In his 1776 book *The Wealth of Nations*, Adam Smith first noted that the operation of a market system creates a curious unity between private interests and social interests. Firms and resource suppliers, seeking to further their own self-interest and operating within the framework of a highly competitive market system, will simultaneously, as though guided by an **"invisible hand,"** promote the public or social interest. For example, we have seen that in a competitive environment, businesses use the least-costly combination of resources to produce a specific output because it is in their self-interest to do so. To act otherwise would be to forgo profit or even to risk business failure. But, at the same time, to use scarce resources in the least-costly (most efficient) way is clearly in the social interest as well.

In our more fruit juice–less milk illustration, it is self-interest, awakened and guided by the competitive market system, that induces responses appropriate to the change in society's wants. Businesses seeking to make higher profits and to avoid losses, and resource suppliers pursuing greater monetary rewards, negotiate changes in the allocation of resources

and end up with the output that society demands. Competition controls or guides self-interest in such a way that it automatically, and quite unintentionally, furthers the best interests of society. The invisible hand ensures that when firms maximize their profits, they also maximize society's output and income.

Of the many virtues of the market system three merit special emphasis:

- ■ *Efficiency*   The basic economic argument for the market system is that it promotes the efficient use of resources, by guiding them into the production of the goods and services most wanted by society. It forces the use of the most efficient techniques in organizing resources for production, and it encourages the development and adoption of new and more efficient production techniques.

- ■ *Incentives*   The market system encourages skill acquisition, hard work, and innovation. Greater work skills and effort mean greater production and higher incomes, which usually translate into a higher standard of living. Similarly, the assuming of risks by entrepreneurs can result in substantial profit incomes. Successful innovations generate economic rewards.

- ■ *Freedom*   The major noneconomic argument for the market system is its emphasis on personal freedom. In contrast to central planning, the market system coordinates economic activity without coercion. The market system permits—indeed, it thrives on—freedom of enterprise and choice. Entrepreneurs and workers are free to further their own self-interest, subject to the rewards and penalties imposed by the market system itself.

QUICK REVIEW 4.3

□   The output mix of the market system is determined by profits, which in turn depend heavily on consumer preferences. Economic profits cause efficient industries to expand; losses cause inefficient industries to contract.

□   Competition forces industries to use the least-costly (most efficient) production methods.

□   In a market economy consumer income and product prices determine how output will be distributed.

□   Competitive markets reallocate resources in response to changes in consumer tastes, technological advances, and changes in supplies of resources.

□   The "invisible hand" of the market system channels the pursuit of self-interest to the good of society.

Shuffling the Deck

Economist Donald Boudreaux Marvels at the Way the Market System Systematically and Purposefully Arranges the World's Tens of Billions of Individual Resources.

In *The Future and Its Enemies,* Virginia Postrel notes the astonishing fact that if you thoroughly shuffle an ordinary deck of 52 playing cards, chances are practically 100 percent that the resulting arrangement of cards has never before existed. *Never.* Every time you shuffle a deck, you produce an arrangement of cards that exists for the first time in history.

The arithmetic works out that way. For a very small number of items, the number of possible arrangements is small. Three items, for example, can be arranged only six different ways. But the number of possible arrangements grows very large very quickly. The number of different ways to arrange five items is 120 . . . for ten items it's 3,628,800 . . . for fifteen items it's 1,307,674,368,000.

The number of different ways to arrange 52 items is 8.066×10^{67}. This is a *big* number. No human can comprehend its enormousness. By way of comparison, the number of possible ways to arrange a mere 20 items is 2,432,902,008,176,640,000— a number larger than the total number of seconds that have elapsed since the beginning of time ten billion years ago—and this number is Lilliputian compared to 8.066×10^{67}.

What's the significance of these facts about numbers? Consider the number of different resources available in the world— my labor, your labor, your land, oil, tungsten, cedar, coffee beans, chickens, rivers, the Empire State Building, Windows 2000, the wharves at Houston, the classrooms at Oxford, the airport at Miami, and on and on and on. No one can possibly count all of the different productive resources available for our use. But we can be sure that this number is at least in the tens of billions.

When you reflect on how incomprehensibly large is the number of ways to arrange a deck containing a mere 52 cards, the mind boggles at the number of different ways to arrange all the world's resources.

If our world were random—if resources combined together haphazardly, as if a giant took them all into his hands and tossed them down like so many [cards]—it's a virtual certainty that the resulting combination of resources would be useless. Unless this chance arrangement were quickly rearranged according to some productive logic, nothing worthwhile would be produced. We would all starve to death. Because only a tiny fraction of possible arrangements serves human ends, any arrangement will be useless if it is chosen randomly or with inadequate knowledge of how each and every resource might be productively combined with each other.

And yet, we witness all around us an arrangement of resources that's productive and serves human goals. Today's arrangement of resources might not be perfect, but it is vastly superior to most of the trillions upon trillions of other possible arrangements.

How have we managed to get one of the minuscule number of arrangements that works? The answer is private property—a social institution that encourages mutual accommodation.

Private property eliminates the possibility that resource arrangements will be random, for each resource owner chooses a course of action only if it promises rewards to the owner that exceed the rewards promised by all other available courses.

[The result] is a breathtakingly complex and productive arrangement of countless resources. This arrangement emerged over time (and is still emerging) as the result of billions upon billions of individual, daily, small decisions made by people seeking to better employ their resources and labor in ways that other people find helpful.

Source: Abridged from Donald J. Boudreaux, "Mutual Accommodation," *Ideas on Liberty,* May 2000, pp. 4–5. Reprinted with permission.

SUMMARY

1. The market system—known also as the private-enterprise system or capitalism—is characterized by the private ownership of resources, including capital, and the freedom of individuals to engage in economic activities of their choice to advance their material well-being. Self-interest is the driving force of such an economy, and competition functions as a regulatory or control mechanism.

2. In the market system, markets and prices organize and make effective the many millions of individual decisions that determine what is produced, the methods of production, and the sharing of output.

3. Specialization, use of advanced technology, and the extensive use of capital goods are common features of market systems.

4. Functioning as a medium of exchange, money eliminates the problems of bartering and permits easy trade and greater specialization, both domestically and internationally.

5. Every economy faces Four Fundamental Questions: (a) What goods and services will be produced? (b) How will the goods and services be produced? (c) Who will get the goods and services? (d) How will the system used accommodate changes in consumer tastes, resource supplies, and technology?

6. The market system produces products whose production and sale yield total revenue sufficient to cover all costs, including a normal profit (a cost). It does not produce products that do not yield a normal profit, or more.

7. Economic profit indicates that an industry is prosperous and promotes its expansion. Losses signify that an industry is not prosperous and hasten its contraction.

8. Consumer sovereignty means that both businesses and resource suppliers are subject to the wants of consumers. Through their dollar votes, consumers decide on the composition of output.

9. Competition forces firms to use the lowest-cost and therefore the most economically efficient production techniques.

10. The prices that a household receives for the resources it supplies to the economy determine that household's income. This income determines the household's claim on the economy's output. Those who have income to spend get the products produced in the market system.

11. By communicating changes in consumer tastes to resource suppliers and entrepreneurs, the market system prompts appropriate adjustments in the allocation of the economy's resources. The market system also encourages technological advance and capital accumulation.

12. Competition, the primary mechanism of control in the market economy, promotes a unity of self-interest and social interests; as though directed by an invisible hand, competition harnesses the self-interest motives of businesses and resource suppliers to further the social interest.

TERMS AND CONCEPTS

private property

freedom of enterprise

freedom of choice

self-interest

competition

roundabout production

specialization

division of labor

medium of exchange

barter

money

Four Fundamental Questions

economic costs

normal profit

economic profit

expanding industry

declining industry

consumer sovereignty

dollar votes

derived demand

guiding function of prices

creative destruction

"invisible hand"

STUDY QUESTIONS

1. Explain each of the following statements:
   a. The market system not only accepts self-interest as a fact of human existence; it relies on self-interest to achieve society's material goals.
   b. The market system provides such a variety of desired goods and services precisely because no single individual or small group is deciding what the economy will produce.

   c. Entrepreneurs and businesses are at the helm of the economy, but their commanders are consumers.

2. Why is private property, and the protection of property rights, so critical to the success of the market system?

3. What are the advantages of "roundabout" production? What is meant by the term "division of labor"?

What are the advantages of specialization in the use of human and material resources? Explain: "Exchange is the necessary consequence of specialization."

4. What problem does barter entail? Indicate the economic significance of money as a medium of exchange. What is meant by the statement "We want money only to part with it."?

5. Evaluate and explain the following statements:
   a. The market system is a profit-and-loss system.
   b. Competition is the indispensable disciplinarian of the market economy.
   c. Production methods that are inferior in the engineering sense may be the most efficient methods in the economic sense, once resource prices are considered.

6. Explain the meaning and implications of the following quotation:

   > The beautiful consequence of the market is that it is its own guardian. If output or prices or certain kinds of remuneration stray away from their socially ordained levels, forces are set into motion to bring them back to the fold. A curious paradox thus ensues: the market, which is the acme of individual economic freedom, is the strictest taskmaster of all. One may appeal the ruling of a planning board or win the dispensation of a [government] minister; but there is no appeal, no dispensation, from the anonymous pressures of the market mechanism. Economic freedom is thus more illusory than at first appears. One can do as one pleases in the market. But if one pleases to do what the market disapproves, the price of individual freedom is economic ruination.[1]

7. **Key Question** Assume that a business firm finds that its profit will be at a maximum when it produces $40 worth of product A. Suppose also that each of the three techniques shown in the following table will produce the desired output:

Resource	Price per Unit of Resource	Technique 1	Technique 2	Technique 3
Labor	$3	5	2	3
Land	4	2	4	2
Capital	2	2	4	5
Entrepreneurial ability	2	4	2	4

The table header "Resource Units Required" spans the three Technique columns.

a. With the resource prices shown, which technique will the firm choose? Why? Will production entail profit or losses? Will the industry expand or contract? When will a new equilibrium output be achieved?
b. Assume now that a new technique, technique 4, is developed. It combines 2 units of labor, 2 of land, 6 of capital, and 3 of entrepreneurial ability. In view of the resource prices in the table, will the firm adopt the new technique? Explain your answer.
c. Suppose that an increase in the labor supply causes the price of labor to fall to $1.50 per unit, all other resource prices remaining unchanged. Which technique will the producer now choose? Explain.
d. "The market system causes the economy to conserve most in the use of resources that are particularly scarce in supply. Resources that are scarcest relative to the demand for them have the highest prices. As a result, producers use these resources as sparingly as is possible." Evaluate this statement. Does your answer to part c, above, bear out this contention? Explain.

8. Suppose the demand for bagels rises dramatically while the demand for breakfast cereal falls. Briefly explain how the competitive market economy will make the needed adjustments to reestablish an efficient allocation of society's scarce resources.

9. **Key Question** Some large hardware stores such as Home Depot boast of carrying as many as 20,000 different products in each store. What motivated the producers of those products—everything from screwdrivers to ladders to water heaters—to make them and offer them for sale? How did the producers decide on the best combinations of resources to use? Who made those resources available, and why? Who decides whether these particular hardware products should continue to get produced and offered for sale?

10. In a single sentence, describe the meaning of the phrase "invisible hand."

11. **(Last Word)** What explains why millions of economic resources tend to get arranged logically and productively rather than haphazardly and unproductively?

12. **Web-Based Question:** *Sparkly things—interested in buying one?* Go to the Internet auction site eBay at www.ebay.com/index.html and click the category Jewelry and Gemstones. How many diamonds are for sale at the moment? How many rubies, sapphires, and opals? Note the wide array of sizes and prices of the gemstones. In what sense is there competition among the sellers in these markets? How does that competition influence prices? In what sense is there

---

[1]Robert L. Heilbroner, *The Worldly Philosophers*, 7th ed. (New York: Simon & Schuster, 1999), pp. 57–58.

competition among buyers? How does that competition influence prices? Do you see something interesting there or elsewhere on eBay? Go ahead and buy it!

13. **Web-Based Question:** *Barter and the IRS* Bartering occurs when goods or services are exchanged without the exchange of money. For some, barter's popularity is that it enables them to avoid paying taxes to the government. How might such avoidance occur? Does the Internal Revenue Service (IRS), www.irs.ustreas.gov/, treat barter as taxable or nontaxable income? (Click Taxpayer Help and Education, then Tele-Tax Topics, and then Types of Income.) How is the value of a barter transaction determined? What are some IRS barter examples? What does the IRS require of the members of so-called barter exchanges?

C H A P T E R

The U.S. Economy
Private and Public Sectors

W̲ᴇ ɴᴏᴡ ᴍᴏᴠᴇ from the general characteristics of the market system to specific information about the U.S. economy. For convenience, we divide the economy into two sectors: the *private sector*, which includes *households* and *businesses*, and the *public sector*, or simply *government*.

■ Households as Income Receivers

The U.S. economy currently has about 105 million households. These households consist of one or more persons occupying a housing unit and are both the ultimate suppliers of all economic resources *and* the major spenders in the economy. We can categorize the income received by households by how it was earned and by how it was divided among households.

The Functional Distribution of Income

The **functional distribution of income** indicates how the nation's earned income is apportioned among wages, rents, interest, and profits, that is, according to the function performed by the income receiver. Wages are paid to labor; rents and interest are paid to owners of property resources; and profits are paid to the owners of corporations and unincorporated businesses.

Figure 5.1 shows the functional distribution of U.S. income earned in 2000. The largest source of income for households is the wages and salaries paid to workers. Notice that the bulk of total U.S. income goes to labor, not to capital. Proprietors' income—the income of doctors, lawyers, small-business owners, farmers, and owners of other unincorporated enterprises—also has a "wage" element. Some of this income is payment for one's own labor, and some of it is profit from one's own business.

The other three types of income are self-evident: Some households own corporate stock and receive dividend incomes on their holdings. Many households also own bonds and savings accounts that yield interest income. And some households receive rental income by providing buildings and natural resources (including land) to businesses and other individuals.

The Personal Distribution of Income

The **personal distribution of income** indicates how the nation's money income is divided among individual households. In Figure 5.2 households are

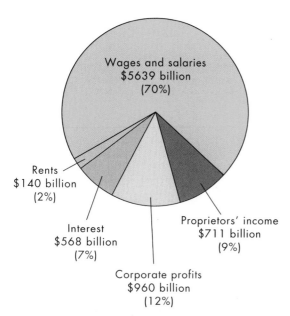

Figure 5.1

The functional distribution of U.S. income, 2000.
More than two-thirds of national income is received as wages and salaries. Income to property owners—corporate profit, interest, and rents—accounts for about one-fifth of total income.
Source: Bureau of Economic Analysis.

divided into five numerically equal groups or quintiles; the heights of the bars show the percentage of total income received by each group. In 1999 the poorest 20 percent of all households received about 4 percent of total personal income, and the richest 20 percent received almost 50 percent. Clearly there is considerable inequality in the personal distribution of U.S. income. **(Key Question 2)**

▌Households as Spenders

How do households dispose of their income? Part of it flows to government as taxes, and the rest is divided between personal savings and personal consumption expenditures. In 2000, households disposed of their total personal income as shown in Figure 5.3.

Personal Taxes

In 2000 households paid $1293 billion in personal taxes, or 16 percent of $8274 billion total income. Personal taxes, of which the personal income tax is the major component, have risen in relative terms since the Second World War. In 1941, households paid just 3 percent of their total income in personal taxes.

Personal Saving

Economists define "saving" as that part of after-tax income that is not spent; hence, households have just two choices about what to do with their income after taxes—use it to consume, or save it. Saving is the portion of income that is not paid in taxes or used to purchase consumer goods but instead flows into bank accounts, insurance policies, bonds and stocks, mutual funds, and other financial assets.

Saving has been very low in the United States in recent years, probably because of the dramatic increase in household wealth caused by the record increases in the value of common stock between 1996 and 1999. Feeling wealthier, households consumed more and saved less. As indicated in Figure 5.3, saving was less than 1 percent of household income in 2000.

Usually, U.S. households save between 5 and 8 percent of their income. Reasons for saving center on *security* and *speculation*. Households save to provide a nest egg for coping with unforeseen contin-

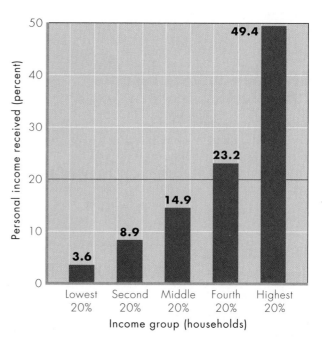

Figure 5.2

The personal distribution of income among U.S. households, 1999. Personal income is unequally distributed in the United States, with the top 20 percent of households receiving about one-half of the total income. In an equal distribution, all five vertical bars would be as high as the horizontal line drawn at 20 percent; then each 20 percent of families would receive 20 percent of the nation's total income.
Source: U.S. Bureau of the Census.

gencies (sickness, accident, and unemployment), for retirement from the workforce, to finance the education of children, or simply for financial security. They may also channel part of their income to purchase stocks, speculating that their investments will increase in value.

The desire to save is not enough in itself, however. You must be able to save, and that depends on the size of your income. If your income is low, you may not be able to save any money at all. If your income is very, very low you may *dissave*—that is, spend more than your after-tax income. You do this by borrowing or by digging into savings you may have accumulated in years when your income was higher.

Both saving and consumption vary directly with income; as households garner more income, they save more and consume more. In fact, the top 10 percent of income receivers account for most of the personal saving in the U.S. economy.

Personal Consumption Expenditures

As Figure 5.3 shows, more than four-fifths of the total income of households flows back into the business sector as personal consumption expenditures—money spent on consumer goods.

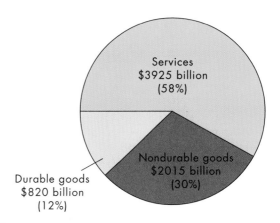

Figure 5.4

The composition of consumer expenditures, 2000.
Consumers divide their spending among durable goods (goods that have lives of 3 years or more), nondurable goods, and services. About 58 percent of consumer spending is for services. *Source:* Bureau of Economic Analysis.

Figure 5.4 shows how consumers divide their expenditures among durable goods, nondurable goods, and services. Twelve percent of consumer expenditures are on **durable goods**—products that have expected lives of 3 years or more. Such goods include automobiles, furniture, and personal computers. Another 30 percent of consumer expenditures are on **nondurable goods**—products that have lives of less than 3 years. Included are such goods as food, clothing, and gasoline. About 58 percent of consumer expenditures are on **services**—the work done for consumers by lawyers, barbers, doctors, lodging personnel, and so on. This high percentage is the reason that the United States is often referred to as a *service-oriented economy*.

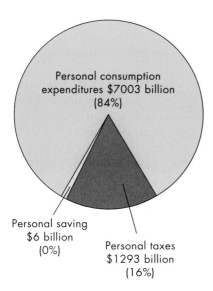

Figure 5.3

The disposition of household income, 2000.
Households apportion their income among taxes, saving, and consumption, with most going to consumption. (The way income is defined in this figure differs slightly from that used in Figure 5.1, accounting for the quantitative discrepancies between the "total income" amounts in the two figures.)
Source: Bureau of Economic Analysis.

QUICK REVIEW 5.1

▪ The functional distribution of income indicates how income is apportioned among wages, rents, interest, and profits; the personal distribution of income indicates how income is divided among families.

▪ Wages and salaries are the major component of the functional distribution of income. The personal distribution of income reveals considerable inequality.

▪ More than 80 percent of household income is consumed; the rest is saved or paid in taxes.

▪ Consumer spending is directed to durable goods, nondurable goods, and services, with nearly 60 percent going to services.

■ The Business Population

Businesses constitute the second major part of the private sector. It will be useful to distinguish among a plant, a firm, and an industry:

■ A **plant** is a physical establishment—a factory, farm, mine, store, or warehouse—that performs one or more functions in fabricating and distributing goods and services.

■ A **firm** is a business organization that owns and operates plants. Some firms operate only one plant, but many own and operate several.

■ An **industry** is a group of firms that produce the same, or similar, products.

The organizational structures of firms are often complex and varied. *Multiplant firms* may be organized horizontally, with several plants performing much the same function. Examples are the multiple bottling plants of Coca-Cola and the many individual Wal-Mart stores. Firms also may be *vertically integrated*, meaning they own plants that perform different functions in the various stages of the production process. For example, oil companies such as Texaco own oil fields, refineries, and retail gasoline stations. Some firms are *conglomerates*, so named because they have plants that produce products in several industries. For example, Pfizer makes not only prescription medicines (Lipitor, Viagra) but also chewing gum (Trident, Dentyne), razors (Schick), cough drops (Halls), breath mints (Clorets, Certs), and antacids (Rolaids).

■ Legal Forms of Businesses

The business population is extremely diverse, ranging from giant corporations such as General Motors, with 1999 sales of $189 billion and more than 600,000 employees, to neighborhood specialty shops and "mom-and-pop" groceries with one or two employees and sales of only $200 to $300 per day. There are three major legal forms of businesses:

■ A **sole proprietorship** is a business owned and operated by one person. Usually, the proprietor (the owner) personally supervises its operation.

■ The **partnership** form of business organization is a natural outgrowth of the sole proprietorship. In a partnership, two or more individuals (the partners) agree to own and operate a business together. Usually they pool their financial

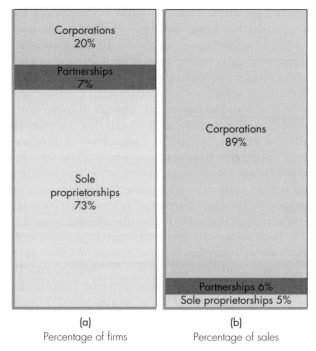

Figure 5.5

The business population and shares of domestic output. (a) Sole proprietorships dominate the business population numerically, but (b) corporations account for almost 90 percent of total sales (output).

resources and business skills. Consequently, they share the risks and the profits or losses.

■ A **corporation** is a legal creation that can acquire resources, own assets, produce and sell products, incur debts, extend credit, sue and be sued, and perform the functions of any other type of enterprise. A corporation is distinct and separate from the individual stockholders who own it. Hired managers run most corporations.

Figure 5.5a shows how the business population is distributed among the three major legal forms. About 73 percent of firms are sole proprietorships, whereas only 20 percent are corporations. But as Figure 5.5b indicates, corporations account for nearly 90 percent of all sales (output).

Advantages and Disadvantages

There are advantages and disadvantages to each form of business enterprise.

Sole Proprietorship

Sole proprietorships are very numerous because they are so easy to set up and organize; there is virtually no complex paper work or legal expense. The proprietor is one's own boss and has substantial freedom of action. Because the proprietor's profit income depends on the enterprise's success, there is strong incentive to manage the business efficiently.

But there are also several disadvantages of sole proprietorships. With rare exceptions, the financial resources of a sole proprietorship are insufficient to permit the firm to grow into a large enterprise. Finances are usually limited to what the proprietor has in the bank and what he or she can borrow. Since proprietorships often fail, commercial banks are not eager to extend them credit.

Also, being totally in charge of an enterprise necessitates that the proprietor carry out all management functions. A proprietor must make decisions on buying, selling, and the hiring and training of personnel, as well as decisions on producing, advertising, and distributing the firm's product. In short, the potential benefits of specialization in business management are not available to the typical small-scale proprietorship.

Finally, and most important, the proprietor is subject to *unlimited liability*. Individuals in business for themselves risk not only the assets of the firm but their personal assets as well. If the assets of an unsuccessful sole proprietorship are insufficient to pay the firm's bills, creditors can file claims against the proprietor's personal property.

Partnership

Like the sole proprietorship, a partnership is easy to organize. Although the partners usually sign a written agreement, there is not much legal red tape or legal expense. Also, greater specialization in management is possible because there are two or more participants. And because there is more than one owner, the financial resources of a partnership are likely to be greater than the resources of a sole proprietorship. Consequently, commercial banks regard partnerships as somewhat better risks than sole proprietorships.

But partnerships have some of the shortcomings of the proprietorship as well as some of their own. Whenever several people participate in management, the divided authority may lead to inconsistent policies or to inaction when action is required. Worse, the partners may disagree on basic policy. And although the finances of partnerships are generally superior to those of sole proprietorships, partnerships are still severely limited. The combined financial resources of three or four partners may not be enough to ensure the growth of a successful enterprise.

The continuity of a partnership is precarious. Generally, when one partner dies or withdraws, the partnership must be dissolved and reorganized, with inevitable disruption of its operations. Finally, unlimited liability plagues a partnership, just as it does a proprietorship. Each partner is liable for all business debts incurred, not only as a result of his or her own performance but also as a result of the performance of any other partner. A wealthy partner risks his or her wealth on the prudence of less affluent partners.

Corporation

The advantages of the corporate form of business enterprise have catapulted it into a dominant position in the United States. Although corporations are relatively small in number, many of them are large in size and in scale of operations. The corporation is by far the most effective form of business organization for raising financial capital (money). The corporation employs unique methods of finance—the selling of stocks and bonds—that enable it to pool the financial resources of large numbers of people. **Stocks** are shares of ownership of a corporation, whereas **bonds** are promises to repay a loan, usually at a set rate of interest. (See the Last Word.)

Financing via sales of stocks and bonds also provides advantages to those who purchase these *securities*. Such financing makes it possible for a household to own a part of the business and to share the expected monetary rewards without actively managing the firm. Moreover, an individual investor can spread risks by buying the securities of several corporations. And it is usually easy for holders of corporate securities to sell their holdings. Organized stock exchanges simplify the transfer of securities from sellers to buyers. This "ease of sale" increases the willingness of savers to make financial investments in corporate securities. Also, corporations have easier access to bank credit than do other types of business organizations. Corporations are better risks and are more likely to become profitable clients of banks. ⚠ 5.1

Corporations have the distinct advantage of **limited liability.** The owners (stockholders) of a corporation risk only what they paid for their stock. Their personal assets are not at stake if the corporation defaults on its debts. Creditors can sue the corporation as a legal person but cannot sue the owners of the corporation as individuals.

Because of their ability to attract financial capital, successful corporations can easily expand the scope of their operations and realize the benefits of expansion. For example, they can take advantage of mass-production technologies and division of labor. A corporation can hire specialists in production, accounting, and marketing functions and thus improve efficiency.

As a legal entity, the corporation has a life independent of its owners and its officers. Legally, at least, corporations are immortal. The transfer of corporate ownership through inheritance or the sale of stock does not disrupt the continuity of the corporation. Corporations have permanence that is conducive to long-range planning and growth.

The corporation's advantages are of tremendous significance and typically override any associated disadvantages. Yet there are certain drawbacks to the corporate form. Some red tape and legal expense are involved in obtaining a corporate charter. And from the social point of view, the corporate form of enterprise lends itself to certain abuses. Because the corporation is a legal entity, unscrupulous business owners can sometimes avoid personal responsibility for questionable business activities by adopting the corporate form of enterprise.

A disadvantage to the owners of corporations is the **double taxation** of some corporate income. Corporate profit that is shared among stockholders as *dividends* is taxed twice—once as corporate profit and again as stockholders' personal income.

Hybrid Structures A number of states have passed legislation authorizing "hybrid" business structures that extend some of the advantages of corporations to firms with one or relatively few owners. Two such structures are the *limited-liability company (LLC)* and the *S corporation*.

The LLC is like an ordinary partnership for tax purposes but resembles a corporation in matters of liability. Like a partnership, an LLC distributes all profit directly to its owners and investors. But like a corporation, an LLC shields the personal assets of owners from liability claims. LLCs have a limited life, typically 30 or 40 years.

The S corporation is a corporation with 75 or fewer shareholders. Because the profit from the corporation passes directly to the owners as if the firm were a sole proprietorship or a partnership, the owners avoid the double taxation on distributed profit. They also enjoy the benefit of limited liability.

The Principal-Agent Problem

Many U.S. corporations are extremely large. In 1999 some 80 U.S. corporations had annual sales of more than $20 billion, and 170 firms had sales of more than $10 billion. General Motors alone sold $189 billion of output in 1999. Only 22 nations in the world had a total annual output that exceeded GM's annual sales!

Large size creates a potential problem. In sole proprietorships and partnerships, the owners of the real and financial assets of the firm enjoy direct control of those assets. But ownership of large corporations is spread over tens or hundreds of thousands of stockholders. The owners of a corporation usually do not manage it—they hire others to do so.

That practice can create a **principal-agent problem.** The *principals* are the stockholders who own the corporation and who hire executives as their agents to run the business on their behalf. But the interests of these managers (the agents) and the wishes of the owners (the principals) do not always coincide. The owners typically want maximum company profit and stock price. The agents, however, may want the power, prestige, and pay that usually accompany control over a large enterprise, independent of its profitability and stock price.

So a conflict of interest may develop. For example, executives may build expensive office buildings, enjoy excessive perks such as corporate jets, and pay too much to acquire other corporations. Consequently, the firm will have bloated costs. Profits and stock prices will not be maximized for the owners. 🔑 5.1

Many corporations have addressed the principal-agent problem by providing a substantial part of executive pay as shares of the companies' stock. The idea is to align the interests of the executives more closely with those of the broader corporate owners. By pursuing high profits and share prices—which benefit the broader owners—the executives enhance their own incomes. On average, high-level U.S. managers now own about 20 percent of their companies' stock. **(Key Question 4)**

■ The Public Sector: Government's Role

The economic activities of the *public sector*—Federal, state, and local government—are extensive. We begin by discussing the economic functions of governments. What is government's role in the economy?

Providing the Legal Structure

Government provides the legal framework and the services needed for a market economy to operate effectively. The legal framework sets the legal status of business enterprises, ensures the rights of private ownership, and allows the making and enforcement of contracts. Government also establishes the legal "rules of the game" that control relationships among businesses, resource suppliers, and consumers. Discrete units of government referee economic relationships, seek out foul play, and impose penalties.

Government intervention is presumed to improve the allocation of resources. By supplying a medium of exchange, ensuring product quality, defining ownership rights, and enforcing contracts, the government increases the volume and safety of exchange. This widens the market and fosters greater specialization in the use of property and human resources. Such specialization promotes a more efficient allocation of resources.

Like the optimal amount of any "good," the optimal amount of regulation is that at which the marginal benefit and marginal cost are equal. Thus, there can be either too little regulation (MB exceeds MC) or too much regulation (MB is less than MC). The task is deciding on the right amount.

Maintaining Competition

Competition is the basic regulatory mechanism in the market system. It is the force that subjects producers and resource suppliers to the dictates of consumer sovereignty. With competition, buyers are the boss, the market is their agent, and businesses are their servants.

It is a different story where a single seller—a **monopoly**—controls an industry. By controlling supply, a monopolist can charge a higher-than-competitive price. Producer sovereignty then supplants consumer sovereignty. In the United States, government has attempted to control monopoly through *regulation* and through *antitrust*.

A few industries are natural monopolies—industries in which technology is such that only a single seller can achieve the lowest possible costs. In some cases government has allowed these monopolies to exist but has also created public commissions to regulate their prices and set their service standards. Examples of *regulated monopolies* are some firms that provide local electricity, telephone, and transportation services.

In nearly all markets, however, efficient production can best be attained with a high degree of competition. The Federal government has therefore enacted a series of antitrust (antimonopoly) laws, beginning with the Sherman Act of 1890, to prohibit certain monopoly abuses and, if necessary, break monopolists up into competing firms.

Redistributing Income

The market system is impersonal and may distribute income more inequitably than society desires. It yields very large incomes to those whose labor, by virtue of inherent ability and acquired education and skills, command high wages. Similarly, those who, through hard work or inheritance, possess valuable capital and land, receive large property incomes.

But many other members of society have less productive ability, have received only modest amounts of education and training, and have accumulated or inherited no property resources.

Moreover, some of the aged, the physically and mentally disabled, and the poorly educated earn small incomes or, like the unemployed, no income at all. Thus society chooses to redistribute a part of total income through a variety of government policies and programs. They are:

- **Transfer payments**   *Transfer payments*, for example, in the form of welfare checks and food stamps, provide relief to the destitute, the dependent, the disabled, and older citizens; unemployment compensation payments provide aid to the unemployed.
- **Market intervention**   Government also alters the distribution of income through *market intervention*, that is, by acting to modify the prices that are or would be established by market forces. Providing farmers with above-market prices for their output and requiring that firms pay minimum wages are illustrations of government interventions designed to raise the income of specific groups.
- **Taxation**   Since the 1930s, government has used the personal income tax to take a larger proportion of the income of the rich than of the poor, thus narrowing the after-tax income difference between high-income and low-income earners.

The *extent* to which government should redistribute income is subject to lively debate. Redistribution involves both benefits and costs. The alleged benefits are greater "fairness," or "economic justice"; the alleged costs are reduced incentives to work, save, invest, and produce, and therefore a loss of total output and income.

Reallocating Resources

Market failure occurs when the competitive market system (1) produces the "wrong" amounts of certain goods and services or (2) fails to allocate any resources whatsoever to the production of certain goods and services whose output is economically justified. The first type of failure results from what economists call *spillovers*, and the second type involves *public goods*. Both kinds of market failure can be corrected by government action.

Spillovers or Externalities
When we say that competitive markets automatically bring about the efficient use of resources, we assume that all the benefits and costs for each product are fully reflected in the market demand and supply curves. That is not always the case. In some markets certain benefits or costs may escape the buyer or seller.

A spillover occurs when some of the costs or the benefits of a good are passed on to or "spill over to" someone other than the immediate buyer or seller. Spillovers are also called *externalities*, because they are benefits or costs that accrue to some third party that is external to the market transaction. 🔑 5.2

Spillover Costs
Production or consumption costs inflicted on a third party without compensation are called **spillover costs.** Environmental pollution is an example. When a chemical manufacturer or a meatpacking plant dumps its wastes into a lake or river, swimmers, fishers, and boaters—and perhaps those who drink the water—suffer spillover costs. When a petroleum refinery pollutes the air with smoke or a paper mill creates obnoxious odors, the community experiences spillover costs for which it is not compensated.

What are the economic effects? Recall that costs determine the position of the firm's supply curve. When a firm avoids some costs by polluting, its supply curve lies farther to the right than it does when the firm bears the full costs of production. As a result, the price of the product is too low and the output of the product is too large to achieve allocative efficiency. A market failure occurs in the form of an overallocation of resources to the production of the good.

Correcting for Spillover Costs
Government can do two things to correct the overallocation of resources. Both solutions are designed to internalize external costs, that is, to make the offending firm pay the costs rather than shift them to others:

- **Legislation**   In cases of air and water pollution, the most direct action is legislation prohibiting or limiting the pollution. Such legislation forces potential polluters to pay for the proper disposal of industrial wastes—here, by installing smoke-abatement equipment or water-purification facilities. The idea is to force potential offenders, under the threat of legal action, to bear *all* the costs associated with production.
- **Specific taxes**   A less direct action is based on the fact that taxes are a cost and therefore a determinant of a firm's supply curve. Government might levy a *specific tax*—that is, a tax confined to a particular product—on each unit of the polluting firm's output. The amount of this tax would roughly equal the estimated

amount of the spillover cost arising from the production of each unit of output. Through this tax, government would pass back to the offending firm a cost equivalent to the spillover cost the firm is avoiding. This would shift the firm's supply curve to the left, reducing equilibrium output and eliminating the overallocation of resources.

Spillover Benefits Sometimes spillovers appear as benefits. The production or consumption of certain goods and services may confer spillover or external benefits on third parties or on the community at large without compensating payment. Immunization against measles and polio results in direct benefits to the immediate consumer of those vaccines. But it also results in widespread substantial spillover benefits to the entire community.

Education is another example of **spillover benefits.** Education benefits individual consumers: Better-educated people generally achieve higher incomes than less well educated people. But education also provides benefits to society, in the form of a more versatile and more productive labor force, on the one hand, and smaller outlays for crime prevention, law enforcement, and welfare programs, on the other.

Spillover benefits mean that the market demand curve, which reflects only private benefits, understates total benefits. The demand curve for the product lies farther to the left than it would if the market took all benefits into account. As a result, a smaller amount of the product will be produced, or, alternatively, there will be an *underallocation* of resources to the product—again a market failure.

Correcting for Spillover Benefits How might the underallocation of resources associated with spillover benefits be corrected? The answer is either to subsidize consumers (to increase demand), to subsidize producers (to increase supply), or, in the extreme, to have government produce the product:

- **Subsidize consumers** To correct the underallocation of resources to higher education, the U.S. government provides low-interest loans to students so that they can afford more education. Those loans increase the demand for higher education.
- **Subsidize suppliers** In some cases government finds it more convenient and administratively simpler to correct an underallocation by subsi-

dizing suppliers. For example, in higher education, state governments provide substantial portions of the budgets of public colleges and universities. Such subsidies lower the costs of producing higher education and increase its supply. Publicly subsidized immunization programs, hospitals, and medical research are other examples.

- **Provide goods via government** A third policy option may be appropriate where spillover benefits are extremely large: Government may finance or, in the extreme, own and operate the industry that is involved. Examples are the U.S. Postal Service and Federal aircraft control systems.

Public Goods and Services

Certain goods called *private goods* are produced through the competitive market system and are said to be *divisible* because they are produced in units small enough to be purchased and used by individual buyers. Examples are the myriad items sold in stores. Private goods are also subject to the **exclusion principle.** Buyers who are willing and able to pay the equilibrium price of the product obtain it, but those who are unable or unwilling to pay are *excluded* from acquiring the product and its benefits.

Certain other goods and services called **public goods** have the opposite characteristics. Public goods are *indivisible;* they must be produced in such large units that they cannot ordinarily be sold to individual buyers. Individuals can buy hamburgers, computers, and automobiles through the market, but they cannot buy aircraft carriers, highways, or space telescopes.

The exclusion principle does not apply to public goods since there is no effective way of excluding individuals from their benefits once such goods come into existence. Obtaining the benefits of private goods requires that they be *purchased;* obtaining the benefits of public goods requires only that they be *available.*

The classic example of a public good is a proposed lighthouse on a treacherous coast. The construction of the lighthouse would be economically justified if its benefits (fewer shipwrecks) exceeded its cost. But the benefits accruing to a single user would not be great enough to justify the purchase of such an indivisible product. Moreover, once it was in operation, the warning light would be a guide to *all* ships; there would be no practical way to exclude any captain from using the light. Economists call this the

free-rider problem, in which people receive benefits from a good without contributing to its cost.

Because the services of the lighthouse cannot be priced and sold, it would be unprofitable for a private firm to devote resources to it. So here we have a service that could yield substantial benefits but to which the market system would allocate no resources. It is a public good, much like national defense, flood control, and public health. Society signals its desire for such goods by voting for particular political candidates who support their provision. The goods themselves must be provided by the public sector and financed by compulsory charges in the form of taxes. ❗ 5.2

Quasi-Public Goods

Government provides many goods that fit the economist's definition of a public good. However, it also provides other goods and services that could be produced and delivered in such a way that the exclusion principle would apply. Such goods, called **quasi-public goods,** include education, streets and highways, police and fire protection, libraries and museums, preventive medicine, and sewage disposal. They could all be priced and provided by private firms through the market system. But, as we noted earlier, because they all have substantial spillover benefits, they would be underproduced by the market system. Therefore, government often provides them to avoid the underallocation of resources that would otherwise occur.

The Reallocation Process

How are resources reallocated from the production of private goods to the production of public and quasi-public goods? If the resources of the economy are fully employed, government must free up resources from the production of private goods and make them available for the production of public and quasi-public goods. It does so by reducing private demand for them. And it does that by levying taxes on households and businesses, taking some of their income out of the circular flow. With lower incomes and hence less purchasing power, households and businesses are obliged to curtail their consumption and investment spending. As a result, the private demand for goods and services declines, as does the private demand for resources. So by diverting purchasing power from private spenders to government, taxes remove resources from private use. (Global Perspective 5.1 shows the extent to which various countries divert labor from the private sector to the public sector.)

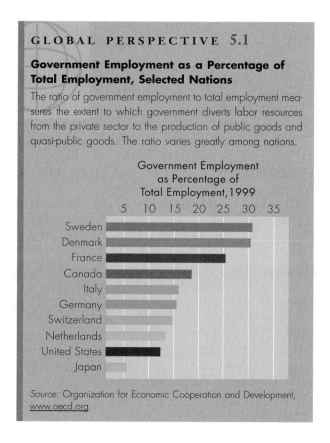

GLOBAL PERSPECTIVE 5.1

Government Employment as a Percentage of Total Employment, Selected Nations

The ratio of government employment to total employment measures the extent to which government diverts labor resources from the private sector to the production of public goods and quasi-public goods. The ratio varies greatly among nations.

Government Employment as Percentage of Total Employment, 1999

Sweden
Denmark
France
Canada
Italy
Germany
Switzerland
Netherlands
United States
Japan

Source: Organization for Economic Cooperation and Development, www.oecd.org.

Government then spends the tax proceeds to provide public and quasi-public goods and services. Taxation releases resources from the production of private consumer goods (food, clothing, television sets) and private investment goods (printing presses, boxcars, warehouses). Government shifts those resources to the production of public and quasi-public goods (post offices, submarines, parks), changing the composition of the economy's total output. **(Key Questions 9 and 10)**

Promoting Stability

An economy's level of output depends on its level of total spending relative to its production capacity. When the level of total spending matches the economy's production capacity, human and property resources are fully employed and prices in general are stable. But sometimes total spending is either inadequate or excessive and the result is either unemployment or inflation. Government promotes stability by addressing these two problems:

■ *Unemployment* When private sector spending is too low, government may try to augment it so that total spending—private plus public—is sufficient to achieve full employment. It does this by increasing government spending or by lowering taxes to stimulate private spending. Also, it often takes actions to lower interest rates, thereby stimulating private borrowing and spending.

■ *Inflation* Inflation is a general increase in the level of prices. Prices of goods and services rise when spenders try to buy more than the economy's capacity to produce. When total spending is excessive and becomes inflationary, government may try to reduce total spending by cutting its own expenditures or by raising taxes to curtail private spending. It may also take actions to increase interest rates to reduce private borrowing and spending.

QUICK REVIEW 5.3

▪ Government enhances the operation of the market system by providing an appropriate legal foundation and promoting competition.

▪ Transfer payments, direct market intervention, and taxation are among the ways in which government can lessen income inequality.

▪ Government can correct for the overallocation of resources associated with spillover costs through legislation or taxes; it can offset the underallocation of resources associated with spillover benefits by granting government subsidies.

▪ Government provides certain public goods because they are indivisible and free-riders can obtain them without payment; government also provides many quasi-public goods because of their large spillover benefits.

▪ Government can stabilize the economy by adjusting spending, tax revenues, and interest rates.

▮ The Circular Flow Revisited

In Figure 5.6 we integrate government into the circular flow model first shown in Figure 2.6. Here flows (1) through (4) are the same as the corresponding flows in that figure. Flows (1) and (2) show business expenditures for the resources provided by households. These expenditures are costs to businesses but represent wage, rent, interest, and profit income to households. Flows (3) and (4) show household expenditures for the goods and services produced by businesses.

Now consider what happens when we add government. Flows (5) through (8) illustrate that government makes purchases in both product and resource markets. Flows (5) and (6) represent government purchases of such products as paper, computers, and military hardware from private businesses. Flows (7) and (8) represent government purchases of resources. The Federal government employs and pays salaries to members of Congress, the armed forces, Justice Department lawyers, meat inspectors, and so on. State and local governments hire and pay teachers, bus drivers, police, and firefighters. The Federal government might also lease or purchase land to expand a military base, and a city might buy land on which to build a new elementary school.

Government then provides public goods and services to both households and businesses, as shown by flows (9) and (10). To finance those public goods and services, businesses and households are required to pay taxes, as shown by flows (11) and (12). These flows are labeled as *net* taxes to indicate that they also include "taxes in reverse" in the form of transfer payments to households and subsidies to businesses. Thus, flow (11) entails various subsidies to farmers, shipbuilders, and airlines as well as income, sales, and excise taxes paid by businesses to government. Most subsidies to business are "concealed" in the form of low-interest loans, loan guarantees, tax concessions, or public facilities provided at prices below their cost. Similarly, flow (12) includes both taxes (personal income taxes, payroll taxes) collected by government directly from households and transfer payments such as welfare payments and social security benefits paid by government.

We can use Figure 5.6 to review how government alters the distribution of income, reallocates resources, and changes the level of economic activity. The structure of taxes and transfer payments significantly affects income distribution. In flow (12) a tax structure that draws tax revenues primarily from well-to-do households, combined with a system of transfer payments to low-income households, reduces income inequality.

Flows (5) through (8) imply that government diverts goods and resources away from private sector consumption or use and directs them to the public

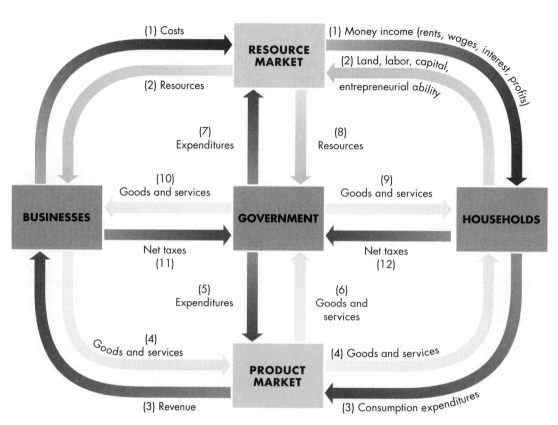

Figure 5.6

The circular flow and the public sector. Government buys products from the product market and employs resources from the re-source market to provide public goods and services to households and businesses. Government finances its expenditures through the net tax revenues (taxes minus transfer payments) it receives from households and businesses.

sector. This resource reallocation is required to produce public goods and services.

Finally, the governmental flows suggest how government might try to stabilize the economy. For example, if the economy had widespread unemployment, government might increase its spending to increase total spending, output, and employment. Similarly, government might reduce taxes or increase transfer payments to increase income available for spending. That would boost private spending and employment. To fight inflation, the opposite policies would be in order: reduced government spending, increased taxes, and reduced transfers.

∎ Government Finance

How large is the U.S. public sector? What are the main expenditure categories of Federal, state, and local governments? How are these expenditures financed?

Government Purchases and Transfers

We can get an idea of the size of government's economic role by examining government purchases of goods and services and government transfer payments. There is a significant difference between these two kinds of outlays:

- **Government purchases** are *exhaustive*; the products purchased directly absorb (require the use of) resources and are part of the domestic output. For example, the purchase of a missile absorbs the labor of physicists and engineers along with steel, explosives, and a host of other inputs.

- **Transfer payments** are *nonexhaustive*; they do not directly absorb resources or create output. Social security benefits, welfare payments, veterans' benefits, and unemployment compensation are examples of transfer payments. Their key characteristic is that recipients make no current contribution to domestic output in return for them.

Federal, state, and local governments spent $2779 billion in 2000. Of that total, government purchases were $1740 billion and government transfers were $1039 billion. Figure 5.7 shows these amounts as percentages of U.S. domestic output for 2000 and compares them to percentages for 1960. Government purchases have declined from about 22 to 17 percent of output since 1960. But transfer payments have doubled as a percentage of output—from 5 percent in 1960 to 10 percent in 2000. Relative to U.S. output, total government spending is thus slightly higher today than it was 40 years ago. This means that the tax revenues required to finance government expenditures are also slightly higher. Today, government spending and the tax revenues needed to finance it are nearly 28 percent of U.S. output.

In 2000 the so-called Tax Freedom Day in the United States was May 3. On that day the average worker had earned enough (from the start of the year) to pay his or her share of the taxes required to finance government spending for the year. Tax Freedom Day arrives even later in several other countries, as implied in Global Perspective 5.2.

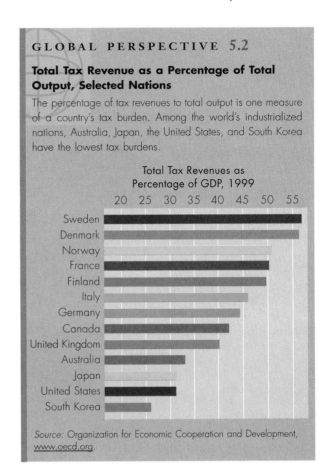

GLOBAL PERSPECTIVE 5.2

Total Tax Revenue as a Percentage of Total Output, Selected Nations

The percentage of tax revenues to total output is one measure of a country's tax burden. Among the world's industrialized nations, Australia, Japan, the United States, and South Korea have the lowest tax burdens.

Total Tax Revenues as Percentage of GDP, 1999

Source: Organization for Economic Cooperation and Development, www.oecd.org.

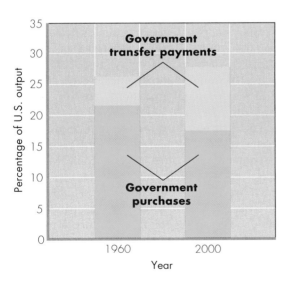

Figure 5.7

Government purchases, transfers, and total spending as percentages of U.S. output, 1960 and 2000. Government purchases have declined as a percent of U.S. output since 1960. Transfer payments, however, have increased, so total government spending (purchases plus transfers) is now about 28 percent of U.S. output.

▌Federal Finance

Now let's look separately at each of the Federal, state, and local units of government in the United States and compare their expenditures and taxes. Figure 5.8 tells the story for the Federal government.

Federal Expenditures

Four areas of Federal spending stand out: (1) pensions and income security, (2) national defense, (3) health, and (4) interest on the public debt. The *pensions and income security* category includes the many income-maintenance programs for the aged, persons with disabilities or handicaps, the unemployed, the retired, and families with no breadwinner. *National defense* accounts for about 16 percent of the Federal budget, underscoring the high cost of military preparedness. *Health* reflects the cost of government health programs for the retired and poor. *Interest on the public debt* is high because the public debt itself is large.

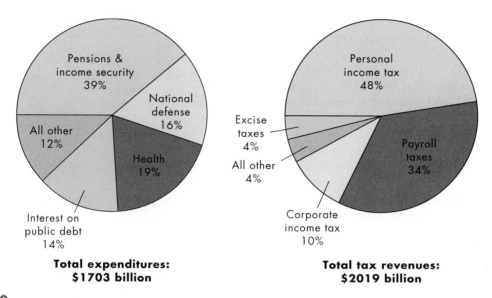

Figure 5.8

Federal expenditures and tax revenues, 1999. Federal expenditures are dominated by spending for pensions and income security and by spending for national defense. A full 82 percent of Federal tax revenue is derived from just two sources: the personal income tax and payroll taxes. The $316 billion difference between revenues and expenditures reflects a budget surplus. *Source:* U.S. Office of Management and Budget.

Federal Tax Revenues

The revenue side of Figure 5.8 shows that the personal income tax, payroll taxes, and the corporate income tax are the basic revenue sources, accounting respectively for 48, 34, and 10 cents of each dollar collected.

Personal Income Tax The **personal income tax** is the kingpin of the Federal tax system and merits special comment. This tax is levied on *taxable income*, that is, on the incomes of households and unincorporated businesses after certain exemptions ($2800 for each household member) and deductions (business expenses, charitable contributions, home mortgage interest payments, certain state and local taxes) are taken into account.

The Federal personal income tax is a *progressive tax*, meaning that people with higher incomes pay a larger percentage of their incomes as taxes than do people with lower incomes. The progressivity is achieved by applying higher tax rates to successive layers or brackets of income.

Columns 1 and 2 in Table 5.1 show the mechanics of the income tax for a married couple filing a joint return in 2000. Note that a 15 percent tax rate applies to all taxable income up to $43,850, a 28 percent rate applies to additional income up to $105,950, and even greater rates apply for three more layers of additional income, the highest rate being 39.6 percent.

The tax rates shown in column 2 in Table 5.1 are marginal tax rates. A **marginal tax rate** is the rate at which the tax is paid on each *additional* unit of taxable income. Thus, if a couple's taxable income is $60,000, they will pay the marginal tax rate of 15 percent on each dollar from $1 to $43,850 and the marginal tax rate of 28 percent on each dollar from $43,851 to $60,000. You should confirm that their total income tax is $11,100.

The marginal tax rates in column 2 overstate the personal income tax bite because the rising rates in that column apply only to the income within each successive tax bracket. To get a better idea of the tax burden, we must consider average tax rates. The **average tax rate** is the total tax paid divided by total taxable income. The couple in our previous example is in the 28 percent tax bracket because they pay a top marginal tax rate of 28 percent on some of their income. But their *average* tax rate is 18.5 percent (=$11,100/$60,000).

A tax whose average rate rises as income increases is a progressive tax. Such a tax claims both a larger absolute amount and a larger proportion of income as income rises. Thus we can say that the Federal personal income tax is progressive. **(Key Question 15)**

Table 5.1
Federal Personal Income Tax Rates, 2000*

(1) Total Taxable Income	(2) Marginal Tax Rate, %	(3) Total Tax on Highest Income in Bracket	(4) Average Tax Rate on Highest Income in Bracket, % (3) ÷ (1)
$1–$43,850	15.0	$ 6,578	15.0
$43,851–$105,950	28.0	23,966	22.6
$105,951–$161,450	31.0	41,171	25.5
$161,451–$288,350	36.0	86,855	30.1
Over $288,350	39.6		

*Data are for a married couple filing a joint return.

Payroll Taxes   Social security contributions are **payroll taxes**—taxes based on wages and salaries—used to finance two compulsory Federal programs for retired workers: social security (an income-enhancement program) and Medicare (which pays for medical services). Employers and employees pay these taxes equally. Improvements in, and extensions of, the social security programs, plus growth of the labor force, have resulted in significant increases in these payroll taxes in recent years. In 2000, employees and employers each paid 7.65 percent on the first $76,200 of an employee's annual earnings and 1.45 percent on all additional earnings.

Corporate Income Tax   The Federal government also taxes corporate income. The **corporate income tax** is levied on a corporation's profit—the difference between its total revenue and its total expenses. For almost all corporations, the tax rate is 35 percent.

Excise Taxes   Taxes on commodities or on purchases take the form of **sales and excise taxes.** The difference between the two is mainly one of coverage. Sales taxes fall on a wide range of products, whereas excises are levied individually on a small, select list of commodities. As Figure 5.8 suggests, the Federal government collects excise taxes (on the sale of such commodities as alcoholic beverages, tobacco, and gasoline) but does not levy a general sales tax; sales taxes are the primary revenue source of most state governments.

▮ State and Local Finance

State and local governments have different mixes of revenues and expenditures than the Federal government has.

State Finances

Note in Figure 5.9 that the primary source of tax revenue for state governments is sales and excise taxes, which account for about 48 percent of all their tax revenue. State personal income taxes, which have much lower rates than the Federal income tax, are the second most important source of state revenue. A tax on corporate income and license fees account for most of the remainder of state tax revenue.

The major expenditures of state governments are for (1) education, (2) public welfare, (3) health and hospitals, and (4) highway maintenance and construction.

Figure 5.9 contains aggregated data, so it tells us little about the finances of individual states. And states vary significantly in the taxes levied. Thus, although personal income taxes are a major source of revenue for all state governments combined, seven states do not levy a personal income tax. Also, there are great variations in the size of tax receipts and disbursements among the states. Thirty-six states augment their tax revenues with state-run lotteries to help close the gap between their tax receipts and expenditures.

The huge gap between state tax revenues and expenditures in Figure 5.9 is largely eliminated when we take nontax sources of income into account. In 1998 the states received $240 billion in intergovernmental grants from the Federal government. They also received significant revenue from miscellaneous sources such as state-owned utilities and liquor stores.

Local Finances

The local level of government includes counties, municipalities, townships, and school districts as well as cities and towns. It is clear from the receipts and expenditures shown in Figure 5.10 that local governments rely heavily on **property taxes.** And they spend most of their revenues on education.

The tax revenues of local governments cover less than one-half of their expenditures. The remaining revenue comes from intergovernmental grants from the Federal and state governments.

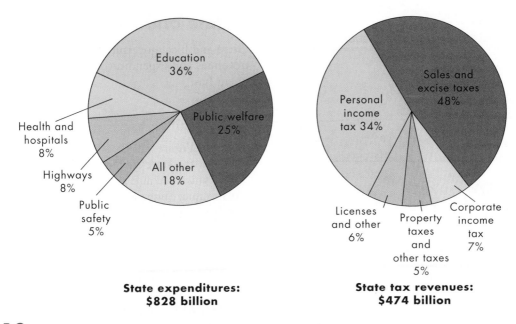

**State expenditures:
$828 billion**

**State tax revenues:
$474 billion**

Figure 5.9

State expenditures and tax revenues, 1998. State governments spend mainly on education and public welfare. Their primary source of tax revenue is sales and excise taxes.
Source: U.S. Bureau of the Census.

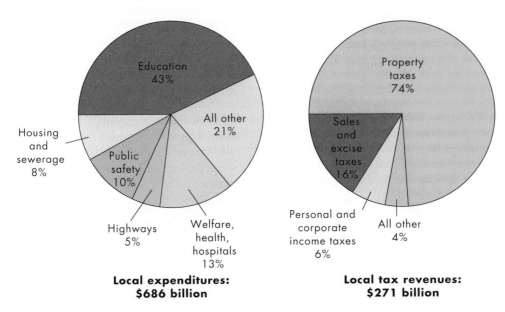

**Local expenditures:
$686 billion**

**Local tax revenues:
$271 billion**

Figure 5.10

Local expenditures and tax revenues, 1996. The expenditures of local governments are largely for education and are financed by property taxes.
Source: U.S. Bureau of the Census.

The Financing of Corporate Operations

One Advantage of Corporations Is Their Ability to Finance Their Operations through the Sale of Stocks and Bonds.

Generally, corporations finance their activities in three ways. First, a very large portion of a corporation's activities is financed internally out of undistributed corporate profits. Second, as do individuals or unincorporated businesses, corporations may borrow from financial institutions. For example, a small corporation planning to build a new plant may obtain the needed funds from a commercial bank, a savings and loan association, or an insurance company. Third, unique to corporations, they can issue common stocks and bonds.

Stocks versus Bonds A common stock represents a share in the ownership of a corporation. The purchaser of a stock certificate has the right to vote for corporate officers and to share in dividends. If you buy 1000 of the 100,000 shares issued by OutTell, Inc. (hereafter OT), then you own 1 percent of the company, are entitled to 1 percent of any dividends declared by the board of directors, and control 1 percent of the votes in the annual election of corporate officials.

In contrast, a bond does not bestow any corporate ownership on the purchaser. A bond purchaser is simply lending money to a corporation. A bond is an IOU, in acknowledgment of a loan, whereby the corporation promises to pay the holder a fixed amount set forth on the bond at some specified future date and other fixed amounts (interest payments) every year up to the bond's maturity date. For example, you might purchase a 10-year OT bond with a face value of $1000 and a 10 percent rate of interest. This means that, in exchange for your $1000, OT guarantees you a $100 interest payment for each of the next 10-years and then repays your $1000 principal at the end of that period.

Differences There are clearly important differences between stocks and bonds. First, as noted above, the bondholder is only a lender,

not an owner of the company. Second, bonds are considered to be less risky than stocks, for two reasons. On the one hand, bondholders have a "legal prior claim" on a corporation's earnings. Dividends cannot be paid to stockholders until all interest payments that are due to bondholders have been paid. On the other hand, holders of OT stock do not know how much their dividends will be or how much they might get for their stock if they decide to sell. If OutTell falls on hard times, stockholders may receive no dividends at all, and the value of their stock may plummet. Provided the corporation does not go bankrupt, the holder of an OT bond is guaranteed a $100 interest payment each year and the return of his or her $1000 at the end of 10 years.

Bond Risks This is not to imply that the purchase of corporate bonds is without risk. The market value of your OT bond may vary over time in accordance with the financial health of the corporation. If OT encounters economic misfortunes that raise questions about its financial integrity, the market value of your bond may fall. Should you sell the bond prior to maturity, you may receive only $600 or $700 for it (rather than $1000) and thereby incur a capital loss.

Changes in the interest rate paid on a bond will also affect the market prices of bonds. An increase in the interest rate will cause the bond price to fall and a decrease in the interest rate will cause the bond price to rise. Assume you purchase a $1000 ten-year OT bond this year when the interest rate is 10 percent. That means that your bond will provide a $100 fixed interest payment each year. But suppose that next year the interest rate jumps to 15 percent. Now OT must guarantee a $150 fixed annual payment on its new $1000 ten-year bonds. Clearly, no sensible person will pay you $1000 for your bond, which pays only $100 of interest income per year, when a new bond can be purchased for $1000 and will pay the holder $150 per year. Hence, if you sell your original bond before it reaches maturity, you may suffer a capital loss.

Bondholders face another source of risk: inflation. If substantial inflation occurs over the 10-year period during which you hold an OT bond, the $1000 principal repaid to you at the end of that period will represent substantially less purchasing power than the $1000 you lent OT 10 years earlier. You will have lent "dear" dollars but will be repaid in "cheap" dollars.

These grants totaled $270 billion in 1996. Also, local governments received $115 billion in proprietary income, that is, revenue from government-owned utilities providing water, electricity, natural gas, and transportation.

Fiscal Federalism

Over the years, the tax collections of both state and local governments have fallen substantially short of their expenditures. Such shortfalls are largely filled by Federal transfers or grants. It is not uncommon for 20 to 25 percent of all revenue received by state and local governments to come from the Federal government. In addition to Federal grants to state and local governments, the states also make grants to local governmental units. This system of intergovernmental transfers is called **fiscal federalism.**

QUICK REVIEW 5.4

■ Government purchases account for about 17 percent of U.S. output; the addition of transfers increases government spending to nearly 28 percent of domestic output.

■ Income security and national defense are the main categories of Federal spending; personal income, payroll, and corporate income taxes are the primary sources of Federal revenue.

■ States rely on sales and excise taxes for revenue; their spending is largely for education and public welfare.

■ Education is the main expenditure for local governments, most of whose revenue comes from property taxes.

SUMMARY

1. The functional distribution of income shows how society's total income is divided among wages, rents, interest, and profit; the personal distribution of income shows how total income is divided among individual households.

2. Households use all their income to pay personal taxes, for saving, and to buy consumer goods. Over half of their consumption expenditures are for services.

3. Sole proprietorships are firms owned and usually operated by single individuals. Partnerships are firms owned and usually operated by just a handful of individuals. Corporations are legal entities, distinct and separate from the individuals who own them. They often have thousands, or even millions, of owners—the stockholders.

4. Government improves the operation of the market system by (a) providing an appropriate legal and social framework and (b) acting to maintain competition.

5. Government alters the distribution of income through the tax-transfer system and through market intervention.

6. Spillovers, or externalities, cause the equilibrium output of certain goods to vary from the socially efficient output. Spillover costs result in an overallocation of resources, which can be corrected by legislation or by specific taxes. Spillover benefits are accompanied by an underallocation of resources, which can be corrected by government subsidies to consumers or producers.

7. Only government is willing to provide public goods, which are indivisible and entail benefits from which nonpaying consumers (free riders) cannot be excluded. Private firms will not produce public goods. Quasi-public goods have some of the characteristics of public goods and some of the characteristics of private goods; government provides them because the private sector would underallocate resources to their production.

8. Government reduces unemployment and inflation by altering its taxation, spending, and interest-rate policies.

9. Government purchases exhaust (use up or absorb) resources; transfer payments do not. Government purchases have declined from about 22 percent of domestic output in 1960 to 17 percent today. Transfer payments, however, have grown significantly. Total government spending now amounts to almost 28 percent of domestic output.

10. The main categories of Federal spending are pensions and income security, national defense, health, and interest on the public debt; Federal revenues come primarily from personal income taxes, payroll taxes, and corporate income taxes.

11. States derive their revenue primarily from sales and excise taxes and personal income taxes; major state expenditures go to education, public welfare, health and hospitals, and highways.

12. Local communities derive most of their revenue from property taxes; education is their most important expenditure.

13. Under the U.S. system of fiscal federalism, state and local tax revenues are supplemented by sizable revenue grants from the Federal government.

TERMS AND CONCEPTS

functional distribution of
   income
personal distribution of
   income
durable goods
nondurable goods
services
plant
firm

industry
sole proprietorship
partnership
corporation
stocks
bonds
limited liability
double taxation
principal-agent problem

monopoly
spillover costs
spillover benefits
exclusion principle
public goods
free-rider problem
quasi-public goods
government purchases
transfer payments

personal income tax
marginal tax rate
average tax rate
payroll taxes
corporate income tax
sales and excise taxes
property taxes
fiscal federalism

STUDY QUESTIONS

1. Distinguish between the functional distribution and personal distribution of income.

2. **Key Question** Assume that the five residents of Econoville receive incomes of $50, $75, $125, $250, and $500. Present the resulting personal distribution of income as a graph similar to Figure 5.2. Compare the incomes of the lowest fifth and the highest fifth of the income receivers.

3. Distinguish between a plant, a firm, and an industry. Contrast a vertically integrated firm, a horizontally organized firm, and a conglomerate.

4. **Key Question** What are the major legal forms of business organization? Briefly state the advantages and disadvantages of each. How do you account for the dominant role of corporations in the U.S. economy?

5. "The legal form an enterprise assumes is dictated primarily by the financial requirements of its particular line of production." Do you agree?

6. Enumerate and briefly discuss the main economic functions of government. Which function do you think is the most controversial? Why?

7. What divergences arise between equilibrium output and efficient output when (a) spillover costs and (b) spillover benefits are present? How might government correct for these divergences? "The presence of spillover costs suggests the underallocation of resources to a particular product and the need for governmental subsidies." Do you agree? Why or why not? Explain how zoning and seat belt laws might be used to deal with a problem of spillover costs.

8. Researchers have concluded that injuries caused by firearms cost more than $500 million a year in hospital expenses alone. Because the majority of persons shot are poor and without insurance, roughly 85 percent of these expenses must be borne by taxpayers. Use your understanding of externalities to recommend appropriate policies.

9. **Key Question** What are the characteristics of public goods? Explain the significance of the exclusion principle. By what means does government provide public goods?

10. **Key Question** Draw a production possibilities curve with public goods on the vertical axis and private goods on the horizontal axis. Assuming the economy is initially operating *on the curve*, indicate how the production of public goods might be increased. How might the output of public goods be increased if the economy is initially operating at a point *inside the curve*?

11. Use your understanding of the characteristics of private and public goods to determine whether the following should be produced through the market system or provided by government: (a) bread; (b) street lighting; (c) bridges; (d) parks; (e) swimming pools; (f) medical care; (g) mail delivery; (h) housing; (i) air traffic control; (j) libraries. State why you answered as you did in each case.

12. Explain how government can manipulate its expenditures and tax revenues to reduce (a) unemployment and (b) the rate of inflation.

13. "Most government actions simultaneously affect the distribution of income, the allocation of resources, and the levels of unemployment and prices." Use the circular flow model to confirm this assertion for each of the following:

    a. The construction of a new high school in Blackhawk County.

    b. A 2 percent reduction in the Federal corporate income tax.

    c. An expansion of preschool programs for disadvantaged children.

    d. A $50 million increase in spending for space research.

    e. The levying of a tax on air polluters.

    f. A $1 increase in the legally required minimum wage.

14. What is the most important source of revenue and the major type of expenditure at the Federal level? At the state level? At the local level?

15. **Key Question** Suppose in Fiscalville there is no tax on the first $10,000 of income, but a 20 percent tax on earnings between $10,000 and $20,000 and a 30 percent tax on income between $20,000 and $30,000. Any income above $30,000 is taxed at 40 percent. If your income is $50,000, how much will you pay in taxes? Determine your marginal and average tax rates. Is this a progressive tax? Explain.

16. **(Last Word)** Describe three ways to finance corporate activity. Make a case arguing that stocks are more risky than bonds for the financial investor.

17. **Web-Based Question:** *Personal distribution of income—what is the trend?* Visit the U.S. Census Bureau website at www.census.gov/hhes/income/midclass/index.html and select Data. Since 1969, how has the share of aggregate household income received by the lowest and highest income quintiles (fifths) changed?

18. **Web-Based Question:** *States taxes and expenditures per capita—where does your state rank?* Go to the Census Bureau site, www.census.gov/govs/www/state.html, and find the table that ranks the states by tax revenue and expenditures per capita for the latest year. Where does your home state rank in each category? Where does the state in which you are attending college, if different, rank? Speculate as to why there is such a gap between the high-ranking and low-ranking states.

C H A P T E R

The United States in the Global Economy

BACKPACKERS IN THE wilderness like to think they are "leaving the world behind," but, like Atlas, they carry the world on their shoulders. Much of their equipment is imported—knives from Switzerland, rain gear from South Korea, cameras from Japan, aluminum pots from England, miniature stoves from Sweden, sleeping bags from China, and compasses from Finland. Moreover, they may have driven to the trailheads in Japanese-made Toyotas or Swedish-made Volvos, sipping coffee from Brazil or snacking on bananas from Honduras. ■ International trade and the global economy affect all of us daily, whether we are hiking in the wilderness, driving our cars, listening to music, or working at our jobs. We cannot "leave the world behind." We are enmeshed in a global web of economic relationships—trading of goods and services, multinational corporations, cooperative ventures among the world's firms, and ties among the world's financial markets. That web is so complex that it is difficult to determine just what is—or isn't—an American product. A Finnish company owns Wilson sporting goods; a Swiss company owns Gerber baby food; and a British corporation owns Burger King. The Buick Regal sedan is manufactured in Canada. Many "U.S." products are made with components from abroad, and, conversely, many "foreign" products contain numerous U.S.-produced parts. (This point is treated humorously in this chapter's Last Word.)

■ International Linkages

Several economic flows link the U.S. economy and the economies of other nations. As identified in Figure 6.1, these flows are:

■ *Goods and services flows* or simply *trade flows.* The United States exports goods and services to other nations and imports goods and services from them.

■ *Capital and labor flows* or simply *resource flows.* U.S. firms establish production facilities—new capital—in foreign countries, and foreign firms establish production facilities in the United States. Labor also moves between nations. Each

93

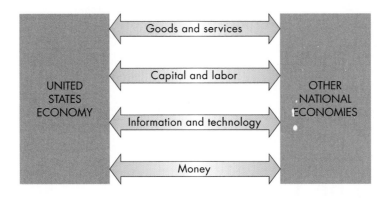

Figure 6.1

International linkages.   The U.S. economy is intertwined with other national economies through goods and services flows (trade flows), capital and labor flows (resource flows), information and technology flows, and financial flows.

year many foreigners immigrate to the United States and some Americans move to other nations.

- **Information and technology flows.** The United States transmits information to other nations about U.S. products, prices, interest rates, and investment opportunities and receives such information from abroad. Firms in other countries use technology created in the United States, and U.S. businesses incorporate technology developed abroad.
- **Financial flows.**   Money is transferred between the United States and other countries for several purposes, for example, paying for imports, buying foreign assets, paying interest on debt, and providing foreign aid.

■ The United States and World Trade

Our main goal in this chapter is to examine trade flows and the financial flows that pay for them. What is the extent and pattern of international trade, and how much has that trade grown? Who are the major participants?

Volume and Pattern

Table 6.1 suggests the importance of world trade for selected countries. Many countries, with restricted resources and limited domestic markets, cannot efficiently produce the variety of goods their citizens want. So they must import goods from other nations. That, in turn, means that they must export, or

sell abroad, some of their own products. For such countries, exports may run from 25 to 35 percent or more of their gross domestic product (GDP)—the market value of all goods and services produced in an economy. Other countries, the United States, for example, have rich and diversified resource bases and large internal markets. Although the total volume of trade is huge in the United States, it constitutes a smaller percentage of GDP than it does in a number of other nations.

Volume   For the United States and for the world as a whole the volume of international trade has been increasing both absolutely and relative to their GDPs. A comparison of the boxed data in Figure 6.2 reveals substantial growth in the dollar amount of

Table 6.1

Exports of Goods and Services as a Percentage of GDP, Selected Countries, 1999

Country	Exports as Percentage of GDP
Netherlands	56
Canada	41
New Zealand	29
United Kingdom	29
France	27
Italy	27
Germany	27
United States	12
Japan	11

Source: IMF, *International Financial Statistics,* 2000.

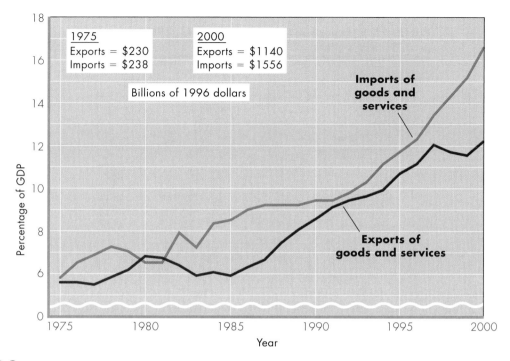

Figure 6.2

U.S. trade as percentage of GDP. U.S. imports and exports have increased in volume and have greatly increased as a percentage of GDP since 1975.
Source: Bureau of Economic Analysis. Data are from the national income accounts and are adjusted for inflation (1996 dollars).

U.S. exports and imports over the past several decades. The graph shows the rapid growth of U.S. exports and imports of goods and services as percentages of GDP. In 2000, U.S. exports and imports were 12 and 17 percent of GDP, respectively.

Even so, the United States now accounts for a diminished percentage of total world trade. In 1947 it supplied about one-third of the world's total exports, compared with about one-eighth today. World trade has increased more rapidly for other nations than it has for the United States. *But in terms of absolute volumes of imports and exports, the United States is still the world's leading trading nation.*

Dependence   The United States is almost entirely dependent on other countries for bananas, cocoa, coffee, spices, tea, raw silk, nickel, tin, natural rubber, and diamonds. Imported goods compete with U.S. goods in many of our domestic markets: Japanese cameras and cars, French and Italian wines, and Swiss and Austrian snow skis are a few examples. Even the "great American pastime" of baseball relies heavily on imported gloves and baseballs.

Of course, world trade is a two-way street. Many U.S. industries rely on foreign markets. Almost all segments of U.S. agriculture rely on sales abroad; for example, exports of rice, wheat, cotton, and tobacco vary from one-fourth to more than one-half of the total output of those crops. The U.S. computer, chemical, semiconductor, aircraft, automobile, machine tool, and coal industries, among many others, sell significant portions of their output in international markets. Table 6.2 shows some of the major commodity exports and imports of the United States.

Trade Patterns   The following facts will give you an overview of U.S. international trade:

■ The United States has a *trade deficit* in goods. In 1999 U.S. imports of goods exceeded U.S. exports of goods by $346 billion.

■ The United States has a *trade surplus* in services (such as accounting services and financial services). In 1999 U.S. exports of services exceeded U.S. imports of services by $81 billion.

■ The United States imports some of the same categories of goods that it exports, specifically,

Table 6.2

Principal U.S. Exports and Imports of Goods, 1999 (in Billions of Dollars)

Exports	Amount	Imports	Amount
Semiconductors	$47.0	Automobiles	$96.3
Computers	46.7	Computers	81.5
Chemicals	46.0	Petroleum	67.8
Consumer durables	37.8	Clothing	55.9
Generating equipment	29.4	Household appliances	44.3
Aircraft	29.0	Semiconductors	37.6
Telecommunications	26.6	Chemicals	30.1
Automobiles	16.5	Consumer electronics	26.2
Grains	13.9	Telecommunications	23.9
Nonferrous metals	13.5	Iron and steel	18.1

Source: Consolidated from Department of Commerce data.

automobiles, computers, chemicals, semiconductors, and telecommunications equipment. (see Table 6.2).

■ As Table 6.3 implies, most U.S. export and import trade is with other industrially advanced nations, not with developing countries. (Although the data in this table are for *goods* only, the same general pattern applies to *services*).

■ Canada is the United States' most important trading partner quantitatively. In 1999, 24 percent of U.S. exported goods were sold to Canadians, who in turn provided 20 percent of U.S. imports of goods (see Table 6.3).

■ The United States has sizable trade deficits with Japan and China. In 1999, U.S. imported goods from Japan exceeded U.S. exported goods to Japan by $75 billion, and U.S. imported goods from China exceeded U.S. exported goods to China by $69 billion (see Table 6.3).

■ The U.S. dependence on foreign oil is reflected in its trade with members of the Organization of Petroleum Exporting Countries (OPEC). In 1999, the United States imported $24 billion of goods (mainly oil) from OPEC members, while exporting $12 billion of goods to those countries (see Table 6.3).

Table 6.3

U.S. Exports and Imports of Goods by Area, 1999*

Exports to	Value, Billions of Dollars	Percentage of Total	Imports from	Value, Billions of Dollars	Percentage of Total
Industrial countries	$398	58	Industrial countries	$ 552	54
Canada	$167	24	Canada	$201	20
Japan	56	8	Japan	131	13
Western Europe	163	24	Western Europe	215	21
Australia	12	2	Australia	5	1
Developing countries	286	42	Developing countries	$ 478	46
Mexico	87	13	Mexico	111	11
China	13	2	China	82	8
Eastern Europe	6	1	Eastern Europe	12	1
OPEC countries	12	2	OPEC countries	24	2
Other	168	24	Other	249	24
Total	$684	100	Total	$1030	100

*Data are on an international transactions basis and exclude military shipments. The import numbers do not add to 100 percent because of rounding.
Source: Survey of Current Business, October 2000.

■ In terms of volume, the most significant U.S. export of *services* is airline transportation provided by U.S. carriers for foreign passengers.

Financial Linkages

International trade requires complex financial linkages among nations. How does a nation such as the United States obtain more goods from others than it provides to them? How does the United States finance its goods and services trade deficit of $265 billion (= +81 in services − $346 in goods)? The answer is by either borrowing from foreigners or by selling real assets (for example, factories, real estate) to them. The United States is the world's largest borrower of foreign funds. Moreover, nations with which the United States has large trade deficits, such as Japan, often "recycle their excess dollars" by buying U.S. real assets.

Rapid Trade Growth

Several factors have propelled the rapid growth of international trade since the Second World War.

Transportation Technology

High transportation costs are a barrier to any type of trade, particularly among traders who are distant from one another. But improvements in transportation have shrunk the globe and have fostered world trade. Airplanes now transport low-weight, high-value items such as diamonds and semiconductors swiftly from one nation to another. We now routinely transport oil in massive tankers, significantly lowering the cost of transportation per barrel. Grain is loaded onto oceangoing ships at modern, efficient grain silos at Great Lakes and coastal ports. Natural gas flows through large-diameter pipelines from exporting to importing countries—for instance, from Russia to Germany and from Canada to the United States.

Communications Technology

Dramatic improvements in communications technology have also advanced world trade. Computers, the Internet, telephones, and fax (facsimile) machines now directly link traders around the world, enabling exporters to access overseas markets and to carry out trade deals. A distributor in New York can get a price quote on 1000 woven baskets in Thailand as quickly as a quotation on 1000 laptop computers in Texas. Money moves around the world in the blink of an eye. Exchange rates, stock prices, and interest rates flash onto computer screens nearly simultaneously in Los Angeles, London, and Lisbon.

General Decline in Tariffs

Tariffs are excise taxes (duties) on imported products. They have had their ups and downs over the years, but since 1940 they have generally fallen. A glance ahead to Figure 6.5 shows that U.S. tariffs as a percentage of imports (on which duties are levied) are now about 4 percent, down from 37 percent in 1940. Many nations still maintain barriers to free trade, but, on average, tariffs have fallen significantly, thus increasing international trade.

Participants in International Trade

All the nations of the world participate to some extent in international trade.

United States, Japan, and Western Europe

As Global Perspective 6.1 indicates, the top participants in world trade by total volume are the United States, Germany, and Japan. In 1999 those three nations had combined exports of $1.6 trillion. Along with Germany, other western European nations such as France, Britain, and Italy

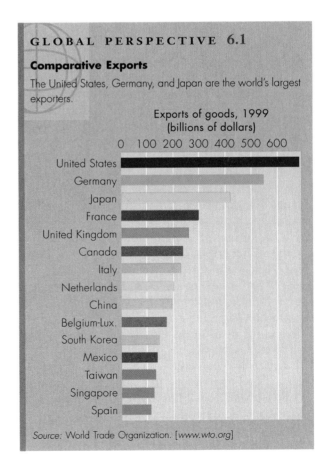

GLOBAL PERSPECTIVE 6.1

Comparative Exports

The United States, Germany, and Japan are the world's largest exporters.

Exports of goods, 1999
(billions of dollars)

Source: World Trade Organization. [www.wto.org]

are major exporters and importers. The United States, Japan, and the western European nations also form the heart of the world's financial system and provide headquarters for most of the world's large **multinational corporations**—firms that have sizable production and distribution activities in other countries. Examples of such firms are Unilever (Netherlands), Nestlé (Switzerland), Coca-Cola (United States), Bayer Chemicals (Germany), and Mitsubishi (Japan).

New Participants Important new participants have arrived on the world trade scene. One group is made up of the newly industrializing Asian economies of Hong Kong (now part of China), Singapore, South Korea, and Taiwan. Although these Asian economies experienced economic difficulties in the 1990s, they have expanded their share of world exports from about 3 percent in 1972 to more than 10 percent today. Together, they export about as much as either Germany or Japan and much more than France, Britain, or Italy. Other economies in southeast Asia, particularly Malaysia and Indonesia, also have expanded their international trade.

China, with its increasing reliance on the market system, is an emerging major trader. Since initiating market reforms in 1978, its annual growth of output has averaged 9 percent (compared with about 3 percent annually over that period in the United States). At this remarkable rate, China's total output nearly doubles every 8 years! An upsurge of exports and imports has accompanied that expansion of output. In 1989 Chinese exports and imports were each about $50 billion. In 1999 each topped $200 billion, with 33 percent of China's exports going to the United States. Also, China has been attracting substantial foreign investment (more than $800 billion since 1990).

The collapse of communism in eastern Europe and the former Soviet Union in the early 1990s has altered world trade patterns. Before that collapse, the eastern European nations of Poland, Hungary, Czechoslovakia, and East Germany traded mainly with the Soviet Union and such political allies as North Korea and Cuba. Today, East Germany is reunited with West Germany, and Poland, Hungary, and the Czech Republic have established new trade relationships with western Europe and the United States.

Russia itself has initiated far-reaching market reforms, including widespread privatization of industry, and has made major trade deals with firms around the globe. Although its transition to capital-

ism has been far from smooth, Russia may one day be a major trading nation. Other former Soviet republics—now independent nations—such as Estonia and Azerbaijan also have opened their economies to international trade and finance.

QUICK REVIEW 6.1

There are four main categories of economic flows linking nations: goods and services flows, capital and labor flows, information and technology flows, and financial flows.

World trade has increased globally and nationally. In terms of volume, the United States is the world's leading international trader. But with exports and imports of only about 12 to 17 percent of GDP, the United States is not as dependent on international trade as some other nations.

Advances in transportation and communications technology and declines in tariffs have all helped expand world trade.

The United States, Japan, and the western European nations dominate world trade. Recent new traders are the Asian economies of Singapore, South Korea, Taiwan, and China (including Hong Kong), the eastern European nations, and the former Soviet states.

Specialization and Comparative Advantage

Given the presence of an *open economy*—one that includes the international sector—the United States produces more of certain goods (exports) and fewer of other goods (imports) than it would otherwise. Thus U.S. labor and other resources are shifted toward export industries and away from import industries. For example, the United States uses more resources to make commercial aircraft and to grow wheat and less to make autos and clothing. So we ask: "Do shifts of resources like these make economic sense? Do they enhance U.S. total output and thus the U.S. standard of living?"

The answers are affirmative. *Specialization and international trade increase the productivity of a nation's resources and allow for greater total output than would otherwise be possible.* This idea is not new. Adam Smith had this to say in 1776:

It is the maxim of every prudent master of a family, never to attempt to make at home what it will cost him more to make than to buy. The taylor does not attempt to make his own shoes, but buys them of the shoemaker. The shoemaker does not attempt to make his own clothes, but employs a taylor. The farmer attempts to make neither the one nor the other, but employs those different artificers. . . .

What is prudence in the conduct of every private family, can scarce be folly in that of a great kingdom. If a foreign country can supply us with a commodity cheaper than we can make it, better buy it of them with some part of the produce of our own industry, employed in a way in which we have some advantage.[1]

Nations specialize and trade for the same reasons as individuals: Specialization and exchange result in greater overall output and income.

Basic Principle

In the early 1800s British economist David Ricardo expanded on Smith's idea by observing that it pays for a person or a country to specialize and trade even if some potential trading partner is more productive in *all* economic activities.

Consider the certified public accountant (CPA) who is also a skilled house painter. Suppose the CPA is a swifter painter than the professional painter she is thinking of hiring. Also suppose she can earn $50 per hour but would have to pay the painter $15 per hour. And say it would take the accountant 30 hours to paint her house but the painter would take 40 hours.

Should the CPA take time from her accounting to paint her own house, or should she hire the painter? The CPA's opportunity cost of painting her house is $1500 (=30 hours of sacrificed CPA time × $50 per CPA hour). The cost of hiring the painter is only $600 (=40 hours of painting × $15 per hour of painting). Although the CPA is better at both accounting and painting, she *will get her house painted at lower cost by specializing in accounting and using some of her earnings from accounting to hire a house painter.*

Similarly, the house painter can reduce his cost of obtaining accounting services by specializing in painting and using some of his income to hire the CPA to prepare his income tax forms. Suppose it would take the painter 10 hours to prepare his tax return, while the CPA could handle the task in 2 hours. The house painter would sacrifice $150 of income (=10 hours of painting time × $15 per hour) to do something he could hire the CPA to do for $100 (=2 hours of CPA time × $50 per CPA hour).

---

[1]Adam Smith, *The Wealth of Nations* (New York: Modern Library, 1937), p. 424. (Originally published in 1776.)

Table 6.4
Mexico's Production Possibilities Table (in Tons)

Product	Production Alternatives				
	A	B	C	D	E
Avocados	0	20	24	40	60
Soybeans	15	10	9	5	0

By using the CPA to prepare his tax return, the painter *lowers the cost of getting his tax return prepared.*

What is true for our CPA and house painter is also true for nations. Specializing enables nations to reduce the cost of obtaining the goods and services they desire.

Comparative Costs

Our simple example shows that the reason specialization is economically desirable is that it results in more efficient production. Now let's put specialization into the context of trading nations and use the familiar concept of the production possibilities table for our analysis. Suppose the production possibilities for one product in Mexico and for one product in the United States are as shown in Tables 6.4 and 6.5. In both tables we assume constant costs. Each country must give up a constant amount of one product to secure a certain increment of the other product. (This assumption simplifies our discussion without impairing the validity of our conclusions.)

Specialization and trade are mutually beneficial or "profitable" to the two nations if the comparative costs of producing the two products within the two nations differ. What are the comparative costs of avocados and soybeans in Mexico? By comparing production alternatives A and B in Table 6.4, we see that 5 tons of soybeans (=15 − 10) must be sacrificed to produce 20 tons of avocados (=20 − 0). Or, more simply, in Mexico it costs 1 ton of soybeans (S) to produce 4 tons of avocados (A); that is, 1S ≡ 4A. Because we assumed constant costs, this domestic

Table 6.5
U.S. Production Possibilities Table (in Tons)

Product	Production Alternatives				
	R	S	T	U	V
Avocados	0	30	33	60	90
Soybeans	30	20	19	10	0

comparative-cost ratio will not change as Mexico expands the output of either product. This is evident from production possibilities B and C, where we see that 4 more tons of avocados (=24 − 20) cost 1 unit of soybeans (=10 − 9).

Similarly, in Table 6.5, comparing U.S. production alternatives R and S reveals that in the United States it costs 10 tons of soybeans (=30 − 20) to obtain 30 tons of avocados (=30 − 0). That is, the domestic comparative-cost ratio for the two products in the United States is 1S ≡ 3A. Comparing production alternatives S and T reinforces this conclusion: an extra 3 tons of avocados (=33 − 30) comes at the sacrifice of 1 ton of soybeans (=20 − 19).

The comparative costs of the two products within the two nations are obviously different. Economists say that the United States has a domestic comparative advantage or, simply, a **comparative advantage** over Mexico in soybeans. The United States must forgo only 3 tons of avocados to get 1 ton of soybeans, but Mexico must forgo 4 tons of avocados to get 1 ton of soybeans. In terms of domestic opportunity costs, soybeans are relatively cheaper in the United States. *A nation has a comparative advantage in some product when it can produce that product at a lower domestic opportunity cost than can a potential trading partner.* Mexico, in contrast, has a comparative advantage in avocados. While 1 ton of avocados costs $\frac{1}{3}$ ton of soybeans in the United States, it costs only $\frac{1}{4}$ ton of soybeans in Mexico. Comparatively speaking, avocados are cheaper in Mexico. We summarize the situation in Table 6.6.

Because of these differences in domestic comparative costs, if both nations specialize, each according to its comparative advantage, each can achieve a larger total output with the same total input of resources. Together they will be using their scarce resources more efficiently. 🔑 6.1

Table 6.6
Comparative-Advantage Example: A Summary

Soybeans	Avocados
Mexico: Must give up 4 tons of avocados to get 1 ton of soybeans	*Mexico:* Must give up $\frac{1}{4}$ ton of soybeans to get 1 ton of avocados
United States: Must give up 3 tons of avocados to get 1 ton of soybeans	*United States:* Must give up $\frac{1}{3}$ ton of soybeans to get 1 ton of avocados
Comparative advantage: United States	Comparative advantage: Mexico

Terms of Trade

The United States can shift production between soybeans and avocados at the rate of 1S for 3A. Thus, the United States would specialize in soybeans only if it could obtain *more than* 3 tons of avocados for 1 ton of soybeans by trading with Mexico. Similarly, Mexico can shift production at the rate of 4A for 1S. So it would be advantageous to Mexico to specialize in avocados if it could get 1 ton of soybeans for *less than* 4 tons of avocados.

Suppose that through negotiation the two nations agree on an exchange rate of 1 ton of soybeans for $3\frac{1}{2}$ tons of avocados. These **terms of trade** are mutually beneficial to both countries, since each can "do better" through such trade than through domestic production alone. The United States can get $3\frac{1}{2}$ tons of avocados by sending 1 ton of soybeans to Mexico, while it can get only 3 tons of avocados by shifting its own resources domestically from soybeans to avocados. Mexico can obtain 1 ton of soybeans at a lower cost of $3\frac{1}{2}$ tons of avocados through trade with the United States, compared to the cost of 4 tons if Mexico produced the ton of soybeans itself.

Gains from Specialization and Trade

Let's pinpoint the gains in total output from specialization and trade. Suppose that, before specialization and trade, production alternative C in Table 6.4 and alternative T in 6.5 were the optimal product mixes for the two countries. That is, Mexico preferred 24 tons of avocados and 9 tons of soybeans (Table 6.4) and the United States preferred 33 tons of avocados and 19 tons of soybeans (Table 6.5) to all other available domestic alternatives. These outputs are shown in column 1 in Table 6.7.

Now assume that both nations specialize according to their comparative advantage, with Mexico producing 60 tons of avocados and no soybeans (alternative E) and the United States producing no avocados and 30 tons of soybeans (alternative R). These outputs are shown in column 2 in Table 6.7. Using our 1S ≡ $3\frac{1}{2}$ A terms of trade, assume that Mexico exchanges 35 tons of avocados for 10 tons of U.S. soybeans. Column 3 in Table 6.7 shows the quantities exchanged in this trade, with a minus sign indicating exports and a plus sign indicating imports. As shown in column 4, after the trade Mexico has 25 tons of avocados and 10 tons of soybeans, while the United States has 35 tons of avocados and 20 tons of

Table 6.7

Specialization According to Comparative Advantage and the Gains from Trade (in Tons)

Country	(1) Outputs before Specialization	(2) Outputs after Specialization	(3) Amounts Traded	(4) Outputs Available after Trade	(5) Gains from Specialization and Trade (4) − (1)
Mexico	24 avocados	60 avocados	−35 avocados	25 avocados	1 avocados
	9 soybeans	0 soybeans	+10 soybeans	10 soybeans	1 soybeans
United States	33 avocados	0 avocados	+35 avocados	35 avocados	2 avocados
	19 soybeans	30 soybeans	−10 soybeans	20 soybeans	1 soybeans

soybeans. Compared with their optimum product mixes before specialization and trade (column 1), *both* nations now enjoy more avocados and more soybeans! Specifically, Mexico has gained 1 ton of avocados and 1 ton of soybeans. The United States has gained 2 tons of avocados and 1 ton of soybeans. These gains are shown in column 5.

Specialization based on comparative advantage improves global resource allocation. The same total inputs of world resources and technology result in a larger global output. If Mexico and the United States allocate all their resources to avocados and soybeans, respectively, the same total inputs of resources can produce more output between them, indicating that resources are being allocated more efficiently.

We noted in Chapter 2 that through specialization and international trade a nation can overcome the production constraints imposed by its domestic production possibilities table and curve. Our discussion of Tables 6.4, 6.5, and 6.7 has shown just how this is done. The domestic production possibilities data (Tables 6.4 and 6.5) of the two countries have not changed, meaning that neither nation's production possibilities curve has shifted. But specialization and trade mean that citizens of both countries can enjoy increased consumption (column 5 of Table 6.7). Thus specialization and trade have the same effect as an increase in resources or in technological progress: they make more goods available to an economy. **(Key Question 4)** 📖 6.1

■ The Foreign Exchange Market

Buyers and sellers, whether individuals, firms, or nations, use money to buy products or to pay for the use of resources. Within the domestic economy, prices are stated in terms of the domestic currency

and buyers use that currency to purchase domestic products. In Mexico, for example, buyers have pesos, and that is what sellers want.

International markets are different. Sellers set their prices in terms of their domestic currencies, but buyers often possess entirely different currencies. How many dollars does it take to buy a truckload of Mexican avocados selling for 3000 pesos, a German automobile selling for 50,000 euros, or a Japanese motorcycle priced at 300,000 yen? Producers in Mexico, Germany, and Japan want payment in pesos, euros, and yen, respectively, so that they can pay their wages, rent, interest, dividends, and taxes. A **foreign exchange market,** *a market in which various national currencies are exchanged for one another,* serves this need. The equilibrium prices in these markets are called **exchange rates.** An exchange rate is the rate at which the currency of one nation can be exchanged for the currency of another nation. (See Global Perspective 6.2.) Two points about the foreign exchange market are particularly noteworthy:

- *A competitive market* Real-world foreign exchange markets conform closely to the markets discussed in Chapter 3. They are competitive markets characterized by large numbers of buyers and sellers dealing in standardized products such as the American dollar, the European euro, the British pound, and the Japanese yen.

- *Linkages to all domestic and foreign prices* The market price or exchange rate of a nation's currency is an unusual price; it links all domestic prices with all foreign prices. Exchange rates enable consumers in one country to translate prices of foreign goods into units of their own currency: they need only multiply the foreign product price by the exchange rate. If the U.S.

GLOBAL PERSPECTIVE 6.2

Exchange Rates: Foreign Currency per U.S. Dollar

The amount of foreign currency that a dollar will buy varies greatly from nation to nation and fluctuates in response to supply and demand changes in the foreign exchange market. The amounts shown here are for January 2001.

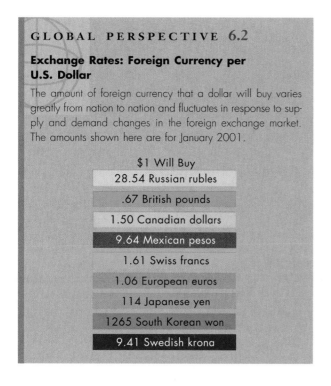

$1 Will Buy
28.54 Russian rubles
.67 British pounds
1.50 Canadian dollars
9.64 Mexican pesos
1.61 Swiss francs
1.06 European euros
114 Japanese yen
1265 South Korean won
9.41 Swedish krona

dollar–yen exchange rate is $.01 (1 cent) per yen, a Sony television set priced at ¥20,000 will cost $200 (=20,000 × $.01) in the United States. If the exchange rate rises to $.02 (2 cents) per yen, it will cost $400 (=20,000 × $.02) in the United States. Similarly, all other Japanese products would double in price to U.S. buyers in response to the altered exchange rate. As you will see, a change in exchange rates has important implications for a nation's level of domestic production and employment. **!** 6.2

Dollar-Yen Market

How does the foreign exchange market work? Let's look briefly at the market for dollars and yen. U.S. firms exporting goods to Japan want payment in dollars, not yen; but the Japanese importers of those U.S. goods possess yen, not dollars. So the Japanese importers supply their yen in exchange for dollars in the foreign exchange market. At the same time, there are U.S. importers of Japanese goods who need to pay the Japanese exporters in yen, not dollars. These importers go to the foreign exchange market as demanders of yen. We then have a market in which the "price" is in dollars and the "product" is yen.

Figure 6.3 shows the supply of yen (by Japanese importers) and the demand for yen (by U.S. importers). The intersection of demand curve D_y and supply curve S_y establishes the equilibrium dollar price of yen. Here the equilibrium price of 1 yen—the dollar-yen exchange rate—is 1 cent per yen, or $.01 = ¥1. At this price, the market for yen clears; there is neither a shortage nor a surplus of yen. The equilibrium $.01 price of 1 yen means that $1 will buy 100 yen or ¥100 worth of Japanese goods. Conversely, 100 yen will buy $1 worth of U.S. goods. **◺** 6.1

Changing Rates: Depreciation and Appreciation

What might cause the exchange rate to change? The determinants of the demand for and supply of yen are similar to the determinants of demand and supply for almost any product. In the United States, several things might increase the demand for—and therefore the dollar price of—yen. Incomes might rise in the United States, enabling residents to buy not only more domestic goods but also more Sony televisions, Nikon cameras, and Nissan automobiles

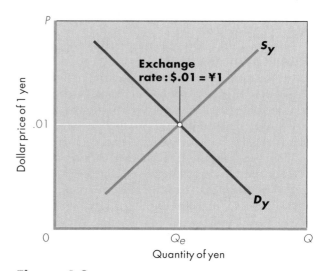

Figure 6.3

The market for yen. U.S. imports from Japan create a demand D_y for yen, while U.S. exports to Japan (Japan's imports) create a supply S_y of yen. The dollar price of 1 yen—the exchange rate—is determined at the intersection of the supply and demand curves. In this case the equilibrium price is $.01, meaning that 1 cent will buy 1 yen.

from Japan. So people in the United States would need more yen, and the demand for yen would increase. Or a change in people's tastes might enhance their preferences for Japanese goods. When gas prices soared in the 1970s, many auto buyers in the United States shifted their demand from gas-guzzling domestic cars to gas-efficient Japanese compact cars. The result was an increased demand for yen.

The point is that an increase in the U.S. demand for Japanese goods will increase the demand for yen and raise the dollar price of yen. Suppose the dollar price of yen rises from $.01 = ¥1 to $.02 = ¥1. When the dollar price of yen increases, we say a **depreciation** of the dollar relative to the yen has occurred. It then takes more dollars (pennies in this case) to buy a single yen. Alternatively stated, the *international value of the dollar* has declined. A depreciated dollar buys fewer yen and therefore fewer Japanese goods; the yen and all Japanese goods have become more expensive to U.S. buyers. Result: Consumers in the United States shift their expenditures from Japanese goods to now less expensive American goods. The Ford Taurus becomes relatively more attractive than the Honda Accord to U.S. consumers. Conversely, because each yen buys more dollars—that is, because the international value of the yen has increased—U.S. goods become cheaper to people in Japan and U.S. exports to Japan rise.

If the opposite event occurred—if the Japanese demanded more U.S. goods—then they would supply more yen to pay for these goods. The increase in the supply of yen relative to the demand for yen would decrease the equilibrium price of yen in the foreign exchange market. For example, the dollar price of yen might decline from $.01 = ¥1 to $.005 = ¥1. A decrease in the dollar price of yen is called an **appreciation** of the dollar relative to the yen. It means that the international value of the dollar has increased. It then takes fewer dollars (or pennies) to buy a single yen; the dollar is worth more because it can purchase more yen and therefore more Japanese goods. Each Sony Walkman becomes less expensive in terms of dollars, so people in the United States purchase more of them. In general, U.S. imports rise. Meanwhile, because it takes more yen to get a dollar, U.S. exports to Japan fall.

Figure 6.4 summarizes these currency relationships. **(Key Question 6)**

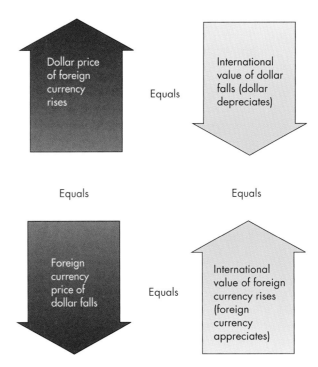

Figure 6.4

Currency appreciation and depreciation. Suppose the dollar price of a certain foreign currency rises (as illustrated by the upper left arrow). That means the international value of the dollar depreciates (upper right arrow). It also means that the foreign currency price of the dollar has declined (lower left arrow) and that the international value of the foreign currency has appreciated (lower right arrow).

QUICK REVIEW 6.2

- A country has a comparative advantage when it can produce a product at a lower domestic opportunity cost than a potential trading partner can.

- Specialization based on comparative advantage increases the total output available for nations that trade with one another.

- The foreign exchange market is a market in which foreign currencies are exchanged.

- An appreciation of the dollar is an increase in the international value of the dollar relative to the currency of some other nation; after appreciation a dollar buys more units of that currency. A depreciation of the dollar is a decrease in the international value of the dollar relative to some other currency; after depreciation a dollar buys fewer units of that currency.

▌Government and Trade

If people and nations benefit from specialization and international exchange, why do governments sometimes try to restrict the free flow of imports or encourage exports? What kinds of world trade barriers can governments erect, and why would they do so?

Trade Impediments and Subsidies

There are four means by which governments commonly interfere with free trade:

- **Protective tariffs** are excise taxes or duties placed on imported goods. Protective tariffs are designed to shield domestic producers from foreign competition. They impede free trade by causing a rise in the prices of imported goods, thereby shifting demand toward domestic products. An excise tax on imported shoes, for example, would make domestically produced shoes more attractive to consumers.
- **Import quotas** are limits on the quantities or total value of specific items that may be imported. Once a quota is "filled," further imports of that product are choked off. Import quotas are more effective than tariffs in retarding international commerce. With a tariff, a product can go on being imported in large quantities; with an import quota, however, all imports are prohibited once the quota is filled.
- **Nontariff barriers** (and, implicitly, *nonquota* barriers) include onerous licensing requirements, unreasonable standards pertaining to product quality, or simply bureaucratic red tape in customs procedures. Some nations require that importers of foreign goods obtain licenses and then restrict the number of licenses issued. Although many nations carefully inspect imported agricultural products to prevent the introduction of potentially harmful insects, some countries use lengthy inspections to impede imports.
- **Export subsidies** consist of government payments to domestic producers of export goods. By reducing production costs, the subsidies enable producers to charge lower prices and thus to sell more exports in world markets. Two examples: Some European governments have

heavily subsidized Airbus Industries, a European firm that produces commercial aircraft, to help Airbus to compete against the American firm Boeing. The United States and other nations have subsidized domestic farmers to boost the domestic food supply. Such subsidies have lowered the market price of food and have artificially lowered export prices on agricultural produce.

Why Government Trade Interventions?

What accounts for the impulse to impede imports, boost exports, and create trade surpluses through government policy when free trade is beneficial to a nation? Why would a nation want to send more output abroad for consumption there than it gains as imported output in return? There are several reasons—some legitimate, most not.

Misunderstanding the Gains from Trade

It is a commonly accepted myth that the greatest benefit to be derived from international trade is greater domestic employment in the export sector. This suggests that exports are "good" because they increase domestic employment, whereas imports are "bad" because they deprive people of jobs at home. Actually, the true benefit created by international trade is the overall increase in output obtained through specialization and exchange. A nation can fully employ its resources, including labor, with or without international trade. International trade, however, enables society to use its resources in ways that increase its total output and therefore its overall well-being.

A nation does not need international trade to operate *on* its production possibilities curve. A closed (nontrading) national economy can have full employment without international trade. However, through world trade an economy can reach a point *beyond* its domestic production possibilities curve. The gain from trade is the extra output obtained from abroad—the imports obtained for less cost than the cost if they were produced at home.

Political Considerations

While a nation as a whole gains from trade, trade may harm particular domestic industries and particular groups of resource suppliers. In our earlier comparative-advantage example, specialization and trade adversely affected the U.S. avocado industry and the Mexican soybean industry. Those industries might seek to preserve their economic positions by persuading their respective governments to protect them from imports—perhaps through tariffs or import quotas.

Those who directly benefit from import protection are few in number but have much at stake. Thus, they have a strong incentive to pursue political activity to achieve their aims. However, the overall cost of tariffs and quotas typically greatly exceeds the benefits. It is not uncommon to find that it costs the public $100,000 or more a year to protect a domestic job that pays less than half that amount. Moreover, because these costs are buried in the price of goods and spread out over millions of citizens, the cost born by each individual citizen is quite small. In the political arena, the voice of the relatively few producers demanding *protectionism* is loud and constant, whereas the voice of those footing the bill is soft or nonexistent.

Indeed, the public may be won over by the apparent plausibility ("Cut imports and prevent domestic unemployment") and the patriotic ring ("Buy American!") of the protectionist arguments. The alleged benefits of tariffs are immediate and clear-cut to the public, but the adverse effects cited by economists are obscure and dispersed over the entire economy. When political deal making is added in—"You back tariffs for the apparel industry in my state, and I'll back tariffs on the auto industry in your state"—the outcome can be a network of protective tariffs, import quotas, and export subsidies.

Costs to Society

Tariffs and quotas benefit domestic producers of the protected products, but they harm domestic consumers, who must pay higher than world prices for the protected goods. They also hurt domestic firms that use the protected goods as inputs in their production processes. For example, a tariff on imported steel would boost the price of steel girders, thus hurting firms that construct large buildings. Also, tariffs and quotas reduce competition in the protected industries. With less competition from foreign producers, domestic firms may be slow to design and implement cost-saving production methods and introduce new or improved products.

▌Multilateral Trade Agreements and Free-Trade Zones

When one nation enacts barriers against imports, the nations whose exports suffer may retaliate with trade barriers of their own. In such a *trade war*, escalating tariffs choke world trade and reduce everyone's economic well-being. The **Smoot-Hawley Tariff Act** of 1930 is a classic example. Although that act was meant to reduce imports and stimulate U.S. production, the high tariffs it authorized prompted adversely affected nations to retaliate with tariffs equally high. International trade fell, lowering the output and income of all nations. Economic historians generally agree that the Smoot-Hawley Tariff Act was a contributing cause of the Great Depression. Aware of that fact, nations have worked to lower tariffs worldwide. Their pursuit of free trade has been aided by powerful domestic interest groups: Exporters of goods and services, importers of foreign components used in "domestic" products, and domestic sellers of imported products all strongly support lower tariffs.

Figure 6.5 makes clear that while the United States has been a high-tariff nation over much of its history, U.S. tariffs have generally declined during the past half-century.

Reciprocal Trade Agreements Act

The **Reciprocal Trade Agreements Act** of 1934 started the downward trend of tariffs. Aimed at reducing tariffs, this act had two main features:

- ▪ *Negotiating authority* It authorized the president to negotiate with foreign nations agreements that would reduce existing U.S. tariffs by up to 50 percent. Those reductions were contingent on the actions other nations took to lower tariffs on U.S. exports.
- ▪ *Generalized reductions* The specific tariff reductions negotiated between the United States and any particular nation were generalized through most-favored-nation clauses, which often accompany such agreements. These clauses

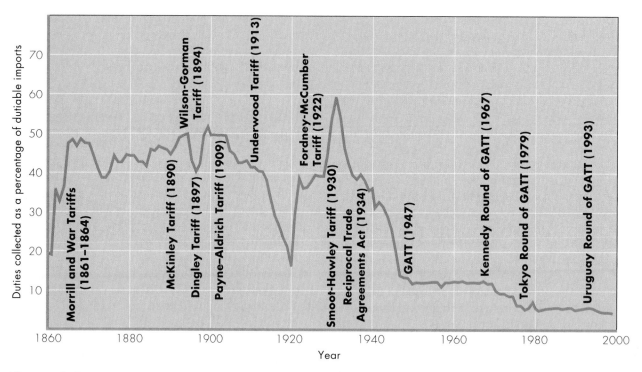

Figure 6.5

U.S. tariff rates, 1860–1999. Historically, U.S. tariff rates have fluctuated. But beginning with the Reciprocal Trade Agreements Act of 1934, the trend has been downward.
Source: U.S. Department of Commerce data.

stipulate that any subsequently reduced U.S. tariffs, resulting from negotiation with any other nation, would apply equally to any nation that signed the original agreement. So if the United States negotiates a reduction in tariffs on wristwatches with, say, France, the lower U.S. tariffs on imported French watches also apply to the imports of the other nations having most-favored-nation status, say, Japan and Switzerland. This way, the reductions in U.S. tariffs automatically apply to many nations.

General Agreement on Tariffs and Trade

The Reciprocal Trade Agreements Act provided only bilateral (between two nations) negotiations. Its approach was broadened in 1947 when 23 nations, including the United States, signed the **General Agreement on Tariffs and Trade (GATT)**. GATT was based on three principles: (1) equal, nondis-

criminatory trade treatment for all member nations, (2) the reduction of tariffs by multilateral negotiation, and (3) the elimination of import quotas. Basically, GATT provided a forum for the negotiation of reduced trade barriers on a multilateral basis among nations.

Since the Second World War, member nations have completed eight "rounds" of GATT negotiations to reduce trade barriers. The eighth and most recent round of negotiations began in Uruguay in 1986. After 7 years of wrangling, in 1993 the 128 member nations reached a new agreement. The *Uruguay Round* agreement took effect on January 1, 1995, and its provisions are to be phased in through 2005.

Under this agreement, tariffs on thousands of products have been eliminated or reduced, with overall tariffs eventually dropping by 33 percent. The agreement also liberalized government rules that in the past impeded the global market for such services as advertising, legal services, tourist services, and financial services. Quotas on imported textiles and apparel were phased out and replaced with tariffs. Other provisions reduced agricultural subsidies paid to farmers and protected intellectual property (patents, trademarks, copyrights) against piracy.

When fully implemented, the Uruguay Round agreement will boost the world's GDP by an estimated $6 trillion, or 8 percent. Consumers in the United States will save more than $30 billion annually.

World Trade Organization

The Uruguay Round agreement established the **World Trade Organization (WTO)** as GATT's successor. Some 140 nations belong to the WTO, with China being one of the latest entrants. The WTO oversees trade agreements reached by the member nations and rules on trade disputes among them. It also provides forums for further rounds of trade negotiations.

GATT and the WTO have been positive forces in the trend toward liberalized world trade. The trade rules agreed upon by the member nations provide a strong and necessary bulwark against the protectionism called for by the special-interest groups in the various nations.

For that reason and others, the WTO is highly controversial. Critics are concerned that rules crafted to expand international trade and investment enable firms to circumvent national laws that protect workers and the environment. What good are minimum-wage laws, worker safety laws, collective bargaining rights, and environmental laws if firms can easily shift their production to nations that have weaker laws or consumers can buy goods produced in those countries?

Proponents of the WTO respond that labor and environmental protections should be pursued directly in nations that have low standards and via international organizations other than the WTO. These issues should not be linked to the process of trade liberalization, which confers widespread economic benefits across nations. Moreover, say proponents of the WTO, many environmental and labor concerns are greatly overblown. Most world trade is among advanced industrial countries, not between them and countries that have lower environmental and labor standards. Moreover, the free flow of goods and resources raises output and income in the developing nations. Historically, such

increases in living standards have engendered stronger, not weaker, protections for the environment and for workers.

The European Union

Countries have also sought to reduce tariffs by creating regional *free-trade zones*—also called *trade blocs.* The most dramatic example is the **European Union (EU),** formerly called the European Economic Community. Initiated as the Common Market in 1958, the EU now comprises 15 western European nations—France, Germany, Italy, Belgium, the Netherlands, Luxembourg, Denmark, Ireland, United Kingdom, Greece, Spain, Portugal, Austria, Finland, and Sweden.

The EU Trade Bloc

The EU has abolished tariffs and import quotas on nearly all products traded among the participating nations and established a common system of tariffs applicable to all goods received from nations outside the EU. It has also liberalized the movement of capital and labor within the EU and has created common policies in other economic matters of joint concern, such as agriculture, transportation, and business practices. The EU is now a strong **trade bloc:** a group of countries having common identity, economic interests, and trade rules.

EU integration has achieved for Europe what the U.S. constitutional prohibition on tariffs by individual states has achieved for the United States: increased regional specialization, greater productivity, greater output, and faster economic growth. The free flow of goods and services has created large markets for EU industries. The resulting economies of large-scale production have enabled these industries to achieve much lower costs than they could have achieved in their small, single-nation markets.

The effects of EU success on nonmember nations, such as the United States, have been mixed. A peaceful and increasingly prosperous EU makes its members better customers for U.S. exports. But U.S. firms and other nonmember firms have been faced with tariffs and other barriers that make it difficult for them to compete against firms within the EU trade bloc. For example, autos produced in Germany and sold in Spain or France face no tariffs, whereas U.S. and Japanese autos sold in those EU countries do. This puts U.S. and Japanese firms at a serious disadvantage. Similarly, EU trade restrictions hamper eastern European exports of metals, textiles, and farm products, goods that the eastern Europeans produce in abundance.

By giving preferences to countries within their free-trade zone, trade blocs such as the EU tend to reduce their members' trade with non-bloc members. Thus, the world loses some of the benefits of a completely open global trading system. Eliminating that disadvantage has been one of the motivations for liberalizing global trade through the World Trade Organization.

The Euro One of the most significant recent accomplishments of the EU is the establishment of the so-called Euro Zone. In 2000, 11 of the 15 EU members shared a common currency—the **euro.** Greece becomes the twelfth member of the Euro Zone on January 1, 2002. Great Britain, Denmark, and Sweden have opted out of the common currency, at least for now.

On January 1, 1999, the euro made its debut for electronic payments such as credit card purchases and transfer of funds among banks. On January 1, 2002, euro notes and coins will begin circulating alongside the existing currencies, and on July 1, 2002, only the euro will be accepted for payment.

Economists expect the euro to raise the standard of living of the Euro Zone members over time. By ending the inconvenience and expense of exchanging currencies, the euro will enhance the free flow of goods, services, and resources among the Euro Zone members. It will also enable consumers and businesses to comparison shop for outputs and inputs, and this will increase competition, reduce prices, and lower costs.

North American Free Trade Agreement

In 1993 Canada, Mexico, and the United States formed a major trade bloc. The **North American Free Trade Agreement (NAFTA)** established a free-trade zone that has about the same combined output as the EU but encompasses a much larger geographic area. NAFTA has greatly reduced tariffs and other trade barriers between Canada, Mexico, and the United States and will eliminate them entirely by 2008.

Critics of NAFTA feared that it would cause a massive loss of U.S. jobs as firms moved to Mexico

to take advantage of lower wages and weaker regulations on pollution and workplace safety. Also, there was concern that Japan and South Korea would build plants in Mexico and transport goods tariff-free to the United States, further hurting U.S. firms and workers.

In retrospect, the critics were much too pessimistic. Employment has increased in the United States by more than 14 million workers since passage of NAFTA, and the unemployment rate has sunk from 6.9 to 4.2 percent. Increased trade between Canada, Mexico, and the United States has enhanced the standard of living in all three countries. **(Key Question 10)**

QUICK REVIEW 6.3

■ Governments curtail imports and promote exports through protective tariffs, import quotas, nontariff barriers, and export subsidies.

■ The General Agreement on Tariffs and Trade (GATT) established multinational reductions in tariffs and import quotas. The Uruguay Round of GATT (1993) reduced tariffs worldwide, liberalized international trade in services, strengthened protections for intellectual property, and reduced agricultural subsidies.

■ The World Trade Organization (WTO)—GATT's successor—rules on trade disputes and provides forums for negotiations on further rounds of trade liberalization.

■ The European Union (EU) and the North American Free Trade Agreement (NAFTA) have reduced internal trade barriers among their members by establishing large free-trade zones. Of the 15 EU members, 11 now have a common currency—the euro.

■ Increased Global Competition

Freer international trade has brought intense competition both within the United States and across the globe. In the United States, imports have gained major shares of many markets, including those for cars, steel, car tires, clothing, sporting goods, electronics, motorcycles, outboard motors, and toys. Nevertheless, hundreds of U.S. firms have prospered in the global marketplace. Such firms as Boeing, McDonald's, Dow Chemicals, Intel, Coca-Cola, Microsoft, AT&T, Monsanto, Procter & Gamble, and Hewlett-Packard have continued to retain high market shares at home and have dramatically expanded their sales abroad. Of course, not all U.S. firms have been so successful. Some have not been able to compete, either because their international competitors make better-quality products, have lower production costs, or both.

Is the heightened competition that accompanies the global economy a good thing? Although some domestic producers *do* get hurt and their workers must find employment elsewhere, foreign competition clearly benefits consumers and society in general. Imports break down the monopoly power of existing firms, thereby lowering product prices and providing consumers with a greater variety of goods. Foreign competition also forces domestic producers to become more efficient and to improve product quality; that has already happened in several U.S. industries, including steel and autos. Most U.S. firms can and do compete quite successfully in the global marketplace.

What about the U.S. firms that cannot compete successfully in open markets? The harsh reality is that they should go out of business, much like an unsuccessful corner boutique. Persistent economic losses mean that scarce resources are not being used efficiently. Shifting those resources to alternative, profitable uses will increase total U.S. output. It will be far less expensive for the United States to provide training and, if necessary, relocation assistance to laid-off workers than to try to protect these jobs from foreign competition.

Buy American: The Global Refrigerator

Humorist Art Buchwald Looks at the Logic of the "Buy American" Campaign.

"There is only one way the country is going to get on its feet," said Baleful.

"How's that?" I asked, as we drank coffee in his office at the Baleful Refrigerator Company.

"The consumer has to start buying American," he said, slamming his fist down on the desk. "Every time an American buys a foreign refrigerator it costs one of my people his job. And every time one of my people is out of work it means he or she can't buy refrigerators."

"It's a vicious circle," I said.

Baleful's secretary came in. "Mr. Thompson, the steel broker is on the phone."

My friend grabbed the receiver. "Thompson, where is that steel shipment from Japan that was supposed to be in last weekend? . . . I don't care about weather. We're almost out of steel, and I'll have to close down the refrigerator assembly line next week. If you can't deliver when you promise, I'll find myself another broker."

"You get your steel from Japan?" I asked Baleful.

"Even with shipping costs, their price is still lower than steel made in Europe. We used to get all our sheets from Belgium, but the Japanese are now giving them a run for their money."

The buzzer on the phone alerted Baleful. He listened for a few moments and then said, "Excuse me, I have a call from Taiwan. Mark Four? Look, R&D designed a new push-button door handle and we're going to send the specs to you. Tell Mr. Chow if his people send us a sample of one and can make it for us "at the same price as the old handle, we'll give his company the order."

A man came in with a plastic container and said, "Mr. Baleful, you said you wanted to see one of these before we ordered them. They are the containers for the ice maker in the refrigerator."

Baleful inspected it carefully and banged it on the floor a couple of times. "What's the price on it?"

"Hong Kong can deliver it at $2 a tray, and Dong-Fu Plastics in South Korea said they can make it for $1.70."

"It's just a plastic tray. Take the South Korea bid. We'll let Hong Kong supply us with the shelves for the freezer. Any word on the motors?"

"There's a German company in Brazil that just came out with a new motor, and it's passed all our tests, so Johnson has ordered 50,000."

"Call Cleveland Motors and tell them we're sorry, but the price they quoted us was just too high."

"Yes, sir," the man said and departed.

The secretary came in again and said, "Harry telephoned and wanted to let you know the defroster just arrived from Finland. They're unloading the box cars now."

"Good. Any word on the wooden crates from Singapore?"

"They're at the dock in Hoboken."

"Thank heaven. Cancel the order from Boise Cascade."

"What excuse should I give them?"

"Tell them we made a mistake in our inventory, or we're switching to plastic. I don't care what you tell them."

Baleful turned to me. "Where were we?"

"You were saying that if the consumer doesn't start buying American, this country is going to be in a lot of trouble."

"Right. It's not only his patriotic duty, but his livelihood that's at stake. I'm going to Washington next week to tell the Senate Commerce Committee that if they don't get on the stick, there isn't going to be a domestic refrigerator left in this country. We're not going to stay in business for our health."

"Pour it to them," I urged him.

Baleful said, "Come out with me into the showroom."

I followed him. He went to his latest model, and opened the door. "This is an American refrigerator made by the American worker, for the American consumer. What do you have to say to that?"

"It's beautiful," I said. "It puts foreign imports to shame."

Source: Art Buchwald, "Being Bullish on Buying American." Reprinted by permission. We discovered this article in *Master Curriculum Guide in Economics: Teaching Strategies for International Trade* (New York: Joint Council on Economic Education, 1988).

SUMMARY

1. Goods and services flows, capital and labor flows, information and technology flows, and financial flows link the United States and other countries.

2. International trade is growing in importance globally and for the United States. World trade is significant to the United States in two respects: (a) The absolute volumes of U.S. imports and exports exceed those of any other single nation. (b) The United States is completely dependent on trade for certain commodities and materials that cannot be obtained domestically.

3. Principal U.S. exports include semiconductors, computers, chemicals, consumer durables, generating equipment, and aircraft; principal U.S. imports include automobiles, computers, petroleum, clothing, and household appliances. Quantitatively, Canada is the United States' most important trading partner.

4. Global trade has been greatly facilitated by (a) improvements in transportation technology, (b) improvements in communications technology, and (c) general declines in tariffs. Although the United States, Japan, and the western European nations dominate the global economy, the total volume of trade has been increased by the contributions of several new trade participants. They include the Asian economies of Singapore, South Korea, Taiwan, and China (including Hong Kong), the eastern European countries (such as the Czech Republic, Hungary, and Poland), and the newly independent countries of the former Soviet Union (such as Estonia, Ukraine, and Azerbaijan).

5. Specialization based on comparative advantage enables nations to achieve higher standards of living through trade with other countries. A trading partner should specialize in products and services for which its domestic opportunity costs are lowest. The terms of trade must be such that both nations can obtain more of some product via trade than they could obtain by producing it at home.

6. The foreign exchange market sets exchange rates between currencies. Each nation's imports create a supply of its own currency and a demand for foreign currencies. The resulting supply–demand equilibrium sets the exchange rate that links the currencies of all nations. Depreciation of a nation's currency reduces its imports and increases its exports; appreciation increases its imports and reduces its exports.

7. Governments influence trade flows through (a) protective tariffs, (b) quotas, (c) nontariff barriers, and (d) export subsidies. Such impediments to free trade result from misunderstandings about the advantages of free trade and from political considerations. By artificially increasing product prices, trade barriers cost U.S. consumers billions of dollars annually.

8. The Reciprocal Trade Agreements Act of 1934 marked the beginning of a trend toward lower U.S. tariffs. Most-favored-nation status allows a nation to export goods into the United States at the United States' lowest tariff level, then or at any later time.

9. In 1947 the General Agreement on Tariffs and Trade (GATT) was formed to encourage nondiscriminatory treatment for all member nations, to reduce tariffs, and to eliminate import quotas. The Uruguay Round of GATT negotiations (1993) reduced tariffs and quotas, liberalized trade in services, reduced agricultural subsidies, reduced pirating of intellectual property, and phased out quotas on textiles.

10. GATT's successor, the World Trade Organization (WTO), has 140 member nations. It implements WTO agreements, rules on trade disputes between members, and provides forums for continued discussions on trade liberalization.

11. Free-trade zones (trade blocs) liberalize trade within regions but may at the same time impede trade with non-bloc members. Two examples of free-trade arrangements are the 15-member European Union (EU) and the North American Free Trade Agreement (NAFTA), comprising Canada, Mexico, and the United States. Eleven of the EU nations have agreed to abandon their national currencies for a common currency called the euro.

12. The global economy has created intense foreign competition in many U.S. product markets, but most U.S. firms are able to compete well both at home and globally.

TERMS AND CONCEPTS

multinational corporations

comparative advantage

terms of trade

foreign exchange market

exchange rates

depreciation

appreciation

protective tariffs

import quotas

nontariff barriers

export subsidies

Smoot-Hawley Tariff Act

Reciprocal Trade Agreements Act

most-favored-nation clauses

General Agreement on Tariffs and Trade (GATT)

World Trade Organization (WTO)

European Union (EU)

trade bloc

euro

North American Free Trade Agreement (NAFTA)

STUDY QUESTIONS

1. Describe the four major economic flows that link the United States with other nations. Provide a specific example to illustrate each flow. Explain the relationships between the top and bottom flows in Figure 6.1.

2. How important is international trade to the U.S. economy? In terms of volume, does the United States trade more with the industrially advanced economies or with developing economies? What country is the United States' most important trading partner, quantitatively?

3. What factors account for the rapid growth of world trade since the Second World War? Who are the major players in international trade today? Besides Japan, what other Asian nations play significant roles in international trade?

4. **Key Question** The following are production possibilities tables for South Korea and the United States. Assume that before specialization and trade the optimal product mix for South Korea is alternative B and for the United States is alternative U.

Product	South Korea's Production Possibilities					
	A	B	C	D	E	F
Radios (in thousands)	30	24	18	12	6	0
Chemicals (in tons)	0	6	12	18	24	30

Product	U.S. Production Possibilities					
	R	S	T	U	V	W
Radios (in thousands)	10	8	6	4	2	0
Chemicals (in tons)	0	4	8	12	16	20

a. Are comparative-cost conditions such that the two areas should specialize? If so, what product should each produce?

b. What is the total gain in radio and chemical output that would result from such specialization?

c. What are the limits of the terms of trade? Suppose actual terms of trade are 1 unit of radios for $1\frac{1}{2}$ units of chemicals and that 4 units of radios are exchanged for 6 units of chemicals. What are the gains from specialization and trade for each nation?

d. Can you conclude from this illustration that specialization according to comparative advantage results in more efficient use of world resources? Explain.

5. Suppose that the comparative-cost ratios of two products—baby formula and tuna fish—are as follows in the hypothetical nations of Canswicki and Tunata:

    Canswicki: 1 can baby formula ≡ 2 cans tuna fish
    Tunata: 1 can baby formula ≡ 4 cans tuna fish

In what product should each nation specialize? Explain why terms of trade of 1 can baby formula ≡ $2\frac{1}{2}$ cans tuna fish would be acceptable to both nations.

6. **Key Question** True or False? "U.S. exports create a demand for foreign currencies; foreign imports of U.S. goods create a supply of foreign currencies." Explain. Would a decline in U.S. consumer income or a weakening of U.S. preferences for foreign products cause the dollar to depreciate or to appreciate? Other things equal, what would be the effects of that depreciation or appreciation on U.S. exports and imports?

7. If the European euro were to decline in value (depreciate) in the foreign exchange market, would it be easier or harder for the French to sell their wine in the United States? Suppose you were planning a trip to Paris. How would depreciation of the euro change the dollar cost of your trip?

8. True or False? "An increase in the American dollar price of the South Korean won implies that the South Korean won has depreciated in value." Explain.

9. What measures do governments take to promote exports and restrict imports? Who benefits and who loses from protectionist policies? What is the net outcome for society?

10. **Key Question** Identify and state the significance of each of the following: (a) WTO; (b) EU; (c) euro; (d) NAFTA. What commonality do they share?

11. Explain: "Free-trade zones such as the EU and NAFTA lead a double life: They can promote free trade among members, but they pose serious trade obstacles for nonmembers." Do you think the net effects of trade blocs are good or bad for world trade? Why? How do the efforts of the WTO relate to these trade blocs?

12. Speculate as to why some U.S. firms strongly support trade liberalization while other U.S. firms favor protectionism. Speculate as to why some U.S. labor unions strongly support trade liberalization while other U.S. labor unions strongly oppose it.

13. **(Last Word)** What point is Art Buchwald making in his humorous essay on the Baleful Refrigerator Company? Why might Mr. Baleful *oppose* tariffs on imported goods even though he wants consumers to buy "American" refrigerators?

14. **Web-Based Question:** *Trade balances with partner countries* The U.S. Census Bureau, at www.census.gov/foreign-trade/www/statistics.html, lists the top trading partners of the United States (imports and exports added together) as well as the top 10 countries with which the United States has a trade surplus and a trade deficit. Using the current year-to-date data, compare the top 10 deficit and surplus countries with the top 10 trading partners. Are deficit and surplus countries equally represented in the top 10 trading partners list, or does one group dominate the list? The top 10 trading partners represent what percent of U.S. imports and what percent of U.S. exports?

15. **Web-Based Question:** *Foreign exchange rates—the yen for dollars* The Federal Reserve System website, www.federalreserve.gov/releases/H10/hist/, provides historical foreign-exchange-rate data for a wide variety of currencies. The information is based on data collected by the Federal Reserve Bank of New York from a sample of market participants. Look at the data for the Japanese yen from 1990 to the present. Assume that you were in Tokyo every New Year's from January 1, 1990, to this year and bought a *bento* (box lunch) for 1000 yen each year. Convert this amount to dollars using the yen-dollar exchange rate for each January since 1990, and plot the dollar price of the *bento* over time. Has the dollar appreciated or depreciated against the yen? What was the least amount in dollars that your box lunch cost? The most?

2

*Microeconomics of
Product Markets*

C H A P T E R

Supply and Demand
Elasticities and Government-Set Prices

MODERN MARKET ECONOMIES rely mainly on the activities of consumers, businesses, and resource suppliers to allocate resources efficiently. Those activities and their outcomes are the subject of *microeconomics*, to which we now turn. We start, in Part 2, by investigating the behaviors and decisions of consumers and businesses. ■ In this chapter we extend our previous discussion of demand and supply. First, we introduce three ideas: *price elasticity*—the buying and selling responses of consumers and producers to price changes; *cross elasticity*—the buying response of consumers of one product when the price of another product changes; and *income elasticity*—the buying response of consumers when their incomes change. Second, we discuss markets in which government sets maximum or minimum prices.

■ Price Elasticity of Demand

The law of demand tells us that consumers will buy more of a product when its price declines and less when its price increases. But how much more or less will they buy? The amount varies from product to product and over different price ranges for the same product. And such variations matter. For example, a firm contemplating a price hike will want to know how consumers will respond. If they remain highly loyal and continue to buy, the firm's revenue and profit will rise. But if consumers defect en masse to other sellers or other products, revenue and profit will tumble.

The responsiveness (or sensitivity) of consumers to a price change is measured by a product's **price elasticity of demand.** For some products—for example, restaurant meals—consumers are highly responsive to price changes. Modest price changes cause very large changes in the quantity purchased. Economists say that the demand for such products is *relatively elastic* or simply *elastic*.

For other products—for example, salt—consumers pay much less attention to price changes. Substantial price changes cause only small changes in the amount purchased. The demand for such products is *relatively inelastic* or simply *inelastic*. ▮ 7.1 ▰ 7.1

The Price-Elasticity Coefficient and Formula

Economists measure the degree of price elasticity or inelasticity of demand with the coefficient E_d, defined as

$$E_d = \frac{\text{percentage change in quantity demanded of product X}}{\text{percentage change in price of product X}}$$

The percentage changes in the equation are calculated by dividing the *change* in quantity demanded by the original quantity demanded and by dividing the *change* in price by the original price. So we can restate the formula as

$$E_d = \frac{\text{change in quantity demanded of X}}{\text{original quantity demanded of X}}$$
$$\div \frac{\text{change in price of X}}{\text{original price of X}}$$

Use of Percentages   Why use percentages rather than absolute amounts in measuring consumer responsiveness? There are two reasons.

First, if we use absolute changes, the choice of units will arbitrarily affect our impression of buyer responsiveness. To illustrate: If the price of a bag of popcorn at the local softball game is reduced from $3 to $2 and consumers increase their purchases from 60 to 100 bags, it will seem that consumers are quite sensitive to price changes and therefore that demand is elastic. After all, a price change of 1 unit has caused a change in the amount demanded of 40 units. But by changing the monetary unit from dollars to pennies (why not?), we find that a price change of 100 units (pennies) causes a quantity change of 40 units. This may falsely lead us to believe that demand is inelastic. We avoid this problem by using percentage changes. This particular price decline is 33 percent whether we measure it in dollars ($1/$3) or pennies (100¢/300¢).

Second, by using percentages, we can correctly compare consumer responsiveness to changes in the prices of different products. It makes little sense to compare the effects on quantity demanded of (1) a $1 increase in the price of a $10,000 used car with (2) a $1 increase in the price of a $1 soft drink. Here the price of the used car has increased by .01 percent while the price of the soft drink is up by 100 percent. We can more sensibly compare the consumer responsiveness to price increases by using some common percentage increase in price for both.

Elimination of Minus Sign   We know from the downsloping demand curve that price and quantity demanded are inversely related. Thus, the price-elasticity coefficient of demand E_d will always be a negative number. As an example, if price declines, then quantity demanded will increase. This means that the numerator in our formula will be positive and the denominator negative, yielding a negative E_d. For an increase in price, the numerator will be negative but the denominator positive, again yielding a negative E_d.

Economists usually ignore the minus sign and simply present the absolute value of the elasticity coefficient to avoid an ambiguity that might otherwise arise. It can be confusing to say that an E_d of -4 is greater than one of -2. This possible confusion is avoided when we say an E_d of 4 reveals greater elasticity than one of 2. So, in what follows, we ignore the minus sign in the coefficient of price elasticity of demand and show only the absolute value. Incidentally, the ambiguity does not arise with supply because price and quantity supplied are positively related.

Interpretations of E_d

We can interpret the coefficient of price elasticity of demand as follows.

Elastic Demand   Demand is **elastic** if a specific percentage change in price results in a larger percentage change in quantity demanded. Then E_d will be greater than 1. Example: Suppose that a 2 percent decline in the price of cut flowers results in a 4 percent increase in quantity demanded. Then demand for cut flowers is elastic and

$$E_d = \frac{.04}{.02} = 2$$

Inelastic Demand   If a specific percentage change in price produces a smaller percentage change in quantity demanded, demand is **inelastic.** Then E_d will be less than 1. Example: Suppose that a 2 percent decline in the price of coffee leads to only a 1 percent increase in quantity demanded. Then demand is inelastic and

$$E_d = \frac{.01}{.02} = .5$$

Unit Elasticity The case separating elastic and inelastic demands occurs where a percentage change in price and the resulting percentage change in quantity demanded are the same. Example: Suppose that a 2 percent drop in the price of chocolate causes a 2 percent increase in quantity demanded. This special case is termed **unit elasticity** because E_d is exactly 1, or unity. In this example,

$$E_d = \frac{.02}{.02} = 1$$

Extreme Cases When we say demand is "inelastic," we do not mean that consumers are completely unresponsive to a price change. In that extreme situation, where a price change results in no change whatsoever in the quantity demanded, economists say that demand is **perfectly inelastic.** The price-elasticity coefficient is zero because there is no response to a change in price. Approximate examples include an acute diabetic's demand for insulin or an addict's demand for heroin. A line parallel to the vertical axis, such as D_1 in Figure 7.1a, shows perfectly inelastic demand graphically.

Conversely, when we say demand is "elastic," we do not mean that consumers are completely responsive to a price change. In that extreme situation, where a small price reduction causes buyers to increase their purchases from zero to all they can obtain, the elasticity coefficient is infinite ($= \infty$) and economists say demand is **perfectly elastic.** A line parallel to the horizontal axis, such as D_2 in Figure 7.1b, shows perfectly elastic demand. You will see in Chapter 10 that such a demand applies to a firm—say, a raspberry grower—that is selling its product in a purely competitive market.

Refinement: Midpoint Formula

Unfortunately, there is an annoying problem that arises in computing the price-elasticity coefficient. To understand this problem and its solution, consider the hypothetical demand data for movie tickets in Table 7.1. To calculate E_d for, say, the \$5–\$4 price range, which price-quantity combination should we use as a point of reference? We have two choices—the \$5–4-unit combination and the \$4–5-unit combination—and our choice will influence the outcome. (In this case, each "unit" represents 1000 tickets: 2 units are 2000, 3 units are 3000, and so on.)

For the \$5–4-unit reference point, the price change is from \$5 to \$4, so the percentage decrease

Figure 7.1

Perfectly inelastic and elastic demands. Demand curve D_1 in (a) represents perfectly inelastic demand ($E_d = 0$). A price increase will result in no change in quantity demanded. Demand curve D_2 in (b) represents perfectly elastic demand. A price increase will cause quantity demanded to decline from an infinite amount to zero ($E_d = \infty$).

in price is 20 percent; the quantity change is from 4 to 5 units, so the percentage increase in quantity is 25 percent. Substituting in the formula, we get $E_d = 25/20$, or 1.25, indicating that demand is somewhat elastic.

But for the \$4–5-unit reference point, the price change is from \$4 to \$5, making the percentage increase in price 25 percent; the quantity change is from 5 to 4 units, or a 20 percent decline in quantity. The elasticity coefficient is therefore 20/25, or .80, meaning that demand for tickets is slightly inelastic. Which is it? Is the hypothetical demand for movie tickets elastic or inelastic?

A solution to this problem is to use averages of the two ticket prices and two quantities as the reference point. For the same \$5–\$4 price range, the price reference is \$4.50, and the quantity reference is 4.5 units. The percentage change in price is now \$1/\$4.50, or about 22 percent, and the percentage change in quantity is 1/4.50, or also about 22 percent, providing an E_d of 1. This solution estimates

Table 7.1

Price Elasticity of Demand for Movie Tickets as Measured by the Elasticity Coefficient and the Total-Revenue Test

(1) Total Quantity of Tickets Demanded per Week, Thousands	(2) Price per Ticket	(3) Elasticity Coefficient (E_d)	(4) Total Revenue, (1) × (2)	(5) Total-Revenue Test
1	$8		$ 8,000	
2	7	5.00	14,000	Elastic
3	6	2.60	18,000	Elastic
4	5	1.57	20,000	Elastic
5	4	1.00	20,000	Unit elastic
6	3	0.64	18,000	Inelastic
7	2	0.38	14,000	Inelastic
8	1	0.20	8,000	Inelastic

elasticity at the midpoint of the relevant price range. We now can state the *midpoint formula* for E_d as

$$E_d = \frac{\text{change in quantity}}{\text{sum of quantities}/2} \div \frac{\text{change in price}}{\text{sum of prices}/2}$$

Substituting data for the $5–$4 price range, we get

$$E_d = \frac{1}{9/2} \div \frac{1}{9/2} = 1$$

This indicates that at the $4.50–4.5-unit midpoint the price elasticity of demand is unity. Here a 1 percent price change will result in a 1 percent change in quantity demanded.

Assignment: Verify the elasticity coefficients for the $1–$2 and $7–$8 ticket price ranges in Table 7.1. The interpretation of E_d for the $1–$2 range is that a 1 percent change in price will change quantity demanded by .20 percent. For the $7–$8 range a 1 percent change in price will change quantity demanded by 5 percent.

Graphical Analysis

We used the hypothetical data for movie tickets in columns 1 and 2, Table 7.1, to plot the demand curve *D* in Figure 7.2a. The curve illustrates that elasticity typically varies over the different price ranges of the same demand schedule or curve. For all straight-line and most other demand curves, demand is more elastic toward the upper left (the $5–$8 price range of *D*) than toward the lower right (the $4–$1 price range of *D*). 7.1

This is the consequence of the arithmetic properties of the elasticity measure. Specifically, in the upper left segment of the demand curve, the percentage change in quantity is large because the original reference quantity is small. Similarly, the percentage change in price is small in that segment because the original reference price is large. The relatively large percentage change in quantity divided by the relatively small change in price yields a large E_d—an elastic demand.

The reverse holds true for the lower right segment of the demand curve. Here the percentage change in quantity is small because the original reference quantity is large; similarly, the percentage change in price is large because the original reference price is small. The relatively small percentage change in quantity divided by the relatively large percentage change in price results in a small E_d—an inelastic demand.

The demand curve in Figure 7.2a also illustrates that the slope of a demand curve—its flatness or steepness—is not a sound basis for judging elasticity. The catch is that the slope of the curve is computed from *absolute* changes in price and quantity, while elasticity involves *relative* or *percentage* changes in price and quantity. The demand curve in Figure 7.2a is linear, which by definition means that the slope is constant throughout. But we have demonstrated that such a curve is elastic in its high-price ($8–$5) range and inelastic in its low-price ($4–$1) range. **(Key Question 2)**

(a)
Demand curve

(b)
Total-revenue curve

Figure 7.2

The relation between price elasticity of demand for movie tickets and total revenue. Demand curve D in (a) is based on Table 7.1 and is marked to show that the hypothetical weekly demand for movie tickets is elastic at higher price ranges and inelastic at lower price ranges. The total-revenue curve TR in (b) is derived from demand curve D. When price falls and TR increases, demand is elastic; when price falls and TR is unchanged, demand is unit-elastic; and when price falls and TR declines, demand is inelastic.

QUICK REVIEW 7.1

■ Price elasticity of demand measures the sensitivity of consumers to changes in the price of a product.

■ The price elasticity of demand coefficient E_d is the ratio of the percentage change in quantity demanded to the percentage change in price. The averages of the prices and quantities are used as references in calculating the percentage changes.

■ When E_d is greater than 1, demand is elastic; when E_d is less than 1, demand is inelastic; when E_d is equal to 1, demand is of unit elasticity.

■ Demand is typically elastic in the high-price (low-quantity) range of the demand curve and inelastic in the low-price (high-quantity) range of the curve.

The Total-Revenue Test

The importance of elasticity for firms relates to the effect of price changes on total revenue and thus on profits (total revenue minus total costs).

Total revenue (TR) is the total amount the seller receives from the sale of a product in a particular time period; it is calculated by multiplying the product price (P) by the quantity demanded and sold (Q). In equation form:

$$TR = P \times Q$$

Total revenue and the price elasticity of demand are related. Indeed, perhaps the easiest way to infer whether demand is elastic or inelastic is to employ the **total-revenue test,** which looks at what happens to total revenue when product price changes.

Elastic Demand If demand is elastic, a decrease in price will increase total revenue. Even though a lesser price is received per unit, enough additional units are sold to more than make up for the lower price. For an example, look at demand curve D in Figure 7.2a, specifically the elastic-demand region at the upper left. (Disregard Figure 7.2b for the moment.) At point a on the curve, price is $8 and quantity demanded is 1 unit, or 1000 tickets. So total revenue, or price times quantity, is $8000 (= $8 × 1000 tickets). Geometrically, total revenue is area $0P_8aQ_1$, found by multiplying one side of the rectangle ($0P_8$) by the other ($0Q_1$).

If the price of movie tickets declines to $7 (point b), the quantity demanded becomes 2 units, and total revenue is \$14,000 (= \$2 × 7000 tickets), or area $0P_7bQ_2$. As a result of the price decline from \$8 to \$7, total revenue has increased from \$8000 to \$14,000. This increase has occurred because the loss in revenue from the lower price per unit (area P_7P_8ac) is less than the gain in revenue from the larger quantity demanded (area Q_1cbQ_2) accompanying the lower price. Specifically, the \$1 price reduction applies to the original 1000 tickets (Q_1), for a loss of \$1000. But the lower price increases quantity demanded by 1000 tickets (Q_1 to Q_2), with a resulting gain in revenue of \$7000. Thus, the movie theater achieves a net increase in total revenue of \$6000 (= \$7000 − \$1000).

The reasoning is reversible: If demand is elastic, a price increase will reduce total revenue. If we shift from b to a on the demand curve, the gain in total revenue caused by the higher ticket price (area P_7P_8ac) is less than the loss in revenue from the drop in sales (area Q_1cbQ_2). Combining these results tells us that demand is elastic if a price change causes total revenue to change in the opposite direction.

Inelastic Demand If demand is inelastic, a price decrease will reduce total revenue. The modest increase in ticket sales will not offset the decline in revenue per unit, and the net result is that total revenue will decline. To see this, look at the lower right of demand curve D in Figure 7.2a, specifically the inelastic-demand region. At point f on the curve, price is \$2 and quantity demanded is 7000 tickets. So total revenue is \$14,000, or area $0P_2fQ_7$. If the price drops to \$1 (point h), quantity demanded increases to 8000 tickets. Total revenue becomes \$8000, which is clearly less than \$14,000; area $0P_1hQ_8$ is smaller than area $0P_2fQ_7$. Total revenue has declined because the loss of revenue from the lower unit price (area P_1P_2fg) is larger than the gain in revenue from the accompanying increase in sales (area Q_7ghQ_8). The \$1 decline in price applies to 7000 tickets, with a consequent revenue loss of \$7000. The sales increase accompanying that lower price is 1000 tickets, which results in a revenue gain of \$1000. The overall result is a net decrease in total revenue of \$6000 (= \$1000 − \$7000).

Again, our analysis is reversible: If demand is inelastic, a price increase will increase total revenue. Together, these results tell us that demand is inelastic if a price change causes total revenue to change in the same direction.

Unit Elasticity In the special case of unit elasticity, an increase or a decrease in price leaves total revenue unchanged. The loss in revenue from a lower unit price is exactly offset by the gain in revenue from the accompanying increase in sales. Conversely, the gain in revenue from a higher unit price is exactly offset by the revenue loss associated with the accompanying decline in the amount demanded.

In Figure 7.2a we find that at the \$5 price, 4000 tickets will be sold, yielding total revenue of \$20,000. At \$4 a total of 5000 tickets will be sold, again resulting in \$20,000 of total revenue. The \$1 price reduction causes the loss of \$4000 in revenue on the 4000 tickets that could have been sold for \$5 each. This is exactly offset by a \$4000 revenue gain that results from the sale of 1000 more tickets at the lower \$4 price.

Price Elasticity and the Total-Revenue Curve

In Figure 7.2b we graphed the total revenue per week to the theater owner that corresponds to each price-quantity combination indicated along demand curve D in Figure 7.2a. The price–quantity-demanded combination represented by point a on the demand curve yields total revenue of \$8000 (= \$8 × 1000 tickets). In Figure 7.2b, we graphed this \$8000 amount vertically at 1 unit (1000 tickets) demanded. Similarly, the price–quantity-demanded combination represented by point b in the upper panel yields total revenue of \$14,000 (= \$7 × 2000 tickets). This amount is graphed vertically at 2 units (2000 tickets) demanded in the lower panel. The ultimate result of such graphing is total-revenue curve TR, which first slopes upward, then reaches a maximum, and finally turns downward.

Comparison of curves D and TR sharply focuses the relationship between elasticity and total revenue. Lowering the ticket price in the elastic range of demand—for example, from \$8 to \$5—increases total revenue. Conversely, increasing the ticket price in that range reduces total revenue. In both cases, price and total revenue change in opposite directions, confirming that demand is elastic.

The \$5–\$4 price range of demand curve D reflects unit elasticity. When price either decreases from \$5 to \$4 or increases from \$4 to \$5, total revenue remains \$20,000. In both cases, price has changed and total revenue has remained constant, confirming that demand is unit-elastic when we consider these particular price changes.

In the inelastic range of demand curve *D*, lowering the price—for example, from $4 to $1—decreases total revenue, as shown in Figure 7.2b. Raising the price boosts total revenue. In both cases, price and total revenue move in the same direction, confirming that demand is inelastic.

So here again is the total-revenue test: Note what happens to total revenue when the price of a product changes. If total revenue changes in the opposite direction from price, demand is elastic. If total revenue changes in the same direction as price, demand is inelastic. If total revenue does not change when price changes, demand is unit-elastic.

Table 7.2 summarizes the characteristics of price elasticity of demand. You should review it carefully. **(Key Questions 4 and 5)**

Determinants of Price Elasticity of Demand

We cannot say just what will determine the price elasticity of demand in each individual situation. However, the following generalizations are often helpful.

Substitutability Generally, *the larger the number of substitute goods that are available, the greater the price elasticity of demand.* We will find later that in a purely competitive market, where by definition there are many perfect substitutes for the product of any specific seller, the demand curve seen by that single seller is perfectly elastic. If one competitive seller of carrots or potatoes raises its price, buyers will turn

to the readily available perfect substitutes provided by its many rivals. Similarly, we would expect the lowering of world trade barriers to increase the elasticity of demand for most products by making more substitutes available. With unimpeded foreign trade, Mercedes and BMWs become effective substitutes for domestic Cadillacs and Lincolns. At the other extreme, we saw earlier that the diabetic's demand for insulin is highly inelastic because there simply are no close substitutes.

The elasticity of demand for a product depends on how narrowly the product is defined. Demand for Reebok sneakers is more elastic than is the overall demand for shoes. Many other brands are readily substitutable for Reebok sneakers, but there are few, if any, good substitutes for shoes.

Proportion of Income Other things equal, *the higher the price of a good relative to consumers' incomes, the greater the price elasticity of demand.* A 10 percent increase in the price of relatively low-priced pencils or chewing gum amounts to a few pennies, and quantity demanded will probably decline only slightly. Thus, price elasticity for such low-priced items tends to be low. But a 10 percent increase in the price of relatively high-priced automobiles or housing means additional expenditures of perhaps $2500 or $15,000, respectively. These price increases are significant fractions of the annual incomes and budgets of most families, and quantities demanded will likely diminish significantly. Price elasticity for such items tends to be high.

Luxuries versus Necessities In general, *the more that a good is considered to be a "luxury" rather*

Table 7.2

Price Elasticity of Demand: A Summary

Absolute Value of Elasticity Coefficient	Demand Is:	Description	Impact on Total Revenue of a: Price Increase	Price Decrease
Greater than 1 ($E_d > 1$)	Elastic or relatively elastic	Quantity demanded changes by a larger percentage than does price	Total revenue decreases	Total revenue increases
Equal to 1 ($E_d = 1$)	Unit or unitary elastic	Quantity demanded changes by the same percentage as does price	Total revenue is unchanged	Total revenue is unchanged
Less than 1 ($E_d < 1$)	Inelastic or relatively inelastic	Quantity demanded changes by a smaller percentage than does price	Total revenue increases	Total revenue decreases

than a "necessity," the greater is the price elasticity of demand. Bread and electricity are generally regarded as necessities; it is difficult to get along without them. A price increase will not significantly reduce the amount of bread consumed or the amount of lighting and power used in a household. (Note the very low price-elasticity coefficient of these goods in Table 7.3.) An extreme case: A person does not decline an operation for acute appendicitis because the physician's fee has just gone up.

On the other hand, travel vacations and jewelry are luxuries, which, by definition, can easily be forgone. If the prices of travel vacations and jewelry rise, a consumer need not buy them and will suffer no great hardship without them.

What about the demand for a common product like salt? It is highly inelastic on three counts: There are few good substitutes available; salt is a negligible item in the family budget; and it is a "necessity" rather than a luxury.

Time Generally, *product demand is more elastic the longer the time period under consideration.* Consumers often need time to adjust to changes in prices. For example, when the price of a product rises, it takes time to find and experiment with other products to see if they are acceptable. Consumers may not immediately reduce their purchases very much when the price of beef rises by 10 percent, but in time they may shift to chicken or fish.

Another consideration is product durability. Studies show that "short-run" demand for gasoline is more inelastic ($E_d = .2$) than is "long-run" demand ($E_d = .7$). In the short run, people are "stuck" with their present cars and trucks, but with rising gasoline prices they eventually replace them with smaller, more fuel-efficient vehicles.

Table 7.3 shows estimated price-elasticity coefficients for a number of products. Each reflects some combination of the elasticity determinants just discussed. As an exercise, you should select two or three of them and explain how they relate to the determinants. (**Key Question 6**)

QUICK REVIEW 7.2

- When the price of a good changes, total revenue will change in the opposite direction if demand for the good is price-elastic, in the same direction if demand is price-inelastic, and not at all if demand is unit-elastic.

- Price elasticity of demand is greater (a) the larger the number of substitutes available; (b) the higher the price of a product relative to one's budget; (c) the greater the extent to which the product is a luxury; and (d) the longer the time period involved.

Applications of Price Elasticity of Demand

The concept of price elasticity of demand has great practical significance, as the following examples suggest.

Table 7.3
Selected Price Elasticities of Demand

Product or Service	Coefficient of Price Elasticity of Demand (E_d)	Product or Service	Coefficient of Price Elasticity of Demand (E_d)
Newspapers	.10	Gasoline	.60
Electricity (household)	.13	Milk	.63
Bread	.15	Household appliances	.63
Major league baseball tickets	.23	Movies	.87
Telephone service	.26	Beer	.90
Sugar	.30	Shoes	.91
Medical care	.31	Motor vehicles	1.14
Eggs	.32	Beef	1.27
Legal services	.37	China, glassware, tableware	1.54
Automobile repair	.40	Restaurant meals	2.27
Clothing	.49	Lamb and mutton	2.65

Source: Compiled from numerous studies and sources reporting price elasticity of demand.

Bumper Crops

The demand for most farm products is highly inelastic; E_d is perhaps .20 or .25. As a result, increases in the output of farm products arising from a good growing season or from increased productivity tend to depress both the prices of farm products and the total revenues (incomes) of farmers. For farmers as a group, the inelastic demand for their products means that a bumper crop may be undesirable. For policymakers it means that achieving the goal of higher total farm income requires that farm output be restricted.

Excise Taxes

The government pays attention to elasticity of demand when it selects goods and services on which to levy excise taxes. If a $1 tax is levied on a product and 10,000 units are sold, tax revenue will be $10,000 (= $1 × 10,000 units sold). If the government raises the tax to $1.50 but the higher price that results reduces sales to 5000 because of elastic demand, tax revenue will decline to $7500 (= $1.50 × 5000 units sold). Because a higher tax on a product with elastic demand will bring in less tax revenue, legislatures tend to seek out products that have inelastic demand—such as liquor, gasoline, and cigarettes—when levying excises. In fact, the Federal government, in its effort to reduce the budget deficit, increased taxes on those very categories of goods in 1991.

But the government sometimes misjudges in such matters. For example, in 1991 Congress also imposed a 10 percent excise tax on yachts costing more than $100,000. Believing the demand for yachts was inelastic, Congress felt that the impact on sales would be small and therefore anticipated that the tax would raise $1.5 billion over 5 years. But demand turned out to be more elastic than the lawmakers thought. Many boat owners reponded by keeping their old boats longer, and some prospective first-time buyers abandoned plans to buy pleasure boats. Sales dropped by nearly 90 percent in Florida, where many prospective buyers avoided the tax by buying their boats in the Bahamas. Government revenue from the tax was further reduced by the 1990–1991 recession, which shifted the demand curve for most durable goods, yachts included, to the left. In 1991 the 10 percent tax raised only $30 million in revenue.

The tax, coupled with the recession, had a devastating effect on boat manufacturers. In the first year of the tax one-third of all U.S. yacht-building companies halted production, and more than 20,000 workers lost their jobs. In 1993 Congress repealed the tax.

Decriminalization of Illegal Drugs

In recent years proposals to legalize drugs have been widely debated. Proponents contend that drugs should be treated like alcohol; they should be made legal for adults and regulated for purity and potency. The current war on drugs, it is argued, has been unsuccessful, and the associated costs—including enlarged police forces, the construction of more prisons, an overburdened court system, and untold human costs—have increased markedly. Legalization would allegedly reduce drug trafficking significantly by taking the profit out of it. Crack cocaine and heroin, for example, are cheap to produce and could be sold at low prices in legal markets. Because the demand of addicts is highly inelastic, the amounts consumed at the lower prices would increase only modestly. Addicts' total expenditures for cocaine and heroin would decline, and so would the street crime that finances those expenditures.

Opponents of legalization say that the overall demand for cocaine and heroin is far more elastic than proponents think. In addition to the inelastic demand of addicts, there is another market segment whose demand is relatively elastic. This segment consists of the occasional users or "dabblers," who use hard drugs when their prices are low but who abstain or substitute, say, alcohol when their prices are high. Thus, the lower prices associated with the legalization of hard drugs would increase consumption by dabblers. Also, removal of the legal prohibitions against using drugs might make drug use more socially acceptable, increasing the demand for cocaine and heroin.

Many economists predict that the legalization of cocaine and heroin would reduce street prices by up to 60 percent, depending on if and how much they were taxed. According to a recent study, price declines of that size would increase the number of occasional users of heroin by 54 percent and the number of occasional users of cocaine by 33 percent. The total quantity of heroin demanded would rise by an estimated 100 percent, and the quantity of cocaine demanded would rise by 50 percent.[1] Moreover, many existing and first-time dabblers might in time become addicts. The overall result, say the opponents of legalization, would be higher social costs, possibly including an increase in street crime.

---

[1]Henry Saffer and Frank Chaloupka, "The Demand for Illegal Drugs," *Economic Inquiry*, July 1999, pp. 401–411.

Minimum Wage In 2001 the Federal minimum wage prohibited employers from paying workers less than $5.15 per hour. Critics say that such a minimum wage, if it is above the equilibrium market wage, moves employers upward along their down-sloping labor demand curves toward lower quantities of labor demanded and consequently causes unemployment, particularly among teenage workers. On the other hand, workers who remain employed at the minimum wage receive higher incomes than they otherwise would. The amount of income lost by the newly unemployed and the amount of income gained by those who keep their jobs depend on the elasticity of demand for teenage labor. Research suggests that the demand for teenage labor is relatively inelastic. If correct, this means that income gains associated with the minimum wage would exceed income losses. The "unemployment argument" made by critics of the minimum wage would be stronger if the demand for teenage workers were elastic.

▌Price Elasticity of Supply

The concept of price elasticity also applies to supply. If producers are relatively responsive to price changes, supply is elastic. If they are relatively insensitive to price changes, supply is inelastic. 🔑 7.2

We measure the degree of price elasticity or inelasticity of supply with the coefficient E_s, defined almost like E_d except that we substitute "percentage change in quantity supplied" for "percentage change in quantity demanded":

$$E_s = \frac{\text{percentage change in quantity supplied of product X}}{\text{percentage change in price of product X}}$$

For reasons explained earlier, the averages, or midpoints, of the before and after quantities supplied and the before and after prices are used as reference points for the percentage changes. Suppose an increase in the price of a good from $4 to $6 increases the quantity supplied from 10 units to 14 units. The percentage change in price would be 2/5, or 40 percent, and the percentage change in quantity would be 4/12, or 33 percent:

$$E_s = \frac{.33}{.40} = .83$$

In this case, supply is inelastic, since the price-elasticity coefficient is less than 1. If E_s is greater than 1, supply is elastic. If it is equal to 1, supply is unit-elastic. Also, E_s is never negative, since price and quantity supplied are directly related. Thus, there are no minus signs to drop, as was necessary with elasticity of demand.

The main determinant of **price elasticity of supply** is the amount of time producers have for responding to a change in product price. A firm's response to, say, an increase in the price of Christmas trees depends on its ability to shift resources from the production of other products (whose prices we assume remain constant) to the production of trees. And shifting resources takes time: The longer the time, the greater the resource "shiftability." So we can expect a greater response, and therefore greater elasticity of supply, the longer a firm has to adjust to a price change.

In analyzing the impact of time on elasticity, economists distinguish among the immediate market period, the short run, and the long run.

Price Elasticity of Supply: The Market Period

The **market period** is the period that occurs when the time immediately after a change in market price is too short for producers to respond with a change in quantity supplied. Suppose the owner of a small farm brings to market one truckload of tomatoes that is the entire season's output. The supply curve for the tomatoes is perfectly inelastic (vertical); the farmer will sell the truckload whether the price is high or low. Why? Because the farmer can offer only one truckload of tomatoes even if the price of tomatoes is much higher than anticipated. He or she might like to offer more tomatoes, but tomatoes cannot be produced overnight. Another full growing season is needed to respond to a higher-than-expected price by producing more than one truckload. Similarly, because the product is perishable, the farmer cannot withhold it from the market. If the price is lower than anticipated, he or she will still sell the entire truckload.

The farmer's costs of production, incidentally, will not enter into this decision to sell. Though the price of tomatoes may fall far short of production costs, the farmer will nevertheless sell out to avoid a total loss through spoilage. During the market period, our farmer's supply of tomatoes is fixed: Only one truckload is offered no matter how high or low the price.

Figure 7.3a shows the farmer's vertical supply curve during the market period. Supply is perfectly inelastic because the farmer does not have time to respond to a change in demand, say, from D_1 to D_2. The resulting price increase from P_0 to P_m simply determines which buyers get the fixed quantity supplied; it elicits no increase in output.

However, not all supply curves need be perfectly inelastic immediately after a price change. If the product is not perishable and the price rises, producers may choose to increase quantity supplied by drawing down their inventories of unsold, stored goods. This will cause the market supply curve to attain some positive slope. For our tomato farmer, the market period may be a full growing season; for producers of goods that can be inexpensively stored, there may be no market period at all.

Price Elasticity of Supply: The Short Run

In the **short run,** the plant capacity of individual producers and of the entire industry is fixed. Even so, firms do have time to use their fixed plants more or less intensively. In the short run, our farmer's plant (land and farm machinery) is fixed. But he does have time in the short run to cultivate tomatoes more intensively by applying more labor and more fertilizer and pesticides to the crop. The result is a somewhat greater output in response to a presumed increase in demand; this greater output is reflected in

a more elastic supply of tomatoes, as shown by S_s in Figure 7.3b. Note now that the increase in demand from D_1 to D_2 is met by an increase in quantity (from Q_0 to Q_s), so there is a smaller price adjustment (from P_0 to P_s) than would be the case in the market period. The equilibrium price is therefore lower in the short-run than in the market period.

Price Elasticity of Supply: The Long Run

The **long run** is a time period long enough for firms to adjust their plant sizes and for new firms to enter (or existing firms to leave) the industry. In the "tomato industry," for example, our farmer has time to acquire additional land and buy more machinery and equipment. Furthermore, other farmers may, over time, be attracted to tomato farming by the increased demand and higher price. Such adjustments create a larger supply response, as represented by the more elastic supply curve S_L in Figure 7.3c. The outcome is a smaller price rise (P_0 to P_l) and a larger output increase (Q_0 to Q_l) in response to the increase in demand from D_1 to D_2. **(Key Question 10)**

There is no total-revenue test for elasticity of supply. Supply shows a positive or direct relationship between price and amount supplied; the supply curve is upsloping. Regardless of the degree of elasticity or inelasticity, price and total revenue always move together.

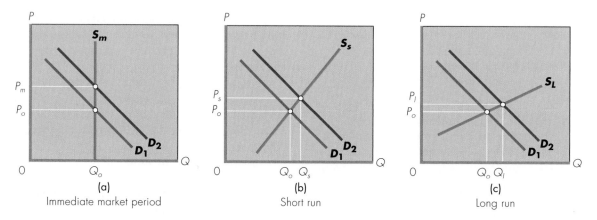

(a)	(b)	(c)
Immediate market period	Short run	Long run

Figure 7.3

Time and the elasticity of supply.   The greater the amount of time producers have to adjust to a change in demand, here from D_1 to D_2, the greater will be their output response. In the immediate market period (a) there is insufficient time to change output, and so supply is perfectly inelastic. In the short run (b) plant capacity is fixed, but changing the intensity of its use can alter output; supply is therefore more elastic. In the long run (c) all desired adjustments, including changes in plant capacity, can be made, and supply becomes still more elastic.

■ Cross Elasticity and Income Elasticity of Demand

Price elasticities measure the responsiveness of the quantity of a product demanded or supplied when its price changes. The consumption of a good also is affected by a change in the price of a related product or by a change in income.

Cross Elasticity of Demand

The **cross elasticity of demand** measures how sensitive consumer purchases of one product (say, X) are to a change in the price of some other product (say, Y). We calculate the coefficient of cross elasticity of demand E_{xy} just as we do the coefficient of simple price elasticity, except that we relate the percentage change in the consumption of X to the percentage change in the price of Y:

$$E_{xy} = \frac{\text{percentage change in quantity}}{\text{percentage change in price}}$$
$$\frac{\text{demanded of product X}}{\text{of product Y}}$$

This cross-elasticity (or cross-price-elasticity) concept allows us to quantify and more fully understand substitute and complementary goods, introduced in Chapter 3.

Substitute Goods

If cross elasticity of demand is positive, meaning that sales of X move in the same direction as a change in the price of Y, then X and Y are substitute goods. An example is Kodak film (X) and Fuji film (Y). An increase in the price of Kodak film causes consumers to buy more Fuji film, resulting in a positive cross elasticity. The larger is the positive cross-elasticity coefficient, the greater the substitutability between the two products.

Complementary Goods

When cross elasticity is negative, we know that X and Y "go together"; an increase in the price of one decreases the demand for the other. So the two are complementary goods. For example, an increase in the price of cameras will decrease the amount of film purchased. The larger the negative cross-elasticity coefficient, the greater is the complementarity between the two goods.

Independent Goods

A zero or near-zero cross elasticity suggests that the two products being considered are unrelated or independent goods. An example is walnuts and film: We would not expect a change in the price of walnuts to have any effect on purchases of film, and vice versa.

Applications

The degree of substitutability of products, measured by the cross-elasticity coefficient, is important to businesses and government. For example, suppose that Coca-Cola is considering whether or not to lower the price of its Sprite brand. Not only will it want to know something about the price elasticity of demand for Sprite (will the price cut increase or decrease total revenue?), but it will also be interested in knowing if the increased sales of Sprite will come at the expense of its Coke brand. How sensitive are the sales of one of its products (Coke) to a change in the price of another of its products (Sprite)? By how much will the increased sales of Sprite "cannibalize" the sales of Coke? A low cross elasticity would indicate that Coke and Sprite are weak substitutes for each other and that a lower price for Sprite would have little effect on Coke sales.

Government also implicitly uses the idea of cross elasticity of demand in assessing whether a proposed merger between two large firms will substantially reduce competition and therefore violate the antitrust laws. For example, the cross elasticity between Coke and Pepsi is high, making them strong substitutes for each other. Consequently, the government would likely block a merger between them because the merger would lessen competition. In contrast, the cross elasticity between film and gasoline is low or zero. A merger between Kodak and Shell would have a minimal effect on competition. So government would let that merger happen.

Income Elasticity of Demand

Income elasticity of demand measures the degree to which consumers respond to a change in their incomes by buying more or less of a particular good. The coefficient of income elasticity of demand E_i is determined with the formula

$$E_i = \frac{\text{percentage change in quantity demanded}}{\text{percentage change in income}}$$

Normal Goods

For most goods, the income-elasticity coefficient E_i is positive, meaning that more of them are demanded as incomes rises. Such goods are called normal or superior goods, which we first described in Chapter 3. But the value of E_i varies greatly among normal goods. For example, income elasticity of demand for automobiles is about +3, while income elasticity for most farm products is only about +.20.

Inferior Goods

A negative income-elasticity coefficient designates an inferior good. Retread tires, cabbage, long-distance bus tickets, used clothing, and muscatel wine are likely candidates. Consumers decrease their purchases of inferior goods as incomes rise.

Insights

Coefficients of income elasticity of demand provide insights into the economy. For example, income elasticity helps explain the expansion and contraction of industries in the United States. On average, total income in the economy has grown 2 to 3 percent annually. As income has expanded, industries producing products for which demand is quite income-elastic have expanded their outputs. Thus automobiles ($E_i = +3$), housing ($E_i = +1.5$), books ($E_i = +1.4$), and restaurant meals ($E_i = +1.4$) have all experienced strong growth of output. Meanwhile, industries producing products for which income elasticity is low or negative have tended to grow less rapidly or to decline. For example, agriculture ($E_i = +.20$) has grown far more slowly than has the economy's total output. We do not eat twice as much when our income doubles.

As another example, when recessions occur and people's incomes decline, grocery stores fare relatively better than stores selling electronic equipment. People do not substantially cut back on their purchases of food when their incomes fall; income elasticity of demand for food is relatively low. But they do substantially cut back on their purchases of electronic equipment; income elasticity on such equipment is relatively high. **(Key Questions 12 and 13)**

In Table 7.4 we provide a convenient synopsis of the cross-elasticity and income-elasticity concepts.

■ Government-Set Prices

This brings us to the second major supply and demand topic of our chapter: the implications of government-set prices. On occasion the general public and the government conclude that supply and demand have resulted in prices that are either unfairly high to buyers or unfairly low to sellers. In such instances the government may intervene by legally limiting how high or low a price may go.

Price Ceilings and Shortages

A **price ceiling** sets the maximum legal price a seller may charge for a product or service. A price at or below the ceiling is legal; a price above it is not. The rationale for establishing price ceilings (or ceiling prices) on specific products is that they purportedly enable consumers to obtain some "essential" good or service that they could not afford at the equilibrium price. Examples are rent controls and usury laws, which specify maximum "prices" in the forms of rent and interest that can be charged to borrowers. Also, the government has at times imposed price ceilings either on all products or on a very wide range of products—so-called price controls—to try to restrain inflation. Price controls were invoked during the Second World War, during the Korean conflict, and in the 1970s.

Graphical Analysis

We can easily demonstrate the effects of price ceilings graphically. Let's suppose that rapidly rising world income boosts the purchase of automobiles and shifts the demand for gasoline to

Table 7.4

Cross- and Income-Elasticities of Demand

Value of Coefficient	Description	Type of Good(s)
Cross elasticity:		
Positive ($E_{wz} > 0$)	Quantity demanded of W changes in same direction as change in price of Z	Substitutes
Negative ($E_{xy} < 0$)	Quantity demanded of X changes in opposite direction from change in price of Y	Complements
Income elasticity:		
Positive ($E_i > 0$)	Quantity demanded of the product changes in same direction as change in income	Normal or superior
Negative ($E_i < 0$)	Quantity demanded of the product changes in opposite direction from change in income	Inferior

the right so that the equilibrium or market price reaches $2.50 per gallon, shown as P_0 in Figure 7.4. The rapidly rising price of gasoline greatly burdens low- and moderate-income households, which pressure government to "do something." To keep gasoline affordable for these households, the government imposes a ceiling price P_c of $2 per gallon. To be effective, a price ceiling must be below the equilibrium price. A ceiling price of $3, for example, would have had no immediate effect on the gasoline market.

What are the effects of this $2 ceiling price? The rationing ability of the free market is rendered ineffective. Because the ceiling price P_c is below the market-clearing price P_0, there is a lasting shortage of gasoline. The quantity of gasoline demanded at P_c is Q_d and the quantity supplied is only Q_s; a persistent excess demand or shortage of amount $Q_d - Q_s$ occurs.

The important point is that the price ceiling P_c prevents the usual market adjustment in which competition among buyers bids up price, including more production and rationing some buyers out of the market. That process would continue until the shortage disappeared at the equilibrium price and quantity, P_0 and Q_0. ▮ **7.2**

By preventing these market adjustments from occurring, the price ceiling poses problems born of the market disequilibrium.

Rationing Problem
How will the government apportion the available supply Q_s among buyers who want the greater amount Q_d? Should gasoline be distributed on a first-come, first-served basis, that is, to those willing and able to get in line the soonest and stay in line? Or should gas stations distribute it on the basis of favoritism? Since an unregulated shortage does not lead to an equitable distribution of gasoline, the government must establish some formal system for rationing it to consumers. One option is to issue ration coupons, which authorize bearers to purchase a fixed amount of gasoline per month. The rationing system would entail first the printing of coupons for Q_s gallons of gasoline and then the equitable distribution of the coupons among consumers so that the wealthy family of four and the poor family of four both receive the same number of coupons.

Black Markets
But ration coupons would not prevent a second problem from arising. The demand curve in Figure 7.4 tells us that many buyers are willing to pay more than the ceiling price P_c. And, of course, it is more profitable for gasoline stations to sell at prices above the ceiling. Thus, despite a sizable enforcement bureaucracy that would have to accompany the price controls, **black markets** in which gasoline is illegally bought and sold at prices above the legal limits will flourish. Counterfeiting of ration coupons will also be a problem. And since the price of gasoline is now "set by government," there would be political pressure on government to set the price even lower.

Rent Controls
About 200 cities in the United States, including New York City, Boston, and San Francisco, have at one time or another enacted rent controls: maximum rents established by law (or, more recently, have set maximum rent increases for existing tenants). Such laws are well intended. Their goals are to protect low-income families from escalating rents caused by perceived housing shortages and to make housing more affordable to the poor.

What have been the actual economic effects? On the demand side, it is true that as long as rents are below equilibrium, more families are willing to consume rental housing; the quantity of rental housing demanded increases at the lower price. The problem occurs on the supply side. Price controls make it less attractive for landlords to offer housing on the rental market. In the short run, owners may sell their rental units or convert them to condominiums. In the long run, low rents make it unprofitable for owners to repair or renovate their rental units. (Rent controls are one cause of the many abandoned apartment buildings found in larger cities.) Also,

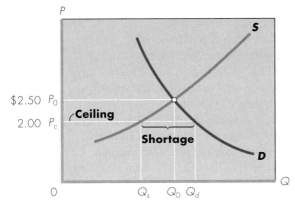

Figure 7.4

A price ceiling results in a persistent shortage. A price ceiling is a maximum legal price such as P_c that is below the equilibrium price. It results in a persistent product shortage, here shown by the distance between Q_d and Q_s.

insurance companies, pension funds, and other potential new investors in housing will find it more profitable to invest in office buildings, shopping malls, or motels, where rents are not controlled.

In brief, rent controls distort market signals and thus resources are misallocated: Too few resources are allocated to rental housing, and too many to alternative uses. Ironically, although rent controls are often legislated to lessen the effects of perceived housing shortages, controls in fact are a primary cause of such shortages. For that reason, most American cities have either abandoned or are in the process of abandoning rent controls. (This chapter's Last Word looks at an ironic side effect of rent controls in New York City.)

Credit Card Interest Ceilings

Over the years there have been many calls for Congress to impose a nationwide interest-rate ceiling on credit card accounts. Several states now have such laws, although some card issuers have circumvented them by moving their national operations to states that do not have such limits (for example, South Dakota). The usual rationale for interest-rate ceilings is that the banks and retail stores issuing such cards are presumably taking unfair advantage of users and, in particular, lower-income users by charging interest rates that average about 18 percent.

What might be the responses to government's imposing a below-equilibrium interest rate on credit cards? The lower interest income associated with a legal interest ceiling would require that the issuers of cards reduce their costs or enhance their revenues:

- Card issuers might tighten credit standards to reduce losses due to nonpayment and collection costs. Then, low-income people and young people who have not yet established their creditworthiness would find it more difficult to obtain credit cards.
- The annual fee charged to cardholders might be increased, as might the fee charged to merchants for processing credit card sales. Similarly, card users might be charged a fee for every transaction.
- Card users now have a postpurchase "grace period" during which the credit provided is interest-free. That period might be shortened or eliminated.
- Certain "enhancements" that accompany some credit cards (for example, extended warranties on products bought with a card) might be eliminated.

- Finally, retail stores that issue their own cards might increase their prices to help offset the decline of interest income. This would mean that customers who pay cash would in effect be subsidizing customers who use credit cards.

Price Floors and Surpluses

Price floors are minimum prices fixed by the government. A price at or above the price floor is legal; a price below it is not. Price floors above equilibrium prices are usually invoked when society feels that the free functioning of the market system has not provided a sufficient income for certain groups of resource suppliers or producers. Formerly supported prices for agricultural products and current minimum wages are two examples of price (or wage) floors. Let's look at the former.

Suppose the equilibrium price for wheat is $2 per bushel and, because of that low price, many farmers have extremely low incomes. The government decides to help out by establishing a legal price floor or price support of $3 per bushel.

What will be the effects? At any price above the equilibrium price, quantity supplied will exceed quantity demanded—that is, there will be a persistent excess supply or surplus of the product. Farmers will be willing to produce and offer for sale more than private buyers are willing to purchase at the price floor. As we saw with a price ceiling, an imposed legal price disrupts the rationing ability of the free market.

Figure 7.5 illustrates the effect of a price floor. Suppose that S and D are the supply and demand curves for corn. Equilibrium price and quantity are P_0 and Q_0, respectively. If the government imposes a price floor of P_f, farmers will produce Q_s but private buyers will purchase only Q_d. The surplus is the excess of Q_s over Q_d. 7.2

The government may cope with the surplus resulting from a price floor in two ways:

- It can restrict supply (for example, by instituting acreage allotments by which farmers agree to take a certain amount of land out of production) or increase demand (for example, by researching new uses for the product involved). These actions may reduce the difference between the equilibrium price and the price floor and thereby reduce the size of the resulting surplus.
- If these efforts are not wholly successful, then the government must purchase the surplus output at the $3 price (thereby subsidizing farmers) and store or otherwise dispose of it.

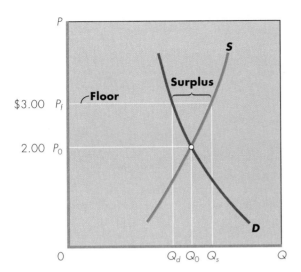

Figure 7.5

A price floor results in a persistent surplus. A price floor is a minimum legal price such as P_f, which results in a persistent product surplus, here shown by the horizontal distance between Q_s and Q_d.

Controversial Tradeoffs

In a free market, the competitive forces match the supply decisions of producers and the demand decisions of buyers. But price ceilings and floors interfere with such an outcome. The government must provide a rationing system to handle product shortages stemming from price ceilings and devise ways to eliminate product surpluses arising from price floors. Legal maximum and minimum prices thus entail controversial tradeoffs. The alleged benefits of price ceilings and floors to consumers and producers, respectively, must be balanced against the costs associated with the consequent shortages and surpluses.

Furthermore, our discussion of price controls, rent controls, and interest-rate ceilings on credit cards shows that government interference with the market can have unintended, undesirable side effects. Price controls, for example, create illegal black markets. Rent controls may discourage housing construction and repair. And instead of protecting low-income families from higher interest charges, interest-rate ceilings may simply deny credit to those families. For all these reasons, economists generally oppose government-imposed prices.

QUICK REVIEW 7.3

Price elasticity of supply measures the sensitivity of suppliers to changes in the price of a product. The price-elasticity-of-supply coefficient E_s is the ratio of the percentage change in quantity supplied to the percentage change in price. The elasticity of supply varies directly with the amount of time producers have to respond to the price change.

The cross-elasticity-of-demand coefficient E_{xy} is computed as the percentage change in the quantity demanded of product X divided by the percentage change in the price of product Y. If the cross-elasticity coefficient is positive, the two products are substitutes; if negative, they are complements.

The income-elasticity coefficient E_i is computed as the percentage change in quantity demanded divided by the percentage change in income. A positive coefficient indicates a normal or superior good. The coefficient is negative for an inferior good.

Government-controlled prices in the form of ceilings and floors stifle the rationing function of prices and cause unintended side effects.

Luxury on $8 a Day

New York City Is Phasing Out Rent Controls by Allowing Landlords to Increase Rents by 20 Percent When Apartments Become Vacant. But as Reported By the *Wall Street Journal*, Rent Controls Have Resulted in Exceptional Bargains for Some Long-Term Tenants.

Some 30 years ago, Lenore Morse checked into a luxury hotel overlooking Central Park and she hasn't checked out yet. Why should she?

Her elegantly appointed one-bedroom suite boasts a kitchenette and an extraordinary view. Room service is available around the clock should she develop a craving for caviar on toast points or some such delicacy. Three newspapers are delivered to her room every day at no charge. And one more thing: The room costs Mrs. Morse only $8 per day.

"It's very pleasant," says the 89-year-old longtime guest at the ITT Luxury Collection hotel, where other guests pay as much as $1,600 a night.

Mrs. Morse pays so little because she is still a tenant of the hotel, formerly the Ritz-Carlton and soon to be the Westin, under New York's decades-old rent control and rent regulation laws. Across the Big Apple, thousands of old-time tenants are still living in some of the city's finest hotels for as little as the price of a bowl of soup in the restaurant downstairs. And unless they check out voluntarily, it will be that way for years.

Some hotels have tried to cajole permanent residents to leave by offering buyouts of as much as $250,000. But guests rarely take the bait. After all, who can put a price on living in a hotel like the Plaza, where the Beatles stayed during their first visit to the United States? And maid service is so hard to find—better leave that to the hotel manager.

Consider Jean van Buuren, who makes her home at the Mark, an elegant boutique hotel on the Upper East Side whose nightly rates run as high as $2,500. Mrs. van Buuren moved into the hotel with her parents shortly after her graduation from high school in the 1940s.

Now, Mrs. van Buuren lives alone in her one-bedroom suite when she isn't off on one of the exotic foreign jaunts she takes three or four times a year. On display are the collectibles she picked up during her travels, including glassware from France, pottery from Japan, sculpture from Zimbabwe. She need not worry about dusting these treasures. The maids see to that, as well as vacuuming the plush carpet, cleaning the bathroom and making the bed each morning. Her monthly rent: less than $500, according to hotel management.

Down the hall is Karen Stark, a retired fashion designer who created the yellow satin inaugural gown worn by Pat Nixon in 1969. Mrs. Stark's three-room apartment is decorated all in white, except for the gleaming piano in one corner of the living room. Staffers at the Mark treat her with all due respect, she says, but she knows they're just waiting for her to "check out." Permanently, that is.

One tenant who doesn't plan to cooperate is John Zoiner, a commercial photographer in his early 50s who lives in the penthouse floor of the sleek Mansfield hotel. Mr. Zoiner answered a classified ad 27 years ago and found himself in a 500-square-foot apartment with a glass wall and ceilings 18 feet high. Since he moved in, the hotel has gone through a major renovation and now features complimentary cappuccino 24 hours a day, free videos and a gleaming chrome-and-marble lobby. Mr. Zoiner, who pays about $440 a month, lets curious tourists ogle his pad.

"I'm not leaving," says Mr. Zoiner. "This is too huge of a bargain."

Source: Nancy Keates, "Only in New York: Luxury at $8 a Day," *Wall Street Journal*, Jan. 23, 1998, p. B9. Abridged and reprinted by permission of the *The Wall Street Journal*, © 1998 Dow Jones & Company, Inc. All rights reserved.

SUMMARY

1. Price elasticity of demand measures consumer response to price changes. If consumers are relatively sensitive to price changes, demand is elastic. If they are relatively unresponsive to price changes, demand is inelastic.

2. The price-elasticity coefficient E_d measures the degree of elasticity or inelasticity of demand. The coefficient is found by the formula

$$E_d = \frac{\text{percentage change in quantity demanded of X}}{\text{percentage change in price of X}}$$

Economists use the averages of prices and quantities under consideration as reference points in determining percentage changes in price and quantity. If E_d is greater than 1, demand is elastic. If E_d is less than 1, demand is inelastic. Unit elasticity is the special case in which E_d equals 1.

3. Perfectly inelastic demand is graphed as a line parallel to the vertical axis; perfectly elastic demand is shown by a line above and parallel to the horizontal axis.

4. Elasticity varies at different price ranges on a demand curve, tending to be elastic in the upper left segment and inelastic in the lower right segment. Elasticity cannot be judged by the steepness or flatness of a demand curve.

5. If total revenue changes in the opposite direction from prices, demand is elastic. If price and total revenue change in the same direction, demand is inelastic. Where demand is of unit elasticity, a change in price leaves total revenue unchanged.

6. The number of available substitutes, the size of an item's price relative to one's budget, whether the product is a luxury or a necessity, and length of time to adjust are all determinants of elasticity of demand.

7. The elasticity concept also applies to supply. The coefficient of price elasticity of supply is found by the formula

$$E_s = \frac{\text{percentage change in quantity supplied of X}}{\text{percentage change in price of X}}$$

The averages of the prices and quantities under consideration are used as reference points for computing percentage changes. Elasticity of supply depends on the ease of shifting resources between alternative uses, which in turn varies directly with the time producers have to adjust to a particular price change.

8. Cross elasticity of demand indicates how sensitive the purchase of one product is to changes in the price of another product. The coefficient of cross elasticity of demand is found by the formula

$$E_{xy} = \frac{\text{percentage change in quantity demanded of X}}{\text{percentage change in price of Y}}$$

Positive cross elasticity of demand identifies substitute goods; negative cross elasticity identifies complementary goods.

9. Income elasticity of demand indicates the responsiveness of consumer purchases to a change in income. The coefficient of income elasticity of demand is found by the formula

$$E_i = \frac{\text{percentage change in quantity demanded of X}}{\text{percentage change in income}}$$

The coefficient is positive for normal goods and negative for inferior goods.

10. Legally fixed prices stifle the rationing function of equilibrium prices. Effective price ceilings result in persistent product shortages, and if an equitable distribution of the product is sought, government must ration the product to consumers. Price floors lead to product surpluses; the government must either purchase these surpluses or eliminate them by imposing restrictions on production or by increasing private demand.

TERMS AND CONCEPTS

price elasticity of demand	perfectly elastic demand	short run	price ceiling
elastic demand	total revenue (TR)	long run	black market
inelastic demand	total-revenue test	cross elasticity of demand	price floor
unit elasticity	price elasticity of supply	income elasticity of demand	
perfectly inelastic demand	market period		

STUDY QUESTIONS

1. Explain why the choice between 1, 2, 3, 4, 5, 6, 7, and 8 "units," or 1000, 2000, 3000, 4000, 5000, 6000, 7000, and 8000 movie tickets, makes no difference in determining elasticity in Table 7.1.

2. **Key Question** Graph the accompanying demand data, and then use the midpoint formula for E_d to determine price elasticity of demand for each of the four possible $1 price changes. What can you conclude about the relationship between the slope of a curve and its elasticity? Explain in a nontechnical way why demand is elastic in the northwest segment of the demand curve and inelastic in the southeast segment.

Product Price	Quantity Demanded
$5	1
4	2
3	3
2	4
1	5

3. Draw two linear demand curves parallel to one another. Demonstrate that for any specific price change demand is more elastic on the curve closer to the origin.

4. **Key Question** Calculate total-revenue data from the demand schedule in question 2. Graph total revenue below your demand curve. Generalize about the relationship between price elasticity and total revenue.

5. **Key Question** How would the following changes in price affect total revenue? That is, would total revenue increase, decline, or remain unchanged?
   a. Price falls and demand is inelastic.
   b. Price rises and demand is elastic.
   c. Price rises and supply is elastic.
   d. Price rises and supply is inelastic.
   e. Price rises and demand is inelastic.
   f. Price falls and demand is elastic.
   g. Price falls and demand is of unit elasticity.

6. **Key Question** What are the major determinants of price elasticity of demand? Use those determinants and your own reasoning in judging whether demand for each of the following products is probably elastic or inelastic: (*a*) bottled water; (*b*) toothpaste; (*c*) Crest toothpaste; (*d*) ketchup; (*e*) diamond bracelets; (*f*) Microsoft Windows operating system.

7. What effect would a rule stating that university students must live in university dormitories have on the price elasticity of demand for dormitory space? What impact might this in turn have on room rates?

8. "If the demand for farm products is highly price-inelastic, a bumper crop may reduce farm incomes." Evaluate and illustrate graphically.

9. You are chairperson of a state tax commission responsible for establishing a program to raise new revenue through excise taxes. Would elasticity of demand be important to you in determining the products on which the taxes should be levied? Explain.

10. **Key Question** In November 1998 Vincent van Gogh's self-portrait sold at auction for $71.5 million. Portray this sale in a demand and supply diagram, and comment on the elasticity of supply. Comedian George Carlin once mused, "If a painting can be forged well enough to fool some experts, why is the original so valuable?" Provide an answer.

11. Because of a legal settlement over state health care claims, in 1999 the U.S. tobacco companies had to raise the average price of a pack of cigarettes from $1.95 to $2.45. The projected decline in cigarette sales was 8 percent. What does this imply for the elasticity of demand for cigarettes? Explain.

12. **Key Question** Suppose the cross elasticity of demand for products A and B is +3.6 and for products C and D is −5.4. What can you conclude about how products A and B are related? Products C and D?

13. **Key Question** The income elasticities of demand for movies, dental services, and clothing have been estimated to be +3.4, +1, and +.5, respectively. Interpret these coefficients. What does it mean if an income elasticity coefficient is negative?

14. A recent study has found that an increase in the price of beer would reduce the amount of marijuana consumed. Is cross elasticity of demand between the two products positive or negative? Are these products substitutes or complements? What might be the logic behind this relationship?

15. Why is it desirable for price ceilings to be accompanied by government rationing? And for price floors to be accompanied by programs that purchase surpluses, restrict output, or increase demand? Show graphically why price ceilings produce shortages and price floors cause surpluses.

16. **(Last Word)** What unusual side effect have rent controls in New York City produced? Use the economic perspective to explain why a substantial "buyout" may not in all cases correct the problem.

17. **Web-Based Question:** *Kmart—determinants of demand elasticities of "Blue Light Specials"* Generally, the elasticity of demand for a product will be greater (a) the larger the number of substitutes, (b)

the greater the proportion of income an item takes, and (c) the less the item is considered to be a necessity. Kmart, at its website, www.kmart.com, posts a weekly sales circular on selected merchandise, organized by department. It must conclude that the demand for these "Blue Light Specials" is elastic: The decrease in price will increase total revenue. Check out this week's specials and, for each item, score 1 point for meeting the criterion of each determinant above. How many specials score a 3? Do any score 0? Why would Kmart include any item that scored less than a 3?

18. **Web-Based Question:** *New York apartments—rent stabilization* In New York City rent control was enacted during the Second World War and then maintained afterward. Today, the control takes the form of rent stabilization. Visit the websites of Tenant Net, at www.tenant.net, and of the NYC Rent Guidelines Board, at www.housingnyc.com, to determine how rent stabilization works. What would be the likely attitude of each of the following groups toward the rent stabilization program: current landlords, current renters, people looking for an apartment to rent in NYC?

C H A P T E R

Consumer Behavior and Utility Maximization

I F   Y O U   W E R E   to compare the shopping carts of almost any two consumers, you would observe striking differences. Why does Paula have potatoes, peaches, and Pepsi in her cart while Sam has sugar, saltines, and 7-Up in his? Why didn't Paula also buy pasta and plums? Why didn't Sam have soup and spaghetti on his grocery list? ■ In this chapter, you will see how individual consumers allocate their incomes among the various goods and services available to them. Given a particular budget, how does a consumer decide what goods and services to buy? Why does the typical consumer buy more of a product when its price falls? As we answer these questions, you will also strengthen your understanding of the law of demand.

■ A Closer Look at the Law of Demand

The law of demand is based on common sense. A high price discourages consumers from buying; a low price encourages them to buy. In Chapter 3 we mentioned two explanations of the downward-sloping demand curve—income and substitution effects and the law of diminishing marginal utility—that backed up that everyday observation. We now want to say more about these explanations in the context of consumer behavior, the subject of this chapter. A third explanation, based on indifference curves, is more advanced and is summarized in the appendix to this chapter.

Income and Substitution Effects

Our first explanation of the downward slope of the demand curve involves the income and substitution effects.

The Income Effect   The **income effect** is the impact that a change in the price of a product has on a consumer's real income and consequently on the quantity demanded of that good. Let's suppose our product is a coffee drink such as a latté or cappuccino. If the price of such drinks declines, the real income or purchasing power of anyone who buys them increases. That is, people are able to buy more with the same money income. The increase in real income will be reflected in increased purchases of many normal goods, including coffee drinks.

For example, with a constant money income of $20 every 2 weeks, you can buy 10 coffee drinks at $2 each. But if the price falls to $1 apiece and you buy 10 of them, you will have $10 per week left over to buy more coffee drinks and other goods. A decline in the price of coffee drinks increases the consumer's real income, enabling him or her to purchase more of them. This is the income effect.

The Substitution Effect The **substitution effect** is the impact that a change in a product's price has on its relative expensiveness and consequently on the quantity demanded. When the price of a product falls, that product becomes cheaper relative to all other products. Consumers will substitute the cheaper product for other products that are now relatively more expensive. In our example, if the prices of other products remain unchanged and the price of coffee drinks falls, lattés and cappuccinos become more attractive to the buyer. Coffee drinks are a "relatively better buy" at $1 than at $2. The lower price will induce the consumer to substitute coffee drinks for some of the now relatively less attractive items in the budget—perhaps colas, bottled water, or iced tea. Because a lower price increases the relative attractiveness of a product, the consumer buys more of it. This is the substitution effect.

The income and substitution effects combine to increase a consumer's *ability* and *willingness* to buy more of a specific good when its price falls. **!** 8.1 **🔑** 8.1

Law of Diminishing Marginal Utility

A second explanation of the downward-sloping demand curve is that, although consumer wants in general may be insatiable, wants for particular commodities can be satisfied. In a specific span of time over which consumers' tastes remain unchanged, consumers can get as much of a particular good or service as they can afford. But the more of that product they obtain, the less they want still more of it.

Consider durable goods, for example. A consumer's desire for an automobile, when he or she has none, may be very strong. But the desire for a second car is less intense; and for a third or fourth, weaker and weaker. Unless they are collectors, even the wealthiest families rarely have more than a half-dozen cars, although their incomes would allow them to purchase a whole fleet of vehicles.

Terminology Evidence indicates that consumers can fulfill specific wants with succeeding units of a commodity but that each added unit provides less utility than the last unit purchased. Recall that a product has utility if it can satisfy a want: **Utility** is want-satisfying power. The utility of a good or service is the satisfaction or pleasure one gets from consuming it. Three characteristics of this concept must be emphasized:

- "Utility" and "usefulness" are not synonymous. Paintings by Picasso may offer great utility to art connoisseurs but are useless functionally (other than for hiding a crack on a wall).
- Implied in the first characteristic is the fact that utility is subjective. The utility of a specific product may vary widely from person to person. A "jacked-up" truck may have great utility to someone who drives off-road but little utility to someone too old to climb into the rig. Eyeglasses have tremendous utility to someone who has poor eyesight but no utility at all to a person with 20-20 vision.
- Because utility is subjective, it is difficult to quantify. But for purposes of illustration we assume that people can measure satisfaction with units called *utils* (units of utility). For example, a particular consumer may get 100 utils of satisfaction from a smoothie, 10 utils of satisfaction from a candy bar, and 1 util of satisfaction from a stick of gum. These imaginary units of satisfaction are convenient for quantifying consumer behavior.

Total Utility and Marginal Utility We must distinguish carefully between total utility and marginal utility. **Total utility** is the total amount of satisfaction or pleasure a person derives from consuming some specific quantity—for example, 10 units—of a good or service. **Marginal utility** is the *extra* satisfaction a consumer realizes from an additional unit of that product—for example, from the eleventh unit. Alternatively, we can say that marginal utility is the change in total utility that results from the consumption of 1 more unit of a product.

Figure 8.1 (Key Graph) and the accompanying table reveal the relation between total utility and marginal utility. We have drawn the curves from the data in the table. Column 2 shows the total utility associated with each level of consumption of this particular product: tacos. Column 3 shows the marginal utility—the change in total utility—that

K E Y   G R A P H

(1) Tacos Consumed per Meal	(2) Total Utility, Utils	(3) Marginal Utility, Utils
0	0	
1	10	10
2	18	8
3	24	6
4	28	4
5	30	2
6	30	0
7	28	−2

(a)
Total utility

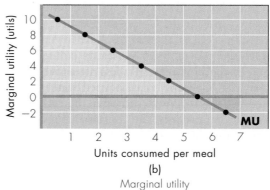

(b)
Marginal utility

Figure 8.1

Total and marginal utility. Curves TU and MU are graphed from the data in the table. (a) As more of a product is consumed, total utility increases at a diminishing rate, reaches a maximum, and then declines. (b) Marginal utility, by definition, reflects the changes in total utility. Thus marginal utility diminishes with increased consumption, becomes zero when total utility is at a maximum, and is negative when total utility declines. As shown by the shaded rectangles in (a) and (b), marginal utility is the change in total utility associated with each additional taco. Or, alternatively, each new level of total utility is found by adding marginal utility to the preceding level of total utility.

Quick Quiz 8.1

1. Marginal utility:
   a. is the extra output a firm obtains when it adds another unit of labor.
   b. explains why product supply curves slope upward.
   c. typically rises as successive units of a good are consumed.
   d. is the extra satisfaction from the consumption of 1 more unit of some good or service.

2. Marginal utility in Figure 8.1b is positive, but declining, when total utility in Figure 8.1a is positive and:
   a. rising at an increasing rate.
   b. falling at an increasing rate.
   c. rising at a decreasing rate.
   d. falling at a decreasing rate.

3. When marginal utility is zero in graph (b), total utility in graph (a) is:
   a. also zero.
   b. neither rising nor falling.
   c. negative.
   d. rising, but at a declining rate.

4. Suppose the person represented by these graphs experienced a diminished taste for tacos. As a result the:
   a. TU curve would get steeper.
   b. MU curve would get flatter.
   c. TU and MU curves would shift downward.
   d. MU curve, but not the TU curve, would collapse to the horizontal axis.

Answers: 1. d; 2. c; 3. b; 4. c

results from the consumption of each successive taco. Starting at the origin in Figure 8.1a, we observe that each of the first 5 units increases total utility (TU), but by a diminishing amount. Total utility reaches a maximum with the addition of the sixth unit and then declines.

So in Figure 8.1b we find that marginal utility (MU) remains positive but diminishes through the first 5 units (because total utility increases at a declining rate). Marginal utility is zero for the sixth unit (because that unit doesn't change total utility). Marginal utility then becomes negative with the seventh unit and beyond (because total utility is falling). Figure 8.1b and table column 3 tell us that each successive taco yields less extra utility, meaning fewer utils, than the preceding one as the consumer's want for tacos comes closer and closer to fulfillment.[1] The principle that marginal utility declines as the consumer acquires additional units of a given product is known as the **law of diminishing marginal utility.** (Key Question 2) ⚠ 8.2 🔎 8.2

Marginal Utility, Demand, and Elasticity

How does the law of diminishing marginal utility explain why the demand curve for a given product slopes downward? The answer is that if successive units of a good yield smaller and smaller amounts of marginal, or extra, utility, then the consumer will buy additional units of a product only if its price falls. The consumer for whom Figure 8.1 is relevant may buy two tacos at a price of $1 each. But because he or she obtains less marginal utility from additional tacos, the consumer will choose not to buy more at that price. The consumer would rather spend additional dollars on products that provide more (or equal) utility, not less utility. Therefore, additional tacos with less utility are not worth buying unless the price declines. (When marginal utility becomes negative, Taco Bell would have to pay you to consume another taco!) Thus, diminishing marginal utility supports the idea that price must decrease in order for quantity demanded to increase. In other words, consumers behave in ways that make demand curves downward-sloping.

Moreover, the amount by which marginal utility declines as more units of a product are consumed helps us determine that product's price elasticity of demand. Other things equal, if marginal utility falls sharply as successive units of a product are consumed, demand is inelastic. A given decline in price will elicit only a relatively small increase in quantity demanded, since the MU of extra units drops off so rapidly. Conversely, modest declines in marginal utility as consumption increases imply an elastic demand. A particular decline in price will entice consumers to buy considerably more units of the product, since the MU of additional units declines so slowly.

QUICK REVIEW 8.1

▪ The law of demand can be explained in terms of the income effect (a decline in price raises the consumer's purchasing power) and the substitution effect (a product whose price falls is substituted for other products).

▪ Utility is the benefit or satisfaction a person receives from consuming a good or a service.

▪ The law of diminishing marginal utility indicates that gains in satisfaction become smaller as successive units of a specific product are consumed.

▪ Diminishing marginal utility provides another rationale for the law of demand, as well as one for differing price elasticities.

▪ Theory of Consumer Behavior

In addition to explaining the law of demand, the idea of diminishing marginal utility explains how consumers allocate their money incomes among the many goods and services available for purchase.

Consumer Choice and Budget Constraint

The typical consumer's situation has the following dimensions.

▪ *Rational behavior* The consumer is a rational person, who tries to use his or her money income to derive the greatest amount of satisfaction, or utility, from it. Consumers want to get "the most for their money" or, technically, to maximize their total utility. They engage in **rational behavior.**

▪ *Preferences* Each consumer has clear-cut preferences for certain of the goods and services that are available in the market. We assume buyers also have a good idea of how much marginal

---

[1]Technical footnote: In Figure 8.1b we graphed marginal utility at half-units. For example, we graphed the marginal utility of 4 utils at $3\frac{1}{2}$ units because "4 utils" refers neither to the third nor the fourth unit per se but to the *addition* or *subtraction* of the fourth unit.

utility they will get from successive units of the various products they might purchase.

■ *Budget constraint*   At any point in time the consumer has a fixed, limited amount of money income. Since each consumer supplies a finite amount of human and property resources to society, he or she earns only limited income. Thus, every consumer faces what economists call a **budget constraint** (budget limitation), even those who earn millions of dollars a year. Of course, budget constraints are more severe for consumers with average incomes than for those with extraordinarily high incomes.

■ *Prices*   Goods are scarce relative to the demand for them, so every good carries a price tag. We assume that the price tags are not affected by the amounts of specific goods each person buys. After all, each person's purchase is a minuscule part of total demand. Moreover, since the consumer has a limited number of dollars, he or she can buy only a limited amount of goods. The consumer cannot buy everything wanted. This point drives home the reality of scarcity to each consumer.

So the consumer must compromise; he or she must choose the most satisfying mix of goods and services. Different individuals will choose different mixes. And as Global Perspective 8.1 shows, the mix may vary from nation to nation.

Utility-Maximizing Rule

Of all the different combinations of goods and services a consumer can obtain within his or her budget, which specific combination will yield the maximum utility or satisfaction? To maximize satisfaction, *the consumer should allocate his or her money income so that the last dollar spent on each product yields the same amount of extra (marginal) utility.* We call this the **utility-maximizing rule.** When the consumer has "balanced his or her margins" using this rule, there is no incentive to alter the expenditure pattern. The consumer is in equilibrium and would be worse off—total utility would decline—if there were any alteration in the bundle of goods purchased, providing there is no change in taste, income, products, or prices.

Numerical Example

An illustration will help explain the utility-maximizing rule. For simplicity our example is limited to two products, but the analysis applies as well if there are

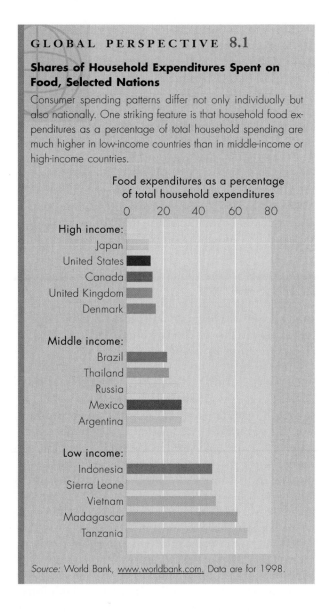

Shares of Household Expenditures Spent on Food, Selected Nations

Consumer spending patterns differ not only individually but also nationally. One striking feature is that household food expenditures as a percentage of total household spending are much higher in low-income countries than in middle-income or high-income countries.

Food expenditures as a percentage of total household expenditures

Source: World Bank, www.worldbank.com. Data are for 1998.

more. Suppose consumer Holly is trying to decide which combination of two products she should purchase with her fixed daily income of $10. These products might be asparagus and breadsticks, apricots and bananas, or apples and broccoli. Let's just call them A and B.

Holly's preferences for products A and B and their prices are the basic data determining the combination that will maximize her satisfaction. Table 8.1 summarizes those data, with column 2a showing the amount of marginal utility she will derive from each successive unit of A and with column 3a showing the same thing for product B. Both columns reflect the law of diminishing marginal util-

Table 8.1

The Utility-Maximizing Combination of Products A and B Obtainable with an Income of $10*

(1) Unit of Product	(2) Product A: Price = $1		(3) Product B: Price = $2	
	(a) Marginal Utility, Utils	(b) Marginal Utility per Dollar (MU/Price)	(a) Marginal Utility, Utils	(b) Marginal Utility per Dollar (MU/Price)
First	10	10	24	12
Second	8	**8**	20	10
Third	7	7	18	9
Fourth	6	6	16	**8**
Fifth	5	5	12	6
Sixth	4	4	6	3
Seventh	3	3	4	2

*It is assumed in this table that the amount of marginal utility received from additional units of each of the two products is independent of the quantity of the other product. For example, the marginal-utility schedule for product A is independent of the amount of B obtained by the consumer.

ity, which is assumed to begin with the second unit of each product purchased.

Marginal Utility per Dollar

Before applying the utility-maximizing rule to these data, we must put the marginal-utility information in columns 2a and 3a on a per-dollar-spent basis. A consumer's choices are influenced not only by the extra utility that successive units of product A will yield but also by how many dollars (and therefore how many units of alternative product B) she must give up to obtain those added units of A.

The rational consumer must compare the extra utility from each product with its added cost (that is, its price). Suppose you prefer a pizza whose marginal utility is, say, 36 utils to a movie whose marginal utility is 24 utils. But if the pizza's price is $12 and the movie costs only $6, you would choose the movie rather than the pizza! Why? Because the marginal utility per dollar spent would be 4 utils for the movie (= 24 utils ÷ $6) compared to only 3 utils for the pizza (= 36 utils ÷ $12). You could see two movies for $12 and, assuming that the marginal utility of the second movie is, say, 16 utils, your total utility would be 40 utils. Clearly, 40 units of satisfaction from two movies are superior to 36 utils from the same $12 expenditure on one pizza.

To make the amounts of extra utility derived from differently priced goods comparable, marginal utilities must be put on a per-dollar-spent basis. We do this in columns 2b and 3b by dividing the marginal-utility data of columns 2a and 3a by the prices of A and B— $1 and $2, respectively.

Decision-Making Process

In Table 8.1 we have Holly's preferences on a unit basis and a per-dollar basis as well as the price tags of A and B. With $10 to spend, in what order should Holly allocate her dollars on units of A and B to achieve the highest degree of utility within the $10 limit imposed by her income? And what specific combination of A and B will she have obtained at the time she uses up her $10?

Concentrating on columns 2b and 3b in Table 8.1, we find that Holly should first spend $2 on the first unit of B, because its marginal utility per dollar of 12 utils is higher than A's 10 utils. But now Holly finds herself indifferent about whether she should buy a second unit of B or the first unit of A because the marginal utility per dollar of both is 10 utils. So she buys both of them. Holly now has 1 unit of A and 2 units of B. Also, the last dollar she spent on each good yielded the same marginal utility per dollar (10 utils). But this combination of A and B does not represent the maximum amount of utility that Holly can obtain. It cost her only $5 [= (1 × $1) + (2 × $2)], so she has $5 remaining, which she can spend to achieve a still higher level of total utility.

Examining columns 2b and 3b again, we find that Holly should spend the next $2 on a third unit of B because marginal utility per dollar for the third unit of B is 9 compared with 8 for the second unit of A. But now, with 1 unit of A and 3 units of B, we find she is again indifferent between a second unit of A and a fourth unit of B because both provide 8 utils per dollar. So Holly purchases 1 more unit of each. Now the last dollar spent on each product provides the same marginal utility per dollar (8 utils), and Holly's money income of $10 is exhausted.

The utility-maximizing combination of goods attainable by Holly is 2 units of A and 4 of B. By summing marginal-utility information from columns 2a and 3a, we find that Holly is obtaining 18 (= 10 + 8) utils of satisfaction from the 2 units of A and 78 (= 24 + 20 + 18 + 16) utils of satisfaction from the 4 units of B. Her $10, optimally spent, yields 96 (= 18 + 78) utils of satisfaction.

Table 8.2, which summarizes our step-by-step process for maximizing Holly's utility, merits careful study. Note that we have implicitly assumed that

Table 8.2

Sequence of Purchases to Achieve Consumer Equilibrium, Given the Data in Table 8.1

Choice Number	Potential Choices	Marginal Utility per Dollar	Purchase Decision	Income Remaining
1	First unit of A	10	First unit of B for $2	$8 = $10 − $2
	First unit of B	12		
2	First unit of A	10	First unit of A for $1 and second unit of B for $2	$5 = $8 − $3
	Second unit of B	10		
3	Second unit of A	8	Third unit of B for $2	$3 = $5 − $2
	Third unit of B	9		
4	Second unit of A	8	Second unit of A for $1 and fourth unit of B for $2	$0 = $3 − $3
	Fourth unit of B	8		

Holly spends her entire income. She neither borrows nor saves. However, saving can be regarded as a "commodity" that yields utility and can be incorporated into our analysis. In fact, we treat it that way in question 4 at the end of this chapter. **(Key Question 4)**

Inferior Options Holly can obtain other combinations of A and B with $10, but none will yield as great a total utility as do 2 units of A and 4 of B. As an example, she can obtain 4 units of A and 3 of B for $10. However, this combination yields only 93 utils, clearly inferior to the 96 utils provided by 2 of A and 4 of B. Furthermore, there are other combinations of A and B (such as 4 of A and 5 of B or 1 of A and 2 of B) in which the marginal utility of the last dollar spent is the same for both A and B. But all such combinations either are unobtainable with Holly's limited money income (as 4 of A and 5 of B) or do not exhaust her money income (as 1 of A and 2 of B) and therefore fail to yield the maximum utility attainable.

Problem: Suppose Holly's money income is $14 rather than $10. What now is the utility-maximizing combination of A and B? Are A and B normal or inferior goods?

Algebraic Restatement

Our allocation rule says that a consumer will maximize her satisfaction when she allocates her money income so that the last dollar spent on product A, the last on product B, and so forth, yield equal amounts of additional, or marginal, utility. The marginal utility per dollar spent on A is indicated by the MU of product A divided by the price of A (column 2b in Table 8.1), and the marginal utility per dollar spent on B by the MU of product B divided by the price of B (column 3b in Table 8.1). Our utility-maximizing rule merely requires that these ratios be equal. Algebraically,

$$\frac{\text{MU of product A}}{\text{price of A}} = \frac{\text{MU of product B}}{\text{price of B}}$$

And, of course, the consumer must exhaust her available income. Table 8.1 shows us that the combination of 2 units of A and 4 of B fulfills these conditions in that

$$\frac{8 \text{ utils}}{\$1} = \frac{16 \text{ utils}}{\$2}$$

and the consumer's $10 income is spent.

If the equation is not fulfilled, then some reallocation of the consumer's expenditures between A and B (from the low to the high marginal-utility-per-dollar product) will increase the consumer's total utility. For example, if the consumer spent $10 on 4 of A and 3 of B, we would find that

$$\frac{\text{MU of A: 6 utils}}{\text{price of A: \$1}} < \frac{\text{MU of B: 18 utils}}{\text{price of B: \$2}}$$

Here the last dollar spent on A provides only 6 utils of satisfaction, and the last dollar spent on B provides 9 (= 18 ÷ $2). So the consumer can increase total satisfaction by purchasing more of B and less of A. As dollars are reallocated from A to B, the marginal utility per dollar of A will increase while the marginal utility per dollar of B will decrease. At some new combination of A and B the two will be equal and consumer equilibrium will be achieved. Here that combination is 2 of A and 4 of B.

▪ Utility Maximization and the Demand Curve

Once you understand the utility-maximizing rule, you can easily see why product price and quantity demanded are inversely related. Recall that the basic determinants of an individual's demand for a specific product are (1) preferences or tastes, (2) money income, and (3) the prices of other goods. The utility data in Table 8.1 reflect our consumer's preferences. We continue to suppose that her money income is $10. And, concentrating on the construction of a simple demand curve for product B, we assume that the price of A, representing "other goods," is still $1.

Deriving the Demand Schedule and Curve

We can derive a single consumer's demand schedule for product B by considering alternative prices at which B might be sold and then determining the quantity the consumer will purchase. We have already determined one such price-quantity combination in the utility-maximizing example: Given tastes, income, and prices of other goods, our rational consumer will purchase 4 units of B at $2.

Now let's assume the price of B falls to $1. The marginal-utility-per-dollar data of column 3b in Table 8.1 will double, because the price of B has been halved; the new data for column 3b are in fact identical to those in column 3a. But the purchase of 2 units of A and 4 of B is no longer an equilibrium combination. By applying the same reasoning we used in the initial utility-maximizing example, we now find that Holly's utility-maximizing combination is 4 units of A and 6 units of B. As summarized in the table in Figure 8.2, Holly will purchase 6 units of B when the price of B is $1. Using the data in this table, we can sketch the downward-sloping demand curve D_B shown in Figure 8.2. This exercise, then, clearly links the utility-maximizing behavior of a consumer and that person's demand curve for a particular product.

Income and Substitution Effects Revisited

At the beginning of this chapter we mentioned that the law of demand can be understood in terms of the substitution and income effects. Our analysis does not let us sort out these two effects quantitatively. However, we can see through utility maximization how each is involved in the increased purchase of product B when the price of B falls.

To see the substitution effect, recall that before the price of B declined, Holly was in equilibrium when purchasing 2 units of A and 4 units of B in that

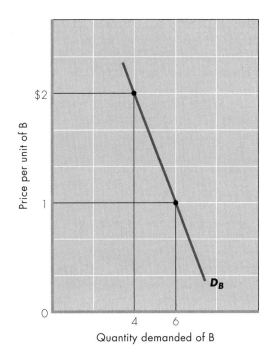

Price per Unit of B	Quantity Demanded
$2	4
1	6

Figure 8.2

Deriving an individual demand curve. At a price of $2 for product B, the consumer represented by the data in the table maximizes utility by purchasing 4 units of product B. The decline in the price of product B to $1 upsets the consumer's initial utility-maximizing equilibrium. The consumer restores equilibrium by purchasing 6 rather than 4 units of product B. Thus, a simple price-quantity schedule emerges, which locates two points on a downward-sloping demand curve.

$MU_A(8)/P_A(\$1) = MU_B(16)/P_B(\$2)$. But after B's price falls from $2 to $1, we have $MU_A(8)/P_A(\$1) < MU_B(16)/P_B(\$1)$; more simply stated, the last dollar spent on B now yields more utility (16 utils) than does the last dollar spent on A (8 utils). This indicates that a switching of purchases from A to B is needed to restore equilibrium; that is, a *substitution* of now cheaper B for A will occur when the price of B drops.

What about the *income effect?* The assumed decline in the price of B from $2 to $1 increases Holly's real income. Before the price decline, Holly was in equilibrium when buying 2 of A and 4 of B. But at the lower $1 price for B, Holly would have to spend only $6 rather than $10 on the same combination of goods. She has $4 left over to spend on more of A, more of B, or more of both. In short, the price decline of B has caused Holly's *real* income to increase, so she can now obtain larger amounts of A and B with the same $10 of *money* income. The portion of the increase in her purchases of B due to this increase in real income is the income effect. **(Key Question 5)**

QUICK REVIEW 8.2

■   The theory of consumer behavior assumes that, with limited income and a set of product prices, consumers make rational choices on the basis of well-defined preferences.

■   A consumer maximizes utility by allocating income so that the marginal utility per dollar spent is the same for every good purchased.

■   We can derive a downward-sloping demand curve by changing the price of one product in the consumer-behavior model and noting the change in the utility-maximizing quantity of that product demanded.

■ Applications and Extensions

Many real-world phenomena can be explained by applying the theory of consumer behavior.

The Compact Disc Takeover

Compact discs (CDs) made their debut in the United States in 1983. The CD revolutionized the retail music industry, pushing the vinyl long-playing record to virtual extinction. In 1983 fewer than 1 million CDs were sold in the United States as compared with almost 210 million LP discs. But by 1999 some 939 million CDs were sold, while the sales of LPs plummeted to 2.9 million.

This swift turnabout resulted from both price and quality considerations. Although the price of CDs has not declined significantly, the price of CD players has nosedived. Costing $1000 or more a decade ago, most players currently sell for under $150. Portable CD players are priced even lower. While CDs and LPs are *substitute* goods, CD players and CDs are *complementary* goods. The lower price for CD players has expanded their sales and greatly increased the demand for CDs. Moreover, CDs hold much more music than LPs and provide a wider range of sound and greater brilliance of musical tone than LPs.

In terms of our analysis, CD players and CDs have higher ratios of marginal utility to price than do LP players and LPs. So the vast majority of consumers have discovered that they can enhance their total utility by substituting CDs for LPs.

The Diamond-Water Paradox

Early economists such as Adam Smith were puzzled by the fact that some "essential" goods had much lower prices than some "unimportant" goods. Why would water, essential to life, be priced below diamonds, which have much less usefulness? The paradox is resolved when we acknowledge that water is in great supply relative to demand and thus has a very low price per gallon. Diamonds, in contrast, are rare and are costly to mine, cut, and polish. Because their supply is small relative to demand, their price is very high per carat.

Moreover, the marginal utility of the last unit of water consumed is very low. The reason follows from our utility-maximizing rule. Consumers (and producers) respond to the very low price of water by using a great deal of it—for generating electricity, irrigating crops, heating buildings, watering lawns, quenching thirst, and so on. Consumption is expanded until marginal utility, which declines as more water is consumed, equals its low price. On the other hand, relatively few diamonds are purchased because of their prohibitively high price, meaning that their marginal utility remains high. In equilibrium:

$$\frac{\text{MU of water (low)}}{\text{price of water (low)}} = \frac{\text{MU of diamonds (high)}}{\text{price of diamonds (high)}}$$

Although the marginal utility of the last unit of water consumed is low and the marginal utility of the last diamond purchased is high, the total utility of water is very high and the total utility of diamonds quite low. The total utility derived from the consumption of water is large because of the enormous amounts of water consumed. Total utility is the sum of the marginal utilities of all the gallons of water consumed, including the trillions of gallons that have far higher marginal utilities than the last unit consumed. In contrast, the total utility derived from diamonds is low since their high price means that relatively few of them are bought. Thus the water-diamond "paradox" is solved: Water has much more total utility (roughly, usefulness) than diamonds even though the price of diamonds greatly exceeds the price of water. These relative prices relate to marginal utility, not total utility. 🔑 8.3

The Value of Time

The theory of consumer behavior has been generalized to account for the economic value of *time*. Both consumption and production take time. Time is a valuable economic commodity; by using an hour in productive work a person can earn $6, $0, $50, or more, depending on her or his education and skills. By using that hour for leisure or in consumption activities, the individual incurs the opportunity cost of forgone income; she or he sacrifices the $6, $0, or $50 that could have been earned by working.

Imagine a self-employed consumer who is considering buying a round of golf, on the one hand, and a concert, on the other. The market price of the golf game is $30 and that of the concert is $40. But the golf game takes more time than the concert. Suppose this consumer spends 4 hours on the golf course but only 2 hours at the concert. If her time is worth $10 per hour, as evidenced by the $10 wage she can obtain by working, then the "full price" of the golf game is $70 (the $30 market price plus $40 worth of time). Similarly, the full price of the concert is $60 (the $40 market price plus $20 worth of time). We find that, contrary to what market prices alone indicate, the full price of the concert is really less than the full price of the golf game.

If we now assume that the marginal utilities derived from successive golf games and concerts are identical, traditional theory would indicate that our consumer should consume more golf games than concerts because the market price of the former ($30) is lower than that of the latter ($40). But when time is taken into account, the situation is reversed and golf games ($70) are more expensive than concerts ($60). So it is rational for this person to consume more concerts than golf games.

By accounting for time, we can explain certain observable phenomena that traditional theory does not explain. It may be rational for the unskilled worker or retiree whose time has little market value to ride a bus from Chicago to Pittsburgh. But the corporate executive, whose time is very valuable, will find it cheaper to fly, even though bus fare is only a fraction of plane fare. It is sensible for the retiree, living on a modest social security check and having ample time, to spend many hours shopping for bargains at the mall or taking long trips in a motor home. It is equally intelligent for the highly paid physician, working 55 hours per week, to buy a new personal computer over the Internet and take short vacations at expensive resorts.

People in other nations often feel affluent Americans are "wasteful" of food and other material goods but "overly economical" in their use of time. Americans who visit developing countries find that time is used casually or "squandered," while material goods are very highly prized and carefully used. These differences are not a paradox or a case of radically different temperaments. The differences are primarily a rational reflection of the fact that the high productivity of labor in an industrially advanced society gives time a high market value, whereas the opposite is true in a low-income, developing country.

Medical Care Purchases

The method of payment for certain goods and services affects their prices at the time we buy them and significantly changes the amount purchased. Let's go back to Table 8.1. Suppose the $1 price for A is its "true" unit value or opportunity cost. But now, for some reason, its price is only, say, $.20. A rational consumer clearly would buy more units at $.20 than at the $1 price.

That is what happens with medical care. People in the United States who have health insurance pay a fixed premium once a month that covers, say, 80 percent of all incurred health care costs. This means that when they actually need health care, its price to them will be only 20 percent of the actual market price. How would you act in such a situation? When you are ill, you would likely purchase a great deal more medical care than you would if you were confronted with the full price. As a result, financing health care through insurance is an important factor in explaining today's high expenditures on health care and the historical growth of such spending as a percentage of domestic output.

Similar reasoning applies to purchases of buffet meals. If you buy a meal at an all-you-can-eat buffet, you will tend to eat more than if you purchased it item by item. Why not eat that second dessert? Its marginal utility is positive and its "price" is zero!

Cash and Noncash Gifts

Marginal-utility analysis also helps us understand why people generally prefer cash gifts to noncash gifts costing the same amount. The reason is simply that the noncash gifts may not match the recipient's preferences and thus may not add as much as cash to total utility. Thought of differently, consumers know their own preferences better than the gift giver does, and the $100 cash gift provides more choices.

Look back at Table 8.1. Suppose Holly has zero earned income but is given the choice of a $2 cash gift or a noncash gift of 2 units of A. Because 2 units of A can be bought with $2, these two gifts are of equal monetary value. But by spending the $2 cash gift on the first unit of B, Holly could obtain 24 utils. The noncash gift of the first 2 units of A would yield only 18 (= 10 + 8) units of utility. Conclusion: The noncash gift yields less utility to the beneficiary than does the cash gift.

Since giving noncash gifts is common, a considerable value of those gifts is potentially lost because they do not match their recipients' tastes. For ex-

ample, Aunt Flo may have paid $15 for the Frank Sinatra CD she gave you for Christmas, but you would pay only $7.50 for it. Thus, a $7.50, or 50 percent, value loss is involved. Multiplied by billions spent on gifts each year, the potential loss of value is large.

But some of that loss is avoided by the creative ways individuals handle the problem. For example, newlyweds set up gift registries for their weddings to help match up their wants to the noncash gifts received. Also, people obtain cash refunds or exchanges for gifts, so they can buy goods that provide more utility. And people have even been known to "recycle gifts" by giving them to someone else at a later time. All three actions support the proposition that individuals take actions to maximize their total utility.

Criminal Behavior

Although Economic Analysis Is Not Particularly Relevant in Explaining Some Crimes of Passion and Violence (For Example, Murder and Rape), It Does Provide Interesting Insights on Such Property Crimes as Robbery, Burglary, and Auto Theft.

Through extension, the theory of rational consumer behavior provides some useful insights on criminal behavior. Both the lawful consumer and the criminal try to maximize their total utility (or net benefit). For example, you can remove a textbook from the campus bookstore by either purchasing it or stealing it. If you *buy* the book, your action is legal; you have fully compensated the bookstore for the product. (The bookstore would rather have your money than the book.) If you *steal* the book, you have broken the law. Theft is outlawed because it imposes uncompensated costs on others. In this case, your action reduces the bookstore's revenue and profit and also may impose costs on other buyers who now must pay higher prices for their textbooks.

Why might someone engage in criminal activity such as stealing? Just like the consumer who compares the marginal utility of a good with its price, the potential criminal compares the marginal benefit from his or her action with the "price" or cost. If the marginal benefit (to the criminal) exceeds the price or marginal cost (also to the criminal), the individual undertakes the criminal activity.

Most people, however, do not engage in theft, burglary, or fraud. Why not? The answer is that they perceive the personal price of engaging in these illegal activities to be too high relative to the marginal benefit. That price or marginal cost to the potential criminal has several facets. First, there are the "guilt costs," which for many people are substantial. Such individuals would not steal from others even if there were no penalties for doing so. Their moral sense of right and wrong would entail too great a guilt cost relative to the benefit from the stolen good. Other types of cost include the direct costs of the criminal activity (supplies and tools) and the forgone income from legitimate activities (the opportunity cost to the criminal).

Unfortunately, guilt costs, direct costs, and forgone income are not sufficient to deter some people from stealing. So society imposes other costs, mainly fines and imprisonment, on lawbreakers. The potential of being fined increases the marginal cost to the criminal. The potential of being imprisoned boosts marginal cost still further. Most people highly value their personal freedom and lose considerable legitimate earnings while incarcerated.

Given these types of cost, the potential criminal estimates the marginal cost and benefit of committing the crime. As a simple example, suppose that the direct cost and opportunity cost of stealing an $80 textbook both are zero. The probability of getting caught is 10 percent and, if apprehended, there will be a $500 fine. The potential criminal will estimate the marginal cost of stealing the book as $50 (= $500 fine × .10 chance of apprehension). Someone who has a guilt cost of zero will choose to steal the book because the marginal benefit of $80 will exceed the marginal cost of $50. In contrast, someone having a guilt cost of, say, $40, will not steal the book. The marginal benefit of $80 will not be as great as the marginal cost of $90 (= $50 of penalty cost + $40 of guilt cost).

This perspective on illegal behavior has some interesting implications. For example, other things equal, crime will rise (more of it will be "bought") when its price falls. This explains, for instance, why some people who do not steal from stores under normal circumstances participate in looting stores during riots, when the marginal cost of being apprehended has substantially declined.

Another implication is that society can reduce unlawful behavior by increasing the "price of crime." It can nourish and increase guilt costs through family, educational, and religious efforts. It can increase the direct costs of crime by using more sophisticated security systems (locks, alarms, video surveillance) so that criminals will have to buy and use more sophisticated tools. It can undertake education and training initiatives to enhance the legitimate earnings of people who might otherwise engage in illegal activity. It can increase policing to raise the probability of being apprehended for crime. And it can impose greater penalties for those who are caught and convicted.

<h1 style="text-align:center">SUMMARY</h1>

1. The income and substitution effects and the law of diminishing marginal utility help explain why consumers buy more of a product when its price drops and less of the product when its price increases.

2. The income effect implies that a decline in the price of a product increases the consumer's real income and enables the consumer to buy more of that product with a fixed money income. The substitution effect implies that a lower price makes a product relatively more attractive and therefore increases the consumer's willingness to substitute it for other products.

3. The law of diminishing marginal utility states that beyond a certain quantity, additional units of a specific good will yield declining amounts of extra satisfaction to a consumer.

4. We assume that the typical consumer is rational and acts on the basis of well-defined preferences. Because income is limited and goods have prices, the consumer cannot purchase all the goods and services he or she might want. The consumer therefore selects the attainable combination of goods that maximizes his or her utility or satisfaction.

5. A consumer's utility is maximized when income is allocated so that the last dollar spent on each product purchased yields the same amount of extra satisfaction. Algebraically, the utility-maximizing rule is fulfilled when

$$\frac{\text{MU of product A}}{\text{price of A}} = \frac{\text{MU of product B}}{\text{price of B}}$$

and the consumer's total income is spent.

6. The utility-maximizing rule and the demand curve are logically consistent. Because marginal utility declines, a lower price is needed to induce the consumer to buy more of a particular product.

<h1 style="text-align:center">TERMS AND CONCEPTS</h1>

income effect

substitution effect

utility

total utility

marginal utility

law of diminishing marginal utility

rational behavior

budget constraint

utility-maximizing rule

<h1 style="text-align:center">STUDY QUESTIONS</h1>

1. Explain the law of demand through the income and substitution effects, using a price increase as a point of departure. Explain the law of demand in terms of diminishing marginal utility.

2. **Key Question** Complete the following table and answer the questions below:

Units Consumed	Total Utility	Marginal Utility
0	0	
1	10	10
2	—	8
3	25	—
4	30	—
5	—	3
6	34	—

   a. At which rate is total utility increasing: a constant rate, a decreasing rate, or an increasing rate? How do you know?

   b. "A rational consumer will purchase only 1 unit of the product represented by these data, since that amount maximizes marginal utility." Do you agree? Explain why or why not.

   c. "It is possible that a rational consumer will not purchase any units of the product represented by these data." Do you agree? Explain why or why not.

3. Mrs. Wilson buys loaves of bread and quarts of milk each week at prices of $1 and 80 cents, respectively. At present she is buying these products in amounts such that the marginal utilities from the last units purchased of the two products are 80 and 70 utils, respectively. Is she buying the utility-maximizing combination of bread and milk? If not, how should she reallocate her expenditures between the two goods?

4. **Key Question** Columns 1 through 4 in the table on the next page show the marginal utility, measured in utils, that Ricardo would get by purchasing various amounts of products A, B, C, and D. Column 5 shows the marginal utility Ricardo gets from saving. Assume that the prices of A, B, C, and D are $18, $6, $4, and $24, respectively, and that Ricardo has an income of $106.

Column 1		Column 2		Column 3		Column 4		Column 5	
Units of A	MU	Units of B	MU	Units of C	MU	Units of D	of MU	Number of Dollars Saved	MU
1	72	1	24	1	15	1	36	1	5
2	54	2	15	2	12	2	30	2	4
3	45	3	12	3	8	3	24	3	3
4	36	4	9	4	7	4	18	4	2
5	27	5	7	5	5	5	13	5	1
6	18	6	5	6	4	6	7	6	$\frac{1}{2}$
7	15	7	2	7	$3\frac{1}{2}$	7	4	7	$\frac{1}{4}$
8	12	8	1	8	3	8	2	8	$\frac{1}{8}$

a. What quantities of A, B, C, and D will Ricardo purchase in maximizing his utility?

b. How many dollars will Ricardo choose to save?

c. Check your answers by substituting them into the algebraic statement of the utility-maximizing rule.

5. **Key Question** You are choosing between two goods, X and Y, and your marginal utility from each is as shown below. If your income is $9 and the prices of X and Y are $2 and $1, respectively, what quantities of each will you purchase to maximize utility? What total utility will you realize? Assume that, other things remaining unchanged, the price of X falls to $1. What quantities of X and Y will you now purchase? Using the two prices and quantities for X, derive a demand schedule (price–quantity-demanded table) for X.

Units of X	MU_x	Units of Y	MU_y
1	10	1	8
2	8	2	7
3	6	3	6
4	4	4	5
5	3	5	4
6	2	6	3

6. How can time be incorporated into the theory of consumer behavior? Explain the following comment: "Want to make millions of dollars? Devise a product that saves Americans lots of time."

7. Explain:

a. "Before economic growth, there were too few goods; after growth, there is too little time."

b. "It is irrational for an individual to take the time to be completely rational in economic decision making."

c. "Telling Santa what you want for Christmas makes sense in terms of utility maximization."

8. In the last decade or so there has been a dramatic expansion of small retail convenience stores (such as Kwik Shops, 7-Elevens, Gas 'N Shops), although their prices are generally much higher than prices in large supermarkets. What explains the success of the convenience stores?

9. Many apartment-complex owners are installing water meters for each apartment and billing the occupants according to the amount of water they use. This is in contrast to the former procedure of having a central meter for the entire complex and dividing up the water expense as part of the rent. Where individual meters have been installed, water usage has declined 10 to 40 percent. Explain that drop, referring to price and marginal utility.

10. **Advanced Analysis** A mathematically "fair bet" is one in which a gambler bets, say, $100, for a 10 percent chance to win $1000 dollars ($100 = .10 × $1000). Assuming diminishing marginal utility of dollars, explain why this is *not* a fair bet in terms of utility. Why is it even a less fair bet when the "house" takes a cut of each dollar bet? So is gambling irrational?

11. **Advanced Analysis** Let $MU_A = z = 10 - x$ and $MU_B = z = 21 - 2y$, where z is marginal utility per dollar measured in utils, x is the amount spent on product A, and y is the amount spent on product B. Assume that the consumer has $10 to spend on A and B—that is, $x + y = 10$. How is the $10 best allocated between A and B? How much utility will the marginal dollar yield?

12. **(Last Word)** In what way is criminal behavior similar to consumer behavior? Why do most people obtain goods via legal behavior as opposed to illegal behavior? What are society's main options for reducing illegal behavior?

13. **Web-Based Question:** *The ESPN Sportszone—to fee or not to fee* The ESPN Sportszone, at espn. go.com/, is a major sports information site. Most of

the content is free, but ESPN has a premium membership (see its "Insider") available for a monthly or an annual fee. Similar, but fee-free, sports content can be found at the websites of CNN/Sports Illustrated, www.cnnsi.com/, and CBS Sports Line, cbs.sportsline.com/. Since ESPN has put a price tag on some of its sports content, it implies that the utility of a premium membership cannot be found at a no-fee site and is therefore worth the price. Is this the case? Use the utility maximization rule to justify your subscribing or not subscribing to the premium membership.

14. **Web-Based Question:** *Here is $300—go spend it at Wal-Mart* Assume that you and several classmates each receive a $300 credit voucher (good for today only) from Wal-Mart Online. Go to www.walmart.com/ and select $300 worth of merchandise. Use Add to Cart to keep a running total, and use Review Cart to print your final selection. Compare your list with your classmates' lists. What explains the differences? Would you have purchased your items if you had received $300 in cash to be spent whenever and wherever you pleased?

Indifference Curve Analysis

A more advanced explanation of consumer behavior and equilibrium is based on (1) budget lines and (2) so-called indifference curves.

The Budget Line: What Is Attainable

A **budget line** (or, more technically, the *budget constraint*) is a schedule or curve that shows various combinations of two products a consumer can purchase with a specific money income. If the price of product A is $1.50 and the price of product B is $1, a consumer could purchase all the combinations of A and B shown in Table 1 with $12 of money income. At one extreme, the consumer might spend all of his or her income on 8 units of A and have nothing left to spend on B. Or, by giving up 2 units of A and thereby "freeing" $3, the consumer could have 6 units of A and 3 of B. And so on to the other extreme, at which the consumer could buy 12 units of B at $1 each, spending his or her entire money income on B with nothing left to spend on A.

Figure 1 shows the same budget line graphically. Note that the graph is not restricted to whole units of A and B as is the table. Every point on the graph represents a possible combination of A and B, including fractional quantities. The slope of the

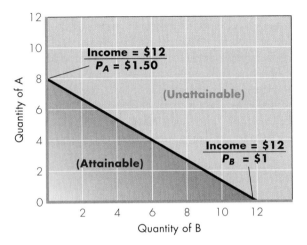

Figure 1

A consumer's budget line. The budget line shows all the combinations of any two products that can be purchased, given the prices of the products and the consumer's money income.

graphed budget line measures the ratio of the price of B to the price of A; more precisely, the absolute value of the slope is $P_B/P_A = \$1.00/\$1.50 = \frac{2}{3}$. This is the mathematical way of saying that the consumer must forgo 2 units of A (measured on the vertical axis) to buy 3 units of B (measured on the horizontal axis). In moving down the budget or price line, 2 units of A (at $1.50 each) must be given up to obtain 3 more units of B (at $1 each). This yields a slope of $\frac{2}{3}$.

The budget line has two other significant characteristics:

- *Income changes* The location of the budget line varies with money income. An increase in money income shifts the budget line to the right; a decrease in money income shifts it to the left. To verify this, recalculate Table 1, assuming that money income is (a) $24 and (b) $6, and plot the new budget lines in Figure 1.

Table 1

The Budget Line: Whole-Unit Combinations of A and B Attainable with an Income of $12

Units of A (Price = $1.50)	Units of B (Price = $1)	Total Expenditure
8	0	$12 (= $12 + $0)
6	3	$12 (= $9 + $3)
4	6	$12 (= $6 + $6)
2	9	$12 (= $3 + $9)
0	12	$12 (= $0 + $12)

■ *Price changes* A change in product prices also shifts the budget line. A decline in the prices of both products—the equivalent of an increase in real income—shifts the curve to the right. (You can verify this by recalculating Table 1 and re-plotting Figure 1 assuming that $P_A = \$.75$ and $P_B = \$.50$.) Conversely, an increase in the prices of A and B shifts the curve to the left. (Assume $P_A = \$3$ and $P_B = \$2$, and rework Table 1 and Figure 1 to substantiate this statement.)

Note what happens if P_B changes while P_A and money income remain constant. In particular, if P_B drops, say, from \$1 to \$.50, the lower end of the budget line fans outward to the right. Conversely, if P_B increases, say, from \$1 to \$1.50, the lower end of the line fans inward to the left. In both instances the line remains "anchored" at 8 units on the vertical axis because P_A has not changed.

Indifference Curves: What Is Preferred

Budget lines reflect "objective" market data, specifically income and prices. They reveal combinations of products A and B that can be purchased, given current money income and prices.

Indifference curves, on the other hand, reflect "subjective" information about consumer preferences for A and B. An indifference curve shows all the combinations of two products A and B that will yield the same total satisfaction or total utility to a consumer. Table 2 and Figure 2 present a hypothetical indifference curve for products A and B. The consumer's subjective preferences are such that he or she will realize the same total utility from each combination of A and B shown in the table or on the curve. So the consumer will be indifferent (will not care) as to which combination is actually obtained. 🔎 **8.4**

Indifference curves have several important characteristics.

Table 2
An Indifference Schedule (Whole Units)

Combination	Units of A	Units of B
j	12	2
k	6	4
l	4	6
m	3	8

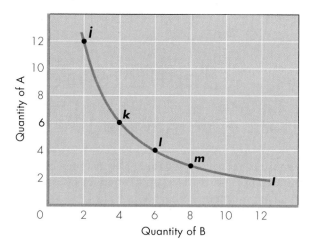

Figure 2
A consumer's indifference curve. Every point on indifference curve *I* represents some combination of products A and B, and all those combinations are equally satisfactory to the consumer. That is, each combination of A and B on the curve yields the same total utility.

Indifference Curves Are Downsloping An indifference curve slopes downward because more of one product means less of the other if total utility is to remain unchanged. Suppose the consumer moves from one combination of A and B to another, say, from *j* to *k* in Figure 2. In so doing, the consumer obtains more of product B, increasing his or her total utility. But because total utility is the same everywhere on the curve, the consumer must give up some of the other product, A, to reduce total utility by a precisely offsetting amount. Thus "more of B" necessitates "less of A," and the quantities of A and B are inversely related. A curve that reflects inversely related variables is downward-sloping.

Indifference Curves Are Convex to the Origin A downward-sloping curve can be concave (bowed outward) or convex (bowed inward) to the origin. A concave curve has an increasing (steeper) slope as one moves down the curve, while a convex curve has a diminishing (flatter) slope as one moves down the curve. Note in Figure 2 that *the indifference curve is convex to the origin*. Its slope diminishes or becomes flatter as we move from *j* to *k* to *l*, and so on down the curve. Technically, the slope of the indifference curve at each point measures the **marginal rate of substitution (MRS)** of the combination represented by that point. The slope or MRS shows the rate at which the consumer who possesses that combination will substitute one good for the other (say, B for A) to remain equally satisfied. The diminishing slope of the indifference curve means the willingness to substitute B for A diminishes as one moves down the curve.

The rationale for this convexity—that is, for a diminishing MRS—is that a consumer's subjective willingness to substitute B for A (or A for B) will depend on the amounts of B and A he or she has to begin with. Consider Table 2 and Figure 2 again, beginning at point *j*. Here, in relative terms, the consumer has a substantial amount of A and very little of B. Within this combination, a unit of B is very valuable (that is, its marginal utility is high), while a unit of A is less valuable (its marginal utility is low). The consumer will then be willing to give up a substantial amount of A to get, say, 2 more units of B. In this case, the consumer is willing to forgo 6 units of A to get 2 more units of B; the MRS is $\frac{6}{2}$, or 3.

But at point *k* the consumer has less A and more B. Here A is somewhat more valuable, and B less valuable, "at the margin." In a move from point *k* to point *l*, the consumer is willing to give up only 2 units of A to get 2 more units of B, so the MRS is only $\frac{2}{2}$, or 1. Having still less of A and more of B at point *l*, the consumer is willing to give up only 1 unit of A in return for 2 more units of B and the MRS falls to $\frac{1}{2}$.

In general, as the amount of B *increases*, the marginal utility of additional units of B *decreases*. Similarly, as the quantity of A *decreases*, its marginal utility *increases*. In Figure 2 we see that in moving down the curve, the consumer will be willing to give up smaller and smaller amounts of A to offset acquiring each additional unit of B. The result is a curve with a diminishing slope, a curve that is convex to the origin. The MRS declines as one moves southeast along the indifference curve.

The Indifference Map

The single indifference curve of Figure 2 reflects some constant (but unspecified) level of total utility or satisfaction. It is possible and useful to sketch a whole series of indifference curves or an **indifference map**, as shown in Figure 3. Each curve reflects a different level of total utility. Specifically, each curve to the right of our original curve (labeled I_3 in Figure 3) reflects combinations of A and B that yield more utility than I_3. Each curve to the left of I_3 reflects less total utility than I_3. As we move out from the origin, each successive indifference curve represents

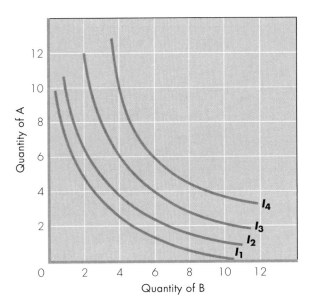

Figure 3

An indifference map. An indifference map is a set of indifference curves. Curves farther from the origin indicate higher levels of total utility. Thus any combination of products A and B represented by a point on I_4 has greater total utility than any combination of A and B represented by a point on I_3, I_2, and I_1.

sents a higher level of utility. To demonstrate this fact, draw a line in a northeasterly direction from the origin; note that its points of intersection with successive curves entail larger amounts of both A and B and therefore higher levels of total utility. ▋ **8.3**

Equilibrium at Tangency

Since the axes in Figures 1 and 3 are identical, we can superimpose a budget line on the consumer's indifference map, as shown in Figure 4. By definition, the budget line indicates all the combinations of A and B that the consumer can attain with his or her money income, given the prices of A and B. Of these attainable combinations, the consumer will prefer the combination that yields the greatest satisfaction or utility. Specifically, the utility-maximizing combination will be the combination lying on the highest attainable indifference curve. It is called the consumer's **equilibrium position.**

In Figure 4 the consumer's equilibrium position is at point *X*, where the budget line is *tangent* to I_3. Why not point *Y*? Because *Y* is on a lower indifference curve, I_2. By moving "down" the budget line—by shifting dollars from purchases of A to purchases of B—the consumer can attain an indifference curve

Figure 4

The consumer's equilibrium position. The consumer's equilibrium position is represented by point X, where the black budget line is tangent to indifference curve I_3. The consumer buys 4 units of A at $1.50 per unit and 6 of B at $1 per unit with a $12 money income. Points Z and Y represent attainable combinations of A and B but yield less total utility, as is evidenced by the fact that they are on lower indifference curves. Point W would entail more utility than X, but it requires a greater income than the $12 represented by the budget line.

farther from the origin and thereby increase the total utility derived from the same income. Why not point Z? For the same reason: Point Z is on a lower indifference curve, I_1. By moving "up" the budget line—by reallocating dollars from B to A—the consumer can get on higher indifference curve I_3 and increase total utility.

How about point W on indifference curve I_4? While it is true that W would yield a greater total utility than X, point W is beyond (outside) the budget line and hence is *not* attainable by the consumer. Point X represents the optimal *attainable* combination of products A and B. Note that, according to the definition of tangency, the slope of the highest attainable indifference curve equals the slope of the budget line. Because the slope of the indifference curve reflects the MRS (marginal rate of substitution) and the slope of the budget line is P_B/P_A, the consumer's optimal or equilibrium position is the point where

$$\text{MRS} = \frac{P_B}{P_A}$$

(You may benefit by trying **Appendix Key Question 3** at this time.)

The Measurement of Utility

There is an important difference between the marginal-utility theory of consumer demand and the indifference curve theory. The marginal-utility theory assumes that utility is *numerically* measurable, that is, that the consumer can say how much extra utility he or she derives from each extra unit of A or B. The consumer needs that information to realize the utility-maximizing (equilibrium) position, as indicated by

$$\frac{\text{marginal utility of A}}{\text{price of A}} = \frac{\text{marginal utility of B}}{\text{price of B}}$$

The indifference curve approach imposes a less stringent requirement on the consumer. He or she need only specify whether a particular combination of A and B will yield more than, less than, or the same amount of utility as some other combination of A and B will yield. The consumer need only say, for example, that 6 of A and 7 of B will yield more (or less) satisfaction than will 4 of A and 9 of B. Indifference curve theory does not require that the consumer specify *how much* more (or less) satisfaction will be realized.

When we compare the equilibrium situations in the two theories, we find that in the indifference curve analysis the MRS equals P_B/P_A at equilibrium; however, in the marginal-utility approach the ratio of marginal utilities equals P_B/P_A. We therefore deduce that at equilibrium the MRS is equivalent in the marginal-utility approach to the ratio of the marginal utilities of the last purchased units of the two products.[2]

The Derivation of the Demand Curve

We noted earlier that with a fixed price for A, an increase in the price of B will cause the bottom of the budget line to fan inward to the left. We can use that fact to derive a demand curve for product B. In Figure 5a we reproduce the part of Figure 4 that shows our initial consumer equilibrium at point X.

---

[2]Technical footnote: If we begin with the utility-maximizing rule, $MU_A/P_A = MU_B/P_B$, and then multiply through by P_B and divide through by MU_A, we obtain $P_B/P_A = MU_B/MU_A$. In indifference curve analysis we know that at the equilibrium position MRS $= P_B/P_A$. Hence, at equilibrium, MRS also equals MU_B/MU_A.

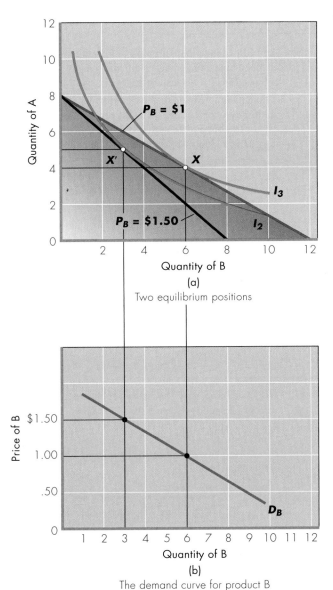

Figure 5

Deriving the demand curve. (a) When the price of product B is increased from $1 to $1.50, the equilibrium position moves from X to X', decreasing the quantity of product B demanded from 6 to 3 units. (b) The demand curve for product B is determined by plotting the $1–6-unit and the $1.50–3-unit price-quantity combinations for product B.

The budget line determining this equilibrium position assumes that money income is $12 and that $P_A = \$1.50$ and $P_B = \$1$. Let's see what happens to the equilibrium position when we increase P_B to $1.50 and hold both money income and the price of A constant.

The result is shown in Figure 5a. The budget line fans to the left, yielding a new equilibrium point X' where it is tangent to lower indifference curve I_2. At X' the consumer buys 3 units of B and 5 of A, compared with 4 of A and 6 of B at X. Our interest is in B, and we now have sufficient information to locate two points on the demand curve for product B. We know that at equilibrium point X the price of B is $1 and 6 units are purchased; at equilibrium point X' the price of B is $1.50 and 3 units are purchased.

These data are shown graphically in Figure 5b as points on the consumer's demand curve for B. Note that the horizontal axes of Figure 5a and 5b are identical; both measure the quantity demanded of B. We can therefore drop vertical reference lines from Figure 5a down to the horizontal axis of Figure 5b. On the vertical axis of Figure 5b we locate the two chosen prices of B. Knowing that these prices yield the relevant quantities demanded, we locate two points on the demand curve for B. By simple manipulation of the price of B in an indifference curve–budget line context, we have obtained a downward-sloping demand curve for B. We have thus again derived the law of demand assuming "other things equal," since only the price of B was changed (the price of A and the consumer's money income and tastes remained constant). But, in this case, we have derived the demand curve without resorting to the questionable assumption that consumers can measure utility in units called "utils." In this indifference curve approach, consumers simply compare combinations of products A and B and determine which combination they prefer, given their incomes and the prices of the two products.

APPENDIX SUMMARY

1. The indifference curve approach to consumer behavior is based on the consumer's budget line and indifference curves.

2. The budget line shows all combinations of two products that the consumer can purchase, given product prices and his or her money income.

3. A change in either product prices or money income moves the budget line.

4. An indifference curve shows all combinations of two products that will yield the same total utility to a consumer. Indifference curves are downward-sloping and convex to the origin.

5. An indifference map consists of a number of indifference curves; the farther from the origin, the higher the total utility associated with a curve.

6. The consumer is in equilibrium (utility is maximized) at the point on the budget line that lies on the highest attainable indifference curve. At that point the budget line and indifference curve are tangent.

7. Changing the price of one product shifts the budget line and determines a new equilibrium point. A downsloping demand curve can be determined by plotting the price-quantity combinations associated with two or more equilibrium points.

APPENDIX TERMS AND CONCEPTS

budget line

indifference curve

marginal rate of
    substitution (MRS)

indifference map

equilibrium position

APPENDIX STUDY QUESTIONS

1. What information is embodied in a budget line? What shifts occur in the budget line when money income (*a*) increases and (*b*) decreases? What shifts occur in the budget line when the price of the product shown on the vertical axis (*a*) increases and (*b*) decreases?

2. What information is contained in an indifference curve? Why are such curves (*a*) downward-sloping and (*b*) convex to the origin? Why does total utility increase as the consumer moves to indifference curves farther from the origin? Why can't indifference curves intersect?

3. **Appendix Key Question** Using Figure 4, explain why the point of tangency of the budget line with an indifference curve is the consumer's equilibrium position. Explain why any point where the budget line intersects an indifference curve is not equilibrium. Explain: "The consumer is in equilibrium where $MRS = P_B/P_A$."

4. Assume that the data in the accompanying table give an indifference curve for Mr. Chen. Graph this curve, putting A on the vertical axis and B on the horizontal

axis. Assuming that the prices of A and B are \$1.50 and \$1, respectively, and that Mr. Chen has \$24 to spend, add his budget line to your graph. What combination of A and B will Mr. Chen purchase? Does your answer meet the $MRS = P_B/P_A$ rule for equilibrium?

Units of A	Units of B
16	6
12	8
8	12
4	24

5. Explain graphically how indifference analysis can be used to derive a demand curve.

6. **Advanced Analysis** Demonstrate mathematically that the equilibrium condition $MRS = P_B/P_A$ is the equivalent of the utility-maximizing rule $MU_A/P_A = MU_B/P_B$.

C H A P T E R

The Costs of Production

Our attention now turns from the behavior of consumers to the behavior of producers. In market economies, a wide variety of businesses produce an even wider variety of goods and services. Each of those businesses requires economic resources in order to produce its products. In obtaining and using resources, a firm makes monetary payments to resource owners (for example, workers) and incurs opportunity costs when using resources it already owns (for example, entrepreneurial talent). Those payments and opportunity costs together make up the firm's *costs of production*, which we discuss in this chapter. ■ Then, in the next several chapters, we bring product demand, product prices, and revenue back into the analysis and explain how firms compare revenues and costs in determining how much to produce. Our ultimate purpose is to show how those comparisons relate to economic efficiency.

■ Economic Costs

Costs exist because resources are scarce, productive, and have alternative uses. When society uses a combination of resources to produce a particular product, it forgoes all alternative opportunities to use those resources for other purposes. The measure of the **economic cost,** or **opportunity cost,** of any resource used to produce a good is the value or worth the resource would have in its best alternative use.

We stressed this view of costs in our analysis of production possibilities in Chapter 2, where we found that the opportunity cost of producing more pizzas is the industrial robots that must be forgone. Similarly, the opportunity cost of the steel used in

constructing office buildings is the value it would have in manufacturing automobiles or refrigerators. The paper used for printing economics textbooks is not available for printing encyclopedias or romance novels. And if an assembly-line worker is capable of assembling either personal computers or washing machines, then the cost to society of employing that worker in a computer plant is the contribution he or she would otherwise have made in producing washing machines.

Explicit and Implicit Costs

Now let's consider costs from the firm's viewpoint. Keeping opportunity costs in mind, we can say that *economic costs are the payments a firm must make, or the incomes it must provide, to attract the resources it needs away from alternative production opportunities.* Those payments to resource suppliers are explicit (revealed and expressed) or implicit (present but not obvious). So in producing products firms incur *explicit costs* and *implicit costs.*

- A firm's **explicit costs** are the monetary payments (or cash expenditures) it makes to those who supply labor services, materials, fuel, transportation services, and the like. Such money payments are for the use of resources owned by others.

- A firm's **implicit costs** are the opportunity costs of using its self-owned, self-employed resources. To the firm, implicit costs are the money payments that self-employed resources could have earned in their best alternative use.

Example: Suppose you are earning $22,000 a year as a sales representative for a T-shirt manufacturer. At some point you decide to open a retail store of your own to sell T-shirts. You invest $20,000 of savings that have been earning you $1000 per year. And you decide that your new firm will occupy a small store that you own and have been renting out for $5000 per year. You hire one clerk to help you in the store, paying her $18,000 annually.

A year after you open the store, you total up your accounts and find the following:

Total sales revenue		$120,000
Cost of T-shirts	$40,000	
Clerk's salary	18,000	
Utilities	5,000	
Total (explicit) costs		63,000
Accounting profit		57,000

Looks good. But unfortunately your accounting profit of $57,000 ignores your implicit costs and thus overstates the economic success of your venture. By providing your own financial capital, building, and labor, you incur implicit costs (forgone incomes) of $1000 of interest, $5000 of rent, and $22,000 of wages. If your entrepreneurial talent is worth, say, $5000 annually in other business endeavors of similar scope, you have also ignored that implicit cost. So:

Accounting profit		$57,000
Forgone interest	$ 1,000	
Forgone rent	5,000	
Forgone wages	22,000	
Forgone entrepreneurial income . . .	5,000	
Total implicit costs		33,000
Economic profit		24,000

Normal Profit as a Cost

The $5000 implicit cost of your entrepreneurial talent in the above example is a **normal profit.** As is true of the forgone rent and forgone wages, the payment you could otherwise receive for performing entrepreneurial functions is indeed an implicit cost. If you did not realize at least this minimum, or normal, payment for your effort, you could withdraw from this line of business and shift to a more attractive endeavor. So a normal profit is a cost of doing business.

The economist includes as costs of production all the costs—explicit and implicit, including a normal profit—required to attract and retain resources in a specific line of production. For economists, a firm's economic costs are the opportunity costs of the resources used, whether those resources are owned by others or by the firm. In our example, economic costs are $96,000 (= $63,000 of explicit costs + $33,000 of implicit costs).

Economic Profit (or Pure Profit)

Obviously, then, economists use the term "profit" differently from the way accountants use it. To the accountant, profit is the firm's total revenue less its explicit costs (or accounting costs). To the economist, **economic profit** is total revenue less economic costs (explicit and implicit costs, the latter including a normal profit to the entrepreneur). So when an economist says a certain firm is earning only enough revenue to cover its costs, this means it is meeting all explicit and implicit costs and the entrepreneur is receiving a payment just large enough to retain his or her talents in the present line of production.

If a firm's total revenue exceeds all its economic costs (explicit + implicit), any residual goes to the entrepreneur. That residual is called an *economic,* or *pure, profit.* In short:

$$\text{Economic profit} = \text{total revenue} - \text{economic cost}$$

In our example, economic profit is $24,000, found by subtracting the $96,000 of economic cost from the $120,000 of revenue. An *economic* profit is not a cost, because it is a return in excess of the normal profit that is required to retain the entrepreneur in this particular line of production. Even if the economic profit is zero, the entrepreneur is still covering all explicit and implicit costs, including a normal profit. In our example, as long as accounting profit is $33,000 or more (so economic profit is zero or more), you will be earning a $5000 normal profit and will therefore continue to operate your T-shirt store.

Figure 9.1 shows the relationship among the various cost and profit concepts that we have just discussed. To test yourself, you might want to enter cost data from our example in the appropriate blocks. **(Key Question 2)**

Short Run and Long Run

When the demand for a firm's product changes, the firm's profitability may depend on how quickly it can adjust the amounts of the various resources it employs. It can easily and quickly adjust the quantities employed of many resources such as hourly labor, raw materials, fuel, and power. It needs much more time, however, to adjust its *plant capacity*—the size of the factory building, the amount of machinery and equipment, and other capital resources. In some heavy industries such as aircraft manufacturing, a firm may need several years to alter plant capacity. Because of these differences in adjustment time, economists find it useful to distinguish between two conceptual periods: the short run and the long run. We will discover that costs differ in these two time periods.

Short Run: Fixed Plant   The **short run** is a period too brief for a firm to alter its plant capacity, yet long enough to permit a change in the degree to which the fixed plant is used. The firm's plant capacity is fixed in the short run. However, the firm can vary its output by applying larger or smaller amounts of labor, materials, and other resources to that plant. It can use its existing plant capacity more or less intensively in the short run.

Long Run: Variable Plant   From the viewpoint of an existing firm, the **long run** is a period long enough for it to adjust the quantities of all the resources that it employs, including plant capacity. From the industry's viewpoint, the long run also includes enough time for existing firms to dissolve and leave the industry or for new firms to be created and enter the industry. While the short run is a "fixed-plant" period, the long run is a "variable-plant" period.

Illustrations   If Boeing hires 100 extra workers for one of its commercial airline plants or adds an entire shift of workers, we are speaking of the short run. If it adds a new production facility and installs more equipment, we are referring to the long run. The first situation is a *short-run adjustment*; the second is a *long-run adjustment*.

The short run and the long run are conceptual periods rather than calendar time periods. In light-manufacturing industries, changes in plant capacity may be accomplished almost overnight. A small T-shirt manufacturer can increase its plant capacity in a matter of days by ordering and installing two or three new cutting tables and several extra sewing machines. But for heavy industry the long run is a different matter. Texaco may require several years to construct a new oil refinery.

Figure 9.1
Economic profit versus accounting profit. Economic profit is equal to total revenue less economic costs. Economic costs are the sum of explicit and implicit costs and include a normal profit to the entrepreneur. Accounting profit is equal to total revenue less accounting (explicit) costs.

> **QUICK REVIEW 9.1**
>
> ■ Explicit costs are money payments a firm makes to outside suppliers of resources; implicit costs are the opportunity costs associated with a firm's use of resources it owns.
>
> ■ Normal profit is the implicit cost of entrepreneurship. Economic profit is total revenue less all explicit and implicit costs, including normal profit.
>
> ■ In the short run, a firm's plant capacity is fixed; in the long run, a firm can vary its plant size and firms can enter or leave the industry.

∎ Short-Run Production Relationships

A firm's costs of producing a specific output depend on the prices of the needed resources and the quantities of resources (inputs) needed to produce that output. Resource supply and demand determine resource prices. The technological aspects of production, specifically the relationships between inputs and output, determine the quantities of resources needed. Our focus will be on the *labor*-output relationship, given a fixed plant capacity. But before examining that relationship, we need to define three terms:

- **Total product (TP)** is the total quantity, or total output, of a particular good produced.
- **Marginal product (MP)** is the extra output or added product associated with adding a unit of a variable resource, in this case labor, to the production process. Thus,

$$\text{Marginal product} = \frac{\text{change in total product}}{\text{change in labor input}}$$

- **Average product (AP),** also called labor productivity, is output per unit of labor input:

$$\text{Average product} = \frac{\text{total product}}{\text{units of labor}}$$

In the short run, a firm can for a time increase its output by adding units of labor to its fixed plant. But by how much will output rise when it adds the labor? Why do we say "for a time"?

Law of Diminishing Returns

The answers are provided in general terms by the **law of diminishing returns,** also called the *law of diminishing marginal product* and the *law of variable proportions*. This law assumes that technology is fixed and thus the techniques of production do not change. It states that *as successive units of a variable resource (say, labor) are added to a fixed resource (say, capital or land), beyond some point the extra, or marginal, product that can be attributed to each additional unit of the variable resource will decline.* For example, if additional workers are hired to work with a constant amount of capital equipment, output will eventually rise by smaller and smaller amounts as more workers are hired. ❗9.1 🔎9.1

Rationale   Suppose a farmer has a fixed resource of 80 acres planted in corn. If the farmer does not cultivate the cornfields (clear the weeds) at all, the yield will be 40 bushels per acre. If he cultivates the land once, output may rise to 50 bushels per acre. A second cultivation may increase output to 57 bushels per acre, a third to 61, and a fourth to 63. Succeeding cultivations will add less and less to the land's yield. If this were not so, the world's needs for corn could be fulfilled by extremely intense cultivation of this single 80-acre plot of land. Indeed, if diminishing returns did not occur, the world could be fed out of a flowerpot. Why not? Just keep adding more seed fertilizer, and harvesters!

The law of diminishing returns also holds true in nonagricultural industries. Assume a wood shop is manufacturing furniture frames. It has a specific amount of equipment such as lathes, planers, saws, and sanders. If this shop hired just one or two workers, total output and productivity (output per worker) would be very low. The workers would have to perform many different jobs, and the advantages of specialization would not be realized. Time would be lost in switching from one job to another, and machines would stand idle much of the time. In short, the plant would be understaffed, and production would be inefficient because there would be too much capital relative to the amount of labor.

The shop could eliminate those difficulties by hiring more workers. Then the equipment would be more fully used, and workers could specialize on doing a single job. Time would no longer be lost switching from job to job. As more workers were added, production would become more efficient and the marginal product of each succeeding worker would rise.

But the rise could not go on indefinitely. If still more workers were added, beyond a certain point, overcrowding would set in. Since workers would then have to wait in line to use the machinery, they would be underused. Total output would increase at a diminishing rate, because, given the fixed size of the plant, each worker would have less capital equipment to work with as more and more labor was hired. The marginal product of additional workers would decline, because there would be more labor in proportion to the fixed amount of capital. Eventually, adding still more workers would cause so much congestion that marginal product would become negative and total product would decline. At the extreme, the addition of more and more labor would exhaust all the standing room, and total product would fall to zero.

Note that the law of diminishing returns assumes that all units of labor are of equal quality. Each successive worker is presumed to have the same innate ability, motor coordination, education, training, and work experience. Marginal product ultimately diminishes, not because successive workers are qualitatively inferior but because more workers are being used relative to the amount of plant and equipment available.

Tabular Example

Table 9.1 is a numerical illustration of the law of diminishing returns. Column 2 shows the total product, or total output, resulting from combining each level of a variable input (labor) in column 1 with a fixed amount of capital.

Column 3 shows the marginal product (MP), the change in total product associated with each additional unit of labor. Note that with no labor input, total product is zero; a plant with no workers will produce no output. The first 3 units of labor reflect increasing marginal returns, with marginal products of 10, 15, and 20 units, respectively. But beginning with the fourth unit of labor, marginal product diminishes continuously, becoming zero with the seventh unit of labor and negative with the eighth.

Average product, or output per labor unit, is shown in column 4. It is calculated by dividing total product (column 2) by the number of labor units needed to produce it (column 1). At 5 units of labor, for example, AP is 14 (= 70/5).

Graphical Portrayal

Figure 9.2 (Key Graph) shows the diminishing-returns data in Table 9.1 graphically and further clarifies the relationships between total, marginal, and average products. (Marginal product in Figure 9.2b is plotted halfway between the units of labor, since it applies to the addition of each labor unit.)

Note first in Figure 9.2a that total product, TP, goes through three phases: It rises initially at an increasing rate; then it increases, but at a diminishing rate; finally, after reaching a maximum, it declines.

Geometrically, marginal product—shown by the MP curve in Figure 9.2b—is the slope of the total-product curve. Marginal product measures the change in total product associated with each succeeding unit of labor. Thus, the three phases of total product are also reflected in marginal product. Where total product is increasing at an increasing rate, marginal product is rising. Here, extra units of labor are adding larger and larger amounts to total product. Similarly, where total product is increasing but at a decreasing rate, marginal product is positive but falling. Each additional unit of labor adds less to total product than did the previous unit. When total product is at a maximum, marginal product is zero. When total product declines, marginal product becomes negative.

Average product, AP (Figure 9.2b), displays the same tendencies as marginal product. It increases, reaches a maximum, and then decreases as more and more units of labor are added to the fixed plant. But note the relationship between marginal product and average product: Where marginal product exceeds average product, average product rises. And where marginal product is less than average product, average product declines. It follows that marginal product intersects average product where average product is at a maximum.

Table 9.1
Total, Marginal, and Average Product: The Law of Diminishing Returns

(1) Units of the Variable Resource (Labor)	(2) Total Product (TP)	(3) Marginal Product (MP), Change in (2)/ Change in (1)	(4) Average Product (AP), (2)/(1)
0	0		—
1	10	10 ⎫ Increasing	10.00
2	25	15 ⎬ marginal	12.50
3	45	20 ⎭ returns	15.00
4	60	15 ⎫ Diminishing	15.00
5	70	10 ⎬ marginal	14.00
6	75	5 ⎭ returns	12.50
7	75	0 ⎫ Negative	10.71
8	70	−5 ⎬ marginal returns	8.75

KEY GRAPH

(a)
Total product

(b)
Marginal and average product

Figure 9.2

The law of diminishing returns. (a) As a variable resource (labor) is added to fixed amounts of other resources (land or capital), the total product that results will eventually increase by diminishing amounts, reach a maximum, and then decline.
(b) Marginal product is the change in total product associated with each new unit of labor. Average product is simply output per labor unit. Note that marginal product intersects average product at the maximum average product.

Quick Quiz 9.2

1. Which of the following is an assumption underlying these figures?
   a. Firms first hire "better" workers and then hire "poorer" workers.
   b. Capital and labor are both variable, but labor increases more rapidly than capital.
   c. Consumers will buy all the output (total product) produced.
   d. Workers are of equal quality.

2. Marginal product is:
   a. the change in total product divided by the change in the quantity of labor.
   b. total product divided by the quantity of labor.
   c. always positive.
   d. unrelated to total product.

3. Marginal product in graph (b) is zero when:
   a. average product in graph (b) stops rising.
   b. the slope of the marginal-product curve in graph (b) is zero.
   c. total product in graph (a) begins to rise at a diminishing rate.
   d. the slope of the total-product curve in graph (a) is zero.

4. Average product in graph (b):
   a. rises when it is less than marginal product.
   b. is the change in total product divided by the change in the quantity of labor.
   c. can never exceed marginal product.
   d. falls whenever total product in graph (a) rises at a diminishing rate.

Answers: 1. d; 2. a; 3. d; 4. a

This relationship is a mathematical necessity. If you add a larger number to a total than the current average of that total, the average must rise. And if you add a smaller number to a total than the current average of that total, the average must fall. You raise your average examination grade only when your score on an additional (marginal) examination is greater than the average of all your past scores. You lower your average when your grade on an additional exam is below your current average. In our production example, when the amount an extra worker adds to total product exceeds the average product of all workers currently employed, average product will rise. Conversely, when an extra worker adds to total product an amount that is less than the current average product, then average product will decrease.

The law of diminishing returns is embodied in the shapes of all three curves. But, as our definition of the law of diminishing returns indicates, economists are most concerned with its effects on marginal product. The regions of increasing, diminishing, and negative marginal product (returns) are shown in Figure 9.2b. **(Key Question 4)** 🔑 9.2

▌Short-Run Production Costs

Production information such as that provided in Table 9.1 and Figure 9.2a and 9.2b must be coupled with resource prices to determine the total and per-

unit costs of producing various levels of output. We know that in the short run some resources, those associated with the firm's plant, are fixed. Other resources, however, are variable. So short-run costs are either fixed or variable.

Fixed, Variable, and Total Costs

Let's see what distinguishes fixed costs, variable costs, and total costs from one another.

Fixed Costs   **Fixed costs** are *those costs that in total do not vary with changes in output.* Fixed costs are associated with the very existence of a firm's plant and therefore must be paid even if its output is zero. Such costs as rental payments, interest on a firm's debts, a portion of depreciation on equipment and buildings, and insurance premiums are generally fixed costs; they do not increase even if a firm produces more. In column 2 in Table 9.2 we assume that the firm's total fixed cost is $100. By definition, this fixed cost is incurred at all levels of output, including zero. The firm cannot avoid paying fixed costs in the short run.

Variable Costs   **Variable costs** are *those costs that change with the level of output.* They include payments for materials, fuel, power, transportation services, most labor, and similar variable resources. In column

Table 9.2
Total-, Average-, and Marginal-Cost Schedules for an Individual Firm in the Short Run

	Total-Cost Data			Average-Cost Data			Marginal Cost
(1) Total Product (Q)	(2) Total Fixed Cost (TFC)	(3) Total Variable Cost (TVC)	(4) Total Cost (TC) TC = TFC + TVC	(5) Average Fixed Cost (AFC) AFC = TFC/Q	(6) Average Variable Cost (AVC) AVC = TVC/Q	(7) Average Total Cost (ATC) ATC = TC/Q	(8) Marginal Cost (MC) MC = change in TC / change in Q
0	$100	$ 0	$ 100				$ 90
1	100	90	190	$100.00	$90.00	$190.00	80
2	100	170	270	50.00	85.00	135.00	70
3	100	240	340	33.33	80.00	113.33	60
4	100	300	400	25.00	75.00	100.00	70
5	100	370	470	20.00	74.00	94.00	80
6	100	450	550	16.67	75.00	91.67	90
7	100	540	640	14.29	77.14	91.43	110
8	100	650	750	12.50	81.25	93.75	130
9	100	780	880	11.11	86.67	97.78	150
10	100	930	1030	10.00	93.00	103.00	

3 of Table 9.2 we find that the total of variable costs changes directly with output. But note that the increases in variable cost associated with succeeding 1-unit increases in output are not equal. As production begins, variable cost will for a time increase by a decreasing amount; this is true through the fourth unit of output in Table 9.2. Beyond the fourth unit, however, variable cost rises by increasing amounts for succeeding units of output.

The reason lies in the shape of the marginal-product curve. At first, as in Figure 9.2b, marginal product is increasing, so smaller and smaller increases in the amounts of variable resources are needed to produce successive units of output. Hence the variable cost of successive units of output decreases. But when, as diminishing returns are encountered, marginal product begins to decline, larger and larger additional amounts of variable resources are needed to produce successive units of output. Total variable cost therefore increases by increasing amounts.

Total Cost

Total Cost is *the sum of fixed cost and variable cost at each level of output.* It is shown in column 4 in Table 9.2. At zero units of output, total cost is equal to the firm's fixed cost. Then for each unit of the 10 units of production, total cost increases by the same amount as variable cost.

Figure 9.3 shows graphically the fixed-, variable-, and total-cost data given in Table 9.2. Observe that total variable cost, TVC, is measured vertically from the horizontal axis at each level of output. The amount of fixed cost, shown as TFC, is added vertically to the total-variable-cost curve to obtain the points on the total-cost curve TC.

The distinction between fixed and variable costs is significant to the business manager. Variable costs can be controlled or altered in the short run by changing production levels. Fixed costs are beyond the business manager's current control; they are incurred in the short run and must be paid regardless of output level.

Per-Unit, or Average, Costs

Producers are certainly interested in their total costs, but they are equally concerned with per-unit, or average, costs. In particular, average-cost data are more meaningful for making comparisons with product price, which is always stated on a per-unit basis. Average fixed cost, average variable cost, and average total cost are shown in columns 5 to 7, Table 9.2.

Figure 9.3

Total cost is the sum of fixed cost and variable cost. Total variable cost (TVC) changes with output. Total fixed cost (TFC) is independent of the level of output. The total cost (TC) at any output is the vertical sum of the fixed cost and variable cost at that output.

AFC

Average fixed cost (AFC) for any output level is found by dividing total fixed cost (TFC) by that output (Q). That is,

$$AFC = \frac{TFC}{Q}$$

Because the total fixed cost is, by definition, the same regardless of output, AFC must decline as output increases. As output rises, the total fixed cost is spread over a larger and larger output. When output is just 1 unit in Table 9.2, TFC and AFC are the same at $100. But at 2 units of output, the total fixed cost of $100 becomes $50 of AFC or fixed cost per unit; then it becomes $33.33 per unit as $100 is spread over 3 units, and $25 per unit when spread over 4 units. This process is sometimes referred to as "spreading the overhead." Figure 9.4 shows that AFC graphs as a continuously declining curve as total output is increased.

AVC

Average variable cost (AVC) for any output level is calculated by dividing total variable cost (TVC) by that output (Q):

$$AVC = \frac{TVC}{Q}$$

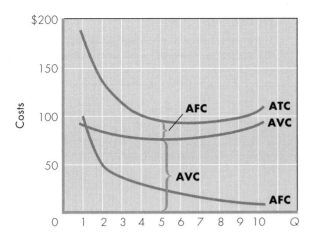

Figure 9.4

The average-cost curves. AFC falls as a given amount of fixed costs is apportioned over a larger and larger output. AVC initially falls because of increasing marginal returns but then rises because of diminishing marginal returns. Average total cost (ATC) is the vertical sum of average variable cost (AVC) and average fixed cost (AFC).

As added variable resources increase output, AVC declines initially, reaches a minimum, and then increases again. A graph of AVC is a U-shaped or saucer-shaped curve, as shown in Figure 9.4.

Because total variable cost reflects the law of diminishing returns, so must AVC, which is derived from total variable cost. Because marginal returns increase initially, it takes fewer and fewer additional variable resources to produce each of the first 4 units of output. As a result, variable cost per unit declines. AVC hits a minimum with the fifth unit of output, and beyond that point AVC rises as diminishing returns require more and more variable resources to produce each additional unit of output.

In simpler terms, at very low levels of output production is relatively inefficient and costly. Because the firm's fixed plant is understaffed, average variable cost is relatively high. As output expands, however, greater specialization and better use of the firm's capital equipment yield more efficiency, and variable cost per unit of output declines. As still more variable resources are added, a point is reached where diminishing returns are incurred. The firm's capital equipment is now staffed more intensively, and therefore each added input unit does not increase output by as much as preceding inputs. This means that AVC eventually increases.

You can verify the U or saucer shape of the AVC curve by returning to Table 9.1. Assume the price of

labor is $10 per unit. By dividing average product (output per labor unit) into $10 (price per labor unit), we determine the labor cost per unit of output. Because we have assumed labor to be the only variable input, the labor cost per unit of output is the variable cost per unit of output, or AVC. When average product is initially low, AVC is high. As workers are added, average product rises and AVC falls. When average product is at its maximum, AVC is at its minimum. Then, as still more workers are added and average product declines, AVC rises. The "hump" of the average-product curve is reflected in the saucer or U shape of the AVC curve. As you will soon see, the two are mirror images of each other.

ATC **Average total cost (ATC)** for any output level is found by dividing total cost (TC) by that output (Q) or by adding AFC and AVC at that output:

$$\text{ATC} = \frac{\text{TC}}{Q} = \frac{\text{TFC}}{Q} + \frac{\text{TVC}}{Q} = \text{AFC} + \text{AVC}$$

Graphically, ATC can be found by adding vertically the AFC and AVC curves, as in Figure 9.4. Thus the vertical distance between the ATC and AVC curves measures AFC at any level of output.

Marginal Cost

One final and very crucial cost concept remains: **Marginal cost (MC)** is *the extra, or additional, cost of producing 1 more unit of output.* MC can be determined for each added unit of output by noting the change in total cost which that unit's production entails:

$$\text{MC} = \frac{\text{change in TC}}{\text{change in } Q}$$

Calculations In column 4, Table 9.2, production of the first unit of output increases total cost from $100 to $190. Therefore, the additional, or marginal, cost of that first unit is $90 (column 8). The marginal cost of the second unit is $80 (= $270 − $190); the MC of the third is $70 (= $340 − $270); and so forth. The MC for each of the 10 units of output is shown in column 8.

MC can also be calculated from the total-variable-cost column, because the only difference between total cost and total variable cost is the constant amount of fixed costs ($100). Thus, the change in total cost and the change in total variable cost associated with each additional unit of output are always the same.

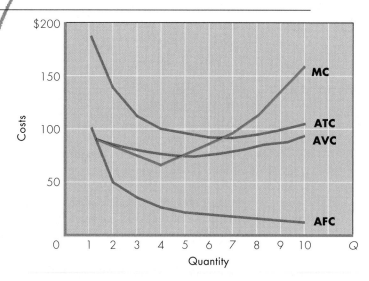

Figure 9.5

The relationship of the marginal-cost curve to the average-total-cost and average-variable-cost curves. The marginal-cost (MC) curve cuts through the average-total-cost (ATC) curve and the average-variable-cost (AVC) curve at their minimum points. When MC is below average total cost, ATC falls; when MC is above average total cost, ATC rises. Similarly, when MC is below average variable cost, AVC falls; when MC is above average variable cost, AVC rises.

Marginal Decisions Marginal costs are costs the firm can control directly and immediately. Specifically, MC designates all the cost incurred in producing the last unit of output. Thus, it also designates the cost that can be "saved" by not producing that last unit. Average-cost figures do not provide this information. For example, suppose the firm is undecided whether to produce 3 or 4 units of output. At 4 units Table 9.2 indicates that ATC is $100. But the firm does not increase its total costs by $100 by producing the fourth unit, nor does it save $100 by not producing that unit. Rather, the change in costs involved here is only $60, as the MC column in Table 9.2 reveals.

A firm's decisions as to what output level to produce are typically marginal decisions, that is, deci-

sions to produce a few more or a few less units. Marginal cost is the change in costs when 1 more or 1 less unit of output is produced. When coupled with marginal revenue (which, as you will see in Chapter 10, indicates the change in revenue from 1 more or 1 less unit of output), marginal cost allows a firm to determine if it is profitable to expand or contract its production. The analysis in the next three chapters focuses on those marginal calculations.

Graphical Portrayal Marginal cost is shown graphically in **Figure 9.5 (Key Graph).** Marginal cost at first declines sharply, reaches a minimum, and then rises rather abruptly. This reflects the fact that variable costs, and therefore total cost, increase first by decreasing amounts and then by increasing amounts (see columns 3 and 4. Table 9.2). ☑ 9.1

MC and Marginal Product

The marginal-cost curve's shape is a consequence of the law of diminishing returns. Looking back at Table 9.1, we can see the relationship between marginal product and marginal cost. If all units of a variable resource (here labor) are hired at the same price, the marginal cost of each extra unit of output will fall as long as the marginal product of each additional worker is rising. This is true because marginal cost is the (constant) cost of an extra worker divided by his or her marginal product. Therefore, in Table 9.1, suppose that each worker can be hired for $10. Because the first worker's marginal product is 10 units of output, and hiring this worker increases the firm's costs by $10, the marginal cost of each of these 10 extra units of output is $1 (= $10 ÷ 10 units). The second worker also increases costs by $10, but the marginal product is 15, so the marginal cost of each of these 15 extra units of output is $.67 (= $10 ÷ 15 units). Similarly, the MC of each of the 20 extra units of output contributed by the third worker is $.50 (= $10 ÷ 20 units). To generalize, as long as marginal product is rising, marginal cost will fall.

But with the fourth worker diminishing returns set in and marginal cost begins to rise. For the fourth worker, marginal cost is $.67 (= $10 ÷ 15 units); for the fifth worker, MC is $1 ($10 ÷ 10 units); for the sixth, MC is $2 (= $10 ÷ 5 units); and so on. If the price (cost) of the variable resource remains constant, increasing marginal returns will be reflected in a declining marginal cost, and diminishing marginal returns in a rising marginal cost. The MC curve is a mirror reflection of the marginal-product curve. As you can see in Figure 9.6, when marginal product is rising, marginal cost is necessarily falling. When marginal product is at its maximum, marginal cost is at its minimum. And when marginal product is falling, marginal cost is rising.

Relation of MC to AVC and ATC

Figure 9.5 shows that the marginal-cost curve MC intersects both the AVC and the ATC curves at their minimum points. As noted earlier, this marginal-average relationship is a mathematical necessity, which a simple illustration will reveal. Suppose a baseball pitcher has allowed his opponents an average of 3 runs per game in the first three games he has pitched. Now, whether his average falls or rises as a result of

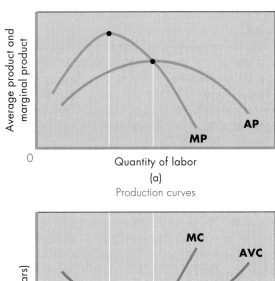

Figure 9.6

The relationship between productivity curves and cost curves. The marginal-cost (MC) curve and the average-variable-cost (AVC) curve in (b) are mirror images of the marginal-product (MP) and average-product (AP) curves in (a). Assuming that labor is the only variable input and that its price (the wage rate) is constant, then when MP is rising, MC is falling, and when MP is falling, MC is rising. Under the same assumptions, when AP is rising, AVC is falling, and when AP is falling, AVC is rising.

pitching a fourth (marginal) game will depend on whether the additional runs he allows in that extra game are fewer or more than his current 3-run average. If in the fourth game he allows fewer than 3 runs, for example, 1, his total runs will rise from 9 to 10 and his average will fall from 3 to $2\frac{1}{2}$ (= 10 ÷ 4). Conversely, if in the fourth game he allows more than 3 runs, say, 7, his total will increase from 9 to 16 and his average will rise from 3 to 4 (= 16 ÷ 4).

So it is with costs. When the amount (the marginal cost) added to total cost is less than the current average total cost, ATC will fall. Conversely, when the marginal cost exceeds ATC, ATC will rise. This means in Figure 9.5 that as long as MC lies below ATC, ATC will fall, and whenever MC lies above ATC, ATC will rise. Therefore, at the point of intersection where MC equals ATC, ATC has just ceased to fall but has not yet begun to rise. This, by definition, is the minimum point on the ATC curve. The marginal-cost curve intersects the average-total-cost curve at the ATC curve's minimum point. **9.2**

Marginal cost can be defined as the addition either to total cost or to total variable cost resulting from 1 more unit of output; thus this same rationale explains why the MC curve also crosses the AVC curve at the AVC curve's minimum point. No such relationship exists between the MC curve and the average-fixed-cost curve, because the two are not related; marginal cost includes only those costs that change with output, and fixed costs by definition are those that are independent of output. **(Key Question 7)**

Shifts of the Cost Curves

Changes in either resource prices or technology will cause costs to change and therefore the cost curves to shift. If fixed costs double from $100 to $200, the AFC curve in Figure 9.5 would be shifted upward. At each level of output, fixed costs are higher. The ATC curve would also move upward, because AFC is a component of ATC. But the positions of the AVC and MC curves would be unaltered, because their locations are based on the prices of variable rather than fixed resources. However, if the price (wage) of labor or some other variable input rose, AVC, ATC, and MC would rise and those cost curves would all shift upward. The AFC curve would remain in place because fixed costs have not changed. And, of course, reductions in the prices of fixed or variable resources would reduce costs and produce shifts of the cost curve exactly opposite to those just described.

The discovery of a more efficient technology would increase the productivity of all inputs. The cost figures in Table 9.2 would all be lower. To illustrate, if labor is the only variable input, if wages are $10 per hour, and if average product is 10 units, then AVC would be $1. But if a technological improvement increases the average product of labor to 20 units, then AVC will decline to $.50. More generally, an upward shift in the productivity curves shown in Figure 9.6a means a downward shift in the cost curves portrayed in Figure 9.6b. (See Global Perspective 9.1.)

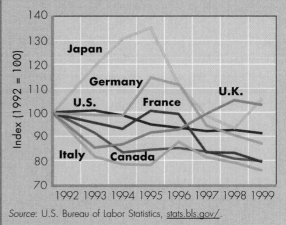
■ Long-Run Production Costs

In the long run an industry and the individual firms it comprises can undertake all desired resource adjustments. That is, they can change the amount of all inputs used. The firm can alter its plant capacity;

it can build a larger plant or revert to a smaller plant than that assumed in Table 9.2. The industry also can change its plant size; the long run allows sufficient time for new firms to enter or for existing firms to leave an industry. We will discuss the impact of the entry and exit of firms to and from an industry in the next chapter; here we are concerned only with changes in plant capacity made by a single firm. Let's couch our analysis in terms of average total cost (ATC), making no distinction between fixed and variable costs because all resources, and therefore all costs, are variable in the long run.

Firm Size and Costs

Suppose a single-plant manufacturer begins on a small scale and, as the result of successful operations, expands to successively larger plant sizes with larger output capacities. What happens to average total cost as this occurs? For a time, successively larger plants will lower average total cost. However, eventually the building of a still larger plant may cause ATC to rise.

Figure 9.7 illustrates this situation for five possible plant sizes. ATC-1 is the short-run average-total-cost curve for the smallest of the five plants, and ATC-5 the curve for the largest. Constructing larger plants will lower the minimum average total costs through plant size 3. But then larger plants will mean higher minimum average total costs.

The Long-Run Cost Curve

The vertical lines perpendicular to the output axis in Figure 9.7 indicate the outputs at which the firm should change plant size to realize the lowest attainable average total costs of production. These are the outputs at which the per-unit costs for a larger plant drop below those for the current, smaller plant. For all outputs up to 20 units, the lowest average total costs are attainable with plant size 1. However, if the firm's volume of sales expands beyond 20 units but less than 30, it can achieve lower per-unit costs by constructing a larger plant, size 2. Although total cost will be higher at the expanded levels of production, the cost per unit of output will be less. For any output between 30 and 50 units, plant size 3 will yield the lowest average total costs. From 50 to 60 units of output, the firm must build the size-4 plant to achieve the lowest unit costs. Lowest average total costs for any output over 60 units require construction of the still larger plant, size 5.

Tracing these adjustments, we find that the long-run ATC curve for the enterprise is made up of segments of the short-run ATC curves for the various plant sizes that can be constructed. The long-run ATC curve shows the lowest average total cost at which *any output level* can be produced after the firm has had time to make all appropriate adjustments in its plant size. In Figure 9.7 the gold, bumpy curve

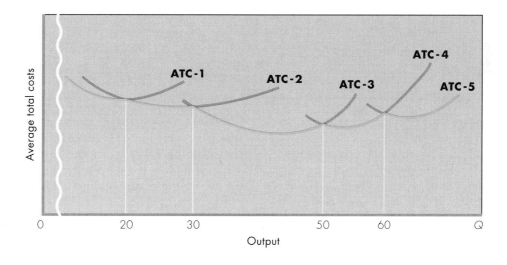

Figure 9.7

The long-run average-total-cost curve: five possible plant sizes.   The long-run average-total-cost curve is made up of segments of the short-run cost curves (ATC-1, ATC-2, etc.) of the various-size plants from which the firm might choose. Each point on the bumpy planning curve shows the lowest unit cost attainable for any output when the firm has had time to make all desired changes in its plant size.

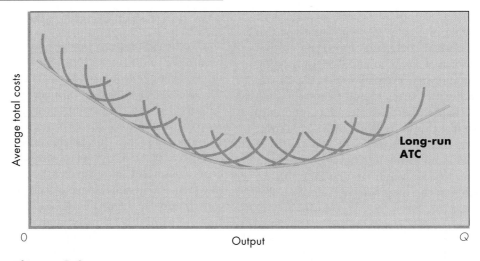

Figure 9.8

The long-run average-total-cost curve: unlimited number of plant sizes. If the number of possible plant sizes is very large, the long-run average-total-cost curve approximates a smooth curve. Economies of scale, followed by diseconomies of scale, cause the curve to be U-shaped.

Quick Quiz 9.8

1. The unlabeled green curves in this figure illustrate the:
   a. long-run average-total-cost curves of various firms constituting the industry.
   b. short-run average-total-cost curves of various firms constituting the industry.
   c. short-run average-total-cost curves of various plant sizes available to a particular firm.
   d. short-run marginal-cost curves of various plant sizes available to a particular firm.

2. The unlabeled green curves in this figure derive their shapes from:
   a. decreasing, then increasing, short-run returns.
   b. increasing, then decreasing, short-run returns.
   c. economies, then diseconomies, of scale.
   d. diseconomies, then economies, of scale.

3. The long-run ATC curve in this figure derives its shape from:
   a. decreasing, then increasing, short-run returns.
   b. increasing, then decreasing, short-run returns.
   c. economies, then diseconomies, of scale.
   d. diseconomies, then economies, of scale.

4. The long-run ATC curve is often called the firm's:
   a. planning curve.
   b. capital-expansion path.
   c. total-product curve.
   d. production possibilities curve.

Answers: 1. c; 2. b; 3. c; 4. a

is the firm's long-run ATC curve or, as it is often called, the firm's *planning curve.*

In most lines of production the choice of plant size is much wider than in our illustration. In many industries the number of possible plant sizes is virtually unlimited, and in time quite small changes in the volume of output will lead to changes in plant size. Graphically, this implies an unlimited number of short-run ATC curves, one for each output level, as suggested by **Figure 9.8 (Key Graph).** Then, rather than being made up of segments of short-run ATC curves as in Figure 9.7, the long-run ATC curve is made up of all the points of tangency of the

unlimited number of short-run ATC curves from which the long-run ATC curve is derived. Therefore, the planning curve is smooth rather than bumpy. Each point on it tells us the minimum ATC of producing the corresponding level of output.

Economies and Diseconomies of Scale

We have assumed that for a time larger and larger plant sizes will lead to lower unit costs but that beyond some point successively larger plants will mean higher average total costs. That is, we have assumed the long-run ATC curve is U-shaped. But why should this be? Note, first, that the law of diminishing returns does not apply in the long run. That's because diminishing returns presume one resource is fixed in supply while the long run means all resources are variable. Also, our discussion assumes resource prices are constant. We can explain the U-shaped long-run average-total-cost curve in terms of economies and diseconomies of large-scale production.

Economies of Scale

Economies of scale, or economies of mass production, explain the downsloping part of the long-run ATC curve, as in-dicated in Figure 9.9, graphs (a), (b), and (c). As plant size increases, a number of factors will for a time lead to lower average costs of production.

Labor Specialization Increased specialization in the use of labor becomes more achievable as a plant increases in size. Hiring more workers means jobs can be divided and subdivided. Each worker may now have just one task to perform instead of five or six. Workers can work full-time on the tasks for which they have special skills. In a small plant, skilled machinists may spend half their time performing un-skilled tasks, leading to higher production costs.

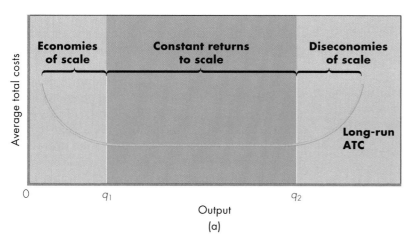

(a)

Figure 9.9

Various possible long-run average-total-cost curves. In (a), economies of scale are rather rapidly obtained as plant size rises, and diseconomies of scale are not en-countered until a considerably large scale of output has been achieved. Thus, long-run aver-age total cost is constant over a wide range of output. In (b), economies of scale are exten-sive, and diseconomies of scale occur only at very large outputs. Average total cost therefore declines over a broad range of output. In (c), economies of scale are exhausted quickly, fol-lowed immediately by diseconomies of scale. Minimum ATC thus occurs at a relatively low output.

(b)

(c)

Further, by working at fewer tasks, workers become proficient at those tasks. The jack-of-all-trades doing five or six jobs is not likely to be efficient in any of them. Concentrating on one task, the same worker may become highly efficient.

Finally, greater labor specialization eliminates the loss of time that accompanies each shift of a worker from one task to another.

Managerial Specialization Large-scale production also means better use of, and greater specialization in, management. A supervisor who can handle 20 workers is underused in a small plant that employs only 10 people. The production staff could be doubled with no increase in supervisory costs.

Small firms cannot use management specialists to best advantage. In a small plant a sales specialist may have to divide his or her time between several executive functions, for example, marketing, personnel, and finance. A larger scale of operations means that the marketing expert can supervise marketing full-time, while specialists perform other managerial functions. Greater efficiency and lower unit costs are the net result.

Efficient Capital Small firms often cannot afford the most efficient equipment. In many lines of production such machinery is available only in very large and extremely expensive units. Furthermore, effective use of the equipment demands a high volume of production, and that again requires large-scale producers.

In the automobile industry the most efficient fabrication method employs robotics and elaborate assembly-line equipment. Effective use of this equipment demands an annual output of perhaps 200,000 to 400,000 automobiles. Only very large-scale producers can afford to purchase and use this equipment efficiently. The small-scale producer is faced with a dilemma. To fabricate automobiles using other equipment is inefficient and therefore more costly per unit. The alternative of purchasing the efficient equipment and underusing it at low levels of output is also inefficient and costly.

Other Factors Many products entail design and development costs, as well as other "start-up" costs, which must be incurred irrespective of projected sales. These costs decline per unit as output is increased. Similarly, advertising costs decline per auto, per computer, per stereo system, and per box of detergent as more units are produced and sold. Also, the firm's production and marketing expertise usually rises as it produces and sells more output. This *learning by doing* is a further source of economies of scale.

All these factors contribute to lower average total costs for the firm that is able to expand its scale of operations. Where economies of scale are possible, an increase in all resources of, say, 10 percent will cause a more-than-proportionate increase in output of, say, 20 percent. The result will be a decline in ATC.

In many U.S. manufacturing industries economies of scale have been of great significance. Firms that have expanded their scale of operations to obtain economies of mass production have survived and flourished. Those unable to expand have become relatively high-cost producers, doomed to a struggle to survive.

Diseconomies of Scale In time the expansion of a firm may lead to diseconomies and therefore higher average total costs.

The main factor causing **diseconomies of scale** is the difficulty of efficiently controlling and coordinating a firm's operations as it becomes a large-scale producer. In a small plant a single key executive may make all the basic decisions for the plant's operation. Because of the firm's small size, the executive is close to the production line, understands the firm's operations, and can digest information and make efficient decisions.

This neat picture changes as a firm grows. There are now many management levels between the executive suite and the assembly line; top management is far removed from the actual production operations of the plant. One person cannot assemble, digest, and understand all the information essential to decision making on a large scale. Authority must be delegated to many vice-presidents, second vice-presidents, and so forth. This expansion of the management hierarchy leads to problems of communication and cooperation, bureaucratic red tape, and the possibility that decisions will not be coordinated. Similarly, decision making may be slowed down to the point that decisions fail to reflect changes in consumer tastes or technology quickly enough. The result is impaired efficiency and rising average total costs.

Also, in massive production facilities workers may feel alienated from their employers and care little about working efficiently. Opportunities to shirk, by avoiding work in favor of on-the-job leisure, may be greater in large plants than in small ones. Countering worker alienation and shirking may require additional worker supervision, which increases costs.

Where diseconomies of scale are operative, an increase in all inputs of, say, 10 percent will cause a less-than-proportionate increase in output of, say, 5 percent. As a consequence, ATC will increase. The rising portion of the long-run cost curves in Figure 9.9 illustrates diseconomies of scale.

Constant Returns to Scale

In some industries there may exist a rather wide range of output between the output at which economies of scale end and the output at which diseconomies of scale begin. That is, there may be a range of **constant returns to scale** over which long-run average cost does not change. The q_1q_2 output range of Figure 9.9a is an example. Here a given percentage increase in all inputs of, say, 10 percent will cause a proportionate 10 percent increase in output. Thus, in this range ATC is constant.

Applications and Illustrations

The business world offers many examples of economies and diseconomies of scale. Here are just a few.

Successful Start-Up Firms

The U.S. economy has greatly benefited over the past few decades by explosive growth of new start-up firms. Where economies of scale are significant, such firms can enjoy years or even decades of growth accompanied by lower average total cost. That has been the case for such firms as Intel (microchips), Starbucks (coffee), Microsoft (software), Dell (personal computers), Yahoo (Internet search engine), Cisco Systems (Internet switching), Federal Express (overnight delivery), and America Online (Internet access).

A major source of these economies of scale is the ability to spread huge product development and advertising costs over a larger and larger number of units of output. These firms also benefit from the greater specialization of labor, management, and capital equipment permitted by larger firm size. And, in some cases, the full exploitation of economies of scale is still continuing. For example, America Online's cost of delivering Internet access to each additional user is very low. Thus, its average total cost probably will continue to fall as it signs up more subscribers.

The Verson Stamping Machine

In 1996 Verson (a U.S. firm located in Chicago) introduced a 49-foot-tall metal stamping machine that is the size of a house and weighs as much as 12 locomotives. This $30 million machine, which cuts and sculpts raw sheets of steel into automobile hoods and fenders, enables automakers to make new parts in just 5 minutes compared with 8 hours for older stamping presses. A single machine is designed to make 5 million auto parts a year. So, to achieve the cost saving from this machine, an auto manufacturer must have sufficient auto production to use all these parts. By allowing the use of this cost-saving piece of equipment, large firm size achieves economies of scale.

The Daily Newspaper

The daily newspaper is undoubtedly one of the economy's great bargains. Think of all the resources that are combined to produce it: reporters, delivery people, photographers, editors, management, printing presses, pulp mills, pulp mill workers, ink manufacturers, forest-product firms, loggers, logging truck drivers, and on and on. Yet for 50 cents you can buy a high-quality newspaper in major cities.

The fundamental reason that newspapers have such low prices is the low costs resulting from economies of scale. If only 100 or 200 people bought the paper each day, the average cost of each paper would be exceedingly high because the overhead (fixed) costs of producing the paper would be spread over so few readers. But when publishers sell thousands or hundreds of thousands of newspapers each day, they spread their overhead costs very widely. They also can fully use expensive but highly efficient printing presses. For both reasons, the average total cost of a paper sinks to a few dimes. Moreover, the greater the number of readers, the larger is the amount of money that advertisers are willing to pay for ad space. That added revenue helps keep the price of the newspaper low.

General Motors

Executives of General Motors, the world's largest auto producer, are well aware of the realities of diseconomies of scale. Experts on the auto industry say GM's large size may be a liability; it is substantially larger than Ford and Daimler-Chrysler and is larger than Toyota and Honda combined. Compared with these competitors, GM has a cost disadvantage that may help explain its substantial decline in long-term market share. Despite billions of dollars of investment in modern equipment, GM still has the lowest productivity and the highest cost per car in the industry.[1]

---

[1]Walter Adams and James W. Brock (eds.) *The Structure of American Industry*, 12th ed. (Upper Saddle River, N.J.: Prentice-Hall, 2001), pp. 123, 128; F. M. Scherer, *Industry Structure, Strategy, and Public Policy* (New York: Harper-Collins, 1996), pp. 324–325; and Jeffrey Ball, "Productivity Improves among U.S. Automakers," *Wall Street Journal*, June 18, 1999, p. A2.

To try to reduce scale diseconomies, GM has taken several actions. It has established joint ventures (combined projects) with smaller foreign rivals such as Toyota to reduce its production costs. It has created Saturn, a separate, stand-alone auto manufacturing company. It has given each of its five automotive divisions (Chevrolet, Buick, Pontiac, Oldsmobile, and Cadillac) greater autonomy with respect to styling, engineering, and marketing decisions to reduce the layers of managerial approval required in decision making. GM has reorganized into a small-car group and a midsize and luxury group to try to cut costs and bring new cars to the market faster. Most recently, it has dismantled its entire Oldsmobile division. Whether these actions will overcome GM's diseconomies of scale remains to be seen.

Minimum Efficient Scale and Industry Structure

Economies and diseconomies of scale are an important determinant of an industry's structure. Here we introduce the concept of **minimum efficient scale (MES)**, which is the lowest level of output at which a firm can minimize long-run average costs. In Figure 9.9a that level occurs at q_1 units of output. Because of the extended range of constant returns to scale, firms producing substantially greater outputs could also realize the minimum attainable average costs. Specifically, firms within the q_1 to q_2 range would be equally efficient. So we would not be surprised to find an industry with such cost conditions to be populated by firms of quite different sizes. The apparel, food processing, furniture, wood products, snowboard, and small-appliance industries are examples. With an extended range of constant returns to scale, relatively large and relatively small firms can coexist in an industry and be equally successful. Another example appears to be banking.

Compare this with Figure 9.9b, where economies of scale prevail over a wide range of outputs and diseconomies of scale appear only at very high levels of output. This pattern of declining long-run average total cost may occur over an extended range of outputs, as in the automobile, aluminum, steel, and other heavy industries. The same pattern holds in several of the new industries related to information technology, for example, computer microchips, operating system software, and Internet service provision.

Given consumer demand, efficient production will be achieved with a few large-scale producers.

Small firms cannot realize the minimum efficient scale and will not be able to compete. In the extreme, economies of scale might extend beyond the market's size, resulting in what is termed **natural monopoly,** a relatively rare market situation in which average total cost is minimized when only one firm produces the particular good or service.

Where economies of scale are few and diseconomies come into play quickly, the minimum efficient size occurs at a low level of output, as shown in Figure 9.9c. In such industries a particular level of consumer demand will support a large number of relatively small producers. Many retail trades and some types of farming fall into this category. So do certain kinds of light manufacturing, such as the baking, clothing, and shoe industries. Fairly small firms are as efficient as, or more efficient than, large-scale producers in such industries.

Our point here is that the shape of the long-run average-total-cost curve is determined by technology and the economies and diseconomies of scale that result. The shape of the long-run ATC curve, in turn, can be significant in determining whether an industry is populated by a relatively large number of small firms or is dominated by a few large producers, or lies somewhere in between.

But we must be cautious in our assessment because industry structure does not depend on cost conditions alone. Government policies, the geographic size of markets, managerial strategy and skill, and other factors must be considered in explaining the structure of a particular industry. **(Key Question 10)** ! 9.3   🔑 9.3

> ### QUICK REVIEW 9.3
>
> ■ Most firms have U-shaped long-run average-total-cost curves, reflecting economies and then diseconomies of scale.
>
> ■ Economies of scale are the consequence of greater specialization of labor and management, more efficient capital equipment, and the spreading of start-up costs among more units of output.
>
> ■ Diseconomies of scale are caused by the problems of coordination and communication that arise in large firms.
>
> ■ Minimum efficient scale is the lowest level of output at which a firm's long-run average total cost is at a minimum.

Irrelevancy of Sunk Costs

Sunk Costs Should Be Disregarded in Decision Making.

There is an old saying: Don't cry over spilt milk. The message is that once you have spilled a glass of milk, there is nothing you can do to recover it, so you should forget about it and "move on from there." This saying has great relevance to what economists call sunk costs. Such costs are like sunken ships on the ocean floor: Once these costs are incurred, they cannot be recovered.

Let's gain an understanding of this idea by applying it first to consumers and then to businesses. Suppose you buy an expensive ticket to an upcoming football game, but the morning of the game you wake up with a bad case of the flu. Feeling miserable, you step outside to find that the wind chill is about −10 degrees. You absolutely do not want to go to the game, but you remind yourself that you paid a steep price for the ticket. You call several people to try to sell the ticket, but you soon discover that no one is interested in it, even at a discounted price. You conclude that everyone who wants a ticket has one.

Should you go to the game? Economic analysis says that you should not take actions for which marginal cost exceeds marginal benefit. And, in this situation, the price you paid for the ticket is irrelevant to the decision. Both marginal or additional cost and marginal or additional benefit are forward-looking. If the marginal cost of going to the game is greater than the marginal benefit, the best decision is to go back to bed. This decision should be the same whether you paid $2, $20, or $200 for the game ticket, because the price that you pay for something does not affect its marginal benefit. Once the ticket has been purchased and cannot be resold, its cost is irrelevant to the decision to attend the game. Since "you absolutely do not want to go," clearly the marginal cost exceeds the marginal benefit of the game.

Here is a second consumer example: Suppose a family is on vacation and stops at a roadside stand to buy some apples. The kids get back into the car and bite into their apples, immediately

pronouncing them "totally mushy" and unworthy of another bite. Both parents agree that the apples are "terrible," but the father continues to eat his, because, as he says, "We paid a premium price for them." One of the older children replies, "Dad, that is irrelevant." Although not stated very diplomatically, the child is exactly right. In making a new decision, you should ignore all costs that are not affected by the decision. The prior bad decision (in retrospect) to buy the apples should not dictate a second decision for which marginal benefit is less than marginal cost.

Now let's apply the idea of sunk costs to firms. Some of a firm's costs are not only fixed (recurring, but unrelated to the level of output) but sunk (unrecoverable). For example, a nonrefundable annual lease payment for the use of a store cannot be recouped once it has been paid. A firm's decision about whether to move from the store to a more profitable location does not depend on the amount of time remaining on the lease. If moving means greater profit, it makes sense to move whether there are 300 days, 30 days, or 3 days left on the lease.

Or, as another example, suppose a firm spends $1 million on R&D to bring out a new product, only to discover that the product sells very poorly. Should the firm continue to produce the product at a loss even when there is no realistic hope for future success? Obviously, it should not. In making this decision, the firm realizes that the amount it has spent in developing the product is irrelevant; it should stop production of the product and cut its losses. In fact, many firms have dropped products after spending millions of dollars on their development. Examples are the quick decision by Coca-Cola to drop its New Coke and the eventual decision by McDonald's to drop its McLean Burger.

Consider a final real-world example: For decades, Boeing and McDonnell Douglas were keen rivals in the worldwide sale of commercial airplanes. Each company spent billions of dollars on R&D and marketing in an attempt to gain competitive advantages over the other. Then, in 1996, they suddenly merged. Many observers wondered how two fierce rivals who had spent such huge amounts to compete could suddenly forget the past and agree to merge. But the past efforts and expenditures were irrelevant to the decision; they were sunk costs. The forward-looking decision led both companies to conclude, each for its own reasons, that the marginal benefit of a merger would outweigh the marginal cost.

In short, if a cost has been incurred and cannot be partly or fully recouped by some other choice, a rational consumer or firm should ignore it. Sunk costs are irrelevant. Or, as the saying goes, don't cry over spilt milk.

SUMMARY

1. Economic costs include all payments that must be received by resource owners to ensure a continued supply of needed resources to a particular line of production. Economic costs include explicit costs, which flow to resources owned and supplied by others, and implicit costs, which are payments for the use of self-owned and self-employed resources. One implicit cost is a normal profit to the entrepreneur. Economic profit occurs when total revenue exceeds total cost (= explicit costs + implicit costs, including a normal profit).

2. In the short run a firm's plant capacity is fixed. The firm can use its plant more or less intensively by adding or subtracting units of variable resources, but it does not have sufficient time in the short run to alter plant size.

3. The law of diminishing returns describes what happens to output as a fixed plant is used more intensively. As successive units of a variable resource, such as labor are added to a fixed plant, beyond some point the marginal product associated with each additional unit of a resource declines.

4. Because some resources are variable and others are fixed, costs can be classified as variable or fixed in the short run. Fixed costs are independent of the level of output; variable costs vary with output. The total cost of any output is the sum of fixed and variable costs at that output.

5. Average fixed, average variable, and average total costs are fixed, variable, and total costs per unit of output. Average fixed cost declines continuously as output increases because a fixed sum is being spread over a larger and larger number of units of production. A graph of average variable cost is U-shaped, reflecting the law of diminishing returns. Average total cost is the sum of average fixed and average variable costs; its graph is also U-shaped.

6. Marginal cost is the extra, or additional, cost of producing 1 more unit of output. It is the amount by which total cost and total variable cost change when 1 more or 1 less unit of output is produced. Graphically, the marginal-cost curve intersects the ATC and AVC curves at their minimum points.

7. Lower resource prices shift cost curves downward, as does technological progress. Higher input prices shift cost curves upward.

8. The long run is a period of time sufficiently long for a firm to vary the amounts of all resources used, including plant size. In the long run all costs are variable. The long-run ATC, or planning, curve is composed of segments of the short-run ATC curves, and it represents the various plant sizes a firm can construct in the long run.

9. The long-run ATC curve is generally U-shaped. Economies of scale are first encountered as a small firm expands. Greater specialization in the use of labor and management, the ability to use the most efficient equipment, and the spreading of start-up costs among more units of output all contribute to economies of scale. As the firm continues to grow, it will encounter diseconomies of scale stemming from the managerial complexities that accompany large-scale production. The output ranges over which economies and diseconomies of scale occur in an industry are often an important determinant of the structure of that industry.

TERMS AND CONCEPTS

economic (opportunity) cost

explicit costs

implicit costs

normal profit

economic profit

short run

long run

total product (TP)

marginal product (MP)

average product (AP)

law of diminishing returns

fixed costs

variable costs

total cost

average fixed cost (AFC)

average variable cost (AVC)

average total cost (ATC)

marginal cost (MC)

economies of scale

diseconomies of scale

constant returns to scale

minimum efficient scale (MES)

natural monopoly

STUDY QUESTIONS

1. Distinguish between explicit and implicit costs, giving examples of each. What are some explicit and implicit costs of attending college? Why does the economist classify normal profit as a cost? Is economic profit a cost of production?

2. **Key Question** Gomez runs a small pottery firm. He hires one helper at $12,000 per year, pays annual rent of $5000 for his shop, and spends $20,000 per year on materials. He has $40,000 of his own funds invested in equipment (pottery wheels, kilns, and so forth) that

could earn him $4000 per year if alternatively invested. He has been offered $15,000 per year to work as a potter for a competitor. He estimates his entrepreneurial talents are worth $3000 per year. Total annual revenue from pottery sales is $72,000. Calculate the accounting profit and the economic profit for Gomez's pottery firm.

3. Which of the following are short-run and which are long-run adjustments?

   a. Wendy's builds a new restaurant.

   b. Acme Steel Corporation hires 200 more production workers.

   c. A farmer increases the amount of fertilizer used on his corn crop.

   d. An Alcoa aluminum plant adds a third shift of workers.

4. **Key Question** Complete the following table by calculating marginal product and average product from the data given.

Inputs of Labor	Total Product	Marginal Product	Average Product
0	0	———	
1	15	———	———
2	34	———	———
3	51	———	———
4	65	———	———
5	74	———	———
6	80	———	———
7	83	———	———
8	82	———	———

Plot the total, marginal, and average products and explain in detail the relationship between each pair of curves. Explain why marginal product first rises, then declines, and ultimately becomes negative. What bearing does the law of diminishing returns have on short-run costs? Be specific. "When marginal product is rising, marginal cost is falling. And when marginal product is diminishing, marginal cost is rising." Illustrate and explain graphically.

5. Why can the distinction between fixed costs and variable costs be made in the short run? Classify the following as fixed or variable costs: advertising expenditures, fuel, interest on company-issued bonds, shipping charges, payments for raw materials, real estate taxes, executive salaries, insurance premiums, wage payments, depreciation and obsolescence charges, sales taxes, and rental payments on leased office machinery. "There are no fixed costs in the long run; all costs are variable." Explain.

6. List several fixed and variable costs associated with owning and operating an automobile. Suppose you are considering whether to drive your car or fly 1000 miles to Florida for spring break. Which costs—fixed, variable, or both—would you take into account in making your decision? Would any implicit costs be relevant? Explain.

7. **Key Question** A firm has fixed costs of $60 and variable costs as indicated in the table below. Complete the table below; check your calculations by referring to question 4 at the end of Chapter 10.

   a. Graph total fixed cost, total variable cost, and total cost. Explain how the law of diminishing returns influences the shapes of the variable-cost and total-cost curves.

   b. Graph AFC, AVC, ATC, and MC. Explain the derivation and shape of each of these four curves and their relationships to one another. Specifically, explain in nontechnical terms why the MC curve intersects both the AVC and the ATC curves at their minimum points.

   c. Explain how the location of each curve graphed in question 7b would be altered if (1) total fixed cost had been $100 rather than $60 and (2) total variable cost had been $10 less at each level of output.

Total Product	Total Fixed Cost	Total Variable Cost	Total Cost	Average Fixed Cost	Average Variable Cost	Average Total Cost	Marginal Cost
0	$ ———	$ 0	$ ———	$ ———	$ ———	$ ———	$ ———
1	———	45	———	———	———	———	———
2	———	85	———	———	———	———	———
3	———	120	———	———	———	———	———
4	———	150	———	———	———	———	———
5	———	185	———	———	———	———	———
6	———	225	———	———	———	———	———
7	———	270	———	———	———	———	———
8	———	325	———	———	———	———	———
9	———	390	———	———	———	———	———
10	———	465	———	———	———	———	———

8. Indicate how each of the following would shift the (1) marginal-cost curve, (2) average-variable-cost curve, (3) average-fixed-cost curve, and (4) average-total-cost curve of a manufacturing firm. In each case specify the direction of the shift.
   a. A reduction in business property taxes.
   b. An increase in the nominal wages of production workers.
   c. A decrease in the price of electricity.
   d. An increase in insurance rates on plant and equipment.
   e. An increase in transportation costs.

9. Suppose a firm has only three possible plant-size options, represented by the ATC curves shown in the accompanying figure. What plant size will the firm choose in producing (*a*) 50, (*b*) 130, (*c*) 160, and (*d*) 250 units of output? Draw the firm's long-run average-cost curve on the diagram and describe this curve.

10. **Key Question** Use the concepts of economies and diseconomies of scale to explain the shape of a firm's long-run ATC curve. What is the concept of minimum efficient scale? What bearing can the shape of the long-run ATC curve have on the structure of an industry?

11. **(Last Word)** What is a sunk cost? Provide an example of a sunk cost other than one from this book. Why are such costs irrelevant in making decisions about future actions?

12. **Web-Based Question:** *The 10 largest U.S. firms— what are their sources of economies of scale?* Check out the Fortune 500 list of the largest U.S. firms at www.fortune.com. From the top 10 list, select three firms from three different industries and discuss the likely sources of the economies of scale that underlie their large size.

13. **Web-Based Question:** *Corporate annual reports— identify fixed and variable costs* Use the Yahoo search engine at www.yahoo.com to locate the home page of a company of your choice. Find and review the company's income statement in its annual report, and classify the nonrevenue items as either fixed or variable costs. Are all costs clearly identifiable as either fixed or variable? What item would be considered accounting profit? Would economic profit be higher or lower than this accounting profit?

10

Pure Competition

I N   C H A P T E R   7 we examined the relationship between product demand and total revenue, and in Chapter 9 we discussed costs of production. Now we want to put revenues and costs together to see how a business decides what price to charge and how much output to produce. But a firm's decisions concerning price and production depend greatly on the character of the industry in which it is operating. There is no "average" or "typical" industry. At one extreme is a single producer that dominates the market; at the other extreme are industries in which thousands of firms each produce a minute fraction of market supply. Between these extremes are many other industries. ■ Since we cannot examine each industry individually, we will focus on several basic *models* of market structure. Together, these models will help you understand how price and output are determined in the many product markets in the economy. They will also help you assess the efficiency or inefficiency of those markets.

▮ Four Market Models

Economists group industries into four distinct market structures: pure competition, pure monopoly, monopolistic competition, and oligopoly. These four market models differ in several respects: the number of firms in the industry, whether those firms produce a standardized product or try to differentiate their products from those of other firms, and how easy or how difficult it is for firms to enter the industry.

Very briefly the four models are as follows:

■ **Pure competition** involves a very large number of firms producing a standardized product (that is, a product identical to that of other produc-

ers, such as corn or cucumbers). New firms can enter or exit the industry very easily.

■ **Pure monopoly** is a market structure in which one firm is the sole seller of a product or service (for example, a local electric utility). Since the entry of additional firms is blocked, one firm constitutes the entire industry. Because the monopolist produces a unique product, it makes no effort to differentiate its product.

■ **Monopolistic competition** is characterized by a relatively large number of sellers producing differentiated products (clothing, furniture, books). There is widespread *nonprice competition*, a selling strategy in which one firm tries to dis-

Table 10.1

Characteristics of the Four Basic Market Models

Characteristic	Pure Competition	Monopolistic Competition	Oligopoly	Pure Monopoly
		Market Model		
Number of firms	A very large number	Many	Few	One
Type of product	Standardized	Differentiated	Standardized or differentiated	Unique; no close substitutes
Control over price	None	Some, but within rather narrow limits	Limited by mutual interdependence; considerable with collusion	Considerable
Conditions of entry	Very easy, no obstacles	Relatively easy	Significant obstacles	Blocked
Nonprice competition	None	Considerable emphasis on advertising, brand names, trademarks	Typically a great deal, particularly with product differentiation	Mostly public relations advertising
Examples	Agriculture	Retail trade, dresses, shoes	Steel, automobiles, farm implements, many household appliances	Local utilities

tinguish its product or service from all competing products on the basis of attributes like design and workmanship (an approach called *product differentiation*). Either entry to or exit from monopolistically competitive industries is quite easy.

■ **Oligopoly** involves only a few sellers of an identical or similar product; consequently, each firm is affected by the decisions of its rivals and must take those decisions into account in determining its own price and output.

Table 10.1 summarizes the characteristics of the four models for easy comparison. In discussing these four market models, we will occasionally distinguish the characteristics of *pure competition* from those of the three other basic market structures, which together we will designate as **imperfect competition.**

■ Pure Competition: Characteristics and Occurrence

Let's take a fuller look at pure competition, the focus of the remainder of this chapter:

■ *Very large numbers*   A basic feature of a purely competitive market is the presence of a large number of independently acting sellers, often offering their products in large national or international markets. Examples: markets for farm commodities, the stock market, and the foreign exchange market.

■ *Standardized product*   Purely competitive firms produce a standardized (identical or ho-

mogeneous) product. As long as the price is the same, consumers will be indifferent about which seller to buy the product from. Buyers view the products of firms B, C, D, and E as perfect substitutes for the product of firm A. Because purely competitive firms sell standardized products, they make no attempt to differentiate their products and do not engage in other forms of nonprice competition.

■ *"Price takers"*   In a purely competitive market individual firms exert no significant control over product price. Each firm produces such a small fraction of total output that increasing or decreasing its output will not perceptibly influence total supply or, therefore, product price. In short, the competitive firm is a **price taker:** It cannot change market price; it can only adjust to it. That means that the individual competitive producer is at the mercy of the market. Asking a price higher than the market price would be futile. Consumers will not buy from firm A at $2.05 when its 9999 competitors are selling an identical product, and therefore a perfect substitute, at $2 per unit. Conversely, because firm A can sell as much as it chooses at $2 per unit, there is no reason for it to charge a lower price, say, $1.95, for to do so would shrink its profit.

■ *Free entry and exit*   New firms can freely enter and existing firms can freely leave purely competitive industries. No significant legal, technological, financial, or other obstacles prohibit new firms from selling their output in any competitive market.

Relevance of Pure Competition

Although pure competition is relatively rare in the real world, this market model is highly relevant. A few industries more closely approximate pure competition than any other market structure. In particular, we can learn much about markets for agricultural goods, fish products, foreign exchange, basic metals, and stock shares by studying the pure-competition model. Also, pure competition is a meaningful starting point for any discussion of price and output determination. Moreover, the operation of a purely competitive economy provides a standard, or norm, for evaluating the efficiency of the real-world economy.

■ Demand as Seen by a Purely Competitive Seller

To develop a tabular and graphical model of pure competition, we first examine demand from a competitive seller's viewpoint and see how it affects revenue. This seller might be a wheat farmer, a strawberry grower, a sheep rancher, a catfish raiser, or the like. Because each purely competitive firm offers only a negligible fraction of total market supply, it must accept the price predetermined by the market; it is a price taker, not a price maker.

Perfectly Elastic Demand $D = MR$

The demand curve of the competitive firm, as represented by columns 1 and 2 in Table 10.2, is perfectly elastic. As shown in the table, the market price is $131. The firm represented cannot obtain a higher price by restricting its output, nor does it need to lower its price to increase its sales volume.

We are *not* saying that *market* demand is perfectly elastic in a competitive market. Rather, market demand graphs as a downsloping curve, as a glance ahead at Figure 10.7b will reveal. In fact, the total-demand curves for most agricultural products are quite inelastic, even though agriculture is the most competitive industry in the U.S. economy. An entire industry (all firms producing a particular product) can affect price by changing industry output. For example, all firms, acting independently but simultaneously, can increase price by reducing output. But the individual firm cannot do that. So the demand schedule faced by the *individual firm* in a purely competitive industry is perfectly elastic at the market price, as demonstrated in Figure 10.1.

Average, Total, and Marginal Revenue

The firm's demand schedule is also its revenue schedule. What appears as price per unit to the purchaser is also revenue per unit, or average revenue, to the seller. To say that all buyers must pay $131 per unit is to say that the revenue per unit, or **average revenue**,

Table 10.2
The Demand and Revenue Schedules for a Purely Competitive Firm

Firm's Demand Schedule		Firm's Revenue Data	
(1) Product Price (P) (Average Revenue)	(2) Quantity Demanded (Q)	(3) Total Revenue (TR), (1) × (2)	(4) Marginal Revenue (MR)
$131	0	$ 0	
131	1	131	$131
131	2	262	131
131	3	393	131
131	4	524	131
131	5	655	131
131	6	786	131
131	7	917	131
131	8	1048	131
131	9	1179	131
131	10	1310	131

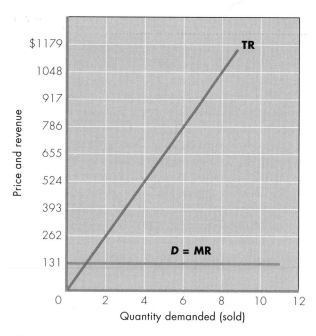

Figure 10.1

Demand, marginal revenue, and total revenue of a purely competitive firm. Because a purely competitive firm can sell additional units of output at the market price, its marginal-revenue curve (MR) coincides with its perfectly elastic demand curve (D). The firm's total-revenue curve (TR) is a straight upward-sloping line.

received by the seller is $131. Price and average revenue are the same thing seen from different viewpoints.

The **total revenue** for each sales level is found by multiplying price by the corresponding quantity the firm can sell. (Column 1 multiplied by column 2 in Table 10.2 yields column 3.) In this case, total revenue increases by a constant amount, $131, for each additional unit of sales. Each unit sold adds exactly its constant price to total revenue.

When a firm is pondering a change in its output, it will consider how its total revenue will change as a result. What will be the additional revenue from selling another unit of output? **Marginal revenue** is the change in total revenue, that is, the extra revenue, that results from selling 1 more unit of output. In column 3, Table 10.2, total revenue is zero when zero units are sold. The first unit of output sold increases total revenue from zero to $131; so marginal revenue for that unit is $131. The second unit sold increases total revenue from $131 to $262, and marginal revenue is again $131. Note in column 4 that, as is price, marginal revenue is a constant $131. In pure competition, marginal revenue and price are equal. **(Key Question 3)**

Graphical Portrayal

Figure 10.1 shows the purely competitive firm's demand curve and total-revenue and marginal-revenue curves. The demand curve (D) is horizontal, indicating perfect price elasticity. The marginal-revenue curve (MR) coincides with the demand curve because the product price (and hence MR) is constant. Total revenue (TR) is a straight line that slopes upward to the right. Its slope is constant because each extra unit of sales increases TR by $131.

■ Profit Maximization in the Short Run

Because the purely competitive firm is a price taker, it can maximize its economic profit (or minimize its loss) only by adjusting its *output*. And, in the short run, the firm has a fixed plant. Thus it can adjust its output only through changes in the amount of variable resources (materials, labor) it uses. It adjusts its variable resources to achieve the output level that maximizes its profit.

There are two ways to determine the level of output at which a competitive firm will realize maximum profit or minimum loss. One method is to compare total revenue and total cost; the other is to compare marginal revenue and marginal cost. Both approaches apply to all firms, whether they are pure competitors, pure monopolists, monopolistic competitors, or oligopolists.[1]

---

[1] To make sure you understand these two approaches, we will apply both of them to output determination under pure competition. But since we want to emphasize the marginal approach, we will limit our graphical application of the total-revenue approach to a situation where the firm maximizes profits. We will then use the marginal approach to examine three cases: profit maximization, loss minimization, and shutdown.

Total-Revenue–Total-Cost Approach: Profit-Maximization Case

Confronted with the market price of its product, the competitive producer will ask: (1) Should we produce this product? (2) If so, in what amount? (3) What economic profit (or loss) will we realize?

Let's demonstrate how a pure competitor answers these questions, given certain cost data and a specific market price. Our cost data are already familiar to you because they are the fixed-cost, variable-cost, and total-cost data in Table 9.2, repeated in columns 1 to 4 in Table 10.3. (Recall that these data reflect explicit and implicit costs, including a normal profit.) Assuming that the market price is $131, the total revenue for each output level is found by multiplying output (total product) by price. Total-revenue data are in column 5. Then in column 6 we find the profit or loss at each output level by subtracting total cost, TC (column 4), from total revenue, TR (column 5).

Should the firm produce? Definitely. It can realize a profit by doing so. How much should it produce? Nine units. Column 6 tells us that this is the output at which total economic profit is at a maximum. What economic profit (or loss) will it realize? A $299 economic profit—the difference between total revenue ($1179) and total cost ($880).

Figure 10.2a compares total revenue and total cost graphically for this profit-maximizing case.

Observe again that the total-revenue curve for a purely competitive firm is a straight line (Table 10.2). Total cost increases with output in that more production requires more resources. But the rate of increase in total cost varies with the relative efficiency of the firm. Specifically, the cost data reflect Chapter 9's law of diminishing marginal returns. From zero to 4 units of output, total cost increases at a decreasing rate as the firm uses its fixed resources more efficiently. With additional output, total cost begins to rise by ever-increasing amounts because of the diminishing returns accompanying more intensive use of the plant.

Total revenue and total cost are equal where the two curves in Figure 10.2a intersect (at roughly 2 units of output). Total revenue covers all costs (including a normal profit, which is included in the cost curve), but there is no economic profit. For this reason economists call this output a **break-even point**: an output at which a firm makes a *normal profit* but not an economic profit. If we extended the data beyond 10 units of output, another break-even point would occur where total cost catches up with total revenue, somewhere between 13 and 14 units of output in Figure 10.2a. Any output within the two break-even points identified in the figure will produce an economic profit. The firm achieves maximum profit, however, where the vertical distance between the total-revenue and total-cost curves is greatest. For our particular data,

Table 10.3

The Profit-Maximizing Output for a Purely Competitive Firm: Total-Revenue–Total-Cost Approach (Price = $131)

(1) Total Product (output) (Q)	(2) Total Fixed Cost (TFC)	(3) Total Variable Cost (TVC)	(4) Total Cost (TC)	(5) Total Revenue (TR)	(6) Profit (+) or Loss (−)
				Price: **$131**	
0	$100	$ 0	$ 100	$ 0	$ −100
1	100	90	190	131	− 59
2	100	170	270	262	− 8
3	100	240	340	393	+ 53
4	100	300	400	524	+124
5	100	370	470	655	+185
6	100	450	550	786	+236
7	100	540	640	917	+277
8	100	650	750	1048	+298
9	100	780	**880**	**1179**	**+299**
10	100	930	1030	1310	+280

(a)
Profit-maximizing case

(b)
Total economic profit

Figure 10.2

Total-revenue–total-cost approach to profit maximization for a purely competitive firm. (a) The firm's profit is maximized at that output (9 units) where total revenue, TR, exceeds total cost, TC, by the maximum amount. (b) The vertical distance between TR and TC in (a) is plotted as a total-economic-profit curve. Maximum economic profit is $299 at 9 units of output.

this is at 9 units of output, where maximum profit is $299.

The profit-maximizing output is easier to see in Figure 10.2b, where total profit is graphed for each level of output. Where the total-revenue and total-cost curves intersect in Figure 10.2a, economic profit is zero, as shown by the total-profit line in Figure 10.2b. Where the vertical distance between TR and TC is greatest in the upper graph, economic profit is at its peak ($299), as shown in the lower graph. This firm will choose to produce 9 units, since that output maximizes its profit.

Marginal-Revenue–Marginal-Cost Approach

In the second approach, the firm compares the amounts that each *additional* unit of output would add to total revenue and to total cost. In other words, the firm compares the *marginal revenue* (MR) and the *marginal cost* (MC) of each successive unit of output. Assuming that producing is preferable to shutting down, the firm should produce any unit of output whose marginal revenue exceeds its marginal cost because the firm would gain more in revenue from selling that unit than it would add to its costs by producing it. Conversely, if the marginal cost of a unit of output exceeds its marginal revenue, the firm should not produce that unit. Producing it would add more to costs than to revenue, and profit would decline or loss would increase.

MR = MC Rule In the initial stages of production, where output is relatively low, marginal revenue will usually (but not always) exceed marginal cost. So it is profitable to produce through this range of output. But at later stages of production, where output is relatively high, rising marginal costs will exceed marginal revenue. Obviously, a profit-maximizing firm will want to avoid output levels in that range. Separating these two production ranges is a unique point at which marginal revenue equals marginal cost. This point is the key to the output-determining rule: *In the short run, the firm will maximize profit or minimize loss by producing the output at which marginal revenue equals marginal cost (as long as producing is preferable to shutting down).* This profit-maximizing guide is known as the **MR = MC rule.** (For most sets of MR and MC data, MR and MC will be precisely equal at a fractional level of output. In such instances the firm should produce the last complete unit of output for which MR exceeds MC.)

Three Characteristics of the MR = MC Rule Keep in mind these three features of the MR = MC rule:

- As noted, the rule applies only if producing is preferable to shutting down. We will show shortly

that if marginal revenue does not equal or exceed average variable cost, the firm will shut down rather than produce the MR = MC output.

- The rule is an accurate guide to profit maximization for all firms whether they are purely competitive, monopolistic, monopolistically competitive, or oligopolistic.
- The rule can be restated as $P = MC$ when applied to a purely competitive firm. Because the demand schedule faced by a competitive seller is perfectly elastic at the going market price, product price and marginal revenue are equal. So under pure competition (and only under pure competition) we may substitute P for MR in the rule: *When producing is preferable to shutting down, the competitive firm that wants to maximize its profit or minimize its loss should produce at that point where price equals marginal cost ($P = MC$).*

Now let's apply the MR = MC rule or, because we are considering pure competition, the $P = MC$ rule, first using the same price as used in our total-revenue–total-cost approach to profit maximization. Then, by considering other prices, we will demonstrate two additional cases: loss minimization and shutdown. *It is crucial that you understand the MR = MC analysis that follows since it reappears in Chapters 11 and 12.*

Profit-Maximizing Case The first five columns in Table 10.4 reproduce the AFC, AVC, ATC, and MC data derived for our product in Table 9.2. It is the marginal-cost data of column 5 that we will

Table 10.4

The Profit-Maximizing Output for a Purely Competitive Firm: Marginal-Revenue–Marginal-Cost Approach (Price = $131)

(1) Total Product (Output)	(2) Average Fixed Cost (AFC)	(3) Average Variable Cost (AVC)	(4) Average Total Cost (ATC)	(5) Marginal Cost (MC)	(6) Price = Marginal Revenue (MR)	(7) Total Economic Profit (+) or Loss (−)
0						$−100
1	$100.00	$90.00	$190.00	$ 90	$131	− 59
2	50.00	85.00	135.00	80	131	− 8
3	33.33	80.00	113.33	70	131	+ 53
4	25.00	75.00	100.00	60	131	+124
5	20.00	74.00	94.00	70	131	+185
6	16.67	75.00	91.67	80	131	+236
7	14.29	77.14	91.43	90	131	+277
8	12.50	81.25	93.75	110	131	+298
9	**11.11**	**86.67**	**97.78**	**130**	**131**	**+299**
10	10.00	93.00	103.00	150	131	+280

compare with price (equals marginal revenue) for each unit of output. Suppose first that the market price, and therefore marginal revenue, is $131, as shown in column 6.

What is the profit-maximizing output? Every unit of output up to and including the ninth unit represents greater marginal revenue than marginal cost of output. Each of the first 9 units therefore adds to the firm's profit and should be produced. The tenth unit, however, should not be produced. It would add more to cost ($150) than to revenue ($131).

Profit Calculations

The economic profit realized by producing 9 units can be calculated from the average-total-cost data. Multiplying price ($131) by output (9), we find that total revenue is $1179. Multiplying average total cost ($97.78) by output (9) gives us total cost of $880.[2] The difference of $299 (= $1179 − $880) is the economic profit. Clearly, this firm will prefer to operate rather than shut down.

Perhaps an easier way to calculate the economic profit is to determine the profit per unit by subtracting the average total cost ($97.78) from the product price ($131) and multiplying the difference

---

[2]Most of the unit-cost data are rounded figures. Therefore, economic profits calculated from them will typically vary by a few cents from the profits determined in the total-revenue–total-cost approach. Here we simply ignore the few-cents differentials to make our answers consistent with the results of the total-revenue–total-cost approach.

(a per-unit profit of $33.22) by output (9). Take some time now to verify the numbers in column 7 in Table 10.4. You will find that any output other than that which adheres to the MR = MC rule will mean either profits below $299 or losses.

Graphical Portrayal

Figure 10.3 (Key Graph) shows price (= MR) and marginal cost graphically. Price equals marginal cost at the profit-maximizing output of 9 units. There the per-unit economic profit is $P − A$, where P is the market price and A is the average total cost for an output of 9 units. The total economic profit is $9 \times (P − A)$, shown by the taupe rectangular area. 10.1

Note that the firm wants to maximize its total profit, not its per-unit profit. Per-unit profit is greatest at 7 units of output, where price exceeds average total cost by $39.57 (= $131 − $91.43). But by producing only 7 units, the firm would be forgoing the production of 2 additional units of output that would clearly contribute to total profit. The firm is happy to accept lower per-unit profits for additional units of output because they nonetheless add to total profit.

Loss-Minimizing Case

Now let's assume that the market price is $81 rather than $131. Should the firm still produce? If so, how much? And what will be the resulting profit or loss? The answers, respectively, are "Yes," "Six units," and "A loss of $64."

The first five columns in Table 10.5 are the same as those in Table 10.4. Column 6 shows the new

Table 10.5

The Loss-Minimizing Outputs for a Purely Competitive Firm: Marginal-Revenue–Marginal-Cost Approach (Prices = $81 and $71)

(1) Total Product (Output)	(2) Average Fixed Cost (AFC)	(3) Average Variable Cost (AVC)	(4) Average Total Cost (ATC)	(5) Marginal Cost (MC)	(6) $81 Price = Marginal Revenue (MR)	(7) Profit (+) or Loss (−), $81 Price	(8) $71 Price = Marginal Revenue (MR)	(9) Profit (+) or Loss (−) $71 Price
0						$ − 100		**$− 100**
1	$100.00	$90.00	$190.00	$ 90	$81	−109	$71	−119
2	50.00	85.00	135.00	80	81	−108	71	−128
3	33.33	80.00	113.33	70	81	− 97	71	−127
4	25.00	75.00	100.00	60	81	− 76	71	−116
5	20.00	74.00	94.00	70	81	− 65	71	−115
6	**16.67**	**75.00**	**91.67**	**80**	**81**	**− 64**	71	−124
7	14.29	77.14	91.43	90	81	− 73	71	−143
8	12.50	81.25	93.75	110	81	−102	71	−182
9	11.11	86.67	97.78	130	81	−151	71	−241
10	10.00	93.00	103.00	150	81	−220	71	−320

KEY GRAPH

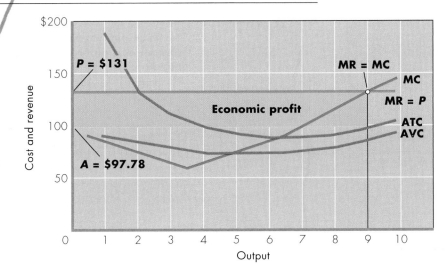

price (equal to MR), $81. Comparing columns 5 and 6, we find that the first unit of output adds $90 to total cost but only $81 to total revenue. One might conclude: "Don't produce—close down!" But that would be hasty. Remember that in the very early stages of production, marginal product is low, making marginal cost unusually high. The price–marginal-cost relationship improves with increased production. For units 2 through 6, price exceeds marginal cost. Each of these 5 units adds more to revenue than to cost, and as shown in column 7, they decrease the total loss. Together they more than compensate for the "loss" taken on the first unit. Beyond 6 units, however, MC exceeds MR (= P). The firm should therefore produce 6 units. In general, the

profit-seeking producer should always compare marginal revenue (or price under pure competition) with the rising portion of the marginal-cost schedule or curve.

Loss Determination Will production be profitable? No, because at 6 units of output the average total cost of $91.67 exceeds the price of $81 by $10.67 per unit. If we multiply that by the 6 units of output, we find the firm's total loss is $64. Alternatively, comparing the total revenue of $486 (= 6 × $81) with the total cost of $550 (= 6 × $91.67), we see again that the firm's loss is $64.

Then why produce? Because this loss is less than the firm's $100 of fixed costs, which is the $100 loss

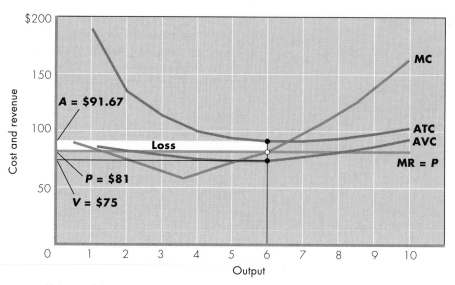

Figure 10.4

The short-run loss-minimizing position of a purely competitive firm. If price P exceeds the minimum AVC (here $74 at Q = 5) but is less than ATC, the MR = MC output (here 6 units) will permit the firm to minimize its losses. In this instance the loss is A − P per unit, where A is the average total cost at 6 units of output. The total loss is shown by the white area and is equal to 6 × (A − P).

the firm would incur in the short run by closing down. The firm receives enough revenue per unit ($81) to cover its average variable costs of $75 and also provide $6 per unit, or a total of $36, to apply against fixed costs. Therefore, the firm's loss is only $64 (= $100 − $36), not $100. ![] 10.1

Graphical Portrayal This loss-minimizing case is shown graphically in Figure 10.4. Wherever price *P* exceeds average variable cost AVC, the firm can pay part, but not all, of its fixed costs by producing. The loss is minimized by producing the output at which MC = MR (here, 6 units). At that output, each unit contributes *P − V* to covering fixed cost, where *V* is the AVC at 6 units of output. The

per-unit loss is *A − P* = $10.67, and the total loss is 6 × (*A − P*), or $64, as shown by the white area.

Shutdown Case   Suppose now that the market yields a price of only $71. Should the firm produce? No, because at every output the firm's average variable cost is greater than the price (compare columns 3 and 8 in Table 10.5). The smallest loss it can incur by producing is greater than the $100 fixed cost it will lose by shutting down (as shown by column 9). The best action is to shut down.

You can see this shutdown situation in Figure 10.5. Price comes closest to covering average variable costs at the MR (= *P*) = MC output of 5 units. But even here, price or revenue per unit

Figure 10.5

The short-run shutdown position of a purely competitive firm. If price P falls below the minimum AVC (here $74 at Q = 5), the competitive firm will minimize its losses in the short run by shutting down. There is no level of output at which the firm can produce and realize a loss smaller than its total fixed cost.

would fall short of average variable cost by $3 (= $74 − $71). By producing at the MR (= *P*) = MC output, the firm would lose its $100 worth of fixed cost plus $15 ($3 of variable cost on each of the 5 units), for a total loss of $115. This compares unfavorably with the $100 fixed-cost loss the firm would incur by shutting down and producing no output. So it will make sense for the firm to shut down rather than produce at a $71 price—or at any price less than the minimum average variable cost of $74.

The shutdown case reminds us of the qualifier to our MR (= *P*) = MC rule. A competitive firm will maximize profit or minimize loss in the short run by producing that output at which MR (= *P*) = MC, *provided that market price exceeds minimum average variable cost.*

Min ATC

▮ Marginal Cost and Short-Run Supply

In the preceding section we simply selected three different prices and asked what quantity the profit-seeking competitive firm, faced with certain costs, would choose to offer in the market at each price. This set of product prices and corresponding quantities supplied constitutes part of the supply schedule for the competitive firm.

Table 10.6 summarizes the supply schedule data for those three prices ($131, $81, and $71) and four others. This table confirms the direct relationship between product price and quantity supplied that we identified in Chapter 3. Note first that the firm will not produce at price $61 or $71, because both are less than the $74 minimum AVC. Then note that quantity supplied increases as price increases. Observe finally that economic profit is higher at higher prices.

Table 10.6

The Supply Schedule of a Competitive Firm Confronted with the Cost Data in Table 10.4

Price	Quantity Supplied	Maximum Profit (+) or Minimum Loss (−)
$151	10	$+480
131	9	+299
111	8	+138
91	7	− 3
81	6	− 64
71	0	−100
61	0	−100

Generalized Depiction

Figure 10.6 (Key Graph) generalizes the MR = MC rule and the relationship between short-run production costs and the firm's supply behavior. The ATC, AVC, and MC curves are shown, along with several marginal-revenue lines drawn at possible market prices. Let's observe quantity supplied at each of these prices:

- Price P_1 is below the firm's minimum average variable cost, so at this price the firm won't operate at all. Quantity supplied will be zero, as it will be at all other prices below P_2.
- Price P_2 is just equal to the minimum average variable cost. The firm will supply Q_2 units of output (where $MR_2 = MC$) and just cover its total variable cost. Its loss will equal its total fixed cost. (Actually, the firm would be indifferent as to shutting down or supplying Q_2 units of output, but we assume it produces.)
- At price P_3 the firm will supply Q_3 units of output to minimize its short-run losses. At any other price between P_2 and P_4 the firm will minimize its losses by producing and supplying the quantity at which MR (= *P*) = MC.
- The firm will just break even at price P_4. There it will supply Q_4 units of output (where $MR_4 = MC$), earning a normal profit but not an economic profit. Total revenue will just cover total cost, including a normal profit, because the revenue per unit ($MR_4 = P_4$) and the total cost per unit (ATC) are the same.
- At price P_5 the firm will realize an economic profit by producing and supplying Q_5 units of output. In fact, at any price above P_4 the firm will obtain economic profit by producing to the point where MR (= *P*) = MC.

Note that each of the MR (= *P*) = MC intersection points labeled *b*, *c*, *d* and *e* in Figure 10.6 indicates a possible product price (on the vertical axis) and the corresponding quantity that the firm would supply at that price (on the horizontal axis). Thus, points such as these are on the upsloping supply curve of the competitive firm. Note too that quantity supplied would be zero at any price below the minimum average variable cost (AVC). We can conclude that the portion of the firm's marginal-cost curve lying above its average-variable-cost curve is its short-run supply curve. In Figure 10.6, the solid segment of the marginal-cost curve MC is this firm's **short-run supply curve.** It tells us the amount of output the firm will supply at each price in a series of prices.

KEY GRAPH

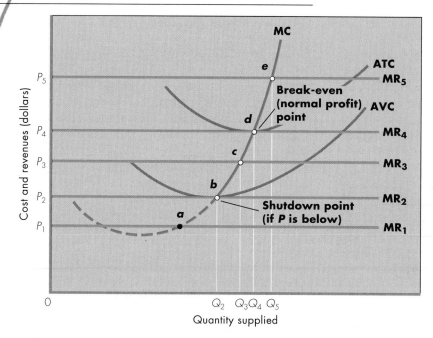

Figure 10.6

The $P = MC$ rule and the competitive firm's short-run supply curve.
Application of the $P = MC$ rule, as modified by the shutdown case, reveals that the (solid) segment of the firm's MC curve that lies above AVC is the firm's short-run supply curve. More specifically, at price P_1, $P = MC$ at point a, but the firm will produce no output because P_1 is less than minimum AVC. At price P_2 the firm will operate at point b, where it produces Q_2 units and incurs a loss equal to its total fixed cost. At P_3 it operates at point c, where output is Q_3 and loss is less than total fixed cost. With the price of P_4, the firm operates at point d; in this case the firm earns a normal profit because at output Q_4 price equals ATC. At price P_5 the firm operates at point e and maximizes its economic profit by producing Q_5 units.

Quick Quiz 10.6

1. Which of the following might increase product price from P_3 to P_5?
   a. An improvement in production technology.
   b. A decline in the price of a substitute good.
   c. An increase in the price of a complementary good.
   d. Rising incomes if the product is a normal good.

2. An increase in price from P_3 to P_5 would:
   a. shift this firm's MC curve to the right.
   b. mean that MR_5 exceeds MC at Q_3 units, inducing the firm to expand output to Q_5.
   c. decrease this firm's average variable costs.
   d. enable this firm to obtain a normal, but not an economic, profit.

3. At P_4:
   a. this firm has no economic profit.
   b. this firm will earn only a normal profit and thus will shut down.
   c. MR_4 will be less than MC at the profit-maximizing output.
   d. the profit-maximizing output will be Q_5.

4. Suppose P_4 is $10, P_5 is $15, Q_4 is 8 units, and Q_5 is 10 units. This firm's:
   a. supply curve is elastic over the Q_4–Q_5 range of output.
   b. supply curve is inelastic over the Q_4–Q_5 range of output.
   c. total revenue will decline if price rises from P_4 to P_5.
   d. marginal-cost curve will shift downward if price falls from P_5 to P_4.

Answers: 1. d; 2. b; 3. a; 4. b

Diminishing Returns, Production Costs, and Product Supply

We have now identified the links between the law of diminishing returns (Chapter 9), production costs, and product supply in the short run. Because of the law of diminishing returns, marginal cost eventually rises as more units of output are produced. And because marginal cost rises with output, a purely competitive firm must get successively higher prices to motivate it to produce additional units of output.

Viewed alternatively, higher product prices and marginal revenue encourage a purely competitive firm to expand output. As its output increases, the firm's marginal costs rise as a result of the law of diminishing returns. At some now greater output, this higher MC equals the new product price and

MR. Profit once again is maximized, but at a greater total amount. Quantity supplied has increased in direct response to an increase in product price and the desire to maximize profit.

Changes in Supply

In Chapter 9 we saw that changes in such factors as the prices of variable inputs or in technology will alter costs and shift the marginal-cost or short-run supply curve to a new location. All else equal, for example, a wage increase would increase marginal cost and shift the supply curve in Figure 10.6 upward as viewed from the horizontal axis (leftward as viewed from the vertical axis). That is, supply would decrease. Similarly, technological progress that increases the productivity of labor would reduce marginal cost and shift the marginal-cost or supply curve downward as viewed from the horizontal axis (rightward as viewed from the vertical axis). This represents an increase in supply.

Firm and Industry: Equilibrium Price

In the preceding section we developed the competitive firm's short-run supply curve by applying the MR (= P) = MC rule. We now determine which of the various possible prices will actually be the market equilibrium price.

From Chapter 3 we know that in a purely competitive market, equilibrium price is determined by total, or market, supply and total demand. To derive total supply, the supply schedules or curves of the individual competitive sellers must be summed. Columns 1 and 3 in Table 10.7 repeat the supply schedule for the individual competitive firm, as derived in Table 10.6. We now assume that there are 1000 competitive firms in this industry, all having the same total and unit costs as the single firm we discussed. This lets us calculate the market supply schedule (columns 2 and 3) by multiplying the quantity-supplied figures of the single firm (column 1) by 1000.

Market Price and Profits

To determine the equilibrium price and output, these total-supply data must be compared with total-demand data. Let's assume that total demand is as shown in columns 3 and 4 in Table 10.7. By comparing the total quantity

Table 10.7
Firm and Market Supply and Market Demand

(1) Quantity Supplied, Single Firm	(2) Total Quantity Supplied, 1000 Firms	(3) Product Price	(4) Total Quantity Demanded
10	10,000	$151	4,000
9	9,000	131	6,000
8	**8,000**	**111**	**8,000**
7	7,000	91	9,000
6	6,000	81	11,000
0	0	71	13,000
0	0	61	16,000

supplied and the total quantity demanded at the seven possible prices, we determine that the equilibrium price is $111 and the equilibrium quantity is 8000 units for the industry—8 units for each of the 1000 identical firms.

Will these conditions of market supply and demand make this a prosperous or an unprosperous industry? Multiplying produce price ($111) by output (8 units), we find that the total revenue of each firm is $888. The total cost is $750, found by looking at column 4 in Table 10.3. The $138 difference is the economic profit of each firm. For the industry, total economic profit is $138,000. This, then, is a prosperous industry.

Another way of calculating economic profit is to determine per-unit profit by subtracting average total cost ($93.75) from product price ($111) and multiplying the difference (per-unit profit of $17.25) by the firm's equilibrium level of output (8). Again we obtain an economic profit of $138 per firm and $138,000 for the industry.

Graphical Portrayal

Figure 10.7 shows this analysis graphically. The individual supply curves of each of the 1000 identical firms—one of which is shown as $s = MC$ in Figure 10.7a—are summed horizontally to get the total-supply curve $S = \Sigma MC$ of Figure 10.7b. With total-demand curve D, it yields the equilibrium price $111 and equilibrium quantity (for the industry) 8000 units. This equilibrium price is given and unalterable to the individual firm; that is, each firm's demand curve is perfectly elastic at the equilibrium price, as

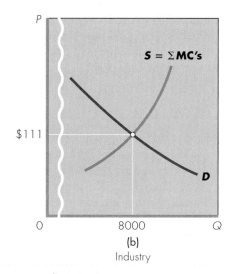

(a)
Single firm

(b)
Industry

Figure 10.7

Short-run competitive equilibrium for (a) a firm and (b) the industry. The horizontal sum of the 1000 firms' individual supply curves (s) determines the industry supply curve (S). Given industry demand (D), the short-run equilibrium price and output for the industry are $111 and 8000 units. Taking the equilibrium price as given, the individual firm establishes its profit-maximizing output at 8 units and, in this case, realizes the economic profit represented by the taupe area.

indicated by *d* in Figure 10.7a. Because the individual firm is a price taker, the marginal-revenue curve coincides with the firm's demand curve *d*. This $111 price exceeds the average total cost at the firm's equilibrium MR = MC output of 8 units, so the firm earns an economic profit represented by the taupe area in Figure 10.7a.

Assuming no changes in costs or market demand, these diagrams reveal a genuine equilibrium in the short run. There are no shortages or surpluses in the market to cause price or total quantity to change. Nor can any firm in the industry increase its profit by altering its output. Note, too, that higher unit and marginal costs, on the one hand, or weaker market demand, on the other, could change the situation so that Figure 10.7a resembles Figure 10.4 or Figure 10.5. In Figure 10.7a and 10.7b, sketch how higher costs or decreased demand could produce short-run losses.

Firm versus Industry   Figure 10.7 underscores a point made earlier: Product price is a given fact to the *individual* competitive firm, but the supply plans of all competitive producers *as a group* are a basic determinant of product price. If we recall the fallacy of composition, we find there is no inconsistency here. Although one firm, supplying a negligible frac-

tion of total supply, cannot affect price, the sum of the supply curves of all the firms in the industry constitutes the industry supply curve, and that curve does have an important bearing on price. **(Key Question 4)**

QUICK REVIEW 10.2

■ Profit is maximized, or loss minimized, at the output at which marginal revenue (or price in pure competition) equals marginal cost, provided that price exceeds average variable cost.

■ If the market price is below the minimum average variable cost, the firm will minimize its losses by shutting down.

■ The segment of the firm's marginal-cost curve that lies above the average-variable-cost curve is its short-run supply curve.

■ Table 10.8 summarizes the MR = MC approach to determining the competitive firm's profit-maximizing output. It also shows the equivalent analysis in terms of total revenue and total cost.

■ Under competition, equilibrium price is a given to the individual firm and simultaneously is the result of the production (supply) decisions of all firms as a group.

Table 10.8

Output Determination in Pure Competition in the Short Run

Question	Answer
Should this firm produce?	Yes, if price is equal to, or greater than, minimum average variable cost. This means that the firm is profitable or that its losses are less than its fixed cost.
What quantity should this firm produce?	Produce where MR (= *P*) = MC; there, profit is maximized (TR exceeds TC by a maximum amount) or loss is minimized.
Will production result in economic profit?	Yes, if price exceeds average total cost (TR will exceed TC). No, if average total cost exceeds price (TC will exceed TR).

■ Profit Maximization in the Long Run

In the short run the industry is composed of a specific number of firms, each with a fixed, unalterable plant. Firms may shut down in the sense that they can produce zero units of output in the short run, but they do not have sufficient time to liquidate their assets and go out of business. By contrast, in the long run firms already in an industry have sufficient time either to expand or to contract their plant capacities. More important, the number of firms in the industry may either increase or decrease as new firms enter or existing firms leave. We now examine how these long-run adjustments modify our conclusions concerning short-run output and price determination.

Assumptions

We make three simplifying assumptions, none of which affects our conclusions:

- ■ *Entry and exit only* The only long-run adjustment is the entry or exit of firms. Moreover, we ignore all short-run adjustments in order to concentrate on the effects of the long-run adjustments.
- ■ *Identical costs* All firms in the industry have identical cost curves. This assumption lets us discuss an "average," or "representative," firm, knowing that all other firms in the industry are similarly affected by any long-run adjustments that occur.
- ■ *Constant-cost industry* The industry is a constant-cost industry. This means that the entry and exit of firms does not affect resource prices or, consequently, the locations of the average-total-cost curves of individual firms.

Goal of Our Analysis

The basic conclusion we seek to explain is this: After all long-run adjustments are completed, product price will be exactly equal to, and production will occur at, each firm's minimum average total cost.

This conclusion follows from two basic facts: (1) Firms seek profits and shun losses, and (2) under pure competition, firms are free to enter and leave an industry. If market price initially exceeds average total costs, the resulting economic profits will attract new firms to the industry. But this industry expansion will increase supply until price is brought back down to equality with minimum average total cost. Conversely, if price is initially less than average total cost, resulting losses will cause firms to leave the industry. As they leave, total supply will decline, bringing the price back up to equality with minimum average total cost.

Long-Run Equilibrium

Consider the average firm in a purely competitive industry that is initially in long-run equilibrium. This firm is represented in Figure 10.8a, where MR = MC and price and minimum average total cost are equal at $50. Economic profit here is zero; the industry is in equilibrium or "at rest" because there is no tendency for firms to enter or to leave. The existing firms are earning normal profits, which, recall, are included in their cost curves. The $50 market price is determined in Figure 10.8b by market or industry demand D_1 and supply S_1. (S_1 is a short-run supply curve; we will develop the long-run industry supply curve in our discussion.)

As shown on the quantity axes of the two graphs, equilibrium output in the industry is 100,000 while equilibrium output for the single firm is 100. If all

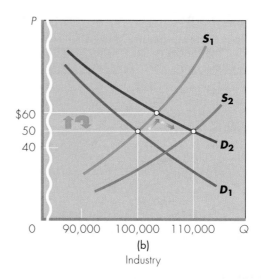

(a)
Single firm

(b)
Industry

Figure 10.8

Temporary profits and the reestablishment of long-run equilibrium in (a) a representative firm and (b) the industry. A favorable shift in demand (D_1 to D_2) will upset the original industry equilibrium and produce economic profits. But those profits will cause new firms to enter the industry, increasing supply (S_1 to S_2) and lowering product price until economic profits are once again zero.

firms in the industry are identical, there must be 1000 firms (= 100,000/100).

Entry Eliminates Economic Profits
Let's upset the long-run equilibrium in Figure 10.8 and see what happens. Suppose a change in consumer tastes increases product demand from D_1 to D_2. Price will rise to $60, as determined at the intersection of D_2 and S_1, and the firm's marginal-revenue curve will shift upward to $60. This $60 price exceeds the firm's average total cost of $50 at output 100, creating an economic profit of $10 per unit. This economic profit will lure new firms into the industry. Some entrants will be newly created firms; others will shift from less prosperous industries.

As firms enter, the market supply of the product increases, pushing the product price below $60. Economic profits persist, and entry continues until short-run supply increases to S_2. Market price falls to $50, as does marginal revenue for the firm. Price and minimum average total cost are again equal at $50. The economic profits caused by the boost in demand have been eliminated, and, as a result, the previous incentive for more firms to enter the industry has disappeared. Long-run equilibrium has been restored.

Observe in Figure 10.8a and 10.8b that total quantity supplied is now 110,000 units and each firm

is producing 100 units. Now 1100 firms rather than the original 1000 populate the industry. Economic profits have attracted 100 more firms.

Exit Eliminates Losses
Now let's consider a shift in the opposite direction. We begin in Figure 10.9b with curves S_1 and D_1 setting the same initial long-run equilibrium situation as in our previous analysis, including the $50 price.

Suppose consumer demand declines from D_1 to D_3. This forces the market price and marginal revenue down to $40, making production unprofitable at the minimum ATC of $50. In time the resulting losses will induce firms to leave the industry. Their owners will seek a normal profit elsewhere rather than accept the below-normal profits (loss) now confronting them. And as capital equipment wears out, some firms will simply go out of business. As this exodus of firms proceeds, however, industry supply decreases, pushing the price up from $40 toward $50. Losses continue and more firms leave the industry until the supply curve shifts to S_3. Once this happens, price is again $50, just equal to the minimum average total cost. Losses have been eliminated and long-run equilibrium is restored.

In Figure 10.9a and 10.9b, total quantity supplied is now 90,000 units and each firm is producing 100 units. Only 900 firms, not the original

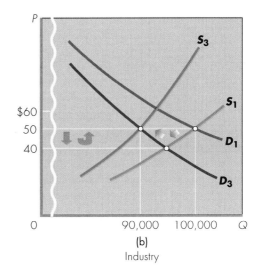

(a)
Single firm

(b)
Industry

Figure 10.9

Temporary losses and the reestablishment of long-run equilibrium in (a) a representative firm and (b) the industry. An unfavorable shift in demand (D_1 to D_3) will upset the original industry equilibrium and produce losses. But those losses will cause firms to leave the industry, decreasing supply (S_1 to S_3) and increasing product price until all losses have disappeared.

1000, populate the industry. Losses have forced 100 firms out.

You may have noted that we have sidestepped the question of which firms will leave the industry when losses occur by assuming that all firms have identical cost curves. In the "real world," of course, entrepreneurial talents differ. Even if resource prices and technology are the same for all firms, inferior entrepreneurs tend to incur higher costs and therefore are the first to leave an industry when demand declines. Similarly, firms with less productive labor forces will be higher-cost producers and likely candidates to quit an industry when demand decreases.

We have now reached an intermediate goal: Our analysis verifies that competition, reflected in the entry and exit of firms, eliminates economic profits or losses by adjusting price to equal minimum long-run average total cost. In addition, this competition forces firms to select output levels at which average total cost is minimized.

Long-Run Supply for a Constant-Cost Industry

Although our analysis has dealt with the long run, we have noted that the market supply curves in Figures 10.8b and 10.9b are short-run curves. What then is the character of the **long-run supply curve**

of a competitive industry? The analysis points us toward an answer. The crucial factor here is the effect, if any, that changes in the number of firms in the industry will have on costs of the individual firms in the industry.

Constant-Cost Industry   In our analysis of long-run competitive equilibrium we assumed that the industry under discussion was a **constant-cost industry.** This means that industry expansion or contraction will not affect resource prices and therefore production costs. Graphically, it means that the entry or exit of firms does not shift the long-run ATC curves of individual firms. This is the case when the industry's demand for resources is small in relation to the total demand for those resources. Then the industry can expand or contract without significantly affecting resource prices and costs.

Perfectly Elastic Long-Run Supply   What does the long-run supply curve of a constant-cost industry look like? The answer is contained in our previous analysis. There we saw that the entry and exit of firms changes industry output but always brings the product price back to its original level, where it is just equal to the constant minimum ATC. Specifically, we discovered that the industry would supply 90,000, 100,000, or 110,000 units of output, all at a price of $50 per unit. In other words, the long-run supply curve of a constant-cost industry is perfectly elastic.

This is demonstrated graphically in Figure 10.10, which uses data from Figures 10.8 and 10.9. Suppose industry demand is originally D_1, industry output is Q_1 (100,000 units), and product price is P_1 ($50). This situation, from Figure 10.8, is one of long-run equilibrium. We saw that when demand increases to D_2, upsetting this equilibrium, the resulting economic profits attract new firms. Because this is a constant-cost industry, entry continues and industry output expands until the price is driven back down to the level of the unchanged minimum ATC. This is at price P_2 ($50) and output Q_2 (110,000).

From Figure 10.9, we saw that a decline in market demand from D_1 to D_3 causes an exit of firms and ultimately restores equilibrium at price P_3 ($50) and output Q_3 (90,000 units). The points Z_1, Z_2, and Z_3 in Figure 10.10 represent these three price-quantity combinations. A line or curve connecting all such points shows the various price-quantity combinations that firms would produce if they had enough time to make all desired adjustments to changes in demand. This line or curve is the industry's long-run supply curve. In a constant-cost industry this curve (straight line) is horizontal, as in Figure 10.10, thus representing perfectly elastic supply.

Long-Run Supply for an Increasing-Cost Industry

Constant-cost industries are a special case. Most industries are **increasing-cost industries,** in which firms' ATC curves shift upward as the industry expands and downward as the industry contracts. Usually, the entry of new firms will increase resource prices, particularly in industries using specialized resources whose supplies are not readily increased in response to an increase in resource demand. Higher resource prices result in higher long-run average total costs for all firms in the industry. These higher costs cause upward shifts in each firm's long-run ATC curve.

Thus, when an increase in product demand results in economic profits and attracts new firms to an increasing-cost industry, a two-way squeeze works to eliminate those profits. As before, the entry of new firms increases market supply and lowers the market price. But now the entire ATC curve shifts upward. The overall result is a higher-than-original equilibrium price. The industry produces a larger output at a higher product price because the industry expansion has increased resource prices and the minimum average total cost. We know that, in the long run, the product price must cover ATC.

Since greater output will be supplied at a higher price, the long-run industry supply curve is upsloping. Instead of supplying 90,000, 100,000, or 110,000 units at the same price of $50, an increasing-cost industry might supply 90,000 units at $45, 100,000 units at $50, and 110,000 units at $55. A higher price is required to induce more production, because costs per unit of output increase as production rises.

We show this in Figure 10.11. Original market demand is D_1 and industry price and output are P_1 ($50) and Q_1 (100,000 units), respectively, at equilibrium point Y_1. An increase in demand to D_2 upsets this equilibrium and leads to economic profits. New firms enter the industry, increasing both market supply and production costs of individual firms. A

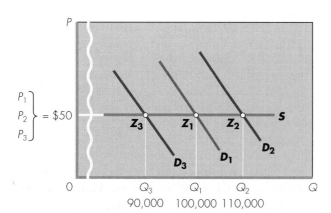

Figure 10.10

The long-run supply curve for a constant-cost industry is horizontal. Because the entry or exodus of firms does not affect resource prices or, therefore, unit costs, an increase in demand (D_1 to D_2) causes an expansion in industry output (Q_1 to Q_2) but no alteration in price ($50). Similarly, a decrease in demand (D_1 to D_3) causes a contraction of output (Q_1 to Q_3) but no change in price. This means that the long-run industry supply curve (S) is horizontal through points Z_1, Z_2 and Z_3.

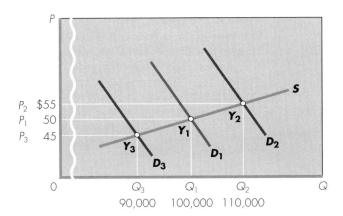

Figure 10.11
The long-run supply curve for an increasing-cost industry is upsloping. In an increasing-cost industry the entry of new firms in response to an increase in demand (D_3 to D_1 to D_2) will bid up resource prices and thereby increase unit costs. As a result, an increased industry output (Q_3 to Q_1 to Q_2) will be forthcoming only at higher prices ($\$55 > \$50 > \$45$). The long-run industry supply curve (S) therefore slopes upward through points Y_3, Y_1, and, Y_2.

new price is established at point Y_2, where P_2 is $55 and Q_2 is 110,000 units.

Conversely, a decline in demand from D_1 to D_3 makes production unprofitable and causes firms to leave the industry. The resulting decline in resource prices reduces the minimum average total cost of production for firms that stay. A new equilibrium price is established at some level below the original price, say, at point Y_3, where P_3 is $45 and Q_3 is 90,000 units. Connecting these three equilibrium positions, we derive the upsloping long-run supply curve S in Figure 10.11.

Long-Run Supply for a Decreasing-Cost Industry

In **decreasing-cost industries,** firms experience lower costs as the industry expands. The personal computer industry is an example. As demand for personal computers increased, new manufacturers of computers entered the industry and greatly increased the resource demand for the components used to build them (for example, memory chips, hard drives, monitors, and operating software). The expanded production of the components enabled the producers of those items to achieve substantial economies of scale. The decreased production costs of the components reduced their prices, which greatly lowered the computer manufacturers' average costs of production. The supply of personal computers increased by more than demand, and the price of personal computers declined.

We urge you to rework the analysis underlying Figure 10.11 to show that the long-run supply curve of a decreasing-cost industry is *downsloping*. (**Key Question 6**)

▌Pure Competition and Efficiency

Our final goal in this chapter is to relate pure competition to efficiency. Whether a purely competitive industry is a constant-cost industry or an increasing-cost industry, the final long-run equilibrium positions of all firms have the same basic characteristics relating to economic efficiency. As shown in **Figure 10.12 (Key Graph),** price (and marginal revenue) will settle where it is equal to minimum average total cost: P (and MR) = minimum ATC. Moreover, since the marginal-cost curve intersects the average-total-cost curve at its minimum point, marginal cost and average total cost are equal: MC = minimum ATC. Thus in long-run equilibrium there is a multiple equality: P (and MR) = MC = minimum ATC.

This triple equality tells us that although a competitive firm may realize economic profit or loss in the short run, it will earn only a normal profit by producing in accordance with the MR (= P) = MC rule in the long run. Also, this triple equality suggests certain conclusions of great social significance concerning the efficiency of a purely competitive economy.

Economists agree that, subject to qualifications discussed in later chapters, an idealized purely competitive economy leads to an efficient use of society's scarce resources. A competitive market economy uses the limited amounts of resources available to society in a way that maximizes the satisfaction of consumers. As we demonstrated in Chapter 2, efficient use of limited resources requires both productive efficiency and allocative efficiency.

Productive efficiency requires that goods be produced in the least costly way. **Allocative efficiency** requires that resources be apportioned among

KEY GRAPH

Figure 10.12

The long-run equilibrium position of a competitive firm: *P* = MC = minimum ATC. The equality of price and minimum average total cost indicates that the firm is using the most efficient known technology and is charging the lowest price *P* and producing the greatest output *Q* consistent with its costs. The equality of price and marginal cost indicates that resources are being allocated in accordance with consumer preferences.

Quick Quiz 10.12

1. We know this firm is a price taker because:
   a. its MC curve slopes upward.
   b. its ATC curve is U-shaped.
   c. its MR curve is horizontal.
   d. MC and ATC are equal at the profit-maximizing output.

2. This firm's MC curve is rising because:
   a. it is a price taker,
   b. of the law of diminishing marginal utility.
   c. wage rates rise as output expands.
   d. of the law of diminishing marginal returns.

3. At this firm's profit-maximizing output:
   a. total revenue equals total cost.
   b. it is earning an economic profit.
   c. allocative, but not necessarily productive, efficiency is achieved.
   d. productive, but not necessarily allocative, efficiency is achieved.

4. The equality of *P*, MC, and minimum ATC:
   a. occurs only in constant-cost industries.
   b. encourages entry of new firms.
   c. means that the "right goods" are being produced in the "right ways."
   d. results in a zero accounting profit.

Answers: 1. c; 2. d; 3. a; 4. c

---

firms and industries so as to yield the mix of products and services that is most wanted by society (consumers). Allocative efficiency has been realized when it is impossible to alter the combination of goods produced and achieve a net gain for society. Let's look at how productive and allocative efficiency would be achieved under purely competitive conditions. 🔒 10.1

Productive Efficiency: *P* = Minimum ATC

In the long run, pure competition forces firms to produce at the minimum average total cost of production and to charge a price that is just consistent with that cost. That is a highly favorable situation from the consumer's point of view. It means that unless firms use the best-available (least-cost) production methods and combinations of inputs, they will not survive. Stated differently, it means that the minimum amount of resources will be used to produce any particular output. Let's suppose that output is cucumbers.

In the final equilibrium position shown in Figure 10.9a, each firm in the cucumber industry is producing 100 units (say, pickup truckloads) of output by using $5000 (equal to average total cost of $50 × 100 units) worth of resources. If one firm produced that same output at a total cost of, say, $7000, its resources would be used inefficiently. Society would be faced with a net loss of $2000 worth of alternative products. But this cannot happen in pure competition; this firm would incur a loss of $2000, requiring it either to reduce its costs or go out of business.

Note, too, that consumers benefit from productive efficiency by paying the lowest product price possible under the prevailing technology and cost conditions.

Allocative Efficiency: P = MC

Productive efficiency alone does not ensure the efficient allocation of resources. Least-cost production must be used to provide society with the "right goods"—the goods that consumers want most. Before we can show that the competitive market system does just that, we must discuss the social meaning of product prices. There are two critical elements here:

- The money price of any product is society's measure of the relative worth of an additional unit of that product—for example, cucumbers. So the price of a unit of cucumbers is the marginal benefit derived from that unit of the product.
- Similarly, recalling the idea of opportunity cost, we see that the marginal cost of an additional unit of a product measures the value, or relative worth, of the other goods sacrificed to obtain it. In producing cucumbers, resources are drawn away from producing other goods. The marginal cost of producing a unit of cucumbers measures society's sacrifice of those other goods.

To understand why $P = MC$ defines allocative efficiency, let's first look at situations where that is not the case.

Underallocation: P > MC

In pure competition, a firm will realize the maximum possible profit only by producing where price equals marginal cost (Figure 10.12). Producing fewer cucumbers such that MR (and thus P) exceeds MC yields less than maximum profit. It also entails, from society's viewpoint, an underallocation of resources to this product. The fact that price still exceeds marginal cost indicates that society values additional units of cucumbers more highly than the alternative products the appropriate resources could otherwise produce.

To illustrate, if the price or marginal benefit of a unit of cucumbers is $100 and its marginal cost is $50, producing an additional unit will cause a net increase in total well-being of $50. Society will gain cucumbers valued at $100, while the alternative products sacrificed by allocating more resources to cucumbers would be valued at only $50. Whenever society can gain something valued at $100 by giving up something valued at $50, the initial allocation of resources must have been inefficient.

Overallocation: P < MC

For similar reasons, the production of cucumbers should not go beyond the output at which price equals marginal cost. To produce where MC exceeds MR (and thus P) would yield less than the maximum profit for the producer and, from the viewpoint of society, would entail an overallocation of resources to cucumbers. Producing cucumbers at a level where marginal cost exceeds price (or marginal benefit) means that society is producing cucumbers by sacrificing alternative goods that society values more highly.

For example, if the price of a unit of cucumbers is $75 and its marginal cost is $100, then the production of 1 less unit of cucumbers would result in a net increase in society's total well-being of $25. Society would lose cucumbers valued at $75, but reallocating the freed resources to their best alternative uses would increase the output of some other good valued at $100. Whenever society is able to give up something of lesser value in return for something of greater value, the original allocation of resources must have been inefficient.

Efficient Allocation

Our conclusion must be that in pure competition, when profit-motivated firms produce each good or service to the point where price (marginal benefit) and marginal cost are equal, society's resources are being allocated efficiently. Each item is being produced to the point at which the value of the last unit is equal to the value of the alternative goods sacrificed by its production. Altering the production of cucumbers would reduce consumer satisfaction. Producing cucumbers beyond the $P = MC$ point would sacrifice alternative goods whose value to society exceeds that of the extra cucumbers. Producing cucumbers short of the $P = MC$ point would sacrifice cucumbers that society values more than the alternative goods its resources could produce. (**Key Question 7**)

Dynamic Adjustments

A further attribute of purely competitive markets is their ability to restore efficiency when disrupted by changes in the economy. A change in consumer tastes, resource supplies, or technology will automatically set in motion the appropriate realignments of resources. For example, suppose that cucumbers and pickles become dramatically more popular. First, the price of cucumbers will increase and so, at current output, the price of cucumbers will exceed their marginal cost. At this point efficiency will be lost, but the higher price will create economic profits in the cucumber industry and stimulate its expansion. The profitability of cucumbers will permit the industry to bid resources away from now less pressing uses, say, watermelons. Expansion of the industry will end only when the price of cucumbers and their marginal cost are equal—that is, when allocative efficiency has been restored.

Similarly, a change in the supply of a particular resource—for example, the field laborers who pick cucumbers—or in a production technique will upset an existing price–marginal-cost equality by either raising or lowering marginal cost. The resulting inequality will cause business managers, in either pursuing profit or avoiding loss, to reallocate resources until price once again equals marginal cost. In so doing, they will correct any inefficiency in the allocation of resources that the original change may have temporarily imposed on the economy.

"Invisible Hand" Revisited Finally, the highly efficient allocation of resources that a purely competitive economy promotes comes about because businesses and resource suppliers seek to further their self-interest. The "invisible hand" (chapter 4) is at work in a competitive market system. The competitive system not only maximizes profits for individual producers but, at the same time, creates a pattern of resource allocation that maximizes consumer satisfaction. The invisible hand thus organizes the private interests of producers in a way that is fully in accord with society's interest in using scarce resources efficiently.

QUICK REVIEW 10.3

■ In the long run, the entry of firms into an industry will compete away any economic profits, and the exit of firms will eliminate losses, so price and minimum average total cost are equal.

■ The long-run supply curves of constant-, increasing-, and decreasing-cost industries are horizontal, upsloping, and downsloping, respectively.

■ In purely competitive markets both productive efficiency (price equals minimum average total cost) and allocative efficiency (price equals marginal cost) are achieved in the long run.

Pure Competition and Consumer Surplus

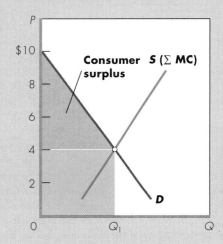

Pure Competition Provides Consumers with the Largest Utility Surplus That Is Consistent with Keeping the Product in Production.

In almost all markets, consumers collectively obtain more utility (total satisfaction) from their purchases than the amount of their expenditures (product price × quantity). This surplus of utility arises because some consumers are willing to pay more than the equilibrium price but need not do so.

Consider the market for oranges depicted in the accompanying figure. The demand curve *D* tells us that some consumers of oranges are willing to pay more than the $4 equilibrium price per bag. For example, assume Bob is willing to pay $9; Barb, $8; Bill, $7; Bart, $6; and Brent, $5. Betty, in contrast, is unwilling to pay one penny more than the $4 equilibrium price.

There are many other consumers besides Bob, Barb, Bill, Bart, and Brent in this market who are willing to pay prices above $4. Only Betty pays exactly the price she is willing to pay; the others receive some amount of utility beyond their expenditures. The difference between that utility value (measured by the vertical height of the points on the demand curve) and the $4 price is called *consumer surplus*. When we add together each buyer's utility surplus, we obtain the consumer surplus for all the consumers in the market. To get the Q_1 bags of oranges, consumers collectively are willing to pay the sum of the amounts represented by the light green triangle and taupe

rectangle. However, they have to pay only the amount represented by the taupe rectangle. The light green triangle thus represents consumer surplus. 🔍 **10.2**

A glance at the figure shows that the amount of consumer surplus—the size of the light green triangle—would be less if the sellers could charge some price above $4. As just one example, at a price of $8, only a very small triangle of consumer surplus would exist. But purely competitive firms cannot charge $8, because they are price takers. Any firm that charged a price above $4 would immediately lose all its business to the other firms.

Moreover, we know that in pure competition the equilibrium price equals the marginal cost of the Q_1 bags of oranges. And, since we are assuming that entry and exit have resulted in this price being equal to the lowest average total cost, each seller is earning only a normal profit. By definition, this profit is just sufficient to continue production of oranges.

The principle that emerges is this: By establishing the lowest price consistent with continued production, pure competition yields the largest sustainable amount of consumer surplus.

SUMMARY

1. Economists group industries into four models based on their market structures: (a) pure competition, (b) pure monopoly, (c) monopolistic competition, and (d) oligopoly.

2. A purely competitive industry consists of a large number of independent firms producing a standardized product. Pure competition assumes that firms and resources are mobile among different industries.

3. In a competitive industry, no single firm can influence market price. This means that the firm's demand curve is perfectly elastic and price equals marginal revenue.

4. We can analyze short-run profit maximization by a competitive firm by comparing total revenue and total cost or by applying marginal analysis. A firm maximizes its short-run profit by producing the output at which total revenue exceeds total cost by the greatest amount.

5. Provided price exceeds minimum average variable cost, a competitive firm maximizes profit or minimizes loss in the short run by producing the output at which price or marginal revenue equals marginal cost. If price is less than average variable cost, the firm minimizes its loss by shutting down. If price is greater than average variable cost but is less than average total cost, the firm minimizes its loss by producing the $P = MC$ output. If price also exceeds average total cost, the firm maximizes its economic profit at the $P = MC$ output.

6. Applying the MR $(= P) = MC$ rule at various possible market prices leads to the conclusion that the segment of the firm's short-run marginal-cost curve that lies above the firm's average-variable-cost curve is its short-run supply curve.

7. In the long run, the market price of a product will equal the minimum average total cost of production. At a higher price, economic profits would cause firms to enter the industry until those profits had been competed away. At a lower price, losses would force the exit of firms from the industry until the product price rose to equal average total cost.

8. The long-run supply curve is horizontal for a constant-cost industry, upsloping for an increasing-cost industry, and downsloping for a decreasing-cost industry.

9. The long-run equality of price and minimum average total cost means that competitive firms will use the most efficient known technology and charge the lowest price consistent with their production costs.

10. The long-run equality of price and marginal cost implies that resources will be allocated in accordance with consumer tastes. The competitive price system will reallocate resources in response to a change in consumer tastes, in technology, or in resource supplies and will thereby maintain allocative efficiency over time.

TERMS AND CONCEPTS

pure competition	price taker	MR = MC rule	decreasing-cost industry
pure monopoly	average revenue	short-run supply curve	productive efficiency
monopolistic competition	total revenue	long-run supply curve	allocative efficiency
oligopoly	marginal revenue	constant-cost industry	
imperfect competition	break-even point	increasing-cost industry	

STUDY QUESTIONS

1. Briefly state the basic characteristics of pure competition, pure monopoly, monopolistic competition, and oligopoly. Under which of these market classifications does each of the following most accurately fit? (*a*) a supermarket in your hometown; (b) the steel industry; (c) a Kansas wheat farm; (d) the commercial bank in which you or your family has an account; (e) the automobile industry. In each case justify your classification.

2. Strictly speaking, pure competition has never existed and probably never will. Then why study it?

3. **Key Question** Use the following demand schedule to determine total revenue and marginal revenue for each possible level of sales:

Product Price	Quantity Demanded	Total Revenue	Marginal Revenue
$2	0	$_____	$_____
2	1	_____	_____
2	2	_____	_____
2	3	_____	_____
2	4	_____	_____
2	5	_____	_____

a. What can you conclude about the structure of the industry in which this firm is operating? Explain.

b. Graph the demand, total-revenue, and marginal-revenue curves for this firm.

c. Why do the demand and marginal-revenue curves coincide?

d. "Marginal revenue is the change in total revenue associated with additional units of output." Explain verbally and graphically, using the data in the table.

4. **Key Question** Assume the following cost data are for a purely competitive producer:

Total Product	Average Fixed Cost	Average Variable Cost	Average Total Cost	Marginal Cost
0				
1	$60.00	$45.00	$105.00	$45
2	30.00	42.50	72.50	40
3	20.00	40.00	60.00	35
4	15.00	37.50	52.50	30
5	12.00	37.00	49.00	35
6	10.00	37.50	47.50	40
7	8.57	38.57	47.14	45
8	7.50	40.63	48.13	55
9	6.67	43.33	50.00	65
10	6.00	46.50	52.50	75

a. At a product price of $56, will this firm produce in the short run? Why or why not? If it is preferable to produce, what will be the profit-maximizing or loss-minimizing output? Explain. What economic profit or loss will the firm realize per unit of output?

b. Answer the relevant questions of 4a assuming product price is $41.

c. Answer the relevant questions of 4a assuming product price is $32.

d. In the table below, complete the short-run supply schedule for the firm (columns 1 and 2) and indicate the profit or loss incurred at each output (column 3).

(1) Price	(2) Quantity Supplied, Single Firm	(3) Profit (+) or Loss (−)	(4) Quantity Supplied, 1500 Firms
$26	____	$____	____
32	____	____	____
38	____	____	____
41	____	____	____
46	____	____	____
56	____	____	____
66	____	____	____

e. Explain: "That segment of a competitive firm's marginal-cost curve that lies above its average-

variable-cost curve constitutes the short-run supply curve for the firm." Illustrate graphically.

f. Now assume that there are 1500 identical firms in this competitive industry; that is, there are 1500 firms, each of which has the cost data shown in the table. Complete the industry supply schedule (column 4).

g. Suppose the market demand data for the product are as follows:

Price	Total Quantity Demanded
$26	17,000
32	15,000
38	13,500
41	12,000
46	10,500
56	9,500
66	8,000

What will be the equilibrium price? What will be the equilibrium output for the industry? For each firm? What will profit or loss be per unit? Per firm? Will this industry expand or contract in the long run?

5. Why is the equality of marginal revenue and marginal cost essential for profit maximization in all market structures? Explain why price can be substituted for marginal revenue in the MR = MC rule when an industry is purely competitive.

6. **Key Question** Using diagrams for both the industry and a representative firm, illustrate competitive long-run equilibrium. Assuming constant costs, employ these diagrams to show how (*a*) an increase and (*b*) a decrease in market demand will upset that long-run equilibrium. Trace graphically and describe verbally the adjustment processes by which long-run equilibrium is restored. Now rework your analysis for increasing- and decreasing-cost industries and compare the three long-run supply curves.

7. **Key Question** In long-run equilibrium, P = minimum ATC = MC. Of what significance for economic efficiency is the equality of P and minimum ATC? The equality of P and MC? Distinguish between productive efficiency and allocative efficiency in your answer.

8. **(Last Word)** Suppose that improved technology causes the supply curve for oranges to shift rightward in the market discussed in this Last Word (see the figure there). Assuming no change in the location of the demand curve, what will happen to consumer surplus? Explain why.

9. **Web-Based Question:** *You are a pure competitor—what was your revenue yesterday?* Suppose that you

operate a purely competitive firm that buys and sells foreign currencies. Also suppose that yesterday your business activity consisted of buying 100,000 Swiss francs at the market exchange rate and selling them for a 3 percent commission. Go to the Federal Reserve website at federalreserve.gov and select, in order, Research and Data, Statistics, and Foreign Exchange Rates. What was your total revenue in dollars yesterday (be sure to include your commission)? Why would your profit for the day be considerably less than this total revenue?

10. **Web-Based Question:** *Entry and exit of firms—where have they occurred?* Go to the Census Bureau website at www.census.gov and select Economic Census, then Comparative Statistics, and then Manufacturing. Identify three manufacturing industries that experienced large percentage increases in the number of firms between 1992 and 1997. Identify three manufacturing industries that experienced large percentage decreases. What single factor is the most likely cause of the entry and exit differences between your two groups? Explain.

CHAPTER 11

Pure Monopoly

W E T U R N N O W from pure competition to pure monopoly, which is at the opposite end of the spectrum of industry structures listed in Table 10.1. You deal with monopolies—sole sellers of products and services—more often than you might think. When you see the logo for Microsoft's Windows on your computer, you are dealing with a monopoly (or, at least, a near-monopoly). When you purchase certain prescription drugs, you are buying monopolized products. When you make a local telephone call, turn on your lights, or subscribe to cable TV, you may be patronizing a monopoly, depending on your location. ■ What precisely do we mean by "pure monopoly," and what conditions enable it to arise and survive? How does a pure monopolist determine its profit-maximizing price and output quantity? Does a pure monopolist achieve the efficiency associated with pure competition? If not, what should the government do about it? A simplified model of pure monopoly will help us answer these questions.

■ An Introduction to Pure Monopoly

Pure monopoly exists when a single firm is the sole producer of a product for which there are no close substitutes. Here are the main characteristics of pure monopoly:

- **Single seller** A pure, or absolute, monopoly is an industry in which a single firm is the sole producer of a specific good or the sole supplier of a service; the firm and the industry are synonymous.
- **No close substitutes** A pure monopoly's product is unique in that there are no close substitutes. The consumer who chooses not to buy the monopolized product must do without it.

- **Price maker** The pure monopolist controls the total quantity supplied and thus has considerable control over price; it is a *price maker*. (Unlike the pure competitor that has no such control and therefore is a *price taker*.) The pure monopolist confronts the usual downward-sloping product demand curve. It can change its product price by changing the quantity of the product it supplies. The monopolist will use this power whenever it is advantageous to do so.
- **Blocked entry** A pure monopolist has no immediate competitors because certain barriers keep potential competitors from entering the industry. Those barriers may be economic, technological, legal, or of some other type. But entry is totally blocked in pure monopoly.

■ *Nonprice competition* The product produced by a pure monopolist may be either standardized (as with natural gas and electricity) or differentiated (as with Windows or Frisbees). Monopolists that have standardized products engage mainly in public relations advertising, whereas those with differentiated products sometimes advertise their products' attributes. 🔑 **11.1**

Examples of Monopoly

Examples of *pure* monopoly are relatively rare, but there are many examples of less pure forms. In most cities, government-owned or government-regulated public utilities—natural gas and electric companies, the water company, the cable TV company, and the local telephone company—are all monopolies or virtually so.

There are also many "near-monopolies" in which a single firm has the bulk of sales in a specific market. Intel, for example, provides 80 percent of the central microprocessors used in personal computers. First Data Corporation, via its Western Union subsidiary, accounts for 80 percent of the market for money order transfers. Brannock Device Company has an 80 percent market share of the shoe sizing devices found in shoe stores. Wham-O, through its Frisbee brand, sells 90 percent of plastic throwing disks. The De Beers diamond syndicate effectively controls 63 percent of the world's supply of rough-cut diamonds (see this chapter's Last Word).

Professional sports teams are, in a sense, monopolies because they are the sole suppliers of specific services in large geographic areas. With a few exceptions, a single major-league team in each sport serves each large American city. If you want to see a live major-league baseball game in St. Louis or Seattle, you must patronize the Cardinals or the Mariners, respectively. Other geographic monopolies exist. For example, a small town may be served by only one airline or railroad. In a small, isolated community, the local bank, movie, or bookstore may approximate a monopoly.

Of course, there is almost always some competition. Satellite television is a substitute for cable, and amateur softball is a substitute for professional baseball. The Linux operating system can substitute for Windows, and so on. But such substitutes are typically either more costly or in some way less appealing.

Dual Objectives of the Study of Monopoly

We want to examine pure monopoly not only for its own sake but also because such a study will help you understand the more common market structures of monopolistic competition and oligopoly, to be discussed in Chapter 12. These two market structures combine, in differing degrees, characteristics of pure competition and pure monopoly.

■ Barriers to Entry

The factors that prohibit firms from entering an industry are called **barriers to entry.** In pure monopoly, strong barriers to entry effectively block all potential competition. Somewhat weaker barriers may permit oligopoly, a market structure dominated by a few firms. Still weaker barriers may permit the entry of a fairly large number of competing firms giving rise to monopolistic competition. And the absence of any effective entry barriers permits the entry of a very large number of firms, which provide the basis of pure competition. So barriers to entry are pertinent not only to the extreme case of pure monopoly but also to other market structures in which there is some degree of monopoly-like conditions and behavior.

Economies of Scale

Modern technology in some industries is such that economies of scale—declining average total cost with added firm size—are extensive. So a firm's long-run average-cost schedule will decline over a wide range of output. Given market demand, only a few large firms or, in the extreme, only a single large firm can achieve low average total costs.

Figure 11.1 indicates economies of scale over a wide range of outputs. If total consumer demand is within that output range, then only a single producer can satisfy demand at least cost. Note, for example, that a monopolist can produce 200 units at a per-unit cost of $10 and a total cost of $2000. If there are two firms in the industry and each produces 100 units, the unit cost is $15 and total cost rises to $3000 (= 200 units × $15). A still more competitive situation with four firms each producing 50 units would boost unit and total cost to $20 and $4000, respectively. Conclusion: When long-run ATC is declining, only a single producer, a monopolist, can produce any particular output at minimum total cost.

Figure 11.1

Economies of scale: the natural monopoly case. A declining long-run average-total-cost curve over a wide range of output quantities indicates extensive economies of scale. A single monopoly firm can produce, say, 200 units of output at lower cost ($10 each) than could two or more firms that had a combined output of 200 units.

If a pure monopoly exists in such an industry, economies of scale will serve as an entry barrier and will protect the monopolist from competition. New firms that try to enter the industry as small-scale producers cannot realize the cost economies of the monopolist and therefore cannot obtain the normal profits necessary for survival or growth. A new firm might try to start out big, that is, to enter the industry as a large-scale producer so as to achieve the necessary economies of scale. But the massive plant facilities required would necessitate huge amounts of financing, which a new and untried enterprise would find difficult to secure. In most cases the financial obstacles and risks to "starting big" are prohibitive. This explains why efforts to enter such industries as automobiles, computer operating software, commercial aircraft, and basic steel are so rare.

In the extreme circumstance, in which the market demand curve cuts the long-run ATC curve where average total costs are still declining, the single firm is called a *natural monopoly*. It might seem that a natural monopolist's lower unit cost would enable it to charge a lower price than if the industry were more competitive. But that won't necessarily happen. A pure monopolist may, instead, set its price far above ATC and obtain substantial economic profit. In that event, the lowest-unit-cost advantage of a natural monopolist would accrue to the monopolist as profit and not as lower prices to consumers. That is why the government regulates some natural monopolies, specifying the price they may charge. We will say more about that later. 🔑 **11.2**

Legal Barriers to Entry: Patents and Licenses

Government also creates legal barriers to entry by awarding patents and licenses.

Patents   A *patent* is the exclusive right of an inventor to use, or to allow another to use, her or his invention. Patents and patent laws aim to protect the inventor from rivals who would use the invention without having shared in the effort and expense of developing it. At the same time, patents provide the inventor with a monopoly position for the life of the patent. The world's nations have agreed on a uniform patent length of 20 years from the time of application. Patents have figured prominently in the growth of modern-day giants such as IBM, Merck, Kodak, Xerox, Polaroid, General Electric, and DuPont.

Research and development (R&D) is what leads to most patentable inventions and products. Firms that gain monopoly power through their own research or by purchasing the patents of others can use patents to strengthen their market position. The profit from one patent can finance the research required to develop new patentable products. In the pharmaceutical industry, patents on prescription drugs have produced large monopoly profits that have helped finance the discovery of new patentable medicines. So monopoly power achieved through patents may well be self-sustaining, even though patents eventually expire and generic drugs then compete with the original brand.

Licenses   Government may also limit entry into an industry or occupation through *licensing*. At the national level, the Federal Communications Commission licenses only so many radio and television stations in each geographic area. In many large cities one of a limited number of municipal licenses is required to drive a taxicab. The consequent restriction of the supply of cabs creates economic profit for cab owners and drivers. New cabs cannot enter the industry to drive down prices and profits. In a few instances the government might "license" itself to provide some product and thereby create a public monopoly. For example, in some states only state-owned retail outlets can sell liquor. Similarly, many states have "licensed" themselves to run lotteries.

Ownership or Control of Essential Resources

A monopolist can use private property as an obstacle to potential rivals. For example, a firm that owns or controls a resource essential to the production process can prohibit the entry of rival firms. At one time the International Nickel Company of Canada (now called Inco) controlled 90 percent of the world's known nickel reserves. A local firm may own all the nearby deposits of sand and gravel. And it is very difficult for new sports leagues to be created because existing professional sports leagues have contracts with the best players and have long-term leases on the major stadiums and arenas.

Pricing and Other Strategic Barriers to Entry

Even if a firm is not protected from entry by, say, extensive economies of scale or ownership of essential resources, entry may effectively be blocked by the way the monopolist responds to attempts by rivals to enter the industry. Confronted with a new entrant, the monopolist may "create an entry barrier" by slashing its price, stepping up its advertising, or taking other strategic actions to make it difficult for the entrant to succeed. Examples: Before its breakup in 1980, AT&T allegedly undertook several entry-deterring actions, including selective price cutting, to maintain its monopoly in the long-distance telephone industry. In 2000 a Federal District Court ruled that Microsoft had engaged in illegal actions to drive Netscape from the Internet browser market. Microsoft had developed its own browser, Internet Explorer, and given it away free. It had also provided price discounts on its Windows operating system to computer manufacturers that featured Microsoft's Internet Explorer rather than Netscape's Navigator.

■ Monopoly Demand

Now that we have explained the sources of monopoly, we want to build a model of pure monopoly so that we can analyze its price and output decisions. Let's start by making three assumptions:

- Patents, economies of scale, or resource ownership secure our monopolist's status.
- No unit of government regulates the firm.
- The firm is a single-price monopolist; it charges the same price for all units of output.

The crucial difference between a pure monopolist and a purely competitive seller lies on the demand side of the market. The purely competitive seller faces a perfectly elastic demand at the price determined by market supply and demand. It is a price taker that can sell as much or as little as it wants at the going market price. Each additional unit sold will add the amount of the constant product price to the firm's total revenue. That means that marginal revenue for the competitive seller is constant and equal to product price. (Refer to Table 10.2 and Figure 10.1 for price, marginal-revenue, and total-revenue relationships for the purely competitive firm.)

The demand curve for the monopolist (and for any imperfectly competitive seller) is very different from that of the pure competitor. Because the pure monopolist *is* the industry, its demand curve is *the market demand curve*. And because market demand is not perfectly elastic, the monopolist's demand curve is downsloping. Columns 1 and 2 in Table 11.1 illustrate this concept. Note that quantity demanded increases as price decreases.

In Chapter 10 we drew separate demand curves for the purely competitive industry and for a single firm in such an industry. But only a single demand curve is needed in pure monopoly. The firm and the industry are one and the same. We have graphed part of the demand data in Table 11.1 as demand curve *D* in Figure 11.2. This is the monopolist's demand curve *and* the market demand curve. The downward-sloping demand curve has three implications that are essential to understanding the monopoly model.

Table 11.1

Revenue and Cost Data of a Pure Monopolist

	Revenue Data				Cost Data		
(1) Quantity of Output	(2) Price (Average Revenue)	(3) Total Revenue, (1) × (2)	(4) Marginal Revenue	(5) Average Total Cost	(6) Total Cost, (1) × (5)	(7) Marginal Cost	(8) Profit (+) or Loss (−)
0	$172	$ 0			$ 100		$−100
1	162	162	$162	$190.00	190	$ 90	− 28
2	152	304	142	135.00	270	80	+ 34
3	142	426	122	113.33	340	70	+ 86
4	132	528	102	100.00	400	60	+128
5	**122**	**610**	**82**	**94.00**	**470**	**70**	**+ 140**
6	112	672	62	91.67	550	80	+122
7	102	714	42	91.43	640	90	+ 74
8	92	736	22	93.75	750	110	− 14
9	82	738	2	97.78	880	130	−142
10	72	720	−18	103.00	1030	150	−310

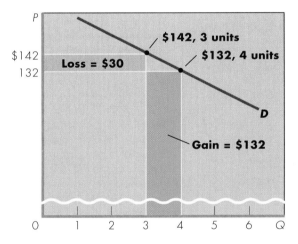

Figure 11.2

Price and marginal revenue in pure monopoly.
A pure monopolist, or any other imperfect competitor with a downsloping demand curve such as *D*, must set a lower price in order to sell more output. Here, by charging $132 rather than $142, the monopolist sells an extra unit (the fourth unit) and gains $132 from that sale. But from this gain must be subtracted $30, which reflects the $10 less the monopolist charged for each of the first 3 units. Thus, the marginal revenue of the fourth unit is $102 (= $132 − $30), considerably less than its $132 price.

Marginal Revenue Is Less Than Price

The monopolist's downward-sloping demand curve means that it can increase sales only by charging a lower price. Consequently, marginal revenue is less than price (average revenue) for every level of output except the first. Why so? The reason is that the lower price applies not only to the extra output sold but also to all prior units of output. The monopolist could have sold these prior units at a higher price if it had not produced and sold the extra output. Each additional unit of output sold increases total revenue by an amount equal to its own price less the sum of the price cuts that apply to all prior units of output.

Figure 11.2 confirms this point. There, we have highlighted two price-quantity combinations from the monopolist's demand curve. The monopolist can sell 1 more unit at $132 than it can at $142 and that way obtain $132 of extra revenue. But to sell that fourth unit for $132, the monopolist must also sell the first 3 units at $132 rather than $142. The $10 reduction in revenue on 3 units results in a $30 revenue loss. The net difference in total revenue from selling a fourth unit is $102: the $132 gain from the fourth unit minus the $30 forgone on the first 3 units. This net gain (marginal revenue) of $102 from the fourth unit is clearly less than the $132 price of the fourth unit.

Column 4 in Table 11.1 shows that marginal revenue is always less than the corresponding product price in column 2, except for the first unit of output. Because marginal revenue is the change in total revenue associated with each additional unit of output, the declining amounts of marginal revenue in column 4 mean that total revenue increases at a diminishing rate (as shown in column 3).

We show the relationship between the monopolist's marginal-revenue curve and total-revenue curve in Figure 11.3. For this figure, we extended the demand and revenue data of columns 1 through 4 in Table 11.1, assuming that successive $10 price cuts each elicit 1 additional unit of sales. That is, the monopolist can sell 11 units at $62, 12 units at $52, and so on.

Note that the monopolist's MR curve lies below the demand curve, indicating that marginal revenue is less than price at every output quantity but the very first unit. Observe also the special relationship between total revenue and marginal revenue. Because marginal revenue is the change in total revenue, marginal revenue is positive while total revenue is increasing. When total revenue reaches its maximum, marginal revenue is zero. When total revenue is diminishing, marginal revenue is negative.

The Monopolist Is a Price Maker

All imperfect competitors, whether pure monopoly, oligopoly, or monopolistic competition, face downward-sloping demand curves. So firms in those industries can to one degree or another influence total supply through their own output decisions. In changing market supply, they can also influence product price. Firms with downward-sloping demand curves are *price makers*.

This is most evident in pure monopoly, where one firm controls total output. The monopolist faces a downsloping demand curve in which each output is associated with some unique price. Thus, in deciding on what volume of output to produce, the monopolist is also indirectly determining the price it will charge. Through control of output, it can "make the price." From columns 1 and 2 in Table 11.1 we

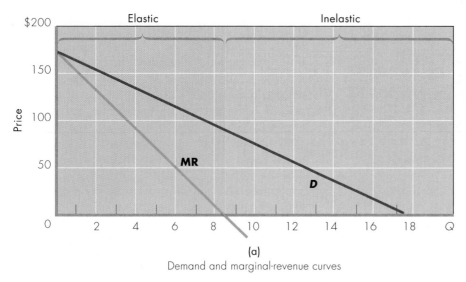

(a)
Demand and marginal-revenue curves

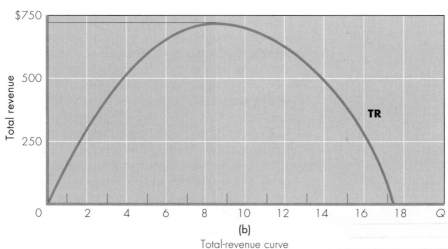

(b)
Total-revenue curve

Figure 11.3

Demand, marginal revenue, and total revenue for an imperfectly competitive firm.

(a) Because it must lower price on all units sold in order to increase its sales, an imperfectly competitive firm's marginal-revenue curve (MR) lies below its downsloping demand curve (D). The elastic and inelastic regions of demand are highlighted. (b) Total revenue (TR) increases at a decreasing rate, reaches maximum, and then declines. Note that in the elastic region, TR is increasing and hence MR is positive. When TR reaches its maximum, MR is zero. In the inelastic region of demand, TR is declining, so MR is negative.

find that the monopolist can charge a price of $72 if it produces and offers for sale 10 units, a price of $82 if it produces and offers for sale 9 units, and so forth.

The Monopolist Sets Prices in the Elastic Region of Demand

The total-revenue test for price elasticity of demand is the basis for our third implication. Recall from Chapter 7 that the total-revenue test reveals that when demand is elastic, a decline in price will increase total revenue. Similarly, when demand is inelastic, a decline in price will reduce total revenue. Beginning at the top of demand curve D in Figure 11.3a, observe that as the price declines from $172 to approximately $82, total revenue increases (and marginal revenue therefore is positive). This means that demand is elastic in this price range. Conversely, for price declines below $82, total revenue decreases (marginal revenue is negative), indicating that demand is inelastic there.

The implication is that a monopolist will never choose a price-quantity combination where price reductions cause total revenue to decrease (marginal revenue to be negative). The profit-maximizing monopolist will always want to avoid the inelastic segment of its demand curve in favor of some price-quantity combination in the elastic region. Here's why: To get into the inelastic region, the monopolist must lower price and increase output. In the inelastic region a lower price means less total revenue. And increased output always means increased total cost. Less total revenue and higher total cost yield lower profit. **(Key Question 4)**

QUICK REVIEW 11.1

A pure monopolist is the sole supplier of a product or service for which there are no close substitutes.

A monopoly survives because of entry barriers such as economies of scale, patents and licenses, the ownership of essential resources, and strategic actions to exclude rivals.

The monopolist's demand curve is downsloping, and its marginal-revenue curve lies below its demand curve.

The downsloping demand curve means that the monopolist is a price maker.

The monopolist will operate in the elastic region of demand since in the inelastic region it can increase total revenue and reduce total cost by reducing output.

■ Output and Price Determination

At what specific price-quantity combination will a profit-maximizing monopolist choose to operate? To answer this question, we must add production costs to our analysis.

Cost Data

On the cost side, we will assume that although the firm is a monopolist in the product market, it hires resources competitively and employs the same technology as Chapter 10's competitive firm does. This lets us use the cost data we developed in Chapter 9 and applied in Chapter 10, so we can compare the price-output decisions of a pure monopoly with those of a pure competitor. Columns 5 through 7 in Table 11.1 restate the pertinent cost data from Table 9.2.

MR = MC Rule

A monopolist seeking to maximize total profit will employ the same rationale as a profit-seeking firm in a competitive industry. If producing is preferable to shutting down, it will produce up to the output at which marginal revenue equals marginal cost (MR = MC).

A comparison of columns 4 and 7 in Table 11.1 indicates that the profit-maximizing output is 5 units, because the fifth unit is the last unit of output whose marginal revenue exceeds its marginal cost. What price will the monopolist charge? The demand schedule shown as columns 1 and 2 in Table 11.1 indicates there is only one price at which 5 units can be sold: $122.

This analysis is shown in **Figure 11.4 (Key Graph)**, where we have graphed the demand, marginal-revenue, average-total-cost, and marginal-cost data of Table 11.1. The profit-maximizing output occurs at 5 units of output (Q_m), where the marginal-revenue (MR) and marginal-cost (MC) curves intersect. There, MR = MC.

To find the price the monopolist will charge, we extend a vertical line from Q_m up to the demand curve D. The unique price P_m at which Q_m units can be sold is $122. In this case, it is the profit-maximizing price. The monopolist sets the quantity at Q_m to charge its profit-maximizing price of $122.

In columns 2 and 5 in Table 11.1 we see that at 5 units of output, the product price ($122) exceeds the average total cost ($94). The monopolist thus

KEY GRAPH

Figure 11.4

The profit-maximizing position of a pure monopolist. The pure monopolist maximizes profit by producing the MR = MC output, here Q_m = 5 units. Then, as seen from the demand curve, it will charge price P_m = $122. Average total cost will be A = $94, meaning that per-unit profit is $P_m - A$ and total profit is $5 \times (P_m - A)$. Total economic profit is thus represented by the taupe rectangle.

Quick Quiz 11.4

1. The MR curve lies below the demand curve in this figure because the:
   a. demand curve is linear (a straight line).
   b. demand curve is highly inelastic throughout its full length.
   c. demand curve is highly elastic throughout its full length.
   d. gain in revenue from an extra unit of output is less than the price charged for that unit of output.

2. The area labeled "Economic profit" can be found by multiplying the difference between P and ATC by quantity. It also can be found by:
   a. dividing profit per unit by quantity.
   b. subtracting total cost from total revenue.
   c. multiplying the coefficient of demand elasticity by quantity.

   d. multiplying the difference between P and MC by quantity.

3. This pure monopolist:
   a. charges the highest price that it could achieve.
   b. earns only a normal profit in the long run.
   c. restricts output to create an insurmountable entry barrier.
   d. restricts output to increase its price and total economic profit.

4. At this monopolist's profit-maximizing output:
   a. price equals marginal revenue.
   b. price equals marginal cost.
   c. price exceeds marginal cost.
   d. profit per unit is maximized.

Answers: 1. d; 2. b; 3. d; 4. c

---

earns an economic profit of $28 per unit, and the total economic profit is then $140 (= 5 units × $28). In Figure 11.4, per-unit profit is $P_m - A$, where A is the average total cost of producing Q_m units. We find total economic profit by multiplying this per-unit profit by the profit-maximizing output Q_m.

Another way we can determine the profit-maximizing output is by comparing total revenue and total cost at each possible level of production and choosing the output with the greatest positive difference. Use columns 3 and 6 in Table 11.1 to verify our conclusion that 5 units is the profit-maximizing output. An accurate graphing of total revenue and total cost against output would also show the greatest difference (the maximum profit) at 5 units of output. Table 11.2 is a step-by-step summary of the process for determining the profit-maximizing output, profit-maximizing price, and economic profit in pure monopoly. **(Key Question 5)** 11.1

Table 11.2

Steps for Graphically Determining the Profit-Maximizing Output, Profit-Maximizing Price, and Economic Profit (if Any) in Pure Monopoly

Step 1. Determine the profit-maximizing output by finding where MR = MC.

Step 2. Determine the profit-maximizing price by extending a vertical line upward from the output determined in step 1 to the pure monopolist's demand curve.

Step 3. Determine the pure monopolist's economic profit using one of two methods:

Method 1. Find profit per unit by substracting the average total cost of the profit-maximizing output from the profit-maximizing price. Then multiply the difference by the profit-maximizing output to determine economic profit (if any).

Method 2. Find total cost by multiplying the average total cost of the profit-maximizing output by that output. Find total revenue by multiplying the profit-maximizing output by the profit-maximizing price. Then subtract total cost from total revenue to determine economic profit (if any).

No Monopoly Supply Curve

Recall that MR equals *P* in pure competition and that the supply curve of a purely competitive firm is determined by applying the MR (= *P*) = MC profit-maximizing rule. At any specific market-determined price the purely competitive seller will maximize profit by supplying the quantity at which MC is equal to that price. When the market price increases or decreases, the competitive firm produces more or less output. Each market price is thus associated with a specific output, and all such price-output pairs define the supply curve. This supply curve turns out to be the portion of the firm's MC curve that lies above the average-variable-cost curve (see Figure 10.6).

At first glance we would suspect that the pure monopolist's marginal-cost curve would also be its supply curve. But that is *not* the case. *The pure monopolist has no supply curve.* There is no unique relationship between price and quantity supplied for a monopolist. Like the competitive firm, the monopolist equates marginal revenue and marginal cost to determine output, but for the monopolist marginal revenue is less than price. Because the monopolist does not equate marginal cost to price, it is possible for different demand conditions to bring about different prices for the same output. To convince yourself of this, refer to Figure 11.4 and pencil in a new, steeper marginal-revenue curve that intersects the marginal-cost curve at the same point as does the present marginal-revenue curve. Then draw in a new demand curve that roughly corresponds with your new marginal-revenue curve. With the new curves, the same MR = MC output of 5 units now corresponds with a higher profit-maximizing price.

Conclusion: There is no single, unique price associated with each output level Q_m, and so there is no supply curve for the pure monopolist.

Misconceptions Concerning Monopoly Pricing

Our analysis exposes two fallacies concerning monopoly behavior.

Not Highest Price Because a monopolist can manipulate output and price, people often believe it "will charge the highest price possible." That is incorrect. There are many prices above P_m in Figure 11.4, but the monopolist shuns them because they yield a smaller-than-maximum total profit. The monopolist seeks maximum total profit, not maximum price. Some high prices that could be charged would reduce sales and total revenue too severely to offset any decrease in total cost.

Total, Not Unit, Profit The monopolist seeks maximum *total* profit, not maximum *unit* profit. In Figure 11.4 a careful comparison of the vertical distance between average total cost and price at various possible outputs indicates that per-unit profit is greater at a point slightly to the left of the profit-maximizing output Q_m. This is seen in Table 11.1, where unit profit at 4 units of output is $32 (= $132 − $100) compared with $28 (= $122 − $94) at the profit-maximizing output of 5 units. Here the monopolist accepts a lower-than-maximum per-unit profit because additional sales more than compensate for the lower unit profit. A profit-seeking monopolist would rather sell 5 units at a profit of $28 per unit (for a total profit of $140) than 4 units at a profit of $32 per unit (for a total profit of only $128).

Possibility of Losses by Monopolist

The likelihood of economic profit is greater for a pure monopolist than for a pure competitor. In the long run the pure competitor is destined to have only a normal profit, whereas barriers to entry mean that any economic profit realized by the monopolist can persist. In pure monopoly there are no new entrants to increase supply, drive down price, and eliminate economic profit.

But pure monopoly does not guarantee profit. The monopolist is not immune from changes in tastes that reduce the demand for its product. Nor is it immune from upward-shifting cost curves caused by escalating resource prices. If the demand and cost situation faced by the monopolist is far less favorable than that in Figure 11.4, the monopolist will incur losses in the short run. Despite its dominance in the market (as, say, a seller of home sewing machines), the monopoly enterprise in Figure 11.5 suffers a loss, as shown, because of weak demand and relatively high costs. Yet it continues to operate for the time being because its total loss is less than its fixed cost. More precisely, at output Q_m the monopolist's

price P_m exceeds its average variable cost V. Its loss per unit is $A - P_m$, and the total loss is shown by the taupe rectangle.

Like the pure competitor, the monopolist will not persist in operating at a loss. Faced with continuing losses, in the long run the firm's owners will move their resources to alternative industries that offer better profit opportunities. Thus we can expect the monopolist to realize a normal profit or better in the long run.

■ Economic Effects of Monopoly

Let's now evaluate pure monopoly from the standpoint of society as a whole. Our reference for this evaluation will be the outcome of long-run efficiency in a purely competitive market, identified by the triple equality $P = MC = $ minimum ATC.

Price, Output, and Efficiency

Figure 11.6 graphically contrasts the price, output, and efficiency outcomes of pure monopoly and a purely competitive *industry*. Starting with Figure 11.6a, we are reminded that the purely competitive industry's market supply curve S is the horizontal sum of the marginal-cost curves of all the firms in the industry. Let's suppose there are 1000 such firms. Comparing their combined supply curves S with market demand D, we get the purely competitive price and output of P_c and Q_c.

Recall that this price-output combination results in both productive efficiency and allocative efficiency. *Productive efficiency* is achieved because free entry and exit forces firms to operate where average total cost is at a minimum. The sum of the minimum-ATC outputs of the 1000 pure competitors is the industry output, here, Q_c. Product price is at the lowest level consistent with minimum average total cost. The *allocative efficiency* of pure competition results because production occurs up to that output at which price (the measure of a product's value or marginal benefit to society) equals marginal cost (the worth of the alternative products forgone by society in producing any given commodity). In short: $P = MC = $ minimum ATC.

Now let's suppose that this industry becomes a pure monopoly (Figure 11.6b) as a result of one firm buying out all its competitors. We also assume that no changes in costs or market demand result from this dramatic change in the industry structure. What were formerly 1000 competing firms are now a single

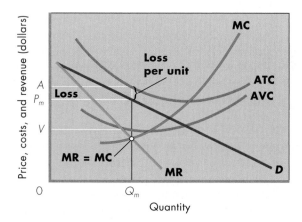

Figure 11.5

The loss-minimizing position of a pure monopolist. If demand D is weak and costs are high, the pure monopolist may be unable to make a profit. Because P_m exceeds V, the average variable cost at the $MR = MC$ output Q_m, the monopolist will minimize losses in the short run by producing at that output. The loss per unit is $A - P_m$, and the total loss is indicated by the taupe rectangle.

Figure 11.6

Inefficiency of pure monopoly relative to a purely competitive industry. (a) In a purely competitive industry, entry and exit of firms ensures that price (P_c) equals marginal cost (MC) and that the minimum average-total-cost output (Q_c) is produced. Both productive efficiency (P = minimum ATC) and allocative efficiency (P = MC) are obtained. (b) In pure monopoly, the MR curve lies below the demand curve. The monopolist maximizes profit at output Q_m, where MR = MC, and charges price P_m. Thus, output is lower (Q_m rather than Q_c) and price is higher (P_m rather than P_c) than they would be in a purely competitive industry. Monopoly is inefficient, since output is less than that required for achieving minimum ATC (here at Q_c) and because the monopolist's price exceeds MC.

pure monopolist consisting of 1000 noncompeting branches.

The competitive market supply curve S has become the marginal-cost curve (MC) of the monopolist, the summation of the MC curves of its many branch plants. (Since the monopolist does not have a supply curve, as such, we have removed the S label.) The important change, however, is on the demand side. From the viewpoint of each of the 1000 individual competitive firms, demand was perfectly elastic, and marginal revenue was therefore equal to price. Each firm equated MR (= price) and MC in maximizing profits. But market demand and individual demand are the same to the pure monopolist. The firm *is* the industry, and thus the monopolist sees the downsloping demand curve D shown in Figure 11.6b.

This means that marginal revenue is less than price, that graphically the MR curve lies below demand curve D. In using the MR = MC rule, the monopolist selects output Q_m and price P_m. A comparison of both graphs in Figure 11.6 reveals that the monopolist finds it profitable to sell a smaller output at a higher price than do the competitive producers. Monopoly yields neither productive nor allocative efficiency. The monopolist's output is less

than Q_c, the output at which average total cost is lowest. And price is higher than the competitive price P_c, which in long-run equilibrium pure competition equals minimum average total cost. Thus the monopoly price *exceeds* minimum average total cost. Also, at the monopolist's Q_m output, product price is considerably higher than marginal cost, meaning that society values additional units of this monopolized product more highly than it values the alternative products the resources could otherwise produce. So the monopolist's profit-maximizing output results in an underallocation of resources. The monopolist finds it profitable to restrict output and therefore employ fewer resources than is justified from society's standpoint. So the monopolist does not achieve allocative efficiency.

In monopoly, then, P exceeds MC and P exceeds minimum ATC.

Income Transfer

In general, monopoly transfers income from consumers to the stockholders who own the monopoly. By virtue of their market power, monopolists charge a higher price than would a purely competitive firm with the same costs. So monopolists in effect levy a "private tax" on consumers and obtain substantial economic profits. These monopolistic profits are not equally distributed, because higher-income groups largely own corporate stock. The owners of monopolistic enterprises thus tend to benefit at the expense of the consumers, who "overpay" for the product. Because, on average, these owners have more income than the buyers, monopoly increases income inequality.

Exception: If the buyers of a monopoly product are wealthier than the owners of the monopoly, the income transfer from consumers to owners may reduce income inequality. But, in general, this is not the case, and we thus conclude that monopoly contributes to income inequality.

Cost Complications

Our evaluation of pure monopoly has led us to conclude that, given identical costs, a purely monopolistic industry will charge a higher price, produce a smaller output, and allocate economic resources less efficiently than a purely competitive industry. These inferior results are rooted in the entry barriers characterizing monopoly.

Now we must recognize that costs may not be the same for purely competitive and monopolistic producers. The unit cost incurred by a monopolist may be either larger or smaller than that incurred by a purely competitive firm. There are four reasons why costs may differ: (1) economies of scale, (2) a factor called "X-inefficiency," (3) the need for monopoly-preserving expenditures, and (4) the "very long run" perspective, which allows for technological advance.

Economies of Scale Once Again Where there are extensive economies of scale, market demand may not be sufficient to support a large number of competing firms, each producing at minimum efficient scale. In such cases, an industry of one or two firms would have a lower average total cost than would the same industry made up of numerous competitive firms. At the extreme, only a single firm—a natural monopoly—might be able to achieve the lowest long-run average total cost.

Some firms relating to new information technologies—for example, computer software, Internet service, and wireless communications—have displayed extensive economies of scale. As these firms have grown, their long-run average total costs have declined because of greater use of specialized inputs,

the spreading of product development costs, and learning by doing. Also, *simultaneous consumption* and *network effects* have reduced costs.

A product's ability to satisfy a large number of consumers at the same time is called **simultaneous consumption** (or *nonrivalous consumption*). Dell Computers needs to produce a personal computer for each customer, but Microsoft needs to produce its Windows program only once. Then, at very low marginal cost, Microsoft delivers its program by disk or Internet to millions of consumers. The same is true for Internet service providers, music producers, and wireless communication firms. Because marginal costs are so low, the average total cost of output declines as more customers are added.

Network effects are increases in the value of a product to each user, including existing users, as the total number of users rise. Good examples are computer software, cell phones, pagers, palm computers, and other products related to the Internet. When other people have Internet service and devices to access it, a person can conveniently send e-mail messages to them. And when they have similar software, documents, spreadsheets, and photos can be attached to the e-mail messages. The greater are the number of persons connected to the system, the more the benefits of the product to each person are magnified.

Such network effects may drive a market toward monopoly because consumers tend to choose standard products that everyone else is using. The focused demand for these products permits their producers to grow rapidly and thus achieve economies of scale. Smaller firms, which have the higher-cost "right" products or the "wrong" products get acquired or go out of business.

Economists generally agree that some new information firms have not yet exhausted their economies of scale. But most economists question whether such firms are truly natural monopolies. Most firms eventually achieve their minimum efficient scale at less than the full size of the market. Even if natural monopoly develops, it's unlikely that the monopolist will pass cost reductions along to consumers as price reductions. So, with perhaps a handful of exceptions, economies of scale do not change the general conclusion that monopolies yield less efficiency than do more competitive industries.

X-Inefficiency In constructing all the average-total-cost curves used in this book, we have assumed that the firm uses the most efficient existing technology. In other words, it uses the technology

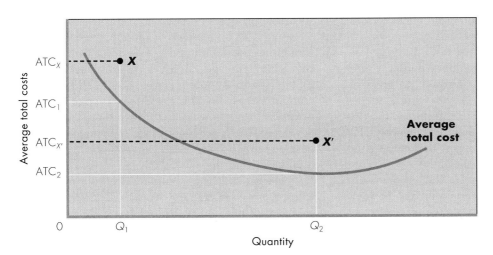

Figure 11.7

X-inefficiency. The average-total-cost curve (ATC) is assumed to reflect the minimum cost of producing each particular unit of output. Any point above this "lowest-cost" ATC curve, such as X or X′, implies X-inefficiency: operation at greater than lowest cost for a particular level of output.

that permits it to achieve the lowest average total cost of whatever level of output it chooses to produce. **X-inefficiency** occurs when a firm's actual cost of producing any output is greater than the lowest possible cost of producing it. In Figure 11.7 X-inefficiency is represented by operation at points X and X′ above the lowest-cost ATC curve. At these points, per-unit costs are ATC_x (as opposed to ATC_1) for output Q_1 and $\text{ATC}_{x'}$ (as opposed to ATC_2) for output Q_2. Any point above the average-total-cost curve in Figure 11.7 is possible but reflects inefficiency or "bad management" by the firm. 🔎 **11.3**

Why is X-inefficiency allowed to occur if it reduces profits? The answer is that managers may have goals, such as corporate growth, an easier work life, avoidance of business risk, or giving jobs to incompetent relatives, that conflict with cost minimization. Or X-inefficiency may arise because a firm's workers are poorly motivated or ineffectively supervised. Or a firm may simply become lethargic and inert, relying on rules of thumb in decision making as opposed to relevant calculations of costs and revenues.

For our purposes the relevant question is whether monopolistic firms tend more toward X-inefficiency than competitive producers do. Presumably they do. Firms in competitive industries are continually under pressure from rivals, forcing them to be internally efficient to survive. But monopolists are sheltered from such competitive forces by entry barriers, and that lack of pressure may lead to X-inefficiency.

There is no indisputable evidence regarding X-inefficiency, but what evidence we have suggests that it increases as competition decreases. A reasonable estimate is that X-inefficiency may be 10 per-

cent or more of costs for monopolists but only 5 percent for an "average" oligopolistic industry in which the four largest firms produce 60 percent of total output.[1] In the words of one authority: "The evidence is fragmentary, but it points in the same direction. X-inefficiency exists, and it is more apt to be reduced when competitive pressures are strong than when firms enjoy insulated market positions."[2]

Rent-Seeking Expenditures   **Rent-seeking behavior** is any activity designed to transfer income or wealth to a particular firm or resource supplier at someone else's, or even society's, expense. We have seen that a monopolist can obtain an economic profit even in the long run. Therefore, it is no surprise that a firm may go to great expense to acquire or maintain a monopoly granted by government through legislation or an exclusive license. Such rent-seeking expenditures add nothing to the firm's output, but they clearly increase its costs. They imply that monopoly involves higher costs and less efficiency than suggested in Figure 11.6b.

Technological Advance   In the very long run, firms can reduce their costs through the discovery and implementation of new technology. If monopolists are more likely than competitive producers to develop more efficient production techniques over time, then the inefficiency of monopoly might be

[1]William G. Shepherd, *The Economics of Industrial Organization*, 4th ed. (Englewood Cliffs, N.J.: Prentice-Hall, 1997), p. 107.

[2]F. M. Scherer and David Ross, *Industrial Market Structure and Economic Performance*, 3d ed. (Chicago: Rand McNally College Publishing, 1990), p. 414.

overstated. Since research and development (R&D) is the topic of Chapter 13, we will provide only a brief assessment here.

The general view of economists is that a pure monopolist will not be technologically progressive. Although its economic profit provides ample means to finance research and development, it has little incentive to implement new techniques (or products). The absence of competitors means that there is no external pressure for technological advance in a monopolized market. Because of its sheltered market position, the pure monopolist can afford to be inefficient and lethargic; there simply is no penalty for being so.

One caveat: Research and technological advance may be one of the monopolist's barriers to entry. Thus, the monopolist may continue to seek technological advance to avoid falling prey to new rivals. In this case technological advance is essential to the maintenance of monopoly. But then it is potential competition, not the monopoly market structure, that is driving the technological advance. By assumption, no such competition exists in the pure monopoly model; entry is completely blocked.

Assessment and Policy Options

For reasons we have discussed, monopoly is a legitimate concern to an economy. Monopolists can charge higher-than-competitive prices that result in an underallocation of resources to the monopolized product. They can stifle innovation, engage in rent-seeking behavior, and foster X-inefficiency. Even when their costs are low because of economies of scale, there is no guarantee that the price they charge will reflect those low costs. The cost savings may simply accrue to the monopoly as greater economic profit.

Fortunately, however, monopoly is not widespread in the economy. Barriers to entry are seldom completely successful. Although research and technological advance may strengthen the market position of a monopoly, technology may also undermine monopoly power. Over time, the creation of new technologies may work to destroy monopoly positions. For example, the development of courier delivery, fax machines, and e-mail has eroded the monopoly power of the U.S. Postal Service. Cable television monopolies are now challenged by satellite TV and by new technologies that permit the transmission of audio and visual signals over the Internet.

Similarly, patents eventually expire, and before they do, the development of new and distinct substitutable products often circumvents existing patent advantages. New sources of monopolized resources sometimes are found and competition from foreign firms may emerge. (See Global Perspective 11.1) Finally, if a monopoly is sufficiently fearful of future competition from new products, it may keep its prices relatively low so as to discourage rivals from developing such products. If so, consumers may pay nearly competitive prices even though competition is currently lacking.

So what should government do about monopoly when it arises in the real world? Economists agree that government needs to look carefully at monopoly on a case-by-case basis. Three general policy options are available:

- If the monopoly is achieved and sustained through anticompetitive actions, creates substantial economic inefficiency, and appears to be long-lasting, the government can file charges against the monopoly under the antitrust laws. If found guilty of monopoly abuse, the firm can either be expressly prohibited from engaging in certain business activities or be broken into two

GLOBAL PERSPECTIVE 11.1

Competition from Foreign Multinational Corporations

Competition from foreign multinational corporations diminishes the market power of firms in the United States. Here are just a few of the hundreds of foreign multinational corporations that compete strongly with U.S. firms in certain American markets.

Company (Country)	Main Products
Bayer (Germany)	chemicals
BP Amoco (United Kingdom)	gasoline
L. M. Ericsson (Sweden)	wireless phones
NEC (Japan)	computers
Nestlé (Switzerland)	food products
Nokia (Finland)	wireless phones
Royal Dutch/Shell (Netherlands)	gasoline
Royal Philips (Netherlands)	electronics
Sony (Japan)	electronics
Toyota (Japan)	automobiles
Unilever (Netherlands)	food products

Source: Compiled from the Fortune 500 listing of the world's largest firms, www.fortune.com.

or more competing firms. This breakup approach is the one that a Federal court established for Microsoft in 2000. Microsoft is currently appealing the decision. (We cite the Internet addresses for access to the actual court decisions in Web-Based Question 13 at the end of this chapter. We discuss the antitrust laws and the Microsoft case in Chapter 19.)

■ If the monopoly is a natural monopoly, society can allow it to continue to expand. If no competition emerges from new products, government may then decide to regulate its prices and operations. (We discuss this option later in this chapter and in Chapter 19.)

■ If the monopoly appears to be unsustainable over a long period of time, say, because of emerging new technology, society can simply choose to ignore it. (In Chapter 13 we discuss the potential for real-world monopoly to collapse in the very long run.)

QUICK REVIEW 11.2

■ The monopolist maximizes profit (or minimizes loss) at the output where MR = MC and charges the price that corresponds to that output on its demand curve.

■ The monopolist has no supply curve, since any of several prices can be associated with a specific quantity of output supplied.

■ Assuming identical costs, a monopolist will be less efficient than a purely competitive industry because the monopolist produces less output and charges a higher price.

■ The inefficiencies of monopoly may be offset or lessened by economies of scale and, less likely, by technological progress, but they may be intensified by the presence of X-inefficiency and rent-seeking expenditures.

■ Price Discrimination

We have assumed in this chapter that the monopolist charges a single price to all buyers. But under certain conditions the monopolist can increase its profit by charging different prices to different buyers. In so doing, the monopolist is engaging in **price discrimination,** the practice of selling a specific product at more than one price when the price differences are not justified by cost differences. 🔑 11.4

Conditions

The opportunity to engage in price discrimination is not readily available to all sellers. Price discrimination is possible when the following conditions are realized:

■ **Monopoly power** The seller must be a monopolist or, at least, must possess some degree of monopoly power, that is, some ability to control output and price.

■ **Market segregation** At relatively low cost to itself, the seller must be able to segregate buyers into distinct classes, each of which has a different willingness or ability to pay for the product. This separation of buyers is usually based on different elasticities of demand, as the examples below will make clear.

■ **No resale** The original purchaser cannot resell the product or service. If buyers in the low-price segment of the market could easily resell in the high-price segment, the monopolist's price-discrimination strategy would create competition in the high-price segment. This competition would reduce the price in the high-price segment and undermine the monopolist's price-discrimination policy. This condition suggests that service industries such as the transportation industry or legal and medical services, where resale is impossible, are candidates for price discrimination.

Examples of Price Discrimination

Price discrimination is widely practiced in the U.S. economy. For example, airlines charge high fares to traveling executives, whose demand for travel is inelastic, and offer lower "Saturday night stayover rates" and "14-day advance purchase fares" to attract vacationers and others whose demands are more elastic.

Electric utilities frequently segment their markets by end uses, such as lighting and heating. The absence of reasonable lighting substitutes means that the demand for electricity for illumination is inelastic and that the price per kilowatt-hour for such use is high. But the availability of natural gas and petroleum for heating makes the demand for electricity for this purpose less inelastic and the price lower.

Movie theaters and golf courses vary their charges on the basis of time (for example, higher evening and weekend rates) and age (for example, lower rates for youths, senior discounts). Railroads vary the rate charged per ton-mile of freight according to the market value of the product being shipped. The shipper of 10 tons of television sets or costume jewelry is charged more than the shipper of 10 tons of gravel or coal.

The issuance of discount coupons, redeemable at purchase, is a form of price discrimination. It permits firms to give price discounts to their most price-sensitive customers who have elastic demand. Less price-sensitive consumers who have less elastic demand are not as likely to undertake the clipping and redeeming of coupons. The firm thus makes a larger profit than if it had used a single-price, no-coupon strategy.

Finally, price discrimination often occurs in international trade. A Russian aluminum producer, for example, might sell aluminum for less in the United States than in Russia. In the United States, this seller faces an elastic demand because several substitute suppliers are available. But in Russia, where the manufacturer dominates the market and trade barriers impede imports, consumers have fewer choices and thus demand is less elastic. ▮ 11.1

Consequences of Price Discrimination

As you will see shortly, a monopolist can increase its profit by practicing price discrimination. At the same time, *perfect price discrimination* results in more output than would be purchased at a single monopoly price. Such price discrimination occurs when the monopolist charges each customer the price that he or she would be willing to pay rather than go without the product.

More Profit   Let's again consider our monopolist's downsloping demand curve in Figure 11.4, this time to see why price discrimination can yield additional profit. In that figure we saw that the profit-maximizing single price is $P_m = \$122$. However, the segment of the demand curve above the economic profit area (in taupe) reveals that some buyers are willing to pay more than $122 rather than forgo the product.

If the monopolist can identify those buyers, segregate them, and charge the maximum price each would be willing to pay, total revenue and economic profit would increase. Observe from columns 1 and 2 in Table 11.1 that buyers of the first 4 units of output would be willing to pay $162, $152, $142, and $132, respectively, for those units. If the seller could practice perfect price discrimination by charging the maximum price for each unit, total revenue would increase from $610 (= $122 × 5) to $710 (= $122 + $132 + $142 +

$152 + $162) and profit would increase from $140 (= $610 − $470) to $240 (= $710 − $470).

More Production   Other things equal, the monopolist practicing perfect price discrimination will produce a larger output than the monopolist that does not. When the nondiscriminating monopolist lowers its price to sell additional output, the lower price not only applies to the additional output but also to all the prior units of output. So the single-price monopolist's marginal revenue falls more rapidly than price and, graphically, its marginal-revenue curve lies below its demand curve. The decline of marginal revenue is a disincentive to increased production.

But when a discriminating monopolist lowers price, the reduced price applies only to the additional unit sold and not to the prior units. Thus, marginal revenue equals price for each unit of output, and the firm's marginal revenue curve and demand curve coincide. The disincentive to increase production is removed.

We can show the outcome through Table 11.1. Because marginal revenue and price are equal, the discriminating monopolist finds it profitable to produce 7 units, not 5 units, of output. The additional revenue from the sixth and seventh units is $214 (= $112 + $102). Thus total revenue for 7 units is $924 (= $710 + $214). Since total cost for 7 units is $640, profit is $284.

Ironically, although perfect price discrimination results in higher monopoly profit than that achieved by a nondiscriminating monopolist, it also results in greater output and thus greater allocative efficiency. In our example, the output level of 7 units matches the output that would have occurred in pure competition. That is, allocative efficiency ($P = MC$) is achieved.

Graphical Portrayal   Figure 11.8 shows the effects of price discrimination graphically. Figure 11.8a merely restates Figure 11.4 in a generalized form to show the position of a nondiscriminating monopolist as a benchmark. The nondiscriminating monopolist produces output Q_1 (where MR = MC) and charges price P_1. Total revenue is area $0bce$ and economic profit is area $abcd$.

The monopolist in Figure 11.8b engages in perfect price discrimination, charging each buyer the highest price he or she is willing to pay. Starting at the very first unit, each additional unit is sold for the price indicated by the corresponding point on the demand curve. This monopolist's demand and

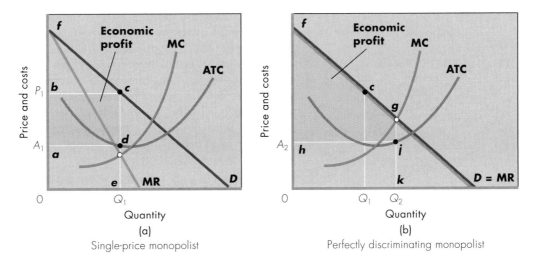

Figure 11.8
Single-price versus perfectly discriminating monopoly pricing. (a) The single-price monopolist produces output Q_1 at which MR = MC, charges price P_1 for all units, incurs an average total cost of A_1, and realizes an economic profit represented by area *abcd*. (b) The perfectly discriminating monopolist has MR = D and, as a result, produces output Q_2 (where MR = MC). It then charges the maximum price for each unit of output, incurs average total cost A_2, and realizes an economic profit represented by area *hfgj*.

marginal-revenue curves coincide, because the monopolist does not cut price on preceding units to sell more output. Thus, the most profitable output is Q_2 (where MR = MC), which is greater than Q_1. Total revenue is area 0*fgk* and total cost is area 0*hjk*. The economic profit of *hfgj* for the discriminating monopolist is clearly larger than the profit of *abcd* for the single-price monopolist.

The impact of price discrimination on consumers is mixed. Those buying each unit out to Q_1 will pay more than the nondiscriminatory price of P_1. But those additional consumers brought into the market by discrimination will pay less than P_1. Specifically, they will pay the various prices shown on segment *cg* of the D = MR curve.

Overall, then, (1) perfect price discrimination results in greater profit and greater output than is the case in single-price monopoly; (2) some consumers pay more than the single price, but other consumers pay less; and (3) perfect price discrimination and pure competition are equally efficient. **(Key Question 6)**

■ Regulated Monopoly

Natural monopolies traditionally have been subject to *rate regulation* (price regulation), although the recent trend has been to deregulate the parts of the

industries where competition seems possible. For example, long-distance telephone, natural gas at the wellhead, wireless communications, cable television, and long-distance electricity transmission have been, to one degree or another, deregulated over the past several decades. And regulators in some states are beginning to allow new entrants to compete with existing local telephone and electricity providers. Nevertheless, state and local regulatory commissions still regulate the prices that most local natural gas distributors, regional telephone companies, and local electricity suppliers can charge.

Let's consider the regulation of a local natural monopoly, for example, a natural gas provider. Figure 11.9 shows the demand and the long-run cost curves facing our firm. Because of extensive economies of scale, the demand curve cuts the natural monopolist's long-run average-total-cost curve at a point where that curve is still falling. It would be inefficient to have several firms in this industry because each would produce a much smaller output, operating well to the left on the long-run average-total-cost curve. In short, each firm's lowest average total cost would be substantially higher than that of a single firm. So efficient, low-cost production requires a single seller.

We know by application of the MR = MC rule that Q_m and P_m are the profit-maximizing output and

Figure 11.9

Regulated monopoly. The socially optimal price P_r, found where D and MC intersect, will result in an efficient allocation of resources but may entail losses to the monopoly. The fair-return price P_f will allow the monopolist to break even but will not fully correct the underallocation of resources.

price that an unregulated monopolist would choose. Because price exceeds average total cost at output Q_m, the monopolist enjoys a substantial economic profit. Furthermore, price exceeds marginal cost, indicating an underallocation of resources to this product or service. Can government regulation bring about better results from society's point of view?

Socially Optimal Price: P = MC

If the objective of a regulatory commission is to achieve allocative efficiency, it should attempt to establish a legal (ceiling) price for the monopolist that is equal to marginal cost. Remembering that each point on the market demand curve designates a price-quantity combination, and noting that the marginal-cost curve cuts the demand curve only at point r, we see that P_r is the only price on the demand curve equal to marginal cost. The maximum or ceiling price effectively causes the monopolist's demand curve to become horizontal (indicating perfectly elastic demand) from zero out to point r, where the regulated price ceases to be effective. Also, out to point r we have MR $= P_r$.

Confronted with the legal price P_r, the monopolist will maximize profit or minimize loss by producing Q_r units of output, because at this output MR $(= P_r) =$ MC. By making it illegal to charge more than P_r per unit, the regulatory agency has removed the monopolist's incentive to restrict output to Q_m to obtain a higher price and greater profit.

In short, the regulatory commission can simulate the allocative forces of pure competition by imposing the legal price P_r and letting the monopolist choose its profit-maximizing or loss-minimizing output. Production takes place where $P_r =$ MC, and this equality indicates an efficient allocation of resources to this product or service. The price that achieves allocative efficiency is called the **socially optimal price.**

Fair-Return Price: P = ATC

But the socially optimal price P_r that equals marginal cost may be so low that average total costs are not covered, as is the case in Figure 11.9. The result is a loss for the firm. The reason lies in the basic character of our firm. Because it is required to meet the heaviest "peak" demands (both daily and seasonally) for natural gas, it has substantial excess production capacity when demand is relatively "normal." Its high level of investment in production facilities and economies of scale mean that its average total cost is likely to be greater than its marginal cost over a very wide range of outputs. In particular, as in Figure 11.9, average total cost is likely to be greater than the price P_r at the intersection of the demand curve and marginal-cost curve. Therefore, forcing the socially optimal price P_r on the regulated monopolist would result in short-run losses and long-run bankruptcy for the utility.

What to do? One option is to provide a public subsidy to cover the loss that marginal-cost pricing would entail. Another possibility is to condone price discrimination and hope that the additional revenue gained will permit the firm to cover costs.

In practice, regulatory commissions have pursued a third option: They modify the objective of allocative efficiency and $P =$ MC pricing. Most regulatory agencies in the United States establish a **fair-return price.** They do so because the courts have ruled that a socially optimal price leading to losses and bankruptcy deprives the monopoly's owners of their private property without due process of law. The Supreme Court has held that regulatory agencies must permit a "fair return" to utility owners.

Remembering that total cost includes a normal or "fair" profit, we see in Figure 11.9 that a fair-return price should be on the average-total-cost curve. Because the demand curve cuts average total cost only at point f, clearly P_f is the only price on the demand curve that permits a fair return. The corresponding output at regulated price P_f will be Q_f. Total revenue of $0afb$ will equal the utility's total cost of the same amount, and the firm will realize a normal profit.

Dilemma of Regulation

Comparing results of the socially optimal price ($P =$ MC) and the fair-return price ($P =$ ATC) suggests a policy dilemma, sometimes termed the *dilemma of regulation*. When its price is set to achieve the most efficient allocation of resources ($P =$ MC), the regulated monopoly is likely to suffer losses. Survival of the firm would presumably depend on permanent public subsidies out of tax revenues. On the other hand, although a fair-return price ($P =$ ATC) allows the monopolist to cover costs, it only partially resolves the underallocation of resources that the unregulated monopoly price would foster. That is, the fair-return price would increase output only from Q_m to Q_f in Figure 11.9, while the socially optimal output is Q_r. Despite this dilemma, regulation can improve on the results of monopoly from the social point of view. Price regulation (even at the fair-

return price) can simultaneously reduce price, increase output, and reduce the economic profits of monopolies. **(Key Question 11)**

QUICK REVIEW 11.3

■ Price discrimination occurs when a firm sells a product at different prices that are not based on cost differences.

■ The conditions necessary for price discrimination are (a) monopoly power, (b) the ability to segregate buyers on the basis of demand elasticities, and (c) the inability of buyers to resell the product.

■ Compared with single pricing by a monopolist, perfect price discrimination results in greater profit and greater output. Many consumers pay higher prices, but other buyers pay prices below the single price.

■ Monopoly price can be reduced and output increased through government regulation.

■ The socially optimal price ($P =$ MC) achieves allocative efficiency but may result in losses; the fair-return price ($P =$ ATC) yields a normal profit but fails to achieve allocative efficiency.

De Beers' Diamonds: Are Monopolies Forever?

De Beers Was One of the World's Strongest and Most Enduring Monopolies. But in Mid-2000 It Announced That It Could No Longer Control the Supply of Diamonds and Thus Would Abandon Its 66-Year Policy of Monopolizing the Diamond Trade.

De Beers, a Swiss-based company controlled by a South African corporation, produces about 50 percent of the world's rough-cut diamonds and purchases for resale a sizable number of the rough-cut diamonds produced by other mines worldwide. As a result, De Beers markets 63 percent of the world's diamonds to a select group of diamond cutters and dealers. But that percentage has declined from 80 percent in the mid-1980s and continues to shrink. Therein lies the company's problem.

Classic Monopoly Behavior

De Beers' past monopoly behavior and results are a classic example of the unregulated monopoly model illustrated in Figure 11.4. No matter how many diamonds it mined or purchased, it sold only the quantity of diamonds that would yield an "appropriate" (monopoly) price. That price was well above production costs, and De Beers and its partners earned monopoly profits.

When demand fell, De Beers reduced its sales to maintain price. The excess of production over sales was then reflected in growing diamond stockpiles held by De Beers. It also attempted to bolster demand through advertising ("Diamonds are forever"). When demand was strong, it increased sales by reducing its diamond inventories.

De Beers used several methods to control the production of many mines it did not own. First, it convinced a number of independent producers that "single-channel" or monopoly marketing through De Beers would maximize their profit. Second, mines that circumvented De Beers often found their market suddenly flooded with similar diamonds from De Beers' vast stockpiles. The resulting price decline and loss of profit often would encourage a "rogue" mine into the De Beers fold. Finally, De Beers simply purchased and stockpiled diamonds produced by independent mines so that their added supplies would not "undercut" the market.

An End of an Era?

Several factors have come together to unravel the monopoly. New diamond discoveries resulted in a growing leakage of diamonds into world markets outside De Beers' control. For example, significant prospecting and trading in Angola occurred. Recent diamond discoveries in Canada's Northwest Territories pose another threat. Although De Beers is a participant in that region, a large uncontrolled supply of diamonds is expected to emerge. Similarly, although Russia is part of the De Beers monopoly, this cash-strapped country is allowed to sell part of its diamond stock directly into the world markets.

If that was not enough, Australian diamond producer Argyle opted to withdraw from the De Beers monopoly. Its annual production of mostly low-grade industrial diamonds accounts for about 6 percent of the global $8 billion diamond market. Moreover, the international media began to focus heavily on the role that diamonds play in financing the bloody civil wars in Africa. Fearing a consumer boycott of diamonds, De Beers pledged not to buy these "conflict" diamonds or do business with any firms that did. These diamonds, however, continue to find their way into the marketplace, eluding De Beers' control.

In mid-2000 De Beers abandoned its attempt to control the supply of diamonds. It announced that it planned to transform itself from a diamond cartel to a modern firm selling "premium" diamonds and other luxury goods under the De Beers label. It therefore would gradually reduce its $4 billion stockpile of diamonds and turn its efforts to increasing the overall demand for diamonds through advertising. De Beers proclaimed that it was changing its strategy to being "the diamond supplier of choice."

With its high market share and ability to control its own production levels, De Beers will still wield considerable influence over the price of rough-cut diamonds. But it turns out that the De Beers monopoly was not forever.

SUMMARY

1. A pure monopolist is the sole producer of a commodity for which there are no close substitutes.

2. The existence of pure monopoly and other imperfectly competitive market structures is explained by barriers to entry in the form of (a) economies of scale, (b) patent ownership and research, (c) ownership or control of essential resources, and (d) pricing and other strategic behavior.

3. The pure monopolist's market situation differs from that of a competitive firm in that the monopolist's demand curve is downsloping, causing the marginal-revenue curve to lie below the demand curve. Like the competitive seller, the pure monopolist will maximize profit by equating marginal revenue and marginal cost. Barriers to entry may permit a monopolist to acquire economic profit even in the long run. However, (a) the monopolist does not charge "the highest price possible"; (b) the price that yields maximum total profit to the monopolist rarely coincides with the price that yields maximum unit profit; (c) high costs and a weak demand may prevent the monopolist from realizing any profit at all; and (d) the monopolist avoids the inelastic region of its demand curve.

4. With the same costs, the pure monopolist will find it profitable to restrict output and charge a higher price than would sellers in a purely competitive industry. This restriction of output causes resources to be misallocated, as is evidenced by the fact that price exceeds marginal cost in monopolized markets.

5. In general, monopoly transfers income from consumers to the owners of the monopoly. Because, on average, consumers of monopolized products have less income than the corporate owners, monopoly increases income inequality.

6. The costs monopolists and competitive producers face may not be the same. On the one hand, economies of scale may make lower unit costs available to monopolists but not to competitors. Also, pure monopoly may be more likely than pure competition to reduce costs via technological advance because of the monopolist's ability to realize economic profit, which can be used to finance research. On the other hand, X-inefficiency—the failure to produce with the least costly combination of inputs—is more common among monopolists than among competitive firms. Also, monopolists may make costly expenditures to maintain monopoly privileges that are conferred by government. Finally, the blocked entry of rival firms weakens the monopolist's incentive to be technologically progressive.

7. A monopolist can increase its profit by practicing price discrimination, provided (a) it can segregate buyers on the basis of elasticities of demand and (b) its product or service cannot be readily transferred between the segregated markets. Other things equal, the perfectly discriminating monopolist will produce a larger output than the nondiscriminating monopolist.

8. Price regulation can be invoked to eliminate wholly or partially the tendency of monopolists to underallocate resources and to earn economic profits. The socially optimal price is determined where the demand and marginal-cost curves intersect; the fair-return price is determined where the demand and average-total-cost curves intersect.

TERMS AND CONCEPTS

pure monopoly
barriers to entry

simultaneous consumption
network effects

X-inefficiency
rent-seeking behavior
price discrimination

socially optimal price
fair-return price

STUDY QUESTIONS

1. "No firm is completely sheltered from rivals; all firms compete for consumer dollars. If that is so, then pure monopoly does not exist." Do you agree? Explain. How might you use Chapter 20's concept of cross elasticity of demand to judge whether monopoly exists?

2. Discuss the major barriers to entry into an industry. Explain how each barrier can foster either monopoly or oligopoly. Which barriers, if any, do you feel give rise to monopoly that is socially justifiable?

3. How does the demand curve faced by a purely monopolistic seller differ from that confronting a purely competitive firm? Why does it differ? Of what significance is the difference? Why is the pure monopolist's demand curve not perfectly inelastic?

4. **Key Question** Use the demand schedule that follows to calculate total revenue and marginal revenue at each quantity. Plot the demand, total-revenue, and marginal-revenue curves and explain the relationships between them. Explain why the marginal revenue of

the fourth unit of output is $3.50, even though its price is $5. Use Chapter 20's total-revenue test for price elasticity to designate the elastic and inelastic segments of your graphed demand curve. What generalization can you make as to the relationship between marginal revenue and elasticity of demand? Suppose the marginal cost of successive units of output was zero. What output would the profit-seeking firm produce? Finally, use your analysis to explain why a monopolist would never produce in the inelastic region of demand.

Price (P)	Quantity Demanded (Q)	Price (P)	Quantity Demanded (Q)
$7.00	0	$4.50	5
6.50	1	4.00	6
6.00	2	3.50	7
5.50	3	3.00	8
5.00	4	2.50	9

5. **Key Question** Suppose a pure monopolist is faced with the demand schedule shown below and the same cost data as the competitive producer discussed in question 4 at the end of Chapter 10. Calculate the missing total-revenue and marginal-revenue amounts, and determine the profit-maximizing price and profit-earning output for this monopolist. What is the monopolist's profit? Verify your answer graphically and by comparing total revenue and total cost.

Price	Quantity Demanded	Total Revenue	Marginal Revenue
$115	0	$_____	$_____
100	1	_____	_____
83	2	_____	_____
71	3	_____	_____
63	4	_____	_____
55	5	_____	_____
48	6	_____	_____
42	7	_____	_____
37	8	_____	_____
33	9	_____	_____
29	10	_____	_____

6. **Key Question** If the firm described in question 5 could engage in perfect price discrimination, what would be the level of output? Of profits? Draw a diagram showing the relevant demand, marginal-revenue, average-total-cost, and marginal-cost curves and the equilibrium price and output for a nondiscriminating monopolist. Use the same diagram to show the equilibrium position of a monopolist that is able to practice perfect price discrimination. Compare equilibrium outputs, total revenues, economic profits, and consumer prices in the two cases. Comment on the economic desirability of price discrimination.

7. Assume that a pure monopolist and a purely competitive firm have the same unit costs. Contrast the two with respect to (a) price, (b) output, (c) profits, (d) allocation of resources, and (e) impact on the distribution of income. Since both monopolists and competitive firms follow the MC = MR rule in maximizing profits, how do you account for the different results? Why might the costs of a purely competitive firm and a monopolist be different? What are the implications of such a cost difference?

8. Critically evaluate and explain each statement:
   a. Because they can control product price, monopolists are always assured of profitable production by simply charging the highest price consumers will pay.
   b. The pure monopolist seeks the output that will yield the greatest per-unit profit.
   c. An excess of price over marginal cost is the market's way of signaling the need for more production of a good.
   d. The more profitable a firm, the greater its monopoly power.
   e. The monopolist has a pricing policy; the competitive producer does not.
   f. With respect to resource allocation, the interests of the seller and of society coincide in a purely competitive market but conflict in a monopolized market.
   g. In a sense the monopolist makes a profit for not producing; the monopolist produces profit more than it does goods.

9. Assume a monopolistic publisher has agreed to pay an author 15 percent of the total revenue from the sales of a text. Will the author and the publisher want to charge the same price for the text? Explain.

10. Explain verbally and graphically how price (rate) regulation may improve the performance of monopolies. In your answer distinguish between (a) socially optimal (marginal-cost) pricing and (b) fair-return (average-total-cost) pricing. What is the "dilemma of regulation"?

11. **Key Question** It has been proposed that natural monopolists should be allowed to determine their profit-maximizing outputs and prices and then government should tax their profits away and distribute them to consumers in proportion to their purchases from the monopoly. Is this proposal as socially desirable as requiring monopolists to equate price with marginal cost or average total cost?

12. **(Last Word)** How was De Beers able to control the world price of diamonds over the past several decades even though it produced only 50 percent of the diamonds? What factors ended its monopoly? What is its new strategy for earning economic profit, rather than just normal profit?

13. **Web-Based Question:** *Is Microsoft a monopoly?— What did the Federal district court conclude?* Use the information at <u>usvms.gpo.gov/conclusions_ index.html</u> to answer the following questions: On what basis did the Federal district court conclude that Microsoft was a monopoly (see the section on monopoly power)? What specific percentage market share did it attribute to Microsoft? Go to <u>usvms.gpo.gov</u> to discover the court's main remedy for reducing Microsoft's monopoly power. Finally,

Microsoft has appealed the district court decision to a higher court. Use the Internet to determine the present status of the appeal. Is the appeal still pending? Has the district court decision been upheld? Overturned?

14. **Web-Based Question:** *Getting to know your state regulatory commission* Go to <u>www.yahoo.com</u> or some other standard search engine and type "public utility commissions" in the search line. Find the utilities commission for the state where you reside (or another state if you cannot find the website for your state commission). What industries does the state commission regulate? How many specific firms are registered or regulated? List the names of ten such specific firms. Why are these and the other firms regulated?

12

Monopolistic Competition
and Oligopoly

MOST MARKET STRUCTURES in the U.S. economy fall between the two extremes of pure competition and pure monopoly. In this chapter we develop models of *monopolistic competition* and *oligopoly* that more closely approximate "real-world" market structures. ■ Monopolistic competition exhibits a considerable amount of competition mixed with a small dose of monopoly power. For example, when you go out to eat, you have an amazing variety of choices. You can get a meal at a fast-food place such as McDonald's, Subway, or Taco Bell. Or you can go to a restaurant with a fuller menu and with table service, say, Applebee's, TGI Fridays, or a locally owned restaurant. For a special meal you can choose an Italian, French, or Japanese fine-food restaurant where your bill may be $20 or more per person. Each of these establishments serves food and beverages, but all have different menus and prices. Competition among them is based not only on price but also on product quality, location, service, and advertising. ■ Oligopoly, in contrast, displays a blend of greater monopoly power, less competition via entry, and more strategic behavior. There are only a few firms in an oligopolistic industry, and entry is difficult. For example, when you fly on a large commercial aircraft, you are probably flying in a plane built by one of two producers: Airbus or Boeing. In many manufacturing, mining, and wholesaling industries there are only a few dominant firms, not the thousands of producers present in pure competition, the many firms in monopolistic competition, or the single firm in monopoly.

■ Monopolistic Competition

Let's begin by examining **monopolistic competition,** which is characterized by (1) a relatively large number of sellers, (2) differentiated products (often promoted by heavy advertising), and (3) easy entry to, and exit from, the industry. The first and third characteristics provide the "competitive" aspect of monopolistic competition; the second characteristic provides the "monopolistic" aspect. In general, however, monopolistically competitive industries are far more competitive than they are monopolistic. 🔑12.1

Relatively Large Number of Sellers

Monopolistic competition is characterized by a fairly large number of firms, say, 25, 35, 60, or 70, not by the hundreds or thousands of firms in pure competition. Consequently, monopolistic competition involves:

- *Small market shares* Each firm has a comparatively small percentage of the total market and consequently has limited control over market price.

- *No collusion* The presence of a relatively large number of firms ensures that collusion by a group of firms to restrict output and set prices is unlikely.

- *Independent action* With numerous firms in an industry, there is no feeling of interdependence among them; each firm can determine its own pricing policy without considering the possible reactions of rival firms. A single firm may realize a modest increase in sales by cutting its price, but the effect of that action on competitors' sales will be nearly imperceptible and will probably trigger no response.

Differentiated Products

In contrast to pure competition, in which there is a standardized product, monopolistic competition is distinguished by **product differentiation.** Monopolistically competitive firms turn out variations of a particular product. They produce products with slightly different physical characteristics, offer varying degrees of customer service, provide varying amounts of locational convenience, or proclaim special qualities, real or imagined, for their products.

Let's examine these aspects of product differentiation in more detail.

Product Attributes Product differentiation may entail physical or qualitative differences in the products themselves. Real differences in functional features, materials, design, and workmanship are vital aspects of product differentiation. Personal computers, for example, differ in terms of storage capacity, speed, graphic displays, and included software. There are dozens of competing principles of economics textbooks that differ in content, organization, presentation and readability, pedagogical aids, and

graphics and design. Most cities have a variety of retail stores selling men's and women's clothes that differ greatly in styling, materials, and quality of work. Similarly, one furniture manufacturer may feature its solid oak furniture, while a competitor stresses its solid maple furniture.

Service Service and the conditions surrounding the sale of a product are forms of product differentiation too. One grocery store may stress the helpfulness of its clerks who bag your groceries and carry them to your car. A warehouse competitor may leave bagging and carrying to its customers but feature lower prices. Customers may prefer 1-day over 3-day dry cleaning of equal quality. The prestige appeal of a store, the courteousness and helpfulness of clerks, the firm's reputation for servicing or exchanging its products, and the credit it makes available are all service aspects of product differentiation.

Location Products may also be differentiated through the location and accessibility of the stores that sell them. Small convenience stores manage to compete with large supermarkets, even though these minimarts have a more limited range of products and charge higher prices. They compete mainly on the basis of location—being close to customers and situated on busy streets. A motel's proximity to an interstate highway gives it a locational advantage that may enable it to charge a higher room rate than nearby motels in less convenient locations.

Brand Names and Packaging Product differentiation may also be created through the use of brand names and trademarks, packaging, and celebrity connections. Most aspirin tablets are very much alike, but many headache sufferers believe that one brand—for example, Bayer, Anacin, or Bufferin—is superior and worth a higher price than a generic substitute. A celebrity's name associated with jeans, perfume, or athletic equipment may enhance the appeal of those products for some buyers. Many customers prefer one style of ballpoint pen to another. Packaging that touts "natural spring" bottled water may attract additional customers.

Some Control over Price Despite the relatively large number of firms, monopolistic competitors do have some control over their product prices because of product differentiation. If consumers prefer the products of specific sellers, then within limits they will pay more to satisfy their preferences. Sellers and buyers are not linked randomly, as in a purely competitive market. But the monopolistic competitor's control over price is quite limited, since there are numerous potential substitutes for its product.

Easy Entry and Exit

Entry into monopolistically competitive industries is relatively easy compared to oligopoly or pure monopoly. Because monopolistic competitors are typically small firms, both absolutely and relatively, economies of scale are few and capital requirements are low. On the other hand, compared with pure competition, financial barriers may result from the need to develop and advertise a product that differs from rivals' products. Some firms may hold patents on their products or copyrights on their brand names, making it difficult and costly for other firms to imitate them.

Exit from monopolistically competitive industries is easier still. Nothing prevents an unprofitable monopolistic competitor from holding a going-out-of-business sale and shutting down.

Advertising

The expense and effort involved in product differentiation would be wasted if consumers were not made aware of product differences. Thus, monopolistic competitors advertise their products, often heavily. The goal of product differentiation and advertising—so-called **nonprice competition**—is to make price less of a factor in consumer purchases and make product differences a greater factor. If successful, the firm's demand curve will shift to the right and will become less elastic.

Monopolistically Competitive Industries

Table 12.1 lists several manufacturing industries that approximate monopolistic competition. (We will explain the data in column 3 later in this chapter.) In addition, many retail establishments in metropolitan areas are monopolistically competitive, including grocery stores, gasoline stations, barbershops, dry cleaners, clothing stores, and restaurants.

■ Price and Output in Monopolistic Competition

We now analyze the price and output decisions of a monopolistically competitive firm. Initially, we assume that each firm in the industry is producing a specific differentiated product and engaging in a particular amount of advertising. Later we'll see how changes in the product and in the amount of advertising modify our conclusions.

The Firm's Demand Curve

Our explanation is based on **Figure 12.1 (Key Graph).** The basic feature of that diagram is the elasticity of demand, as shown by the individual firm's demand curve. The demand curve faced by a

Table 12.1

Percentage of Output Produced by Firms in Selected Low-Concentration U.S. Manufacturing Industries

(1) Industry	(2) Percentage of Industry Output* Produced by the Four Largest Firms	(3) Herfindahl Index	(1) Industry	(2) Percentage of Industry Output* Produced by the Four Largest Firms	(3) Herfindahl Index
Manufactured ice	24	264	Textile bags	17	164
Plastic pipe	23	268	Bolts, nuts, and rivets	17	134
Book publishing	23	251	Jewelry	16	95
Paperboard boxes	23	237	Typesetting	16	106
Curtains and draperies	22	184	Asphalt paving	15	103
Textile machinery	21	197	Sawmills	14	78
Leather goods	21	196	Women's dresses	11	61
Lighting fixtures	21	191	Sheet metal work	9	34
Wood furniture	20	167	Wood pallets	6	14
Wooden kitchen cabinets	19	156			

*As measured by value of shipments. Data are for 1992. Data for 1997 will be released in the second half of 2001. See www.census.gov/epcd/www/concentration. html. *Source:* Bureau of Census, Census of Manufacturers, 1992.

(a)
Short-run profits

(b)
Short-run losses

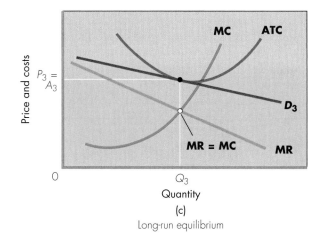

(c)
Long-run equilibrium

Figure 12.1

A monopolistically competitive firm: short run and long run. The monopolistic competitor maximizes profit or minimizes loss by producing the output at which MR = MC. The economic profit shown in (a) will induce new firms to enter, eventually eliminating economic profit. The loss shown in (b) will cause an exit of firms until normal profit is restored. After such entry and exit, the price will settle in (c) to where it just equals average total cost at the MR = MC output. At this price P_3 and output Q_3, the monopolistic competitor earns only a normal profit, and the industry is in long-run equilibrium.

Quick Quiz 12.1

1. Price exceeds MC in:
   a. graph (a) only.
   b. graph (b) only.
   c. graphs (a) and (b) only.
   d. graphs (a), (b), and (c).

2. Price exceeds ATC in:
   a. graph (a) only.
   b. graph (b) only.
   c. graphs (a) and (b) only.
   d. graphs (a), (b), and (c).

3. The firm represented by Figure 12.1c is:
   a. making a normal profit.
   b. incurring a loss.

   c. producing at the same level of output as a purely competitive firm.
   d. producing a standardized product.

4. Which of the following pairs are both "competition-like elements" in monopolistic competition?
   a. Price exceeds MR; standardized product.
   b. Entry is relatively easy; only a normal profit in the long run.
   c. Price equals MC at the profit-maximizing output; economic profits are likely in the long run.
   d. The firms' demand curve is downsloping; differentiated products.

Answers: 1. d; 2. a; 3. a; 4. b

monopolistically competitive seller is highly, but not perfectly, elastic. It is precisely this feature that distinguishes monopolistic competition from pure monopoly and pure competition. The monopolistic competitor's demand is more elastic than the demand faced by a pure monopolist, because the monopolistically competitive seller has many competitors producing closely substitutible goods. The pure monopolist has no rivals at all. Yet, for two reasons, the monopolistic competitor's demand is not perfectly elastic like that of the pure competitor. First, the monopolistic competitor has fewer rivals; second, its products are differentiated, so they are not perfect substitutes.

The price elasticity of demand faced by the monopolistically competitive firm depends on the number of rivals and the degree of product differentiation. The larger the number of rivals and the weaker the product differentiation, the greater the price elasticity of each seller's demand, that is, the closer monopolistic competition will be to pure competition.

The Short Run: Profit or Loss

The monopolistically competitive firm maximizes its profit or minimizes its loss in the short run just as do the other firms we have discussed: by producing the output at which marginal revenue equals marginal cost (MR = MC). In Figure 12.1a the firm produces output Q_1, where MR = MC. As shown by demand curve D_1, it then can charge price P_1. It realizes an economic profit, shown by the taupe area [= $(P_1 - A_1) \times Q_1$].

But with less favorable demand or costs, the firm may incur a loss in the short run. We show this possibility in Figure 12.1b, where the firm's best strategy is to minimize its loss. It does so by producing output Q_2 (where MR = MC) and, as determined by demand curve D_2, by charging price P_2. Because price P_2 is less than average total cost A_2, the firm incurs a per-unit loss of $A_2 - P_2$ and a total loss represented as the taupe area [= $(A_2 - P_2) \times Q_2$].

The Long Run: Only a Normal Profit

In the long run, firms will enter a profitable monopolistically competitive industry and leave an unprofitable one. So a monopolistic competitor will earn only a normal profit in the long run or, in other words, will only break even. (Remember that the cost curves include both explicit and implicit costs, including a normal profit.)

Profits: Firms Enter In the case of short-run profit (Figure 12.1a), economic profits attract new rivals, because entry to the industry is relatively easy. As new firms enter, the demand curve faced by the typical firm shifts to the left (falls). Why? Because each firm has a smaller share of total demand and now faces a larger number of close-substitute products. This decline in the firm's demand reduces its economic profit. When entry of new firms has reduced demand to the extent that the demand curve is tangent to the average-total-cost curve at the profit-maximizing output, the firm is just making a normal profit. This situation is shown in Figure 12.1c, where demand is D_3 and the firm's long-run equilibrium output is Q_3. As Figure 12.1c indicates, any greater or lesser output will entail an average total cost that exceeds product price P_3, meaning a loss for the firm. At the tangency point between the demand curve and ATC, total revenue equals total costs. With the economic profit gone, there is no further incentive for additional firms to enter.

Losses: Firms Leave When the industry suffers short-run losses, as in Figure 12.1b, some firms will exit in the long run. Faced with fewer substitute products and blessed with an expanded share of total demand, the surviving firms will see their demand curves shift to the right (rise), as to D_3. Their losses will disappear and give way to normal profits (Figure 12.1c). (For simplicity we have assumed constant costs; shifts in the cost curves as firms enter or leave would complicate our discussion slightly but would not alter our conclusions.)

Complications The representative firm in the monopolistic competition model earns only a normal profit in the long run. That outcome may not always occur, however, in the real world of small firms as opposed to the theoretical model.

■ Some firms may achieve sufficient product differentiation such that other firms cannot duplicate them, even over time. One hotel in a major city may have the best location relative to business and tourist activities. Or a firm may have developed a well-known brand name that gives it a slight but very long-lasting advantage over imitators. Such firms may have sufficient monopoly power to realize modest economic profits even in the long run.

■ Entry to some monopolistically competitive industries is not as free in reality as it is in theory. Because of product differentiation, there are likely to be greater financial barriers to entry than there would be if the product were standardized. This suggests some monopoly power, with small economic profits continuing even in the long run.

With all things considered, however, the normal profit outcome—the long-run equilibrium—shown in Figure 12.1c is a reasonable portrayal of reality. 📐 **12.1**

▌Monopolistic Competition and Efficiency

We know from Chapter 10 that economic efficiency requires the triple equality $P = MC = $ minimum ATC. The equality of price and minimum average total cost yields *productive efficiency*. The good is be-

ing produced in the least costly way, and the price is just sufficient to cover average total cost, including a normal profit. The equality of price and marginal cost yields *allocative efficiency*. The right amount of output is being produced, and thus the right amount of society's scarce resources is being devoted to this specific use.

How efficient is monopolistic competition, as measured against this triple equality?

Neither Productive nor Allocative Efficiency

In monopolistic competition, neither productive nor allocative efficiency occurs in long-run equilibrium. We show this in Figure 12.2, which includes an enlargement of part of Figure 12.1c. First note that the profit-maximizing price P_3 slightly exceeds the lowest average total cost, A_4. Therefore, in producing the profit-maximizing output Q_3, the firm's average total cost is slightly higher than optimal from society's perspective—productive efficiency is not

Figure 12.2

The inefficiency of monopolistic competition. In long-run equilibrium a monopolistic competitor achieves neither productive nor allocative efficiency. Productive efficiency is not realized because production occurs where the average total cost A_3 exceeds the minimum average total cost A_4. Allocative efficiency is not realized because the product price P_3 exceeds the marginal cost M_3. The result is an underallocation of resources and excess productive capacity of $Q_4 - Q_3$.

achieved. Also note that the profit-maximizing price P_3 exceeds marginal cost (here M_3), meaning that monopolistic competition causes an underallocation of resources. Society values each unit of output between Q_3 and Q_4 more highly than the goods it would have to forgo to produce those units. Thus, to a modest extent, monopolistic competition also fails the allocative-efficiency test. Consumers pay a higher-than-competitive price and obtain a less-than-optimal output. Indeed, monopolistic competitors must charge a higher-than-competitive price in the long run in order to achieve a normal profit.

Excess Capacity

In monopolistic competition, the gap between the minimum-ATC output and the profit-maximizing output identifies **excess capacity:** plant and equipment that are underused because firms are producing less than the minimum-ATC output. We show this gap as the distance between Q_4 and Q_3 in Figure 12.2. If each monopolistic competitor could profitably produce at the minimum-ATC output, fewer firms could produce the same total output, and the product could be sold at a lower price. Monopolistically competitive industries thus are overcrowded with firms, each operating below its optimal capacity. This situation is typified by many kinds of retail establishments. For example, in most cities there is an abundance of small motels and restaurants that operate well below half capacity. **(Key Question 2)**

∎ Product Variety

The situation portrayed in Figures 12.1c and 12.2 is not very satisfying to monopolistic competitors, since it foretells only a normal profit. But the profit-realizing firm of Figure 12.1a need not stand by and watch new competitors eliminate its profit by imitating its product, matching its customer service, and copying its advertising. Each firm has a product that is distinguishable in some way from those of the other producers. So the firm can attempt to stay ahead of competitors and sustain its profit through further product differentiation and better advertising. By developing or improving its product, it may be able to postpone, at least for a while, the outcome of Figure 12.1c.

Although product differentiation and advertising will add to the firm's costs, they can also increase the demand for its product. If demand increases by more than enough to compensate for the added costs, the firm will have improved its profit position. As Figure 12.2 suggests, the firm has little or no prospect of increasing profit by price cutting. So why not engage in nonprice competition?

Benefits of Product Variety

The product variety and product improvement that accompany the drive to maintain economic profit in monopolistic competition are a benefit for society—one that may offset the cost of the inefficiency associated with monopolistic competition. Consumers have a wide diversity of tastes: Some like regular fries, others like curly fries; some like contemporary furniture, others like traditional furniture. If a product is differentiated, then at any time the consumer will be offered a wide range of types, styles, brands, and quality gradations of that product. Compared with pure competition, this provides an advantage to the consumer. The range of choice is widened, and producers more fully meet the wide variation in consumer tastes.

The product improvement promoted by monopolistic competition further differentiates products and expands choices. And a successful product improvement by one firm obligates rivals to imitate or improve on that firm's temporary market advantage or else lose business. So society benefits from better products.

In fact, product differentiation creates a tradeoff between consumer choice and productive efficiency. The stronger the product differentiation, the greater is the excess capacity and, hence, the greater is the productive inefficiency. But the greater the product differentiation, the more likely the firms will satisfy the great diversity of consumer tastes. The greater is the excess-capacity problem, the wider the range of consumer choice.

Further Complexity

Finally, the ability to engage in nonprice competition makes the market situation of a monopolistic competitor more complex than Figure 12.1 indicates. That figure assumes a given (unchanging) product and a given level of advertising expenditures. But we know that, in practice, product attributes and advertising are not fixed. The monopolistically competitive firm juggles three factors—price, product, and advertising—in seeking maximum profit. It must determine what variety of product, selling at what price, and supplemented by what level of advertising will result in the greatest profit. This complex situation is not easily expressed in a simple, meaningful economic model. At best, we can say that each possible combination of price, product, and advertising poses a different demand and cost (production cost plus advertising cost) situation for the firm and that one combination yields the maximum profit. In practice, this optimal combination cannot be readily forecast but must be found by trial and error.

> ### QUICK REVIEW 12.1
>
> ▪ Monopolistic competition involves a relatively large number of firms operating in a noncollusive way and producing differentiated products with easy industry entry and exit.
>
> ▪ In the short run, a monopolistic competitor will maximize profit or minimize loss by producing that output at which marginal revenue equals marginal cost.
>
> ▪ In the long run, easy entry and exit of firms cause monopolistic competitors to earn only a normal profit.
>
> ▪ A monopolistic competitor's long-run equilibrium output is such that price exceeds the minimum average total cost (implying that consumers do not get the product at the lowest price attainable) and price exceeds marginal cost (indicating that resources are underallocated to the product).

▌ Oligopoly

In terms of competitiveness, the spectrum of market structures reaches from pure competition, to monopolistic competition, to oligopoly, to pure monopoly (review Table 10.1). We now direct our attention to **oligopoly,** a market dominated by a few large producers of a homogeneous or differentiated product. Because of their "fewness," oligopolists have considerable control over their prices, but each must consider the possible reaction of rivals to its own pricing, output, and advertising decisions.

A Few Large Producers

The phrase "a few large producers" is necessarily vague because the market model of oligopoly covers much ground, ranging between pure monopoly, on the one hand, and monopolistic competition, on the other. Oligopoly encompasses the U.S. aluminum

industry, in which three huge firms dominate an entire national market, and the situation in which four or five much smaller auto-parts stores enjoy roughly equal shares of the market in a medium-size town. Generally, however, when you hear a term such as "Big Three," "Big Four," or "Big Six," you can be sure it refers to an oligopolistic industry.

Homogeneous or Differentiated Products

An oligopoly may be either a **homogeneous oligopoly** or a **differentiated oligopoly,** depending on whether the firms in the oligopoly produce standardized or differentiated products. Many industrial products (steel, zinc, copper, aluminum, lead, cement, industrial alcohol) are virtually standardized products that are produced in oligopolies. Alternatively, many consumer goods industries (automobiles, tires, household appliances, electronics equipment, breakfast cereals, cigarettes, and many sporting goods) are differentiated oligopolies. These differentiated oligopolies typically engage in considerable nonprice competition supported by heavy advertising.

Control over Price, but Mutual Interdependence

Because firms are few in oligopolistic industries, each firm is a "price maker"; like the monopolist, it can set its price and output levels to maximize its profit. But unlike the monopolist, which has no rivals, the oligopolist must consider how its rivals will react to any change in its price, output, product characteristics, or advertising. Oligopoly is thus characterized by **mutual interdependence:** a situation in which each firm's profit depends not entirely on its own price and sales strategies but also on those of its rivals. Example: In deciding whether to increase the price of its baseball gloves, Rawlings will try to predict the response of the other major producers, such as Wilson. Second example: In deciding on its advertising strategy, Burger King will take into consideration how McDonald's might react.

Entry Barriers

The same barriers to entry that create pure monopoly also contribute to the creation of oligopoly. Economies of scale are important entry barriers in a number of oligopolistic industries, such as the aircraft, rubber, and cement industries. In those industries, three or four firms might each have sufficient sales to achieve economies of scale, but new firms would have such a small market share that they could not do so. They would then be high-cost producers, and as such they could not survive. A closely related barrier is the large expenditure for capital—the cost of obtaining necessary plant and equipment—required for entering certain industries. The jet engine, automobile, commercial aircraft, and petroleum-refining industries, for example, are all characterized by very high capital requirements.

The ownership and control of raw materials help explain why oligopoly exists in many mining industries, including gold, silver, and copper. In the electronics, chemicals, photographic equipment, office equipment, and pharmaceutical industries, patents have served as entry barriers. Moreover, oligopolists can preclude the entry of new competitors through preemptive and retaliatory pricing and advertising strategies.

Mergers

Some oligopolies have emerged mainly through the growth of the dominant firms in a given industry (examples: breakfast cereals, chewing gum, candy bars). But for other industries the route to oligopoly has been through mergers (examples: steel, in its early history, and, more recently, airlines, banking, and entertainment). The merging, or combining, of two or more competing firms may substantially increase their market share, and this in turn may allow the new firm to achieve greater economies of scale.

Another motive underlying the "urge to merge" is the desire for monopoly power. The larger firm that results from a merger has greater control over market supply and thus the price of its product. Also, since it is a larger buyer of inputs, it will probably be able to demand and obtain lower prices (costs) on its production inputs.

Measures of Industry Concentration

Several means are used to measure the degree to which oligopolistic industries are concentrated in the "hands" of their largest firms. The most-often-used measures are *concentration ratios* and the *Herfindahl index.*

Concentration Ratio
A **concentration ratio** reveals the percentage of total output produced and sold by an industry's largest firms. Column 2 in

Table 12.2 lists the four-firm concentration ratio—the percentage of total industry sales accounted for by the four largest firms—for a number of oligopolistic industries. For example, the four largest U.S. producers of breakfast cereals manufacture 85 percent of all breakfast cereals produced in the United States.

When the largest four firms in an industry control 40 percent or more of the market (as in Table 12.2), that industry is considered oligopolistic. Using this benchmark, about one-half of all U.S. manufacturing industries are oligopolies.

Although concentration ratios provide useful insights into the competitiveness or monopoly power of various industries, they have three shortcomings.

Localized Markets
Concentration ratios pertain to the nation as a whole, whereas the markets for some products are highly localized because of high transportation costs. For example, the four-firm concentration ratio for ready-mix concrete is only 6 percent, suggesting a highly competitive industry. But the sheer bulk of this product limits the relevant market to a specific town or metropolitan area, and in such localized markets we often find oligopolistic concrete producers.

Interindustry Competition
Since definitions of industries are somewhat arbitrary, we must be aware of **interindustry competition**—that is, competition between two products associated with different industries. The high concentration ratio for the copper industry shown in Table 12.2 understates the competition in that industry, because aluminum competes with copper in many applications (for example, in the market for electric transmission lines).

World Trade
The data in Table 12.2 are only for products produced in the United States and may overstate concentration because they do not account for the **import competition** of foreign suppliers. The motorcycle and bicycle industry is a good example. Although Table 12.2 shows that four U.S. firms produce 65 percent of the domestic output of those goods, it ignores the fact that a very large portion of the motorcycles and bicycles bought in the United States are imports. Many of the world's largest corporations are foreign, and many of them do business in the United States.

Herfindahl Index
The concentration-ratio shortcomings listed above actually apply to many

Table 12.2

Percentage of Output Produced by Firms in Selected High-Concentration U.S. Manufacturing Industries

(1) Industry	(2) Percentage of Industry Output* Produced by the Four Largest Firms	(3) Herfindahl Index	(1) Industry	(2) Percentage of Industry Output* Produced by the Four Largest Firms	(3) Herfindahl Index
Primary copper	98	2827	Aircraft	79	2711
Cigarettes	93	ND[†]	Photo equipment and supplies	78	2408
Beer	90	ND	Gypsum products	75	2078
Electric light bulbs	86	2702	Men's slacks	75	2338
Breakfast cereals	85	2253	Tires and inner tubes	70	1743
Motor vehicles	84	2676	Roasted coffee	66	1501
Greeting cards	84	2922	Motorcycles and bicycles	65	1419
Glass containers	84	2162	Soap and detergents	63	1584
Small-arms ammunition	84	ND[†]	Lawn and garden equipment	62	1085
Household refrigerators and freezers	82	1891			
Flat glass	81	1988			
Turbines and generators	79	2549			

*As measured by value of shipments. Data are for 1992. Data for 1997 will be released in the second half of 2001. See www.census.gov/epcd/www/concentration. html.

[†]ND = not disclosed.

Source: Bureau of Census, Census of Manufacturers, 1992.

measures of concentration, but one of those shortcomings can be eliminated: Suppose that in industry X one firm produces all the market output. In a second industry, Y, there are four firms, of which each has 25 percent of the market. The concentration ratio is 100 percent for both these industries. But industry X is a pure monopoly, while industry Y is an oligopoly that may be facing significant economic rivalry. Most economists would agree that monopoly power (or market power) is substantially greater in industry X than in industry Y, a fact disguised by their identical 100 percent concentration ratios.

The **Herfindahl index** addresses this problem. This index is the sum of the squared percentage market shares of all firms in the industry. In equation form:

$$\text{Herfindahl index} = (\%S_1)^2 + (\%S_2)^2 + (\%S_3)^2 + \cdots + (\%S_n)^2$$

where $\%S_1$ is the percentage market share of firm 1, $\%S_2$ is the percentage market share of firm 2, and so on for each firm in the industry. By squaring the percentage market shares of all firms in the industry, the Herfindahl index gives much greater weight to larger, and thus more powerful, firms than to smaller ones. In the case of the single-firm industry X, the index would be at its maximum of 100^2 or 10,000,

indicating an industry with complete monopoly power. For our supposed four-firm industry Y, the index would be $25^2 + 25^2 + 25^2 + 25^2$, or 2500, indicating much less market power. (For a purely competitive industry, the index would approach zero, since each firm's market share—$\%S$ in the equation—is extremely small.)

To generalize, the larger the Herfindahl index, the greater the market power within an industry. Note in Table 12.2 that the four-firm concentration ratios for the glass-container industry and the greeting-card industry are both 84 percent. But the Herfindahl index of 2922 for the greeting-card industry suggests greater market power than the 2162 index for the glass-container industry. Also, contrast the much larger Herfindahl indexes in Table 12.2 with those for the low-concentration industries in Table 12.1. **(Key Question 7)**

▌Oligopoly Behavior: A Game-Theory Overview

Oligopoly pricing behavior has the characteristics of certain games of strategy, such as poker, chess, and bridge. The best way to play such a game depends on the way one's opponent plays. Players (and oligopolists) must pattern their actions according to the actions and expected reactions of rivals. The study of how people behave in strategic situations is called *game theory*. And we will use a simple **game-theory model** to analyze the pricing behavior of oligopolists. We assume a duopoly, or two-firm oligopoly, producing athletic shoes. Each of the two firms—let's call them RareAir and Uptown—has a choice of two pricing strategies: price high or price low. The profit each firm earns will depend on the strategy it chooses and the strategy its rival chooses. 🔎 12.2

There are four possible combinations of strategies for the two firms, and a lettered cell in Figure 12.3 represents each combination. For example, cell C represents a low-price strategy for Uptown along with a high-price strategy for RareAir. Figure 12.3 is called a *payoff matrix*, because each cell shows the payoff (profit) to each firm that would result from each combination of strategies. Cell C shows that if Uptown adopts a low-price strategy and RareAir a high-price strategy, then Uptown will earn $15 million (green portion) and RareAir will earn $6 million (gold portion).

RareAir's price strategy

Figure 12.3
Profit payoff (in millions) for a two-firm oligopoly.
Each firm has two possible pricing strategies. RareAir's strategies are shown in the top margin, and Uptown's in the left margin. Each lettered cell of this four-cell payoff matrix represents one combination of a RareAir strategy and an Uptown strategy and shows the profit that combination would earn for each firm.

Mutual Interdependence Revisited

The data in Figure 12.3 are hypothetical, but their relationships are typical of real situations. Recall that oligopolistic firms can increase their profits, and influence their rivals' profits, by changing their pricing strategies. Each firm's profit depends on its own pricing strategy and that of its rivals. This mutual interdependence of oligopolists is the most obvious point demonstrated by Figure 12.3. If Uptown adopts a high-price strategy, its profit will be $12 million provided that RareAir also employs a high-price strategy (cell A). But if RareAir uses a low-price strategy against Uptown's high-price strategy (cell B), RareAir will increase its market share and boost its profit from $12 to $15 million. RareAir's higher profit will come at the expense of Uptown, whose profit will fall from $12 to $6 million. Uptown's high-price strategy is a good strategy only if RareAir also employs a high-price strategy.

Collusive Tendencies

Figure 12.3 also suggests that oligopolists often can benefit from **collusion**—that is, cooperation with rivals. To see the benefits of collusion, first suppose that both firms in Figure 12.3 are acting independently and following high-price strategies. Each realizes a $12 million profit (cell A).

Note that either RareAir or Uptown could increase its profit by switching to a low-price strategy (cell B or C). The low-price firm would increase its profit to $15 million, and the high-price firm's profit would fall to $6 million. The high-price firm would be better off if it, too, adopted a low-price policy. Doing so would increase its profit from $6 million to $8 million (cell D). The effect of all this independent strategy shifting would be the reduction of both firms' profits from $12 million (cell A) to $8 million (cell D).

In real situations, too, independent action by oligopolists may lead to mutual "competitive" low-price strategies: Independent oligopolists compete with respect to price, and this leads to lower prices and lower profits. This outcome is clearly beneficial to consumers but not to the oligopolists, whose profits decrease.

How could oligopolists avoid the low-profit outcome of cell D? The answer is that they could collude, rather than establish prices competitively or independently. In our example, the two firms could agree to establish and maintain a high-price policy.

So each firm will increase its profit from $8 million (cell D) to $12 million (cell A).

Incentive to Cheat

The payoff matrix also explains why an oligopolist might be strongly tempted to cheat on a collusive agreement. Suppose Uptown and RareAir agree to maintain high-price policies, with each earning $12 million in profit (cell A). Both are tempted to cheat on this collusive pricing agreement, because either firm can increase its profit to $15 million by lowering its price. If Uptown secretly cheats on the agreement by charging low prices, the payoff moves from cell A to cell C. Uptown's profit rises to $15 million, and RareAir's falls to $6 million. If RareAir cheats, the payoff moves from cell A to cell B, and RareAir gets the $15 million. **(Key Question 8)** 12.1

> ### QUICK REVIEW 12.2
>
> An oligopoly is made up of relatively few firms producing either homogeneous or differentiated products; these firms are mutually interdependent.
>
> Barriers to entry such as scale economies, control of patents or strategic resources, or the ability to engage in retaliatory pricing characterize oligopolies. Oligopolies may result from internal growth of firms, mergers, or both.
>
> The four-firm concentration ratio shows the percentage of an industry's sales accounted for by its four largest firms; the Herfindahl index measures the degree of market power in an industry by summing the squares of the percentage market shares held by the individual firms in the industry.
>
> Game theory reveals that (a) oligopolies are mutually interdependent in their pricing policies; (b) collusion enhances oligopoly profits; and (c) there is a temptation for oligopolists to cheat on a collusive agreement.

■ Three Oligopoly Models

To gain further insight into oligopolistic pricing and output behavior, we will examine three distinct pricing models: (1) the kinked-demand curve, (2) collusive pricing, and (3) price leadership.

Why not a single model, as in our discussions of the other market structures? There are two reasons:

■ *Diversity of oligopolies* Oligopoly encompasses a greater range and diversity of market

situations than do other market structures. It includes the *tight* oligopoly, in which two or three firms dominate an entire market, and the *loose* oligopoly, in which six or seven firms share, say, 70 or 80 percent of a market while a "competitive fringe" of firms shares the remainder. It includes both differentiated and standardized products. It includes cases in which firms act in collusion and those in which they act independently. It embodies situations in which barriers to entry are very strong and situations in which they are not quite so strong. In short, the diversity of oligopoly does not allow us to explain all oligopolistic behaviors with a single market model.

■ *Complications of interdependence* The mutual interdependence of oligopolistic firms complicates matters significantly. Because firms cannot predict the reactions of their rivals with certainty, they cannot estimate their own demand and marginal-revenue data. Without such data, firms cannot determine their profit-maximizing price and output, even in theory, as we will see.

Despite these analytical difficulties, two interrelated characteristics of oligopolistic pricing have been observed. First, if the macroeconomy is generally stable, oligopolistic prices are typically inflexible (or "rigid" or "sticky"). Prices change less frequently under oligopoly than under pure competition, monopolistic competition, and, in some instances, pure monopoly. Second, when oligopolistic prices do change, firms are likely to change their prices together, suggesting that there is a tendency to act in concert, or collusively, in setting and changing prices (as we mentioned in the preceding section). The diversity of oligopolies and the presence of mutual interdependence are reflected in the models that follow.

Kinked-Demand Theory: Noncollusive Oligopoly

Imagine an oligopolistic industry made up of three hypothetical firms (Arch, King, and Dave's), each having about one-third of the total market for a differentiated product. Assume that the firms are "independent," meaning that they do not engage in collusive price practices. Assume, too, that the going price for Arch's product is P_0 and its current sales are Q_0, as shown in **Figure 12.4a (Key Graph)**.

Now the question is, "What does the firm's demand curve look like?" Mutual interdependence and the uncertainty about rivals' reactions make this

KEY GRAPH

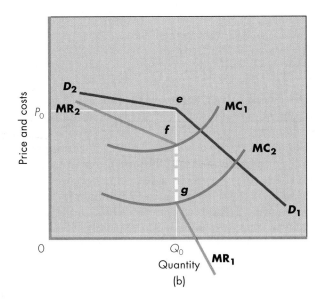

(a)

(b)

Figure 12.4

The kinked-demand curve. (a) The slope of a noncollusive oligopolist's demand and marginal-revenue curves depends on whether its rivals match (straight lines D_1 and MR_1) or ignore (straight lines D_2 and MR_2) any price changes that it may initiate from the current price P_0. (b) In all likelihood an oligopolist's rivals will ignore a price increase but follow a price cut. This causes the oligopolist's demand curve to be kinked (D_2eD_1) and the marginal-revenue curve to have a vertical break, or gap (fg). Because any shift in marginal costs between MC_1 and MC_2 will cut the vertical (dashed) segment of the marginal-revenue curve, no change in either price P_0 or output Q_0 will result from such a shift.

Quick Quiz 12.4

1. Suppose Q_0 in this figure represents annual sales of 5 million units for this firm. The other two firms in this three-firm industry sell 3 million and 2 million units, respectively. The Herfindahl index for this industry is:
   a. 100 percent.
   b. 400.
   c. 10.
   d. 3800

2. The D_2e segment of the demand curve D_2eD_1 in graph (b) implies that:
   a. this firm's total revenue will fall if it increases its price above P_0.
   b. other firms will match a price increase above P_0.
   c. the firm's relevant marginal-revenue curve will be MR_1 for price increases above P_0.

   d. the product in this industry is necessarily standardized.

3. By matching a price cut, this firm's rivals can:
   a. increase their market shares.
   b. increase their marginal revenues.
   c. maintain their market shares.
   d. lower their total costs.

4. A shift of the marginal-cost curve from MC_2 to MC_1 in graph (b) would:
   a. increase the "going price" above P_0.
   b. leave price at P_0, but reduce this firm's total profit.
   c. leave price at P_0, but reduce this firm's total revenue.
   d. make this firm's demand curve more elastic.

Answers: 1. d; 2. a; 3. c; 4. b

question hard to answer. The location and shape of an oligopolist's demand curve depend on how the firm's rivals will react to a price change introduced by Arch. There are two plausible assumptions about the reactions of Arch's rivals:

■ ***Match price changes*** One possibility is that King and Dave's will exactly match any price change initiated by Arch. In this case, Arch's demand and marginal-revenue curves will look like the straight lines labeled D_1 and MR_1 in Figure 12.4a. Why are they so steep? Reason: If Arch cuts its price, its sales will increase only modestly because its two rivals will also cut their prices to prevent Arch from gaining an advantage over them. The small increase in sales that Arch (and its two rivals) will realize is at the expense of other industries; Arch will gain no sales from King and Dave's. If Arch raises its price, its sales will fall only modestly, because King and Dave's will match its price increase. The industry will lose sales to other industries, but Arch will lose no customers to King and Dave's.

■ ***Ignore price changes*** The other possibility is that King and Dave's will ignore any price change by Arch. In this case, the demand and marginal-revenue curves faced by Arch will resemble the straight lines D_2 and MR_2 in Figure 12.4a. Demand in this case is considerably more elastic than it was under the previous assumption. The reasons are clear: If Arch lowers its price and its rivals do not, Arch will gain sales significantly at the expense of its two rivals because it will be underselling them. Conversely, if Arch raises its price and its rivals do not, Arch will lose many customers to King and Dave's, which will be underselling it. Because of product differentiation, however, Arch's sales will not fall to zero when it raises its price; some of Arch's customers will pay the higher price because they have a strong preference for Arch's product.

A Combined Strategy

Now, which is the most logical assumption for Arch to make about how its rivals will react to any price change it might initiate? The answer is, "It depends on the direction of price." Common sense and observation of oligopolistic industries suggest that a firm's rivals will match price declines below P_0 as they act to prevent the price cutter from taking their customers. But they will ignore price increases above P_0, because the rivals of

the price-increasing firm stand to gain the business lost by the price booster. In other words, the dark-green left-hand segment of the "rivals ignore" demand curve D_2 seems relevant for price increases, and the dark-green right-hand segment of the "rivals follow" demand curve D_1 seems relevant for price cuts. It is logical, then, or at least a reasonable assumption, that the noncollusive oligopolist faces the **kinked-demand curve** D_2eD_1, as shown in Figure 12.4b. Demand is highly elastic above the going price P_0 but much less elastic or even inelastic below that price.

Note also that if it is correct to suppose that rivals will follow a price cut but ignore an increase, the marginal-revenue curve of the oligopolist will also have an odd shape. It, too, will be made up of two segments: the taupe left-hand part of marginal-revenue curve MR_2 in Figure 12.4a and the taupe right-hand part of marginal-revenue curve MR_1. Because of the sharp difference in elasticity of demand above and below the going price, there is a gap, or what we can simply treat as a vertical segment, in the marginal-revenue curve. We show this gap as the dashed segment in the combined marginal-revenue curve MR_2fgMR_1 in Figure 12.4b.

Price Inflexibility

This analysis helps explain why prices are generally stable in noncollusive oligopolistic industries. There are both demand and cost reasons.

On the demand side, the kinked-demand curve gives each oligopolist reason to believe that any change in price will be for the worse. If it raises its price, many of its customers will desert it. If it lowers its price, its sales at best will increase very modestly, since rivals will match the lower price. Even if a price cut increases the oligopolist's total revenue somewhat, its costs may increase by a greater amount. And if its demand is inelastic to the right of Q_0, as it may well be, then the firm's profit will surely fall. A price decrease in the inelastic region lowers the firm's total revenue, and the production of a larger output increases its total costs.

On the cost side, the broken marginal-revenue curve suggests that even if an oligopolist's costs change substantially, the firm may have no reason to change its price. In particular, all positions of the marginal-cost curve between MC_1 and MC_2 in Figure 12.4b will result in the firm's deciding on exactly the same price and output. For all those positions, MR equals MC at output Q_0; at that output, it will charge price P_0.

Criticisms of the Model The kinked-demand analysis has two shortcomings. First, it does not explain how the going price gets to be at P_0 in Figure 12.4 in the first place. It only helps explain why oligopolists tend to stick with an existing price. The kinked-demand curve explains price inflexibility but not price itself.

Second, when the macroeconomy is unstable, oligopoly prices are not as rigid as the kinked-demand theory implies. During inflationary periods, many oligopolists have raised their prices often and substantially. And during downturns (recessions), some oligopolists have cut prices. In some instances these price reductions have set off a **price war:** *successive and continuous rounds of price cuts by rivals as they attempt to maintain their market shares.* **(Key Question 9)**

Cartels and Other Collusion

Our game-theory model demonstrated that oligopolists might benefit from collusion. We can say that collusion occurs whenever firms in an industry reach an agreement to fix prices, divide up the market, or otherwise restrict competition among themselves. The disadvantages and uncertainties of noncollusive, kinked-demand oligopolies are obvious. There is always the danger of a price war breaking out, especially during a general business recession. Then each firm finds that, because of unsold goods and excess capacity, it can reduce per-unit costs by increasing market share. Then, too, a new firm may surmount entry barriers and initiate aggressive price cutting to gain a foothold in the market. In addition, the kinked-demand curve's tendency toward rigid prices may adversely affect profits if general inflationary pressures increase costs. However, by controlling price through collusion, oligopolists may be able to reduce uncertainty, increase profits, and perhaps even prohibit the entry of new rivals.

Price and Output Assume once again that there are three hypothetical oligopolistic firms (Gypsum, Sheetrock, and GSR) producing, in this instance, gypsum Sheetrock for finishing interior walls. All three firms produce a homogeneous product and have identical cost curves. Each firm's demand curve is indeterminate unless we know how its rivals will react to any price change. Therefore, we suppose each firm assumes that its two rivals will match either a price cut or a price increase. In other words, each firm has a demand curve like the straight line

D_1 in Figure 12.4a. And since they have identical cost data, and the same demand and thus marginal-revenue data, we can say that Figure 12.5 represents the position of each of our three oligopolistic firms.

What price and output combination should, say, Gypsum select? If Gypsum were a pure monopolist, the answer would be clear: Establish output at Q_0, where marginal revenue equals marginal cost, charge the corresponding price P_0, and enjoy the maximum profit attainable. However, Gypsum does have two rivals selling identical products, and if Gypsum's assumption that its rivals will match its price of P_0 proves to be incorrect, the consequences could be disastrous for Gypsum. Specifically, if Sheetrock and GSR actually charge prices below P_0, then Gypsum's demand curve D will shift sharply to the left as its potential customers turn to its rivals, which are now selling the same product at a lower price. Of course, Gypsum can retaliate by cutting its price too, but this will move all three firms down their demand curves, lowering their profits. It may even drive them to a point where average total cost exceeds price and losses are incurred.

So the question becomes, "Will Sheetrock and GSR want to charge a price below P_0?" Under our assumptions, and recognizing that Gypsum has little choice except to match any price they may set below

Figure 12.5

Collusion and the tendency toward joint-profit maximization. If oligopolistic firms face identical or highly similar demand and cost conditions, they may collude to limit their joint output and to set a single, common price. Thus each firm acts as if it were a pure monopolist, setting output at Q_0 and charging price P_0. This price and output combination maximizes each oligopolist's profit (taupe area) and thus their combined or joint profit.

P_0, the answer is no. Faced with the same demand and cost circumstances, Sheetrock and GSR will find it in their interest to produce Q_0 and charge P_0. This is a curious situation; each firm finds it most profitable to charge the same price, P_0, but only if its rivals actually do so! How can the three firms ensure the price P_0 and quantity Q_0 solution in which each is keenly interested? How can they avoid the less profitable outcomes associated with either higher or lower prices?

The answer is evident: They can collude. They can get together, talk it over, and agree to charge the same price, P_0. In addition to reducing the possibility of price wars, this will give each firm the maximum profit. (But it will also subject them to antitrust prosecution if they are caught!) For society, the result will be the same as would occur if the industry were a pure monopoly composed of three identical plants.

Overt Collusion: The OPEC Cartel

Collusion may assume a variety of forms. The most comprehensive form of collusion is the **cartel,** *a group of producers that typically creates a formal written agreement specifying how much each member will produce and charge.* Output must be controlled—the market must be divided up—in order to maintain the agreed-upon price. The collusion is overt, or open to view.

Undoubtedly the most significant international cartel is the Organization of Petroleum Exporting Countries (OPEC), comprising 11 oil-producing nations (see Global Perspective 12.1.) OPEC produces 40 percent of the world's oil and supplies 60 percent of all oil traded internationally. In the late 1990s it reacted vigorously to very low oil prices by greatly restricting supply. Some non-OPEC producers supported the cutback in production, and within a 15-month period the price of oil shot up from $11 a barrel to $34 a barrel. Gasoline prices in the United States rose by as much as $1 a gallon in some markets. Fearing a global political and economic backlash from the major industrial nations, OPEC upped the production quotas for its members in mid-2000. The increases in oil supply that resulted reduced oil prices somewhat. It is clear that the OPEC cartel has sufficient market power to hold the price of oil substantially above its marginal cost of production.

Covert Collusion: Relatively Recent Examples

Cartels are illegal in the United States, and hence any collusion that exists is covert or se-

GLOBAL PERSPECTIVE 12.1

The 11 OPEC Nations, Daily Oil Production, 2001

The OPEC nations produce about 40 percent of the world's oil and 60 percent of the oil sold in world markets.

OPEC Country	Barrels of Oil
Saudi Arabia	8,189,000
Iran	3,698,000
Venezuela	2,902,000
UAE	2,201,000
Nigeria	2,075,000
Kuwait	2,021,000
Libya	1,350,000
Indonesia	1,307,000
Algeria	805,000
Qatar	653,000
Iraq	(U.N. embargo)

Source: OPEC, www.opec.org/.

cret. Yet there are numerous examples, as shown by evidence from antitrust (antimonopoly) cases. In 1993 the Borden, Pet, and Dean food companies, among others, either pleaded guilty or were convicted of rigging bids on the prices of milk products sold to schools and military bases. By phone or at luncheons, company executives agreed in advance on which firm would submit the low bid for each school district or military base. In 1996 American agribusiness Archer Daniels Midland and three Japanese and South Korean firms were found to have conspired to fix the worldwide price and sales volume of a livestock feed additive. Executives for the firms secretly met in Hong Kong, Paris, Mexico City, Vancouver, and Zurich to discuss their plans. **!** 12.2

In many other instances collusion is even subtler. **Tacit understandings** (historically called "gentlemen's agreements") are frequently made at cocktail parties, on golf courses, through phone calls, or at trade association meetings. In such agreements, competing firms reach a verbal understanding on product price, leaving market shares to be decided by nonprice competition. Although these agreements, too, violate antitrust laws—and can result in severe personal and corporate penalties—the elusive character of tacit understandings makes them more difficult to detect.

Obstacles to Collusion Normally, cartels and similar collusive arrangements are difficult to establish and maintain. Here are several barriers to collusion:

Demand and Cost Differences When oligopolists face different costs and demand curves, it is difficult for them to agree on a price. This is particularly the case in industries where products are differentiated and change frequently. Even with highly standardized products, firms usually have somewhat different market shares and operate with differing degrees of productive efficiency. Thus it is unlikely that even homogeneous oligopolists would have the same demand and cost curves.

In either case, differences in costs and demand mean that the profit-maximizing price will differ among firms; no single price will be readily acceptable to all, as we assumed was true in Figure 12.5. So price collusion depends on compromises and concessions that are not always easy to obtain and hence act as an obstacle to collusion.

Number of Firms Other things equal, the larger the number of firms, the more difficult it is to create a cartel or some other form of price collusion. Agreement on price by three or four producers that control an entire market may be relatively easy to accomplish. But such agreement is more difficult to achieve where there are, say, 10 firms, each with roughly 10 percent of the market, or where the Big Three have 70 percent of the market while a competitive fringe of 8 or 10 smaller firms battles for the remainder.

Cheating As the game-theory model makes clear, there is a temptation for collusive oligopolists to engage in secret price cutting to increase sales and profit. The difficulty with such cheating is that buyers who are paying a high price for a product may become aware of the lower-priced sales and demand similar treatment. Or buyers receiving a price concession from one producer may use the concession as a wedge to get even larger price concessions from a rival producer. Buyers' attempts to play producers against one another may precipitate price wars among the producers. Although secret price concessions are potentially profitable, they threaten collusive oligopolies over time. Collusion is more likely to succeed when cheating is easy to detect and punish. Then the conspirators are less likely to cheat on the price agreement.

Recession Long-lasting recession usually serves as an enemy of collusion, because slumping markets increase average total cost. In technical terms, as the oligopolists' demand and marginal-revenue curves shift to the left in Figure 12.5 in response to a recession, each firm moves leftward and upward to a higher operating point on its average-total-cost curve. Firms find they have substantial excess production capacity, sales are down, unit costs are up, and profits are being squeezed. Under such conditions, businesses may feel they can avoid serious profit reductions (or even losses) by cutting price and thus gaining sales at the expense of rivals.

Potential Entry The greater prices and profits that result from collusion may attract new entrants, including foreign firms. Since that would increase market supply and reduce prices and profits, successful collusion requires that colluding oligopolists block the entry of new producers.

Legal Obstacles: Antitrust Law U.S. antitrust laws prohibit cartels and price-fixing collusion. So less obvious means of price control have evolved in this country.

Price Leadership Model

Price leadership entails a type of implicit understanding by which oligopolists can coordinate prices without engaging in outright collusion based on formal agreements and secret meetings. Rather, a practice evolves whereby the "dominant firm"—usually the largest or most efficient in the industry—initiates price changes and all other firms more or less automatically follow the leader. Many industries, including farm machinery, cement, copper, newsprint, glass containers, steel, beer, fertilizer, cigarettes, and tin, are practicing, or have in the recent past practiced, price leadership.

Leadership Tactics An examination of price leadership in a variety of industries suggests that the price leader is likely to observe the following tactics.

Infrequent Price Changes Because price changes always carry the risk that rivals will not follow the lead, price adjustments are made only infrequently. The price leader does not respond to minuscule day-to-day changes in costs and demand. Price is changed only when cost and demand conditions have been altered significantly and on an industrywide basis as the result of, for example, industrywide wage increases, an increase in excise taxes, or an increase in the price of some basic input such as energy. In the automobile industry, price adjustments traditionally have been made when new models are introduced each fall.

Communications The price leader often communicates impending price adjustments to the industry through speeches by major executives, trade publication interviews, or press releases. By publicizing "the need to raise prices," the price leader seeks agreement among its competitors regarding the actual increase.

Limit Pricing The price leader does not always choose the price that maximizes short-run profits for the industry because the industry may want to discourage new firms from entering. If the cost advantages (economies of scale) of existing firms are a major barrier to entry, new entrants could surmount that barrier if the price leader and the other firms set product price high enough. New firms that are relatively inefficient because of their small size might survive and grow if the industry sets price very high. So, in order to discourage new competitors and to maintain the current oligopolistic structure of the industry, the price leader may keep price below the short-run profit-maximizing level. The strategy of establishing a price that blocks the entry of new firms is called *limit pricing*.

Breakdowns in Price Leadership: Price Wars

Price leadership in oligopoly occasionally breaks down, at least temporarily, and sometimes results in a price war. An example of disruption of price leadership occurred in the breakfast cereal industry, in which Kellogg traditionally had been the price leader. General Mills countered Kellogg's leadership in 1995 by reducing the prices of its cereals by 11 percent. In 1996 Post responded with a 20 percent price cut, which Kellogg then followed. Not to be outdone, Post reduced its prices by another 11 percent.

Most price wars eventually run their course. When all firms recognize that low prices are severely reducing their profits, they again yield price leadership to one of the industry's leading firms. That firm then begins to raise prices, and the other firms willingly follow suit.

▮ Oligopoly and Advertising

We have noted that oligopolists would rather not compete on the basis of price and may become involved in price collusion. Nonetheless, each firm's share of the total market is typically determined through product development and advertising, for two reasons:

■ Product development and advertising campaigns are less easily duplicated than price cuts. Price cuts can be quickly and easily matched by a firm's rivals to cancel any potential gain in sales derived from that strategy. Product improvements and successful advertising, however, can produce more permanent gains in market share because they cannot be duplicated as quickly and completely as price reductions.

■ Oligopolists have sufficient financial resources to engage in product development and advertising. For most oligopolists, the economic profits earned in the past can help finance current advertising and product development.

Product development (or, more broadly, "research and development") is the subject of the next chapter, so we will confine our present discussion to advertising. In recent years, U.S. advertising has exceeded $215 billion annually, and worldwide advertising, $420 billion. *Advertising is prevalent in both monopolistic competition and oligopoly.* Table 12.3 lists the 10 leading U.S. advertisers in 1999.

Table 12.3

The Largest U.S. Advertisers, 1999

Company	Advertising Spending, Millions of $
General Motors Corp.	$4040
Procter & Gamble	2612
Philip Morris Cos.	2202
Pfizer	2142
AT&T	1951
DaimlerChrysler	1804
Ford Motor Co.	1640
Sears, Roebuck & Co.	1505
PepsiCo	1318
Verizon	1313

Source: Advertising Age, www.adage.com/.

Advertising may affect prices, competition, and efficiency both positively and negatively, depending on the circumstances. While our focus here is on advertising by oligopolists, the analysis is equally applicable to advertising by monopolistic competitors.

Positive Effects of Advertising

In order to make rational (efficient) decisions, consumers need information about product characteristics and prices. Advertising may be a low-cost means of providing that information. Suppose you are in the market for a high-quality camera and there is advertising of such a product in newspapers or magazines. To make a rational choice, you may have to spend several days visiting stores to determine the prices and features of various brands. This search entails both direct costs (gasoline, parking fees) and indirect costs (the value of your time). Advertising reduces your search time and minimizes these costs.

By providing information about the various competing goods that are available, advertising diminishes monopoly power. In fact, advertising is frequently associated with the introduction of new products designed to compete with existing brands. Could Toyota and Honda have so strongly challenged U.S. auto producers without advertising? Could Federal Express have sliced market share away from UPS and the U.S. Postal Service without advertising?

Viewed this way, advertising is an efficiency-enhancing activity. It is a relatively inexpensive means of providing useful information to consumers and

thus lowering their search costs. By enhancing competition, advertising results in greater economic efficiency. By facilitating the introduction of new products, advertising speeds up technological progress. By increasing output, advertising can reduce long-run average total cost by enabling firms to obtain economies of scale.

Potential Negative Effects of Advertising

Not all the effects of advertising are positive, of course. Much advertising is designed simply to manipulate or persuade consumers—that is, to alter their preferences in favor of the advertiser's product. A television commercial that indicates that a popular personality drinks a particular brand of soft drink—and therefore that you should too—conveys little or no information to consumers about price or quality. In addition, advertising is sometimes based on misleading and extravagant claims that confuse consumers rather than enlighten them. Indeed, in some cases advertising may well persuade consumers to pay high prices for much-acclaimed but inferior products, forgoing better but unadvertised products selling at lower prices. Example: *Consumer Reports* has found that heavily advertised premium motor oils and fancy additives provide no better engine performance and longevity than do cheaper brands.

Firms often establish substantial brand-name loyalty and thus achieve monopoly power via their advertising (see Global Perspective 12.2). As a consequence, they are able to increase their sales, expand their market shares, and enjoy greater profits. Larger profit permits still more advertising and further enlargement of the firm's market share and profit. In time, consumers may lose the advantages of competitive markets and face the disadvantages of monopolized markets. Moreover, new entrants to the industry need to incur large advertising costs in order to establish their products in the marketplace; thus, advertising costs may be a barrier to entry. **(Key Question 11)**

Advertising can also be self-canceling. The advertising campaign of one fast-food hamburger chain may be offset by equally costly campaigns waged by rivals, so each firm's demand actually remains unchanged. Few, if any, extra burgers will be purchased, and each firm's market share will stay the same. But because of the advertising, the cost and hence the price of hamburgers will be higher.

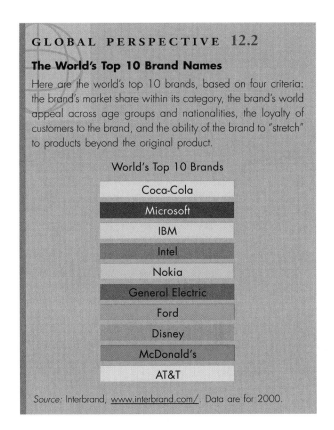

Source: Interbrand, www.interbrand.com/. Data are for 2000.

When advertising either leads to increased monopoly power or is self-canceling, economic inefficiency results.

Oligopoly and Efficiency

Is oligopoly, then, an efficient market structure from society's standpoint? How do the price and output decisions of the oligopolist measure up to the triple equality $P = MC = $ minimum ATC that occurs in pure competition?

Productive and Allocative Efficiency

Many economists believe that the outcome of some oligopolistic markets is approximately as shown in Figure 12.5. This view is bolstered by evidence that many oligopolists sustain sizable economic profits year after year. In that case, the oligopolist's production occurs where price exceeds marginal cost and average total cost. Moreover, production is below the output at which average total cost is minimized.

In this view, neither productive efficiency ($P = $ minimum ATC) nor allocative efficiency ($P = MC$) is likely to occur under oligopoly.

A few observers assert that oligopoly is actually less desirable than pure monopoly, because government usually regulates pure monopoly in the United States to guard against abuses of monopoly power. Informal collusion among oligopolists may yield price and output results similar to those under pure monopoly yet give the outward appearance of competition involving independent firms.

Qualifications

We should note, however, three qualifications to this view:

- *Increased foreign competition* In the past decade, foreign competition has increased rivalry in a number of oligopolistic industries—steel, automobiles, photographic film, electric shavers, outboard motors, and copy machines, for example. This has helped to break down such cozy arrangements as price leadership and to stimulate more competitive pricing.

- *Limit pricing* Recall that some oligopolists may purposely keep prices below the short-run profit-maximizing level in order to bolster entry barriers. In essence, consumers and society may get some of the benefits of competition—prices closer to marginal cost and minimum average total cost—even without the competition that free entry would provide.

- *Technological advance* Over time, oligopolistic industries may foster more rapid product development and greater improvement of production techniques than would be possible if they were purely competitive. Oligopolists have large economic profits from which they can fund expensive research and development (R&D). Moreover, the existence of barriers to entry may give the oligopolist some assurance that it will reap the rewards of successful R&D. Thus, the short-run economic inefficiencies of oligopolists may be partly or wholly offset by the oligopolists' contributions to better products, lower prices, and lower costs over time. We will have more to say about these more dynamic aspects of rivalry in Chapter 13.

Oligopoly in the Beer Industry

The Beer Industry Was Once Populated by Hundreds of Firms and an Even Larger Number of Brands. But It Now Is an Oligopoly Dominated by a Handful of Producers.

The brewing industry has undergone profound changes since the Second World War that have increased the degree of concentration in the industry. In 1947 more than 400 independent brewing companies existed in the United States. By 1967 there were 124, and by 1980 only 33. While the five largest brewers sold only 19 percent of the nation's beer in 1947, the Big Four brewers (Anheuser-Busch, Miller, Coors, and Pabst) currently sell 87 percent of the nation's domestically produced beer. The Big Two—Anheuser-Busch (at 47 percent) and Miller (at 22 percent)—produce 69 percent. The industry is clearly an oligopoly.

Changes on the demand side of the market have contributed to the "shakeout" of small brewers from the industry. First, consumer tastes have generally shifted from the stronger-flavored beers of the small brewers to the light products of the larger brewers. Second, there has been a shift from the consumption of beer in taverns to consumption of it in the home. The significance of this change is that taverns were usually supplied with kegs from local brewers to avoid the relatively high cost of shipping kegs. But the acceptance of aluminum cans for home consumption made it possible for large, distant brewers to compete with the local brewers, because the former could now ship their products by truck or rail without breakage.

Developments on the supply side of the market have been even more profound. Technological advances speeded up the bottling and canning lines. Today, large brewers can fill and close 2000 cans per line per minute. Large plants are also able to reduce labor costs through the automating of brewing and warehousing. Furthermore, plant construction costs per barrel are about one-third less for a 4.5-million-barrel plant than for a 1.5-million-barrel plant. As a consequence of these and other factors, the minimum efficient scale in brewing is a plant size of about 4.5 million barrels, with multiple plants. Because the construction cost of a modern brewery of that size is $300 million, economies of scale may now constitute a significant barrier to entry.

"Blindfold" taste tests confirm that most mass-produced American beers taste alike. So brewers greatly emphasize advertising. And here Anheuser-Busch, Miller, and Coors, which sell national brands, enjoy major cost advantages over producers such as Pabst that have many regional brands (for example, Lonestar, Rainer, Schaefer, and Schmidts). The reason is because national television advertising is less costly *per viewer* than local spot TV advertising.

Although mergers have occurred in the brewing industry, they have not been a fundamental cause of the rising concentration. Rather, they largely have been the result of failing smaller breweries (such as Heileman) selling out. Dominant firms have expanded by heavily advertising their main brands and by creating new brands such as Lite, Bud Light, Genuine Draft, Keystone, and Icehouse rather than acquiring other brewers. This has sustained significant product differentiation, despite the declining number of major brewers.

SUMMARY

1. The distinguishing features of monopolistic competition are (a) there are enough firms in the industry to ensure that each firm has only limited control over price, mutual interdependence is absent, and collusion is nearly impossible; (b) products are characterized by real or perceived differences so that economic rivalry entails both price and nonprice competition; and (c) entry to the industry is relatively easy. Many aspects of retailing, and some manufacturing industries in which economies of scale are few, approximate monopolistic competition.

2. Monopolistically competitive firms may earn economic profits or incur losses in the short run. The easy entry and exit of firms result in only normal profits in the long run.

3. The long-run equilibrium position of the monopolistically competitive producer is less socially desirable than that of the pure competitor. Under monopolistic competition, price exceeds marginal cost, suggesting an underallocation of resources to the product, and price exceeds minimum average total cost, indicating that consumers do not get the product at the lowest price that cost conditions might allow.

4. Nonprice competition provides a means by which monopolistically competitive firms can offset the long-run tendency for economic profit to fall to zero. Through product differentiation, product development, and advertising, a firm may strive to increase the demand for its product more than enough to cover the added cost of such nonprice competition. Consumers benefit from the wide diversity of product choice that monopolistic competition provides.

5. In practice, the monopolistic competitor seeks the specific combination of price, product, and advertising that will maximize profit.

6. Oligopolistic industries are characterized by the presence of few firms, each having a significant fraction

The rise of the Miller Brewing Company from the seventh- to the second-largest producer in the 1970s was due in large measure to advertising and product differentiation. When the Philip Morris Company acquired Miller in 1970, the new management made two big changes. First, it "repositioned" Miller High Life beer into that segment of the market where potential sales were the greatest. Sold previously as the "champagne of beers," High Life had appealed heavily to upper-income consumers and to occasional women beer drinkers. Miller's new television ads featured young blue-collar workers, who were inclined to be greater beer consumers. Second, Miller then developed its low-calorie Lite beer, which was extensively promoted with Philip Morris advertising dollars. Lite proved to be the most popular new product in the history of the beer industry. Miller later introduced its Genuine Draft beer, which found its place within the top 10 brands.

But the story of the last two decades has been not Miller but, rather, Anheuser-Busch (A-B), which has greatly expanded its market share. A-B now makes the nation's top two brands, Budweiser and Bud Light, and within 3 to 5 years is expected to produce one-half the beer sold in the United States. Part of A-B's success owes to the demise of regional competitors. But part also is the result of A-B's strategic prowess. It has constructed state-of-the-art breweries, created effective advertising campaigns, and forged strong relationships with regional distributors.

Imported beers such as Beck, Corona, Foster's, and Guinness constitute about 9 percent of the market, with individual brands seeming to wax and wane in popularity. Some local or regional microbreweries such as Samuel Adams and Pyramid, which brew specialty beers and charge super-premium prices, have slightly whittled into the sales of the major brewers. A-B and Miller have taken notice, responding with specialty brands of their own (for example, Redwolf, Elk Mountain, Crossroads, Red Dog, Icehouse) and bought stakes in microbrewers Redhook Ale and Celis. Overall, however, it appears that imports may pose more of a threat to the majors than the microbreweries do.

Sources: Based on Kenneth G. Elzinga, "Beer," in Walter Adams and James Brock (eds.), *The Structure of American Industry*, 10th ed. (Upper Saddle River, N.J.: Prentice-Hall, 2001), pp. 85–113; and Douglas F. Greer, "Beer: Causes of Structural Change," in Larry Duetsch (ed.), *Industry Studies*, 2d ed. (New York: M. E. Sharpe, 1998), pp. 28–64. Authors' updates.

of the market. Firms thus situated are mutually interdependent: The behavior of any one firm directly affects, and is affected by, the actions of rivals. Products may be either virtually uniform or significantly differentiated. Various barriers to entry, including economies of scale, underlie and maintain oligopoly.

7. Concentration ratios are a measure of oligopoly (monopoly) power. By giving more weight to larger firms, the Herfindahl index is designed to measure market dominance in an industry.

8. Game theory (a) shows the interdependence of oligopolists' pricing policies, (b) reveals the tendency of oligopolists to collude, and (c) explains the temptation of oligopolists to cheat on collusive arrangements.

9. Noncollusive oligopolists may face a kinked-demand curve. This curve and the accompanying marginal-revenue curve help explain the price rigidity that often characterizes oligopolies; they do not, however, explain how the actual prices of products were first established.

10. The uncertainties inherent in oligopoly promote collusion. Collusive oligopolists such as cartels maximize joint profits—that is, they behave like pure monopolists. Demand and cost differences, a "large" number of firms, cheating through secret price concessions, recessions, and the antitrust laws are all obstacles to collusive oligopoly.

11. Price leadership is an informal means of collusion whereby one firm, usually the largest or most efficient, initiates price changes and the other firms in the industry follow the leader.

12. Market shares in oligopolistic industries are usually determined on the basis of product development and advertising. Oligopolists emphasize nonprice competition because (a) advertising and product variations are less easy for rivals to match and (b) oligopolists frequently have ample resources to finance nonprice competition.

13. Advertising may affect prices, competition, and efficiency either positively or negatively. Positive: It can provide consumers with low-cost information about

competing products, help introduce new competing products into concentrated industries, and generally reduce monopoly power and its attendant inefficiencies. Negative: It can promote monopoly power via persuasion and the creation of entry barriers. Moreover, it can be self-canceling when engaged in by rivals by boosting costs and increasing economic inefficiency while accomplishing little else.

14. Neither productive nor allocative efficiency is realized in oligopolistic markets, but oligopoly may be superior to pure competition in promoting research and development and technological progress.

TERMS AND CONCEPTS

monopolistic competition	homogeneous oligopoly	import competition	price war
product differentiation	differentiated oligopoly	Herfindahl index	cartel
nonprice competition	mutual interdependence	game-theory model	tacit understandings
excess capacity	concentration ratio	collusion	price leadership
oligopoly	interindustry competition	kinked-demand curve	

STUDY QUESTIONS

1. How does monopolistic competition differ from pure competition in its basic characteristics? From pure monopoly? Explain fully what product differentiation may involve. Explain how the entry of firms into its industry affects the demand curve facing a monopolistic competitor and how that, in turn, affects its economic profit.

2. **Key Question** Compare the elasticity of the monopolistic competitor's demand with that of a pure competitor and a pure monopolist. Assuming identical long-run costs, compare graphically the prices and outputs that would result in the long run under pure competition and under monopolistic competition. Contrast the two market structures in terms of productive and allocative efficiency. Explain: "Monopolistically competitive industries are characterized by too many firms, each of which produces too little."

3. "Monopolistic competition is monopolistic up to the point at which consumers become willing to buy close-substitute products and competitive beyond that point." Explain.

4. "Competition in quality and service may be just as effective as price competition in giving buyers more for their money." Do you agree? Why? Explain why monopolistically competitive firms frequently prefer nonprice competition to price competition.

5. Critically evaluate and explain:
   a. "In monopolistically competitive industries economic profits are competed away in the long run; hence, there is no valid reason to criticize the performance and efficiency of such industries."
   b. "In the long run, monopolistic competition leads to a monopolistic price but not to monopolistic profits."

6. Why do oligopolies exist? List five or six oligopolists whose products you own or regularly purchase. What distinguishes oligopoly from monopolistic competition?

7. **Key Question** Answer the following questions, which relate to measures of concentration:
   a. What is the meaning of a four-firm concentration ratio of 60 percent? 90 percent? What are the shortcomings of concentration ratios as measures of monopoly power?
   b. Suppose that the five firms in industry A have annual sales of 30, 30, 20, 10, and 10 percent of total industry sales. For the five firms in industry B the figures are 60, 25, 5, 5, and 5 percent. Calculate the Herfindahl index for each industry and compare their likely competitiveness.

8. **Key Question** Explain the general meaning of the following profit payoff matrix for oligopolists C and D. All profit figures are in thousands.

C's possible prices

		$40	$35
D's possible prices	$40	$57 / $60	$59 / $55
	$35	$50 / $69	$55 / $58

   a. Use the payoff matrix to explain the mutual interdependence that characterizes oligopolistic industries.
   b. Assuming no collusion between C and D, what is the likely pricing outcome?

c. In view of your answer to 8*b*, explain why price collusion is mutually profitable. Why might there be a temptation to cheat on the collusive agreement?

9. **Key Question** What assumptions about a rival's response to price changes underlie the kinked-demand curve for oligopolists? Why is there a gap in the oligopolist's marginal-revenue curve? How does the kinked-demand curve explain price rigidity in oligopoly? What are the shortcomings of the kinked-demand model?

10. Why might price collusion occur in oligopolistic industries? Assess the economic desirability of collusive pricing. What are the main obstacles to collusion? Speculate as to why price leadership is legal in the United States, whereas price fixing is not.

11. **Key Question** Why is there so much advertising in monopolistic competition and oligopoly? How does such advertising help consumers and promote efficiency? Why might it be excessive at times?

12. **Advanced Analysis** Construct a game-theory matrix involving two firms and their decisions on high versus low advertising budgets and the effects of each on profits. Show a circumstance in which both firms select high advertising budgets even though both would be more profitable with low advertising budgets. Why won't they unilaterally cut their advertising budgets?

13. **(Last Word)** What firm dominates the beer industry? What demand and supply factors have contributed to "fewness" in this industry?

14. **Web-Based Question:** *Bookselling on the Internet —how do sellers differentiate identical books?* Upstart company Amazon introduced bookselling on the Web through its site at www.amazon.com. Amazon's success enticed a long-time bookseller, Barnes & Noble, to go online with a major website, www.barnesandnoble.com. Search both sites for Viktor Frankl's *Man's Search for Meaning* (paperback). Find the price delivered to your address. Is one cheaper? Identify the nonprice competition that might lead you to order from one company rather than the other.

15. **Web-Based Question:** *Market shares—top 10 lists Advertising Age*, at adage.com, compiles statistics on the market shares of many familiar products. Go to "Ad Age Dataplace" to find 100 leading national advertisers. Then scroll down and select the top 10 lists for five separate products. In general, do the very top sellers in the top 10 lists advertise more or less than the sellers toward the bottoms of the lists? Are there exceptions? Do you think the top 10 lists would get turned upside down if the pattern of advertising were turned upside down? Why or why not?

CHAPTER

13

Technology, R&D, and Efficiency

- "Just do it!" In 1968 two entrepreneurs in Oregon developed a lightweight sport shoe and formed a new company called Nike, incorporating a "swoosh" logo (designed by a graduate student for $35). Today, Nike employs more than 20,000 workers and sells more than $9 billion worth of athletic shoes, hiking boots, and sports apparel annually.

- "Intel inside." Intel? In 1967 neither this company nor its product existed. Today it is the world's largest producer of microprocessors for personal computers, with 67,500 employees and more than $29 billion in annual sales.

- When Wal-Mart arrives, "Look for falling prices." Expanding from a single store in 1962 to more than 2600 stores today, Wal-Mart employs about 650,000 full- and part-time workers and has greater annual revenues than Ford Motor, IBM, or AT&T.

- In 1996 Palm introduced its Palm Pilot, a palm-size personal computer that now also has wireless Internet capabilities. A novel idea? Apparently so. Microsoft, Handspring, OmniSky, and others have followed with similar products, and cell phone makers are incorporating Internet functionality into some of their new phones.

Each of these brief descriptions entails some elements of **technological advance,** broadly defined as *new and better goods and services and new and better ways of producing or distributing them.* In this chapter, we want to look at some of the microeconomics of technological advance. Who motivates and implements technological advance? What determines a firm's optimal amount of research and development (R&D)? What are the extent and implications of the imitation problem that innovators face? Are certain market structures more conducive to technological advance than others? And how does technological advance relate to efficiency?

Technological Advance: Invention, Innovation, and Diffusion

For economists, technological advance occurs over a theoretical time period called the *very long run*, which can be as short as a few months or as long as many years. Recall that in our four market models (pure competition, monopolistic competition, oligopoly, and pure monopoly), the short run is a period in which technology and plant and equipment are fixed. In the long run, technology is constant but firms can change their plant sizes and are free to enter or exit industries. In contrast, the **very long run** is a period in which technology can change and in which firms can develop and offer entirely new products.

In Chapter 2 we saw that technological advance shifts an economy's production possibilities curve outward, enabling the economy to obtain more goods and services. Technological advance is a three-step process of invention, innovation, and diffusion.

Invention

The basis of technological advance is **invention:** *the discovery of a product or process through the use of imagination, ingenious thinking, and experimentation and the first proof that it will work.* Invention is a process, and the result of the process is also called an invention. The prototypes (basic working model) of the telephone, the automobile, and the microchip are inventions. Invention usually is based on scientific knowledge and is the product of individuals, either working on their own or as members of corporate R&D staffs. Later on you will see how governments encourage invention by providing the inventor with a **patent,** an exclusive right to sell any new and useful process, machine, or product for a set period of time. In 2000 the five firms that secured the most U.S. patents were IBM (2922 patents), NEC (2034), Canon (1897), Samsung (1442), and Lucent (1442). Such patents have a worldwide duration of 20 years from the time of application for the patent.

Innovation

Innovation draws directly on invention. While invention is the "discovery and first proof of workability," **innovation** is *the first successful commercial introduction of a new product, the first use of a new method, or the creation of a new form of business enterprise.*

Innovation is of two types: **product innovation,** which refers to new and improved products or services; and **process innovation,** which refers to new and improved methods of production or distribution.

Unlike inventions, innovations cannot be patented. Nevertheless, innovation is a major factor in competition, since it sometimes enables a firm to "leapfrog" competitors by rendering their products or processes obsolete. For example, personal computers coupled with software for word processing pushed some major typewriter manufacturers into obscurity. More recently, innovations in hardware retailing (large warehouse stores such as Home Depot) have threatened the existence of smaller, more traditional hardware stores.

But innovation need not weaken or destroy existing firms. Aware that new products and processes may threaten their survival, existing firms have a powerful incentive to engage continuously in R&D of their own. Innovative products and processes often enable such firms to maintain or increase their profit. The aluminum cans introduced by Reynolds, disposable contact lenses by Johnson & Johnson, and scientific calculators by Hewlett-Packard are good examples. Thus, innovation can either diminish or strengthen market power.

Diffusion

Diffusion is the spread of an innovation through imitation or copying. To take advantage of new profit opportunities or to slow the erosion of profit, both new and existing firms emulate the successful innovations of others. Years ago McDonald's successfully introduced the fast-food hamburger; Burger King, Wendy's, and other firms soon copied that idea. Alamo greatly increased its auto rentals by offering customers unlimited mileage, and Hertz, Avis, Budget, and others eventually followed. Daimler-Chrysler profitably introduced a luxury version of its Jeep Grand Cherokee; other manufacturers, including Acura, Mercedes, and Lexus, countered with luxury sport-utility vehicles of their own. In each of these cases, innovation led eventually to widespread imitation—that is, to diffusion.

R&D Expenditures

As related to *businesses,* the term "research and development" is used loosely to include direct efforts toward invention, innovation, and diffusion.

However, *government* also engages in R&D, particularly R&D having to do with national defense. In 2000 *total* U.S. R&D expenditures (business *plus* government) were $264 billion. Relative to GDP that amount was 2.64 percent, which is a reasonable measure of the emphasis the U.S. economy puts on technological advance. As shown in Global Perspective 13.1, this is a high percentage of GDP compared to several other nations.

American businesses spent $199 billion on R&D in 2000. Figure 13.1 shows how these R&D expenditures were allocated. Observe that U.S. firms collectively channeled 72 percent of their R&D expenditures to "development" (innovation and imitation, the route to diffusion). They spent another 22 percent on applied research, or on pursuing invention. For reasons we will mention later, only 6 percent of business R&D expenditures went for basic research, the search for general scientific principles. Of course, industries, and firms within industries, vary greatly in the amount of emphasis they place on these three processes.

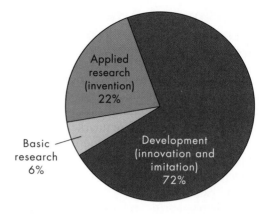

Figure 13.1

The composition of business R&D outlays in the United States, 2000. Firms channel the bulk of their R&D spending to innovation and imitation, because both have direct commercial value; less to applied research, that is, invention; and a relatively small amount to basic scientific research.

Source: National Science Foundation.

Modern View of Technological Advance

For decades most economists regarded technological advance as being external to the economy—a random outside force to which the economy adjusted. From time to time fortuitous advances in scientific and technological knowledge occurred, paving the way for major new products (automobiles, airplanes) and new production processes (assembly lines). Firms and industries, each at its own pace, then incorporated the new technology into their products or processes to enhance or maintain their profit. Then, after making the appropriate adjustments, they settled back into new long-run equilibrium positions. Although technological advance has been vitally important to the economy, economists believed it was rooted in the independent advance of science, which is largely external to the market system.

Most contemporary economists have a different view. They see capitalism itself as the driving force of technological advance. In their view, invention, innovation, and diffusion occur in response to incentives within the economy, meaning that technological advance is *internal* to capitalism. Specifically, technological advance arises from intense rivalry among individuals and firms that motivates them to seek and exploit new profit opportunities or to expand existing opportunities. That rivalry occurs both among

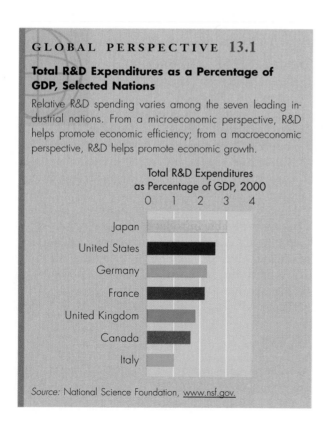

existing firms and between existing firms and new firms. Moreover, many advances in "pure" scientific knowledge are motivated, at least in part, by the prospect of commercial applicability and eventual profit. In the modern view, entrepreneurs and other innovators are at the heart of technological advance.

■ Role of Entrepreneurs and Other Innovators

It will be helpful to distinguish between "entrepreneurs" and "other innovators":

- ■ *Entrepreneurs* Recall that the entrepreneur is an initiator, innovator, and risk bearer—the catalyst who combines land, labor, and capital resources in new and unique ways to produce new goods and services. In the past a single individual, for example, Andrew Carnegie in steel, Henry Ford in automobiles, Levi Strauss in blue jeans, carried out the entrepreneurial role. Such advances as air conditioning, the ballpoint pen, cellophane, the jet engine, insulin, xerography, and the helicopter all have an individualistic heritage. But in today's more technologically complex economy, entrepreneurship is just as likely to be carried out by entrepreneurial teams. Such teams may include only two or three people working "as their own bosses" on some new product idea or it may consist of larger groups of entrepreneurs who have pooled their financial resources.

- ■ *Other innovators* This designation includes other key people involved in the pursuit of innovation who do not bear personal financial risk. Among them are key executives, scientists, and other salaried employees engaged in commercial R&D activities. (They are sometimes referred to as *intrapreneurs*, since they provide the spirit of entrepreneurship within existing firms.)

Forming Start-Ups

Entrepreneurs often form small new companies called **start-ups** that focus on creating and introducing a new product or employing a new production or distribution technique. Two people, working out of their garages, formed such a start-up in the mid-1970s. Since neither of their employers—Hewlett-Packard and Atari, the developer of Pong (the first video game)—was interested in their prototype personal computer, they founded their own company: Apple Computers. Other examples of successful start-ups are Amgen, a biotechnology firm specializing in new medical treatments; Starbucks, a seller of gourmet coffee; and Amazon, an Internet retailer.

Innovating within Existing Firms

Innovators are also at work within existing corporations, large and small. Such innovators are salaried workers, although many firms have pay systems that provide them with substantial bonuses or shares of the profit. Examples of firms known for their skillful internal innovators are 3M Corporation, the U.S. developer of Scotch tape, Post-it Note Pads, and Thinsulate insulation; and Canon, the Japanese developer of the "laser engine" for personal copiers and printers. R&D work in major corporations has produced significant technological improvements in such products as television sets, telephones, home appliances, automobiles, automobile tires, and sporting equipment.

Some large firms, aware that excessive bureaucracy can stifle creative thinking and technological advance, have separated part of their R&D and manufacturing divisions to form new, more flexible, innovative firms. Three significant examples of such "spin-off firms" are Lucent Technologies, a telephone equipment and R&D firm created by AT&T; Imation, a high-technology firm spun off by the 3M Corporation; and Palm, a maker of hand-held computers, spun off by 3Com.

Anticipating the Future

Some 50 years ago a writer for *Popular Mechanics* magazine boldly predicted, "Computers in the future may weigh no more than 1.5 tons." Today's notebook computers weigh less than 4 pounds. It is difficult to anticipate the future, but that is what innovators try to do. Those with strong anticipatory ability and determination have a knack for introducing new and improved products or services at just the right time. The rewards are both monetary and nonmonetary. Product innovation and development are creative endeavors, with such intangible rewards as personal satisfaction. Also, many people simply enjoy participating in the competitive "contest." Of course, the "winners" can reap huge monetary rewards in the form of economic profits, stock appreciation, or large bonuses. Extreme examples are Bill Gates and Paul Allen, who founded Microsoft in 1975, and had a net worth in 2000 of $85 billion and $40 billion, respectively, mainly in the form of Microsoft stock.

Past successes often give entrepreneurs and innovative firms access to resources for further innovations that anticipate consumer wants. Although they may not succeed a second time, the market tends to entrust the production of goods and services to businesses that have consistently succeeded in filling consumer wants. And the market does not care whether these "winning" entrepreneurs and innovative firms are American, Brazilian, Japanese, German, or Swiss. Entrepreneurship and innovation are global in scope.

Exploiting University and Government Scientific Research

In Figure 13.1 we saw that only 6 percent of business R&D spending in the United States goes to basic scientific research. The reason the percentage is so small is that scientific principles, as such, cannot be patented, nor do they usually have immediate commercial uses. Yet new scientific knowledge is highly important to technological advance. For that reason, entrepreneurs study the scientific output of university and government laboratories to identify discoveries with commercial applicability.

Government and university labs have been the scene of many technological breakthroughs, including hybrid seed corn, nuclear energy, satellite communications, the computer "mouse," genetic engineering, and the Internet. Entire high-tech industries such as computers and biotechnology have their roots in major research universities and government laboratories. And nations with strong scientific communities tend to have the most technologically progressive firms and industries.

Also, firms increasingly help fund university research that relates to their products. Business funding of R&D at universities has grown rapidly, rising to more than $2.2 billion in 2000. Today, the separation between university scientists and innovators is narrowing; scientists and universities increasingly realize that their work may have commercial value and are teaming up with innovators to share in the potential profit. A few firms, of course, find it profitable to conduct basic scientific research on their own. New scientific knowledge can give them a head start in creating an invention or a new product. This is particularly true in the pharmaceutical industry, where it is not uncommon for firms to parlay new scientific knowledge generated in their corporate labs into new, patentable drugs.

■ A Firm's Optimal Amount of R&D

How does a firm decide on its optimal amount of research and development? That amount depends on the firm's perception of the marginal benefit and marginal cost of R&D activity. The decision rule here flows from basic economics: To earn the greatest profit, expand a particular activity until its marginal benefit (MB) equals its marginal cost (MC). A firm that sees the marginal benefit of a particular R&D activity, say, innovation, as exceeding the marginal cost should expand that activity. In contrast, an activity whose marginal benefit promises to be less than its marginal cost should be cut back. But the R&D spending decision is complex, since it involves a present sacrifice for a future expected gain. While the cost of R&D is immediate, the expected benefits occur at some future time and are highly uncertain. So estimating those benefits is often more art than science. Nevertheless, the MB = MC way of thinking remains relevant for analyzing R&D decisions.

Interest-Rate Cost of Funds

Firms have several ways of obtaining the funds they need to finance R&D activities:

■ *Bank loans* Some firms are able to obtain a loan from a bank or other financial institution. Then the cost of using the funds is the interest paid to the lender. The marginal cost is the cost per extra dollar borrowed, which is simply the market interest rate for borrowed funds.

- *Bonds* Established, profitable firms may be able to borrow funds for R&D by issuing bonds and selling them in the bond market. In this case, the cost is the interest paid to the lenders— the bondholders. Again the marginal cost of using the funds is the interest rate. (We discussed bonds in Chapter 5's Last Word.)

- *Retained earnings* A large, well-established firm may be able to draw on its own corporate savings to finance R&D. Typically, such a firm retains part of its profit rather than paying it all out as dividends to corporate owners. Some of the undistributed corporate profit, called *retained earnings*, can be used to finance R&D activity. The marginal cost is the rate at which those funds could have earned interest as deposits in a financial institution.

- *Venture capital* A smaller start-up firm might be able to attract venture capital to finance its R&D projects. Venture capital is financial capital, or simply money, not real capital. **Venture capital** consists of that part of household saving used to finance high-risk business ventures in exchange for shares of the profit if the ventures succeed. The marginal cost of venture capital is the share of expected profit that the firm will have to pay to those who provided the money. This can be stated as a percentage of the venture capital, so it is essentially an interest rate.

- *Personal savings* Finally, individual entrepreneurs might draw on their own savings to finance the R&D for a new venture. The marginal cost of the financing is again the forgone interest rate.

Thus, whatever the source of the R&D funds, we can state the marginal cost of these funds as an interest rate i. For simplicity, let's assume that this interest rate is the same no matter how much financing is required. Further, we assume that a certain firm called MedTech must pay an interest rate of 8 percent, the least expensive funding available to it. Then a graph of the marginal cost of each funding amount for this firm is a horizontal line at the 8 percent interest rate, as shown in Figure 13.2. Such a graph is called an **interest-rate cost-of-funds curve**. This one tells us that MedTech can borrow $10, $10,000, $10,000,000, or more at the 8 percent interest rate. The table accompanying the graph contains the data used to construct the graph and tells us much the same thing.

With these data in hand, MedTech wants to determine how much R&D to finance in the coming year.

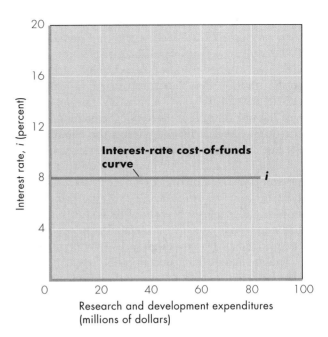

R&D, millions	Interest-rate cost of funds, %
$10	8
20	8
30	8
40	8
50	8
60	8
70	8
80	8

Figure 13.2
The interest-rate cost-of-funds schedule and curve.
As it relates to R&D, a firm's interest-rate cost-of-funds schedule (the table) and curve (the graph) show the interest rate the firm must pay to obtain any particular amount of funds to finance R&D. Curve i indicates the firm can finance as little or as much R&D as it wants at a constant 8 percent rate of interest.

Expected Rate of Return

A firm's marginal benefit from R&D is its expected profit (or return) from the last (marginal) dollar spent on R&D. That is, the R&D is expected to result in a new product or production method that will increase revenue, reduce production costs, or both (in ways we will soon explain). This return is expected, not certain—there is risk in R&D decisions. Let's suppose that after considering such risks, MedTech anticipates that an R&D expenditure of $1 million will result in a new product that will yield a one-time added profit of $1.2 million a year later. The expected rate of return r on the $1 million R&D expenditure (after the $1 million has been repaid) is 20 percent (= $200,000/$1,000,000). This is the marginal benefit of the first $1 million of R&D. (Stretching the return over several years complicates the computation of r, but it does not alter the basic analysis.)

MedTech can use this same method to estimate the expected rates of return for R&D expenditures of $2 million, $3 million, $4 million, and so on. Suppose those marginal rates of return are the ones indicated in the table in Figure 13.3, where they are also graphed as the **expected-rate-of-return curve**. This curve shows the expected rate of return, which is the marginal benefit of each dollar of expenditure on R&D. The curve slopes downward because of diminishing returns to R&D expenditures. A firm will direct its initial R&D expenditures to the highest expected-rate-of-return activities and then use additional funding for activities with successively lower expected rates of return. That is, as the firm increases R&D spending, it uses it to finance R&D activities with lower and lower expected rates of return.

Optimal R&D Expenditures

Figure 13.4 combines the interest-rate cost-of-funds curve (Figure 13.2) and the expected-rate-of-return curve (Figure 13.3). The curves intersect at MedTech's **optimal amount of R&D**, which is $60 million. This amount can also be determined from the table as the amount of funding for which the expected rate of return and the interest cost of borrowing are equal (here, 8 percent). Both the curve and the table tell us that at $60 million of R&D expenditures, the marginal benefit and marginal cost of the last dollar spent on R&D are equal. MedTech should undertake all R&D expenditures up to $60 million, since those outlays yield a higher marginal benefit or expected rate of return, r, than the 8 percent marginal cost or interest-rate cost of borrowing, i. But it should not undertake R&D expenditures beyond $60 million; for these outlays, r (marginal benefit) is less than i (marginal cost). Only at $60 million do we have $r = i$, telling us that MedTech will spend $60 million on R&D.

Our analysis reinforces two important points:

- ***Optimal versus affordable R&D*** From earlier

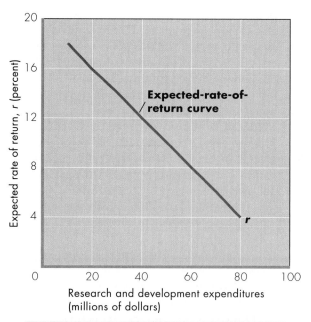

R&D, millions	Expected rate of return, %
$10	18
20	16
30	14
40	12
50	10
60	8
70	6
80	4

Figure 13.3

The expected-rate-of-return schedule and curve. As they relate to R&D, a firm's expected-rate-of-return schedule (the table) and curve (the graph) show the firm's expected gain in profit, as a percentage of R&D spending, for each level of R&D spending. Curve r slopes downward because the firm assesses its potential R&D projects in descending order of expected rates of return.

discussions we know there can be too much, as well as too little, of a "good thing." So it is with R&D and technological advance. Figure 13.4 shows that R&D expenditures make sense to a firm only as long as the expected return from the outlay equals or exceeds the cost of obtaining the funds needed to finance it. Many R&D expenditures may be affordable but not worthwhile, because their marginal benefit is likely to be less than their marginal cost.

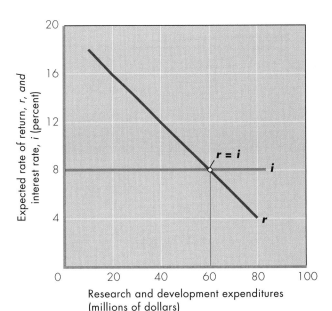

Expected rate of return, %	R&D, millions	Interest-rate cost of funds, %
18	$10	8
16	20	8
14	30	8
12	40	8
10	50	8
8	**60**	**8**
6	70	8
4	80	8

Figure 13.4

A firm's optimal level of R&D expenditures. The firm's optimal level of R&D expenditures ($60 million) occurs where its expected rate of return equals the interest-rate cost of funds, as shown in both the table and the graph. At $60 million of R&D spending, the firm has taken advantage of all R&D opportunities for which the expected rate of return, *r*, exceeds or equals the 8 percent interest cost of borrowing, *i*.

■ *Expected, not guaranteed, returns* The outcomes from R&D are expected, not guaranteed. With 20-20 hindsight, a firm can always look back and decide whether a particular expenditure for R&D was worthwhile. But that assessment is irrelevant to the original decision. At the time of the decision, the expenditure was thought to be worthwhile, on the basis of existing information and expectations. Some R&D decisions may be more like an informed gamble

than the typical business decision. Invention and innovation, in particular, carry with them a great deal of risk. For every successful outcome, there are scores of costly disappointments. **(Key Questions 4 and 5)**

■ Increased Profit via Innovation

In discussing how a firm determines its optimal amount of R&D spending, we sidestepped the question of how technological change can increase a firm's profit. Although the answer may seem obvious—by increasing revenue or reducing production costs—there are insights to be gained by exploring these two potential outcomes in some detail.

Increased Revenue via Product Innovation

Firms here and abroad have profitably introduced hundreds of new products in the past two or three decades. Examples include roller blades, microwave popcorn, cordless drills, digital cameras, camcorders, and projection TVs. Other new products are snowboards, cellular phones, telephone pagers, and automobile air bags. All these items reflect technological advance in the form of product innovation.

How do such new products gain consumer acceptance? As you know from Chapter 8, to maximize their satisfaction, consumers purchase products that have the highest marginal utility per dollar. They determine which products to buy in view of their limited money incomes by comparing the ratios of MU/price for the various goods. They first select the unit of the good with the highest MU/price ratio, then the one with the next highest, and so on, until their incomes are used up.

The first five columns of Table 13.1 repeat some of the information in Table 8.1. Before the introduction of new product C, the consumer maximized total utility from $10 of income by buying 2 units of A at $1 per unit and 4 units of B at $2 per unit. The total $10 budget was thus expended, with $2 spent on A and $8 on B. As shown in columns 2b and 3b, the marginal utility per dollar spent on the last unit of each product was 8 (= 8/$1 = 16/$2). The total utility, derived from columns 2a and 3a, was 96 utils (= 10 + 8 from the first 2 units of A plus 24 + 20 + 18 + 16 from the first 4 units of B). (If you are

Table 13.1

Utility Maximization with the Introduction of a New Product (Income = $10)*

(1) Unit of Product	(2) Product A: Price = $1		(3) Product B: Price = $2		(4) New Product C: Price = $4	
	(a) Marginal Utility, Utils	(b) Marginal Utility per Dollar (MU/Price)	(a) Marginal Utility, Utils	(b) Marginal Utility per Dollar (MU/Price)	(a) Marginal Utility, Utils	(b) Marginal Utility per Dollar (MU/Price)
First	10	10	24	***12***	52	13
Second	8	***8***	20	10	48	***12***
Third	7	7	18	9	44	11
Fourth	6	6	16	***8***	36	9
Fifth	5	5	12	6	32	8

*It is assumed in this table that the amount of marginal utility received from additional units of each of the three products is independent of the quantity purchased of the other products. For example, the marginal-utility schedule for product C is independent of the amount of A and B purchased by the consumer.

uncertain about this outcome, please review the discussion of Table 8.1.)

Now suppose an innovative firm offers new product C (columns 4a and 4b in Table 13.1), priced at $4 per unit. Note that the first unit of C has a higher marginal utility per dollar (13) than any unit of A and B and that the second unit of C and the first unit of B have equal MU/price ratios of 12. To maximize satisfaction, the consumer now buys 2 units of C at $4 per unit, 1 unit of B at $2 per unit, and zero units of A. Our consumer has spent the entire $10 of income ($8 on C and $2 on B), and the MU/price ratios of the last units of B and C are equal at 12. But as determined via columns 3a and 4a, the consumer's total utility is now 124 utils (= 24 from the first unit of B plus 52 + 48 from the first 2 units of C). Total utility has increased by 28 utils (= 124 utils − 96 utils), and that is why product C was purchased. *Consumers will buy a new product only if it increases the total utility they obtain from their limited incomes.*

From the innovating firm's perspective, these "dollar votes" represent new product demand that yields increased revenue. When per-unit revenue exceeds per-unit cost, the product innovation creates per-unit profit. Total profit rises by the per-unit profit multiplied by the number of units sold. As a percentage of the original R&D expenditure, the rise in total profit is the return on that R&D expenditure. It was the basis for the expected-rate-of-return curve *r* in Figure 13.4.

Other related points:

- **_Importance of price_** Consumer acceptance of a new product depends on both its marginal utility and its price. (Confirm that the consumer represented in Table 13.1 would buy zero units of new product C if its price were $8 rather than $4.) To be successful, a new product must not only deliver utility to consumers but do so at an acceptable price.

- **_Unsuccessful new products_** For every successful new product, there are hundreds that do not succeed; the expected return that motivates product innovation is not always realized. Examples of colossal product flops are Ford's Edsel automobile, 3-D movies, quadraphonic stereo, New Coke by Coca-Cola, Kodak disc cameras, and McDonald's McLean burger. Less dramatic failures include the hundreds of "dot-com" firms that have recently gone out of business. In each case, millions of dollars of R&D and promotion expense ultimately resulted in loss, not profit.

- **_Product improvements_** Most product innovation consists of incremental improvements to existing products rather than radical inventions. Examples: more fuel-efficient automobile engines, new varieties of pizza, lighter-weight shafts for golf clubs, more flavorful bubble-gum, "rock shocks" for mountain bikes, and clothing made of wrinkle-free fabrics. (**Key Question 6**)

Reduced Cost via Process Innovation

The introduction of better methods of producing products—process innovation—is also a path toward enhanced profit and a positive return on R&D expenditures. Suppose a firm introduces a new and better production process, say, assembling its product by teams rather than by a standard assembly line. Alternatively, suppose this firm replaces old equipment with more productive equipment embodying technological advance. In either case, the innovation yields an upward shift in the firm's total-product curve from TP_1 to TP_2 in Figure 13.5a. Now more units of output can be produced at each level of resource usage. Note from the figure, for example, that this firm can now produce 2500 units of output, rather than 2000 units, when using 1000 units of labor. So its average product has increased from 2 (= 2000 units of output ÷ 1000 units of labor) to 2.5 (= 2500 units of output ÷ 1000 units of labor).

The result is a downward shift in the firm's average-total-cost curve, from ATC_1 to ATC_2 in Figure 13.5b. To understand why, let's assume this firm pays $1000 for the use of its capital and $9 for

each unit of labor. Since it uses 1000 units of labor, its labor cost is $9000 (= $9 × 1000); its capital cost is $1000; and thus its total cost is $10,000. When its output increases from 2000 to 2500 units as a result of the process innovation, its total cost remains $10,000. So its average total cost declines from $5 (= $10,000/2000) to $4 (= $10,000/2500). Alternatively, the firm could produce the original 2000 units of output with fewer units of labor at an even lower average total cost.

This reduction in average total cost enhances the firm's profit. As a percentage of the R&D expenditure that fostered it, this extra profit is the expected return r, the basis for the rate-of-return-curve in Figure 13.3. In this case, the expected rate of return arose from the prospect of lower production costs through process innovation.

Example: Computer-based inventory control systems, such as those pioneered by Wal-Mart, enabled innovators to reduce the number of people keeping track of inventories and placing reorders of sold goods. They also enabled firms to keep goods arriving "just in time," reducing the cost of storing inventories. The consequence? Significant increases in sales per worker, declines in average total cost, and increased profit. **(Key Question 8)**

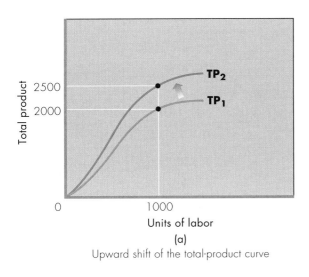

(a)
Upward shift of the total-product curve

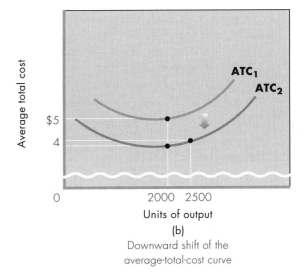

(b)
Downward shift of the average-total-cost curve

Figure 13.5

Process innovation, total product, and average total cost. (a) Process innovation shifts a firm's total-product curve upward from TP_1 to TP_2, meaning that with a given amount of capital the firm can produce more output at each level of labor input. As shown, with 1000 units of labor it can produce 2500 rather than 2000 units of output. (b) The upward shift in the total-product curve results in a downward shift in the firm's average-total-cost curve, from ATC_1 to ATC_2. This means the firm can produce any particular unit of output at a lower average total cost than it could previously. For example, the original 2000 units can be produced at less than $4 per unit, versus $5 per unit originally. Or 2500 units can now be produced at $4 per unit.

∎ Imitation and R&D Incentives

Our analysis of product and process innovation explains how technological advance enhances a firm's profit. But it also hints at a potential **imitation problem:** A firm's rivals may be able to imitate its new product or process, greatly reducing the originator's profit from its R&D effort. As just one example, in the 1980s U.S. auto firms took apart Japanese Honda Accords, piece by piece, to discover the secrets of their high quality. This reverse engineering—which ironically was perfected earlier by the Japanese—helped the U.S. firms incorporate innovative features into their own cars. This type of imitation is perfectly legitimate and fully anticipated; it is often the main path to widespread diffusion of an innovation.

In fact, a dominant firm that is making large profits from its existing products may let smaller firms in the industry incur the high costs of product innovation while it closely monitors their successes and failures. The dominant firm then moves quickly to imitate any successful new product; its goal is to become the second firm to embrace the innovation. In using this so-called **fast-second strategy,** the dominant firm counts on its own product-improvement abilities, marketing prowess, or economies of scale to prevail.

Examples abound: Royal Crown introduced the first diet cola, but Diet Coke and Diet Pepsi dominate diet-cola sales today. Meister-Brau introduced the first low-calorie beer, but Miller popularized the product with its Miller Lite. Gillette moved quickly with its own stainless-steel razor blade only after a smaller firm, Wilkinson, introduced this product innovation.

Benefits of Being First

Imitation and the fast-second strategy raise an important question: What incentive is there for any firm to bear the expenses and risks of innovation if competitors can imitate its new or improved product? Why not let others bear the costs and risks of product development and then just imitate the successful innovations? Although we have seen that this may be a plausible strategy in some situations, there are several protections for, and potential advantages to, taking the lead.

Patents Some technological breakthroughs, specifically inventions, can be patented. Once patented, they cannot be legally imitated for two decades. The purpose of patents is, in fact, to reduce imitation and its negative effect on the incentive for engaging in R&D. Example: Polaroid's patent of its instant camera enabled it to earn high economic profits for many years. When Kodak "cloned" the camera, Polaroid won a patent-infringement lawsuit against its rival. Kodak not only had to stop producing its version of the camera but had to buy back the Kodak instant cameras it had sold and pay millions of dollars in damages to Polaroid.

There are hundreds of other examples of long-run profits based on U.S. patents; they involve products from prescription drugs to pop-top cans to weed trimmers. As shown in Global Perspective 13.2, foreign citizens and firms hold U.S. patents along with American citizens and firms.

Copyrights and Trademarks *Copyrights* protect publishers of books, computer software, movies, videos, and musical compositions from having their works copied. *Trademarks* give the original innovators of products the exclusive right to use a particular product name ("M&Ms," "Barbie Doll," "Wheaties"). By reducing the problem of direct copying, these legal protections increase the incentive for product innovation. They have been

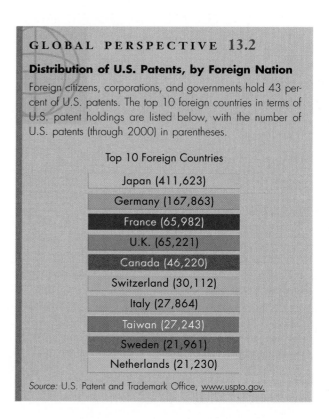

GLOBAL PERSPECTIVE 13.2

Distribution of U.S. Patents, by Foreign Nation

Foreign citizens, corporations, and governments hold 43 percent of U.S. patents. The top 10 foreign countries in terms of U.S. patent holdings are listed below, with the number of U.S. patents (through 2000) in parentheses.

Top 10 Foreign Countries

Japan (411,623)
Germany (167,863)
France (65,982)
U.K. (65,221)
Canada (46,220)
Switzerland (30,112)
Italy (27,864)
Taiwan (27,243)
Sweden (21,961)
Netherlands (21,230)

Source: U.S. Patent and Trademark Office, www.uspto.gov.

strengthened worldwide through recent international trade agreements. ⚠ **13.1**

Brand-Name Recognition

Along with trademark protection, brand-name recognition may give the original innovator a major marketing advantage for years or even decades. Consumers often identify a new product with the firm that first introduced and popularized it in the mass market. Examples: Levi's blue jeans, Kleenex soft tissues, Johnson and Johnson's Band-Aids, Sony's Walkman, and Kellogg's Corn Flakes.

Trade Secrets and Learning by Doing

Some innovations involve trade secrets, without which competitors cannot imitate the product or process. Example: Coca-Cola has successfully kept its formula for Coke a secret from potential rivals. Many other firms have perfected special production techniques known only to them. In a related advantage, a firm's head start with a new product often allows it to achieve substantial cost reductions through learning by doing. The innovator's lower cost may enable it to continue to profit even after imitators have entered the market. ⚠ **13.2**

Time Lags

Time lags between innovation and diffusion often enable innovating firms to realize a substantial economic profit. It takes time for an imitator to gain knowledge of the properties of a new innovation. And once it has that knowledge, the imitator must design a substitute product, gear up a factory for its production, and conduct a marketing campaign. Various entry barriers, such as large financial requirements, economies of scale, and price-cutting, may extend the time lag between innovation and imitation. In practice, it may take years or even decades before rival firms can successfully imitate a profitable new product and cut into the market share of the innovator. In the meantime, the innovator continues to profit.

Profitable Buyouts

A final advantage of being first arises from the possibility of a buyout (outright purchase) of the innovating firm by a larger firm. Here, the innovative entrepreneurs take their rewards immediately, as cash or as shares in the purchasing firm, rather than waiting for perhaps uncertain long-run profits from their own production and marketing efforts.

Two examples: Once the popularity of cellular communications became evident, AT&T bought out McCaw Communications, an early leader in this new technology. When Minnetonka's Softsoap became a huge success, it sold its product to Colgate-Palmolive. More recently, German media giant Bertelsmann bought out Napster, a start-up that helped pioneer the digital delivery of music over the Internet. Such buyouts are legal under current antitrust laws as long as they do not substantially lessen competition in the affected industry. For this to be the case, there must be other strong competitors in the market. That was not true, for example, when Microsoft tried to buy out Intuit (maker of Quicken, the best-selling financial software). That buyout was disallowed because Intuit and Microsoft were the two main suppliers of financial software for personal computers.

In short, despite the imitation problem, there are significant protections and advantages that enable most innovating firms to profit from their R&D efforts, as implied by the continuing high levels of R&D spending by firms year after year. As shown in Figure 13.6, business R&D spending in the United States not only remains substantial but has grown over the past quarter-century. The high levels of spending simply would not continue if imitation consistently and severely depressed rates of return on R&D expenditures.

> **QUICK REVIEW 13.2**
>
> ▪ A firm's optimal R&D expenditure is the amount at which the expected rate of return (marginal benefit) from the R&D expenditure just equals the interest-rate cost of borrowing (marginal cost) required to finance it.
>
> ▪ Product innovation can entice consumers to substitute a new product for existing products to increase their total utility, thereby increasing the innovating firm's revenue and profit.
>
> ▪ Process innovation can lower a firm's production costs and increase its profit by increasing total product and decreasing average total cost.
>
> ▪ A firm faces reduced profitability from R&D if competitors can successfully imitate its new product or process. Nevertheless, there are significant potential protections and benefits to being first, including patents, copyrights, and trademarks; brand-name recognition; trade secrets; cost reductions from learning by doing; and major time lags between innovation and imitation.

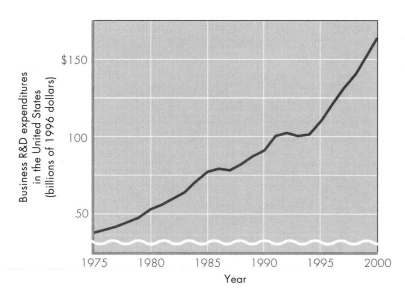

Figure 13.6
The growth of business R&D expenditures in the United States, 1975–2000.
Inflation-adjusted R&D expenditures by firms are substantial and growing, suggesting that R&D continues to be profitable for firms, even in the face of possible imitation.
Source: National Science Foundation, www.nsf.gov/.

▌ Role of Market Structure

In view of our discussion of market structures in the last three chapters, it is logical to ask whether there is some particular market structure or firm size that is best suited to technological progress. Is a highly competitive industry consisting of thousands of relatively small firms preferable to an industry comprising only two or three large firms? Or is some intermediate structure best?

Market Structure and Technological Advance

As a first step toward answering these questions, we survey the strengths and shortcomings of our four market models as related to technological advance.

Pure Competition
Does a pure competitor have a strong incentive and strong ability to undertake R&D? On the positive side, strong competition provides a reason for such firms to innovate; competitive firms tend to be less complacent than monopolists. If a pure competitor does not seize the initiative, one or more rivals may introduce a new product or cost-reducing production technique that could drive it from the market. As a matter of short-term profit and long-term survival, the pure competitor is under continual pressure to improve products and lower costs through innovation. Also, where there are many competing firms, there is less chance that an idea for improving a product or process will be overlooked by a single firm.

On the negative side, the expected rate of return on R&D may be low or even negative for a pure competitor. Because of easy entry, its profit rewards from innovation may quickly be competed away by existing or entering firms that also produce the new product or adopt the new technology. Also, the small size of competitive firms and the fact that they earn only a normal profit in the long run lead to serious questions as to whether they can finance substantial R&D programs. Observers have noted that the high rate of technological advance in the purely competitive agricultural industry, for example, has come not from the R&D of individual farmers but from government-sponsored research and from the development of fertilizers, hybrid seed, and farm implements by oligopolistic firms.

Monopolistic Competition
Like pure competitors, monopolistic competitors cannot afford to be complacent. But unlike pure competitors, which sell standardized products, monopolistic competitors have a strong profit incentive to engage in product development. This incentive to differentiate products from those of competitors stems from the fact that sufficiently novel products may create monopoly power and thus economic profit. There are many examples of innovative firms (McDonald's, Blockbuster Video, Krispy Crème Donuts) that started out as monopolistic competitors in localized markets but soon gained considerable national market power, with the attendant economic profit.

For the typical firm, however, the shortcomings of monopolistic competition in relation to technological advance are the same as those of pure competition. Most monopolistic competitors remain small, which limits their ability to secure inexpensive financing for R&D. In addition, monopolistic competitors find it difficult to extract large profits from technological advances. Any economic profits from innovation are usually temporary, because entry to monopolistically competitive industries is relatively easy. In the long run, new entrants with similar goods reduce the demand for the innovator's product, leaving the innovator with only a normal profit. Monopolistic competitors therefore usually have relatively low expected rates of return on R&D expenditures.

Oligopoly Many of the characteristics of oligopoly are conducive to technological advance. First, the large size of oligopolists enables them to finance the often large R&D costs associated with major product or process innovation. In particular, the typical oligopolist realizes ongoing economic profits, a part of which is retained. This undistributed profit serves as a major source of readily available, relatively low-cost funding for R&D. Moreover, the existence of barriers to entry gives the oligopolist some assurance that it can maintain any economic profit it gains from innovation. Then, too, the large sales volume of the oligopolist enables it to spread the cost of specialized R&D equipment and teams of specialized researchers over a great many units of output. Finally, the broad scope of R&D activity within oligopolistic firms helps them offset the inevitable R&D "misses" with more-than-compensating R&D "hits." Thus, oligopolists clearly have the means and incentive to innovate.

But there is also a negative side to R&D in oligopoly. In many instances, the oligopolist's incentive to innovate may be far less than we have implied above, because oligopoly tends to breed complacency. An oligopolist may reason that it makes little sense to introduce costly new technology and produce new products when it currently is earning a sizable economic profit without them. The oligopolist wants to maximize its profit by exploiting fully all its capital assets. Why rush to develop a new product (say, batteries for electric automobiles) when that product's success will render obsolete much of the firm's current equipment designed to produce its existing product (say, gasoline engines)? It is not difficult to cite oligopolistic industries in which the largest firms' interest in R&D has been quite modest. Examples: the steel, cigarette, and aluminum industries.

Pure Monopoly In general, the pure monopolist has little incentive to engage in R&D; it maintains its high profit through entry barriers that, in theory, are complete. The only incentive for the pure monopolist to engage in R&D is defensive: to reduce the risk of being blindsided by some new product or production process that destroys its monopoly. If such a product is out there to be discovered, the monopolist may have an incentive to find it. By so doing, it can either exploit the new product or process for continued monopoly profit or suppress the product until the monopolist has extracted the maximum profit from its current capital assets. But, in general, economists agree that pure monopoly is the market structure least conducive to innovation.

Inverted-U Theory

Analysis like this has led some experts on technological progress to postulate a so-called **inverted-U theory** of the relationship between market structure and technological advance. This theory is illustrated in Figure 13.7, which relates R&D spending as a percentage of a firm's sales (vertical axis) to the industry's four-firm concentration ratio (horizontal axis). The "inverted-U" shape of the curve suggests that R&D effort is at best weak in both very low concentration industries (pure competition) and very high concentration industries (pure monopoly). Starting from the lowest concentrations, R&D spending as a percentage of sales rises with concentration until a concentration ratio of 50 percent or so is reached, meaning that the four largest firms account for about one-half the total industry output. Beyond that, relative R&D spending decreases as concentration rises.

The logic of the inverted-U theory follows from our discussion. Firms in industries with very low concentration ratios are mainly competitive firms. They are small, and this makes it difficult for them to finance R&D. Moreover, entry to these industries is easy, making it difficult to sustain economic profit from innovations that are not supported by patents. As a result, firms in these industries spend little on R&D relative to their sales. At the other end (far right) of the curve, where concentration is exceptionally high, monopoly profit is already high and innovation will not add much more profit. Furthermore, innovation typically requires costly retooling of very large factories, which will cut into whatever additional profit is realized. As a result, the expected rate of return from R&D is quite low, as are expenditures

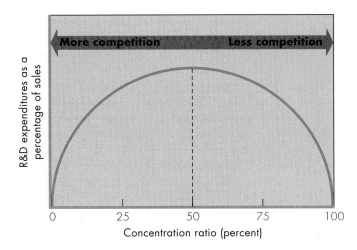

Figure 13.7
The inverted-U theory of R&D expenditures. The inverted-U theory suggests that R&D expenditures as a percentage of sales rise with industry concentration until the four-firm concentration ratio reaches about 50 percent. Further increases in industry concentration are associated with lower relative R&D expenditures.

for R&D relative to sales. Finally, the lack of rivals makes the monopolist quite complacent about R&D.

The optimal industry structure for R&D is one in which expected returns on R&D spending are high and funds to finance it are readily available and inexpensive. From our discussion, those factors seem to occur in industries where a few firms are absolutely and relatively large but where the concentration ratio is not so high as to prohibit vigorous competition by smaller rivals. Rivalry among the larger oligopolistic firms and competition between the larger and the smaller firms then provide a strong incentive for R&D. The inverted-U theory, as represented by Figure 13.7, also points toward this "loose" oligopoly as the optimal structure for R&D spending.

Market Structure and Technological Advance: The Evidence

Dozens of industry studies have tried to pin down the relationship between market structure and technological advance. Because those studies dealt with different industries and time periods, and used different methodologies, they are not easy to compare and summarize. Nevertheless, they provide general support for the inverted-U theory.[1] Other things equal, the optimal market structure for technological advance seems to be an industry in which there is a mix of large oligopolistic firms (a 40 to 60 percent concentration ratio), with several highly innovative smaller firms.

But our "other-things-equal" qualification is quite important here. Whether or not a particular industry is highly technical may well be a more important determinant of R&D than its structure. While some concentrated industries (electronics, aircraft, and petroleum) devote large quantities of resources to R&D and are very innovative, others (cigarettes, aluminum, gypsum products) are not. The level of R&D spending within an industry seems to depend as much on its technical character and "technological opportunities" as on its market structure. There simply may be more opportunities to innovate in the computer and pharmaceutical industries, for example, than in the brick-making and coal-mining industries.

Conclusion: The inverted-U curve shown in Figure 13.7 is a useful depiction of the general relationship between R&D spending and market structure, other things equal.

▌Technological Advance and Efficiency

Technological advance contributes significantly to economic efficiency. New and better processes and products enable society to produce more output, as well as a higher-valued mix of output.

Productive Efficiency

Technological advance as embodied in process innovation improves *productive efficiency* by increasing the productivity of inputs (as indicated in Figure 13.5a) and by reducing average total costs (as in Figure 13.5b). In other words, it enables society to pro-

---

[1]Douglas F. Greer, *Industrial Organization and Public Policy*, 3d ed. (New York: Macmillan, 1992), pp. 680–687.

duce the same amount of a particular good or service while using fewer scarce resources, thereby freeing the unused resources to produce other goods and services. Or if society desires more of the now less expensive good, process innovation enables it to have that greater quantity without sacrificing other goods. Viewed either way, process innovation enhances productive efficiency: It reduces society's per-unit cost of whatever mix of goods and services it chooses. It thus is an important means of shifting an economy's production possibilities curve rightward.

Allocative Efficiency

Technological advance as embodied in *product* (or service) innovation enhances allocative efficiency by giving society a more preferred mix of goods and services. Recall from our earlier discussion that consumers buy a new product rather than an old product only when buying the new one increases the total utility obtained from their limited incomes. Obviously, then, the new product—and the new mix of products it implies—creates a higher level of total utility for society.

In terms of markets, the demand for the new product rises and the demand for the old product declines. The high economic profit engendered by the new product attracts resources away from less valued uses and to the production of the new product. In theory, such shifting of resources continues until the price of the new product equals its marginal cost.

There is a caveat here, however. Innovation (either product or process) can create monopoly power through patents or through the many advantages of being first. When new monopoly power results from an innovation, society may lose part of the improved efficiency it otherwise would have gained from that innovation. The reason is that the profit-maximizing monopolist restricts output to keep its product price above marginal cost. Possible example: Microsoft has used an early innovation in computer software (its DOS operating system) to achieve a commanding presence in some parts of the software industry. It has built its monopoly power partly on a strategy of continual, identifiable product upgrades, from MS-DOS to Windows to Windows XP, with new versions in between. These product improvements are often announced well in advance and contain more and more features of competing software. Moreover, Microsoft has extended some of its monopoly power to related software products (Word,

PowerPoint). So although society has benefited greatly from the surge of product improvements flowing from Microsoft, another result has been rising entry barriers and monopoly in the software industry. Also, Microsoft continues to have economic profit far above the long-run normal profit associated with allocative efficiency. Concerned about this inefficiency, in 2000 a Federal court found Microsoft guilty of violating the antitrust laws and ordered it broken into two competing firms. Microsoft has appealed the verdict and breakup order to a higher court.

On the other hand, innovation can reduce or even destroy monopoly power by providing competition where previously there was none. Economic efficiency is enhanced when that happens, because the new competition helps push prices down closer to marginal cost and minimum average total cost. Innovation that leads to greater competition within an industry reduces the inefficiency associated with reduced restriction of output and monopoly prices. In the Microsoft example, the new technology of the Internet has, at least temporarily, reduced Microsoft's dominance in some emerging areas of the software industry. Specifically, firms such as Sun Microsystems have pioneered new software relating to the Internet (Java programming language), leaving Microsoft working hard to catch up. So it is difficult to judge whether Microsoft's monopoly power has hindered or abetted innovation. At the time of the Federal district court antitrust verdict in 2000, it was spending $2 billion per year on research.

Creative Destruction

Innovation may even generate **creative destruction,** where the creation of new products and new production methods simultaneously destroys the monopoly market positions of firms committed to existing products and old ways of doing business. As stated many years ago by Joseph Schumpeter, who championed this view:

> In capitalist reality . . . it is . . . competition from the new commodity, the new technology, the new source of supply, the new type of business organization—competition which commands a decisive cost or quality advantage and which strikes not at the margins of profits of the existing firms but at their foundation and their very lives. This kind of competition is . . . so . . . important that it becomes a matter of comparative indifference whether competition in the

On the Path to the Personal Computer and Internet

Technological Advance Is Clearly Evident in the Development of the Modern Personal Computer and the Emergence of the Internet. Here Is a Brief History of Those Events.

1945 Grace Murray Hopper finds a dead moth between relay contacts in the experimental Mark II computer at Harvard University. Whenever the computer subsequently malfunctions, workers set out to "debug" the device.

1946 ENIAC is revealed. A precursor to the modern-day computer, it relies on 18,000 vacuum tubes and fills 3000 cubic feet of space.

1947 AT&T scientists invent the "transfer resistance device," later known as the transistor. It replaces the less reliable vacuum tubes in computers.

1961 Bob Noyce (who later founded Intel Corporation) and Jack Kilby invent the first integrated circuit, which miniaturizes electronic circuitry onto a single silicon chip.

1964 IBM introduces the System/360 computer. Configured as a system, it takes up nearly the same space as two tennis courts.

1965 Digital Equipment Corporation unveils its PDP-8, the first relatively small-size computer (a "minicomputer").

1969 A networking system called ARPANET is born; it is the beginning of the Internet.

1971 Intel introduces its 4004 processor (a "microprocessor"). The $200 chip is the size of a thumbnail and has as much computing capability as the earlier ENIAC.

1975 Xerox markets Alto, the first personal computer (a "microcomputer"). Bill Gates and Paul Allen found Microsoft. MITS Corporation's Altair 8800 arrives on the scene. It contains Intel's 8080 microprocessor that Intel developed a year earlier to control traffic lights.

1977 Apple II, Commodore's PET, and Tandy Radio Shack TRS-80 go on sale, setting the stage for the personal computer revolution.

1981 IBM enters the market with its personal computer powered by the Intel 8800 chip and operated by the Microsoft Disc Operating System (MS-DOS). Osborne Computer markets the Osborne 1, the first self-contained microcomputer, but within 2 years the firm declares bankruptcy. Logitech commercializes the "X-Y Position Indicator for a Display System," invented earlier by Douglas Engelbart in a government-funded research lab. Someone dubs it a "computer mouse" because it appears to have a tail.

1982 Compaq Computer "clones" the IBM machines; others do the same. Eventually Compaq becomes the leading seller of personal computers.

1984 Apple introduces its Macintosh computer, with its "user-friendly" icons, attached mouse, and preloaded software. College student Michael Dell founds Dell Computers, which builds per-

ordinary sense functions more or less promptly; the powerful lever that in the [very] long run expands output and brings down prices is in any case made of other stuff.[2]

There are many examples of creative destruction: In the 1800s wagons, ships, and barges were the only means of transporting freight until the railroads broke up their monopoly; the dominant market position of the railroads was, in turn, undermined by trucks and, later, by airplanes. Movies brought new competition to live theater, at one time the "only show in town," but movies were later challenged by television. Vinyl long-playing records supplanted acetate 78-rpm phonograph records; cassettes then challenged LP records; and compact discs undermined cassettes. Now Internet music-recording technology found on sites such as MP3 and Napster threaten sales of traditional CDs. Aluminum cans and plastic bottles have displaced glass bottles in many uses. E-mail has challenged the postal service. Mass discounters such as Wal-Mart and Costco have gained market share at the expense of Sears and Montgomery Ward. 🔑 **13.1**

According to Schumpeter, an innovator will automatically displace any monopolist that no longer delivers superior performance. But many contemporary economists think this notion reflects more wish-

[2]Joseph A. Schumpeter, *Capitalism, Socialism, and Democracy*, 3d ed. (New York: Harper & Row, 1950), pp. 84–85.

sonal computers and sells them through mail order. IBM, Sears Roebuck, and CBS team up to launch Prodigy Services, the first online computer business.

1985 Microsoft releases its Windows graphical interface operating system that improves upon MS-DOS. Ted Waitt starts a mail-order personal computer business (Gateway 2000) out of his South Dakota barn.

1990 Microsoft introduces Windows 3.0, which, like Macintosh, features windows, icons, and pull-down menus. Apple sues Microsoft for copyright infringement.

1991 The World Wide Web (an Internet system) is invented.

1993 Intel introduces its first of several Pentium chips, which greatly speed up computing. The courts reject Apple's claim that Microsoft violated its copyrights on its Macintosh operating system.

1994 Marc Andreessen starts up Netscape Communications and markets Netscape Navigator, which quickly becomes the leading software browser for the emerging Internet. David Filo and Jerry Yang develop Yahoo, a system for locating material stored on the Internet.

1995 Microsoft releases the Windows 95 operating system, which becomes the dominant operating system of personal computers (90 percent market share). Microsoft is now well established as the world's leading software producer. Sun Microsystems introduces Java, an Internet programming language.

1996 Playing catch-up with Netscape, Microsoft develops Microsoft Internet Explorer and gives it away free.

1999 Netscape's market share plunges and it merges with America Online. More than 100 million personal computers are manufactured worldwide this year alone.

2000 A Federal court rules that Microsoft is an abusive monopoly and orders that it be broken into two companies, one that sells its operating system and another that sells its applications. Microsoft appeals the case to a higher court. Sixty percent of American households have access to the Internet either at home or at work, and the Internet spreads worldwide. Internet commerce in the United States reaches $300 billion and an estimated 1.2 million U.S. jobs are Internet-related.

Source: Based partly on Diedtra Henderson, "Moore's Law Still Reigns," *Seattle Times,* Nov. 24, 1996. Augmented and updated.

---

ful thinking than fact. In this view, the idea that creative destruction is automatic

> . . . neglects the ability of powerful established firms to erect private storm shelters—or lobby government to build public storm shelters for them—in order to shield themselves from the Schumpeterian gales of creative destruction. It ignores the difference between the legal freedom of entry and the economic reality deterring the entry of potential newcomers into concentrated industries.[3]

That is, some dominant firms may be able to use strategies such as selective price cutting, buyouts, and massive advertising to block entry and competition from even the most innovative new firms and existing rivals. Moreover, rent-seeking dominant firms have been known to persuade government to give them tax breaks, subsidies, and tariff protection that strengthen their market power.

In short, while innovation in general enhances economic efficiency, in some cases it may lead to entrenched monopoly power. Further innovation may eventually destroy that monopoly power, but the process of creative destruction is neither automatic nor inevitable. On the other hand, rapid technological change, innovation, and efficiency clearly are not necessarily inconsistent with possession of monopoly power.

[3]Walter Adams and James Brock, *The Structure of American Industry,* 10th ed. (Upper Saddle River, N.J.: Prentice-Hall, 2001), pp. 363–364.

SUMMARY

1. Technological advance is evidenced by new and improved goods and services and new and improved production or distribution processes. In economists' models, technological advance occurs only in the *very long run*.

2. *Invention* is the discovery of a product or process through the use of imagination, ingenuity, and experimentation. *Innovation* is the first successful commercial introduction of a new product, the first use of a new method, or the creation of a new form of business enterprise. *Diffusion* is the spread of an earlier innovation among competing firms. Firms channel a majority of their R&D expenditures to innovation and imitation, rather than to basic scientific research and invention.

3. Historically, most economists viewed technological advance as a random, external force to which the economy adjusted. Many contemporary economists see technological advance as occurring in response to profit incentives within the economy and thus as an integral part of capitalism.

4. Entrepreneurs and other innovators try to anticipate the future. They play a central role in technological advance by initiating changes in products and processes. Entrepreneurs often form start-up firms that focus on creating and introducing new products. Sometimes, innovators work in the R&D labs of major corporations. Entrepreneurs and innovative firms often rely heavily on the basic research done by university and government scientists.

5. A firm's optimal amount of R&D spending occurs where its expected return (marginal benefit) from the R&D equals its interest-rate cost of funds (marginal cost) to finance the R&D. Entrepreneurs and firms use several sources to finance R&D, including (a) bank loans, (b) bonds, (c) venture capital (funds lent in return for a share of the profits if the business succeeds), (d) undistributed corporate profits (retained earnings), and (e) personal savings.

6. *Product innovation*, the introduction of new products, succeeds when it provides consumers with higher marginal utility per dollar spent than do existing products. The new product enables consumers to obtain greater total utility from a given income. From the firm's perspective, product innovation increases net revenue sufficiently to yield a positive rate of return on the R&D spending that produced the innovation.

7. *Process innovation* can lower a firm's production costs by improving its internal production techniques. Such improvement increases the firm's total product, thereby lowering its average total cost and increasing its profit. The added profit provides a positive rate of return on the R&D spending that produced the process innovation.

8. *Imitation* poses a potential problem for innovators, since it threatens their returns on R&D expenditures. Some dominant firms use a fast-second strategy, letting smaller firms initiate new products and then quickly imitating the successes. Nevertheless, there are significant protections and potential benefits for firms that take the lead with R&D and innovation, including (a) patent protection, (b) copyrights and trademarks, (c) lasting brand-name recognition, (d) benefits from trade secrets and learning by doing, (e) high economic profits during the time lag between a product's introduction and its imitation, and (f) the possibility of lucrative buyout offers from larger firms.

9. Each of the four basic market structures has potential strengths and weaknesses regarding the likelihood of R&D and innovation. The *inverted-U theory* holds that a firm's R&D spending as a percentage of its sales rises with its industry four-firm concentration ratio, reaches a peak at a 50 percent concentration ratio, and then declines as concentration increases further. Empirical evidence is not clear-cut but lends general support to this theory. For any specific industry, however, the technological opportunities that are available may count more than market structure in determining R&D spending and innovation.

10. In general, technological advance enhances both productive and allocative efficiency. But in some situations patents and the advantages of being first with an innovation can increase monopoly power. While in some cases *creative destruction* eventually destroys monopoly, most economists doubt that this process is either automatic or inevitable.

TERMS AND CONCEPTS

technological advance	product innovation	interest-rate cost-of-funds curve	imitation problem
very long run	process innovation		fast-second strategy
invention	diffusion	expected-rate-of-return curve	inverted-U theory of R&D
patent	start-ups		
innovation	venture capital	optimal amount of R&D	creative destruction

STUDY QUESTIONS

1. What is meant by technological advance, as broadly defined? How does technological advance enter into the definition of the very long run? Which of the following are examples of technological advance, and which are not: an improved production process; entry of a firm into a profitable purely competitive industry; the imitation of a new production process by another firm; an increase in a firm's advertising expenditures?

2. Listed below are several possible actions by firms. Write "INV" beside those that reflect invention, "INN" beside those that reflect innovation, and "DIF" beside those that reflect diffusion.

   a. An auto manufacturer adds "heated seats" as a standard feature in its luxury cars to keep pace with a rival firm whose luxury cars already have this feature.

   b. A television production company pioneers the first music video channel.

   c. A firm develops and patents a working model of a self-erasing whiteboard for classrooms.

   d. A lightbulb firm is the first to produce and market lighting fixtures with halogen lamps.

   e. A rival toy maker introduces a new Jenny doll to compete with Mattel's Barbie doll.

3. Contrast the older and the modern views of technological advance as they relate to the economy. What is the role of entrepreneurs and other innovators in technological advance? How does research by universities and government affect innovators and technological advance? Why do you think some university researchers are becoming more like entrepreneurs and less like "pure scientists"?

4. **Key Question** Suppose a firm expects that a $20 million expenditure on R&D will result in a new product that will increase its revenue by a total of $30 million 1 year from now. The firm estimates that the production cost of the new product will be $29 million.

   a. What is the expected rate of return on this R&D expenditure?

   b. Suppose the firm can get a bank loan at 6 percent interest to finance its $20 million R&D project. Will the firm undertake the project? Explain why or why not.

   c. Now suppose the interest-rate cost of borrowing, in effect, falls to 4 percent because the firm decides to use its own retained earnings to finance the R&D. Will this lower interest rate change the firm's R&D decision? Explain.

5. **Key Question** Answer the following lettered questions on the basis of the information in this table:

Amount of R&D, Millions	Expected Rate of Return on R&D, %
$10	16
20	14
30	12
40	10
50	8
60	6

   a. If the interest-rate cost of funds is 8 percent, what will be the optimal amount of R&D spending for this firm?

   b. Explain why $20 million of R&D spending will not be optimal.

   c. Why won't $60 million be optimal either?

6. **Key Question** Refer to Table 13.1 and suppose the price of new product C is $2 instead of $4. How does this affect the optimal combination of products A, B, and C for the person represented by the data? Explain: "The success of a new product depends not only on its marginal utility but also on its price."

7. Learning how to use software takes time. So once customers have learned to use a particular software package, it is easier to sell them software upgrades than to convince them to switch to new software. What implications does this have for expected rates of return on R&D spending for software firms developing upgrades versus firms developing imitative products?

8. **Key Question** Answer the following questions on the basis of this information for a single firm: total cost of capital = $1000; price paid for labor = $12 per labor unit; price paid for raw materials = $4 per raw-material unit.

   a. Suppose the firm can produce 5000 units of output by combining its fixed capital with 100 units of labor and 450 units of raw materials. What are the total cost and average total cost of producing the 5000 units of output?

   b. Now assume the firm improves its production process so that it can produce 6000 units of output by combining its fixed capital with 100 units of labor and 450 units of raw materials. What are the total cost and average cost of producing the 6000 units of output?

   c. Refer to your answers to 8a and 8b and explain how process innovation can improve economic efficiency.

9. Why might a firm making a large economic profit from its existing product employ a fast-second

strategy in relationship to new or improved products? What risks does it run in pursuing this strategy? What incentive does a firm have to engage in R&D when rivals can imitate its new product?

10. Do you think the overall level of R&D would increase or decrease over the next 20 to 30 years if the lengths of new patents were extended from 20 years to, say, "forever"? What if the duration were reduced from 20 years to, say, 3 years?

11. Make a case that neither pure competition nor pure monopoly is conducive to a great deal of R&D spending and innovation. Why might oligopoly be more favorable to R&D spending and innovation than either pure competition or pure monopoly? What is the inverse-U theory, and how does it relate to your answers to these questions?

12. Evaluate: "Society does not need laws outlawing monopolization and monopoly. Inevitably, monopoly causes its own self-destruction, since its high profit is the lure for other firms or entrepreneurs to develop substitute products."

13. **(Last Word)** Identify a specific example of each of the following in this chapter's Last Word: (*a*) entrepreneurship, (*b*) invention, (*c*) innovation, and (*d*) diffusion.

14. **Web-Based Question:** *The National Science Foundation R&D statistics—what's happening?* The Division of Science Resource Studies website, www.nsf.gov/sbe/srs/stats.htm, provides information on the nation's science, engineering, and technology sectors. Under "Publications and Data" review the current report (in PDF format) titled "National Patterns of Research and Development Resources." Determine if the following R&D figures have increased, remained constant, or decreased over the last 5 years listed: (*a*) Total U.S. R&D expenditures in constant dollars, (*b*) Federal support for R&D in constant dollars, (*c*) R&D as a percentage of U.S. GDP, and (*d*) Federal support of R&D as a percentage of GDP. What are the technological implications of these figures for the United States?

15. **Web-Based Question:** *NASA—are there commercial spin-offs?* Visit the website of NASA's Technology Transfer Office, at www.sti.nasa.gov/tto, to identify significant commercial benefits from secondary use of NASA technology. Search the database to find and describe five such spin-offs. How does the NASA Commercial Technology Network (nctn.hq.nasa.gov/) move technology from the lab to the marketplace?

3

*Microeconomics of
Resource Markets*

14

The Demand for Resources

W E N O W T U R N from the pricing and production of *goods and services* to the pricing and employment of *resources*. Although firms come in various sizes and operate under highly different market conditions, they each have a demand for productive resources. They obtain those resources from households—the direct or indirect owners of land, labor, capital, and entrepreneurial resources. So, referring to the circular flow model (Figure 2.6, page 35), we shift our attention from the bottom loop of the diagram (where businesses supply products that households demand) to the top loop (where businesses demand resources that households supply). ■ This chapter looks at the *demand* for economic resources. Although the discussion is couched in terms of labor, the principles we develop also apply to land, capital, and entrepreneurial ability. In Chapter 15 we will combine resource (labor) demand with labor *supply* to analyze wage rates. Then in Chapter 16 we will use resource demand and resource supply to examine the prices of, and returns to, other productive resources.

■ Significance of Resource Pricing

There are several good reasons to study resource pricing:

■ *Money-income determination* Resource prices are a major factor in determining the income of households. The expenditures that firms make in acquiring economic resources flow as wage, rent, interest, and profit incomes to the households that supply those resources.

■ *Resource allocation* Just as product prices allocate finished goods and services to consumers, resource prices allocate resources among industries and firms. In a dynamic economy, where technology and tastes often change, the efficient allocation of resources over time calls for the continuing shift of resources from one use to another. Resource pricing is a major factor in producing those shifts.

■ *Cost minimization* To the firm, resource prices are costs. And to realize maximum profit, the firm must produce the profit-maximizing output with the most efficient (least costly) combination of resources. Resource prices play the main role in determining the quantities of land, labor, capital, and entrepreneurial ability that will be combined in producing each good or service (see Table 4.1).

- *Ethical questions and policy issues*   There are many ethical questions and public policy issues surrounding the resource market. What degree of income inequality is acceptable? Should the Federal government levy a special tax on the "excess" pay of corporate executives? Should it increase the legal minimum wage? Does it make sense for the government to provide subsidies to farmers? The facts, ethics, and debates relating to income distribution are all grounded on resource pricing.

Marginal Productivity Theory of Resource Demand

To make things simple, we will first assume that a firm hires a certain resource in a purely competitive resource market and sells its output in a purely competitive product market. The simplicity of this situation is twofold: In a competitive product market the firm is a "price taker" and can dispose of as little or as much output as it chooses at the market price. The firm is selling such a negligible fraction of total output that it exerts no influence on product price. Similarly, in the competitive resource market, the firm is a "wage taker." It hires such a negligible fraction of the total supply of the resource that it cannot influence the resource price.

Resource Demand as a Derived Demand

The demand for resources is a **derived demand**: It is derived from the products that they help produce. Resources usually do not directly satisfy customer wants but do so indirectly through their use in producing goods and services. No one wants to consume an acre of land, a John Deere tractor, or the labor services of a farmer, but households do want to consume the food and fiber products that these resources help produce. Similarly, the demand for airplanes generates a demand for assemblers, and the demands for such services as income-tax preparation, haircuts, and child care create derived demands for accountants, barbers, and child care workers. Global Perspective 14.1 demonstrates that the global demand for labor is derived.

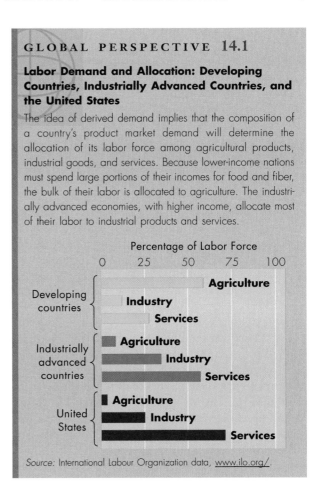

Marginal Revenue Product

The derived nature of resource demand means that the strength of the demand for any resource will depend on

- the productivity of the resource in helping to create a good.
- the market value or price of the good it helps produce.

A resource that is highly productive in turning out a highly valued commodity will be in great demand. On the other hand, a relatively unproductive resource that is capable of producing only a slightly valued commodity will be in little demand. And there will be no demand at all for a resource that is phenomenally efficient in producing something that no one wants to buy.

Productivity   Table 14.1 shows the roles of productivity and product price in determining resource demand. Here we assume that a firm adds one

Table 14.1
The Demand for Labor: Pure Competition in the Sale of the Product

(1) Units of Resource	(2) Total Product (Output)	(3) Marginal Product (MP)	(4) Product Price	(5) Total Revenue, (2) × (4)	(6) Marginal Revenue Product (MRP)
0	0		$2	$ 0	
		7			$14
1	7		2	14	
		6			12
2	13		2	26	
		5			10
3	18		2	36	
		4			8
4	22		2	44	
		3			6
5	25		2	50	
		2			4
6	27		2	54	
		1			2
7	28		2	56	

variable resource, labor, to its fixed plant. Columns 1 and 2 give the number of units of the resource applied to production and the resulting total product (output). Column 3 provides the **marginal product (MP),** or additional output, resulting from each additional resource unit. Columns 1 through 3 remind us that the law of diminishing returns applies here, causing the marginal product of labor to fall beyond some point. For simplicity, we assume that those diminishing marginal returns—those declines in marginal product—begin with the first worker hired.

Product Price   But the derived demand for a resource depends also on the price of the commodity it produces. Column 4 in Table 14.1 adds this price information. Product price is constant, in this case at $2, because we are assuming a competitive product market. The firm is a price taker and will sell units of output only at this market price.

Multiplying column 2 by column 4 gives us the total-revenue data of column 5. These are the amounts of revenue the firm realizes from the various levels of resource usage. From these total-revenue data we can compute **marginal revenue product (MRP)**—*the change in total revenue resulting from the use of each additional unit of a resource* (labor, in this case). In equation form,

$$\text{Marginal revenue product} = \frac{\text{change in total revenue}}{\text{unit change in resource quantity}}$$

The MRPs are listed in column 6 in Table 14.1.

Rule for Employing Resources: MRP = MRC

The MRP schedule, shown as columns 1 and 6, is the firm's demand schedule for labor. To explain why, we must first discuss the rule that guides a profit-seeking firm in hiring any resource: *To maximize profit, a firm should hire additional units of a specific resource as long as each successive unit adds more to the firm's total revenue than it adds to total cost.*

Economists use special terms to designate what each additional unit of labor or other variable resource adds to total cost and what it adds to total revenue. We have seen that MRP measures how much each successive unit of a resource adds to total revenue. The amount that each additional unit of a resource adds to the firm's total (resource) cost is called its **marginal resource cost (MRC).**

In equation form,

$$\text{Marginal resource cost} = \frac{\text{change in total (resource) cost}}{\text{unit change in resource quantity}}$$

So we can restate our rule for hiring resources as follows: It will be profitable for a firm to hire additional units of a resource up to the point at which that resource's MRP is equal to its MRC. If the number of workers a firm is currently hiring is such that the MRP of the last worker exceeds his or her MRC, the firm can profit by hiring more workers. But if the number being hired is such that the MRC of the last worker exceeds his or her MRP, the firm is hiring workers who are not "paying their way" and it can increase its profit by discharging some workers. You may have recognized that this **MRP = MRC rule** is similar to the MR = MC profit-maximizing rule employed throughout our discussion of price and output determination. The rationale of the two rules is the same, but the point of reference is now *inputs* of a resource, not *outputs* of a product.

MRP as Resource Demand Schedule

In a purely competitive labor market, market supply and market demand establish the wage rate. Because each firm hires such a small fraction of market supply, it cannot influence the market wage rate; it is a wage taker, not a wage maker. This means that for each additional unit of labor hired, total resource cost increases by exactly the amount of the constant market wage rate. The MRC of labor exactly equals the market wage rate. Thus, resource "price" (the market wage rate) and resource "cost" (marginal resource cost) are equal for a firm that hires a resource in a competitive labor market. Then the MRP = MRC rule tells us that, in pure competition, the firm will hire workers up to the point at which the market *wage rate* (its MRC) is equal to its MRP.

In terms of the data in columns 1 and 6 in Table 14.1, if the market wage rate is, say, $13.95, the firm will hire only one worker. This is so because the first worker adds $14 to total revenue and slightly less—$13.95—to total cost. In other words, because MRP exceeds MRC for the first worker, it is profitable to hire that worker. For each successive worker, however, MRC (= $13.95) exceeds MRP (= $12 or less), indicating that it will not be profitable to hire any of those workers. If the wage rate is $11.95, by the same reasoning we discover that it will pay the firm to hire both the first and second workers. Similarly, if the wage rate is $9.95, three will be hired. If it is $7.95, four. If it is $5.95, five. And so forth. Hence *the MRP schedule constitutes the firm's demand for labor, because each point on this schedule (or curve) indicates the number of workers the firm would hire at each possible wage rate.* In Figure 14.1, we show the D = MRP curve based on the data in Table 14.1.

The logic here will be familiar to you: In Chapter 10 we applied the price-equals-marginal-cost (P = MC) rule for the profit-maximizing output

Figure 14.1

The purely competitive seller's demand for a resource.   The MRP curve is the resource demand curve; each of its points relates a particular resource price (= MRP when profit is maximized) with a corresponding quantity of the resource demanded. Under pure competition, product price is constant; therefore, the downward slope of the D = MRP curve is due solely to the decline in the resource's marginal product (law of diminishing marginal returns).

to discover that the portion of the purely competitive firm's short-run marginal-cost curve lying above the AVC curve is the short-run product supply curve. Here, we are applying the MRP = MRC (= resource price) rule for the profit-maximizing input to discover that the purely competitive firm's MRP curve is its *resource demand* curve.   ⚠ **14.1**

Resource Demand under Imperfect Product Market Competition

Our analysis of labor demand becomes more complex when the firm is selling its product in an imperfectly competitive market, one in which the firm is a price maker. Pure monopoly, oligopoly, and monopolistic competition in the product market all mean that the firm's product demand curve is downsloping; the firm must set a lower price to increase its sales.

The productivity data in Table 14.1 are retained in columns 1 to 3 in Table 14.2. But here we show in column 4 that product price must be lowered to sell the marginal product of each successive worker. The MRP of the purely competitive seller of Table 14.1 falls for one reason: Marginal product diminishes.

Table 14.2
The Demand for Labor: Imperfect Competition in the Sale of the Product

(1) Units of Resource	(2) Total Produuct (Output)	(3) Marginal Product (MP)	(4) Product Price	(5) Total Revenue, (2) × (4)	(6) Marginal Revenue Product (MRP)
0	0		$2.80	$ 0	
		7			$18.20
1	7		2.60	18.20	
		6			13.00
2	13		2.40	31.20	
		5			8.40
3	18		2.20	39.60	
		4			4.40
4	22		2.00	44.00	
		3			2.25
5	25		1.85	46.25	
		2			1.00
6	27		1.75	47.25	
		1			−1.05
7	28		1.65	46.20	

But the MRP of the imperfectly competitive seller of Table 14.2 falls for two reasons: Marginal product diminishes *and* product price falls as output increases.

We emphasize that the lower price accompanying each increase in output (total product) applies not only to the marginal product of each successive worker but also *to all prior output units that otherwise could have been sold at a higher price.* Observe that the marginal product of the second worker is 6 units of output. These 6 units can be sold for $2.40 each, or, as a group, for $14.40. But this is not the MRP of the second worker. To sell these 6 units, the firm must take a 20-cent price cut on the 7 units produced by the first worker—units that otherwise could have been sold for $2.60 each. Thus, the MRP of the second worker is only $13 [= $14.40 − (7 × 20 cents)], as shown.

Similarly, the third worker adds 5 units to total product, and these units are worth $2.20 each, or $11 total. But to sell these 5 units, the firm must take a 20-cent price cut on the 13 units produced by the first two workers. So the third worker's MRP is only $8.40 [= $11 − (13 × 20 cents)]. The other figures in column 6 are derived similarly.

The result is that the MRP curve—the resource demand curve—of the imperfectly competitive producer is less elastic than that of the purely competitive producer. At a wage rate or MRC of $11.95, both the purely competitive and the imperfectly competitive sellers will hire two workers. But at a $9.95 wage the competitive firm will hire three, and the imperfectly competitive firm only two workers. And at $7.95 the purely competitive firm will employ four employees, and the imperfect competitor only three. You can see this difference in elasticity of resource demand when we graph the MRP data in

Table 14.2 and compare the graph with Figure 14.1, as we do in Figure 14.2.[1]

It is not surprising that the imperfectly competitive producer is less responsive to resource price cuts than the purely competitive producer. The imperfect competitor's relative reluctance to employ more resources, and produce more output, when resource prices fall reflects the imperfect competitor's tendency to restrict output in the product market. Other things equal, the imperfectly competitive seller produces less of a product than a purely competitive seller. In producing that smaller output, it demands fewer resources.

But there is one important qualification. We noted in Chapter 12 that the market structure of oligopoly *might* lead to technological progress and greater production, more employment, and lower prices in the very long run than would a purely competitive market. The resource demand curve in these cases would lie farther to the right than it would if output were restricted as a result of monopoly power. **(Key Question 2)**

Market Demand for a Resource

We have now explained the individual firm's demand curve for a resource. Recall that the total, or market, demand curve for a *product* is found by summing horizontally the demand curves of all individual buy-

---

[1]Note that we plot the points in Figures 14.1 and 14.2 halfway between succeeding numbers of resource units, because MRP is associated with the addition of 1 more unit. Thus, in Figure 14.2, for example, we plot the MRP of the second unit ($13) not at 1 or 2 but at $1\frac{1}{2}$. This "smoothing" enables us to sketch a continuously downsloping curve rather than one that moves downward in discrete steps as each new unit of labor is hired.

Figure 14.2

The imperfectly competitive seller's demand curve for a resource. An imperfectly competitive seller's resource demand curve *D* (solid) slopes downward because both marginal product and product price fall as resource employment and output rise. This downward slope is greater than that for a purely competitive seller (dashed resource demand curve) because the pure competitor can sell the added output at a constant price.

ers in the market. The market demand curve for a particular *resource* is derived in essentially the same way—by summing the individual demand or MRP curves for all firms hiring that resource.

QUICK REVIEW 14.1

■ To maximize profit, a firm will use a resource in an amount at which the resource's marginal revenue product equals its marginal resource cost (MRP = MRC).

■ Application of the MRP = MRC rule to a firm's MRP curve demonstrates that the MRP curve is the firm's resource demand curve. In a purely competitive resource market, resource price (the wage rate) equals MRC.

■ The resource demand curve of a purely competitive seller is downsloping solely because the marginal product of the resource diminishes; the resource demand curve of an imperfectly competitive seller is downsloping because marginal product diminishes and product price falls as output is increased.

Determinants of Resource Demand

What will alter the demand for a resource—that is, shift the resource demand curve? The fact that resource demand is derived from *product demand* and depends on *resource productivity* suggests two "resource demand shifters." Also, our analysis of how changes in the prices of other products can shift a product's demand curve (Chapter 3) suggests another factor: changes in the prices of other *resources*.

Changes in Product Demand

Other things equal, *an increase in the demand for a product that uses a particular resource will increase the demand for the resource, whereas a decrease in product demand will decrease the resource demand.*

Let's see how this works. The first thing to recall is that a change in the demand for a product will change its price. In Table 14.1, let's assume that an increase in product demand boosts product price from $2 to $3. You should calculate the new resource demand schedule (columns 1 and 6) that would result, and plot it in Figure 14.1 to verify that the new resource demand curve lies to the right of the old demand curve. Similarly, a decline in the product demand (and price) will shift the resource demand curve to the left. This effect—resource demand changing along with product demand—demonstrates that resource demand is derived from product demand.

Changes in Productivity

Other things equal, *an increase in the productivity of a resource will increase the demand for the resource and a decrease in productivity will reduce the resource demand.* If we doubled the MP data of column 3 in Table 14.1, the MRP data of column 6 would also double, indicating an increase (rightward shift) in the resource demand curve.

The productivity of any resource may be altered in several ways:

■ **Quantities of other resources** The marginal productivity of any resource will vary with the quantities of the other resources used with it. The greater the amount of capital and land resources used with, say, labor, the greater will be labor's marginal productivity and, thus, labor demand.

■ *Technological progress* Technological improvements that increase the quality of other resources, such as capital, have the same effect. The better the *quality* of capital, the greater the productivity of labor used with it. Dockworkers employed with a specific amount of real capital in the form of unloading cranes are more productive than dockworkers with the same amount of real capital embodied in older conveyor-belt systems.

■ *Quality of the variable resource* Improvements in the quality of the variable resource, such as labor, will increase its marginal productivity and therefore its demand. In effect, there will be a new demand curve for a different, more skilled, kind of labor.

All these considerations help explain why the average level of (real) wages is higher in industrially advanced nations (for example, the United States, Germany, Japan, and France) than in developing nations (for example, India, Ethiopia, Angola, and Cambodia). Workers in industrially advanced nations are generally healthier, better educated, and better trained than are workers in developing countries. Also, in most industries they work with a larger and more efficient stock of capital goods and more abundant natural resources. This creates a strong demand for labor. On the supply side of the market, labor is *relatively* scarce compared with that in most developing nations. A strong demand and a relatively scarce supply of labor result in high wage rates in the industrially advanced nations.

Changes in the Prices of Other Resources

Just as changes in the prices of other products will change the demand for a specific product, changes in the prices of other resources will change the demand for a specific resource. Also recall that the effect of a change in the price of product X on the demand for product Y depends on whether X and Y are substitutes or complements *in consumption.* Similarly, the effect of a change in the price of resource A on the demand for resource B depends on their substitutability or their complementarity *in production.*

Substitute Resources Suppose the technology in a certain production process is such that labor and capital are substitutable. A firm can produce some specific amount of output using a relatively

small amount of labor and a relatively large amount of capital, or vice versa. Now assume that the price of machinery (capital) falls. The effect on the demand for labor will be the net result of two opposed effects: the substitution effect and the output effect.

■ *Substitution effect* The decline in the price of machinery prompts the firm to substitute machinery for labor. This allows the firm to produce its output at lower cost. So at the fixed wage rate, smaller quantities of labor are now employed. This **substitution effect** decreases the demand for labor. More generally, the substitution effect indicates that a firm will purchase more of an input whose relative price has declined and, conversely, use less of an input whose relative price has increased.

■ *Output effect* Because the price of machinery has fallen, the costs of producing various outputs must also decline. With lower costs, the firm finds it profitable to produce and sell a greater output. The greater output increases the demand for all resources, including labor. So this **output effect** increases the demand for labor. More generally, the output effect means that the firm will purchase more of one particular input when the price of the other input falls and less of that particular input when the price of the other input rises.

■ *Net effect* The substitution and output effects are both present when the price of an input changes, but they work in opposite directions. For a decline in the price of capital, the substitution effect decreases the demand for labor and the output effect increases it. The net change in labor demand depends on the relative sizes of the two effects: *If the substitution effect outweighs the output effect, a decrease in the price of capital decreases the demand for labor. If the output effect exceeds the substitution effect, a decrease in the price of capital increases the demand for labor.*

Complementary Resources Recall from Chapter 3 that certain products, such as cameras and film or computers and software, are complementary goods; they "go together" and are jointly demanded. Resources may also be complementary; an increase in the quantity of one of them used in the production process requires an increase in the amount used of the other as well, and vice versa. Suppose a small design firm does computer-assisted design (CAD) with relatively expensive personal computers as its basic piece of capital equipment. Each computer requires a single design engineer to operate it; the machine is not automated—it will not run itself—and a second engineer would have nothing to do.

Now assume that a technological advance in the production of these computers substantially reduces their price. There can be no substitution effect, because labor and capital must be used in *fixed proportions*, one person for one machine. Capital cannot be substituted for labor. But there *is* an output effect. Other things equal, the reduction in the price of capital goods means lower production costs. It will therefore be profitable to produce a larger output. In doing so, the firm will use both more capital and more labor. *When labor and capital are complementary, a decline in the price of capital increases the demand for labor through the output effect.*

We have cast our analysis of substitute resources and complementary resources mainly in terms of a decline in the price of capital. In Table 14.3 we summarize the effects of an *increase* in the price of capital on the demand for labor. We urge you to study it carefully.

Now that we have discussed the full list of the determinants of labor demand, let's again review their effects. Stated in terms of the labor resource, the demand for labor will increase (the labor demand curve will shift rightward) when:

- The demand for (and therefore the price of) the product produced by that labor *increases*.
- The productivity (MP) of labor *increases*.
- The price of a substitute input *decreases*, provided the output effect exceeds the substitution effect.

- The price of a substitute input *increases*, provided the substitution effect exceeds the output effect.
- The price of a complementary input *decreases*.

Be sure that you can "reverse" these effects to explain a *decrease* in labor demand.

Table 14.4 provides several illustrations of the determinants of labor demand, listed by the categories of determinants we have discussed. You will benefit by giving them a close look.

Occupational Employment Trends

Changes in labor demand have considerable significance since they affect wage rates and employment in specific occupations. Increases in labor demand for certain occupational groups result in increases in their employment, and decreases in labor demand result in decreases in their employment. For illustration, let's look at occupations that are growing in demand. (Wage rates are the subject of the next chapter.)

The Fastest-Growing Occupations Table 14.5 lists the 10 fastest-growing U.S. occupations, for 1998 to 2008, as measured by percentage changes and projected by the Bureau of Labor Statistics. It is no coincidence that the service occupations dominate the list. In general, the demand for service workers is rapidly outpacing the demand for manufacturing, construction, and mining workers.

Of the 10 fastest-growing occupations in percentage terms, the top 5 are directly related to computers. The increase in the demand for computer engineers, computer support specialists, systems analysts, database managers, and desktop

Table 14.3
The Effect of an Increase in the Price of Capital on the Demand for Labor, D_L

(1) Relationship of Inputs	(2) Increase in the Price of Capital		
	(a) Substitution Effect	(b) Output Effect	(c) Combined Effect
Substitutes in production	Labor substituted for capital	Production costs up, output down, and less of both capital and labor used	D_L increases if the substitution effect exceeds the output effect; D_L decreases if the output effect exceeds the substitution effect
Complements in production	No substitution of labor for capital	Production costs up, output down, and less of both capital and labor used	D_L decreases

Table 14.4

Determinants of Labor Demand: Factors That Shift the Labor Demand Curve

Determinant	Examples
Change in product demand	Gambling increases in popularity, increasing the demand for workers at casinos.
	Consumers decrease their demand for leather coats, decreasing the demand for tanners.
	The Federal government reduces spending on the military, reducing the demand for military personnel.
Change in productivity	An increase in the skill levels of physicians increases the demand for their services.
	Computer-assisted graphic design increases the productivity of, and demand for, graphic artists.
Change in the price of another resource	An increase in the price of electricity increases the cost of producing aluminum and reduces the demand for aluminum workers.
	The price of security equipment used by businesses to protect against illegal entry falls, decreasing the demand for night guards.
	The price of telephone switching equipment decreases, greatly reducing the cost of telephone service; this in turn increases the demand for telemarketers.
	Health-insurance premiums rise, and firms substitute part-time workers who are not covered by insurance for covered full-time workers who are.

publishing specialists relates to the rapid rise in the demand for computers, computer services, and the Internet. It also relates to the rising productivity of these particular workers, given the vastly improved quality of the computer and communications equipment they work with. Moreover, price declines on such equipment have had stronger output effects than substitution effects, increasing the demand for these kinds of labor.

Three of the other fastest-growing occupations relate to health care: personal care and home health care aides, medical assistants, and physician assistants. The growing demands for these types of labor are derived from the growing demand for health services, caused by several factors. The aging of the U.S. population has brought with it more medical problems, the rising standard of income has led to greater expenditures on health care, and the grow-

Table 14.5

The 10 Fastest-Growing Occupations in Percentage Terms, 1998–2008

Occupation	Employment Thousands of Jobs		Percentage Increase
	1998	2008	
Computer engineers	299	622	108%
Computer support specialists	429	869	103
Systems analysts	617	1194	94
Database administrators	87	155	78
Desktop publishing specialists	26	44	69
Paralegals and legal assistants	136	220	62
Personal care and home health aides	746	1179	58
Medical assistants	252	396	57
Social and human service assistants	268	410	53
Physician assistants	66	98	48

Source: Bureau of Labor Statistics, "Employment Projections," stats.bls.gov.

Table 14.6

The 10 Occupations with the Largest Absolute Job Growth (Thousands of Jobs), 1998–2008

Occupation	Employment 1998	Employment 2008	Number of New Jobs
Systems analysts	617	1194	577
Retail salespersons	4056	4620	564
Cashiers	3198	3754	556
Managers and executives	3362	3913	551
Truck drivers	2970	3463	493
Office clerks	3021	3484	463
Registered nurses	2079	2530	451
Computer support specialists	429	869	440
Personal care and home health aides	746	1179	433
Teacher assistants	1192	1567	375

Source: Bureau of Labor Statistics, "Employment Projections," stats.bls.gov.

ing presence of private and public insurance has allowed people to buy more health care than most could afford individually.

The Occupations with the Greatest Absolute Job Growth

Of course, a large growth percentage may mean a large or small increase in the absolute number of new jobs, depending on the initial employment size of the occupation. Where will the most new jobs actually be added?

Table 14.6 lists the 10 occupations with the greatest projected growth in the absolute number of new jobs between 1998 and 2008. Here the occupations are more varied than in the previous table, although computer- and health care–related occupations are again present. But also included are retail salespersons, cashiers, managers and executives, truck drivers, office clerks, and teacher assistants.

▌ Elasticity of Resource Demand

The employment changes we have just discussed have resulted from shifts in the locations of resource demand curves. Such changes in demand must be distinguished from changes in the quantity of a resource demanded caused by a change in the price of the specific resource under consideration. Such a change is caused not by a shift of the demand curve but, rather, by a movement from one point to another on a fixed resource demand curve. Example: In Figure 14.1 we note that an increase in the wage rate from $5 to $7 will reduce the quantity of labor demanded from 5 to 4 units. This is a change in the *quantity of labor demanded* as distinct from a *change in demand*.

The sensitivity of producers to changes in resource prices is measured by the **elasticity of resource demand.** In coefficient form,

$$E_{rd} = \frac{\text{percentage change in resource quantity}}{\text{percentage change in resource price}}$$

When E_{rd} is greater than 1, resource demand is elastic; when E_{rd} is less than 1, resource demand is inelastic; and when E_{rd} equals 1, resource demand is unit-elastic. What determines the elasticity of resource demand? Several factors are at work. 🔑 **14.1**

Rate of MP Decline

A purely technical consideration is the rate at which the marginal product of the particular resource declines. If the marginal product of one resource declines slowly as it is added to a fixed amount of other resources, the demand (MRP) curve for that resource declines slowly and tends to be highly elastic. A small decline in the price of such a resource will yield a relatively large increase in the amount demanded. Conversely, if the marginal product of the resource declines sharply as more of it is added, the resource demand curve also declines rapidly. This means that a relatively large decline in the wage rate will be accompanied by a modest increase in the amount of labor hired; labor demand is inelastic.

Ease of Resource Substitutability

The degree to which resources are substitutable is also a determinant of elasticity. *The larger the number of satisfactory substitute resources available, the greater the elasticity of demand for a particular resource.* If a furniture manufacturer finds that five or six different types of wood are equally satisfactory in making coffee tables, a rise in the price of any one type of wood may cause a sharp drop in the amount demanded as the producer substitutes one of the other woods. At the other extreme, there may be no reasonable substitutes; bauxite is absolutely essential in the production of aluminum ingots. Thus, the demand for bauxite by aluminum producers is inelastic.

Time can play a role in the input substitution process. For example, a firm's truck drivers may obtain a substantial wage increase with little or no immediate decline in employment. But over time, as the firm's trucks wear out and are replaced, that wage increase may motivate the company to purchase larger trucks and in that way deliver the same total output with fewer drivers. Another example: New commercial aircraft have been designed to require only two cockpit personnel rather than the customary three, again indicating some substitutability between labor and capital if there is enough time.

Elasticity of Product Demand   The elasticity of demand for any resource depends on the elasticity of demand for the product it helps produce. *The greater the elasticity of product demand, the greater the elasticity of resource demand.* The derived nature of resource demand leads us to expect this relationship. A small rise in the price of a product with great elasticity of demand will sharply reduce output, bringing about a relatively large decline in the amounts of various resources demanded. This means that the demand for the resource is elastic.

Remember that the resource demand curve in Figure 14.1 is more elastic than the resource demand curve shown in Figure 14.2. The difference arises because in Figure 14.1 we assume a perfectly elastic product demand curve, while Figure 14.2 is based on a downsloping or less than perfectly elastic product demand curve.

Ratio of Resource Cost to Total Cost   *The larger the proportion of total production costs accounted for by a resource, the greater the elasticity of demand for that resource.* In the extreme, if labor cost is the only production cost, then a 20 percent increase in wage rates will shift all the firm's cost curves upward by 20 percent. If product demand is elastic, this substantial increase in costs will cause a relatively large decline in sales and a sharp decline in the amount of labor demanded. So labor demand is highly elastic. But if labor cost is only 50 percent of production cost, then a 20 percent increase in wage rates will increase costs by only 10 percent. With the same elasticity of product demand, this will cause a relatively small decline in sales and therefore in the amount of labor demanded. In this case the demand for labor is much less elastic. **(Key Question 3)**

> **QUICK REVIEW 14.2**
>
> ■   A resource demand curve will shift because of changes in product demand, changes in the productivity of the resource, and changes in the prices of other inputs.
>
> ■   If resources A and B are substitutable, a decline in the price of A will decrease the demand for B provided the substitution effect exceeds the output effect. But if the output effect exceeds the substitution effect, the demand for B will increase.
>
> ■   If resources C and D are complements, a decline in the price of C will increase the demand for D.
>
> ■   Elasticity of resource demand measures the extent to which producers change the quantity of a resource they hire when its price changes.
>
> ■   The elasticity of resource demand will be less the more rapid the decline in marginal product, the smaller the number of substitutes, the smaller the elasticity of product demand, and the smaller the proportion of total cost accounted for by the resource.

■ Optimal Combination of Resources

So far, our main focus has been on one variable input, labor. But in the long run firms can vary the amounts of all the resources they use. That's why we need to consider what combination of resources a firm will choose when *all* its inputs are variable. While our analysis is based on two resources, it can be extended to any number of inputs.

We will consider two interrelated questions:

■   What combination of resources will minimize costs at a specific level of output?

■   What combination of resources will maximize profit?

The Least-Cost Rule

A firm is producing a specific output with the **least-cost combination of resources** *when the last dollar spent on each resource yields the same marginal product.* That is, the cost of any output is minimized when the ratios of marginal product to price of the last units of resources used are the same for each resource. In competitive resource markets, recall, marginal resource cost is the market resource price; the firm can hire as many or as few units of the resource as it wants at that price. Then, with just two resources, labor and capital, a competitive firm minimizes its total cost of a specific output when

$$\frac{\text{marginal product}}{\text{of labor (MP}_L\text{)}}_{\text{price of labor (}P_L\text{)}} = \frac{\text{marginal product}}{\text{of capital (MP}_C\text{)}}_{\text{price of capital (}P_C\text{)}} \quad (1)$$

Throughout, we will refer to the marginal products of labor and capital as MP_L and MP_C, respectively, and symbolize the price of labor by P_L and the price of capital by P_C.

A concrete example shows why fulfilling the condition in equation (1) leads to least-cost production. Assume that the price of both capital and labor is $1 per unit but that they are currently employed in such amounts that the marginal product of labor is 10 and the marginal product of capital is 5. Our equation immediately tells us that this is not the least costly combination of resources:

$$\frac{\text{MP}_L = 10}{P_L = \$1} > \frac{\text{MP}_C = 5}{P_C = \$1}$$

Suppose the firm spends $1 less on capital and shifts that dollar to labor. It loses 5 units of output produced by the last dollar's worth of capital, but it gains 10 units of output from the extra dollar's worth of labor. Net output increases by 5 (= 10 − 5) units for the same total cost. More such shifting of dollars from capital to labor will push the firm *down* along its MP curve for labor and *up* along its MP curve for capital, increasing output and moving the firm toward a position of equilibrium where equation (1) is fulfilled. At that equilibrium position, the MP per dollar for the last unit of both labor and capital might be, for example, 7. And the firm will be producing a greater output for the same (original) cost.

Whenever the same total-resource cost can result in a greater total output, the cost per unit—and therefore the total cost of any specific level of output—can be reduced. Being able to produce a *larger* output with a *specific* total cost is the same as being able to produce a *specific* output with a *smaller* total cost. If the firm in our example buys $1 less of capital, its output will fall by 5 units. If it spends only $.50 of that dollar on labor, the firm will increase its output by a compensating 5 units (= $\frac{1}{2}$ of the MP per dollar). Then the firm will realize the same total output at a $.50 lower total cost.

The cost of producing any specific output can be reduced as long as equation (1) does not hold. But when dollars have been shifted between capital and labor to the point where equation (1) holds, no additional changes in the use of capital and labor will reduce costs further. The firm is now producing that output using the least-cost combination of capital and labor.

All the long-run cost curves developed in Chapter 9 and used thereafter assume that the least-cost combination of inputs has been realized at each level of output. Any firm that combines resources in violation of the least-cost rule would have a higher-than-necessary average total cost at each level of output. That is, it would incur *X-inefficiency*, as discussed in Figure 11.7.

The producer's least-cost rule is analogous to the consumer's utility-maximizing rule described in Chapter 8. In achieving the utility-maximizing combination of goods, the consumer considers both his or her preferences as reflected in diminishing-marginal-utility data and the prices of the various products. Similarly, in achieving the cost-minimizing combination of resources, the producer considers both the marginal-product data and the price (costs) of the various resources.

The Profit-Maximizing Rule

Minimizing cost is not sufficient for maximizing profit. A firm can produce any level of output in the least costly way by applying equation (1). But there is only one unique level of output that maximizes profit. Our earlier analysis of product markets showed that this profit-maximizing output occurs where marginal revenue equals marginal cost (MR = MC). Near the beginning of this chapter we determined that we could write this profit-maximizing condition as MRP = MRC as it relates to resource inputs.

In a purely competitive resource market the marginal resource cost (MRC) is exactly equal to the resource price *P*. Thus, for any competitive resource market, we have as our profit-maximizing equation

MRP (resource) = *P* (resource)

This condition must hold for every variable resource, and in the long run all resources are variable. In competitive markets, a firm will therefore achieve its **profit-maximizing combination of resources** when each resource is employed to the point at which its marginal revenue product equals its price. For two resources, labor and capital, we need both

$$P_L = \text{MRP}_L \qquad \text{and} \qquad P_C = \text{MRP}_C$$

We can combine these conditions by dividing both sides of each equation by their respective prices and equating the results to get

$$\frac{MRP_L}{P_L} = \frac{MRP_C}{P_C} = 1 \qquad (2)$$

Note in equation (2) that it is not sufficient that the MRPs of the two resources be *proportionate* to their prices; the MRPs must be *equal* to their prices and the ratios therefore equal to 1. For example, if $MRP_L = \$15$, $P_L = \$5$, $MRP_C = \$9$, and $P_C = \$3$, the firm is underemploying both capital and labor even though the ratios of MRP to resource price are identical for both resources. The firm can expand its profit by hiring additional amounts of both capital and labor until it moves down their downsloping MRP curves to the points at which $MRP_L = \$5$ and $MRP_C = \$3$. The ratios will then be 5/5 and 3/3 and equal to 1.

The profit-maximizing position in equation (2) includes the cost-minimizing condition of equation (1). That is, if a firm is maximizing profit according to equation (2), then it must be using the least-cost combination of inputs to do so. However, the converse is not true: A firm operating at least cost according to equation (1) may not be operating at the output that maximizes its profit.

Numerical Illustration

A numerical illustration will help you understand the least-cost and profit-maximizing rules. In columns 2, 3, 2′, and 3′ in Table 14.7 we show the total products and marginal products for various amounts of labor and capital that are assumed to be the only inputs needed in producing some product, say, key chains. Both inputs are subject to diminishing returns.

We also assume that labor and capital are supplied in competitive resource markets at $8 and $12, respectively, and that key chains sell competitively at $2 per unit. For both labor and capital we can determine the total revenue associated with each input level by multiplying total product by the $2 product price. These data are shown in columns 4 and 4′. They enable us to calculate the marginal revenue product of each successive input of labor and capital as shown in columns 5 and 5′, respectively.

Producing at Least Cost What is the least-cost combination of labor and capital to use in producing, say, 50 units of output? The answer, which we can obtain by trial and error, is 3 units of labor and 2 units of capital. Columns 2 and 2′ indicate that this combination of labor and capital does, indeed, result in the required 50 (= 28 + 22) units of output. Now, note from columns 3 and 3′ that hiring 3 units of labor gives us $MP_L/P_L = \frac{6}{8} = \frac{3}{4}$ and hiring 2 units of capital gives us $MP_C/P_C = \frac{9}{12} = \frac{3}{4}$. So equation (1) is fulfilled. How can we verify that costs are actually minimized? First, we see that the total cost of employing 3 units of labor and 2 of capital is $48 [= (3 × \$8) + (2 × \$12)].

Other combinations of labor and capital will also yield 50 units of output, but at a higher cost than

Table 14.7

Data for Finding the Least-Cost and Profit-Maximizing Combination of Labor and Capital*

	Labor (Price = $8)					Capital (Price = $12)			
(1) Quantity	(2) Total Product (Output)	(3) Marginal Product	(4) Total Revenue	(5) Marginal Revenue Product	(1′) Quantity	(2′) Total Product (Output)	(3′) Marginal Product	(4′) Total Revenue	(5′) Marginal Revenue Product
0	0		$ 0		0	0		$ 0	
		12		$24			13		$26
1	12		24		1	13		26	
		10		20			9		18
2	22		44		2	22		44	
		6		12			6		**12**
3	28		56		**3**	28		56	
		5		10			4		8
4	33		66		4	32		64	
		4		**8**			3		6
5	37		74		5	35		70	
		3		6			2		4
6	40		80		6	37		74	
		2		4			1		2
7	42		84		7	38		76	

*To simplify, it is assumed in this table that the productivity of each resource is independent of the quantity of the other. For example, the total and marginal products of labor are assumed not to vary with the quantity of capital employed.

$48. For example, 5 units of labor and 1 unit of capital will produce 50 (= 37 + 13) units, but total cost is higher, at $52 [= (5 × $8) + (1 × $12)]. This comes as no surprise, because 5 units of labor and 1 unit of capital violate the least-cost rule— $MP_L/P_L = \frac{4}{8}$, $MP_C/P_C = \frac{13}{12}$. Only the combination (3 units of labor and 2 units of capital) that minimizes total cost will satisfy equation (1). All other combinations capable of producing 50 units of output violate the cost-minimizing rule, and therefore cost more than $48.

Maximizing Profit

Will 50 units of output maximize the firm's profit? No, because the profit-maximizing terms of equation (2) are not satisfied when the firm employs 3 units of labor and 2 of capital. To maximize profit, each input should be employed until its price equals its marginal revenue product. But for 3 units of labor, labor's MRP in column 5 is $12 while its price is only $8. This means the firm could increase its profit by hiring more labor. Similarly, for 2 units of capital, we see in column 5′ that capital's MRP is $18 and its price is only $12. This indicates that more capital should also be employed. By producing only 50 units of output (even though they are produced at least cost), labor and capital are being used in less-than-profit-maximizing amounts. The firm needs to expand its employment of labor and capital, thereby increasing its output.

Table 14.7 shows that the MRPs of labor and capital are equal to their prices, so equation (2) is fulfilled, when the firm is employing 5 units of labor and 3 units of capital. So this is the profit-maximizing combination of inputs.[2] The firm's total cost will be $76, made up of $40 (= 5 × $8) of labor and $36 (= 3 × $12) of capital. Total revenue will be $130, found either by multiplying the total output of 65 (= 37 + 28) by the $2 product price or by summing the total revenues attributable to labor ($74) and to capital ($56). The difference between total revenue and total cost in this instance is $54 (= $130 − $76). Experiment with other combinations of labor and capital to demonstrate that they yield an economic profit of less than $54.

Note that the profit-maximizing combination of 5 units of labor and 3 units of capital is also a least-cost combination for this particular level of output. Using these resource amounts satisfies the least-cost requirement of equation (1) in that $MP_L/P_L = \frac{4}{8} = \frac{1}{2}$ and $MP_C/P_C = \frac{6}{12} = \frac{1}{2}$. **(Key Questions 4 and 5)**

■ Marginal Productivity Theory of Income Distribution

Our discussion of resource pricing is the cornerstone of the controversial view that fairness and economic justice are one of the outcomes of a competitive capitalist economy. Table 14.7 tells us, in effect, that workers receive income payments (wages) equal to the marginal contributions they make to their employers' outputs and revenues. In other words, workers are paid according to the value of the labor services that they contribute to production. Similarly, owners of the other resources receive income based on the value of the resources they supply in the production process.

In this **marginal productivity theory of income distribution,** income gets distributed according to contribution to society's output. So, if you are willing to accept the ethical proposition "To each according to what he or she creates," income payments based on marginal revenue product seem to provide a fair and equitable distribution of society's income. 🄿 14.2

This sounds fair enough, but there are serious criticisms of this theory of income distribution:

■ ***Inequality*** Critics argue that the distribution of income resulting from payment according to marginal productivity may be highly unequal because productive resources are very unequally distributed in the first place. Aside from their differences in mental and physical attributes, individuals encounter substantially different opportunities to enhance their productivity through education and training and the use of more and better equipment. Some people may not be able to participate in production at all because of mental or physical disabilities, and they would obtain no income under a system of distribution based solely on marginal productivity. Ownership of property resources is also highly unequal. Many landlords and capitalists obtain their property by inheritance rather than through their own productive effort. Hence, income from inherited property resources conflicts with the

---

[2]Because we are dealing with discrete (nonfractional) units of the two outputs here, the use of 4 units of labor and 2 units of capital is equally profitable. The fifth unit of labor's MRP and its price (cost) are equal at $8, so that the fifth labor unit neither adds to nor subtracts from the firm's profit; similarly, the third unit of capital has no effect on profit.

Input Substitution: The Case of ATMs

Banks Are Using More Automatic Teller Machines (ATMs) and Employing Fewer Human Tellers.

As you have learned from this chapter, a firm achieves its least-cost combination of inputs when the last dollar it spends on each input makes the same contribution to total output. This raises an interesting real-world question: What happens when technological advance makes available a new, highly productive capital good for which MP/P is greater than it is for other inputs, say, a particular type of labor? The answer is that the least-cost mix of resources abruptly changes, and the firm responds accordingly. If the new capital is a substitute for labor (rather than a complement), the firm replaces the particular type of labor with the new capital. That is exactly what is happening in the banking industry, in which ATMs are replacing human bank tellers.

ATMs made their debut about 30 years ago when Diebold, a U.S. firm, introduced the product. Today, Diebold and NCR (also a U.S. firm) dominate global sales, with the Japanese firm Fujitsu being a distant third. The number of ATMs and their usage has exploded, and currently there are more than 230,000 ATMs in the United States. In 1975, about 10 *million* ATM transactions occurred in the United States. In contrast, since 1995 there have been more than 10 *billion* U.S. ATM transactions each year. There are now 709,000 ATMs worldwide.

ATMs are highly productive: A single machine can handle hundreds of transactions daily, thousands weekly, and millions over the course of several years. ATMs can not only handle cash withdrawals but also accept deposits and facilitate switches of funds between various accounts. Although ATMs are expensive for banks to buy and install, they are available 24 hours a day, and their cost per transaction is one-fourth the cost for human tellers. They rarely get "held up," and they do not quit their jobs (turnover among human tellers is nearly 50 percent per year). Moreover, ATMs are highly convenient; unlike human tellers, they are located not only at banks but also at busy street corners, workplaces, universities, and shopping malls. The same bank card that enables you to withdraw cash from your local ATM also enables you to withdraw pounds from an ATM in London, yen from an ATM in Tokyo, and even rubles from an ATM in Moscow. (All this, of course, assumes that you have money in your checking account.)

In the terminology of this chapter, the more productive, lower-priced ATMs have reduced the demand for a substitute in production—human tellers. Between 1990 and 2000, an estimated 80,000 human teller positions were eliminated, and even more positions will disappear in the coming decade. Where will the people holding these jobs go? Most will eventually move to other occupations. Although the lives of individual tellers are disrupted, society clearly wins. Society gets more convenient banking services as well as the other goods that these "freed-up" labor resources help produce.

Source: Based partly on Ben Craig, "Where Have All the Tellers Gone?" Federal Reserve Bank of Cleveland, *Economic Commentary*, Apr. 15, 1997; and statistics provided by the American Bankers Association.

"To each according to what he or she creates" idea. This reasoning calls for government policies that modify the income distributions made strictly according to marginal productivity.

■ *Market imperfections* The marginal productivity theory rests on the assumptions of competitive markets. Yet labor markets, for example, are riddled with imperfections, as you will see in Chapter 28. Some employers exert pricing power in hiring workers. And some workers, through labor unions, professional associations, and occupational licensing laws, wield monopoly power in selling their services. Even the process of collective bargaining over wages suggests a power struggle over the division of income. In this struggle, market forces—and income shares based on marginal productivity—may get pushed into the background. In addition, discrimination in the labor market can distort earnings patterns. In short, because of real-world market imperfections, wage rates and other resource prices frequently are not based solely on contributions to output.

SUMMARY

1. Resource prices act as a determinant of money incomes, and they simultaneously ration resources to various industries and firms.

2. The demand for any resource is derived from the product it helps produce. That means the demand for a resource will depend on its productivity and on the market value (price) of the good it is producing.

3. Marginal revenue product is the extra revenue a firm obtains when it employs 1 more unit of a resource. The marginal revenue product curve for any resource is the demand curve for that resource, because the firm equates resource price and MRP in determining its profit-maximizing level of resource employment. Thus each point on the MRP curve indicates how many resource units the firm will hire at a specific resource price.

4. The firm's demand curve for a resource slopes downward, because the marginal product of additional units declines in accordance with the law of diminishing returns. When a firm is selling in an imperfectly competitive market, the resource demand curve falls for a second reason: Product price must be reduced for the firm to sell a larger output. We can derive the market demand curve for a resource by summing horizontally the demand curves of all the firms hiring that resource.

5. The demand curve for a resource will shift as the result of (a) a change in the demand for, and therefore the price of, the product the resource is producing; (b) changes in the productivity of the resource; and (c) changes in the prices of other resources.

6. If resources A and B are substitutable for each other, a decline in the price of A will decrease the demand for B provided the substitution effect is greater than the output effect. But if the output effect *exceeds* the substitution effect, a decline in the price of A will increase the demand for B.

7. If resources C and D are complementary or jointly demanded, there is only an output effect; a change in the price of C will change the demand for D in the opposite direction.

8. The majority of the 10 fastest-growing occupations in the United States relate to computers or health care

(see Table 14.5); the occupations with the greatest absolute growth in employment, however, are more mixed (see Table 14.6).

9. The elasticity of demand for a resource measures the responsiveness of producers to a change in the resource's price. The coefficient of the elasticity of resource demand is

$$E_{\mathrm{rd}} = \frac{\text{percentage change in resource quantity}}{\text{percentage change in resource price}}$$

When E_{rd} is greater than 1, resource demand is elastic; when E_{rd} is less than 1, resource demand is inelastic; and when E_{rd} equals 1, resource demand is unit-elastic.

10. The elasticity of demand for a resource will be greater (a) the more slowly the marginal product of the resource declines, (b) the larger the number of good substitute resources available, (c) the greater the elasticity of demand for the product, and (d) the larger the proportion of total production costs attributable to the resource.

11. Any specific level of output will be produced with the least costly combination of variable resources when the marginal product per dollar's worth of each input is the same—that is, when

$$\frac{\text{MP of labor}}{\text{price of labor}} = \frac{\text{MP of capital}}{\text{price of capital}}$$

12. A firm is employing the profit-maximizing combination of resources when each resource is used to the point where its marginal revenue product equals its price. In terms of labor and capital, that occurs when the MRP of labor equals the price of labor and the MRP of capital equals the price of capital—that is, when

$$\frac{\text{MRP of labor}}{\text{price of labor}} = \frac{\text{MRP of capital}}{\text{price of capital}} = 1$$

13. The marginal productivity theory of income distribution holds that all resources are paid according to their marginal contribution to output. Critics assert that such an income distribution is too unequal and that real-world market imperfections result in pay above and below marginal contributions to output.

TERMS AND CONCEPTS

derived demand

marginal product (MP)

marginal revenue product (MRP)

marginal resource cost (MRC)

MRP = MRC rule

substitution effect

output effect

elasticity of resource demand

least-cost combination of resources

profit-maximizing combination of resources

marginal productivity theory of income distribution

STUDY QUESTIONS

1. What is the significance of resource pricing? Explain how the factors determining resource demand differ from those determining product demand. Explain the meaning and significance of the fact that the demand for a resource is a derived demand. Why do resource demand curves slope downward?

2. **Key Question** At the bottom of the page, complete the labor demand table for a firm that is hiring labor competitively and selling its product in a competitive market.

   a. How many workers will the firm hire if the market wage rate is $27.95? $19.95? Explain why the firm will not hire a larger or smaller number of units of labor at each of these wage rates.

   b. Show in schedule form and graphically the labor demand curve of this firm.

   c. Now again determine the firm's demand curve for labor, assuming that it is selling in an imperfectly competitive market and that, although it can sell 17 units at $2.20 per unit, it must lower product price by 5 cents in order to sell the marginal product of each successive labor unit. Compare this demand curve with that derived in question 2b. Which curve is more elastic? Explain.

3. **Key Question** What factors determine the elasticity of resource demand? What effect will each of the following have on the elasticity or the location of the demand for resource C, which is being used to produce commodity X? Where there is any uncertainty as to the outcome, specify the causes of that uncertainty.

   a. An increase in the demand for product X.

   b. An increase in the price of substitute resource D.

   c. An increase in the number of resources substitutable for C in producing X.

   d. A technological improvement in the capital equipment with which resource C is combined.

   e. A fall in the price of complementary resource E.

   f. A decline in the elasticity of demand for product X due to a decline in the competitiveness of the product market.

4. **Key Question** Suppose the productivity of capital and labor are as shown in the accompanying table. The output of these resources sells in a purely competitive market for $1 per unit. Both capital and labor are hired under purely competitive conditions at $3 and $1, respectively.

Units of Capital	MP of Capital	Units of Labor	MP of Labor
0		0	
1	24	1	11
2	21	2	9
3	18	3	8
4	15	4	7
5	9	5	6
6	6	6	4
7	3	7	1
8	1	8	$\frac{1}{2}$

   a. What is the least-cost combination of labor and capital the firm should employ in producing 80 units of output? Explain.

   b. What is the profit-maximizing combination of labor and capital the firm should use? Explain. What is the resulting level of output? What is the economic profit? Is this the least costly way of producing the profit-maximizing output?

5. **Key Question** In each of the following four cases, MRP_L and MRP_C refer to the marginal revenue products of labor and capital, respectively, and P_L and P_C refer to their prices. Indicate in each case whether the conditions are consistent with maximum profits for the firm. If not, state which resource(s) should be used in larger amounts and which resource(s) should be used in smaller amounts.

   a. $MRP_L = \$8$; $P_L = \$4$; $MRP_C = \$8$; $P_C = \$4$

   b. $MRP_L = \$10$; $P_L = \$12$; $MRP_C = \$14$; $P_C = \$9$

   c. $MRP_L = \$6$; $P_L = \$6$; $MRP_C = \$12$; $P_C = \$12$

   d. $MRP_L = \$22$; $P_L = \$26$; $MRP_C = \$16$; $P_C = \$19$

Units of Labor	Total Product	Marginal Product	Product Price	Total Revenue	Marginal Revenue Product
0	0		$2	$_____	
1	17	_____	2	_____	$_____
2	31	_____	2	_____	_____
3	43	_____	2	_____	_____
4	53	_____	2	_____	_____
5	60	_____	2	_____	_____
6	65	_____	2	_____	_____

6. **(Last Word)** Explain the economics of the substitution of ATMs for human tellers. Some banks are beginning to assess transaction fees when customers use human tellers rather than ATMs. What are these banks trying to accomplish?

7. Florida citrus growers say that the recent crackdown on illegal immigration is increasing the market wage rates necessary to get their oranges picked. Some are turning to $100,000 to $300,000 mechanical harvesters known as "trunk, shake, and catch" pickers, which vigorously shake oranges from the trees. If widely adopted, what will be the effect on the demand for human orange pickers? What does that imply about the relative strengths of the substitution and output effects?

8. **Web-Based Question:** *Selected occupations—what are their employment outlooks?* Use the A to Z index in the Bureau of Labor Statistics *Occupational Outlook*, at www.bls.gov/oco/, to determine the general and specific employment outlooks for (a) textile machinery operators, (b) financial managers, (c) computer operators, and (d) dental hygienists. Why do these job outlooks differ?

9. **Web-Based Question:** *The overall demand for labor—in which countries has it increased the most?* In countries where real wages are steady or rising, increases in total employment reflect increases in labor demand. Go to the Bureau of Labor Statistics website, www.bls.gov/data/top20.htm, and select International Labor Statistics (at the bottom). Find the percentage increases in employment for the United States, Japan, Germany, France, Great Britain, Italy, and Canada for the most recent 10-year period. Which three countries have had the fastest growth of labor demand, as measured by the percentage change in employment? Which three the slowest?

CHAPTER 15

Wage Determination

NEARLY **136 MILLION** of us go to work each day in the United States. We work at an amazing variety of jobs for thousands of different firms and receive considerable differences in pay. What determines our hourly wage or annual salary? Why is the salary for, say, a topflight major league baseball player $15 million or more a year, whereas the pay for a first-rate schoolteacher is $50,000? Why are starting salaries for college graduates who major in engineering and accounting so much higher than those for graduates majoring in journalism and sociology? ■ Having explored the major factors that underlie labor demand, we now bring *labor supply* into our analysis to help answer these questions. Generally speaking, labor supply and labor demand interact to determine the level of hourly wage rates or annual salaries in each occupation. Collectively, those wages and salaries make up 70 percent of the national income.

▋ Labor, Wages, and Earnings

Economists use the term "labor" broadly to apply to (1) blue- and white-collar workers of all varieties; (2) professional people such as lawyers, physicians, dentists, and teachers; and (3) owners of small businesses, including barbers, plumbers, and a host of retailers who provide labor as they carry on their own businesses.

Wages are the price that employers pay for labor. Wages may take the form of weekly or monthly salaries, bonuses, royalties, or commissions. Our references to "wages" include not only direct money payments but also fringe benefits such as paid vacations, health insurance, and pensions. Here we will use the term "wages" to mean the wage rate per

hour, per day, and so forth. That will remind us that a wage rate is a price paid per unit of labor services. It will also let us distinguish between the wage rate and labor earnings, the latter being determined by multiplying the number of hours worked per week, per month, or per year by the hourly wage or wage rate.

We must also distinguish between nominal wages and real wages. A **nominal wage** is the amount of money received per hour, per day, and so on. A **real wage** is the quantity of goods and services a worker can obtain with nominal wages; real wages reveal the "purchasing power" of nominal wages.

Your real wage depends on your nominal wage and the prices of the goods and services you purchase. Suppose you receive an 8 percent increase in your nominal wage during a certain year but in that same year the price level increases by 5 percent. Then your real wage has increased by 3 percent (= 8 percent − 5 percent). Unless otherwise indicated, we will assume that the overall level of prices remains constant. In other words, we will discuss only *real* wages.

■ General Level of Wages

Wages differ among nations, regions, occupations, and individuals. Wage rates are much higher in the United States than in China or India. They are slightly higher in the north and east of the United States than in the south. Plumbers are paid less than NFL punters. And physician Adam may earn twice as much as physician Bennett for the same number of hours of work. Wage rates also differ by gender, race, and ethnic background.

The general, or average, level of wages, like the general level of prices, includes a wide range of different wage rates. It includes the wages of bakers, barbers, brick masons, and brain surgeons. By averaging such wages, we can more easily compare wages among regions and among nations.

As Global Perspective 15.1 suggests, the general level of real wages in the United States is relatively high—although not the highest in the world.

The simplest explanation for the high real wages in the United States and other industrially advanced economies (referred to hereafter as advanced economies) is that the demand for labor in those nations is relatively large compared to the supply of labor.

Role of Productivity

We know from the previous chapter that the demand for labor, or for any other resource, depends on its productivity. In general, the greater the productivity of labor, the greater is the demand for it. And if the total supply of labor is fixed, then the stronger the demand for labor, the higher is the average level of real wages. The demand for labor in the United States and the other major advanced economies is large because labor in those countries is highly productive. There are several reasons for that high productivity:

■ *Plentiful capital* Workers in the advanced economies have access to large amounts of physical capital equipment (machinery and buildings). In the United States there is $75,000 of physical capital available, on average, for each worker.

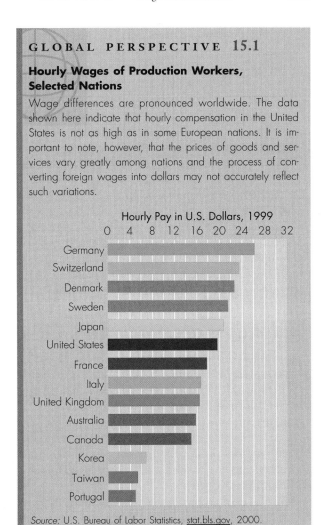

GLOBAL PERSPECTIVE 15.1

Hourly Wages of Production Workers, Selected Nations

Wage differences are pronounced worldwide. The data shown here indicate that hourly compensation in the United States is not as high as in some European nations. It is important to note, however, that the prices of goods and services vary greatly among nations and the process of converting foreign wages into dollars may not accurately reflect such variations.

Hourly Pay in U.S. Dollars, 1999

Germany
Switzerland
Denmark
Sweden
Japan
United States
France
Italy
United Kingdom
Australia
Canada
Korea
Taiwan
Portugal

Source: U.S. Bureau of Labor Statistics, stat.bls.gov, 2000.

■ *Access to abundant natural resources* In advanced economies, natural resources tend to be abundant in relation to the size of the labor force. Some of those resources are available domestically and others are imported from abroad. The United States, for example, is richly endowed with arable land, mineral resources, and sources of energy for industry.

■ *Advanced technology* The level of technological progress is generally high in advanced economies. Not only do workers in these economies have more capital equipment to work with, but that equipment is technologically superior to the equipment available to the vast majority of workers worldwide. Moreover, work methods in the advanced economies are steadily being improved through scientific study and research.

- *Labor quality* The health, vigor, education, and training of workers in advanced economies are generally superior to those in developing nations. This means that, even with the same quantity and quality of natural and capital resources, workers in advanced economies tend to be more efficient than many of their foreign counterparts.

- *Intangible factors* Less tangible factors also may underlie the high productivity in some of the advanced economies. In the United States, for example, such factors include (a) the efficiency and flexibility of management; (b) a business, social, and political environment that emphasizes production and productivity; and (c) the vast size of the domestic market, which enables firms to engage in mass production.

Real Wages and Productivity

Figure 15.1 shows the close long-run relationship between output per hour of work and real hourly earnings in the United States. Because real income and real output are two ways of viewing the same thing, real income (earnings) per worker can increase only at about the same rate as output per worker. When workers produce more real output per hour, more real income is available to distribute to them for each hour worked.

In the real world, however, suppliers of land, capital, and entrepreneurial talent also share in the income from production. Real wages therefore do not always rise in lockstep with gains in produc-

tivity over short spans of time. But over long periods, productivity and real wages tend to rise together.

Secular Growth of Real Wages

Basic supply and demand analysis helps explain the long-term trend of real-wage growth in the United States. The nation's labor force has grown significantly over the decades. But, as a result of the productivity-increasing factors we have mentioned, labor demand has increased more rapidly than labor supply. Figure 15.2 shows several such increases in labor supply and labor demand. The result has been a long-run, or secular, increase in wage rates and employment.

▌A Purely Competitive Labor Market

We now turn from the average level of wages to specific wage rates. What determines the wage rate paid for some specific type of labor? Demand and supply analysis again is revealing. Let's begin by examining labor demand and labor supply in a **purely competitive labor market.** In this type of market:

- Many firms compete with one another in hiring a specific type of labor.
- Each of numerous qualified workers with identical skills supplies that type of labor.
- Individual firms and individual workers are "wage takers," since neither can exert any control over the market wage rate.

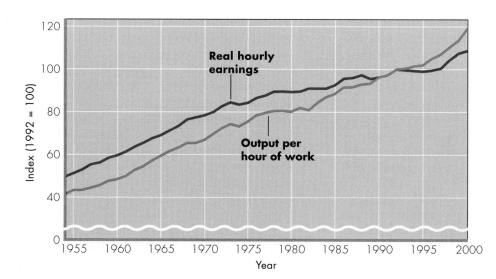

Figure 15.1

Output per hour and real hourly earnings in the United States. Over long periods of years there is a close relationship between output per hour of work and real hourly earnings.

Source: Bureau of Labor Statistics, stat.bls.gov.

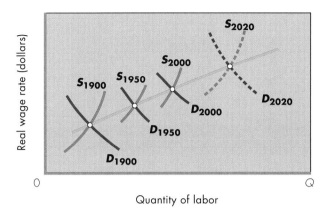

Figure 15.2

The long-run trend of real wages in the United States.   The productivity of U.S. labor has increased substantially over the long run, causing the demand for labor D to shift rightward (that is, to increase) more rapidly than increases in the supply of labor S. The result has been increases in real wages.

Market Demand for Labor

Suppose 200 firms demand a particular type of labor, say, carpenters. These firms need not be in the same industry; industries are defined according to the products they produce and not the resources they employ. Thus, firms producing wood-framed furniture, wood windows and doors, houses and apartment buildings, and wood cabinets will demand carpenters. To find the total, or market, labor demand curve for a particular labor service, we sum horizontally the labor demand curves (the marginal revenue product curves) of the individual firms, as indicated in **Figure 15.3 (Key Graph).** The horizontal summing of the 200 labor demand curves like *d* in Figure 15.3b yields the market labor demand curve *D* in Figure 15.3a.

Market Supply of Labor

On the supply side of a purely competitive labor market, we assume that there is no union and that workers individually compete for available jobs. The supply curve for each type of labor slopes upward, indicating that employers as a group must pay higher wage rates to obtain more workers. This is so because they must bid workers away from other industries, occupations, and localities. Within limits, workers have alternative job opportunities. For example, they may work in other industries in the same locality, or

they may work in their present occupations in different cities or states, or they may work in other occupations.

Firms that want to hire these workers (here, carpenters) must pay higher wage rates to attract them away from the alternative job opportunities available to them. They must also pay higher wages to induce people who are not currently in the labor force—who are perhaps doing household activities or enjoying leisure—to seek employment. In short, assuming that wages are constant in other labor markets, higher wages in a particular labor market entice more workers to offer their labor services in that market—a fact confirmed by the upward-sloping market supply-of-labor curve *S* in Figure 15.3a.

Labor Market Equilibrium

The intersection of the market labor demand curve and the market supply curves determines the equilibrium wage rate and level of employment in purely competitive labor markets. In Figure 15.3a the equilibrium wage rate is W_c ($10), and the number of workers hired is Q_c (1000). To the individual firm the market wage rate W_c is given. Each of the many firms employs such a small fraction of the total available supply of this type of labor that none of them can influence the wage rate. The supply of this labor is perfectly elastic to the individual firm, as shown by horizontal line *s* in Figure 15.3b.

Each individual firm will find it profitable to hire this type of labor up to the point at which marginal revenue product is equal to marginal resource cost. This is merely an application of the MRP = MRC rule we developed in Chapter 14.

As Table 15.1 indicates, when the price of a resource is given to the individual competitive firm, the marginal cost of that resource (MRC) is constant and is equal to the resource price. Here, MRC is constant and is equal to the wage rate. Each additional worker hired adds precisely his or her own wage rate ($10 in this case) to the firm's total resource cost. So the firm in a purely competitive labor market maximizes its profit by hiring workers to the point at which its wage rate equals MRP. In Figure 15.3b this firm will hire q_c (five) workers, paying each of them the market wage rate W_c ($10). So, too, will the other 199 firms (not shown) that are hiring workers in this labor market.

To determine a firm's total revenue from employing a particular number of labor units, we

KEY GRAPH

Figure 15.3
Labor supply and labor demand in (a) a purely competitive labor market and (b) a single competitive firm.
In a purely competitive labor market (a) the equilibrium wage rate W_c and the number of workers Q_c are determined by labor supply S and labor demand D. Because this market wage rate is given to the individual firm (b) hiring in this market, its labor supply curve $s = MRC$ is perfectly elastic. Its labor demand curve is its MRP curve (here labeled mrp). The firm maximizes its profit by hiring workers up to where $MRP = MRC$. Area $0abc$ represents both the firm's total revenue and its total cost. The gold area is its total wage cost; the green area is its nonlabor costs, including a normal profit—that is, the firm's payments to the suppliers of land, capital, and entrepreneurship.

Quick Quiz 15.3

1. The supply-of-labor curve S slopes upward in graph (a) because:
  - a. the law of diminishing marginal utility applies.
  - b. the law of diminishing returns applies.
  - c. workers can afford to "buy" more leisure when their wage rates rise.
  - d. higher wages are needed to attract workers away from other labor markets, household activities, and leisure.

2. This firm's labor demand curve d in graph (b) slopes downward because:
  - a. the law of diminishing marginal utility applies.
  - b. the law of diminishing returns applies.
  - c. the firm must lower its price to sell additional units of its product.
  - d. the firm is a competitive employer, not a monopsonist.

3. In employing five workers, the firm represented in graph (b):
  - a. has a total wage cost of $6000.
  - b. is adhering to the general principle of undertaking all actions for which the marginal benefit exceeds the marginal cost.
  - c. uses less labor than would be ideal from society's perspective.
  - d. experiences increasing marginal returns.

4. A rightward shift of the labor supply curve in graph (a) would shift curve:
  - a. $d = mrp$ leftward in graph (b).
  - b. $d = mrp$ rightward in graph (b).
  - c. $s = MRC$ upward in graph (b).
  - d. $s = MRC$ downward in graph (b).

Answers: 1. d; 2. b; 3. b; 4. d

Table 15.1

The Supply of Labor: Pure Competition in the Hire of Labor

(1) Units of Labor	(2) Wage Rate	(3) Total Labor Cost (Wage Bill)	(4) Marginal Resource (Labor) Cost
0	$10	$ 0	
1	10	10	$10
2	10	20	10
3	10	30	10
4	10	40	10
5	10	50	10
6	10	60	10

sum the MRPs of those units. For example, if a firm employs 3 labor units with marginal revenue products of $14, $13, and $12, respectively, then the firm's total revenue is $39 (= $14 + $13 + $12). In Figure 15.3b, where we are not restricted to whole units of labor, total revenue is represented by area $0abc$ under the MRP curve to the left of q_c. And what area represents the firm's total cost, including a normal profit? Answer: For q_c units, the same area—$0abc$. The gold rectangle represents the firm's total wage cost ($0q_c \times 0W_c$). The green triangle (total revenue minus total wage cost) represents the firm's nonlabor costs—its explicit and implicit payments to land, capital, and entrepreneurship. Thus, in this case, total cost (wages plus other income payments) equals total revenue. This firm and others like it are earning only a normal profit. Figure 15.3b represents a long-run equilibrium for a firm that is selling its product in a purely competitive product market and "buying" its labor in a purely competitive labor market. **(Key Questions 3 and 4)**

■ Monopsony Model

In the purely competitive labor market described in the preceding section, each employer hires too small an amount of labor to influence the wage rate. Each firm can hire as little or as much labor as it needs, but only at the market wage rate, as reflected in its horizontal labor supply curve. The situation is quite different in **monopsony,** a market in which a single employer of labor has substantial buying (hiring)

power. Labor market monopsony has the following characteristics:
- There is only a single buyer of a particular type of labor.
- This type of labor is relatively immobile, either geographically or because workers would have to acquire new skills.
- The firm is a "wage maker," because the wage rate it must pay varies directly with the number of workers it employs.

As is true of monopoly power, there are various degrees of monopsony power. In *pure* monopsony such power is at its maximum, because there is only a single employer in the labor market. The best real-world examples are probably the labor markets in some towns that depend almost entirely on one major firm. For example, a silver-mining concern may be almost the only source of employment in a remote Idaho or Colorado town. A New England textile mill, a Wisconsin paper mill, or a farm-belt food processor may provide most of the employment in its locale. Maytag (the maker of home appliances) is the dominant employer in Newton, Iowa.

In other cases three or four firms may each hire a large portion of the supply of labor in a certain market and therefore have some monopsony power. Moreover, if they tacitly or openly act in concert in hiring labor, they greatly enhance their monopsony power. 🔎 15.1

Upward-Sloping Labor Supply to Firm

When a firm hires most of the available supply of a particular type of labor, its decision to employ more or fewer workers affects the wage rate it pays to those workers. Specifically, if a firm is large in relation to the size of the labor market, it will have to pay a higher wage rate to obtain more labor. Suppose there is only one employer of a particular type of labor in a certain geographic area. In that extreme case, the labor supply curve for that firm and the total supply curve for the labor market are identical. This supply curve is upward-sloping, indicating that the firm must pay a higher wage rate to attract more workers. The supply curve, S in Figure 15.4, is also the average-cost-of-labor curve for the firm; each point on it indicates the wage rate (cost) per worker that must be paid to attract the corresponding number of workers.

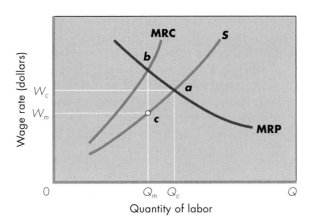

Figure 15.4

The wage rate and level of employment in a monopsonistic labor market. In a monopsonistic labor market the employer's marginal resource (labor) cost curve (MRC) lies above the labor supply curve S. Equating MRC with MRP at point b, the monopsonist hires Q_m workers (compared with Q_c under competition). As indicated by point c on S, it pays only wage rate W_m (compared with the competitive wage W_c).

MRC Higher than the Wage Rate

When a monopsonist pays a higher wage to attract an additional worker, it must pay that higher wage to all the workers it is currently employing at a lower wage. If not, labor morale will deteriorate, and the employer will be plagued with labor unrest because of wage-rate differences existing for the same job. Paying a uniform wage to all workers means that the cost of an extra worker—the marginal resource (labor) cost (MRC)—is the sum of that worker's wage rate and the amount necessary to bring the wage rate of all current workers up to the new wage level.

Table 15.2 illustrates this point. One worker can be hired at a wage rate of $6. But hiring a second worker forces the firm to pay a higher wage rate of $7. The marginal resource (labor) cost of the second worker is $8—the $7 paid to the second worker plus a $1 raise for the first worker. From another viewpoint, total labor cost is now $14 (= 2 × $7), up from $6. So the MRC of the second worker is $8 (= $14 − $6), not just the $7 wage rate paid to that worker. Similarly, the marginal labor cost of the third worker is $10—the $8 that must be paid to attract this worker from alternative employment plus $1 raises, from $7 to $8, for the first two workers.

Table 15.2

The Supply of Labor: Monopsony in the Hire of Labor

(1) Units of Labor	(2) Wage Rate	(3) Total Labor Cost (Wage Bill)	(4) Marginal Resource (Labor) Cost
0	$ 5	$ 0	
1	6	6	$ 6
2	7	14	8
3	8	24	10
4	9	36	12
5	10	50	14
6	11	66	16

The important point is that to the monopsonist, marginal resource (labor) cost exceeds the wage rate. Graphically, the MRC curve lies above the average-cost-of-labor curve, or labor supply curve S, as is clearly shown in Figure 15.4.

Equilibrium Wage and Employment

How many units of labor will the monopsonist hire, and what wage rate will it pay? To maximize profit, the monopsonist will employ the quantity of labor Q_m in Figure 15.4, because at that quantity MRC and MRP are equal (point b).[1] The monopsonist next determines how much it must pay to attract these Q_m workers. From the supply curve S, specifically point c, it sees that it must pay wage rate W_m.

---

[1]The fact that MRC exceeds resource price when resources are hired or purchased under imperfectly competitive (monopsonistic) conditions calls for adjustments in Chapter 14's least-cost and profit-maximizing rules for hiring resources. [See equations (1) and (2) in the "Optimal Combination of Resources" section of Chapter 14.] Specifically, we must substitute MRC for resource price in the denominators of our two equations. That is, with imperfect competition in the hiring of both labor and capital, equation (1) becomes

$$\frac{\text{MP}_L}{\text{MRC}_L} = \frac{\text{MP}_C}{\text{MRC}_C} \qquad (1')$$

and equation (2) is restated as

$$\frac{\text{MRP}_L}{\text{MRC}_L} = \frac{\text{MRP}_C}{\text{MRC}_C} = 1 \qquad (2')$$

In fact, equations (1) and (2) can be regarded as special cases of (1′) and (2′) in which firms happen to be hiring under purely competitive conditions and resource price is therefore equal to, and can be substituted for, marginal resource cost.

Clearly, it need not pay a wage equal to MRP; it can attract exactly the number of workers it wants (Q_m) with wage rate W_m. And that is what it will pay.

Contrast these results with those that would prevail in a competitive labor market. With competition in the hiring of labor, the level of employment would be greater (at Q_c) and the wage rate would be higher (at W_c). Other things equal, the monopsonist maximizes its profit by hiring a smaller number of workers and thereby paying a less-than-competitive wage rate.[2] Society gets a smaller output, and workers get a wage rate that is less by *bc* than their marginal revenue product. Just as a monopolistic seller finds it profitable to restrict product output to realize an above-competitive price for its goods, the monopsonistic employer of resources finds it profitable to restrict employment in order to depress wage rates and therefore costs, that is, to realize wage rates below those that would occur under competitive conditions.[3]

Examples of Monopsony Power

Monopsonistic labor markets are not common in the U.S. economy; typically, many potential employers compete for most workers, particularly for workers who are occupationally and geographically mobile. Also, where monopsony labor market outcomes might have otherwise occurred, unions have sprung up to counteract that power by forcing firms to negotiate wages. Nevertheless, economists have found evidence of monopsony power in such diverse labor markets as the markets for nurses, professional athletes, public school teachers, newspaper employees, and some building-trade workers.

In the case of nurses, the major employers in most locales are a relatively small number of hospitals. Further, the highly specialized skills of nurses are not readily transferable to other occupations. It has been found, in accordance with the monopsony model, that, other things equal, the smaller the number of hospitals in a town or city (that is, the greater the degree of monopsony), the lower the beginning salaries of nurses.

Professional sports leagues also provide a good example of monopsony, particularly as it relates to the pay of first-year players. The National Football League, the National Basketball Association, and Major League Baseball assign first-year players to teams through "player drafts." That device prohibits other teams from competing for the player's services, at least for several years, until the player becomes a "free agent." In this way the league exercises monopsony power, which results in lower salaries than would occur under competitive conditions. **(Key Question 6).**

QUICK REVIEW 15.1

▪ Real wages have increased historically in the United States because labor demand has increased relative to labor supply.

▪ Over the long term, real wages per worker have increased at approximately the same rate as worker productivity.

▪ The competitive employer is a wage taker and employs workers at the point where the wage rate (= MRC) equals MRP.

▪ The labor supply curve to a monopsonist is upward-sloping, causing MRC to exceed the wage rate for each worker. Other things equal, the monopsonist, hiring where MRC = MRP, will employ fewer workers and pay a lower wage rate than would a purely competitive employer.

■ Three Union Models

We have assumed so far that workers compete with one another in selling their labor services. In some labor markets, however, workers sell their labor services collectively through unions. When a union is formed in an otherwise competitive labor market, it bargains with a relatively large number of employers. It has many goals, the most important of which is to raise wage rates. It can pursue that objective in several ways.

Demand-Enhancement Model

From the union's viewpoint, the most desirable technique for raising wage rates is to increase the demand for labor. As Figure 15.5 shows, an increase in

---

[2]This is analogous to the monopolist's restricting output as it sets product price and output on the basis of marginal revenue, not product demand. In this instance, resource price is set on the basis of marginal labor (resource) cost, not resource supply.

[3]A monopsonistic employer may or may not be a monopolistic seller in the product market. The New England textile mill may be a monopsonistic employer yet face severe domestic and foreign competition in selling its product. In other cases—for example, the commercial aircraft and professional sports industries—firms have both monopsony and monopoly power.

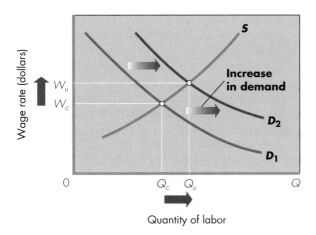

Figure 15.5
Unions and demand-enhancement.   When unions can increase the demand for labor (say, from D_1 to D_2), they can realize higher wage rates (W_c to W_u) and more jobs (Q_c to Q_u).

labor demand will create both higher wage rates and more jobs. How great those increases will be depends on the elasticity of labor supply. The less elastic the labor supply, the greater will be the wage increase; the more elastic the labor supply, the greater will be the employment increase.

To increase labor demand, the union might alter one or more of the determinants of demand. For example, a union can attempt to increase the demand for the product or service it is producing, enhance the productivity of labor, or alter the prices of other inputs.

Increase Product Demand
To increase the demand for the products they help produce—and thus to increase the derived demand for labor services—unions may resort to advertising, political lobbying, or requiring that employers hire redundant labor.

You may have seen ads placed by unions urging consumers to "look for the union label." On occasion, unions have joined with employers to finance advertising campaigns designed to bolster demand for the products its members help produce. The Communications Workers of America (CWA) once helped finance a $2 million "Call or Buy Union" campaign to convince telephone users to choose the long-distance services and equipment of AT&T and Western Union Corporation, which together provided almost 100,000 CWA jobs.

On the political front construction unions have lobbied for new highway, mass-transit, and sta-

dium projects. Teachers' unions and associations have pushed for increased public spending on education. Unions in the aerospace industry have lobbied to increase spending on the military and on space exploration. And the steelworkers' union has at times supported employers in seeking protective tariffs designed to exclude competing foreign steel. The steelworkers recognize that an increase in the price of imported steel through tariffs or international agreements will increase the demand for highly substitutable domestically made steel, boosting the derived demand for U.S. steelworkers.

Increase Productivity
Many decisions affecting labor productivity—for example, decisions concerning the quantity and quality of real capital used by workers—are made unilaterally by management. There is a growing tendency, however, to set up joint labor-management committees designed to increase labor productivity.

Raise the Price of Other Inputs
Unions sometimes have tried to strengthen the demand for their labor by working to increase the price of substitute resources. For example, although union members are generally paid significantly more than the minimum wage, unions have strongly supported increases in the minimum wage. The purpose may be to raise the price of low-wage, nonunion labor, which in some cases is substitutable for union labor. A higher minimum wage for nonunion workers will discourage employers from substituting such workers for union workers and will thereby bolster the demand for union members.

Similarly, unions have sometimes sought to increase the demand for their labor by supporting public actions that will reduce the price of a complementary resource. For example, unions in industries that use large amounts of energy might oppose rate increases proposed by electric or natural-gas utilities. Where labor and energy are complementary, a price increase for energy might reduce the demand for labor through Chapter 14's output effect.

Unions recognize that their ability to influence the demand for labor is very limited. Consequently, they are more likely to try to prevent declines in labor demand than they are to promote increases. So it is not surprising that union efforts to raise wage rates have concentrated on the supply side of the labor market.

Exclusive or Craft Union Model

One way in which unions can boost wage rates is to reduce the supply of labor, and over the years organized labor has favored policies to do just that. For example, labor unions have supported legislation that has (1) restricted immigration, (2) reduced child labor, (3) encouraged compulsory retirement, and (4) enforced a shorter workweek.

Moreover, certain types of workers have adopted techniques designed to restrict the number of workers who can join their union. This is especially true of *craft unions*, whose members possess a particular skill, such as carpenters or brick masons or plumbers. Craft unions have frequently forced employers to agree to hire only union members, thereby gaining virtually complete control of the labor supply. Then, by following restrictive membership policies—for example, long apprenticeships, very high initiation fees, and limits on the number of new members admitted—they have artificially restricted labor supply. As indicated in Figure 15.6, such practices result in higher wage rates and constitute what is called **exclusive unionism.** By excluding workers from unions and therefore from the labor supply, craft unions succeed in elevating wage rates.

This craft union model is also applicable to many professional organizations, such as the American Medical Association, the National Education Association, the American Bar Association, and hundreds of others. Such groups seek to limit competition for their services from less qualified labor suppliers. One way to accomplish that is through **occupational licensing.** Here a group of workers in a given occupation pressure Federal, state, or municipal government to pass a law that says that some occupational group (for example, barbers, physicians, lawyers, plumbers, cosmetologists, egg graders, pest controllers) can practice their trade only if they meet certain requirements. Those requirements might include level of education, amount of work experience, the passing of an examination, and personal characteristics ("the practitioner must be of good moral character"). Members of the licensed occupation typically dominate the licensing board that administers such laws. The result is self-regulation, which often leads to policies that serve only to restrict entry to the occupation and reduce labor supply.

The purpose of licensing is supposedly to protect consumers from incompetent practitioners—surely a worthy goal. But such licensing, if abused, results in above-competitive wages and earnings for those in the licensed occupation (Figure 15.6). Moreover, licensing requirements often include a residency requirement, which inhibits the interstate movement of qualified workers. Some 600 occupations are now licensed in the United States.

Inclusive or Industrial Union Model

Instead of trying to limit their membership, however, most unions seek to organize all available workers. This is especially true of the *industrial unions*, such as those of the automobile workers and steelworkers. Such unions seek as members all available unskilled, semiskilled, and skilled workers in an industry. A union can afford to be exclusive when its members are skilled craftspersons for whom there are few substitutes. But for a union composed of unskilled and semiskilled workers, a policy of limited membership would make available to the employers numerous nonunion workers who are highly substitutable for the union workers.

An industrial union that includes virtually all available workers in its membership can put firms under great pressure to agree to its wage demands. Because of its legal right to strike, such a union can threaten to deprive firms of their entire labor supply. And an actual strike can do just that.

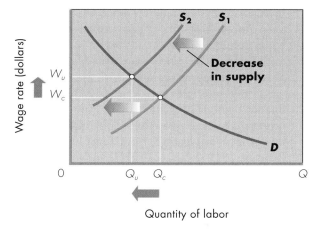

Figure 15.6

Exclusive or craft unionism.   By reducing the supply of labor (say, from S_1 to S_2) through the use of restrictive membership policies, exclusive unions achieve higher wage rates (W_c to W_u). However, restriction of the labor supply also reduces the number of workers employed (Q_c to Q_u).

We illustrate such **inclusive unionism** in Figure 15.7. Initially, the competitive equilibrium wage rate is W_c and the level of employment is Q_c. Now suppose an industrial union is formed that demands a higher, above-equilibrium wage rate of, say, W_u. That wage rate W_u would create a perfectly elastic labor supply over the range ae in Figure 15.7. If firms wanted to hire any workers in this range, they would have to pay the union-imposed wage rate. If they decide against meeting this wage demand, the union will supply no labor at all, and the firms will be faced with a strike. If firms decide it is better to pay the higher wage rate than to suffer a strike, they will cut back on employment from Q_c to Q_u.

By agreeing to the union's W_u wage demand, individual employers become wage takers. Because labor supply is perfectly elastic over range ae, the marginal resource (labor) cost is equal to the wage rate W_u over this range. The Q_u level of employment is the result of employers' equating this MRC (now equal to the wage rate) with MRP, according to our profit-maximizing rule.

Note from point e on labor supply curve S that Q_e workers desire employment at wage W_u. But as indicated by point b on labor demand curve D, only Q_u workers are employed. The result is a surplus of labor of $Q_e - Q_u$ (also shown by distance eb). In a purely competitive labor market without the union, the effect of a surplus of unemployed workers would be lower wages. Specifically, the wage rate would fall to the equilibrium level W_c, where the quantity of labor supplied equals the quantity of labor demanded (each Q_c). But this drop in wages does not happen, because workers are acting collectively through their union. Individual workers cannot offer to work for less than W_u; nor can employers pay less than that.

Wage Increases and Unemployment

Have U.S. unions been successful in raising the wages of their members? Evidence suggests that union members on average achieve a 15 percent wage advantage over nonunion workers.

As Figures 15.6 and 15.7 suggest, the effect of wage-raising actions achieved by both exclusive and inclusive unionism is reduced employment. A union's success in achieving above-equilibrium wage rates thus tends to be accompanied by a decline in the number of workers employed. That result acts as a restraining influence on union wage demands. A union cannot expect to maintain solidarity within its ranks if it seeks a wage rate so high that joblessness will result for, say, 20 or 30 percent of its members.

The unemployment effect created by union-induced wage increases may be reduced in two ways:

- **Growth**   The normal growth of the economy increases the demand for most kinds of labor over time. This continual rightward shift of the labor demand curves in Figures 15.6 and 15.7 might offset, or more than offset, the unemployment effect associated with the indicated wage increases. In that event, the increases in unemployment prompted by the unions would tend to *slow* the growth of job opportunities but would not reduce total employment by firms.

- **Elasticity**   The size of the unemployment effect resulting from union-induced wage increase depends on the elasticity of demand for labor. The more inelastic that demand, the smaller is the amount of unemployment that accompanies a given wage-rate increase. And if unions have sufficient bargaining strength, they may be able to win provisions in their collective bargaining agreements that reduce the elasticity of demand for union labor by reducing the substitutability

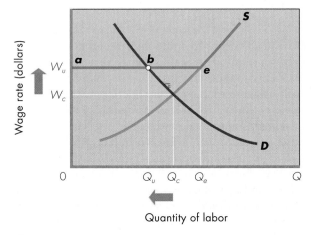

Figure 15.7

Inclusive or industrial unionism.   By organizing virtually all available workers in order to control the supply of labor, inclusive industrial unions may impose a wage rate, such as W_u, which is above the competitive wage rate W_c. In effect, this changes the labor supply curve from S to aeS. At wage rate W_u, employers will cut employment from Q_c to Q_u.

of other inputs for that labor. For example, a union may force employers to accept rules slowing the introduction of new machinery and equipment. Or the union may bargain successfully for severance pay or layoff pay, which increases the cost to the firm of substituting capital for labor when wage rates are increased. Similarly, the union may gain a contract provision prohibiting the firm from subcontracting production to nonunion (lower-wage) firms or from relocating work to low-wage workers overseas, thereby restricting the substitution of cheaper labor for union workers.

▌Bilateral Monopoly Model

Suppose a strong industrial union is formed in a labor market that is monopsonistic rather than competitive, creating a combination of the monopsony model and the inclusive unionism model. The result is called **bilateral monopoly** because in its pure form there is a single seller and a single buyer. The union is a monopolistic "seller" of labor that controls labor supply and can influence wage rates, but it faces a monopsonistic "buyer" of labor that can also affect wages by altering its employment. This is not an uncommon case, particularly in less pure forms in which a single union confronts two, three, or four large employers. Examples: steel, automobiles, construction equipment, professional sports, and commercial aircraft.

Indeterminate Outcome of Bilateral Monopoly

We show this situation in Figure 15.8, where we superimpose Figure 15.7 onto Figure 15.4. The monopsonistic employer will seek the below-competitive-equilibrium wage rate W_m, and the union presumably will press for some above-competitive-equilibrium wage rate such as W_u. Which will be the outcome? We cannot say with certainty. The outcome is "logically indeterminate" because the bilateral monopoly model does not explain what will happen at the collective bargaining table. We can expect the wage outcome to lie somewhere between W_m and W_u. Beyond that, about all we can say is that the party with the greater bargaining power and the more effective bargaining strategy will probably get a wage closer to the one it seeks.

Figure 15.8

Bilateral monopoly in the labor market. A monopsonist seeks to hire Q_m workers (where MRC = MRP) and pay wage rate W_m corresponding to quantity Q_m on labor supply curve S. The inclusive union it faces seeks the above-equilibrium wage rate W_u. The actual outcome cannot be predicted by economic theory.

Desirability of Bilateral Monopoly

The wage and employment outcomes in this situation might be more socially desirable than the term "bilateral monopoly" implies. The monopoly on one side of the market might in effect cancel out the monopoly on the other side, yielding competitive or near-competitive results. If either the union or management prevailed in this market—that is, if the actual wage rate were determined at either W_u or W_m—employment would be restricted to Q_m (where MRP = MRC), which is below the competitive level.

But now suppose the monopoly power of the union roughly offsets the monopsony power of management, and the union and management agree on wage rate W_c, which is the competitive wage. Once management accepts this wage rate, its incentive to restrict employment disappears; no longer can it depress wage rates by restricting employment. Instead, management hires at the most profitable resource quantity, where the bargained wage rate W_c (which is now the firm's MRC) is equal to the MRP. It hires Q_c workers. Thus, with monopoly on both sides of the labor market, the resulting wage rate and level of employment may be closer to competitive levels than would be the case if monopoly existed on only one side of the market. **(Key Question 7)**

QUICK REVIEW 15.2

■ In the demand-enhancement union model, a union increases the wage rate by increasing labor demand through actions that increase product demand, raise labor productivity, or alter the prices of related inputs.

■ In the exclusive (craft) union model, a union increases wage rates by artificially restricting labor supply, through, say, long apprenticeships or occupational licensing.

■ In the inclusive (industrial) union model, a union raises the wage rate by gaining control over a firm's labor supply and threatening to withhold labor via a strike unless a negotiated wage is obtained.

■ Bilateral monopoly occurs in a labor market where a monopsonist bargains with an inclusive, or industrial, union. Wage and employment outcomes are determined by collective bargaining in this situation.

■ The Minimum-Wage Controversy

Since the passage of the Fair Labor Standards Act in 1938, the United States has had a Federal **minimum wage.** That wage has ranged between 35 and 50 percent of the average wage paid to manufacturing workers and was $5.15 per hour in 2001. The purpose of the minimum wage is to provide a "living wage" that will allow less skilled workers to earn enough for them and their children to escape poverty.

Case against the Minimum Wage

Critics, reasoning in terms of Figure 15.7, contend that an above-equilibrium minimum wage (say, W_u) will simply push employers back up their labor demand curves, causing them to hire fewer workers. The higher labor costs may even force some firms out of business. Then some of the poor, low-wage workers whom the minimum wage was designed to help will find themselves out of work. Critics point out that a worker who is *unemployed* at a minimum wage of $5.15 per hour is clearly worse off than he or she would be if *employed* at a market wage rate of, say, $4.85 per hour.

A second criticism of the minimum wage is that it is "poorly targeted" to reduce household poverty. Critics point out that much of the benefit of the

minimum wage accrues to workers, including many teenagers, who do not live in poverty households. Direct government wage subsidies to workers living in poverty households, say the critics, would have a far greater impact on reducing poverty.

Case for the Minimum Wage

Advocates of the minimum wage say that critics analyze its impact in an unrealistic context. Figure 15.7, advocates claim, assumes a competitive, static market. But in a more real, low-pay labor market where there is some monopsony power (Figure 15.8), the minimum wage can increase wage rates without causing unemployment. Indeed, a higher minimum wage may even produce more jobs by eliminating the motive that monopsonistic firms have for restricting employment. For example, a minimum-wage floor of W_c in Figure 15.8 would change the firm's labor supply curve to $W_c aS$ and prompt the firm to increase its employment from Q_m workers to Q_c workers.

Moreover, a minimum wage may increase labor productivity, shifting the labor demand curve to the right and offsetting any reduced employment that the minimum wage might cause. For example, the higher wage rate might prompt firms to find more productive tasks for low-paid workers, thereby raising their productivity. Alternatively, the minimum wage may reduce *labor turnover* (the rate at which workers voluntarily quit). With fewer low-productive trainees, the *average* productivity of the firm's workers would rise. In either case, the higher labor productivity would justify paying the higher minimum wage. So the alleged negative employment effects of the minimum wage might not occur.

Evidence and Conclusions

Which view is correct? Unfortunately, there is no clear answer. All economists agree there is some minimum wage so high that it would severely reduce employment. Consider $20 an hour, as an absurd example. But no current consensus exists on the employment effects of the present level of the minimum wage. Evidence in the 1980s suggested that minimum-wage hikes reduced employment of minimum-wage workers, particularly teenagers (16- to 19-year-olds). The consensus then was that a 10 percent increase in the minimum wage would reduce teenage employment by about 1 to 3 percent. But the minimum-wage hikes in 1991, 1996, and 1997 seemed to produce smaller, and perhaps zero, employment declines among teenagers.[4]

The overall effect of the minimum wage is thus uncertain. On the one hand, the employment and unemployment effects of the minimum wage do not appear to be as great as many critics fear. On the other hand, because a large part of its effect is dissipated on nonpoverty families, the minimum wage is not as strong an antipoverty tool as many supporters contend.

It is clear, however, that the minimum wage has strong political support. Perhaps this stems from two realities: (1) More workers are helped by the minimum wage than are hurt, and (2) the minimum wage gives society some assurance that employers are not "taking undo advantage" of vulnerable, low-skilled workers.

▎Wage Differentials

Hourly wage rates and annual salaries differ greatly among occupations. In Table 15.3 we list average annual salaries for a number of occupations to illustrate such occupational **wage differentials.** For example, observe that surgeons on average earn

Table 15.3

Average Annual Wages in Selected Occupations, 1999

Occupation	Average Annual Wages
Surgeons	$135,660
Aircraft pilots	98,280
Petroleum engineers	72,780
Law professors	70,860
Commercial divers	70,420
Financial managers	69,100
Dental hygienists	48,150
Detectives	47,620
Registered nurses	44,470
Electricians	42,180
Travel agents	24,660
Barbers	20,970
Retail salespersons	19,210
Recreation workers	18,500
Teacher aides	17,400
Fast-food cooks	13,610

Source: Bureau of Labor Statistics, stat.bls.gov, 2001.

---

[4]Alan Krueger, "Teaching the Minimum Wage in Econ 101 in Light of the New Economics of the Minimum Wage," *Journal of Economic Education,* Summer 2001.

seven times as much as retail salespersons. Not shown, there are also large wage differentials within some of the occupations listed. For example, some highly experienced surgeons earn several times as much income as surgeons just starting their careers. And, although average wages for retail salespersons are relatively low, some top salespersons selling on commission make several times the average wages listed for their occupation.

What explains wage differentials such as these? Once again, the forces of demand and supply are revealing. As we demonstrate in Figure 15.9, wage differentials can arise on either the supply or the demand side of labor markets. Figure 15.9a and 15.9b represent labor markets for two occupational groups that have identical *labor supply curves.* Labor market (a) has a relatively high equilibrium wage (W_a) because labor demand is very strong. In labor market (b) the equilibrium wage is relatively low (W_b) because labor demand is weak. Clearly, the wage differential between occupations (a) and (b) results solely from differences in the magnitude of labor demand.

Contrast that situation with Figure 15.9c and 15.9d, where the *labor demand curves* are identical. In labor market (c) the equilibrium wage is relatively high (W_c) because labor supply is highly restricted. In labor market (d) labor supply is highly abundant, so the equilibrium wage (W_d) is relatively low. The wage differential between (c) and (d) results solely from the differences in the magnitude of labor supply.

Although Figure 15.9 provides a good starting point for understanding wage differentials, we need to know *why* demand and supply conditions differ in various labor markets. There are several reasons.

Marginal Revenue Productivity

The strength of labor demand—how far rightward the labor demand curve is located—differs greatly among occupations due to differences in how much various occupational groups contribute to their employer's revenue. This revenue contribution, in turn, depends on the workers' productivity and the strength of the demand for the products they are helping to produce. Where labor is highly productive and product demand is strong, labor demand also is strong and, other things equal, pay is high. Top professional athletes, for example, are highly productive at producing sports entertainment, for which millions of people are willing to pay billions

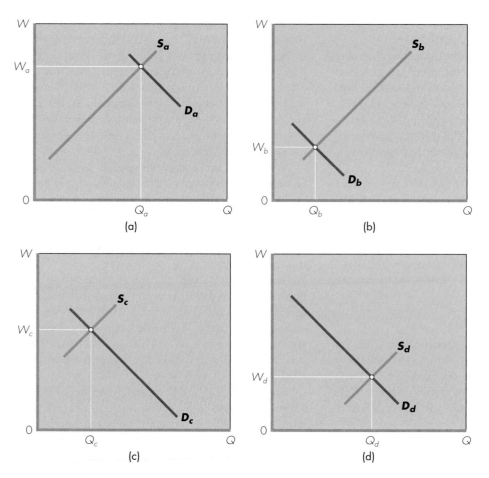

Figure 15.9
Labor demand, labor supply, and wage differentials. The wage differential between labor markets (a) and (b) results solely from differences in labor demand. In labor markets (c) and (d), differences in labor supply are the sole cause of the wage differential.

of dollars over the course of a season. So the **marginal revenue productivity** of these top players is exceptionally high, as are their salaries (as represented in Figure 15.9a). In contrast, in most occupations workers generate much more modest revenue for their employers, so their pay is lower (as in Figure 15.9b).

Noncompeting Groups

On the supply side of the labor market, workers are not homogeneous; they differ in their mental and physical capacities and in their education and training. At any given time the labor force is made up of many **noncompeting groups** of workers, each representing several occupations for which the members of a particular group qualify. In some groups qualified workers are relatively few, whereas in others they are highly abundant. And workers in one group do not qualify for the occupations of other groups.

Ability Only a few workers have the ability or physical attributes to be brain surgeons, concert violinists, top fashion models, research chemists, or professional athletes. Because the supply of these particular types of labor is very small in relation to labor demand, their wages are high (as in Figure 15.9c). The members of these and similar groups do not compete with one another or with other skilled or semiskilled workers. The violinist does not compete with the surgeon, nor does the surgeon compete with the violinist or the fashion model.

The concept of noncompeting groups can be applied to various subgroups and even to specific individuals in a particular group. Some especially skilled violinists can command higher salaries than colleagues who play the same instrument. A handful of top corporate executives earn 10 to 20 times as much as the average chief executive officer. In each of these cases, the supply of top talent is highly limited, since less talented colleagues are only imperfect substitutes.

Education and Training   Another source of wage differentials has to do with differing amounts of investment in human capital. An **investment in human capital** is *an expenditure on education or training that improves the skills and therefore the productivity of workers.* Like expenditures on machinery and equipment, expenditures on education or training that increase a worker's productivity can be regarded as investments. In both cases, current costs are incurred with the intention that they will lead to a greater *future* flow of earnings.   **!** **15.1**   🔑 **15.2**

Figure 15.10 indicates that workers who have made greater investments in education achieve higher incomes during their careers. The reason is twofold: (1) There are fewer such workers, so their supply is limited relative to less educated workers, and (2) more educated workers tend to be more productive and thus in greater demand. Figure 15.10 also indicates that the earnings of better-educated workers rise more rapidly than those of poorly edu-cated workers. The primary reason is that employ-ers provide more on-the-job training to the better-educated workers, boosting their marginal revenue productivity and therefore their earnings.

Although education yields higher incomes, it carries substantial costs. A college education involves not only direct costs (tuition, fees, books) but indirect or opportunity costs (forgone earnings) as well. Does the higher pay received by better-educated workers compensate for these costs? The answer is yes. Rates of return are estimated to be 10 to 13 per-cent for investments in secondary education and 8 to 12 percent for investments in college education. One generally accepted estimate is that each year of schooling raises a worker's wage by about 8 percent. Also, the pay gap between college graduates and high school graduates increased sharply between 1980 and 2000. Specifically, it has risen from 37 to 66 percent for women and from 34 to 60 percent for men.

Compensating Differences

If the workers in a particular noncompeting group are equally capable of performing several different jobs, you might expect the wage rates to be identical for all these jobs. Not so. A group of high school graduates may be equally capable of becoming sales-clerks or unskilled construction workers. But these jobs pay different wages. In virtually all locales, con-struction laborers receive much higher wages than salesclerks. These wage differentials are called **com-pensating differences,** because they must be paid to compensate for nonmonetary differences in various jobs.

The construction job involves dirty hands, a sore back, the hazard of accidents, and irregular employ-ment, both seasonally and cyclically. The retail sales job means clean clothing, pleasant air-conditioned surroundings, and little fear of injury or layoff. Other things equal, it is easy to see why workers would rather pick up a credit card than a shovel. So labor supply is more limited to construction firms (as in Figure 15.9c) than to retail shops (as in Figure 15.9d). Construction firms must pay higher wages than retailers to compensate for the unattractive non-monetary aspects of construction jobs.

Compensating differences play an important role in allocating society's scarce labor resources. If very few workers want to be garbage collectors, then so-ciety must pay high wages to garbage collectors to get the garbage collected. If many more people want

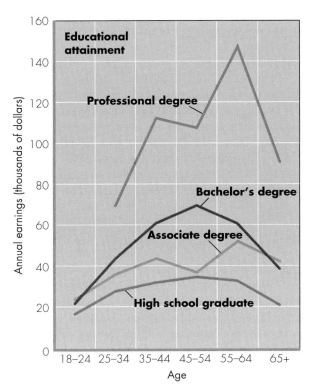

Figure 15.10

Education levels and individual annual earnings.

Annual earnings by age are higher for workers with more educa-tion than less. Investment in education yields a return in the form of earnings differences enjoyed through one's work life.

Source: U.S. Bureau of the Census. Data are for males in 1998.

to be salesclerks, then society need not pay them as much as it pays garbage collectors to get those services performed.

Market Imperfections

The ideas of marginal revenue productivity, noncompeting groups, and differences in nonmonetary aspects of jobs explain many of the wage differentials in the economy. But other persistent differentials result from several types of market imperfections that impede workers from moving from their current jobs to take higher-paying jobs.

Lack of Job Information
Workers may simply be unaware of job opportunities and wage rates in other geographic areas and in other jobs for which they qualify. Consequently, the flow of qualified labor from lower-paying to higher-paying jobs—and thus the adjustments in labor supply—may not be sufficient to equalize wages within occupations.

Geographic Immobility
Workers take root geographically. Many are reluctant to move to new places, to leave friends, relatives, and associates, to force their children to change schools, to sell their houses, or to incur the costs and inconveniences of adjusting to a new job and a new community. As Adam Smith noted over two centuries ago, "A [person] is of all sorts of luggage the most difficult to be transported." The reluctance or inability of workers to move enables geographic wage differentials within the same occupation to persist.

Unions and Government Restraints
Wage differentials may be reinforced by artificial restrictions on mobility imposed by unions and government. We have noted that craft unions find it to their advantage to restrict membership. After all, if carpenters and bricklayers become too plentiful, the wages they can command will decline. Thus the low-paid nonunion carpenter of Brush, Colorado, may be willing to move to Chicago in the pursuit of higher wages. But her chances for succeeding are slim. She may be unable to get a union card, and no card means no job. Similarly, an optometrist or lawyer qualified to practice in one state may not meet licensing requirements of other states, so his or her ability to move is limited. Other artificial barriers involve pension plans, health insurance benefits, and seniority rights that might be jeopardized by moving from one job to another.

Discrimination
Despite legislation to the contrary, discrimination sometimes results in lower wages being paid to women and minority workers than to white males doing virtually identical work. Also, women and minorities may be crowded into certain low-paying occupations, driving down wages there and raising them elsewhere. If discrimination keeps qualified women and minorities from taking higher-paying jobs, then differences in pay will persist. (We discuss discrimination in Chapter 22.)

All four considerations—differences in marginal revenue productivity, noncompeting groups, nonmonetary differences, and market imperfections—come into play in explaining actual wage differentials. For example, the differential between the wages of a physician and those of a construction worker can be explained on the basis of marginal revenue productivity and noncompeting groups. Physicians generate considerable revenue because of their high productivity and the strong willingness of consumers (via insurance) to pay for health care. Physicians also fall into a noncompeting group where, because of stringent training requirements, only relatively few persons qualify. So the supply of labor is small in relation to demand.

In construction work, where training requirements are much less significant, the supply of labor is great relative to demand. So wages are much lower for construction workers than for physicians. However, if not for the unpleasantness of the construction worker's job and the fact that his or her craft union observes restrictive membership policies, the differential would be even greater than it is.

■ Pay for Performance

The models of wage determination we have described in this chapter assume that worker pay is always a standard amount for each hour's work, for example, $15 per hour. But pay schemes are often more complex than that both in composition and in purpose. For instance, many workers receive annual salaries rather than hourly pay. And workers receive differing proportions of fringe benefits (health insurance, life insurance, paid vacations, paid sick-leave days, pension contributions, and so on) as part of their pay. Finally, some pay plans are designed to elicit a desired level of performance from workers. This last aspect of pay plans requires further elaboration.

The Principal-Agent Problem Revisited

In Chapter 4 we identified the *principal-agent problem* as it relates to possible differences in the interests of corporate stockholders (principals) and the executives (agents) they hire. This problem extends to all workers. Firms hire workers because they are needed to help produce the goods and services the firms sell for a profit. Workers are the firms' agents; they are hired to advance the interest (profit) of the firms. The principals are the firms; they hire agents to advance their goals. Firms and workers have one interest in common: They both want the firm to survive and thrive. That will ensure profit for the firm and continued employment and wages for the workers. 🔑 15.3

But the interests of the firm and of workers are not identical. A principal-agent problem arises when those interests diverge. Workers may seek to increase their utility by shirking on the job, that is, by providing less than the agreed-upon effort or by taking unauthorized breaks. They may improve their well-being by increasing their leisure during paid work hours, without forfeiting income. The night security guard in a warehouse may leave work early or spend time reading a novel rather than making the assigned rounds. A salaried manager may spend time away from the office visiting with friends rather than attending to company business.

Firms (principals) have a profit incentive to reduce or eliminate shirking. One option is to monitor workers, but monitoring is difficult and costly. Hiring another worker to supervise or monitor the security guard might double the cost of maintaining a secure warehouse. Another way of resolving a principal-agent problem is through some sort of **incentive pay plan** that ties worker compensation more closely to worker output or performance. Such incentive pay schemes include piece rates; commissions and royalties; bonuses, stock options, and profit sharing; and efficiency wages.

Piece Rates

Piece rates consist of compensation paid according to the number of units of output a worker produces. If a principal pays fruit pickers by the bushel or typists by the page, it need not be concerned with shirking or with monitoring costs.

Commissions or Royalties

Unlike piece rates, commissions and royalties tie compensation to the value of sales. Employees who sell products or services—including real estate agents, insurance agents, stockbrokers, and retail salespersons—commonly receive *commissions* that are computed as a percentage of the monetary value of their sales. Recording artists and authors are paid *royalties*, computed as a certain percentage of sales revenues from their works. Such types of compensation link the financial interests of the salespeople, artists, and authors to the profit interest of the firms.

Bonuses, Stock Options, and Profit Sharing

Bonuses are payments in addition to one's annual salary that are based on some factor such as the performance of the individual worker, or of a group of workers, or of the firm itself. A professional baseball player may receive a bonus based on a high batting average, the number of home runs hit, or the number of runs batted in. A business manager may receive a bonus based on the profitability of her or his unit. *Stock options* allow workers to buy shares of their employer's stock at a fixed, lower price when the stock price rises. Such options are part of the compensation packages of top corporate officials, as well as many workers in relatively new high-technology firms. *Profit-sharing plans* allocate a percentage of a firm's profit to its employees. Such plans have in recent years resulted in large annual payments to many U.S. autoworkers.

Efficiency Wages

The rationale behind *efficiency wages* is that employers will enjoy greater effort from their workers by paying them above-equilibrium wage rates. Glance back at Figure 15.3, which shows a competitive labor market in which the equilibrium wage rate is $10. What if an employer decides to pay an above-equilibrium wage of $12 per hour? Rather than putting the firm at a cost disadvantage compared with rival firms paying only $10, the higher wage might improve worker effort and productivity so that unit labor costs actually fall. For example, if each worker produces 10 units of output per hour at the $12 wage rate compared with only 6 units at the $10 wage rate, unit labor costs for the high-wage firm will be only $1.20 (= $12 ÷ 10) compared to $1.67 (= $10 ÷ 6) for firms paying the equilibrium wage.

An above-equilibrium wage may enhance worker efficiency in several ways. It enables the firm to attract higher-quality workers. It lifts worker morale. And it lowers turnover, resulting in a more experienced workforce, greater worker productivity, and lower recruitment and training costs. Because the opportunity cost of losing a higher-wage job is greater, workers are more likely to put forth their best efforts with less supervision and monitoring. In fact, efficiency wage payments have proved effective for many employers. ❗ 15.2 🔑 15.4

Addenda: Negative Side Effects of Pay for Performance

Although pay for performance may help overcome the principal-agent problem and enhance worker productivity, such plans may have negative side effects and require careful design. Here are a few examples:

■ The rapid production pace that piece rates encourage may result in poor product quality and may compromise the safety of workers. Such outcomes can be costly to the firm over the long run.

■ Commissions may cause some salespeople to engage in questionable or even fraudulent sales practices, such as making exaggerated claims about products or recommending unneeded repairs. Such practices may lead to private lawsuits or government legal action.

■ Bonuses based on personal performance may disrupt the close cooperation needed for maximum team production. A professional basketball player who receives a bonus for points scored may be reluctant to pass the ball to teammates.

■ Since profit sharing is usually tied to the performance of the entire firm, less energetic workers can "free ride" by obtaining their profit share on the basis of hard work by others.

■ There may be a downside to the reduced turnover resulting from above-market wages: Firms that pay efficiency wages have fewer opportunities to hire new workers and suffer the loss of new blood that sometimes energizes the workplace.

QUICK REVIEW 15.3

▨ Proponents of the minimum wage argue that it is needed to assist the working poor and to counter monopsony where it might exist; critics say that it is poorly targeted to reduce poverty and reduces employment.

▨ Wage differentials are attributable in general to the forces of supply and demand, influenced by differences in workers' marginal revenue productivity, education, and skills and by nonmonetary differences in jobs. But several labor market imperfections also play a role.

▨ As it applies to labor, the principal-agent problem is one of workers pursuing their own interests to the detriment of the employer's profit objective.

▨ Pay-for-performance plans (piece rates, commissions, royalties, bonuses, stock options, profit sharing, and efficiency wages) are designed to improve worker productivity by overcoming the principal-agent problem.

Of African-Style Hairbraiders and Stodgy Economists

Newspaper Columnist Michelle Malkin Finds a Connection between Textbook Economics and Real-World Barriers to Occupational Entry.

What do African-style hairbraiders and stodgy economists have in common? More than you ever might have imagined.

According to economics professors, stringent licensing requirements that are passed under the guise of protecting the "public interest" often simply benefit special interests by erecting barriers to entry into a particular labor market.

Economists make their case with painstaking analytical rigor in obscure academic journals. But some of the most convincing teachers of this basic lesson in law and economics don't wear tweed and don't need textbook formulas to prove the point. In urban neighborhoods and inner-city storefronts from Washington state to Washington, D.C., African-style hairbraiders are battling the effects of restrictive business regulations.

And they're winning.

Take Taalib-Din Uqdah, owner of Cornrows Co., in the District of Columbia. Uqdah's tough course in the politics of regulation began four years ago when city inspectors demanded that he obtain an occupational license in cosmetology to run his hair-braiding business. The license required a year of training in everything from manicures to eyebrow arching at a cost of thousands of dollars—but none of the classes covered hairbraiding techniques and other African styles.

"I don't have any problem with government wanting to protect public health and safety," Uqdah explained to me last week. "But the city's code required me to go to an expensive cosmetology school for a year and learn chemical techniques and practices that have nothing to do with what we do. Complying would have killed my company—and pushed many other law-abiding minority business owners underground."

Uqdah is blunt when asked why the city would crack down on hairbraiders: "We're new, we're popular, we're a threat. Licensing is a way for old-line cosmetologists to squash a growing cottage industry of people who are skilled in a cultural art form that's foreign to them."

Uqdah and his wife successfully challenged the city's outdated cosmetology code with legal help from the nonprofit Institute

for Justice based in D.C. As a result, the D.C. government deregulated the cosmetology industry and allowed hairbraiders to obtain a separate operating license with sensible training requirements.

To spread the word, Uqdah founded the American Hairbraiders and Natural Hair Care Association. One member in Memphis, Tenn., pushed successfully for creation of a "natural hair styling" license that requires one-third the hours of instruction required of cosmetologists. And in San Diego this month, the association and the Institute for Justice moved forward with a federal civil-rights suit against the state cosmetology board on behalf of African-American studies professor and hairbraider JoAnne Cornwell.

Cornwell, who has been braiding hair since she was a young girl, sees this as a fight not only for the "economic liberty rights of hairbraiders," but for many other working poor immigrants and minorities struggling to enter the workforce. A victory looks promising. Two weeks ago, federal court judge Rudi Brewster rejected a motion to dismiss the lawsuit. Observing that only 4 percent of the required curriculum actually relates to health and safety—the state's supposed "compelling interest" in regulating hairbraiding—Brewster concluded that the rules place "an almost insurmountable barrier in front of anyone who seeks to practice African hair styling," the effect of which "is to force African hair stylists out of business in favor of mainstream hair stylists and barbers."

Economist Milton Friedman wrote in *Capitalism and Freedom*, "In practice, the considerations taken into account in determining who shall get a license often involve matters that, so far as a layman can see, have no relation whatsoever to professional competence."

Shari Hamilton, owner of Sista's United of Styles in Seattle, says it better. "They don't teach you nothing about nothing. I think it's more of a money and power thing." Hamilton wishes she could have used some of the money she "spent on useless training to hire a few more employees instead." Straight up.

Critics of welfare reform complain there aren't enough jobs to absorb new entrants into the marketplace. But Uqdah of the American Hairbraiders and Natural Hair Care Association has a message for politicians: "Open your eyes! I alone could put 3,000 people to work if we got rid of all the insane barriers and rules that keep people from earning an honest living."

The message is easy to discount when delivered by ivory-tower intellectuals—but impossible to ignore when sounded by small-business owners fighting for their livelihoods, off the chalkboards, out of the theoretical realm, in living color.

Source: Michelle Malkin, "Braiders' Protest Breathes Life into Textbook Economics," *Seattle Times*, May 20, 1997, p. 4. Abridged and reprinted by permission of the author.

SUMMARY

1. The term "labor" encompasses all people who work for pay. The wage rate is the price paid per unit of time for labor. Labor earnings comprise total pay and are found by multiplying the number of hours worked by the hourly wage rate. The nominal wage rate is the amount of money received per unit of time; the real wage rate is the purchasing power of the nominal wage.

2. The long-run growth of real hourly earnings—the average real wage—roughly matches that of productivity, with both increasing over the long run.

3. Global comparisons suggest that real wages in the United States are relatively high, but not the highest, internationally. High real wages in the advanced industrial countries stem largely from high labor productivity.

4. Specific wage rates depend on the structure of the particular labor market. In a competitive labor market the equilibrium wage rate and level of employment are determined at the intersection of the labor supply curve and labor demand curve. For the individual firm, the market wage rate establishes a horizontal labor supply curve, meaning that the wage rate equals the firm's constant marginal resource cost. The firm hires workers to the point where its MRP equals its MRC.

5. Under monopsony the marginal resource cost curve lies above the resource supply curve because the monopsonist must bid up the wage rate to hire extra workers and must pay that higher wage rate to all workers. The monopsonist hires fewer workers than are hired under competitive conditions, pays less-than-competitive wage rates (has lower labor costs), and thus obtains greater profit.

6. A union may raise competitive wage rates by (a) increasing the derived demand for labor, (b) restricting the supply of labor through exclusive unionism, or (c) directly enforcing an above-equilibrium wage rate through inclusive unionism.

7. In many industries the labor market takes the form of bilateral monopoly, in which a strong union "sells" labor to a monopsonistic employer. The wage-rate outcome of this labor market model depends on union and employer bargaining power.

8. On average, unionized workers realize wage rates 15 percent higher than comparable nonunion workers.

9. Economists disagree about the desirability of the minimum wage as an antipoverty mechanism. While it causes unemployment for some low-income workers, it raises the incomes of those who retain their jobs.

10. Wage differentials are largely explainable in terms of (a) marginal revenue productivity of various groups of workers; (b) noncompeting groups arising from differences in the capacities and education of different groups of workers; (c) compensating wage differences, that is, wage differences that must be paid to offset nonmonetary differences in jobs; and (d) market imperfections in the form of lack of job information, geographic immobility, union and government restraints, and discrimination.

11. The principal-agent problem arises when workers provide less-than-expected effort. Firms may combat this by monitoring workers or by creating incentive pay schemes that link worker compensation to effort.

TERMS AND CONCEPTS

nominal wage

real wage

purely competitive labor market

monopsony

exclusive unionism

occupational licensing

inclusive unionism

bilateral monopoly

minimum wage

wage differentials

marginal revenue productivity

noncompeting groups

investment in human capital

compensating differences

incentive pay plan

STUDY QUESTIONS

1. Explain why the general level of wages is high in the United States and other industrially advanced countries. What is the single most important factor underlying the long-run increase in average real-wage rates in the United States?

2. Why is a firm in a purely competitive labor market a *wage taker?* What would happen if it decided to pay less than the going market wage rate?

3. **Key Question** Describe wage determination in a labor market in which workers are unorganized and many firms actively compete for the services of labor. Show this situation graphically, using W_1 to indicate the equilibrium wage rate and Q_1 to show the number of workers hired by the firms as a group. Show the labor supply curve of the individual firm, and compare it with that of the total market. Why

the differences? In the diagram representing the firm, identify total revenue, total wage cost, and revenue available for the payment of nonlabor resources.

4. **Key Question** Complete the following labor supply table for a firm hiring labor competitively:

Units of Labor	Wage Rate	Total Labor Cost (Wage Bill)	Marginal Resource (Labor) Cost
0	$14	$ _____	
1	14	_____	$ _____
2	14	_____	_____
3	14	_____	_____
4	14	_____	_____
5	14	_____	_____
6	14	_____	

  a. Show graphically the labor supply and marginal resource (labor) cost curves for this firm. Explain the relationship of these curves to one another.
  b. Plot the labor demand data of question 2 in Chapter 14 on the graph used in part *a* above. What are the equilibrium wage rate and level of employment? Explain.

5. Suppose the formerly competing firms in question 3 form an employers' association that hires labor as a monopsonist would. Describe verbally the effect on wage rates and employment. Adjust the graph you drew for question 3, showing the monopsonistic wage rate and employment level as W_2 and Q_2, respectively. Using this monopsony model, explain why hospital administrators sometimes complain about a "shortage" of nurses. How might such a shortage be corrected?

6. **Key Question** Assume a firm is a monopsonist that can hire its first worker for $6 but must increase the wage rate by $3 to attract each successive worker. Draw the firm's labor supply and marginal resource cost curves and explain their relationships to one another. On the same graph, plot the labor demand data of question 2 in Chapter 14. What are the equilibrium wage rate and level of employment? Why do these differ from your answer to question 4?

7. **Key Question** Assume a monopsonistic employer is paying a wage rate of W_m and hiring Q_m workers, as indicated in Figure 15.8. Now suppose an industrial union is formed that forces the employer to accept a wage rate of W_c. Explain verbally and graphically why in this instance the higher wage rate will be accompanied by an increase in the number of workers hired.

8. Have you ever worked for the minimum wage? If so, for how long? Would you favor increasing the minimum wage by a dollar? By two dollars? By five dollars? Explain your reasoning.

9. "Many of the lowest-paid people in society—for example, short-order cooks—also have relatively poor working conditions. Hence, the notion of compensating wage differentials is disproved." Do you agree? Explain.

10. What is meant by investment in human capital? Use this concept to explain (*a*) wage differentials, and (*b*) the long-run rise of real wage rates in the United States.

11. What is the principal-agent problem? Have you ever worked in a setting where this problem has arisen? If so, do you think increased monitoring would have eliminated the problem? Why don't firms simply hire more supervisors to eliminate shirking?

12. **(Last Word)** Do you think that African-style hair-braiders should be allowed to braid hair without a cosmetology license? If so, do you think that you would have the same view if you were a licensed cosmetologist?

13. **Web-Based Question: *Real wages and productivity—are workers' paychecks keeping up?*** Over the long run, real wages grow at about the same pace as labor productivity. Go to the Bureau of Labor Statistics website, stats.bls.gov, and select Data and then Most Requested Data for current information on percentage changes in output per hour of all persons in the business sector (labor productivity) and percentage changes in real compensation per hour. Has real compensation per hour kept up with output per hour over the latest 3 years shown?

14. **Web-Based Question: *Men's and women's earnings in professional golf—why the differences?*** Go to espn.go.com/golfonline and select Tours, Rankings, and Money Leaders. What are the annual earnings to date of the top 10 men golfers on the PGA tour? What are the earnings of the top 10 women golfers on the LPGA tour? Why the general differences in earnings between the men and the women golfers?

16

Rent, Interest, and Profit

H OW DO LAND prices and rents get established, and why do they differ? For example, why do 20 acres of land in the middle of the Nevada desert sell for $5000 while 20 prime acres along the Las Vegas strip might command $100 million or more? ■ What factors determine interest rates and cause them to change? For example, why were interest rates on 3-month bank certificates of deposit only 4.9 percent in the United States in April 1999 but 6.7 percent in July 2000? ■ What are the sources of profits and losses? Why do profits change over time? For example, why did Internet switching provider Cisco Systems see its profit jump by 55 percent in 1999, whereas appliance maker Sunbeam lost $300 million that year? ■ In Chapter 15 we focused on wages and salaries, which account for about 70 percent of national income in the United States. In this chapter we examine the other resource payments—rent, interest, and profit—that constitute the remaining 30 percent of national income. We begin by looking at rent.

■ Economic Rent

To most people, "rent" means the money one must pay for the use of an apartment or a dormitory room. To the business executive, "rent" is a payment made for the use of a factory building, machine, or warehouse facility. Such definitions of rent can be confusing and ambiguous, however. Dormitory room rent, for example, may include other payments as well: interest on money the university borrowed to finance the dormitory, wages for custodial services, utility payments, and so on.

Economists use "rent" in a much narrower sense. **Economic rent** is *the price paid for the use of land and other natural resources that are completely fixed in total*

supply. As you will see, this fixed overall supply distinguishes rental payments from wage, interest, and profit payments.

Let's examine this idea and some of its implications through supply and demand analysis. We first assume that all land is of the same grade or quality, meaning that each arable (tillable) acre of land is as productive as every other acre. We assume, too, that all land has a single use, for example, producing wheat. And we suppose that land is rented or leased in a competitive market in which many producers are demanding land and many landowners are offering land in the market.

In Figure 16.1, curve *S* represents the supply of arable land available in the economy as a whole, and

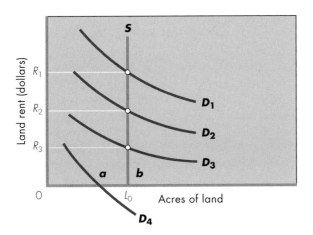

Figure 16.1

The determination of land rent. Because the supply S of land (and other natural resources) is perfectly inelastic, demand is the sole active determinant of land rent. An increase in demand from D_2 to D_1 or a decrease in demand from D_2 to D_3 will cause a considerable change in rent: from R_2 to R_1 in the first instance and from R_2 to R_3 in the second. But the amount of land supplied will remain at L_0. If demand is very weak (D_4) relative to supply, land will be a "free good," commanding no rent.

curve D_2 represents the demand of producers for use of that land. As with all economic resources, this demand is derived from the demand for the product being produced. The demand curve for land is downward-sloping because of diminishing returns and because, for producers as a group, product price must be reduced in order to sell additional units of output.

Perfectly Inelastic Supply

The unique feature of our analysis is on the supply side. For all practical purposes the supply of land is perfectly inelastic (in both the short run and the long run), as reflected in supply curve S. Land has no production cost; it is a "free and nonreproducible gift of nature." The economy has only so much land, and that's that. Of course, within limits any parcel of land can be made more usable by clearing, drainage, and irrigation. But these are capital improvements and not changes in the amount of land itself. Moreover, increases in the usability of land affect only a small fraction of the total amount of land and do not change the basic fact that land and other natural resources are fixed in supply.

Changes in Demand

Because the supply of land is fixed, demand is the only active determinant of land rent; supply is passive. And what determines the demand for land? The factors we discussed in Chapter 14: the price of the product produced on the land, the productivity of land (which depends in part on the quantity and quality of the resources with which land is combined), and the prices of the other resources that are combined with land.

If the demand for land in Figure 16.1 increased from D_2 to D_1, land rent would rise from R_2 to R_1. On the other hand, if the demand for land declined from D_2 to D_3, land rent would fall from R_2 to R_3. But, in either case, the amount of land supplied would remain the same at quantity L_0. Changes in economic rent have no effect on the amount of land available, because the supply of land cannot be augmented. If the demand for land were only D_4, land rent would be zero. Land would be a *free good*—a good for which demand is so weak relative to supply that there is an excess supply of it even if the market price is zero. In Figure 16.1, we show this excess supply as distance $b - a$ at rent of zero. This essentially was the situation in the free-land era of U.S. history.

The ideas underlying Figure 16.1 help answer one of our chapter-opening questions. Land prices and rents are so high along the Las Vegas strip because the demand for that land is tremendous. It is capable of producing exceptionally high revenue from gambling, lodging, and entertainment. In contrast, the demand for isolated land in the middle of the desert is highly limited because very little revenue can be generated from its use. (It is an entirely different matter, of course, if gold can be mined from the land, as is true of some isolated lands in Nevada!)

Land Rent: A Surplus Payment

The perfectly inelastic supply of land must be contrasted with the relatively elastic supply of capital, such as apartment buildings, machinery, and warehouses. In the long run, capital is *not* fixed in total supply. A higher price gives entrepreneurs the incentive to construct and offer larger quantities of property resources. Conversely, a decline in price induces suppliers to allow existing facilities to depreciate and not be replaced. The supply curves of these nonland resources are upward-sloping, meaning that the prices paid to such resources provide an **incentive function.** A high price provides an incentive to offer more of the resource, whereas a low price prompts resource suppliers to offer less.

Not so with land. Rent serves no incentive function, because the total supply of land is fixed. Whether rent is $10,000, $500, $1, or $0 per acre, the same amount of land is available to society for use in production. This is why economists consider rent a *surplus payment* not necessary to ensure that land is available to the economy as a whole.

Application: A Single Tax on Land

If land is a gift of nature, costs nothing to produce, and would be available even without rental payments, why should rent be paid to those who by historical accident, by inheritance, or by crook happen to be landowners? Socialists have long argued that all land rents are unearned incomes. They urge that land should be nationalized (owned by the state) so that any payments for its use can be used by the government to further the well-being of the entire population rather than being used by a landowning minority.

Henry George's Proposal
In the United States, criticism of rental payments has taken the form of a **single-tax movement,** which gained significant support in the late nineteenth century. Spearheaded by Henry George's provocative book *Progress and Poverty* (1879), supporters of this reform movement held that economic rent could be heavily taxed, or even taxed away, without diminishing the available supply of land or, therefore, the productive potential of the economy as a whole.

George observed that as population grew and the geographic frontier closed, landowners enjoyed larger and larger rents from their landholdings. That increase in rents was the result of a growing demand for a resource whose supply was perfectly inelastic. Some landlords were receiving fabulously high incomes, not through any productive effort but solely through their owning advantageously located land. George insisted that these increases in land rent belonged to the economy; he held that land rents should be heavily taxed and the revenue spent for public uses. In seeking popular support for his ideas on land taxation, George proposed that taxes on rental income be the *only* tax levied by government.

George's case for taxing land was based not only on equity or fairness but also on efficiency. That is, a tax on land is efficient because, unlike virtually every other tax, it does not alter the use of the resource being taxed. A tax on wages reduces after-tax wages and may weaken the incentive to work; an individual who decides to work for a $10 before-tax wage may decide to retire when an income tax reduces the wage to an after-tax $8. Similarly, a property tax on buildings lowers returns to investors in such property and might cause some to look for other investments. But no such reallocations of resources occur when land is taxed. The most profitable use of land before it is taxed remains the most profitable use after it is taxed. Of course, a landlord could withdraw land from production when a tax is imposed, but that would mean no rental income at all. And some rental income, no matter how small, is better than none.

Criticisms There are very few remaining advocates of a single tax on land. Critics of the idea have pointed out that:
- Current levels of government spending are such that a land tax alone would not bring in enough revenue; it is unrealistic to consider it as a single tax.
- Most income payments consist of a mixture of such elements as interest, rent, wages, and profits. Land is typically improved in some way, and economic rent cannot be readily disentangled from payments for such improvements. So in practice it would be difficult to determine how much of any specific income payment actually amounted to economic rent.
- So-called *unearned income* accrues to many people other than landowners, especially when the economy is growing. For example, consider the capital gain income received by someone who, some 20 or 25 years ago, chanced to purchase (or inherit) stock in a firm that has experienced rapid profit growth. Is such income more "earned" than the rental income of the landowner?
- Historically, a piece of land is likely to have changed ownership many times. Former owners may have been the beneficiaries of past increases in the value of the land (and in land rent). It would hardly be fair to impose a heavy tax on current owners who paid the competitive market price for the land.

Productivity Differences and Rent Differences

So far we have assumed that all units of land are of the same grade. That is plainly not so. Different pieces of land vary greatly in productivity, depending on soil fertility and on such climatic factors as rainfall and temperature. Such factors explain, for example, why Kansas soil is excellently suited to wheat production, why the sagebrush plains of Wyoming are much less well suited, and why the desert of Arizona is nearly incapable of wheat production. Such productivity differences are reflected in resource demand and prices. Competitive bidding by producers will establish a high rent for highly productive Kansas land; less productive Wyoming land will command a much lower rent; and Arizona desert land may command no rent at all.

Location itself may be just as important in explaining differences in land rent. Other things equal, renters will pay more for a unit of land that is strategically located with respect to materials, transportation, labor, and customers than they will for a unit of land whose location is remote from these things. Examples: the enormously high land prices in major ski resorts and the high price of land that contains oil beneath it.

Figure 16.1, viewed from a slightly different perspective, reveals the rent differentials from quality differences in land. Assume, again, that only wheat can be produced on four grades of land, each of which is available in the fixed amount L_0. When combined with identical amounts of labor, capital, and entrepreneurial talent, the productivity or, more specifically, the marginal revenue product of each of the four grades of land is reflected in demand curves D_1, D_2, D_3, and D_4. Grade 1 land is the most productive, as shown by D_1, while grade 4 is the least productive, as shown by D_4. The resulting economic rents for grades 1, 2, and 3 land will be R_1, R_2, and R_3, respectively; the rent differential will mirror the differences in productivity of the three grades of land. Grade 4 land is so poor in quality that, given its supply S, farmers won't pay anything to use it. It will be a free good because it is not sufficiently scarce in relation to the demand for it to command a price or a rent.

Alternative Uses of Land

We have assumed that land has only one use. Actually, we know that land normally has alternative uses. An acre of Kansas farmland may be useful for

raising not only wheat but corn, oats, barley, and cattle; or it may be useful for building a house or a highway or as a factory site. In other words, any particular use of land involves an opportunity cost—the forgone production from the next best use of the resource. Where there are alternative uses, individual firms must pay rent to cover those opportunity costs in order to secure the use of land for their particular purposes. To the individual firm, rent is a cost of production, just as are wages and interest.

Recall that, as viewed by society, economic rent is not a cost. Society would have the same amount of land with or without the payment of economic rent. From society's perspective, economic rent is a surplus payment above that needed to gain the use of a resource. But individual firms do need to pay rent to attract land resources away from alternative uses. For firms, rental payments are a *cost*. **(Key Question 2)**

QUICK REVIEW 16.1

■ Economic rent is the price paid for resources such as land whose supply is perfectly inelastic.

■ Land rent is a surplus payment, because land would be available to society even if this rent were not paid.

■ The surplus nature of land rent served as the basis for Henry George's single-tax movement.

■ Differential rents allocate land among alternative uses.

▮ Interest

Interest is the price paid for the use of money. It is the price that borrowers need to pay lenders for transferring purchasing power from the present to the future. It can be thought of as the amount of money that must be paid for the use of $1 for 1 year. ▮ **16.1**

■ *Interest is stated as a percentage.* Interest is paid in kind; that is, money (interest) is paid for the loan of money. For that reason, interest is typically stated as a percentage of the amount of money borrowed rather than as a dollar amount. It is less clumsy to say that interest is "12 percent annually" than to say that interest is "$120 per year per $1000." Also, stating interest as a percentage makes it easier to compare the interest paid on loans of different amounts. By expressing interest as a percentage, we can immediately compare an interest payment of, say, $432 per year per $2880 with one of $1800 per year per $12,000. Both interest payments are 15 percent per year, which is not obvious from the actual dollar figures. This interest of 15 percent per year is referred to as a 15 percent interest rate.

- **■ *Money is not a resource.*** Money is *not* an economic resource. In the form of coins, paper currency, or checking accounts, money is not productive; it cannot produce goods and services. However, businesses "buy" the use of money because it can be used to acquire capital goods such as factories, machinery, warehouses, and so on. Such facilities clearly do contribute to production. Thus, in "hiring" the use of money capital, business executives are indirectly buying the use of real capital goods.

Loanable Funds Theory of Interest

In *macroeconomics* the interest rate is often viewed through the lens of the economy's total supply of and demand for money. But because our present focus is on microeconomics, it will be useful to consider a more micro-based theory of interest here. Specifically, the **loanable funds theory of interest** explains the interest rate not in terms of the total supply of and demand for *money* but, rather, in terms of the supply of and demand for *funds available for lending (and borrowing)*. As Figure 16.2 shows, the equilibrium interest rate (here, 8 percent) is the rate at which the quantities of loanable funds supplied and demanded are equal. ☑ **16.1**

Let's first consider the loanable funds theory in simplified form. Specifically, assume households or consumers are the sole suppliers of loanable funds and businesses are the sole demanders. Also assume that lending occurs directly between households and businesses; there are no intermediate financial institutions.

Supply of Loanable Funds

The supply of loanable funds is represented by curve *S* in Figure 16.2. Its upward slope indicates that households will make available a larger quantity of funds at high interest rates than at low interest rates. Most people prefer to use their incomes to purchase pleasurable goods and services *today*, rather than delay purchases to sometime in the *future*. For people to delay consumption and increase their saving, they must be "bribed" or compensated by an interest payment. The larger the

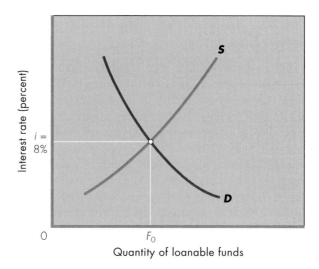

Figure 16.2
The market for loanable funds. The upsloping supply curve *S* for loanable funds reflects the idea that at higher interest rates, households will defer more of their present consumption (save more), making more funds available for lending. The downsloping demand curve *D* for loanable funds indicates that businesses will borrow more at lower interest rates than at higher interest rates. At the equilibrium interest rate (here, 8 percent), the quantities of loanable funds lent and borrowed are equal (here, F_O each).

amount of that payment, the greater the deferral of household consumption and thus the greater the amount of money made available for loans.

There is disagreement among economists as to how much the quantity of loanable funds made available by suppliers changes in response to changes in the interest rate. Most economists view saving as being relatively insensitive to changes in the interest rate. The supply curve of loanable funds may therefore be more inelastic than *S* in Figure 16.2 implies.

Demand for Loanable Funds

Businesses borrow loanable funds primarily to add to their stocks of capital goods, such as new plants or warehouses, machinery, and equipment. Assume that a firm wants to buy a machine that will increase output and sales such that the firm's total revenue will rise by $110 for the year. Also assume that the machine costs $100 and has a useful life of just 1 year. Comparing the $10 earned with the $100 cost of the machine, we find that the expected rate of return on this investment is 10 percent (= $10/$100) for the 1 year.

To determine whether the investment would be profitable and whether it should be made, the firm must compare the interest rate—the price of loanable funds—with the 10 percent expected rate of return. If funds can be borrowed at some rate less than the rate of return, say, at 8 percent, as in Figure 16.2, then the investment is profitable and should be made. But if funds can be borrowed only at an interest rate above the 10 percent rate of return, say, at 14 percent, the investment is unprofitable and should not be made.

Why is the demand for loanable funds down-sloping, as in Figure 16.2? At higher interest rates fewer investment projects will be profitable and hence a smaller quantity of loanable funds will be demanded. At lower interest rates, more investment projects will be profitable and therefore more loanable funds will be demanded. Indeed, as we have just seen, it is profitable to purchase the $100 machine if funds can be borrowed at 8 percent but not if the firm must borrow at 14 percent.

Extending the Model

We now make this simple model more realistic in several ways.

Financial Institutions
Households rarely lend their savings directly to businesses that are borrowing funds for investment. Instead, they place their savings in banks (and other financial institutions). The banks pay interest to savers in order to attract loanable funds and in turn lend those funds to businesses. Businesses borrow the funds from the banks, paying them interest for the use of the money. Financial institutions profit by charging borrowers higher interest rates than the interest rates they pay savers. Both interest rates, however, are based on the supply of and demand for loanable funds.

Changes in Supply
Anything that causes households to be thriftier will prompt them to save more at each interest rate, shifting the supply curve rightward. For example, if interest earned on savings were to be suddenly exempted from taxation, we would expect the supply of loanable funds to increase and the equilibrium interest rate to decrease.

Conversely, a decline in thriftiness would shift the supply-of-loanable-funds curve leftward and increase the equilibrium interest rate. Illustration: If the government expanded social insurance to cover the costs of hospitalization, prescription drugs, and retirement living more fully, the incentive of households to save might diminish.

Changes in Demand
On the demand side, anything that increases the rate of return on potential investments will increase the demand for loanable funds. Let's return to our earlier example, where a firm would receive additional revenue of $110 by purchasing a $100 machine and, therefore, would realize a 10 percent return on investment. What factors might increase or decrease the rate of return? Suppose a technological advance raised the productivity of the machine such that the firm's total revenue increased by $120 rather than $110. The rate of return would then be 20 percent, not 10 percent. Before the technological advance, the firm would have demanded zero loanable funds at, say, an interest rate of 14 percent. But now it will demand $100 of loanable funds at that interest rate, meaning that the demand curve for loanable funds has been shifted to the right.

Similarly, an increase in consumer demand for the firm's product will increase the price of its product. So even though the productivity of the machine is unchanged, its potential revenue will rise from $110 to perhaps $120, increasing the firm's rate of return from 10 to 20 percent. Again the firm will be willing to borrow more than previously at our presumed 8 or 14 percent interest rate, implying that the demand curve for loanable funds has shifted rightward. This shift in demand increases the equilibrium interest rate.

Conversely, a decline in productivity or in the price of the firm's product would shift the demand curve for loanable funds leftward, reducing the equilibrium interest rate.

Other Participants
We must recognize that there are more participants on both the demand and the supply sides of the loanable funds market. For example, while households are suppliers of loanable funds, many are also demanders of such funds. Households borrow to finance expensive purchases such as housing, automobiles, furniture, and household appliances. Governments also are on the demand side of the loanable funds market when they borrow to finance budgetary deficits. And businesses that have revenues in excess of their current expenditures may offer some of those revenues in the market for loanable funds. Thus, like households, businesses operate on both the supply and the demand sides of the market.

Finally, in addition to gathering and making available the savings of households, banks and other financial institutions also increase funds through the lending process and decrease funds when loans are paid back and not lent back out. The Federal Reserve (the nation's central bank) controls the amount of this bank activity and thus influences interest rates.

This fact helps answer one of our chapter opening questions: Why did the interest rate on 3-month certificates of deposit rise from 4.9 percent in April 1999 to 6.7 percent in July 1999. There are two reasons: (1) The demand for loanable funds increased because businesses desired to purchase more capital goods, and (2) the Federal Reserve, fearing inflation, took monetary actions that reduced the supply of loanable funds. **(Key Question 4)**

Range of Interest Rates

Although economists often speak in terms of a single interest rate, there are actually a number of interest rates. Table 16.1 lists several interest rates often referred to in the media. These rates range from 5 to 16 percent. Why the differences?

- *Risk*   Loans to different borrowers for different purposes carry varying degrees of risk. The greater the chance that the borrower will not repay the loan, the higher the interest rate the lender will charge to compensate for that risk.
- *Maturity*   The time length of a loan or its *maturity* (when it needs to be paid back) also affects the interest rate. Other things equal, longer-term loans command higher interest rates than shorter-term loans. The long-term lender suffers the inconvenience and possible financial sacrifice of forgoing alternative uses of his or her money for a greater period.
- *Loan size*   If there are two loans of equal maturity and risk, the interest rate on the smaller of the two loans usually will be higher. The costs of issuing a large loan and a small loan are about the same in dollars, but the cost is greater *as a percentage* of the smaller loan.
- *Taxability*   Interest on certain state and municipal bonds is exempt from Federal income taxation. Because lenders are interested in their after-tax rate of interest, borrowing by states and local governments can attract lenders even though the borrowers pay low interest rates. Consider a high-income lender who pays a 39.6 percent Federal income tax (2001) on marginal income. He or she may prefer a 6 percent interest rate on a tax-exempt municipal bond to an

Table 16.1

Selected Interest Rates, February 2001

Type of Interest Rate	Annual Percentage
30-year Treasury bond rate (interest rate on Federal government security used to finance the public debt)	5.52%
90-day Treasury Bill rate (interest rate on Federal government security used to finance the public debt)	4.88
Prime interest rate (interest rate charged by banks to their best corporate customers)	8.50
30-year mortgage rate (fixed-interest rate on loans for houses)	6.98
4-year automobile loan rate (interest rate for new autos by automobile finance companies)	8.97
Tax-exempt state and municipal bond rate (interest rate paid on a low-risk bond issued by a state or local government)	5.21
Federal funds rate (interest rate on overnight loans between banks)	5.52
Consumer credit card rate (interest rate charged for credit card purchases)	17.08

Sources: Federal Reserve, www.federalreserve.gov and Bankrate.com, www.bankrate.com.

8 percent taxable interest rate on a corporate bond.

- *Market imperfections*   Market imperfections also explain some interest-rate differentials. The small-town bank that monopolizes local lending may charge high interest rates on consumer loans because households find it inconvenient and costly to "shop around" at banks in distant cities. The large corporation, on the other hand, can survey a number of rival lenders to float a new bond issue and secure the lowest obtainable rate.

Pure Rate of Interest

Economists and financial specialists talk of "the" interest rate to simplify the cluster of rates (Table 16.1). When they do so, they usually have in mind the **pure rate of interest.** The pure rate is best approximated by the interest paid on long-term, virtually riskless securities such as long-term bonds of the U.S. government (30-year Treasury bonds). This interest payment can be thought of as being made solely for the use of money over an extended time period, because risk and administrative costs are negligible and the interest rate on these bonds is not distorted by market imperfections. In spring 2001 the pure rate of interest in the United States was 5.5 percent.

Role of the Interest Rate

The interest rate is a critical price that affects the *level* and *composition* of investment goods production, as well as the *amount* of R&D spending.

Interest and Total Output
A lower equilibrium interest rate encourages businesses to borrow more for investment. As a result, total spending in the economy rises, and if the economy has unused resources, so does total output. Conversely, a higher equilibrium interest rate discourages business from borrowing for investment, thereby reducing investment and total spending. Such a decrease in spending may be desirable if an economy is experiencing inflation.

The Federal Reserve often manipulates the interest rate to try to expand investment and output, on the one hand, or to reduce investment and inflation, on the other. It affects the interest rate by changing the supply of money. Increases in the money supply increase the supply of loanable funds, causing the equilibrium interest rate to fall. This boosts investment spending and expands the economy. In contrast, decreases in the money supply decrease the supply of loanable funds, boosting the equilibrium interest rate. As a result, investment is constrained and so is the economy.

Interest and the Allocation of Capital
Prices are rationing devices. The price of money—the interest rate—is certainly no exception. The interest rate rations the available supply of loanable funds to investment projects that have expected rates of return at or above the interest rate cost of the borrowed funds.

If, say, the computer industry expects to earn a return of 12 percent on the money it invests in phys-

ical capital and it can secure the required funds at an interest rate of 8 percent, it can borrow and expand its physical capital. If the expected rate of return on additional capital in the steel industry is only 6 percent, that industry will find it unprofitable to expand its capital at 8 percent interest. The interest rate allocates money, and ultimately physical capital, to the industries in which it will be most productive and therefore most profitable. Such an allocation of capital goods benefits society.

But the interest rate does not perfectly ration capital to its most productive uses. Large oligopolistic borrowers may be better able than competitive borrowers to pass interest costs on to consumers, because they can change prices by controlling output. Also, the size, prestige, and monopsony power of large corporations may help them obtain funds on more favorable terms than can smaller firms, even when the smaller firms have similar rates of profitability.

Interest and R&D Spending
Recall from Chapter 13 that, like the investment decision, the decision on how much to spend on R&D depends on the cost of borrowing funds in relationship to the expected rate of return. Other things equal, the lower the interest rate and thus the lower the cost of borrowing funds for R&D, the greater the amount of R&D spending that is profitable. The higher the interest rate, the less is the amount of R&D spending.

Also, the interest rate allocates R&D funds to firms and industries for which the expected rate of return on R&D is the greatest. Ace Microcircuits may have an expected rate of return of 16 percent on an R&D project, while Glow Paints has only a 2 percent expected rate of return on its R&D project. With the interest rate at 8 percent, loanable funds will flow to Ace, not to Glow. Society will benefit by having R&D spending allocated to projects that have high enough expected rates of return to justify using scarce resources for R&D rather than for other purposes.

Nominal and Real Interest Rates
This discussion of the role of interest in investment decisions and in R&D decisions assumes that there is no inflation. If inflation exists, we must distinguish between nominal and real interest rates, just like we needed to distinguish between nominal and real

wages in Chapter 15. The **nominal interest rate** is the rate of interest expressed in dollars of current value. The **real interest rate** is the rate of interest expressed in purchasing power—dollars of inflation-adjusted value. (For a comparison of nominal interest rates on bank loans in selected countries, see Global Perspective 16.1.)

Example: Suppose the nominal interest rate and the rate of inflation are both 10 percent. If you borrow $100, you must pay back $110 a year from now. However, because of 10 percent inflation, each of these 110 dollars will be worth 10 percent less. Thus, the real value or purchasing power of your $110 at the end of the year is only $100. In inflation-adjusted dollars you are borrowing $100 and at year's end you are paying back $100. While the nominal interest rate is 10 percent, the real interest rate is zero. We determine the real interest rate by subtracting the 10 percent inflation rate from the 10 percent nominal interest rate.

It is the real interest rate, not the nominal rate, that affects investment and R&D decisions. **(Key Question 6)**

GLOBAL PERSPECTIVE 16.1

Short-Term Nominal Interest Rates, Selected Nations

These data show the short-term nominal interest rates (those on 3-month loans) in various countries in 2000. Because these are nominal rates, much of the variation reflects differences in rates of inflation. But differences in central bank monetary policies and in risk of default also explain the variations.

Short-term Interest Rate, 2000
0 10 20 30 40 50 60 70 80

Turkey
Mexico
Hungary
Poland
Greece
South Korea
United Kingdom
United States
Canada
Sweden
Japan

Source: Organization for Economic Cooperation and Development, www.oecd.org/.

Application: Usury Laws

A number of states have passed **usury laws,** which specify a maximum interest rate at which loans can be made. Such rates are a special case of *price ceilings,* discussed in Chapter 7. The purpose of usury laws is to hold down the interest cost of borrowing, particularly for low-income borrowers. ("Usury" simply means exorbitant interest.)

Figure 16.2 helps us assess the impact of such legislation. The equilibrium interest rate there is 8 percent, but suppose a usury law specifies that lenders cannot charge more than 6 percent. The effects are as follows:

- *Nonmarket rationing* At 6 percent, the quantity of loanable funds demanded exceeds the quantity supplied: There is a shortage of loanable funds. Because the market interest rate no longer can ration the available loanable funds to borrowers, lenders (banks) have to do the rationing. We can expect them to make loans only to the most creditworthy borrowers (mainly wealthy, high-income people), thus defeating the goal of the usury law. Low-income, riskier borrowers are excluded from the market and may be forced to turn to loan sharks who charge illegally high interest rates.

- *Gainers and losers* Creditworthy borrowers gain from usury laws, because they pay below-market interest rates. Lenders (ultimately bank shareholders) are losers, because they receive 6 percent rather than 8 percent on each dollar lent.

- *Inefficiency* We have just seen how the equilibrium interest rate allocates money to the investments and the R&D projects whose expected rates of return are greatest. Under usury laws, funds are much less likely to be allocated by banks to the most productive projects. Suppose Mendez has a project so promising she would pay 10 percent for funds to finance it. Chen has a less promising investment, and he would be willing to pay only 7 percent for financing. If the market were rationing funds, Mendez's highly productive project would be funded and Chen's would not. That allocation of funds would be in the interest of both Mendez and society. But with a 6 percent usury rate, Chen may get to the bank before Mendez and receive the loanable funds at 6 percent. So Mendez may not get funded. Legally controlled interest rates may thus inefficiently ration funds to less productive investments or R&D projects.

Economic Profit

We have seen in previous chapters that economists define profit narrowly. To accountants, "profit" is what remains of a firm's total revenue after it has paid individuals and other firms for the materials, capital, and labor they have supplied to the firm. To the economist, this definition overstates profit. The reason is that the accountant's view of profit considers only **explicit costs:** payments made by the firm to outsiders. It ignores **implicit costs:** the monetary income the firm sacrifices when it uses resources that it owns, rather than supplying those resources to the market. The economist considers implicit costs to be opportunity costs, and hence to be real costs that must be accounted for in determining profit. **Economic,** or **pure, profit** is what remains after all costs—both explicit and implicit costs, the latter including a normal profit—have been subtracted from a firm's total revenue. Economic profit may be either positive or negative (a loss).

For example, suppose a shopkeeper owns her own bagel shop, including the land, building, and equipment, and provides her own labor. As economists see it, she grossly overstates her economic profit if she merely subtracts from her total revenue the payments she makes to outsiders for, say, baking ingredients, electricity, and insurance. She has not yet subtracted the cost of the resources *she* has contributed. Those costs are the rent, interest, and wage payments she could have received by making her land, labor, and capital resources available for alternative uses. They are her implicit costs, and they must be taken into account in determining her economic profit. She certainly would have to pay those costs if outsiders supplied these resources to her bagel shop.

Role of the Entrepreneur

The economist views profit as the return to a particular type of human resource: entrepreneurial ability. We know from earlier chapters that the entrepreneur (1) combines resources to produce a good or service, (2) makes basic, nonroutine policy decisions for the firm, (3) introduces innovations in the form of new products or new production processes, and (4) bears the economic risks associated with all those functions.

Part of the entrepreneur's return is a **normal profit.** This is the minimum payment necessary to retain the entrepreneur in his or her current line of production. We saw in Chapter 9 that normal profit is a cost—the cost of using entrepreneurial ability for a particular purpose. We saw also that a firm's total revenue may exceed its total cost; the excess revenue above all costs is its economic profit. This *residual profit* also goes to the entrepreneur. The entrepreneur is the *residual claimant:* the resource that receives what is left after all costs are paid.

Why should there be residual profit? We next examine three possible reasons, two relating to the risks involved in business and one based on monopoly power.

Sources of Economic Profit

Let's first construct an artificial economic environment in which economic profit would be zero. Then, by noting how the real world differs from such an environment, we will see where economic profit arises.

We begin with a purely competitive, static economy. A **static economy** is one in which the basic forces such as resource supplies, technological knowledge, and consumer tastes are constant and unchanging. As a result, all cost and supply data, on the one hand, and all demand and revenue data, on the other, are constant.

Given the nature of these data, the economic future is perfectly certain and foreseeable; there is no uncertainty. The outcome of any price or production policy can be accurately predicted. Furthermore, no product or production process is ever improved. Under pure competition any economic profit or loss that might have existed in an industry will disappear with the entry or exit of firms in the long run. All costs, explicit and implicit, are just covered in the long run, so there is no economic profit in our static economy.

The idea of zero economic profit in a static competitive economy suggests that profit is linked to the dynamic nature of real-world capitalism and its accompanying uncertainty. Moreover, it indicates that economic profit may arise from a source other than the directing, innovating, and risk-bearing functions of the entrepreneur. That source is the presence of some amount of monopoly power.

Risk and Profit
In a real, dynamic economy the future is not certain and predictable; there is uncertainty. This means that the entrepreneur must assume risks. Some or all of economic profit may be a reward for assuming risks.

In linking economic profit with uncertainty and risk bearing, we must distinguish between risks that are insurable and risks that are not. Some types of risk such as fire, floods, theft, and accidents to employees are measurable; that is, their frequency of occurrence can be estimated accurately. Firms can avoid losses due to **insurable risks** by paying an annual fee (an insurance premium) to an insurance company. The entrepreneur need not bear such risks.

However, the entrepreneur must bear the uninsurable risks of business, and those risks are a potential source of economic profit. **Uninsurable risks** are mainly the uncontrollable and unpredictable changes in the demand and supply conditions facing the firm (and hence its revenues and costs). Uninsurable risks stem from three general sources:

- ■ *Changes in the general economic environment* A downturn in business (a recession), for example, can lead to greatly reduced demand, sales, and revenues, and thus to business losses. An otherwise-prosperous firm may experience such losses through no fault of its own.
- ■ *Changes in the structure of the economy* Consumer tastes, technology, resource availability, and prices change constantly in the real world, bringing changes in production costs and revenues. For example, an airline earning

economic profit one year may find its profit plunging the next year as the result of a significant increase in the price of jet fuel.
- ■ *Changes in government policy* A newly instituted regulation, the removal of a tariff, or a change in national defense policy may significantly alter the cost and revenue data of the affected industry and firms.

Regardless of how such revenue and cost changes come about, they are risks that the firm and entrepreneur must take in order to stay in business. *Some or all of the economic profit in a real, dynamic economy may be compensation for taking risks.*

Innovations and Profit
Such uncertainties are beyond the control of the individual firm or industry and thus external to it. One dynamic feature of capitalism, however—innovation—occurs at the initiative of the entrepreneur. Business firms deliberately introduce new methods of production to affect their costs favorably and new products to affect their revenues favorably. The entrepreneur purposely undertakes to upset existing cost and revenue data in a way that promises to be profitable.

But again, uncertainty enters the picture. Despite exhaustive market surveys, new products or modifications of existing products may be economic failures. Similarly, of the many new novels, textbooks, movies, and compact discs that appear every year, only a handful garners large profits. Nor is it known with certainty whether new production machinery will actually yield projected cost economies. Thus, innovations undertaken by entrepreneurs entail uncertainty and the possibility of losses, not just the potential for increased profit. *Some of the economic profit in an innovative economy may be compensation for dealing with the uncertainty of innovation.*

Monopoly and Profit
So far, we have linked economic profit with the uncertainties surrounding (1) the dynamic environment to which enterprises are exposed and (2) the dynamic business processes they initiate themselves. *The existence of monopoly power is a final source of economic profit.* Because a monopolist can restrict output and deter entry, it may persistently enjoy above-competitive prices and economic profit if demand is strong relative to cost.

Economic uncertainty and monopoly are closely intertwined as sources of economic profit. A firm with some monopoly power can reduce business risk, or at least manipulate it enough to reduce its adverse effects, and thus increase and prolong economic profit. Furthermore, a firm can use innovation as a source of monopoly power and a means of sustaining itself and its economic profit.

An important distinction between profit stemming from uncertainty and profit resulting from monopoly has to do with the social desirability of these two sources of profit. Bearing business risk and undertaking innovation in an uncertain economic environment are socially desirable functions. Obtaining monopoly profit is not socially desirable, because it is typically founded on reduced output, above-competitive prices, and economic inefficiency. **(Key Question 8)**

Functions of Profit

Economic profit is the main energizer of the capitalistic economy. It influences both the level of economic output and the allocation of resources among alternative uses.

Profit and Total Output
The expectation of economic profit motivates firms to innovate. Innovation stimulates new investment, thereby increasing total output and employment. Thus, the pursuit of profit enhances economic growth by promoting innovation.

Profit and Resource Allocation
Profit also helps allocate resources among alternative lines of production. Entrepreneurs seek profit and shun losses. The occurrence of economic profit in an industry is a signal that society wants that particular industry to expand. It attracts resources from industries that are not profitable. But the rewards of profit are more than an inducement for an industry to expand; they also attract the financing that firms need for expansion. In contrast, losses penalize businesses that fail to adjust their productive efforts to the goods and services most preferred by customers. Losses signal society's desire for the afflicted industries to contract.

So, in terms of our chapter-opening question, Cisco Systems experienced a large profit increase in 1999 because it was selling Internet switching devices that society greatly wanted. The profit increase signaled that society wanted more of its scarce resources allocated to that use. Sunbeam, in contrast, was not providing products equivalent in value to the costs of the resources used to provide them—the

firm therefore suffered a loss. The loss signaled that society would benefit from a reallocation of all or a part of those resources to some other use.

Profits and losses do not, however, result in an allocation of resources that is perfectly attuned to consumer preferences. The presence of monopoly, for example, impedes the movement of firms and resources from industry to industry in response to economic profit.

QUICK REVIEW 16.3

- Pure or economic profit is what remains after all explicit and implicit costs (including a normal profit) are subtracted from a firm's total revenue.
- Economic profit has three sources: the bearing of uninsurable risk, the uncertainty of innovation, and monopoly power.
- Profit and profit expectations affect the levels of investment, total spending, and domestic output; profit and loss also allocate resources among alternative uses.

■ Income Shares

Our discussion in this and in the preceding chapter would not be complete without a brief reexamination of how U.S. national income is distributed among wages, rent, interest, and profit.

It will be worth your while to look back at Figure 5.1, page 74. Although the income categories shown in that chart do not neatly fit the economic definitions of wages, rent, interest, and profits, they do provide insights about income shares in the United States. Note the dominant role of the labor resource and thus labor income in the U.S. economy. Even with labor income defined narrowly as "wages and salaries," labor receives about 70 percent of national income. But some economists contend that the income of proprietors is largely composed of implicit wages and salaries and therefore should be added to the "wages and salaries" category to determine labor income. When we use this broad definition, labor's share rises to nearly 80 percent of national income, a percentage that has been remarkably stable in the United States since 1900. That leaves about 20 percent for capitalists in the form of rent, interest, and profit. Ironically, capitalist income is a relatively small share of the U.S. economy, which we call a capitalist system.

Determining the Price of Credit

A Variety of Lending Practices May Cause the Effective Interest Rate to Be Quite Different from What It Appears to Be.

Borrowing and lending—receiving and granting credit—are a way of life. Individuals receive credit when they negotiate a mortgage loan and when they use their credit cards. Individuals make loans when they open a savings account in a commercial bank or buy a government bond.

It is sometimes difficult to determine exactly how much interest we pay and receive when we borrow and lend. Let's suppose that you borrow $10,000 that you agree to repay plus $1000 of interest at the end of 1 year. In this instance, the interest rate is 10 percent per year. To determine the interest rate i, we compare the interest paid with the amount borrowed:

$$i = \frac{\$1000}{\$10,000} = 10\%$$

But in some cases a lender—say, a bank—will discount the interest payment at the time the loan is made. Thus, instead of giving the borrower $10,000, the bank discounts the $1000 interest payment in advance, giving the borrower only $9000. This increases the interest rate:

$$i = \frac{\$1000}{\$9000} = 11\%$$

While the absolute amount of interest paid is the same, in the second case the borrower has only $9000 available for the year.

An even more subtle point is that, to simplify their calculations, many financial institutions assume a 360-day year (twelve 30-day months). This means the borrower has the use of the lender's funds for 5 days less than the normal year. This use of a "short year" also increases the actual interest rate paid by the borrower.

The interest rate paid may change dramatically if a loan is repaid in installments. Suppose a bank lends you $10,000 and charges interest in the amount of $1000 to be paid at the end of the year. But the loan contract requires that you repay the $10,000 loan in 12 equal monthly installments. In effect, then, the average amount of the loan outstanding during the year is only $5000. Therefore:

$$i = \frac{\$1000}{\$5000} = 20\%$$

Here interest is paid on the total amount of the loan ($10,000) rather than on the outstanding balance (which averages $5000 for the year), making for a much higher interest rate.

Another factor that influences the effective interest rate is whether or not interest is compounded. Suppose you deposit $10,000 in a savings account that pays a 10 percent interest rate compounded semiannually. In other words, interest is paid on your "loan" to the bank twice a year. At the end of the first 6 months, $500 of interest (10 percent of $10,000 for half a year) is added to your account. At the end of the year, interest is calculated on $10,500 so that the second interest payment is $525 (10 percent of $10,500 for half a year). Thus:

$$i = \frac{\$1025}{\$10,000} = 10.25\%$$

This means that a bank advertising a 10 percent interest rate compounded semiannually is actually paying more interest to its customers than is a competitor paying a simple (noncompounded) interest rate of 10.2 percent.

Two pieces of legislation have attempted to clarify interest charges and payments. The Truth in Lending Act of 1968 requires that lenders state the costs and terms of consumer credit in concise and uniform language, in particular, as an annual percentage rate (APR). More recently, the Truth in Savings Act of 1991 requires that all advertisements of deposit accounts by banks and other financial institutions disclose all fees connected with such accounts and the interest rate and annual percentage return on each account. Nevertheless, some check-cashing firms that lend money to people in return for postdated personal checks have been found to receive interest equivalent to 261 to 913 percent a year. These interest rates prompted calls for state legislators to protect consumers from "predatory lenders." "Let the borrower (or depositor) beware" remains a fitting motto in the world of credit.

SUMMARY

1. Economic rent is the price paid for the use of land and other natural resources whose total supplies are fixed.

2. Rent is a surplus payment that is socially unnecessary because land would be available to the economy even without rental payments. The idea of land rent as a surplus payment gave rise to the single-tax movement of the late 1800s.

3. Differences in land rent result from differences in the fertility and climatic features of the land and differences in location.

4. Although land rent is a surplus payment rather than a cost to the economy as a whole, to individual firms and industries, rental payments are correctly regarded as costs. These payments must be made to gain the use of land, which has alternative uses.

5. Interest is the price paid for the use of money. In the loanable funds theory, the equilibrium interest rate is determined by the demand for and supply of loanable funds. Other things equal, an increase in the supply of loanable funds reduces the equilibrium interest rate, whereas a decrease in supply increases it; increases in the demand for loanable funds raise the equilibrium interest rate, whereas decreases in demand reduce it.

6. Interest rates vary in size because loans differ as to risk, maturity, amount, and taxability. Market imperfections cause additional variations. The pure rate of interest is the interest rate on long-term, virtually riskless, 30-year U.S. Treasury bonds.

7. The equilibrium interest rate influences the level of investment and helps ration financial and physical capital to specific firms and industries. Similarly, this rate influences the size and composition of R&D spending. The *real interest rate*, not the nominal rate, is critical to investment and R&D decisions.

8. Although designed to make funds available to low-income borrowers, usury laws tend to allocate credit to high-income persons, subsidize high-income borrowers at the expense of lenders, and lessen the efficiency with which loanable funds are allocated.

9. Economic, or pure, profit is the difference between a firm's total revenue and the sum of its explicit and implicit costs, the latter including a normal profit. Profit accrues to entrepreneurs for assuming the uninsurable risks associated with organizing and directing economic resources and for innovating. Profit also results from monopoly power.

10. Profit expectations influence innovating and investment activities and therefore the economy's levels of employment and economic growth. The basic function of profits and losses, however, is to allocate resources in accord with consumers' preferences.

11. The largest share of national income—about 70 percent—goes to labor, a share narrowly defined as "wages and salaries." When labor's share is more broadly defined to include "proprietors' income," it rises to about 80 percent of national income, leaving about 20 percent as capital's share.

TERMS AND CONCEPTS

economic rent	pure rate of interest	explicit costs	static economy
incentive function	nominal interest rate	implicit costs	insurable risks
single-tax movement	real interest rate	economic or pure profit	uninsurable risks
loanable funds theory of interest	usury laws	normal profit	

STUDY QUESTIONS

1. How does the economist's use of the term "rent" differ from everyday usage? Explain: "Though rent need not be paid by society to make land available, rental payments are very useful in guiding land into the most productive uses."

2. **Key Question** Explain why economic rent is a surplus payment when viewed by the economy as a whole but a cost of production from the standpoint of individual firms and industries. Explain: "Rent performs no 'incentive function' in the economy."

3. If money is not an economic resource, why is interest paid and received for its use? What considerations account for the fact that interest rates differ greatly on various types of loans? Use those considerations to explain the relative sizes of the interest rates on the following:

   a. A 10-year $1000 government bond.

   b. A $20 pawnshop loan.

   c. A 30-year mortgage loan on a $145,000 house.

   d. A 24-month $12,000 commercial bank loan to finance the purchase of an automobile.

e. A 60-day $100 loan from a personal finance company.

4. **Key Question** Why is the supply of loanable funds upsloping? Why is the demand for loanable funds downsloping? Explain the equilibrium interest rate. List some factors that might cause it to change.

5. What are the major economic functions of the interest rate? How might the fact that many businesses finance their investment activities internally affect the efficiency with which the interest rate performs its functions?

6. **Key Question** Distinguish between nominal and real interest rates. Which is more relevant in making investment and R&D decisions? If the nominal interest rate is 12 percent and the inflation rate is 8 percent, what is the real rate of interest?

7. Historically, usury laws that put below-equilibrium ceilings on interest rates have been used by some states to make credit available to poor people who could not otherwise afford to borrow. Critics contend that poor people are those most likely to be hurt by such laws. Which view is correct?

8. **Key Question** How do the concepts of accounting profit and economic profit differ? Why is economic profit smaller than accounting profit? What are the three basic sources of economic profit? Classify each of the following according to those sources:

a. A firm's profit from developing and patenting a new medication that greatly reduces cholesterol and thus diminishes the likelihood of heart disease and stroke.

b. A restaurant's profit that results from the completion of a new highway past its door.

c. The profit received by a firm due to an unanticipated change in consumer tastes.

9. Why is the distinction between insurable and uninsurable risks significant for the theory of profit? Carefully evaluate: "All economic profit can be traced to either uncertainty or the desire to avoid it." What are the major functions of economic profit?

10. Explain the absence of economic profit in a purely competitive, static economy. Realizing that the major function of profit is to allocate resources according to

consumer preferences, describe the allocation of resources in such an economy.

11. What is the rent, interest, and profit share of national income if proprietors' income is included within the labor (wage) share?

12. **(Last Word)** Assume that you borrow $5000 and pay back the $5000 plus $250 in interest at the end of the year. Assuming no inflation, what is the real interest rate? What would the interest rate be if the $250 of interest had been discounted at the time the loan was made? What would the interest rate be if you were required to repay the loan in 12 equal monthly installments?

13. **Web-Based Question:** *How high is the real interest rate?* The real interest rate is the nominal rate less the rate of inflation. Assume that the consumer price index (CPI) is a proxy for the inflation rate and that 1-year interest rates on Treasury bills represent the nominal interest rate. Find the current CPI at www.bls.gov/cpi (Percent Changes in CPI for Urban Consumers, unadjusted 12 month ending with the most current month), and then subtract it from the current 1-year U.S. Treasury bill rate, found at www.federalreserve.gov/ (Research and Data; Statistics: Releases and Historical Data). Repeat the process for 3-month Treasury bills and the rate of change of the CPI for the past 3 months (compounded annually). Is there a difference between the 3-month and the 12-month real interest rates? If so, why?

14. **Web-Based Question:** *Corporate profits—which industries are making the most?* The Bureau of Economic Analysis provides profit data for various industries in the United States. Go to www.bea.doc. gov/briefrm/tables/ebr7.htm. Based on current figures, which of the following categories of industry classifications has the greatest profits: (*a*) financial or nonfinancial; (*b*) manufacturing, transportation, wholesale trade, or retail trade; (*c*) durable goods or nondurable goods? During the past year, which sectors had the largest and smallest percentage increases in profit? Which sectors, if any, experienced losses? What are the implications of the profit changes for expansion or contraction of the particular industries?

4

Microeconomics of Government

17

Government and Market Failure

The economic activities of government affect your well-being every day. If you drive to work or classes, you are using publicly provided highways and streets. If you attend a public college or university, taxpayers subsidize your education. When you receive a check from your part-time or summer job, you see deductions for income taxes and social security taxes. Government antipollution laws affect the air you breathe. Laws requiring seat belts, motorcycle helmets, and the sprinkler system in college dormitories are all government mandates. ■ In this chapter we examine *market failure*—a circumstance in which private markets do not bring about the allocation of resources that best satisfies society's wants. Where private markets fail, an economic role for government may arise. In this chapter we want to examine how government responds to three types of market failure: public goods, externalities, and information asymmetries. Our discussion of externalities in turn opens the way for a discussion of pollution and pollution policies. ■ In Chapter 18 our discussion of the microeconomics of government continues with an analysis of potential government inefficiencies—called *government failure*—and the economics of taxation.

▌ Public Goods

Recall from Chapter 5 that a private good is *divisible* since it comes in units small enough for individual buyers to afford. It is also subject to the *exclusion principle:* people unwilling or unable to pay for the product are barred from obtaining its benefits. Because of these characteristics, the demand for a private good gets expressed in the marketplace, and profit-seeking suppliers satisfy that demand. In contrast, a public good is *indivisible* and does not fit the exclusion principle. Once a producer has provided a

public good, it cannot bar those who don't pay from obtaining the benefits. Consequently, the demand for the good gets understated in the marketplace, and firms thus lack a profit incentive to offer it for sale. If the good is to exist at all, government will have to provide it. Two simple examples will help clarify these ideas.

The market demand for a private good is the horizontal summation of the demand curves representing all individual buyers (review Table 3.2 and Figure 3.2). Suppose there are just two people in society who enjoy hot dogs, which cost $.80 each to produce. If Adams wants to buy three hot dogs at $1 each and Benson wants to buy two hot dogs at that same price, the market demand curve will reflect that five hot dogs are demanded at a $1 price. A seller charging $1 for each hot dog can gain $5 of revenue and earn $1 of profit [$5 of total revenue minus $4 (= $.80 × 5) of cost].

The situation is different with public goods. Suppose an enterprising sculptor creates a piece of art costing $600 and places it in the town square. Also suppose that Adams gets $300 of enjoyment from the art and Benson gets $400. Sensing this enjoyment and hoping to make a profit, the sculptor approaches Adams for a donation equal to his satisfaction. Adams falsely says that, unfortunately, he doesn't much like the piece. The sculptor then tries Benson, hoping to get $400 or so. Same deal: Benson professes not to like the piece either. Adams and Benson have become *free riders*. Although feeling a bit guilty, both reason that it makes no sense to pay for something when you can receive the benefits without paying for them. The artist is a quick learner; he vows never to try anything like that again.

Generalization: Because of the free-rider problem, the market demand for a public good is nonexistent or significantly understated. Where a producer cannot exclude those who do not pay from receiving the benefits from a good, it is difficult, if not impossible, for the producer to profitably offer the good for sale. Government will have to provide it.

Demand for Public Goods

If consumers need not reveal their true demand for a public good in the marketplace, then how can the optimal amount of that good be determined? The answer is that the government has to try to estimate the demand for a public good through surveys or public votes. Suppose Adams and Benson are the only two people in the society, and their marginal willingness to pay for a public good, this time national defense, is as shown in columns 1 and 2 and columns 1 and 3 in Table 17.1. Economists might have discovered these schedules through a survey asking hypothetical questions about how much each citizen was willing to pay for various types and amounts of public goods rather than go without them.

Notice that the schedules in Table 17.1 are price-quantity schedules, implying that they are demand schedules. Rather than depicting demand in the usual

Table 17.1

Demand for a Public Good, Two Individuals

(1) Quantity of Public Good	(2) Adams' Willingness to Pay (Price)		(3) Benson's Willingness to Pay (Price)		(4) Collective Willingness to Pay (Price)
1	$4	+	$5	=	$9
2	3	+	4	=	7
3	2	+	3	=	5
4	1	+	2	=	3
5	0	+	1	=	1

way—the quantity of a product someone is willing to buy at each possible price—these schedules show the price someone is willing to pay for the marginal unit of each possible quantity. That is, Adams is willing to pay $4 for the first unit of the public good, $3 for the second, $2 for the third, and so on.

Suppose the government produces 1 unit of this public good. Because the exclusion principle does not apply, Adams' consumption of the good does not preclude Benson from also consuming it, and vice versa. So both consume the good, and neither volunteers to pay for it. But from Table 17.1 we can find the amount these two people would be willing to pay, together, rather than do without this 1 unit of the good. Columns 1 and 2 show that Adams would be willing to pay $4 for the first unit of the public good; columns 1 and 3 show that Benson would be willing to pay $5 for it. So the two people are jointly willing to pay $9 (= $4 + $5) for this unit.

For the second unit of the public good, the collective price they are willing to pay is $7 (= $3 from Adams + $4 from Benson); for the third unit they will pay $5 (= $2 + $3); and so on. By finding the collective willingness to pay for each additional unit (column 4), we can construct a collective demand schedule (a willingness-to-pay schedule) for the public good. Here we are not adding the quantities demanded at each possible price, as we do when we determine the market demand for a private good. Instead, we are adding *the prices that people are willing to pay for the last unit of the public good at each possible quantity demanded*.

Figure 17.1 shows the same adding procedure graphically, using the data from Table 17.1. Note that we sum Adams' and Benson's willingness-to-pay curves *vertically* to derive the collective willingness-to-pay curve (demand curve). For example, the

(c)
Collective demand and supply

(b)
Benson

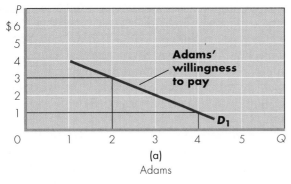

(a)
Adams

Figure 17.1

The optimal amount of a public good. The collective demand curve for a public good, as shown by D_c in (c), is found by summing vertically the individual willingness-to-pay curves D_1 in (a) and D_2 in (b) of Adams and Benson, the only two people in the economy. The supply curve of the public good represented in (c) slopes upward and to the right, reflecting rising marginal costs. The optimal amount of the public good is 3 units, determined by the intersection of D_c and S. At that output, marginal benefit (reflected in the collective demand curve D_c) equals marginal cost (reflected in the supply curve S).

height of the collective demand curve D_c at 2 units of output is $7, the sum of the amounts that Adams and Benson are each willing to pay for the second unit (= $3 + $4). Likewise, the height of the collective demand curve at 4 units of the public good is $3 (= $1 + $2).

What does it mean in Figure 17.1a that, for example, Adams is willing to pay $3 for the second unit of the public good? It means that Adams expects to receive $3 of extra benefit or utility from that unit. And we know from the law of diminishing marginal utility that successive units of any good yield less and less added benefit. This is also true for public goods, explaining the downward slope of the willingness-to-pay curves of both Adams and Benson, and of the collective demand curve. These curves, in essence, are marginal-benefit curves. **(Key Question 1)**

Supply of Public Goods

The supply curve for any good, private or public, is its marginal-cost curve. Marginal cost rises as more of a good is produced. The reason is the law of diminishing returns, which applies whether a society is making missiles (a public good) or mufflers (a private good). In the short run, government has fixed resources (public capital) with which to "produce" public goods such as national defense. As it adds more units of a variable resource (labor) to these fixed resources, total product eventually rises at a diminishing rate. That means that marginal product falls and marginal cost rises, explaining why curve S in Figure 17.1c slopes upward.

Optimal Quantity of a Public Good

We can now determine the optimal quantity of the public good. The collective demand curve D_c in Figure 17.1c measures society's marginal benefit of each unit of this particular good. The supply curve S in that figure measures society's marginal cost of each unit. The optimal quantity of this public good occurs where marginal benefit equals marginal cost, or where the two curves intersect. In Figure 17.1c that point is 3 units of the public good, where the collective willingness to pay for the last (third) unit—the marginal benefit—just matches that unit's marginal cost ($5 = $5). As we saw in Chapter 2, equating marginal benefit and marginal cost efficiently allocates society's scarce resources. **(Key Question 2)**

Cost-Benefit Analysis

The above example suggests a practical means, called **cost-benefit analysis,** for deciding whether to provide a particular public good and how much of it to provide. Like our example, cost-benefit analysis (or marginal-benefit–marginal-cost analysis) involves a comparison of marginal costs and marginal benefits.

Concept   Suppose the Federal government is contemplating a highway construction plan. Because the economy's resources are limited, any decision to use more resources in the public sector will mean fewer resources for the private sector. There will be both a cost and a benefit. The cost is the loss of satisfaction resulting from the accompanying decline in the production of private goods; the benefit is the extra satisfaction resulting from the output of more public goods. Should the needed resources be shifted from the private to the public sector? The answer is yes if the benefit from the extra public goods exceeds the cost that results from having fewer private goods. The answer is no if the cost of the forgone private goods is greater than the benefit associated with the extra public goods.

Cost-benefit analysis, however, can indicate more than whether a public program is worth doing. It can also help the government decide on the extent to which a project should be pursued. Real economic questions cannot usually be answered simply by "yes" or "no" but, rather, by questions such as "how much" or "how little."

Illustration   Although a few private toll roads exist, highways clearly have public goods characteristics because the benefits are widely diffused and the exclusion principle is not easily applied. Should the Federal government expand the Federal highway system? If so, what is the proper size or scope for the overall project?

Table 17.2 lists a series of increasingly ambitious and increasingly costly highway projects: widening existing two-lane highways; building new two-lane highways; building new four-lane highways; building new six-lane highways. The extent to which government should undertake highway construction depends on the costs and benefits. The costs are largely the costs of constructing and maintaining the highways; the benefits are an improved flow of people and goods throughout the nation.

The table shows that total annual benefit (column 4) exceeds total annual cost (column 2) for Plans A, B, and C, indicating that some highway construction is economically justifiable. We see this directly in column 6, where total costs (column 2) are subtracted from total annual benefits (column 4). Net benefits are positive for plans A, B, and C. Plan D is not economically justifiable because net benefits are negative.

But the question of optimal size or scope for this project remains. Comparing the additional, or marginal, cost and the additional, or marginal, benefit relating to each plan determines the answer. The guideline is well known to you from previous discussions: Increase an activity, project, or output as long as the marginal benefit (column 5) exceeds the marginal cost (column 3). Stop the activity at, or as close as possible to, the point at which the marginal benefit equals the marginal cost. Do not undertake a project for which marginal cost exceeds marginal benefit.

In this case plan C (building new four-lane highways) is the best plan. Plans A and B are too modest; the marginal benefits exceed the marginal costs. Plan D's marginal cost ($10 billion) exceeds the marginal benefit ($3 billion) and therefore cannot be

Table 17.2

Cost-Benefit Analysis for a National Highway Construction Project (in Billions)

(1) Plan	(2) Total Cost of Project	(3) Marginal Cost	(4) Total Benefit	(5) Marginal Benefit	(6) Net Benefit, (4) − (2)
No new construction	$ 0		$ 0		$ 0
		$ 4		$ 5	
A: Widen existing highways	4		5		1
		6		8	
B: New 2-lane highways	10		13		3
		8		**10**	
C: New 4-lane highways	**18**		**23**		**5**
		10		3	
D: New 6-lane highways	28		26		−2

justified; it overallocates resources to the project. Plan C is closest to the theoretical optimum because its marginal benefit ($10 billion) still exceeds marginal cost ($8 billion) but approaches the MB = MC (or MC = MB) ideal.

This **marginal-cost–marginal-benefit rule** actually tells us which plan provides the maximum excess of total benefits over total costs or, in other words, the plan that provides society with the maximum net benefit. You can confirm directly in column 6 that the maximum net benefit (of $5 billion) is associated with plan C.

Cost-benefit analysis shatters the myth that "economy in government" and "reduced government spending" are synonymous. "Economy" is concerned with using scarce resources efficiently. If the cost of a proposed government program exceeds its benefits, then the proposed public program should not be undertaken. But if the benefits exceed the cost, then it would be uneconomical or "wasteful" not to spend on that government program. Economy in government does not mean minimization of public spending. It means allocating resources between the private and public sectors to achieve maximum net benefit. **(Key Question 3)**

QUICK REVIEW 17.1

▓ The demand (marginal-benefit) curve for a public good is found by vertically adding the prices all the members of society are willing to pay for the last unit of output at various output levels.

▓ The socially optimal amount of a public good is the amount at which the marginal cost and marginal benefit of the good are equal.

▓ Cost-benefit analysis is the method of evaluating alternative projects or sizes of projects by comparing the marginal cost and marginal benefit and applying the MC = MB rule.

■ Externalities Revisited

In performing its allocation function, government not only produces public goods but also corrects for a market failure called **externalities,** or spillovers. Recall from Chapter 5 that a spillover is a cost or a benefit accruing to an individual or group—a third party—that is *external* to a market transaction. An example of a spillover cost or a negative externality is the cost of breathing polluted air; an example of a spillover benefit or a positive externality is the benefit

of having everyone else inoculated against some disease. When there are spillover costs, an overproduction of the related product occurs and there is an overallocation of resources to this product. Conversely, underproduction and underallocation of resources result when spillover benefits are present. We can demonstrate both graphically.

Spillover Costs

Figure 17.2a illustrates how spillover costs affect the allocation of resources. When producers shift some of their costs onto the community as spillover costs, producers' marginal costs are lower than otherwise. So their supply curves do not include or "capture" all the costs legitimately associated with the production of their goods. A polluting producer's supply curve such as S in Figure 17.2a therefore understates the total cost of production. The firm's supply curve lies to the right of (or below) the full-cost supply curve S_t, which would include the spillover cost. Through polluting and thus transferring cost to society, the firm enjoys lower production costs and has the supply curve S.

The outcome is shown in Figure 17.2a, where equilibrium output Q_e is larger than the optimal output Q_o. This means that resources are overallocated to the production of this commodity; too many units of it are produced. ◿ 17.1

Spillover Benefits

Figure 17.2b shows the impact of spillover benefits on resource allocation. When spillover benefits occur, the market demand curve D lies to the left of (or below) the full-benefits demand curve. That is, D does not include the spillover benefits of the product, whereas D_t does. Consider inoculations against a communicable disease. Watson and Weinberg benefit when they get vaccinated, but so do their associates Alvarez and Anderson who are less likely to contract the disease from them. The market demand curve reflects only the direct, private benefits to Watson and Weinberg. It does not reflect the spillover benefits—the positive externalities—to Alvarez and Anderson, which are included in D_t.

The outcome is that the equilibrium output Q_e is less than the optimal output Q_o. The market fails to produce enough vaccinations, and resources are underallocated to this product.

Economists have explored several approaches to the problems of spillover costs and benefits. Let's

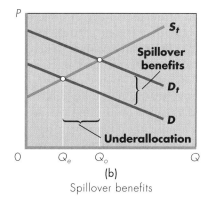

Figure 17.2

Spillover costs and spillover benefits. (a) With spillover costs borne by society, the producers' supply curve S is to the right of (below) the full-cost curve S_t. Consequently, the equilibrium output Q_e is greater than the optimal output Q_o. (b) When spillover benefits accrue to society, the market demand curve D is to the left of (below) the full-benefit demand curve D_t. As a result, the equilibrium output Q_e is less than the optimal output Q_o.

first look at situations where government intervention is not needed and then at some possible government solutions.

Individual Bargaining: Coase Theorem

In the **Coase theorem,** conceived by economist Ronald Coase at the University of Chicago, government is not needed to remedy spillover costs or benefits where (1) property ownership is clearly defined, (2) the number of people involved is small, and (3) bargaining costs are negligible. Under these circumstances the government should confine its role to encouraging bargaining between affected individuals or groups. Property rights place a price tag on an externality, creating opportunity costs for all parties. Because the economic self-interests of the parties are at stake, bargaining will enable them to find a mutually acceptable solution to the externality problem. 🔎 **17.1**

Example of the Coase Theorem Suppose the owner of a large parcel of forestland is considering a plan to clear-cut (totally level) thousands of acres of mature fir trees. The complication is that the forest surrounds a lake with a popular resort on its shore. The resort is on land owned by the resort. The unspoiled beauty of the general area attracts vacationers from all over the nation to the resort, and the resort owner is against the clear-cutting. Should

state or local government intervene to allow or prevent the tree cutting?

According to the Coase theorem, the forest owner and the resort owner can resolve this situation without government intervention. As long as one of the parties to the dispute has property rights to what is at issue, an incentive will exist for both parties to negotiate a solution acceptable to each. In our example, the owner of the timberland holds the property rights to the land to be logged and thus has the right to clear-cut it. The owner of the resort therefore has an economic incentive to negotiate with the forest owner to reduce the logging impact. Excessive logging of the forest surrounding the resort will reduce tourism and revenues to the resort owner.

But what is the economic incentive to the forest owner to negotiate with the resort owner? The answer draws directly on the idea of opportunity cost. One cost incurred in logging the forest is the forgone payment that the forest owner could obtain from the resort owner for agreeing not to clear-cut the fir trees. The resort owner might be willing to make a lump-sum or annual payment to the owner of the forest to avoid or minimize the spillover cost. Or perhaps the resort owner might be willing to buy the forested land to prevent the logging. As viewed by the forest owner, a payment for not clear-cutting or a purchase price above the prior market value of the land is an opportunity cost of logging the land.

It is likely that both parties would regard a negotiated agreement as better than clear-cutting the firs.

Limitations Unfortunately, many externalities involve large numbers of affected parties, high bargaining costs, and community property such as air and water. In such situations private bargaining cannot be used as a remedy. As an example, the global-warming problem affects millions of people in many nations. The vast number of affected parties could not individually negotiate an agreement to remedy this problem. Instead, they must rely on their governments to represent the millions of affected parties and find an acceptable solution.

Nevertheless, the Coase theorem reminds us that in many situations bargaining between private parties can be useful in remedying spillover costs and spillover benefits.

Liability Rules and Lawsuits

Although private negotiation may not be a realistic solution to many externality problems, clearly established property rights may help in another way. The government has erected a framework of laws that define private property and protect it from damage done by other parties. Those laws, and the damage recovery system to which they give rise, permit parties suffering spillover costs to sue for compensation.

Suppose the Ajax Degreaser Company regularly dumps leaky barrels containing solvents into a nearby canyon owned by Bar Q Ranch. Bar Q eventually discovers this dump site and, after tracing the drums to Ajax, immediately contacts its lawyer. Soon after, Bar Q sues Ajax. Not only will Ajax have to pay for the cleanup; it may also have to pay Bar Q additional damages for ruining its property.

Clearly defined property rights and government liability laws thus help remedy some externality problems. They do so directly by forcing the perpetrator of the harmful externality to pay damages to those injured. They do so indirectly by discouraging firms and individuals from generating spillover costs for fear of being sued. It is not surprising, then, that many spillovers do not involve private property but rather property held in common by society. It is the public bodies of water, the public lands, and the public air, where ownership is less clear, that often bear the brunt of spillovers.

Caveat: Like private negotiations, private lawsuits to resolve externalities have their own limitations. Large legal fees and major time delays in the court system are commonplace. Also, the uncertainty associated with the court outcome reduces the effectiveness of this approach. Will the court accept your claim that your emphysema has resulted from the smoke emitted by the factory next door, or will it conclude that your ailment is unrelated to the plant's pollution? Can you prove that a specific firm in the area is the source of the contamination of your well? What happens to Bar Q's suit if Ajax Degreaser goes out of business during the litigation?

Government Intervention

Government intervention may be needed to achieve economic efficiency when externalities affect large numbers of people or when community interests are at stake. Government can use direct controls and taxes to counter spillover costs; it may provide subsidies or public goods to deal with spillover benefits.

Direct Controls The direct way to reduce spillover costs from a certain activity is to pass legislation limiting that activity. Such direct controls force the offending firms to incur the actual costs of the offending activity. To date, this approach has dominated public policy in the United States. Historically, direct controls in the form of uniform emission standards—limits on allowable pollution—have dominated American air pollution policy. For example, the Clean Air Act of 1990 (1) forced factories and businesses to install "maximum achievable control technology" to reduce emissions of 189 toxic chemicals by 90 percent between 1990 and 2000; (2) required a 30 to 60 percent reduction in tailpipe emissions from automobiles by 2000; (3) mandated a 50 percent reduction in the use of chlorofluorocarbons (CFCs), which deplete the ozone layer (CFCs are used widely as a coolant in refrigeration, a blowing agent for foam, and a solvent in the electronics industry); and (4) forced coal-burning utilities to cut their emissions of sulfur dioxide by about 50 percent to reduce the acid-rain destruction of lakes and forests. Clean-water legislation limits the amount of heavy metals, detergents, and other pollutants firms can discharge into rivers and bays. Toxic-waste laws dictate special procedures and dump sites for disposing of contaminated soil and solvents. Violating these laws means fines and, in some cases, imprisonment.

Direct controls raise the marginal cost of production because the firms must operate and maintain pollution-control equipment. The supply curve S in Figure 17.3b, which does not reflect the spillover costs, shifts leftward (upward) to the full-cost supply curve, S_t. Product price increases, equi-

(a)
Spillover costs

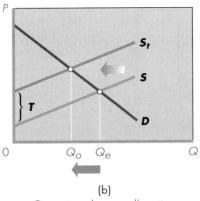

(b)
Correcting the overallocation
of resources via direct controls
or via a tax

Figure 17.3

Correcting for spillover costs (negative externalities). (a) Spillover costs result in an overallocation of resources. (b) Government can correct this overallocation in two ways: (1) use of direct controls, which would shift the supply curve from S to S_t and reduce output from Q_e to Q_o, or (2) imposition of a specific tax T, which would also shift the supply curve from S to S_t, eliminating the overallocation of resources.

librium output falls from Q_e to Q_o, and the initial overallocation of resources shown in Figure 17.3a is corrected.

Specific Taxes

A second policy approach to spillover costs is for government to levy taxes or charges specifically on the related good. For example, the government has placed a manufacturing excise tax on CFCs, which deplete the stratospheric ozone layer protecting the earth from excessive solar ultraviolet radiation. Facing such an excise tax, manufacturers must decide whether to pay the tax or expend additional funds to purchase or develop substitute products. In either case, the tax raises the marginal cost of producing CFCs, shifting the private supply curve for this product leftward (or upward).

In Figure 17.3b, a tax equal to T per unit increases the firm's marginal cost, shifting the supply curve from S to S_t. The equilibrium price rises, and the equilibrium output declines from Q_e to the economically efficient level Q_o. The tax thus eliminates the initial overallocation of resources.

Subsidies and Government Provision

Where spillover benefits are large and diffuse, as in our earlier example of inoculations, government has three options for correcting the underallocation of resources:

■ **Subsidies to buyers** Figure 17.4a again shows the supply-demand situation for spillover benefits. Government could correct the underallocation of resources, for example, to inoculations, by subsidizing consumers of the product. It could give each new mother in the United States a discount coupon to be used to obtain a series of

inoculations for her child. The coupon would reduce the "price" to the mother by, say, 50 percent. As shown in Figure 17.4b, this program would shift the demand curve for inoculations from too low D to the appropriate D_t. The number of inoculations would rise from Q_e to the economically optimal Q_o, eliminating the underallocation of resources shown in Figure 17.4a.

■ **Subsidies to producers** A subsidy to producers is a specific tax in reverse. Taxes impose an extra cost on producers, while subsidies reduce producers' costs. As shown in Figure 17.4c, a subsidy of U per inoculation to physicians and medical clinics would reduce their marginal costs and shift their supply curve rightward from S_t to S_t'. The output of inoculations would increase from Q_e to the optimal level Q_o, correcting the underallocation of resources shown in Figure 17.4a.

■ **Government provision** Finally, where spillover benefits are extremely large, the government may decide to provide the product as a public good. The U.S. government largely eradicated the crippling disease polio by administering free vaccines to all children. India ended smallpox by paying people in rural areas to come to public clinics to have their children vaccinated. **(Key Question 4)**

A Market-Based Approach to Spillover Costs

One novel approach to spillover costs involves only limited government action. The idea is to create a market for externality rights. But before describing

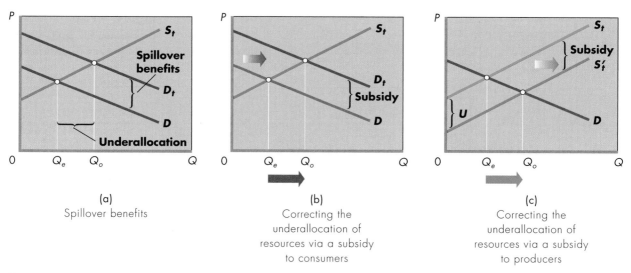

(a)
Spillover benefits

(b)
Correcting the
underallocation of
resources via a subsidy
to consumers

(c)
Correcting the
underallocation of
resources via a subsidy
to producers

Figure 17.4

Correcting for spillover benefits (positive externalities). (a) Spillover benefits result in an underallocation of resources. (b) This underallocation can be corrected by a subsidy to consumers, which shifts market demand from D to D_t and increases output from Q_e to Q_o. (c) Alternatively, the underallocation can be eliminated by providing producers with a subsidy of U, which shifts their supply curve from S_t to S_t', increasing output from Q_e to Q_o.

that approach, we first need to understand the idea called the **tragedy of the commons.**

The Tragedy of the Commons   The air, rivers, lakes, oceans, and public lands, such as parks and streets, are all objects for pollution because the rights to use those resources are held "in common" by society. No private individual or institution has a monetary incentive to maintain the purity or quality of such resources.

We maintain the property we own—for example, we paint and repair our homes periodically—in part because we will recoup the value of these improvements at the time of sale. But as long as "rights" to air, water, and certain land resources are commonly held and are freely available, there is no incentive to maintain them or use them carefully. As a result, these natural resources are overused and thereby degraded or polluted.

For example, a common pasture in which anyone can graze cattle will quickly be overgrazed because each rancher has an incentive to graze as many cattle as possible. Similarly, commonly owned resources such as rivers, lakes, oceans, and the air get used beyond their capacity to absorb pollution. Manufacturers will choose the least-cost combination of inputs and bear only unavoidable costs. If they can dump waste chemicals into rivers and lakes rather than pay for proper disposal, some businesses

will be inclined to do so. Firms will discharge smoke into the air if they can, rather than purchase expensive abatement facilities. Even Federal, state, and local governments sometimes discharge inadequately treated waste into rivers, lakes, or oceans to avoid the expense of constructing expensive treatment facilities. Many individuals avoid the costs of proper refuse pickup and disposal by burning their garbage or dumping it in the woods.

The problem is mainly one of incentives. There is no incentive to incur internal costs associated with reducing or eliminating pollution when those costs can be transferred externally to society. The fallacy of composition also comes into play. Each person and firm reasons their individual contribution to pollution is so small that it is of little or no overall consequence. But their actions, multiplied by hundreds, thousands, or millions, overwhelm the absorptive capacity of the common resources. Society ends up with a degradation or pollution problem.

A Market for Externality Rights   This outcome gives rise to a novel policy approach to spillover costs—one that is market-oriented. The idea is that the government can create a **market for externality rights.** We confine our discussion to pollution, although the same approach might be used with other externalities.

Operation of the Market   In this market approach, an appropriate pollution-control agency would determine the amount of pollutants that firms can discharge into the water or air of a specific region annually while maintaining the water or air quality at some acceptable level. Suppose the agency ascertains that 500 tons of pollutants can be discharged into Metropolitan Lake and "recycled" by nature each year. Then 500 pollution rights, each entitling the owner to dump 1 ton of pollutants into the lake in 1 year, are made available for sale to producers each year. The supply of these pollution rights is fixed and therefore perfectly inelastic, as shown in Figure 17.5.

The demand for pollution rights, represented by D_{2002} in the figure, takes the same downsloping form as the demand for any other input. At higher prices there is less pollution, as polluters either stop polluting or pollute less by acquiring pollution-abatement equipment. An equilibrium market price for pollution rights, here $100, will be determined at which the environment-preserving quantity of pollution rights is rationed to polluters. Figure 17.5 shows that if the use of the lake as a dump site for pollutants were instead free, 750 tons

of pollutants would be discharged into the lake; it would be "overconsumed," or polluted, in the amount of 250 tons.

Over time, as human and business populations expand, demand will increase, as from D_{2002} to D_{2012}. Without a market for pollution rights, pollution in 2012 would be 1000 tons, 500 tons beyond what can be assimilated by nature. With the market for pollution rights, the price would rise from $100 to $200, and the amount of pollutants would remain at 500 tons—the amount that the lake can recycle.

Advantages   This scheme has several advantages over direct controls. Most important, it reduces society's costs by allowing pollution rights to be bought and sold. Suppose it costs Acme Pulp Mill $20 a year to reduce a specific noxious discharge by 1 ton while it costs Zemo Chemicals $8000 a year to accomplish the same 1-ton reduction. Also assume that Zemo wants to expand production, but doing so will increase its pollution discharge by 1 ton.

Without a market for pollution rights, Zemo would have to use $8000 of society's scarce resources to keep the 1-ton pollution discharge from occurring. But with a market for pollution rights, Zemo has a better option: It buys 1 ton of pollution rights for the $100 price shown in Figure 17.5. Acme is willing to sell Zemo 1 ton of pollution rights for $100 because that amount is more than Acme's $20 cost of reducing its pollution by 1 ton. Zemo increases its discharge by 1 ton; Acme reduces its discharge by 1 ton. Zemo benefits (by $8000 − $100), Acme benefits (by $100 − $20), and society benefits (by $8000 − $20). Rather than using $8000 of its scarce resources to hold the discharge at the specified level, society uses only $20 of those resources.

Market-based plans have other advantages. Potential polluters have a monetary incentive not to pollute, because they must pay for the right to discharge effluent. Conservation groups can fight pollution by buying up and withholding pollution rights, thereby reducing pollution below governmentally determined standards. As the demand for pollution rights increases over time, the growing revenue from the sale of a fixed quantity of pollution rights could be devoted to environmental improvement. At the same time, the rising price of pollution rights should stimulate the search for improved pollution-control techniques.

Real-World Examples   Administrative and political problems have kept the government from replacing direct controls—such as uniform emission

Figure 17.5

A market for pollution rights. The supply of pollution rights S is set by the government, which determines that a specific body of water can safely recycle 500 tons of waste. In 2002, the demand for pollution rights is D_{2002} and the 1-ton price is $100. The quantity of pollution is 500 tons, not the 750 tons it would have been without the pollution rights. Over time, the demand for pollution rights increases to D_{2012} and the 1-ton price rises to $200. But the amount of pollution stays at 500 tons, rather than rising to 1000 tons.

limits—with a full-scale market for pollution rights. But the Environmental Protection Agency (EPA) established a system of pollution rights, or "tradeable emission allowances," in the 1980s as part of a plan to reduce the sulfur dioxide emitted by coal-burning public utilities. Those emissions are the major source of acid rain. The market for such rights was greatly expanded by legislation in the 1990s.

The Clean Air Act of 1990 established a limited market for pollution rights, similar to that shown in Figure 17.5, by allowing utilities to trade emission credits provided by government. Utilities can obtain credits by reducing sulfur-dioxide emissions by more than the specified amount. They can then sell their emission credits to other utilities that find it less costly to buy the credits than to install additional pollution-control equipment.

This market for sulfur-dioxide-emission credits complements other air pollution policies that also permit the exchange of pollution rights. The EPA now allows firms to exchange pollution rights internally and externally. Polluters are allowed to transfer air pollution internally between individual sources within their plants. That is, as long as it meets the overall pollution standard assigned to it, a firm may increase one source of pollution by offsetting it with reduced pollution from another part of its operations.

The EPA also permits external trading of pollution rights. It has set targets for reducing air pollution in regions where the minimum standards are not being met. Previously, new pollution sources could not enter these regions unless existing polluters went out of business. But under the system of external trading rights, the EPA allows firms that reduce their pollution below set standards to sell their

pollution rights to other firms. A new firm that wants to locate in the Los Angeles area, for example, might be able to buy rights to emit 20 tons of nitrous oxide annually from an existing firm that has reduced its emissions below its allowable limit. The price of emission rights depends on their supply and demand.

Table 17.3 reviews the major methods for correcting externalities.

Society's Optimal Amount of Externality Reduction

Negative externalities such as pollution reduce the utility of those affected, rather than increase it. These spillovers are not economic goods but economic "bads." If something is bad, shouldn't society eliminate it? Why should society allow firms or municipalities to discharge *any* impure waste into public waterways or to emit *any* pollution into the air?

Reducing a negative externality has a "price." Society must decide how much of a reduction it wants to "buy." Eliminating pollution might not be desirable, even if it were technologically feasible. Because of the law of diminishing returns, cleaning up the last 10 percent of pollutants from an industrial smokestack normally is far more costly than cleaning up the prior 10 percent. Eliminating the next 10 percent is likely to be more costly than cleaning up the previous 10 percent, and so on.

The marginal cost (MC) to the firm and hence to society—the opportunity cost of the extra resources used—rises as pollution is reduced more and more. At some point MC may rise so high that it exceeds society's marginal benefit (MB) of further pollution abatement (reduction). Additional actions to

Table 17.3
Methods for Dealing with Externalities

Problem	Resource Allocation Outcome	Ways to Correct
Spillover costs (negative externalities)	Overallocation of resources	1. Individual bargaining 2. Liability rules and lawsuits 3. Tax on producers 4. Direct controls 5. Market for externality rights
Spillover benefits (positive externalities)	Underallocation of resources	1. Individual bargaining 2. Subsidy to consumers 3. Subsidy to producers 4. Government provision

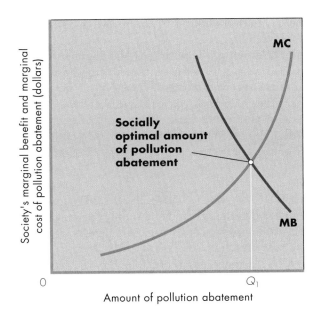

Figure 17.6
Society's optimal amount of pollution abatement.
The optimal amount of externality reduction—in this case, pollution abatement—occurs at Q_1, where society's marginal cost MC and marginal benefit MB of reducing the spillover are equal.

reduce pollution will therefore lower society's well-being; total cost will rise more than total benefit.

MC, MB, and Equilibrium Quantity

Figure 17.6 shows both the rising marginal-cost curve, MC, for pollution reduction and the downsloping marginal-benefit curve, MB, for this outcome. MB slopes downward because of the law of diminishing marginal utility: The more pollution reduction society accomplishes, the lower the utility (and benefit) of the next unit of pollution reduction.

The **optimal reduction of an externality** occurs when society's marginal cost and marginal benefit of reducing that externality are equal (MC = MB). In Figure 17.6 this optimal amount of pollution abatement is Q_1 units. When MB exceeds MC, additional abatement moves society toward economic efficiency; the added benefit of cleaner air or water exceeds the benefit of any alternative use of the required resources. When MC exceeds MB, additional abatement reduces economic efficiency; there would be greater benefits from using resources in some other way than to further reduce pollution.

In reality, it is difficult to measure the marginal costs and benefits of pollution control. Nevertheless, Figure 17.6 demonstrates that some pollution may

be economically efficient. This is so not because pollution is desirable but because beyond some level of control, further abatement may reduce society's net well-being.

Shifts in Locations of Curves The locations of the marginal-cost and marginal-benefit curves in Figure 17.6 are not forever fixed. They can, and probably do, shift over time. For example, suppose that the technology of pollution-control equipment were to improve noticeably. We would expect the cost of pollution abatement to fall, society's MC curve to shift rightward, and the optimal level of abatement to rise. Or suppose that society were to decide that it wanted cleaner air and water because of new information about the adverse health effects of pollution. The MB curve in Figure 17.6 would shift rightward, and the optimal level of pollution control would increase beyond Q_1. Test your understanding of these statements by drawing the new MC and MB curves in Figure 17.6. **(Key Question 7)**

QUICK REVIEW 17.2

▪ Policies for coping with the overallocation of resources caused by spillover costs are (a) private bargaining, (b) liability rules and lawsuits, (c) direct controls, (d) specific taxes, and (e) markets for externality rights.

▪ Policies for correcting the underallocation of resources associated with spillover benefits are (a) private bargaining, (b) subsidies to producers, (c) subsidies to consumers, and (d) government provision.

▪ The optimal amount of negative-externality reduction occurs where society's marginal cost and marginal benefit of reducing the externality are equal.

Solid-Waste Disposal and Recycling

One externality problem that has received widespread attention in the United States is solid-waste disposal. The root cause of the problem can be envisioned through the **law of conservation of matter and energy.** This law holds that matter can be transformed to other matter or into energy but can never vanish. All inputs (fuels, raw materials, water, and so forth) used in the economy's production processes will ultimately result in an equivalent amount of waste. For example, unless it is continuously recycled, the cotton found in a T-shirt ultimately will be abandoned in a closet, buried in a dump, or burned in an incinerator. Even if it is burned, it will not vanish; instead, it will be transformed into heat, smoke, and ash.

The law of conservation of matter and energy is most apparent in solid-waste disposal. The 165 million tons of garbage that accumulate annually in U.S. landfills (trash dumps) are a growing externality problem. Landfills in the northeast, in particular, are either completely full or rapidly filling up. Garbage from there and elsewhere is now being transported hundreds of miles across state lines to dumps in other states.

On the receiving end, people in rural areas near newly expanding dumps are understandably upset about the increased truck traffic on their highways and the growing mounds of smelly garbage in local dumps. Moreover, some landfills are producing serious water-supply pollution.

The high opportunity cost of urban and suburban land and the negative externalities created by dumps make landfills increasingly expensive. An alternative policy is to incinerate garbage in plants that produce electricity. But people object to having garbage incinerators, with their accompanying truck traffic and air pollution, close to their homes. Is

there a better solution to the growing problem of solid waste?

Although garbage dumps and incinerators remain the primary garbage disposal methods, recycling has received increased attention. According to the EPA, 90 percent of lead-acid batteries, 63 percent of aluminum cans, 45 percent of corrugated boxes, 30 percent of newspapers, 21 percent of plastic soft-drink bottles, and 25 percent of glass bottles are now being recycled.

Market for Recyclable Inputs Figure 17.7a, which shows the demand and supply curves for some recyclable product, such as glass, suggests the incentives for recycling.

The demand for recyclable glass derives from manufacturers that use recycled glass as a resource in producing new glass. This demand curve slopes downward, telling us that manufacturers will increase their purchases of recyclable glass as its price falls.

The location of the demand curve in Figure 17.7a depends partly on the demand for the products for which the recycled glass is used. The greater the demand for those products, the greater is the demand for the recyclable input. The location of the curve also depends on the technology and

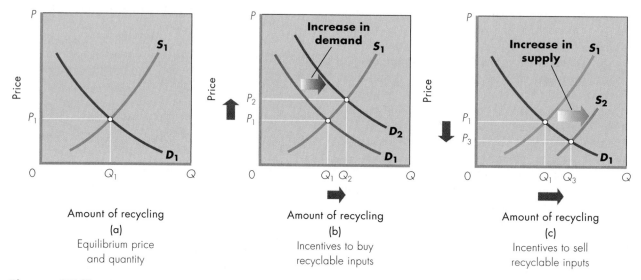

Figure 17.7

The economics of recycling. (a) The equilibrium price and amount of materials recycled are determined by supply S_1 and demand D_1. (b) Policies that increase the incentives for producers to buy recyclable inputs shift the demand curve rightward, say, to D_2, and raise both the equilibrium price and the amount of recycling. (c) Policies that encourage households to recycle shift the supply curve rightward, say, to S_2, and expand the equilibrium amount of recycling. These policies, however, also reduce the equilibrium price of the recycled inputs.

thus the cost of using original raw materials rather than recycled glass in the production process. The more costly it is to use original materials relative to recycled glass, the farther to the right will be the demand curve for recyclable glass.

The supply curve for recyclable glass slopes upward, because higher prices increase the incentive for households to recycle. The location of the supply curve depends on such factors as the attitudes of households toward recycling and the cost to them of alternative disposal.

The equilibrium price P_1 and quantity Q_1 in Figure 17.7a are determined at the intersection of the supply and demand curves. At price P_1 the market clears; there is neither a shortage nor a surplus of recyclable glass.

Policy   Suppose the government wants to encourage recycling as an alternative to land dumps or incineration. It could do that in one of two ways.

Demand Incentives   The government could increase recycling by increasing the demand for recycled inputs. If the demand curve in Figure 17.7b shifts from D_1 rightward to D_2, the equilibrium price and quantity of recycled glass will increase to P_2 and Q_2; more recycling will occur. A policy that might increase demand would be to place taxes on the inputs that are substitutable for recycled glass in the production process. Such taxes would encourage firms to use more of the untaxed recycled glass and less of the taxed inputs. Or the government could shift its purchases toward goods produced with recycled inputs and require that its contractors do the same. Example: In 1993 the Federal government announced a new policy requiring 20 percent or more recycled content in every piece of writing and copying paper purchased by Federal agencies.

Also, environmental awareness by the public can contribute to rightward shifts of the demand curve for recycled resources. Many large firms that produce waste-intensive goods have concluded that it is in their interest to support recycling, for fear of a consumer backlash against their products. Examples: Procter & Gamble (disposable diapers) and McDonald's (packaging of fast foods) have undertaken multimillion-dollar campaigns to use recycled plastic and paper.

Supply Incentives   As shown in Figure 17.7c, government can also increase recycling by shifting the supply curve rightward, as from S_1 to S_2. The equi-

librium price would fall from P_1 to P_3, but the equilibrium quantity—of, in this case, recyclable glass—would rise from Q_1 to Q_3. That is, more recycling would occur. Many local governments have implemented specific policies to do so. For example, they encourage recycling by providing curbside pickup of recyclable goods such as glass, aluminum cans, and newspapers at a lower monthly fee than that for the pickup of other garbage.

In a few cases, supply incentives for recyclables have been so effective that the price of a recycled item has fallen to zero. You can envision this outcome by shifting the supply curve in Figure 17.7c farther rightward. Some cities now are paying users of recyclable inputs such as mixed paper to truck them away from the recycling center; this means that these items have a negative price. If the cost of paying firms to take away recyclable products is lower than the cost of alternative methods, even such paid-for recycling will promote economic efficiency. However, if it is more costly to recycle trash than to bury or incinerate it, even when externalities are considered, such recycling will reduce efficiency rather than increase it. Again we are reminded that there can be either too little or too much of a good thing.

The government's task is to find the optimal amount of recycling compared with the alternative disposal of garbage. It can do this by estimating and comparing the marginal benefit and marginal cost of recycling. And, incidentally, consumers as a group can reduce the accumulation of garbage by buying products that have minimal packaging.

Global Warming

The United States has made significant progress in cleaning its air. According to the EPA, between 1990 and 2000 clean-air laws and antipollution efforts by businesses and local governments have reduced concentrations of carbon monoxide by 36 percent, lead by 60 percent, nitrogen dioxide by 10 percent, smog by 4 percent, particulate matter by 18 percent, and sulfur dioxide by 36 percent.

But significant air pollution problems remain. Some 62 million Americans live in areas that have unhealthy air because of at least one of six major air pollutants. Moreover, the United States and the other nations of the world face the risks of *global warming*. The balance of scientific evidence suggests that carbon dioxide and other gas emissions from factories, power plants, and automobiles are accumulating in the atmosphere and creating a greenhouse effect. As a result, many scientists predict that average temperatures will rise by 2 to 5 degrees Fahrenheit by 2100. In turn, almost all regions of the world will experience noticeable climatic changes. Ocean levels will gradually rise by several inches, and rainfall patterns will change. Snow accumulations will decline in some regions and rise in others. Violent storms such as tornadoes, typhoons, and hurricanes could increase in frequency and severity. But the economic effects of global warming will not be uniform. Cool and temperate regions and nations may economically benefit, and hot and dry regions and nations may be harmed. (Global Perspective 17.1 lists carbon dioxide emissions on a per capita basis for selected nations.)

The world's nations have responded to the global-warming problem by promising to limit the growth of carbon dioxide and other greenhouse emissions. Specifically, the industrially advanced nations agreed in the Kyoto Protocol of 1997 to cut their greenhouse gas emissions 6 to 8 percent below 1990 levels by 2012. The United States committed to a 7 percent reduction below 1990 levels by 2012.

GLOBAL PERSPECTIVE 17.1

Carbon Dioxide Emissions, Tons per Capita, Selected Nations

Carbon dioxide emissions, the major type of greenhouse gas emissions, vary per capita by nation primarily because of different degrees of industrialization and energy production from fossil fuels (coal, oil, and natural gas). The burning of such fuels is the major contributor to global warming.

Carbon Dioxide Emissions, tons per Capita, 1999

United States
Australia
Canada
Czech Republic
Germany
United Kingdom
Japan
Italy
Spain
France

Source: OECD environmental data, Compendium 1999, www.oecd.org.

Many contentious issues remain to be resolved through further meetings and negotiations. For example, to what extent should developing nations such as China and India, currently exempt from the limits, participate in reducing emissions? Should all industrial countries be forced to make, say, at least half their agreed-upon reduction at home, rather than buying tradeable emissions credits from other nations and making no reductions at home? Such credits were established as part of the Kyoto Protocol.

Economists stress that global-warming policies that reduce greenhouse gas emissions and thus slow or eliminate global warming create costs as well as benefits. Therefore it is imperative to consider the marginal costs and marginal benefits carefully in making policy decisions. Greenhouse gas limits should not be so stringent that they end up costing society more than the value of the benefits they produce. But limits should not be so lenient that society forgoes substantial potential benefits that it would have otherwise achieved.

Economists also stress that the market mechanism, through its system of prices and profits and losses, will make appropriate adjustments based on new climatic realities. Air-conditioner sales will rise; snow shovel sales will fall. Some agricultural lands will be deserted; others farther north will be cultivated. The maple syrup industry in New England may shift to Canada. Nevertheless, the *transition costs*—the costs associated with making economic adjustments—of global warming will undoubtedly be very high if no actions are taken to reduce greenhouse gases. The reduction or elimi-

QUICK REVIEW 17.3

◾ The ultimate reason for pollution is the law of conservation of matter and energy, which holds that matter can be transformed into other matter or into energy but does not vanish.

◾ Society's pollution problem has largely resulted from increasing population, rising per capita consumption, certain changes in technology, and the so-called tragedy of the commons.

◾ The government can encourage recycling through demand and supply incentives; its task is to determine the optimal amount of recycling.

◾ Under terms of the 1997 Kyoto Protocol, the industrial nations agreed to cut emissions of greenhouse gases by 6 to 8 percent of the 1990 levels by 2012.

nation of these transition costs is part of the benefit of slowing or eliminating the greenhouse effect. Such benefits must be fully considered in the cost-benefit analysis.

▮ Information Failures

Thus far we have added new detail and insights concerning two types of market failure: public goods and externalities. There is another, subtler, market failure. This one results when either buyers or sellers have incomplete or inaccurate information and their cost of obtaining better information is prohibitive. Technically stated, this market failure occurs because of **asymmetric information**—unequal knowledge possessed by the parties to a market transaction. Buyers and sellers do not have identical information about price, quality, or some other aspect of the good or service.

Sufficient market information normally is available to ensure that goods and services are produced and purchased efficiently. But in some cases inadequate information makes it difficult to distinguish trustworthy from untrustworthy sellers or trustworthy from untrustworthy buyers. In these markets, society's scarce resources may not be used efficiently, thus implying that the government should intervene by increasing the information available to the market participants. Under rare circumstances the government may itself supply a good for which information problems have prohibited efficient production. ▮ 17.1 ▮ 17.2

Inadequate Information Involving Sellers

Inadequate information about sellers and their products can cause market failure in the form of underallocation of resources. Examining the markets for gasoline and for the services of surgeons will show us how this comes about.

Example: Gasoline Market

Assume an absurd situation: Suppose there is no system of weights and measures established by law, no government inspection of gasoline pumps, and no law against false advertising. Each gas station can use whatever measure it chooses; it can define a gallon of gas as it pleases. A station can advertise that its gas is 87 octane when in fact it is only 75. It can rig its pumps to indicate that it is providing more gas than the amount being delivered.

Obviously, the consumer's cost of obtaining reliable information under such chaotic conditions is exceptionally high, if not prohibitive. Customers or their representatives would have to buy samples of gas from various gas stations, have them tested for octane level, and test the accuracy of calibrations at the pump. And these activities would have to be repeated regularly, since a station owner could alter the product quality and the accuracy of the pump at will.

Because of the high costs of obtaining information about the seller, many customers would opt out of this chaotic market. One tankful of a 50 percent solution of gasoline and water would be enough to discourage most motorists from further driving. More realistically, the conditions in this market would encourage consumers to vote for political candidates who promise to provide a government solution. The oil companies and honest gasoline stations would not object to government intervention. They would realize that accurate information, by enabling this market to work, would expand their total sales and profit.

The government has in fact intervened in the market for gasoline and other markets with similar potential information difficulties. It has established a system of weights and measures, employed inspectors to check the accuracy of gasoline pumps, and passed laws against fraudulent claims and misleading advertising. There can be no doubt that these government activities have produced net benefits for society.

Example: Licensing of Surgeons

Suppose now that anyone could hang out a shingle and claim to be a surgeon, much as anyone can become a house painter. The market would eventually sort out the true surgeons from those who are "learning by doing" or are fly-by-night operators who move into and out of an area. As people died from unsuccessful surgery, lawsuits for malpractice eventually would eliminate the medical impostors. People needing surgery for themselves or their loved ones could obtain information from newspaper reports or from people who have undergone similar operations.

But this process of obtaining information for those needing surgery would take considerable time and would impose unacceptably high human and economic costs. There is a fundamental difference between getting an amateurish paint job on one's house and being on the receiving end of heart surgery by a bogus physician. The marginal cost of obtaining information about sellers in the surgery market would be excessively high. The risk of proceeding without good information would result in much less surgery than desirable—an underallocation of resources to surgery.

The government has remedied this market failure through a system of qualifying tests and licensing. The licensing provides consumers with inexpensive information about a service they only infrequently buy. The government has taken a similar role in several other areas of the economy. For example, it approves new medicines, regulates the securities industry, and requires warnings on containers of potentially hazardous substances. It also requires warning labels on cigarette packages and disseminates information about communicable diseases. And it issues warnings about unsafe toys and inspects restaurants for health-related violations.

Inadequate Information Involving Buyers

Just as inadequate information involving sellers can keep markets from achieving economic efficiency, so can inadequate information relating to buyers. The buyers may be consumers who buy products or firms that buy resources.

Moral Hazard Problem

Private markets may underallocate resources to a particular good or service for which there is a severe **moral hazard problem**. The moral hazard problem is the tendency of one party to a contract to alter her or his behavior, after the contract is signed, in ways that could be costly to the other party.

Suppose a firm offers an insurance policy that pays a set amount of money per month to people who suffer divorces. The attractiveness of such insurance is that it would pool the economic risk of divorce among thousands of people and, in particular, would protect spouses and children from the economic hardship that divorce often brings. Unfortunately, the moral hazard problem reduces the likelihood that insurance companies can profitably provide this type of insurance.

After taking out such insurance, some people would alter their behavior in ways that impose heavy costs on the insurer. For example, married couples would have less of an incentive to get along and to iron out marital difficulties. At the extreme, some

people might be motivated to obtain a divorce, collect the insurance, and then continue to live together. Such insurance could even promote more divorces, the very outcome it is intended to protect against. The moral hazard problem would force the insurer to charge such high premiums for this insurance that few policies would be bought. If the insurer could identify in advance those people most prone to alter their behavior, the firm could exclude them from buying it. But the firm's marginal cost of getting such information is too high compared with the marginal benefit. Thus, this market would fail.

Although divorce insurance is not available in the marketplace, society recognizes the benefits of insuring against the hardships of divorce. It has corrected for this underallocation of "hardship insurance" through child-support laws that dictate payments to the spouse who retains the children, when the economic circumstances warrant them. Alimony laws also play a role.

Since, unlike private firms, the government does not have to earn a profit when supplying services, it provides "divorce insurance" of sorts through the Temporary Assistance to Needy Families (TANF) program. If a divorce leaves a spouse with children destitute, the family is eligible for TANF payments for a period of time. Government intervention does not eliminate the moral hazard problem, but it does offset the problem's adverse effects.

The moral hazard problem is also illustrated in the following statements:

- Drivers may be less cautious because they have car insurance.
- Medical malpractice insurance may increase the amount of malpractice.
- Guaranteed contracts for professional athletes may reduce the quality of their performance.
- Unemployment compensation insurance may lead some workers to shirk.
- Government insurance on bank deposits may encourage banks to make risky loans.

Adverse Selection Problem

Another information problem resulting from inadequate information involving buyers is the **adverse selection problem**. This problem arises when information known by the first party to a contract is not known by the second and, as a result, the second party incurs major costs. Unlike the moral hazard problem, which arises after a person signs a contract, the adverse selection problem arises at the time a person signs a contract.

In insurance, the adverse selection problem is that people who are most likely to need insurance payouts are those who buy insurance. For example, those in poorest health will seek to buy the most generous health insurance policies. Or, at the extreme, a person planning to hire an arsonist to "torch" his failing business has an incentive to buy fire insurance.

Our hypothetical divorce insurance sheds further light on the adverse selection problem. If the insurance firm sets the premiums on the basis of the average divorce rate, many married couples who are about to obtain a divorce will buy insurance. An insurance premium based on average probabilities will make a great buy for those about to get divorced. Meanwhile, those in highly stable marriages will not buy it.

The adverse selection problem thus tends to eliminate the pooling of low and high risks, which is the basis of profitable insurance. Insurance rates then must be so high that few people would want to (or be able to) buy such insurance.

Where private firms underprovide insurance because of information problems, the government often establishes some type of social insurance. It can require that everyone in a particular group take the insurance and thereby can overcome the adverse selection problem. Example: Although the social security system in the United States is partly insurance and partly an income transfer program, in its broadest sense it is insurance against poverty during old age. The social security insurance program requires nearly universal participation: People who are most likely to need the minimum benefits that social security provides are automatically participants in the program. So, too, are those not likely to need the benefits. There is, then, no adverse selection problem.

Workplace Safety

The labor market also provides an example of how inadequate information about buyers (employers) can produce market failures.

For several reasons employers have an economic incentive to provide safe workplaces. A safe workplace reduces the amount of disruption of the production process created by job accidents and lowers the costs of recruiting, screening, training, and retaining new workers. It also reduces a firm's worker compensation insurance premiums (legally required insurance against job injuries).

But a safe workplace is expensive: Safe equipment, protective gear, and a slower work pace all entail costs. The firm will decide how much safety to provide by comparing the marginal cost and marginal benefit of providing a safer workplace. Will this amount of job safety achieve economic efficiency, as well as maximize the firm's profit?

The answer is yes if the labor and product markets are competitive and if workers are fully aware of the job risks at various places of employment. With full information, workers will avoid employers having unsafe workplaces. The supply of labor to these establishments will be greatly restricted, forcing them to boost their wages to attract a workforce. The higher wages will then give these employers an incentive to provide increased workplace safety; safer workplaces will reduce wage expenses. Only firms that find it very costly to provide safer workplaces will choose to pay high compensating wage differentials rather than reduce workplace hazards.

But a serious problem arises when workers do not know that particular occupations or workplaces are unsafe. Because information involving the buyer—that is, about the employer and the workplace—is inadequate, the firm may not need to pay a wage premium to attract its workforce. Its incentive to remove safety hazards therefore will be diminished, and its profit-maximizing level of workplace safety will be less than economically desirable. In brief, the labor market will fail because of asymmetric information—in this case, sellers (workers) having less information than buyers (employers).

The government has several options for remedying this information problem:

■ It can directly provide information to workers about the injury experience of various employers, much as it publishes the on-time performance of airlines.

■ It can require that firms provide information to workers about known workplace hazards.

■ It can establish standards of workplace safety and enforce them through inspections and penalties.

Although the Federal government has mainly employed the standards and enforcement approach to improve workplace safety, some critics contend that an information strategy might be less costly and more effective. **(Key Question 13)**

Qualification

People have found many ingenious ways to overcome information difficulties without government intervention. For example, many firms offer product warranties to overcome the lack of information about themselves and their products. Franchising also helps overcome this problem. When you visit a McDonald's or a Marriott, you know precisely what you are going to get, as opposed to stopping at Bob's Hamburger Shop or the Bates Motel.

Also, some private firms and organizations specialize in providing information to buyers and sellers. *Consumer Reports* and the *Mobil Travel Guide* provide product information; labor unions collect and disseminate information about job safety; and credit bureaus provide information to insurance companies. Brokers, bonding agencies, and intermediaries also provide information to clients.

Economists agree, however, that the private sector cannot remedy all information problems. In some situations, government intervention is desirable to promote an efficient allocation of society's scarce resources.

QUICK REVIEW 17.4

Asymmetric information is a source of potential market failure, causing society's scarce resources to be allocated inefficiently.

Inadequate information about sellers and their products may lead to an underallocation of resources to those products.

The moral hazard problem is the tendency of one party to a contract to alter its behavior in ways that are costly to the other party; for example, a person who buys insurance may willingly incur added risk.

The adverse selection problem arises when one party to a contract has less information than the other party and incurs a cost because of that asymmetrical information. For example, an insurance company offering "no-medical-exam-required" life insurance policies may attract customers who have life-threatening diseases.

Lojack: A Case of Positive Externalities

Economists Ian Ayres and Steven Levitt Find That an Auto Antitheft Device Called Lojack Produces Large Spillover Benefits.

Private expenditures to reduce crime are estimated to be $300 billion annually and are growing at a faster rate than is spending on public crime prevention. Unfortunately, some forms of private crime prevention simply redistribute crime rather than reduce it. For example, car alarm systems that have red blinking warning lights may simply divert professional auto thieves to vehicles that do not have such lights and alarms. The owner of a car with such an alarm system benefits through reduced likelihood of theft but imposes a cost on other car owners who do not have such alarms. Their cars are more likely to be targeted for theft by thieves because other cars have visible security systems.

Some private crime prevention measures, however, actually reduce crime, rather than simply redistribute it. One such measure is installation of a Lojack (or some similar) car retrieval system. Lojack is a tiny radio transmitter that is hidden in one of many possible places within the car. When an owner reports a stolen car, the police can remotely activate the transmitter. Police then can determine the car's precise location and track its subsequent movements.

The owner of the car benefits because the 95 percent retrieval rate on cars with the Lojack system is higher than the 60 percent retrieval rate for cars without the system. But, according to a study by Ayres and Levitt, the benefit to the car owner is only 10 percent of the total benefit. Ninety percent of the total benefit is external; it is a spillover benefit to other car owners in the community.

There are two sources of this positive externality. First, the presence of the Lojack device sometimes enables police to intercept the car while the thief is still driving it. For example, in California the arrest rate for cars with Lojack was three times greater than that for cars without it. The arrest puts the car thief out of commission for a time and thus reduces subsequent car thefts in the community. Second, and far more important, the device enables police to trace cars to "chop shops," where crooks disassemble cars for resale of the parts. When police raid the chop shop, they put the entire theft ring out of business. In Los Angeles alone, Lojack has eliminated 45 chop shops in just a few years. The purging of the chop shop and theft ring reduces auto theft in the community. So auto owners who do not have Lojack devices in their cars benefit from car owners who do. Ayres and Levitt estimate the *marginal social benefit* of Lojack—the marginal benefit to the Lojack car owner *plus* the spillover benefit to other car owners—is 15 times greater than the marginal cost of the device.

We saw in Figure 17.4a that the existence of positive externalities causes an insufficient quantity of a product and thus an underallocation of scarce resources to its production. The two general ways to correct the outcome are to subsidize the consumer, as shown in Figure 17.4b, or to subsidize the producer, as shown in Figure 17.4c. Currently, there is only one form of government intervention in place: state-mandated insurance discounts for people who install auto retrieval systems such as Lojack. Those discounts on insurance premiums, in effect, subsidize the consumer by lowering the "price" of the system to consumers. The lower price raises the number of systems installed. But, on the basis of their research, Ayres and Levitt contend that the current levels of insurance discounts are far too small to correct the underallocation that results from the positive externalities created by Lojack.

Source: Based on Ian Ayres and Steven D. Levitt, "Measuring Positive Externalities from Unobservable Victim Precaution: An Empirical Analysis of Lojack," *Quarterly Journal of Economics*, February 1998, pp. 43–77. The authors point out that Lojack did not fund their work in any way, nor do they have any financial stake in Lojack.

SUMMARY

1. Graphically, the collective demand curve for a particular public good can be found by summing vertically the individual demand curves for that good. The demand curve resulting from this process indicates the collective willingness to pay for the last unit of any given amount of the public good.

2. The optimal quantity of a public good occurs where the combined willingness to pay for the last unit—the marginal benefit of the good—equals the good's marginal cost.

3. Cost-benefit analysis can provide guidance as to the economic desirability and most efficient scope of public goods output.

4. Spillovers or externalities cause the equilibrium output of certain goods to vary from the optimal output. Spillover costs (negative externalities) result in an overallocation of resources that can be corrected by legislation or specific taxes. Spillover benefits (positive externalities) are accompanied by an underallocation of resources that can be corrected by subsidies to consumers, subsidies to producers, or government provision.

5. According to the Coase theorem, private bargaining is capable of solving potential externality problems where (a) the property rights are clearly defined, (b) the number of people involved is small, and (c) bargaining costs are negligible.

6. Clearly established property rights and liability rules permit some spillover costs to be prevented or remedied through private lawsuits. Lawsuits, however, can be costly, time-consuming, and uncertain as to their results.

7. Direct controls and specific taxes can improve resource allocation in situations where negative externalities affect many people and community resources. Both direct controls (for example, smokestack emission standards) and specific taxes (for example, taxes on firms producing toxic chemicals) increase production costs and hence product price. As product price rises, the externality is reduced, since less of the output is bought and sold.

8. Markets for pollution rights, where firms can buy and sell the right to discharge a fixed amount of pollution, put a price on pollution and encourage firms to reduce or eliminate it.

9. The socially optimal amount of externality abatement occurs where society's marginal cost and marginal benefit of reducing the externality are equal. This optimal amount of pollution abatement is likely to be less than a 100 percent reduction. Changes in technology or changes in society's attitudes toward pollution can affect the optimal amount of pollution abatement.

10. The law of conservation of matter and energy is at the heart of the pollution problem. Matter can be transformed into other matter or into energy but does not disappear. If not recycled, all production will ultimately end up as waste. Recycling is a recent response to the growing garbage disposal problem. The equilibrium price and quantity of recyclable inputs depend on their demand and supply. The government can encourage recycling through either demand or supply incentives.

11. The global-warming problem is caused by excessive accumulation of carbon dioxide and other greenhouse gases in the earth's atmosphere. In the Kyoto Protocol of 1997 the world's nations agreed to reduce their emissions of greenhouse gases to 6 to 8 percent below 1990 levels by 2012.

12. Asymmetric information between sellers and buyers can cause markets to fail. The moral hazard problem occurs when people alter their behavior after they sign a contract, imposing costs on the other party. The adverse selection problem occurs when one party to a contract takes advantage of the other party's inadequate information, resulting in an unanticipated loss to the latter party.

TERMS AND CONCEPTS

cost-benefit analysis

marginal-cost–marginal-benefit rule

externalities

Coase theorem

tragedy of the commons

market for externality rights

optimal reduction of an externality

law of conservation of matter and energy

asymmetric information

moral hazard problem

adverse selection problem

STUDY QUESTIONS

1. **Key Question** On the basis of the three individual demand schedules on the next page, and assuming these three people are the only ones in the society, determine (a) the market demand schedule on the assumption that the good is a private good and (b) the collective demand schedule on the assumption that the good is a public good. Explain the differences, if any, in your schedules.

Individual 1		Individual 2		Individual 3	
P	Q_d	P	Q_d	P	Q_d
$8	0	$8	1	$8	0
7	0	7	2	7	0
6	0	6	3	6	1
5	1	5	4	5	2
4	2	4	5	4	3
3	3	3	6	3	4
2	4	2	7	2	5
1	5	1	8	1	6

2. **Key Question** Use your demand schedule for a public good, determined in question 1, and the following supply schedule to ascertain the optimal quantity of this public good. Why is this the optimal quantity?

P	Q_s
$19	10
16	8
13	6
10	4
7	2
4	1

3. **Key Question** The following table shows the total costs and total benefits in billions for four different antipollution programs of increasing scope. Which program should be undertaken? Why?

Program	Total Cost	Total Benefit
A	$ 3	$ 7
B	7	12
C	12	16
D	18	19

4. **Key Question** Why are spillover costs and spillover benefits also called negative and positive externalities? Show graphically how a tax can correct for a spillover cost and how a subsidy to producers can correct for a spillover benefit. How does a subsidy to consumers differ from a subsidy to producers in correcting for a spillover benefit?

5. An apple grower's orchard provides nectar to a neighbor's bees, while the beekeeper's bees help the apple grower by pollinating the apple blossoms. Use Figure 17.2b to explain why this situation might lead to an underallocation of resources to apple growing and to beekeeping. How might this underallocation get resolved via the means suggested by the Coase theorem?

6. Explain: "Without a market for pollution rights, dumping pollutants into the air or water is costless; in the presence of the right to buy and sell pollution rights, dumping pollution creates an opportunity cost for the polluter." What is the significance of this opportunity cost to the search for better technology to reduce pollution?

7. **Key Question** Explain the following statement, using the MB curve in Figure 17.6 to illustrate: "The optimal amount of pollution abatement for some substances, say, water from storm drains, is very low; the optimal amount of abatement for other substances, say, cyanide poison, is close to 100 percent."

8. Relate the law of conservation of matter and energy to (a) the air pollution problem and (b) the solid-waste disposal problem. What is the tragedy of the commons, as it relates to pollution?

9. What is the global-warming problem? How is it being addressed? Using an example other than one in the text, explain how global warming might hurt one industry, particular region, or country but help another.

10. Explain how marketable emission credits add to overall economic efficiency, compared to across-the-board limitations on maximum discharges of air pollutants by firms?

11. Explain why there may be insufficient recycling of products when the externalities associated with landfills and garbage incinerators are not considered. What demand and supply incentives might the government provide to promote more recycling? Explain how there could be too much recycling in some situations.

12. Why is it in the interest of new homebuyers and builders of new homes to have government building codes and building inspectors?

13. **Key Question** Place an "M" beside the items in the following list that describe a moral hazard problem and an "A" beside those that describe an adverse selection problem:
    a. A person with a terminal illness buys several life insurance policies through the mail.
    b. A person drives carelessly because he or she has automobile insurance.
    c. A person who intends to "torch" his warehouse takes out a large fire insurance policy.
    d. A professional athlete who has a guaranteed contract fails to stay in shape during the off-season.
    e. A woman who anticipates having a large family takes a job with a firm that offers exceptional child care benefits.

14. **(Last Word)** Explain how a global-positioning anti-theft device installed by one car owner can produce a positive spillover to thousands of others in a city.

15. **Web-Based Question:** *Clean water and government intervention.* Go to www.epa.gov/ow/ to learn

about the Clean Water Act by selecting Laws and Regulations and then Clean Water Act Summary. How does the Office of Water enforce the Act? In 1972 only one-third of the nation's waters were safe for fishing and swimming, wetland losses were estimated at about 460,000 acres annually, and sewage-treatment plants served only 85 million people. Have the Clean Water Act and the Office of Water been successful in improving these numbers?

16. **Web-Based Question:** *Workplace safety—OSHA's role.* Visit the Occupational Safety and Health Administration's website at www.osha.gov. Select The Workers' Page. What is OSHA's general-duty clause? Where is the nearest OSHA office to you? List three categories of information available to workers that might help them learn more about possible work hazards relating to their jobs.

18

Public Choice Theory and the Economics of Taxation

WHY ARE SO many Americans disenchanted with government? Perhaps one reason is the apparent failure of costly government programs to resolve socioeconomic ills. For example, despite billions of dollars spent on the problem, widespread poverty and homelessness in the United States persist. And although per-pupil education spending has dramatically increased in public education, the academic performance of U.S. students on standardized tests compares unfavorably with that of students in many other nations. ■ Critics charge that government agencies are bogged down in paperwork; that the public bureaucracy produces trivial regulations and great duplication of effort; that obsolete programs survive; that various agencies work at cross purposes; that special-interest groups disproportionately influence congressional decisions; and so on. ■ Just as there are *market failures* that impede economic efficiency in the private sector, it would seem there are *government failures* that impede economic efficiency in the public sector. In this chapter we examine some of those impediments. Our two main topics are (1) **public choice theory**—the economic analysis of government decision making—and (2) the economics of taxation. We end the chapter with a brief discussion of conservative and liberal stances on government and economic freedom. 🔑 18.1

■ Revealing Preferences through Majority Voting

Which public goods should government produce and in what amounts? How should the tax burden of financing government be apportioned?

Decisions like these are made collectively in the United States through a democratic process that relies heavily on majority voting. Candidates for office offer alternative policy packages, and citizens elect people who they think will make the best decisions on their collective behalf. Voters "retire" officials who do not adequately represent their collective wishes and elect persons they think do. Also, citizens periodically have opportunities at the state and local levels to vote directly on public expenditures or new legislation.

Although the democratic process does a reasonably good job of revealing society's preferences, it is imperfect. Public choice theory demonstrates that majority voting can produce inefficiencies and inconsistencies.

Inefficient Voting Outcomes

Society's well-being is enhanced when government provides a public good whose total benefit exceeds its total cost. Unfortunately, majority voting does not always produce that outcome. Voters may defeat a proposal to provide a public good even though it may yield total benefits that exceed its total cost. Conversely, majority voting may result in the provision of a public good that costs more than the benefits it yields.

Illustration: Inefficient "No" Vote
Assume that the government can provide a public good, say, national defense, at a total expense of $900. Also assume that there are only three individuals—Adams, Benson, and Conrad—in the society and that they will share the $900 tax expense equally, each being taxed $300 if the proposed public good is provided. And assume, as Figure 18.1a illustrates, that Adams would receive $700 worth of benefits from having this public good; Benson, $250; and Conrad, $200.

What will be the result if a majority vote determines whether or not this public good is provided? Although people do not always vote strictly according to their own economic interest, it is likely Benson and Conrad will vote "no" because they will incur tax costs of $300 each while gaining benefits of only

$250 and $200, respectively. Adams will vote "yes." So the majority vote will defeat the proposal even though the total benefit of $1150 (= $700 for Adams + $250 for Benson + $200 for Conrad) exceeds the total cost of $900. Resources should be devoted to this good, but they will not be. There will be too little of this public good.

Illustration: Inefficient "Yes" Vote
Now consider a situation in which the majority favors a public good even though its total cost exceeds its total benefit. Figure 18.1b shows the details. Again, Adams, Benson, and Conrad will equally share the $900 cost of the public good; they will each be taxed $300. But since Adams' benefit now is only $100 from the public good, she will vote against it. Meanwhile, Benson and Conrad will benefit by $350 each. They will vote for the public good because that benefit ($350) exceeds their tax payments ($300). The majority vote will provide a public good costing $900 that produces total benefits of only $800 (= $100 for Adams + $350 for Benson + $350 for Conrad). Society's resources will be inefficiently allocated to this public good. There will be too much of it.

Conclusion
So an inefficient outcome may occur as either an overproduction or an underproduction of a specific public good, and therefore as an overallocation or underallocation of resources for that

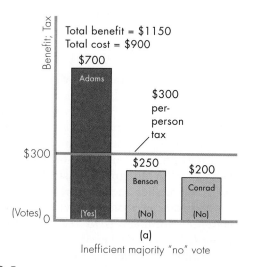

(a)
Inefficient majority "no" vote

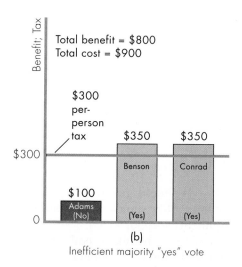

(b)
Inefficient majority "yes" vote

Figure 18.1

Inefficient voting outcomes. Majority voting can produce inefficient decisions. (a) Majority voting leads to rejection of a public good that would entail a greater total benefit than total cost. (b) Majority voting results in acceptance of a public good that has a higher total cost than total benefit.

particular use. In Chapter 30 we saw that government can improve economic efficiency by providing public goods that the market system will not make available. Now we have extended that analysis to reveal that government might fail to provide some public goods whose production is economically justifiable while providing other goods that are not economically warranted.

In our examples, each person has only a single vote, no matter how much he or she might gain or lose from a public good. In the first example (inefficient "no" vote), Adams would be willing to purchase a vote from either Benson or Conrad if buying votes were legal. That way Adams could be assured of obtaining the national defense he so highly values. But since buying votes is illegal, many people with strong preferences for certain public goods may have to go without them.

When individual consumers have a strong preference for a specific *private good*, they usually can find that good in the marketplace even though it may be unpopular with the majority of consumers. A consumer can buy beef tongue, liver, and squid in some supermarkets, although it is doubtful that these products would be available if majority voting stocked the shelves. But a person cannot easily "buy" a *public good* such as national defense once the majority has decided against it.

On the other hand, a consumer in the marketplace can decide not to buy a particular product, even a popular one. But although you may not want national defense, you must "buy" it through your tax payments when it is favored by the majority.

Conclusion: *Because majority voting fails to incorporate the strength of the preferences of the individual voter, it may produce economically inefficient outcomes.*

Interest Groups and Logrolling

There are avenues for resolving the inefficiencies associated with majority voting. Two examples follow.

Interest Groups Those who have a strong preference for a public good may band together into interest groups and use advertisements, mailings, and direct persuasion to convince others of the merits of that public good. Adams might try to persuade Benson and Conrad that it is in their best interest to vote for national defense—that national defense is much more valuable to them than their $250 and $200 valuations. Such appeals are common in democratic politics. Sometimes they are successful; sometimes they are not.

Political Logrolling **Logrolling**—the trading of votes to secure favorable outcomes—can also turn an inefficient outcome into an efficient one. In our first example (Figure 18.1a), perhaps Benson has a strong preference for a different public good, for example, a new road, which Adams and Conrad do not think is worth the tax expense. That would provide an opportunity for Adams and Benson to trade votes to ensure provision of both national defense and the new road. That is, Adams and Benson would each vote "yes" on both measures. Adams would get the national defense and Benson would get the road. Without the logrolling, both public goods would have been rejected. Moreover, the logrolling will add to society's well-being if, as was true for national defense, the road creates a greater overall benefit than cost.

But logrolling need not increase economic efficiency. Even if national defense and the road each cost more than the total benefit each produces, both might still be provided because of the vote trading. Adams and Benson might still engage in logrolling if each expects to secure a sufficient net gain from her or his favored public good, even though the gains would come at the clear expense of Conrad.

Logrolling is very common in state legislatures and Congress. It can either increase or diminish economic efficiency, depending on the circumstances.

Paradox of Voting

Another difficulty with majority voting is the **paradox of voting**, *a situation in which society may not be able to rank its preferences consistently through paired-choice majority voting.* 🔎 18.2

Preferences Consider Table 18.1, in which we again assume a community of three voters: Adams, Benson, and Conrad. Suppose the community has three alternative public goods from which to choose: national defense, a road, and a weather warning system. We expect that each member of the community prefers the three alternatives in a certain order. For example, one person might prefer national defense to a road and a road to a weather warning system. We can attempt to determine the preferences of the community through paired-choice majority voting. Specifically, a vote can be held between any two of the public goods, and the winner of that vote can then be matched against the third public good in another vote.

The three goods and the assumed individual preferences of the three voters are listed in the top part

Table 18.1

Paradox of Voting

Public Good	Preferences		
	Adams	Benson	Conrad
National defense	1st choice	3d choice	2d choice
Road	2d choice	1st choice	3d choice
Weather warning system	3d choice	2d choice	1st choice

Election	Voting Outcomes: Winner
1. National defense vs. road	National defense (preferred by Adams and Conrad)
2. Road vs. weather warning system	Road (preferred by Adams and Benson)
3. National defense vs. weather warning system	Weather warning system (preferred by Benson and Conrad)

of Table 18.1. The data indicate that Adams prefers national defense to the road and the road to the weather warning system. This implies also that Adams prefers national defense to the weather warning system. Benson values the road more than the weather warning system and the warning system more than national defense. Conrad's order of preference is weather warning system, national defense, and road.

Voting Outcomes   The lower part of Table 18.1 shows the outcomes of three hypothetical elections decided through majority vote. In the first, national defense wins against the road, because a majority of voters (Adams and Conrad) prefer national defense to the road. In the second election, to see whether this community wants a road or a weather warning system, a majority of voters (Adams and Benson) prefer the road.

We have determined that the majority of people in this community prefer national defense to a road and prefer a road to a weather warning system. It seems logical to conclude that the community prefers national defense to a weather warning system. But it does not!

To demonstrate this conclusion, we hold a direct election between national defense and the weather warning system. Row 3 shows that a majority of voters (Benson and Conrad) prefer the weather warning system to national defense. As listed in Table 18.1, then, the three paired-choice majority votes imply

that this community is irrational: It seems to prefer national defense to a road and a road to a weather warning system, but would rather have a weather warning system than national defense.

The problem is not irrational community preferences but rather a flawed procedure for determining those preferences. We see that the outcome from paired-choice majority voting may depend on the order in which the votes are taken up. Under some circumstances majority voting fails to make consistent choices that reflect the community's underlying preferences. As a consequence, government may find it difficult to provide the "correct" public goods by acting in accordance with majority voting. Important note: This critique is not meant to suggest that there is some better procedure. Majority voting is much more likely to reflect community preferences than decisions by, say, a dictator or a group of self-appointed leaders. **(Key Question 2)**

Median-Voter Model

One final aspect of majority voting reveals insights into real-world phenomena. The **median-voter model** suggests that, under majority rule and consistent voting preferences, the median voter will in a sense determine the outcomes of elections. The median voter is the person holding the middle position on an issue: Half the other voters have stronger preferences for a public good, amount of taxation, or degree of government regulation, and half have weaker or negative preferences. The extreme voters on each side of an issue prefer the median choice rather than the other extreme position, so the median voter's choice predominates.

Example   Suppose a society composed of Adams, Benson, and Conrad has reached agreement that as a society it needs a weather warning system. Each person independently is to submit a total dollar amount he or she thinks should be spent on the warning system, assuming each will be taxed one-third of that amount. An election will determine the size of the system. Because each person can be expected to vote for his or her own proposal, no majority will occur if all the proposals are placed on the ballot at the same time. Thus, the group decides on a paired-choice vote: They will first vote between two of the proposals and then match the winner of that vote against the remaining proposal.

The three proposals are as follows: Adams desires a $400 system; Benson wants an $800 system;

Conrad opts for a $300 system. Which proposal will win? The median-voter model suggests it will be the $400 proposal submitted by the median voter, Adams. Half the other voters favor a more costly system; half favor a less costly system. To understand why the $400 system will be the outcome, let's conduct the two elections.

First, suppose that the $400 proposal is matched against the $800 proposal. Adams naturally votes for her $400 proposal, and Benson votes for his own $800 proposal. Conrad, who proposed the $300 expenditure for the warning system, votes for the $400 proposal because it is closer to his own. So Adams' $400 proposal is selected by a 2-to-1 majority vote.

Next, we match the $400 proposal against the $300 proposal. Again the $400 proposal wins. It gets a vote from Adams and one from Benson, who proposed the $800 expenditure and for that reason prefers a $400 expenditure to a $300 one. Adams, the median voter in this case, is in a sense the person who has decided the level of expenditure on a weather warning system for this society.

Real-World Applicability Although our illustration is a simple one, it explains a great deal. We do note a tendency for public choices to match most closely the median view. Political candidates, for example, take one set of positions to win the nomination of their political parties; in so doing, they tend to appeal to the median voter within the party to get the nomination. They then shift their views more closely to the political center when they square off against opponents from the opposite political party. In effect, they redirect their appeal toward the median voter within the total population. They also try to label their opponents as being too liberal, or too conservative, and out of touch with "mainstream America." And they conduct polls and adjust their positions on issues accordingly.

Implications The median-voter model has two important implications:

■ Many people will be dissatisfied by the extent of government involvement in the economy. The size of government will largely be determined by the median preference, leaving many people desiring a much larger, or a much smaller, public sector. In the marketplace you can buy zero zucchinis, 2 zucchinis, or 200 zucchinis, depending on how much you enjoy them. In the public sector you get the number of Stealth bombers and interstate highways the median voter prefers.

■ Some people may "vote with their feet" by moving into political jurisdictions where the median voter's preferences are closer to their own. They may move from the city to a suburb where the level of government services, and therefore taxes, is lower. Or they may move into an area known for its excellent, but expensive, school system.

For these reasons, and because our personal preferences for government activity are not static, the median preference shifts over time. Moreover, information about people's preferences is imperfect, leaving much room for politicians to misjudge the true median position. When they do, they may have a difficult time getting reelected. (**Key Question 3**)

■ Government Failure

We have seen that the economic results of the marketplace are not always satisfactory and that government actions can help correct them. Economists agree that government has a legitimate function in dealing with instances of market failure. They advocate the use of cost-benefit analysis to make efficient decisions, including provision of public goods and services, adjustments for widespread externalities, provision of appropriate market information, and so on.

But as implied in our discussion of voting problems, government does not always perform its economic functions effectively and efficiently. In fact, public choice theory reveals that inherent shortcomings within the public sector can produce inefficient outcomes. Such shortcomings may result in **government failure**—inefficiency due to certain characteristics of the public sector. Let's consider some of these characteristics and outcomes.

Special Interests and Rent Seeking

Casual reflection suggests there may be a significant gap between "sound economics" and "good politics." Sound economics calls for the public sector to pursue various programs as long as marginal benefits exceed marginal costs. Good politics, however, suggests that politicians support programs and policies that will maximize their chance of getting elected and staying in office. The result may be that the government will promote the goals of groups of voters that have special interests to the detriment of the larger public. In the process, economic inefficiency may result.

Special-Interest Effect

Efficient public decision making is often impaired by the **special-interest effect.** This is any outcome of the political process whereby a small number of people obtain a government program or policy that gives them large gains at the expense of a much greater number of persons who individually suffer small losses.

The small group of potential beneficiaries is well informed and highly vocal on the issue in question, and they press politicians for approval. The large numbers facing very small individual losses, however, are generally uninformed on the issue. Politicians feel they will lose the campaign contributions and votes of the small special-interest group that backs the issue if they legislate against it but will not lose the support of the large group of uninformed voters, who are likely to evaluate the politicians on other issues of greater importance to them.

The special-interest effect is also evident in so-called *pork-barrel politics,* a means of securing a government project that yields benefits mainly to a single political district and its political representative. In this case, the special-interest group comprises local constituents, while the larger group consists of relatively uninformed taxpayers scattered across a much larger geographic area. Politicians clearly have a strong incentive to secure public goods ("pork") for their local constituents. Such goods win political favor because they are highly valued by constituents and the much larger group of relatively uninformed taxpayers bears the cost. Moreover, logrolling typically enters the picture. "Vote for my special local project and I will vote for yours" become part of the overall strategy for securing "pork" and remaining elected.

Finally, a politician's inclination to support the smaller group of special beneficiaries is enhanced because special-interest groups are often quite willing to help finance the campaigns of "right-minded" politicians and politicians who "bring home the pork." The result is that politicians may support special-interest programs and projects that cannot be justified on economic grounds.

Rent-Seeking Behavior

The appeal to government for special benefits at taxpayers' or someone else's expense is called **rent seeking.** To economists, "rent" is a payment beyond what is necessary to keep a resource supplied in its current use. Corporations, trade associations, labor unions, and professional organizations employ vast resources to secure favorable government policies that result in rent—higher profit or income than would occur under competi-tive market conditions. The government is able to dispense such rent directly or indirectly through laws, rules, hiring, and purchases. Elected officials are willing to provide such rent because they want to be responsive to key constituents, who in turn help them remain in office.

Here are some examples of "rent-providing" legislation or policies: tariffs on foreign products that limit competition and raise prices to consumers; tax breaks that benefit specific corporations; government construction projects that create union jobs but cost more than the benefits they yield; occupational licensing that goes beyond what is needed to protect consumers; and large subsidies to farmers by taxpayers. None of these is justified by economic efficiency. ▮ 18.1

Clear Benefits, Hidden Costs

Some critics say that vote-seeking politicians will not weigh objectively all the costs and benefits of various programs, as economic rationality demands in deciding which to support and which to reject. Because political officeholders must seek voter support every few years, they favor programs that have immediate and clear-cut benefits and vague or deferred costs. Conversely, politicians will reject programs with immediate and easily identifiable costs but with less measurable but very high long-term benefits.

Such biases may lead politicians to reject economically justifiable programs and to accept programs that are economically irrational. Example: A proposal to construct or expand mass-transit systems in large metropolitan areas may be economically rational on the basis of cost-benefit analysis. But if (1) the program is to be financed by immediate increases in highly visible income or sales taxes and (2) benefits will occur only years from now when the project is completed, then the vote-seeking politician may oppose the program.

Assume, on the other hand, that a program of Federal aid to municipal police forces is not justifiable on the basis of cost-benefit analysis. But if the cost is paid for from budget surpluses, the program's modest benefits may seem so large that it will gain approval.

Limited and Bundled Choice

Public choice theorists point out that the political process forces citizens and their elected representatives to be less selective in choosing public goods and services than they are in choosing private goods and services.

In the marketplace, the citizen as a consumer can exactly satisfy personal preferences by buying certain goods and not buying others. However, in the public sector the citizen as a voter is confronted with, say, only two or three candidates for an office, each representing a different "bundle" of programs (public goods and services). None of these bundles of public goods is likely to fit exactly the preferences of any particular voter. Yet the voter must choose one of them. The candidate who comes closest to voter Smith's preference may endorse national health insurance, increases in social security benefits, subsidies to tobacco farmers, and tariffs on imported goods. Smith is likely to vote for that candidate even though Smith strongly opposes tobacco subsidies.

In other words, the voter must take the bad with the good. In the public sector, people are forced to "buy" goods and services they do not want. It is as if, in going to a sporting-goods store, you were forced to buy an unwanted pool cue to get a wanted pair of running shoes. This is a situation where resources are not being used efficiently to satisfy consumer wants. In this sense, the provision of public goods and services is inherently inefficient.

Congress is confronted with a similar limited-choice, bundled-goods problem. Appropriations legislation combines hundreds, even thousands, of spending items into a single bill. Many of these spending items may be completely unrelated to the main purpose of the legislation. Yet congressional representatives must vote the entire package—yea or nay. Unlike consumers in the marketplace, they cannot be selective. **(Key Question 4)**

Bureaucracy and Inefficiency

Some economists contend that public agencies are generally less efficient than private businesses. The reason is not that lazy and incompetent workers somehow end up in the public sector while ambitious and capable people gravitate to the private sector. Rather, it is that the market system creates incentives and pressures for internal efficiency that are absent from the public sector. Private enterprises have a clear goal—profit. Whether a private firm is in a competitive or monopolistic market, efficient management means lower costs and higher profit. The higher profit not only benefits the firm's owners but enhances the promotion prospects of managers. Moreover, part of the managers' pay may be

tied to profit via profit-sharing plans, bonuses, and stock options. There is no similar gain to government agencies and their managers—no counterpart to profit—to create a strong incentive to achieve efficiency.

The market system imposes a very obvious test of performance on private firms: the test of profit and loss. An efficient firm is profitable and therefore successful; it survives, prospers, and grows. An inefficient firm is unprofitable and unsuccessful; it declines and in time goes bankrupt and ceases to exist. But there is no similar, clear-cut test with which to assess the efficiency or inefficiency of public agencies. How can anyone determine whether a public hydroelectricity provider, a state university, a local fire department, the Department of Agriculture, or the Bureau of Indian Affairs is operating efficiently?

Cynics even argue that a public agency that inefficiently uses its resources is likely to survive and grow! In the private sector, inefficiency and monetary loss lead to the abandonment of certain activities or products or even firms. But the government, they say, does not like to abandon activities in which it has failed. Some suggest that the typical response of the government to a program's failure is to increase its budget and staff. This means that public sector inefficiency just continues on a larger scale.

Furthermore, economists assert that government employees, together with the special-interest groups they serve, often gain sufficient political clout to block attempts to pare down or eliminate their agencies. Politicians who attempt to reduce the size of huge Federal bureaucracies such as those relating to agriculture, education, health and welfare, and national defense incur sizable political risk because bureaucrats and special-interest groups will team up to defeat them.

Finally, critics point out that there is a tendency for government bureaucrats to justify their continued employment by looking for and eventually finding new problems to solve. It is not surprising that social "problems," as defined by government, tend to persist or even expand.

The Last Word at the end of this chapter highlights several recent media-reported examples of the special-interest effect, the problem of limited and bundled choices, and problems of government bureaucracy. You might read through these examples now, relating each to the section just completed.

Imperfect Institutions

It is possible to argue that such criticisms of public sector inefficiency are exaggerated and cynical. Perhaps they are. Nevertheless, they do tend to shatter the concept of a benevolent government that responds with precision and efficiency to the wants of its citizens. The market system of the private sector is far from perfectly efficient, and government's economic function is mainly to correct that system's shortcomings. But the public sector too is subject to deficiencies in fulfilling its economic function. "The relevant comparison is not between perfect markets and imperfect governments, nor between faulty markets and all-knowing, rational, benevolent governments, but between inevitably imperfect institutions."[1]

Because the market system and public agencies are both imperfect, it is sometimes difficult to determine whether a particular activity can be performed with greater success in the private sector or in the public sector. It is easy to reach agreement on opposite extremes: National defense must lie with the public sector, while computer production can best be accomplished by the private sector. But what about health insurance? Parks and recreation areas? Fire protection? Garbage collection? Housing? Education? It is hard to assess every good or service and to say absolutely that it should be assigned to either the public sector or the private sector. Evidence: All the goods and services just mentioned are provided in part by *both* private enterprises and public agencies.

> **QUICK REVIEW 18.1**
>
> ▪ Majority voting can produce voting outcomes that are inefficient; projects having greater total benefits than total costs may be defeated, and projects having greater total costs than total benefits may be approved.
>
> ▪ The paradox of voting occurs when voting by majority rule does not provide a consistent ranking of society's preferences for public goods and services.
>
> ▪ The median-voter model suggests that under majority rule and consistent voting preferences, the voter who has the middle preference will determine the outcome of an election.
>
> ▪ Government failure allegedly occurs as a result of rent seeking, pressure by special-interest groups, shortsighted political behavior, limited and bundled choices, and bureaucratic inefficiency.

[1]Otto Eckstein, *Public Finance*, 3d ed. (Englewood Cliffs, N.J.: Prentice-Hall, 1973), p. 17.

▪ Apportioning the Tax Burden

We now turn from the difficulties of making collective decisions about public goods to the difficulties of deciding how those goods should be financed.

It is difficult to measure precisely how the benefits of public goods are apportioned among individuals and institutions. We cannot accurately determine how much citizen Mildred Moore benefits from military installations, a network of highways, a public school system, the national weather bureau, and local police and fire protection.

The situation is different when it comes to paying for those benefits. Studies reveal with reasonable clarity how the overall tax burden is apportioned. (By "tax burden" we mean the total cost of taxes imposed on society.) This apportionment question affects each of us. The overall level of taxes is important, but the average citizen is much more concerned with his or her part of the overall tax burden.

Benefits Received versus Ability to Pay

There are two basic philosophies on how the economy's tax burden should be apportioned.

Benefits-Received Principle The **benefits-received principle** of taxation asserts that households and businesses should purchase the goods and services of government in the same way they buy other commodities. Those who benefit most from government-supplied goods or services should pay the taxes necessary to finance them. A few public goods are now financed on this basis. For example, money collected as gasoline taxes is typically used to finance highway construction and repairs. Thus people who benefit from good roads pay the cost of those roads. Difficulties immediately arise, however, when we consider widespread application of the benefits-received principle:

▪ How will the government determine the benefits that individual households and businesses receive from national defense, education, the court system, and police and fire protection? Recall that public goods provide widespread spillover benefits and that the exclusion principle does not apply. Even in the seemingly straightforward case of highway financing it is difficult to measure benefits. Owners of cars benefit in different degrees from good roads. But others also benefit. For example, businesses benefit because good roads bring them customers.

- The benefits-received principle cannot logically be applied to income redistribution programs. It would be absurd and self-defeating to ask poor families to pay the taxes needed to finance their welfare payments. It would be ridiculous to think of taxing only unemployed workers to finance the unemployment compensation payments they receive.

Ability-to-Pay Principle

The **ability-to-pay principle** of taxation asserts that the tax burden should be apportioned according to taxpayers' income and wealth. In the United States this means that individuals and businesses with larger incomes should pay more taxes in both absolute and relative terms than those with smaller incomes.

What is the rationale of ability-to-pay taxation? Proponents argue that each additional dollar of income received by a household yields a smaller amount of satisfaction or marginal utility when it is spent. Because consumers act rationally, the first dollars of income received in any time period will be spent on high-urgency goods that yield the greatest marginal utility. Successive dollars of income will go for less urgently needed goods and finally for trivial goods and services. This means that a dollar taken through taxes from a poor person who has few dollars represents a greater utility sacrifice than a dollar taken through taxes from a rich person who has many dollars. To balance the sacrifices that taxes impose on income receivers, taxes should be apportioned according to the amount of income a taxpayer receives.

This argument is appealing, but application problems arise here too. Although we might agree that the household earning $100,000 per year has a greater ability to pay taxes than a household receiving $10,000, we don't know exactly how much more ability to pay the first family has. Should the wealthier family pay the *same* percentage of its larger income, and hence a larger absolute amount, as taxes? Or should it be made to pay a *larger* fraction of its income as taxes? And how much larger should that fraction be?

There is no scientific way of measuring someone's ability to pay taxes—and that's the main problem. In practice, the solution hinges on guesswork, the tax views of the political party in power, expediency, and how urgently the government needs revenue.

Progressive, Proportional, and Regressive Taxes

Any discussion of taxation leads ultimately to the question of tax rates. Recall from Chapter 5 that an *average tax rate* is the total tax paid divided by some base against which the tax is compared.

Definitions

Taxes are classified as progressive, proportional, or regressive, depending on the relationship between average tax rates and taxpayer incomes. We focus on incomes because all taxes, whether on income or on a product or a building or a parcel of land, are ultimately paid out of someone's income.

- A tax is **progressive** if its average rate increases as income increases. Such a tax claims not only a larger absolute (dollar) amount but also a larger percentage of income as income increases.
- A tax is **regressive** if its average rate declines as income increases. Such a tax takes a smaller proportion of income as income increases. A regressive tax may or may not take a larger absolute amount of income as income increases. (You may want to derive an example to substantiate this conclusion.)
- A tax is **proportional** if its average rate *remains the same* regardless of the size of income.

We can illustrate these ideas with the personal income tax. Suppose tax rates are such that a household pays 10 percent of its income in taxes regardless of the size of its income. This is a *proportional* income tax. Now suppose the rate structure is such that a household with an annual taxable income of less than $10,000 pays 5 percent in income taxes; a household with an income of $10,000 to $20,000 pays 10 percent; one with a $20,000 to $30,000 income pays 15 percent; and so forth. This is a *progressive* income tax. Finally, suppose the rate declines as taxable income rises: You pay 15 percent if you earn less than $10,000; 10 percent if you earn $10,000 to $20,000; 5 percent if you earn $20,000 to $30,000; and so forth. This is a *regressive* income tax.

In general, progressive taxes are those that fall relatively more heavily on people with high incomes; regressive taxes are those that fall relatively more heavily on the poor. **(Key Question 7)**

Applications

Let's examine the progressivity, or regressivity, of several taxes.

Personal Income Tax

We noted in Chapter 5 that the Federal personal income tax is progressive, with marginal tax rates (those assessed on additional income) ranging from 15 to 39.6 percent in 2000. Rules that allow individuals to deduct from income interest on home mortgages and property taxes and that exempt interest on state and local bonds from taxation tend to make the tax less progressive than these marginal rates suggest. Nevertheless, average tax rates rise with income.

Sales Taxes   At first thought, a general sales tax with, for example, a 5 percent rate would seem to be proportional. But in fact it is regressive with respect to income. A larger portion of a low-income person's income is exposed to the tax than is the case for a high-income person; the rich pay no tax on the part of income that is saved, whereas the poor are unable to save. Example: "Low-income" Smith has an income of $15,000 and spends it all. "High-income" Jones has an income of $300,000 but spends only $200,000 and saves the rest. Assuming a 5 percent sales tax applies to all expenditures of each individual, we find that Smith pays $750 (5 percent of $15,000) in sales taxes and Jones pays $10,000 (5 percent of $200,000). But Smith pays $750/$15,000, or 5 percent of income, as sales taxes, while Jones pays $10,000/$300,000, or 3.3 percent of income. The general sales tax therefore is regressive.

Corporate Income Tax   The Federal corporate income tax is essentially a proportional tax with a flat 35 percent tax rate. But this assumes that corporation owners (shareholders) bear the tax. Some tax experts argue that at least part of the tax is passed through to consumers in the form of higher product prices. To the extent that this occurs, the tax is like a sales tax and is thus regressive.

Payroll Taxes   Payroll (social security and medicare) taxes are regressive because the social security tax applies to only a fixed amount of income. For example, in 2000, the social security tax rate was 6.2 percent, but only of the first $76,200 of a person's wage income. The Medicare tax was 1.45 of all wage income. Someone earning exactly $76,200 would pay $5829.30, or 7.65 percent (= 6.2 percent + 1.45 percent), of his or her $76,200 income. Someone with twice that income, or $152,400, would pay $6934.20 (= $4724.40 of social security tax and $2209.80 of Medicare tax), which is only 4.55 percent of his or her wage income. So the average payroll tax rate falls as income rises, confirming that the payroll tax is regressive.

Moreover, government does not collect payroll taxes on nonwage income (such as interest, dividends, or rents). This makes them even more regressive. If our individual with the $152,400 of wage income also received $147,600 in nonwage income, then the payroll tax would be only 2.31 percent (= $6934.20/$300,000) of his or her total $300,000 income.

Property Taxes   Most economists conclude that property taxes on buildings are regressive for the same reasons as are sales taxes. First, property owners add the tax to the rents that tenants are charged. Second, property taxes, as a percentage of income, are higher for low-income families than for high-income families because the poor must spend a larger proportion of their incomes for housing. This alleged regressivity of property taxes may be increased by differences in property-tax rates from locality to locality. In general, property-tax rates are higher in poorer areas, to make up for lower property values.

■ Tax Incidence and Efficiency Loss

Determining whether a particular tax is progressive, proportional, or regressive is complicated, because those on whom taxes are levied do not always pay the taxes. We therefore need to try to locate the final resting place of a tax, or the **tax incidence.** The tools of elasticity of supply and demand will help. Let's focus on a hypothetical excise tax levied on wine producers. Do the producers really pay this tax, or do they shift it to wine consumers?

Elasticity and Tax Incidence

In Figure 18.2, *S* and *D* represent the pretax market for a certain domestic wine; the no-tax equilibrium price and quantity are $8 per bottle and 15 million bottles. Suppose that government levies an excise tax of $2 per bottle at the winery. Who will actually pay this tax?

Division of Burden   Since the government imposes the tax on the sellers (suppliers), we can view the tax as an addition to the marginal cost of the product. Now sellers must get $2 more for each bottle to receive the same per-unit profit they were getting before the tax. While sellers are willing to offer, for example, 5 million bottles of untaxed wine at $4 per bottle, they must now receive $6 per bottle

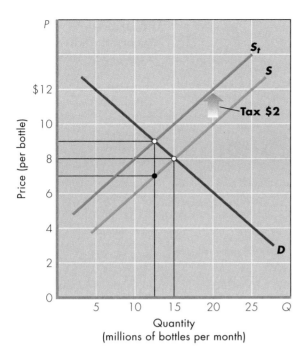

Figure 18.2

The incidence of an excise tax. An excise tax of a specified amount, here $2 per unit, shifts the supply curve upward by the amount of the tax per unit: the vertical distance between S and S_t. This results in a higher price (here $9) to consumers and a lower after-tax price (here $7) to producers. Thus consumers and producers share the burden of the tax in some proportion (here equally at $1 per unit).

(= $4 + $2 tax) to offer the same 5 million bottles. The tax shifts the supply curve upward (leftward) as shown in Figure 18.2, where S_t is the "after-tax" supply curve.

The after-tax equilibrium price is $9 per bottle, whereas the before-tax equilibrium price was $8.

So, in this case, consumers pay half the $2 tax as a higher price; producers pay the other half in the form of a lower after-tax per-unit revenue. That is, after remitting the $2 tax per unit to government, producers receive $7, or $1 less than the $8 before-tax price. So, in this case, consumers and producers share the burden of the tax equally: Producers shift half the tax to consumers in the form of a higher price and bear the other half themselves.

Note also that the equilibrium quantity declines because of the tax levy and the higher price that it imposes on consumers. In Figure 18.2 that decline in quantity is from 15 million bottles to 12.5 million bottles per month. 📐 18.1

Elasticities If the elasticities of demand and supply were different from those shown in Figure 18.2, the incidence of tax would also be different. Two generalizations are relevant.

With a specific supply, the more inelastic the demand for the product, the larger is the portion of the tax shifted to consumers. To verify this, sketch graphically the extreme cases in which demand is perfectly elastic and perfectly inelastic. In the first case, the incidence of the tax is entirely on sellers; in the second, the tax is shifted entirely to consumers.

Figure 18.3 contrasts the more usual cases where demand is either relatively elastic or relatively inelastic in the relevant price range. With elastic demand (Figure 18.3a), a small portion of the tax $(P_e - P_1)$ is shifted to consumers and most of the tax $(P_1 - P_a)$ is borne by the producers. With inelastic demand (Figure 18.3b), most of the tax $(P_i - P_1)$ is shifted to consumers and only a small amount $(P_1 - P_b)$ is paid by producers. In both graphs the per-unit tax is represented by the vertical distance between S_t and S.

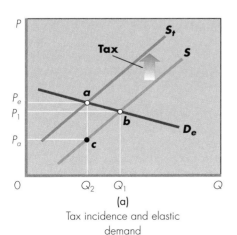

(a)
Tax incidence and elastic demand

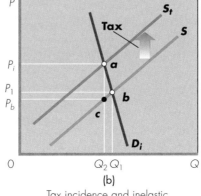

(b)
Tax incidence and inelastic demand

Figure 18.3

Demand elasticity and the incidence of an excise tax.

(a) If demand is elastic in the relevant price range, price rises modestly $(P_1$ to $P_e)$ when an excise tax is levied. Hence, the producer bears most of the tax burden. (b) If demand is inelastic, the price to the buyer increases substantially $(P_1$ to $P_i)$ and most of the tax is shifted to consumers.

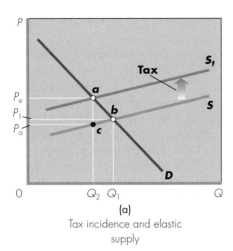

(a)
Tax incidence and elastic
supply

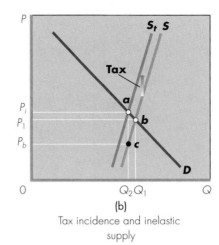

(b)
Tax incidence and inelastic
supply

Figure 18.4

Supply elasticity and the incidence of an excise tax. (a) With elastic supply, an excise tax results in a large price increase (P_1 to P_e) and the tax is therefore paid mainly by consumers. (b) If supply is inelastic, the price rise is small (P_1 to P_i) and sellers bear most of the tax.

Note also that the decline in equilibrium quantity ($Q_1 - Q_2$) is smaller when demand is more inelastic. This is the basis of our previous applications of the elasticity concept: Revenue-seeking legislatures place heavy excise taxes on liquor, cigarettes, automobile tires, telephone service, and other products whose demand is thought to be inelastic. Since demand for these products is relatively inelastic, the tax does not reduce sales by much, so the tax revenue stays high.

The second generalization is that, *with a specific demand, the more inelastic the supply, the larger is the portion of the tax borne by producers.* When supply is elastic (Figure 18.4a), the producers shift most of the tax ($P_e - P_1$) to consumers and bear only a small portion ($P_1 - P_a$) themselves. But where supply is inelastic (Figure 18.4b), the reverse is true: The major portion of the tax ($P_1 - P_b$) falls on sellers, and a relatively small amount ($P_i - P_1$) is shifted to buyers. The equilibrium quantity also declines less with an inelastic supply than it does with an elastic supply.

Gold is an example of a product with an inelastic supply and therefore one where the burden of an excise tax (such as an extraction tax) would mainly fall on producers. On the other hand, because the supply of baseballs is relatively elastic, producers would pass on to consumers much of an excise tax on baseballs.

Efficiency Loss of a Tax

We just observed that producers and consumers typically each bear part of an excise tax levied on producers. Let's now look more closely at the overall economic effect of the excise tax. Consider Figure 18.5, which is identical to Figure 18.2 but contains the additional detail we need for our discussion.

Tax Revenues   In our example, a $2 excise tax on wine increases its market price from $8 to $9 per bottle and reduces the equilibrium quantity from 15 million bottles to 12.5 million. Government tax revenue is $25 million (= $2 × 12.5 million bottles), an amount shown as the rectangle *efac* in Figure 18.5. The elasticities of supply and demand in this

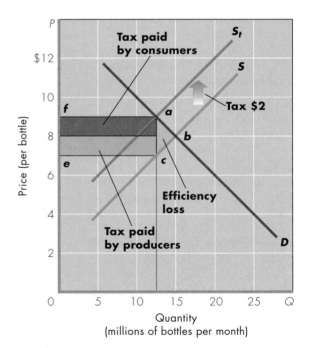

Figure 18.5

Efficiency loss of a tax.   The levy of a $2 tax per bottle of wine increases the price per bottle from $8 to $9 and reduces the equilibrium quantity from 15 million to 12.5 million. Tax revenue to the government is $25 million (area *efac*). The efficiency loss of the tax arises from the 2.5 million decline in output; the amount of that loss is shown as triangle *abc*.

case are such that consumers and producers each pay half this total amount, or $12.5 million apiece (= $1 × 12.5 million bottles). The government uses this $25 million of tax revenue to provide public goods and services. So this transfer of dollars from consumers and producers to government involves no loss of well-being to society.

Efficiency Loss

The $2 tax on wine does more than require consumers and producers to pay $25 million of taxes; it also reduces the equilibrium amount of wine produced and consumed by 2.5 million bottles. The fact that consumers and producers demanded and supplied 2.5 million more bottles of wine before the tax means that those 2.5 million bottles provided benefits in excess of their production costs. This is clear from the following analysis.

Segment *ab* of demand curve *D* in Figure 18.5 indicates the willingness to pay—the marginal benefit—associated with each of the 2.5 million bottles consumed before (but not after) the tax. Segment *cb* of supply curve *S* reflects the marginal cost of each of the bottles of wine. For all but the very last one of these 2.5 million bottles, the marginal benefit (shown by a point on *ab*) exceeds the marginal cost (shown by a point on *cb*). Not producing all 2.5 million bottles of wine reduces well-being by an amount represented by the triangle *abc*. The area of this triangle identifies the **efficiency loss of the tax** (also called the *deadweight loss of the tax*). This loss is society's sacrifice of net benefit, because the tax reduces production and consumption of the product below their levels of economic efficiency, where marginal benefit and marginal cost are equal.

Role of Elasticities

Most taxes create some degree of efficiency loss, but just how much depends on the supply and demand elasticities. Glancing back at Figure 18.3, we see that the efficiency loss area *abc* is greater in Figure 18.3a, where demand is relatively elastic, than in Figure 18.3b, where demand is relatively inelastic. Similarly, area *abc* is greater in Figure 18.4a than in Figure 18.4b, indicating a larger efficiency loss where supply is more elastic. *Other things equal, the greater the elasticities of supply and demand, the greater the efficiency loss of a particular tax.*

Two taxes yielding equal revenues do not necessarily impose equal costs on society. The government must keep this fact in mind in designing a tax system to finance beneficial public goods and services. In general, it should minimize the efficiency loss of the tax system in raising any specific dollar amount of tax revenue.

Qualifications

We must acknowledge, however, that there may be other tax goals as important as, or even more important than, minimizing efficiency losses from taxes. Here are two examples:

- **Redistributive goals**   Government may wish to impose progressive taxes as a way to redistribute income. The 10 percent excise tax the Federal government placed on selected luxuries in 1990 was an example. Because the demand for luxuries is elastic, substantial efficiency losses from this tax were to be expected. However, Congress apparently concluded that the benefits from the redistribution effects of the tax would exceed the efficiency losses.

  Ironically, in 1993 Congress repealed the luxury taxes on personal airplanes and yachts, mainly because the taxes had reduced quantity demanded so much that widespread layoffs of workers were occurring in those industries. But the 10 percent tax on luxury automobiles remained.

- **Reducing negative externalities**   The government may have intended the $2 tax on wine in Figure 18.5 to reduce the consumption of wine by 2.5 million bottles. It may have concluded that such consumption of alcoholic beverages produces certain negative externalities. Therefore, it might have purposely levied this tax to shift the market supply curve such that the price of wine increased and the amount of resources allocated to wine declined (as in Figure 18.3b). **(Key Question 9)**

Probable Incidence of U.S. Taxes

Let's look now at the probable incidence of each of the major sources of tax revenue in the United States.

Personal Income Tax

The incidence of the personal income tax generally is on the individual, because there is little chance for shifting it. But there might be exceptions. Individuals and groups who can control the price of their labor services may be able to shift a part of the tax. Doctors, dentists, lawyers, and other professional people who can readily increase their fees may do so because of the tax. Unions might regard personal income taxes as part of the cost of living and, as a result, strengthen their bargaining resolve for higher wages when personal income tax rates rise. If they are successful, they may shift part of the tax from workers to employers, who, by increasing prices, shift the wage increase to the public. Generally, however, the individual on whom the tax is initially levied bears the burden of the personal income tax. The same ordinarily holds true for payroll and inheritance taxes.

Corporate Income Tax The incidence of the corporate income tax is much less certain. The traditional view is that a firm currently charging the profit-maximizing price and producing the profit-maximizing output will have no reason to change price or output when a tax on corporate income (profit) is imposed. The price and output combination yielding the greatest profit before the tax will still yield the greatest profit after a fixed percentage of the firm's profit is taken away via an income tax. In this view, the company's stockholders (owners) must bear the burden of the tax through lower dividends or a smaller amount of retained earnings.

However, economists recognize that where a small number of firms control a market, producers may be able to shift part of their corporate income tax to consumers through higher prices and to resource suppliers through lower prices and wages. That is, some firms may be able to use their monopoly power as sellers and monopsony power as buyers to reduce the actual amount of the tax paid by their corporate stockholders.

There simply is no consensus among experts on the overall incidence of the corporate income tax. Stockholders, customers, and resource suppliers may share the tax burden in some unknown proportion.

Sales and Excise Taxes A *sales tax* is a general excise tax levied on a full range of consumer goods and services, whereas a *specific excise tax* is one levied only on a particular product. Sales taxes are usually transparent to the buyer, whereas excise taxes are often "hidden" in the price of the product. Sellers often shift both taxes partly or largely to consumers through higher product prices. There may be some difference in the extent to which sales taxes and excise taxes are shifted, however. Because a sales tax covers a much wider range of products than an excise tax, there is little chance for consumers to resist the price boosts that sales taxes entail. They cannot reallocate their expenditures to untaxed, lower-priced products. Therefore, sales taxes tend to be shifted from producers in their entirety to consumers.

Excise taxes, however, fall on a select list of goods. Therefore, the possibility of consumers turning to

substitute goods and services is greater. An excise tax on theater tickets that does not apply to other types of entertainment might be difficult to pass on to consumers via price increases. Why? The answer is provided in Figure 18.3a, where demand is elastic. A price boost to cover the excise tax on theater tickets might cause consumers to substitute alternative types of entertainment. The higher price would reduce sales so much that a seller would be better off to bear all, or a large portion of, the excise tax.

With other products, modest price increases to cover taxes may have smaller effects on sales. The excise taxes on gasoline, cigarettes, and alcoholic beverages provide examples. Here there are few good substitute products to which consumers can turn as prices rise. For these goods, the seller is better able to shift nearly all the excise tax to consumers. Example: Prices of cigarettes have gone up nearly in lockstep with the recent, substantial increases in excise taxes on cigarettes.

As indicated in Global Perspective 18.1, the United States depends less on sales and excise taxes for tax revenue than do several other nations.

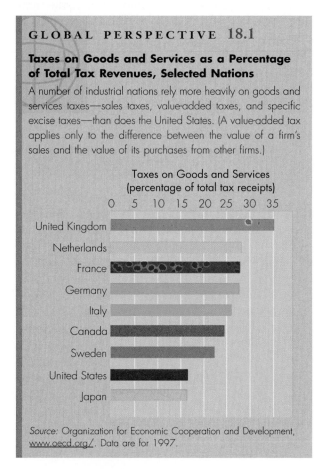

GLOBAL PERSPECTIVE 18.1

Taxes on Goods and Services as a Percentage of Total Tax Revenues, Selected Nations

A number of industrial nations rely more heavily on goods and services taxes—sales taxes, value-added taxes, and specific excise taxes—than does the United States. (A value-added tax applies only to the difference between the value of a firm's sales and the value of its purchases from other firms.)

Taxes on Goods and Services
(percentage of total tax receipts)

United Kingdom
Netherlands
France
Germany
Italy
Canada
Sweden
United States
Japan

Source: Organization for Economic Cooperation and Development, www.oecd.org/. Data are for 1997.

Table 18.2

The Probable Incidence of Taxes

Type of Tax	Probable Incidence
Personal income tax	The household or individual on which it is levied.
Corporate income tax	Some economists conclude the firm on which it is levied bears the tax; others conclude the tax is shifted, wholly or in part, to consumers and resource suppliers.
Sales tax	Consumers who buy the taxed products.
Specific excise taxes	Consumers, producers, or both, depending on elasticities of demand and supply.
Property taxes	Owners in the case of land and owner-occupied residences; tenants in the case of rented property; consumers in the case of business property.

Property Taxes   Many property taxes are borne by the property owner, because there is no other party to whom they can be shifted. This is typically true for taxes on land, personal property, and owner-occupied residences. Even when land is sold, the property tax is not likely to be shifted. The buyer will understand that future taxes will have to be paid on it, and this expected taxation would be reflected in the price the buyer is willing to offer for the land.

Taxes on rented and business property are a different story. Taxes on rented property can be, and usually are, shifted wholly or in part from the owner to the tenant by the process of boosting the rent. Business property taxes are treated as a business cost and are taken into account in establishing product price; hence such taxes are ordinarily shifted to the firm's customers.

Table 18.2 summarizes this discussion of the shifting and incidence of taxes.

The U.S. Tax Structure

Is the overall U.S. tax structure—Federal, state, and local taxes combined—progressive, proportional, or regressive? This question is difficult to answer, because estimates of the distribution of the total tax burden depend on the assumptions we make regarding tax incidence. The extent to which the various taxes are shifted and who bears the ultimate burden are subject to dispute. We have already noted, for example, that there is no consensus among experts as to who actually pays the corporate income tax.

But the majority view of experts can be summarized as follows:

- **The Federal tax system is progressive.**   In 1999, the 20 percent of families with the lowest income paid an average Federal tax rate (on Federal income, payroll, and excise taxes) of only 4.6 percent. The 20 percent with the highest income paid a 29.1 percent average rate; the top 10 percent paid 30.6 percent; and the top 1 percent paid 34.4 percent.[2]

    In 1999 the top 5 percent of all taxpayers paid 50 percent of the total Federal income tax collected. (Because wealthy Americans earn a disproportionately high amount of the total income, they pay a disproportionately high amount of the total tax. This would be true even for a proportional tax system.)

- **The state and local tax structures are largely regressive.**   As a percentage of income, property taxes and sales taxes fall as income rises. Also, state income taxes are generally less progressive than the Federal income tax.

- **The overall U.S. tax system is slightly progressive.**   This means that the tax system alone only slightly redistributes income from the wealthy to the poor. Caution: While the U.S. tax system does not substantially alter the distribution of income, the system of transfer payments does considerably reduce income inequality. Transfer payments to the poorest fifth of U.S. households almost quadruple their collective incomes. The tax-transfer system redistributes income by much more than does the tax system alone.

[2]Henry J. Aaron, William Gale, and James Sly, *Setting National Priorities: The 2000 Election and Beyond* (Washington, D.C.: Brookings Institution, 1999), p. 224. Congressional Budget Office data.

∎ The Issue of Freedom

We end our discussion of government decision making by considering a question that has an elusive answer: What is the relationship between individual freedom and the size and power of government? We make no attempt here to answer this question; we merely outline two opposing views.

The Conservative Position

Many conservative economists feel that, in addition to the economic costs of an expanding public sector, there is a cost in the form of diminished individual freedom. Here's why.

First, there is the "power corrupts" argument. "Freedom is a rare and delicate plant . . . history confirms that the great threat to freedom is the concentration of power . . . by concentrating power in political hands, [government] is . . . a threat to freedom."[3]

Second, we can be selective in the market system of the private sector, using our income to buy precisely what we choose and rejecting unwanted commodities. But, as noted previously, in the public sector—even assuming a high level of political democracy—conformity and coercion are inherent. If the majority decides in favor of certain governmental actions—to build a reservoir, to establish a system of national health insurance, to eliminate the Federal estate tax—the minority must conform. The "use of political channels, while inevitable, tends to strain the social cohesion essential for a stable society."[4] Because individuals through markets can render decisions selectively, the need for conformity and coercion is lessened and the "strain" is reduced when decisions are made in the marketplace. The scope of government should be strictly limited.

Finally, centralization of the power and activities of government into bigger government eliminates at least one check on government:

> If government is to exercise power, better in the county than in the state, better in the state than in Washington, D.C. If I do not like what my local community does, be it in sewage disposal, or zoning, or schools, I can move to another local community, and though few may take this step, the mere possibility acts as a check. If I

do not like what my state does, I can move to another. If I do not like what Washington imposes, I have few alternatives in this world of jealous nations.[5]

The Liberal Position

But liberal economists are skeptical of the conservative position. They say the conservative view is based on the **fallacy of limited decisions.** That is, conservatives implicitly assume that during any particular period there is a limited, or fixed, number of decisions to be made in the operation of the economy. If government makes more of these decisions in performing its functions, the private sector of the economy will necessarily have fewer decisions left to make "freely." Liberal economists regard this as fallacious reasoning. By sponsoring the production of public goods, government is extending the range of free choice by permitting society to enjoy goods and services that would not be available without governmental provision.

We can argue that it is largely through the economic functions of government that we have freed ourselves in some measure from ignorance, unemployment, poverty, disease, crime, discrimination, and other ills. In providing most public goods, government does not typically undertake production itself but, rather, purchases those goods through private enterprise. When government decides to build an interstate highway, private concerns are given the responsibility of making many specific decisions and choices in connection with carrying out this decision.

A leading U.S. economist has summarized the liberal view in these words:

> Traffic lights coerce me and limit my freedom. Yet in the midst of a traffic jam on the unopen road, was I really "free" before there were lights? And has the algebraic total of freedom, for me or the representative motorist or the group as a whole, been increased or decreased by the introduction of well-engineered stop lights? Stop lights, you know, are also go lights. . . . When we introduce the traffic light, we have, although the arch individualist may not like the new order, by cooperation and coercion created . . . greater freedom.[6]

---

[3]Milton Friedman, *Capitalism and Freedom* (Chicago: University of Chicago Press, 1962), p. 2.

[4]Ibid., p. 23.

[5]Ibid., p. 3.

[6]Paul A. Samuelson, "Personal Freedoms and Economic Freedoms in the Mixed Economy," in Earl F. Cheit (ed.), *The Business Establishment* (New York: Wiley, 1964), p. 219.

"Government Failure" in the News

The Media Continually Report Instances of the Special-Interest Effect, Limited and Bundled Choices, and Government Bureaucratic Inefficiency.

Examples:

- It took 23 Federal employees to approve the purchase of laptop computers bought for $3500 each. These computers were priced at $1500 each at the local retail computer store. (*Newsweek*)

- In 1997 the Federal government built a two-hole restroom facility costing $333,000 in a national recreation area in Pennsylvania. The toilets are $13,000 composting models that will not work in the winter. (Knight-Ridder Newspapers)

- In late 1998 Congress contracted to buy 20 C-130 transport planes for $1 billion that the Air Force had not requested. The planes will be built in the district of the then House Speaker (now retired), and many will be stationed in the home state of the Senate Majority Leader. (*New York Times*)

- As part of a radiation cleanup project in Pennsylvania in the late 1990s, the Environmental Protection Agency spent an average of $651,700 to custom-build 10 new houses for homeowners. This was in addition to the cleanup costs. The old houses were worth an average of $147,000 each. (Gannet News Service)

- New and past provisions requiring purchases from American firms added an estimated $5.5 billion to annual defense spending. For example, government departments and their contractors must buy all security locks for government buildings from a single firm, which is located in a state formerly represented by a powerful Senator. (Senator McCain's Congressional "Pork" Internet site)

- Emergency legislation in 1999 to finance the U.S. bombing in Yugoslavia and help rebuild homes destroyed by Hurricane Mitch contained several unrelated "riders" including the approval of an open-pit gold mine in Eastern Washington. The legislation overturned the decisions of two Federal agencies. (*Washington Post*)

- The omnibus appropriations bill for fiscal 1999 was 4000 pages long and weighed over 40 pounds. (Associated Press)

- Appropriations bills for 2000 contained hundreds of special projects that bypassed the appropriate budgetary review process. Just two examples: (a) $1.75 million for manure handling and distribution in five states (Mississippi, Iowa, Nebraska, Texas, and Arizona); (b) $5 million for the International Law Enforcement Center for the Western Hemisphere in Roswell, New Mexico. Also in the bills were hundreds of other special provisions. Examples: (c) language preventing the Coast Guard from decommissioning 11 harbor tugs that provide ice-breaking services for mid-Atlantic and New England ports; (d) language that prohibits the establishment of a national wildlife refuge in the Kankakee watershed in Indiana and Illinois; (e) designation of funding for the 2000 census as "emergency spending," which removed it from congressional spending limitations. (Senator McCain's Congressional "Pork" Internet site)

SUMMARY

1. Majority voting creates a possibility of (a) an under-allocation or an overallocation of resources to a particular public good and (b) inconsistent voting outcomes. the median-voter model predicts that, under majority rule, the person holding the middle position on an issue will determine the outcome of an election involving that issue.

2. Public choice theorists cite reasons why government might be inefficient in providing public goods and services. (a) There are strong reasons for politicians to support special-interest legislation. (b) Politicians may be biased in favor of programs with immediate and clear-cut benefits and difficult-to-identify costs and against programs with immediate and easily identified costs and vague or deferred benefits. (c) Citizens as voters and congressional representatives face limited and bundled choices as to public goods and services, whereas consumers in the private sector can be highly selective in their choices. (d) Government bureaucracies have less incentive to operate efficiently than do private businesses.

3. The benefits-received principle of taxation states that those who receive the benefits of goods and services provided by government should pay the taxes required to finance them. The ability-to-pay principle states that those who have greater income should be taxed more, absolutely and relatively, than those who have less income.

4. The Federal personal income tax is progressive. The corporate income tax is roughly proportional. General sales, excise, payroll, and property taxes are regressive.

5. Excise taxes affect supply and therefore equilibrium price and quantity. The more inelastic the demand for a product, the greater is the portion of an excise tax that is shifted to consumers. The greater the inelasticity of supply, the larger is the portion of the tax that is borne by the seller.

6. Taxation involves the loss of some output whose marginal benefit exceeds its marginal cost. The more elastic the supply and demand curves, the greater is the efficiency loss resulting from a particular tax.

7. Sales taxes normally are shifted to consumers; personal income taxes are not shifted. Specific excise taxes may or may not be shifted to consumers, depending on the elasticities of demand and supply. There is disagreement as to whether corporate income taxes are shifted. Property taxes on owner-occupied property are borne by the owner; those on rental property are borne by tenants.

8. The Federal tax structure is progressive; the state and local tax structure is regressive; and the overall tax structure is slightly progressive.

9. Conservatives believe that individual freedom shrinks as government grows in size or power; liberals believe it does not.

TERMS AND CONCEPTS

public choice theory	government failure	ability-to-pay principle	tax incidence
logrolling	special-interest effect	progressive tax	efficiency loss of a tax
paradox of voting	rent seeking	regressive tax	fallacy of limited decisions
median-voter model	benefits-received principle	proportional tax	

STUDY QUESTIONS

1. Explain how affirmative and negative majority votes can sometimes lead to inefficient allocations of resources to public goods. Is this problem likely to be greater under a benefits-received or under an ability-to-pay tax system? Use the information in Figure 18.1a and 18.1b to show how society might be better off if Adams were allowed to buy votes.

2. **Key Question** Explain the paradox of voting through reference to the accompanying table, which shows the ranking of three public goods by voters Larry, Curley, and Moe:

Public good	Rankings		
	Larry	Curley	Moe
Courthouse	2d choice	1st choice	3d choice
School	3d choice	2d choice	1st choice
Park	1st choice	3d choice	2d choice

3. **Key Question** Suppose there are only five people in a society and each favors one of the five highway construction options in Table 17.2 (include no highway construction as one of the options). Explain which of these highway options will be selected using a majority paired-choice vote. Will this option be the optimal size of the project from an economic perspective?

4. **Key Question** How does the problem of limited and bundled choice in the public sector relate to economic efficiency? Why are public bureaucracies alleged to be less efficient than private enterprises?

5. Explain: "Politicians would make more rational economic decisions if they weren't running for re-election every few years."

6. Distinguish between the benefits-received and the ability-to-pay principles of taxation. Which philosophy is more evident in our present tax structure? Justify your answer. To which principle of taxation do you subscribe? Why?

7. **Key Question** Suppose a tax is such that an individual with an income of $10,000 pays $2000 of tax, a person with an income of $20,000 pays $3000 of tax, a person with an income of $30,000 pays $4000 of tax, and so forth. What is each person's average tax rate? Is this tax regressive, proportional, or progressive?

8. What is meant by a progressive tax? A regressive tax? A proportional tax? Comment on the progressivity or regressivity of each of the following taxes, indicating in each case where you think the tax incidence lies: (*a*) the Federal personal income tax; (*b*) a 4 percent state general sales tax; (*c*) a Federal excise tax on automobile tires; (*d*) a municipal property tax on real estate; (*e*) the Federal corporate income tax.

9. **Key Question** What is the incidence of an excise tax when demand is highly inelastic? Elastic? What effect does the elasticity of supply have on the incidence of an excise tax? What is the efficiency loss of a tax, and how does it relate to elasticity of demand and supply?

10. **Advanced Analysis** Suppose the equation for the demand curve for some product X is $P = 8 - .6Q$ and the supply curve is $P = 2 + .4Q$. What are the equilibrium price and quantity? Now suppose an excise tax is imposed on X such that the new supply equation is $P = 4 + .4Q$. How much tax revenue will this excise tax yield the government? Graph the curves, and label the area of the graph that represents the tax collection "TC" and the area that represents the efficiency loss of the tax "EL." Briefly explain why area EL is the efficiency loss of the tax but TC is not.

11. **(Last Word)** How do the concepts of pork-barrel politics and logrolling relate to the items listed in the Last Word?

12. **Web-Based Question:** *Bureaucracy and inefficiency—the post office versus UPS* Some economists contend that public agencies generally are less efficient than private businesses. United Parcel Service (UPS) competes directly with the U.S. Postal Service for express mail and packages. Assume you need to send an express letter and a three-pound package from your address to either New York City or Los Angeles. On the basis of their interactive rate and options calculators at www.ups.com and www.usps.com, which service is more competitive as to price and delivery? Does a lower rate with greater delivery options mean greater efficiency? Why or why not?

13. **Web-Based Question:** *Federal Tax-Rate Cuts—Did They Occur?* In spring 2001 the Bush Administration proposed sizable cuts in personal income tax rates. The internal Revenue Service (IRS) provides current tax tables online at www.irs.ustreas.gov. Select Tax Info for You and Tax Tables. Compare the rates shown with the 2000 tax rates listed in Table 5.1 on page 87 of this book. Did Congress reduce Federal income tax rates? If so, update Table 5.1.

5

Microeconomic
Issues and Policies

19

Antitrust Policy and Regulation

IN THE SPIRIT of the TV show *Do You Want to Be a Millionaire?* try to answer these questions:

- Which one of the following companies did a Federal District Court find guilty of violating U.S. antitrust laws? (a) Napster, (b) Microsoft, (c) J. C. Nickels, (d) Colgate-Palmolive. Final answer?

- Business firms subject to *industrial regulation* are often called (a) unnatural monopolies, (b) monopolistic competitors, (c) monopsonists, (d) public utilities. Final answer?

- The requirement that businesses make reasonable accommodations for disabled workers and customers is an example of (a) antitrust policy, (b) industrial policy, (c) social regulation, (d) economies of scale. Final answer?

The answers, in order, are (b), (d), and (c). ■ The five chapters that constitute Part 5 examine selected microeconomic issues and policies. In this chapter we look at three sets of government policies toward business: antitrust policy, industrial regulation, and social regulation. **Antitrust policy** consists of the laws and government actions designed to prevent monopoly and promote competition. **Industrial regulation** consists of government regulation of firms' prices (or "rates") within selected industries. **Social regulation** is government regulation of the conditions under which goods are produced, the physical characteristics of goods, and the impact of the production and consumption of goods on society. ■ Then, in the four chapters that follow, we discuss issues and policies relating to agriculture, income inequality, labor markets (unions, discrimination, and immigration), and health care.

■ The Antitrust Laws

The underlying purpose of antitrust policy (antimonopoly policy) is to prevent monopolization, promote competition, and achieve allocative efficiency. Although all economists would agree that these are meritorious goals, there is sharp conflict of opinion about the effectiveness of U.S. antitrust policy. As we will see, antitrust policy over the years has been neither clear-cut nor consistent.

Historical Background

Just after the U.S. Civil War (1861–1865), local markets widened into national markets because of improved transportation facilities, mechanized production methods, and sophisticated corporate structures. In the 1870s and 1880s "trusts" (monopolies) emerged in several industries, including the petroleum, meatpacking, railroad, sugar, lead, coal, whiskey, and tobacco industries.

Firms often used questionable tactics to monopolize these industries and then charged monopoly prices to customers and extracted price concessions from resource suppliers. Farmers and owners of small businesses were particularly vulnerable to the power of large corporate monopolies and were among the first to oppose them. Consumers, labor unions, and economists were not far behind in their opposition.

The main economic case against monopoly is familiar to you from Chapter 11. Monopolists tend to produce less output and charge higher prices than would be the case if their industries were competitive. With pure competition, production occurs where $P = MC$. This equality represents an efficient allocation of resources because P measures the marginal benefit to society of an extra unit of output while marginal cost MC reflects the cost of an extra unit. When $P = MC$, society cannot gain by producing 1 more or 1 less unit of the product. In contrast, a monopolist maximizes profit by equating marginal revenue (not price) with marginal cost. At this $MR = MC$ point, price exceeds marginal cost, meaning that society would obtain more benefit than it would incur cost by producing extra units. There is an underallocation of resources to the monopolized product, and so the economic well-being of society is less than it would be with greater competition.

Government concluded in the late 1800s and early 1900s that market forces in monopolized industries did not provide sufficient control to protect consumers, achieve fair competition, and achieve allocative efficiency. So it instituted two alternative means of control as substitutes for, or supplements to, market forces:

- *Regulatory agencies* In the few markets where the nature of the product or technology creates a *natural monopoly*, the government established public regulatory agencies to control economic behavior.

- *Antitrust laws* In most other markets, social control took the form of antitrust (antimonopoly) legislation designed to inhibit or prevent the growth of monopoly.

Four particular pieces of Federal legislation, as refined and extended by various amendments, constitute the basic law relating to monopoly structure and conduct.

Sherman Act of 1890

The public resentment of trusts that emerged in the 1870s and 1880s culminated in the **Sherman Act** of 1890. This cornerstone of antitrust legislation is surprisingly brief and, at first glance, directly to the point. The core of the act resides in two provisions:

- *Section 1* Every contract, combination in the form of a trust or otherwise, or conspiracy, in restraint of trade or commerce among the several states, or with foreign nations is hereby declared to be illegal.

- *Section 2* Every person who shall monopolize, or attempt to monopolize, or combine or conspire with any person or persons, to monopolize any part of the trade or commerce among the several states, or with foreign nations, shall be deemed guilty of a felony (as later amended from "misdemeanor").

The Sherman Act thus outlawed *restraints of trade* (for example, collusive price fixing and dividing up markets) as well as *monopolization*. Today, the U.S. Department of Justice, the Federal Trade Commission, injured private parties, or state attorney generals can file antitrust suits against alleged violators of the act. The courts can issue injunctions to prohibit anticompetitive practices or, if necessary, break up monopolists into competing firms. Courts can also fine and imprison violators. Further, parties injured by illegal combinations and conspiracies can sue the perpetrators for *treble damages*—awards of three times the amount of the monetary injury done to them.

The Sherman Act seemed to provide a sound foundation for positive government action against business monopolies. However, early court interpretations limited the scope of the act and created ambiguities of law. It became clear that a more explicit statement of the government's antitrust sentiments was needed. The business community itself sought a clearer statement of what was legal and what was illegal.

Clayton Act of 1914

The **Clayton Act** of 1914 contained the desired elaboration of the Sherman Act. Four sections of the act, in particular, were designed to strengthen and make explicit the intent of the Sherman Act:

- Section 2 outlaws *price discrimination* when such discrimination is not justified on the basis of cost differences and when it reduces competition.
- Section 3 forbids **tying contracts,** whereby a producer would sell a desired product only on condition that the buyer acquires other products from the same producer.
- Section 7 prohibits the acquisition of stocks of competing corporations when the outcome would be less competition.
- Section 8 prohibits the formation of **interlocking directorates**—situations where a director of one firm is also a board member of a competing firm—in large corporations where the effect would be reduced competition.

The Clayton Act simply sharpened and clarified the general provisions of the Sherman Act. It also sought to outlaw the techniques that firms might use to develop monopoly power and, in that sense, was a preventive measure. Section 2 of the Sherman Act, by contrast, was aimed more at breaking up existing monopolies.

Federal Trade Commission Act of 1914

The **Federal Trade Commission Act** created the five-member Federal Trade Commission (FTC), which has joint Federal responsibility with the U.S. Justice Department for enforcing the antitrust laws. The act gave the FTC the power to investigate unfair competitive practices on its own initiative or at the request of injured firms. It can hold public hearings on such complaints and, if necessary, issue **cease-and-desist orders** in cases where it discovers "unfair methods of competition in commerce."

The **Wheeler-Lea Act** of 1938 gave the FTC the additional responsibility of policing "deceptive acts or practices in commerce." In so doing, the FTC tries to protect the public against false or misleading advertising and the misrepresentation of products. So the Federal Trade Commission Act, as modified by the Wheeler-Lea Act, (1) established the FTC as an independent antitrust agency and (2) made unfair and deceptive sales practices illegal.

Celler-Kefauver Act of 1950

The **Celler-Kefauver Act** amended the Clayton Act, Section 7, which prohibits a firm from merging with a competing firm (and thereby lessening competition) by acquiring its stock. Firms could evade Section 7, however, by instead acquiring the physical assets (plant and equipment) of competing firms. The Celler-Kefauver Act closed that loophole by prohibiting one firm from obtaining the physical assets of another firm when the effect would be reduced competition. Section 7 of the Clayton Act now prohibits anticompetitive mergers no matter how they are undertaken. **(Key Question 2)**

▌ Antitrust Policy: Issues and Impacts

The effectiveness of any law depends on how the courts interpret it and on the vigor of government enforcement. The courts have been inconsistent in interpreting the antitrust laws. At times, they have applied them vigorously, adhering closely to their spirit and objectives. At other times, their interpretations have rendered certain laws nearly powerless. The Federal government itself has varied considerably in its willingness to apply the antitrust laws. Administrations holding a laissez-faire philosophy about monopoly have sometimes ignored them or have reduced the budgets of the enforcement agencies.

Issues of Interpretation

Differences in judicial interpretations have led to vastly different applications of the antitrust laws. Two questions, in particular, have arisen: (1) Should the focus of antitrust policy be on monopoly behavior or on monopoly structure? (2) How broadly should markets be defined in antitrust cases?

Monopoly Behavior versus Monopoly Structure A comparison of two landmark Supreme Court decisions reveals two distinct interpretations of Section 2 of the Sherman Act as it relates to monopoly behavior and structure.

In the 1920 **U.S. Steel case** the courts applied the **rule of reason,** saying that not every monopoly is illegal. Only monopolies that "unreasonably" restrain trade—so-called "bad trusts"—are subject to antitrust action. The Supreme Court held in this case that size alone was not an offense. Although

U.S. Steel clearly possessed monopoly power, it was innocent of "monopolizing," because it had not resorted to illegal acts against competitors in obtaining that power nor had it unreasonably used its monopoly power.

In the **Alcoa case** of 1945 the courts touched off a 20-year turnabout. The Supreme Court sent the case to the U.S. court of appeals in New York because four of the Supreme Court justices had been involved with litigation of the case before their appointments. Led by Judge Hand the court of appeals held that, even though a firm's behavior might be legal, the mere possession of monopoly power (Alcoa held 90 percent of the aluminum ingot market) violated the antitrust laws. So Alcoa was found guilty of violating the Sherman Act.

These two cases point to a controversy in antitrust policy. Should a firm be judged by its behavior (as in the U.S. Steel case) or by its structure, or market share (as in the Alcoa case)?

"Structuralists" say that a firm with a very high market share will behave like a monopolist. Since the economic performance of such firms will be undesirable, they are legitimate targets for antitrust action. Changes in the structure of the industry, say, by splitting the monopolist into several smaller firms, will improve behavior and performance.

"Behavioralists" assert that the relationship between structure, behavior, and performance is tenuous and unclear. They feel a monopolized or highly concentrated industry may be technologically progressive and have a good record of providing products of increasing quality at reasonable prices. If a firm has served society well and has engaged in no anticompetitive practices, it should not be accused of antitrust violation just because it has an extraordinarily large market share. That share may be the product of superior technology, superior products, and economies of scale. "Why use antitrust laws to penalize efficient, technologically progressive, well-managed firms?" they ask.

Over the past 20 years, the courts have returned to the rule of reason, and most contemporary economists and antitrust enforcers reject strict structuralism. For instance, in 1982 the government dropped its 13-year-long monopolization case against IBM on the grounds that IBM had not unreasonably restrained trade. More recently, the government has made no attempt to break up Intel's monopoly in the sale of microcircuits for personal computers. And in prosecuting the Microsoft case (the subject of this chapter's Last Word), the Federal government made it clear that the behavior used by Microsoft to maintain and extend its monopoly, not the presence of its large market share, violated the Sherman Act. That is, the goverment in effect declared Microsoft "a bad monopoly."

The Relevant Market   Courts often decide whether or not market power exists by considering the share of the market held by the dominant firm. If the market is defined broadly to include a wide range of somewhat similar products, the firm's market share will appear small. If the market is defined narrowly to exclude such products, the market share will seem large. The Supreme Court's task is to determine how broadly to define relevant markets, and it has not always been consistent.

In the Alcoa case, the Court used a narrow definition of the relevant market: the aluminum ingot market. But in the **DuPont cellophane case** of 1956 the Court defined the market very broadly. The government contended that DuPont, along with a licensee, controlled 100 percent of the cellophane market. But the Court accepted DuPont's contention that the relevant market included all "flexible packaging materials"—waxed paper, aluminum foil, and so forth, in addition to cellophane. Despite DuPont's monopoly in the "cellophane market," it controlled only 20 percent of the market for "flexible wrapping materials." The Court ruled that this did not constitute a monopoly.

Issues of Enforcement: Tradeoffs among Goals

Promoting competition is only one of society's goals, and strict enforcement of the antitrust laws may sometimes conflict with some other goal. Below are three examples.

Balance of Trade   Large U.S. trade deficits have led the government to seek ways to increase exports. Antitrust actions that undo a merger between two chemical suppliers, break up a dominant aircraft manufacturer, or dissolve a microchip or software monopolist might weaken the targeted firm, thereby reducing its competitiveness and sales abroad. Consequently, U.S. exports might decline and thus increase the nation's trade deficit. Should government strictly enforce antitrust laws, even when significant amounts of U.S. exports are at stake? Or should the antitrust goal of efficiency be superseded by the goal of balancing exports and imports?

Defense Cutbacks
Cutbacks in defense spending over the past decade have reduced government purchases of military equipment, placing some major defense suppliers in financial jeopardy. Should the government allow defense firms to merge in order to bolster sagging profits and thus reduce the number of worker layoffs that would result if one or both firms went out of business? Or should the government block such mergers as violations of Section 7 of the Clayton Act and simply let the market sort matters out, perhaps through bankruptcies? In 1994 the Defense Department and antitrust regulators reached an informal agreement, easing the way for consolidation of the defense industry via mergers. Several large mergers quickly followed.

Emerging New Technologies
Occasionally, new technologies combine to create new products and services. A current example is the meshing of computers and communications technologies relating to the Internet. This interactive network has improved the communications capabilities of households, businesses, and governments across the globe. It also enables people to access unprecedented amounts of information and directly buy and sell goods and services. The emergence of this new technology has set off a spate of "megamergers" among entertainment companies, telecommunication companies, computer manufacturers, and software producers.

Should the government strictly enforce the Clayton Act to block some of those mergers, specifically ones that produce dominant firms and threaten to reduce competition? Or should the government temporarily suspend antitrust rules to encourage the restructuring of industries and speed the expansion of this new technology? Hastening the advance of Internet-related technologies might also increase U.S. exports of "electronic services" and decrease the large U.S. trade deficit.

Each of these enforcement tradeoffs, by itself, triggers controversy. Some argue that the gains from an antitrust policy must be weighed against the effects of the policy on conflicting objectives. Others contend that selective enforcement of antitrust laws dangerously interferes with the market process. Obviously, different policymakers and different administrations may view such considerations and tradeoffs differently.

Effectiveness of Antitrust Laws

Have the antitrust laws been effective? Although this question is difficult to answer, we can at least observe how the laws have been applied to existing market structures, mergers, price fixing, and tying contracts.

Existing Market Structures
On the basis of the rule of reason, the government generally has been lenient in applying antitrust laws to market structures that have already developed or to firms that have expanded their market shares "naturally." Generally, a firm will be sued only if it has more than 60 percent of the relevant market and there is evidence suggesting that it used abusive conduct to achieve, maintain, or extend its market dominance.

Since 1980 there have been two noteworthy actions aimed at altering existing market structures. The first was the 1982 out-of-court settlement between the government and AT&T. That firm was charged with violating the Sherman Act by engaging in anticompetitive actions designed to maintain its domestic telephone monopoly. As part of the settlement, AT&T agreed to divest itself of its 22 regional telephone-operating companies.

The second significant action was the Federal district court ruling in 2000 that Microsoft violated the Sherman Act through a series of unlawful actions designed to maintain and extend its monopoly of computer operating software. The court's remedy was to split Microsoft into two competing firms and to prohibit either of the two firms from engaging in certain anticompetitive behaviors. Microsoft has appealed the court decision to a higher court.

Mergers
The treatment of mergers, or combinations of existing firms, varies with the type of merger and its effect on competition.

Merger Types There are three basic types of merger, as represented in Figure 19.1. This figure shows two stages of production (the input stage and the output, or final-product, stage) for two distinct final-goods industries (autos and blue jeans). Each rectangle (A, B, C, . . . X, Y, Z) represents a particular firm.

A **horizontal merger** is *a merger between two competitors that sell similar products in the same geographic market.* In Figure 19.1 this type of merger is shown as a combination of glass producers T and U.

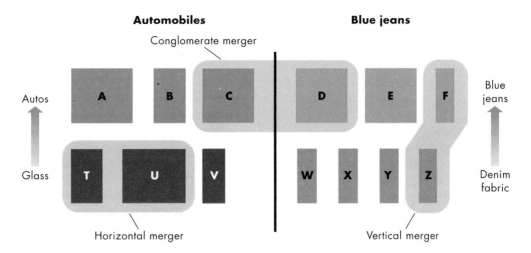

Figure 19.1

Types of mergers. Horizontal mergers (T + U) bring together firms selling the same product in the same geographic market; vertical mergers (F + Z) connect firms having a buyer-seller relationship; and conglomerate mergers (C + D) join firms in different industries or firms operating in different geographic areas.

Actual examples of such mergers include Chase Manhattan's merger with Chemical Bank, Boeing's merger with McDonnell Douglas, and Exxon's merger with Mobil.

A **vertical merger** is *a merger between firms at different stages of the production process.* In Figure 19.1, the merger between firm Z, a producer of denim fabric, and firm F, a producer of blue jeans, is a vertical merger. Vertical mergers are mergers between firms that have buyer-seller relationships. Actual examples of such mergers are PepsiCo's mergers with Pizza Hut, Taco Bell, and Kentucky Fried Chicken. PepsiCo supplies soft drinks to each of these fast-food outlets. (In 1997, PepsiCo spun off these entities into a separate company called Tricon Global Restaurants.)

A **conglomerate merger** is officially defined as *any merger that is not horizontal or vertical; in general, it is the combination of firms in different industries or firms operating in different geographic areas.* Conglomerate mergers can extend the line of products sold, extend the territory in which products are sold, or combine totally unrelated companies. In Figure 19.1, the merger between firm C, an auto manufacturer, and firm D, a blue jeans producer, is a conglomerate merger. Real-world examples of conglomerate mergers include the merger between Walt Disney Company (movies) and the American Broadcasting Company (radio

and television) and the merger between America Online (Internet service provider) and Time Warner (communications).

Merger Guidelines: The Herfindahl Index The Federal government has established very loose merger guidelines based on the Herfindahl index. Recall from Chapter 12 that this measure of concentration is the sum of the squared percentage market shares of the firms within an industry. An industry of only four firms, each with a 25 percent market share, has a Herfindahl index of 2500 ($= 25^2 + 25^2 + 25^2 + 25^2$). In pure competition, where each firm's market share is minuscule, the index approaches 0 ($= 0^2 + 0^2 + \cdots + 0^2$). In pure monopoly, the index for that single firm is 10,000 ($= 100^2$).

The U.S. government uses Section 7 of the Clayton Act to block horizontal mergers that will substantially lessen competition. It is likely to challenge a horizontal merger if the postmerger Herfindahl index would be high (above 1800) and if the merger has substantially increased the index (added 200 or more points). However, other factors, such as economies of scale, the degree of foreign competition, and the ease of entry of new firms, are also considered. Furthermore, horizontal mergers are usually allowed if one of the merging firms is suffering major and continuing losses. (This is one reason Boeing was allowed to acquire McDonnell

Douglas in 1996: MD was losing money in producing its commercial airplanes.)

In recent years, the Federal government has blocked several proposed horizontal mergers. For example, it blocked the mergers between Staples and Office Depot, two major office-supply retailers, and between WorldCom and Sprint, two competing telecommunications firms.

Most *vertical mergers* escape antitrust prosecution because they do not substantially lessen competition in either of the two markets. (In Figure 19.1 neither the Herfindahl index in the industry producing denim fabric nor the index in the blue jeans industry changes when firms Z and F merge vertically.) However, a vertical merger between large firms in highly concentrated industries may be challenged. For example, in 1999 the threat of FTC action spurred Barnes & Noble to abandon its merger with Ingram Book group, the nation's largest book wholesaler. The merger would have enabled Barnes & Noble to set the wholesale price of books charged to its direct retail competitors such as Borders and Amazon.com.

Conglomerate mergers are generally permitted. If an auto manufacturer acquires a blue jeans producer, no antitrust action is likely, since neither firm has increased its own market share as a result. That means the Herfindahl index remains unchanged in each industry. **(Key Question 5)**

Price Fixing   Price fixing is treated strictly. Evidence of price fixing, even by small firms, will bring antitrust action, as will other collusive activities such as scheming to rig bids on government contracts or dividing up sales in a market. In antitrust law, these activities are known as **per se violations;** they are "in and of themselves" illegal, and therefore are *not* subject to the rule of reason. To gain a conviction, the government or other party making the charge need show only that there was a conspiracy to fix prices, rig bids, or divide up markets, not that the conspiracy succeeded or caused serious damage to other parties. ☒ 19.1

Price-fixing investigations and court actions are common. Recent examples include:

- Archer Daniels Midland (ADM) and other agribusinesses admitted fixing the prices of an additive to livestock feed, a sweetener made from corn, and citric acid.
- ConAgra and Hormel agreed to pay more than $21 million to settle their roles in a nationwide price-fixing case involving catfish.

- Reebok agreed to pay nearly $10 million in damages to settle a lawsuit in which it was accused of fixing the minimum price retailers could charge for its footwear.
- The Justice Department fined UCAR International $110 million for scheming with competitors to fix prices and divide the world market for graphite electrodes that are used in steel mills.
- Seven international makers of common vitamins agreed to pay $1.2 billion to corporate buyers of bulk vitamins to settle a lawsuit that alleged the producers engaged in a 9-year conspiracy to artificially inflate the price of vitamins.

Tying Contracts   The Federal government has strictly enforced the prohibition of tying contracts, seeing them as a violation of either the Clayton Act or Section 1 of the Sherman Act. For example, it has stopped movie distributors from forcing theaters to "buy" the projection rights to a full package of films as a condition of showing a blockbuster movie. More recently, the government argued successfully that Microsoft illegally tied Internet Explorer (IE) to Windows and entered into contracts with personal computer makers that required them to feature IE, rather than Netscape Navigator, on the personal computer desktop.

What then can we conclude about the overall effectiveness of antitrust laws? Antitrust policy has not been very effective in restricting the rise of or in breaking up monopolies or oligopolies resulting from legally undertaken internal expansions of firms. But most economists do not deem that to be a flaw. The antitrust laws have been used more effectively against predatory or abusive monopoly, but that effectiveness has been diminished by the slow legal process and consequently long time between the filing of charges and the implementation of remedies. In contrast, antitrust policy *has* been effective in blocking blatantly anticompetitive mergers and in identifying and prosecuting price fixing and tying contracts.

Most economists conclude that, overall, U.S. antitrust policy has been moderately effective in achieving its goal of promoting competition and efficiency. Some, however, think that enforcement of antitrust laws has been too weak. Others believe that U.S. antitrust policy is anachronistic in an era of rapidly changing technology that continuously undermines existing monopoly power.

The Sherman Act of 1890 outlaws restraints of trade and monopolization; the Clayton Act of 1914 as amended by the Celler-Kefauver Act of 1950 outlaws price discrimination, tying contracts, anticompetitive mergers, and interlocking directorates.

The Federal Trade Commission Act of 1914 as bolstered by the Wheeler-Lea Act of 1938 created the Federal Trade Commission (FTC) and gave it authority to investigate unfair methods of competition and deceptive acts or practices in commerce.

"Structuralists" say highly concentrated industries will behave like monopolists; "behaviorists" hold that the relationship between industry structure and firm behavior is uncertain.

Enforcement of antitrust laws may be moderated when other government goals might be affected.

Currently, government treats existing monopoly relatively leniently, as long as it is not abusive; blocks most horizontal mergers between dominant, profitable firms in highly concentrated industries; and vigorously prosecutes price fixing and tying contracts engaged in by firms of all sizes.

■ Industrial Regulation

Antitrust policy assumes that society will benefit if monopoly is prevented from evolving or if it is dissolved where it already exists. We now return to a special situation in which there is an economic reason for an industry to be organized monopolistically.

Natural Monopoly

A **natural monopoly** exists when economies of scale are so extensive that a single firm can supply the entire market at a lower unit cost than could a number of competing firms. Clear-cut circumstances of natural monopoly are relatively rare, but such conditions exist for many *public utilities*, such as local electricity, water, natural gas, and telephone providers. As we discussed in Chapter 11, large-scale operations in some cases are necessary to obtain low unit costs and a low product price. Where there is natural monopoly, competition is uneconomical. If the market were divided among many producers, economies of scale would not be achieved and unit costs and prices would be higher than necessary.

There are two possible alternatives for promoting better economic outcomes where natural monopoly exists. One is public ownership, and the other is public regulation.

Public ownership or some approximation of it has been established in a few instances. Examples: the Postal Service, the Tennessee Valley Authority, and Amtrak at the national level and mass transit, water supply systems, and garbage collection at the local level.

But *public regulation*, or what economists call *industrial regulation*, has been the preferred option in the United States. In this type of regulation, government commissions regulate the prices (usually called "rates") charged by natural monopolists. Table 19.1 lists the two major Federal regulatory commissions and their jurisdictions. It also notes that all 50 states have commissions that regulate the intrastate activities and "utility rates" of remaining natural monopolies.

The economic objective of industrial regulation is embodied in the **public interest theory of regulation.** According to that theory, industrial regulation is necessary to keep a natural monopoly from charging monopoly prices and thus harming consumers and society. The goal of such regulation is to garner for society at least part of the cost reductions associated with natural monopoly while avoiding the restrictions of output and high prices associated with unregulated monopoly. If competition is inappropriate or impractical, society should allow or even encourage a monopoly but regulate its prices. Regulation should then be structured so that ratepayers benefit from the economies of scale—the lower per-unit costs—that natural monopolists are able to achieve.

Table 19.1

The Main Regulatory Commissions Providing Industrial Regulation

Commission (Year Established)	Jurisdiction
Federal Energy Regulatory Commission (1930)*	Electricity, gas, gas pipelines, oil pipelines, water-power sites
Federal Communications Commission (1934)	Telephones, television, cable television, radio, telegraph, CB radios, ham operators, etc.
State public utility commissions (50 states)	Electricity, gas, telephones

*Originally called the Federal Power Commission; renamed in 1977.

In practice, regulators seek to establish rates that will cover production costs and yield a "fair" return to the enterprise. The goal is to set price equal to average total cost so that the regulated firm receives a normal profit, as described in the "Regulated Monopoly" section of Chapter 11. In particular, you should carefully review Figure 11.9.

Problems with Industrial Regulation

There is considerable disagreement on the effectiveness of industrial regulation. Let's examine two criticisms.

Costs and Inefficiency

Costs and Inefficiency An unregulated firm has a strong incentive to reduce its costs at each level of output because that will increase its profit. The regulatory commission, however, confines the regulated firm to a normal profit or a "fair return" on the value of its assets. If a regulated firm lowers its operating costs, the rising profit eventually will lead the regulatory commission to require that the firm lower its rates in order to return its profits to normal. The regulated firm therefore has little or no incentive to reduce its operating costs.

Worse yet, higher costs do not result in lower profit. Because the regulatory commission must allow the public utility a fair return, the regulated monopolist can simply pass through higher production costs to consumers by charging higher rates. A regulated firm may reason that it might as well have high salaries for its workers, opulent working conditions for management, and the like, since the "return" is the same in percentage terms whether costs are minimized or not. So, although a natural monopoly reduces cost through economies of scale, industrial regulation fosters considerable X-inefficiency (Figure 11.7). Due to the absence of competition, the potential cost savings from natural monopoly may never actually materialize.

Perpetuating Monopoly A second general problem with industrial regulation is that it sometimes perpetuates monopoly long after the conditions of natural monopoly have evaporated.

Technological change often creates the potential for competition in at least some or all portions of the regulated industry. Examples: Trucks began competing with railroads; transmission of voice and data by microwave and satellites began competing with transmission over telephone wires; satellite television began competing with cable television; and cell phones began competing with regular phones. But spurred by the firms they regulate, and believing the regulated firms are natural monopolies, commissions often protect the regulated firms from new competition by either blocking entry or extending regulation to competitors. The rationale usually is that the competitors simply want to "skim the cream" from selected highly profitable portions of the regulated industry but do not want to offer the universal service required of the regulated firm. By losing the highly profitable portion of the business, the regulated firms would have to increase rates for services that do not pay their own way in order to continue to receive a fair rate of return on their assets.

But where regulators block entry or extend regulation to competitive firms, industrial regulation may perpetuate a monopoly that is no longer a natural monopoly and would otherwise erode. Ordinary monopoly, protected by government, may then supplant natural monopoly. If so, then the regulated prices may be higher than they would be with competition. The beneficiaries of outdated regulation are the regulated firms, their employees, and perhaps consumers of some services. The losers are all other consumers and the potential competitors that are barred from entering the industry.

Example: Regulation of the railroads by the Interstate Commerce Commission (ICC) was justified in the late 1800s and early 1900s. But by the 1930s, with the emergence of a network of highways, the trucking industry had seriously undermined the monopoly power of the railroads. That is, for the transport of many goods over many routes, railroad service was no longer a natural monopoly. At that time it would have been desirable to dismantle the ICC and let railroads and truckers, along with barges and airlines, compete with one another. Instead, in the 1930s the ICC extended regulation of rates to interstate truckers. The ICC remained in place until its elimination in 1996.

Second example: Until very recently, unregulated long-distance telephone companies such as AT&T and WorldCom have been prohibited from offering local telephone services in competition with regulated local and regional telephone companies. But the very fact that these and other firms wish to try to compete with regulated monopolies calls into question whether those local providers are in fact natural monopolies or, rather, are government-protected monopolies. **(Key Question 10)**

Legal Cartel Theory

The regulation of potentially competitive industries has produced the **legal cartel theory of regulation.** In place of having socially minded officials forcing regulation on natural monopolies to protect consumers, holders of this view see practical politicians "supplying" regulation to local, regional, and national firms that fear the impact of competition on their profits or even on their long-term survival. These firms desire regulation because it yields a legal monopoly that can guarantee a profit. Specifically, the regulatory commission performs such functions as blocking entry (for example, in local telephone service). Or, where there are several firms, the commission divides up the market much like an illegal cartel (for example, prior to airline deregulation, the Civil Aeronautics Board assigned routes to specific airlines). The commission may also restrict potential competition by enlarging the "cartel" (for example, the ICC's addition of trucking to its regulatory domain).

While private cartels are illegal and unstable and often break down, the special attraction of a government-sponsored cartel under the guise of regulation is that it endures. The legal cartel theory of regulation suggests that regulation results from the rent-seeking activities of private firms and the desire of politicians to be responsive (Chapter 18).

Proponents of the legal cartel theory of regulation note that the Interstate Commerce Commission was welcomed by the railroads and that the trucking and airline industries both supported the extension of ICC regulation to their industries, arguing that unregulated competition was severe and destructive.

Occupational licensing is a labor market application of the legal cartel theory. Certain occupational groups—barbers, dentists, hairstylists, interior designers, dietitians, lawyers—demand stringent licensing on the grounds that it protects the public from charlatans and quacks. But skeptics say the real reason may be to limit entry into the oc-

cupational group so that practitioners can receive monopoly incomes. It is not surprising to these skeptics that a recent study found that, other things equal, dental fees were about 15 percent higher and dentists' income 10 percent higher in states with the most restrictive licensing laws compared to states with the least restricitive laws. The quality of dentistry apparently was not affected.[1]

▍Deregulation

Beginning in the 1970s, the legal cartel theory, evidence of inefficiency in regulated industries, and the contention that the government was regulating potentially competitive industries all contributed to a wave of deregulation. Since then, Congress and some state legislatures have passed legislation that has deregulated in varying degrees the airline, trucking, banking, railroad, natural gas, electricity, and television broadcasting industries. Deregulation has also occurred in the telecommunications industry, where antitrust authorities dismantled the regulated monopoly known as the Bell System (AT&T). Deregulation in the 1970s and 1980s was one of the most extensive experiments in economic policy to take place during the last 50 years.

Controversy

Deregulation was controversial, and the nature of the controversy was predictable. Proponents of deregulation, basing their arguments on erosion of natural monopoly and the legal cartel theory, contended that deregulation would lower prices, increase output, and eliminate bureaucratic inefficiencies.

Some critics of deregulation, embracing the view of continued natural monopoly and the public interest theory, argued that deregulation would result in destructive price wars and eventual remonopolization of some of the deregulated industries by a single firm. They predicted higher prices, diminished output, and deteriorating service. Still other critics were concerned that deregulation would lead to industry instability and that vital services (for example, transportation) would be withdrawn from smaller communities. Still others stressed that as

---

[1]Morris Kleiner and Robert Kudrle, "Does Regulation Affect Economic Outcomes? The Case of Dentistry," *Journal of Law and Economics,* October 2000, pp. 547–582.

increased competition reduced the revenues of each firm, firms would lower their safety standards to reduce costs and remain profitable.

Outcomes of Deregulation

While there are still some critics of deregulation, most economists believe that deregulation has clearly benefited consumers and the economy. According to studies, deregulation of formerly regulated industries is now contributing more than $50 billion annually to society's well-being through lower prices, lower costs, and increased output.[2] Most of those gains are accruing in three industries: airlines, railroads, and trucking. Airfares (adjusted for inflation) have declined by about one-third, and airline safety has continued to improve. Trucking and railroad freight rates (again, adjusted for inflation) have dropped by about one-half. Significant efficiency gains have occurred in long-distance telecommunications, and there have been slight efficiency gains in cable television, stock brokerage services, and the natural gas industry. Moreover, deregulation has unleashed a wave of technological advances that have resulted in such new and improved products and services as fax machines, cellular phones, fiber-optic cable, microwave systems in communications, and the Internet.

The success of past deregulation has led to further calls for deregulation. The latest industry to begin the deregulation process is electricity. Deregulation is now occurring at the wholesale level, where firms are free to build generating facilities and sell electricity at market prices. The Federal government's goal is for all consumers to have a choice among competing power suppliers by 2010. Several states have now deregulated electricity rates and opened competition to alternative suppliers. Some have experienced lower electricity costs and rate reductions. But deregulation of wholesale electricity rates (but not retail rates) in California contributed to an energy crisis in the winter of 2001 and large financial losses for California electric utilities. It is too soon in the process to declare deregulation of electricity either a success or a failure.

---

[2]Clifford Winston, "Economic Deregulation: Days of Reckoning for Microeconomists," *Journal of Economic Literature*, September 1993, p. 1284; and Robert Crandall and Jerry Ellig, "Economic Deregulation and Consumer Choice," Center for Market Processes, Fairfax, Virginia.

QUICK REVIEW 19.2

■ Natural monopoly occurs where economies of scale are so extensive that only a single firm can produce the product at minimum average total cost.

■ The public interest theory of regulation says that government must regulate natural monopolies to prevent abuses arising from monopoly power. Regulated firms, however, have less incentive than competitive firms to reduce costs. That is, regulated firms tend to be X-inefficient.

■ The legal cartel theory of regulation suggests that some firms seek government regulation to reduce price competition and ensure stable profits.

■ Deregulation initiated by government in the past three decades has yielded large annual efficiency gains for society.

■ Social Regulation

The industrial regulation discussed in the preceding section has focused on the regulation of prices (or rates) in natural monopolies. But in the early 1960s a new type of regulation began to emerge. This *social regulation* is concerned with the conditions under which goods and services are produced, the impact of production on society, and the physical qualities of the goods themselves.

The Federal government carries out most of the social regulation, although states also play a role. In Table 19.2 we list the main Federal regulatory commissions engaged in social regulation.

Distinguishing Features

Social regulation differs from industrial regulation in several ways.

First, social regulation applies to far more firms than does industrial regulation. Social regulation is often applied "across the board" to all industries and directly affects more producers than does industrial regulation. For instance, while the industrial regulation of the Federal Energy Regulatory Commission (FERC) applies to a relatively small number of firms, Occupational Safety and Health Administration (OSHA) rules and regulations apply to firms in all industries.

Second, social regulation intrudes into the day-to-day production process to a greater extent than

Table 19.2

The Main Federal Regulatory Commissions Providing Social Regulation

Commission (Year Established)	Jurisdiction
Food and Drug Administration (1906)	Safety and effectiveness of food, drugs, and cosmetics
Equal Employment Opportunity Commission (1964)	Hiring, promotion, and discharge of workers
Occupational Safety and Health Administration (1971)	Industrial health and safety
Environmental Protection Agency (1972)	Air, water, and noise pollution
Consumer Product Safety Commission (1972)	Safety of consumer products

industrial regulation. While industrial regulation focuses on rates, costs, and profits, social regulation often dictates the design of products, the conditions of employment, and the nature of the production process. As examples, the Consumer Product Safety Commission (CPSC) regulates the design of potentially unsafe products, and the Environmental Protection Agency (EPA) regulates the amount of pollution allowed during production.

Finally, social regulation has expanded rapidly during the same period in which industrial regulation has waned. Between 1970 and 1980, the U.S. government created 20 new social regulatory agencies. More recently, Congress has established new social regulations to be enforced by existing regulatory agencies. For example, the Equal Employment Opportunity Commission, which is responsible for enforcing laws against workplace discrimination on the basis of race, gender, age, or religion, has been given the added duty of enforcing the Americans with Disabilities Act of 1990. Under this social regulation, firms must provide reasonable accommodations for qualified workers and job applicants with disabilities. Also, sellers must provide reasonable access for customers with disabilities.

The names of the regulatory agencies in Table 19.2 suggest the reasons for their creation and growth: As much of our society had achieved a fairly affluent standard of living by the 1960s, attention shifted to improvement in the nonmaterial quality of life. That focus called for safer products, less pollution, improved working conditions, and greater equality of economic opportunity.

The Optimal Level of Social Regulation

While economists agree on the need for social regulation, they disagree on whether or not the current level of such regulation is optimal. Recall that an activity should be expanded as long as its marginal benefit (MB) exceeds its marginal cost (MC). If the MB of social regulation exceeds its MC, then there is too little social regulation. But if MC exceeds MB, there is too much (review Figure 17.6). Unfortunately, the marginal costs and benefits of social regulation are not always easy to measure and therefore may be illusive. So ideology about the proper size and role of government often drives the debate over social regulation as much as, or perhaps more than, economic cost-benefit analysis.

In Support of Social Regulation Defenders of social regulation say that it has achieved notable successes and, overall, has greatly enhanced society's well-being. They point out that the problems that social regulation confronts are serious and substantial. According to the National Safety Council, about 5000 workers die annually in job-related accidents and 3.8 million workers suffer injuries that force them to miss a day or more of work. Air pollution continues to cloud major U.S. cities, imposing large costs in terms of reduced property values and increased health care expense. Numerous children and adults die each year because of poorly designed or manufactured products (for example, car tires) or tainted food (for example, *E. coli* in beef). Discrimination against some ethnic and racial minorities, persons with disabilities, and older workers reduces their earnings and imposes heavy costs on society.

Proponents of social regulation acknowledge that social regulation is costly. But they correctly point out that a high "price" for something does not necessarily mean that it should not be purchased. They say that the appropriate economic test should be not whether the costs of social regulation are high or low but, rather, whether the benefits of social regulation exceed the costs. After decades of neglect, they further assert, society cannot expect to cleanse the environment, enhance the safety of the workplace, and promote economic opportunity for all without incurring substantial costs. So statements about the huge costs of social regulation are irrelevant, say defenders, since the benefits are even greater. The public often underestimates those benefits, since they are more difficult to measure than costs and often become apparent only after some time has passed (for example, the benefits of reducing global warming).

Proponents of social regulation point to its many specific benefits. Here are just a few examples: It is estimated that highway fatalities would be 40 percent greater annually in the absence of auto safety features mandated through regulation. Compliance with child safety-seat and seat belt laws has significantly reduced the auto fatality rate for small children. The national air quality standards set by law have been reached in nearly all parts of the nation for sulfur dioxide, nitrogen dioxide, and lead. Moreover, recent studies clearly link cleaner air, other things equal, with increases in the values of homes. Affirmative action regulations have increased the labor demand for racial and ethnic minorities and females. The use of childproof lids has resulted in a 90 percent decline in child deaths caused by accidental swallowing of poisonous substances.

Some defenders of social regulation say there are many remaining areas in which greater regulation would generate net benefits to society. For instance, some call for greater regulation of the meat, poultry, and seafood industries to improve food safety. Others favor greater regulation of health care organizations and insurance companies to ensure "patients' rights" for consumers of health care services. Still others say that more regulation is needed to ensure that violent movies, CDs, and video games are not marketed to children.

Advocates of social regulation say that the benefits of such regulation are well worth the considerable costs. The costs are simply the price we must pay to create a hospitable, sustainable, and just society. **(Key Question 12)**

Criticisms of Social Regulation
Critics of social regulation contend that, in many instances, it has been expanded to the point where the marginal costs exceed the marginal benefits. In this view, society would achieve net benefits by cutting back on mettlesome social regulation. Critics say that many social regulation laws are poorly written, making regulatory objectives and standards difficult to understand. As a result, regulators pursue goals well

beyond the original intent of the legislation. Businesses complain that regulators often press for additional increments of improvement, unmindful of costs.

Also, decisions must often be made and rules formed on the basis of inadequate information. Examples: Consumer Product Safety Commission (CPSC) officials may make decisions about certain cancer-causing ingredients in products on the basis of limited laboratory experiments with animals. Or government agencies may establish costly pollution standards to attack the global-warming problem without knowing for certain whether pollution is the main cause of the problem. These efforts, say critics, lead to excessive regulation of business.

Moreover, critics argue that social regulations produce many unintended and costly side effects. For instance, the Federal gas mileage standard for automobiles has been blamed for an estimated 2000 to 3900 traffic deaths a year because auto manufacturers have reduced the weight of vehicles to meet the higher miles-per-gallon standards. Other things equal, drivers of lighter cars have a higher fatality rate than drivers of heavier vehicles.

Finally, opponents of social regulation say that the regulatory agencies may attract overzealous workers who are hostile toward the market system and "believe" too fervently in regulation. For example, the EPA staff allegedly sees all pollution as bad and all polluters as "bad guys." They have been accused of avoiding the challenge of trying to identify the optimal amount of pollution based on a careful analysis of marginal costs and marginal benefits.

Two Reminders

The debate over the proper amount of social regulation will surely continue. We leave both proponents and opponents of social regulation with pertinent economic "reminders."

There Is No Free Lunch
On the one hand, fervent supporters of social regulation need to remember that "there is no free lunch." Social regulation can produce higher prices, stifle innovation, and reduce competition.

Social regulation raises product prices in two ways. It does so directly because compliance costs normally get passed on to consumers, and it does so indirectly by reducing labor productivity. Resources invested in making workplaces accessible to disabled workers, for example, are not available for investment in new machinery designed to increase output per worker. Where the wage rate is fixed, a drop in labor productivity increases the marginal and average total costs of production. In effect, the supply curve for the product shifts leftward, causing the price of the product to rise.

Social regulation may have a negative impact on the rate of innovation. Technological advance may be stifled by, say, the fear that a new plant will not meet EPA guidelines or that a new medicine will require years of testing before being approved by the Food and Drug Administration (FDA).

Social regulation may weaken competition, since it usually places a relatively greater burden on small firms than on large ones. The costs of complying with social regulation are, in effect, fixed costs. Because smaller firms produce less output over which to distribute those costs, their compliance costs per unit of output put them at a competitive disadvantage with their larger rivals. Social regulation is more likely to force smaller firms out of business, thus contributing to the increased concentration of industry.

Less Government Is Not Always Better than More

On the other hand, fervent opponents of social regulation need to remember that less government is not always better than more government. While the market system is a powerful engine of producing goods and services and generating income, it has its flaws. Through social regulation gov-

ernment can clearly increase economic efficiency and thus society's well-being. Ironically, by "taking the rough edges off of capitalism," social regulation may be a strong pro-capitalist force. Properly conceived and executed, social regulation helps maintain political support for the market system. Such support could quickly wane should there be a steady drumbeat of reports of unsafe workplaces, unsafe products, discriminatory hiring, choking pollution, ill-served medical patients, and the like. Social regulation helps the market system deliver not only goods and services but also a "good society."

QUICK REVIEW 19.3

Social regulation is concerned with the conditions under which goods and services are produced, the effects of production on society, and the physical characteristics of the goods themselves.

Defenders of social regulation point to the benefits arising from policies that keep dangerous products from the marketplace, reduce workplace injuries and deaths, contribute to clean air and water, and reduce employment discrimination.

Critics of social regulation say uneconomical policy goals, inadequate information, unintended side effects, and overzealous personnel create excessive regulation, for which regulatory costs exceed regulatory benefits.

The Microsoft Antitrust Case

In 2000 a U.S. District Court Found Microsoft Guilty of Violating the Sherman Act. What Were the Charges and Specific Findings? What Remedy Did the Court Propose?

The Charges In May 1998 the U.S. Justice Department, 19 individual states, and the District of Columbia (hereafter, "the government") filed antitrust charges against Microsoft under the Sherman Antitrust Act. The government charged that Microsoft had violated Section 2 of the act by taking a series of unlawful actions designed to maintain its "Windows" monopoly. It also charged that some of those specific actions violated Section 1 of the Sherman Act.

Microsoft denied the charges, arguing that it had achieved its success through product innovation and lawful business practices. Microsoft argued that it should not be penalized for its superior foresight, business acumen, and technological prowess. It also pointed out that its monopoly was highly transitory because of rapid technological advance.

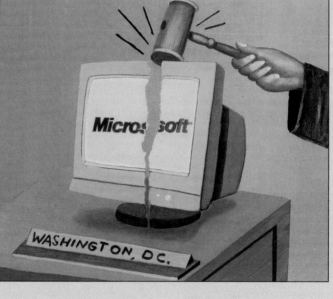

The Findings In June 2000 the district court ruled that the relevant market was that of software used to operate Intel-compatible personal computers (PCs). Microsoft's 95 percent share of that market clearly gave it monopoly power. The court pointed out, however, that being a monopoly is not illegal. The violation of the Sherman Act occurred because Microsoft used anticompetitive means to maintain and broaden its monopoly power.

According to the court, Microsoft feared that the success of Netscape's Navigator, which allowed people to browse the Internet, might allow Netscape to expand its software to include a competitive PC operating system—software that would threaten the Windows monopoly. It also feared that Sun's Internet applications of its Java programming language might eventually threaten Microsoft's Windows monopoly.

To counter these and similar threats, Microsoft illegally tied Internet Explorer (Microsoft's Internet browser) to Windows and provided Internet Explorer at no charge. It also signed contracts with PC makers that required them to feature Internet Explorer on the PC desktop and penalized companies that promoted software prod-

ucts that competed with Microsoft products. Moreover, it gave friendly companies coding that linked Windows to software applications and withheld it from companies featuring Netscape. Finally, under license from Sun, Microsoft developed Windows-related Java software that made Sun's own software incompatible with Windows.

The court concluded:

> Microsoft mounted a deliberate assault upon entrepreneurial efforts, that, left to rise or fall on their own merits could well have enabled the introduction of competition into the market for Intel-compatible PC operating systems. . . . More broadly, Microsoft's anticompetitive actions trammeled the competitive process through which the computer software industry generally stimulates innovation and conduces to the optimum benefit of consumers.*

The Remedy The district court ordered that Microsoft be split into two companies, one selling the Windows operating system and the other selling Microsoft applications (such as Word, Hotmail, MSN, PowerPoint, and Internet Explorer). Also, both companies are expressly prohibited from entering into joint ventures with one another, licensing or selling products to one another at more favorable terms than those given to other firms, or engaging in any of the activities that Microsoft had used to thwart competition and maintain its monopoly. Both companies are free, however, to develop new products that compete with each other, and both can derive those products from the intellectual property embodied in the common products existing at the time of the divestiture. The rights to Internet Explorer, however, reside with the applications company.

The Appeal Stunned by the verdict and the perceived harshness of the remedy, in late 2000 Microsoft appealed the district court decision to a U.S. court of appeals. Microsoft claimed that the government had not proved its case and that District Court Judge Thomas Jackson evidenced bias against Microsoft throughout the case. A decision from the appeals court was still pending at the time of publication of this book. We urge you to update the status of the Microsoft case via an Internet search.

United States v. Microsoft (Conclusions of Law), April 2000, p. 9.

Source: United States v. Microsoft (Conclusions of Law, April 2000; Final Order, June 2000) and Reuters News Service.

SUMMARY

1. The cornerstones of antitrust policy are the Sherman Act of 1890 and the Clayton Act of 1914. The Sherman Act specifies that "every contract, combination . . . or conspiracy in the restraint of interstate trade . . . is . . . illegal" and that any person who monopolizes or attempts to monopolize interstate trade is guilty of a felony.

2. The Clayton Act was designed to bolster and make more explicit the provisions of the Sherman Act. It declares that price discrimination, tying contracts, intercorporate stock acquisitions, and interlocking directorates are illegal when their effect is to reduce competition.

3. The Federal Trade Commission Act of 1914 created the Federal Trade Commission to investigate antitrust violations and to prevent the use of "unfair methods of competition." Empowered to issue cease-and-desist orders, the commission also serves as a watchdog agency over false and deceptive representation of products.

4. The Celler-Kefauver Act of 1950 prohibits one firm from acquiring the assets of another firm when the result will curtail competition.

5. Issues in applying antitrust laws include (a) determining whether an industry should be judged by its structure or by its behavior; (b) defining the scope and size of the dominant firm's market; and (c) balancing the gains from antitrust against other desirable goals, such as balancing exports and imports, consolidating the defense industry, and encouraging new technologies.

6. Antitrust officials are more likely to challenge price fixing, tying contracts, and horizontal mergers than they are to break up existing market structures. Nevertheless, antitrust suits by the Federal government led to the breakup of the AT&T monopoly and the proposed breakup of Microsoft.

7. The objective of industrial regulation is to protect the public from the market power of natural monopolies by regulating prices and quality of service.

8. Critics of industrial regulation contend that it can lead to inefficiency and rising costs and that in many instances it constitutes a legal cartel for the regulated firms. Legislation passed in the late 1970s and the 1980s has brought about varying degrees of deregulation in the airline, trucking, banking, railroad, and television broadcasting industries. Studies indicate that deregulation is producing sizable annual gains to society through lower prices, lower costs, and increased output. The latest U.S. industry to begin the deregulation process is electricity.

9. Social regulation is concerned with product safety, working conditions, and the effects of production on society. Whereas industrial regulation is on the wane, social regulation continues to expand. The optimal amount of social regulation occurs where MB = MC.

10. Those who support social regulation point to its numerous specific successes and assert that it has greatly enhanced society's well-being. Critics of social regulation contend that businesses are excessively regulated to the point where marginal costs exceed marginal benefits. They also say that social regulation often produces unintended and costly side effects.

TERMS AND CONCEPTS

antitrust policy
industrial regulation
social regulation
Sherman Act
Clayton Act
tying contracts

interlocking directorates
Federal Trade
    Commission Act
cease-and-desist order
Wheeler-Lea Act
Celler-Kefauver Act

U.S. Steel case
rule of reason
Alcoa case
DuPont cellophane case
horizontal merger
vertical merger

conglomerate merger
per se violations
natural monopoly
public interest theory of
    regulation
legal cartel theory of
    regulation

STUDY QUESTIONS

1. Both antitrust policy and industrial regulation deal with monopoly. What distinguishes the two approaches? How does government decide to use one form of remedy rather than the other?

2. **Key Question** Describe the major provisions of the Sherman and Clayton acts. What government entities are responsible for enforcing those laws? Are firms permitted to initiate antitrust suits on their own against other firms?

3. Identify the basic issue involved in the U.S. Steel, Alcoa, and DuPont cellophane cases. What issues in antitrust enforcement are implicit in these cases?

4. Explain how strict enforcement of the antitrust laws might conflict with (*a*) promoting exports to achieve a balance of trade, (*b*) easing the burdens of cutbacks in the defense industry, and (*c*) encouraging new technologies. Do you see any dangers in using selective antitrust enforcement as part of a broader policy to increase exports?

5. **Key Question** How would you expect antitrust authorities to react to:
   a. A proposed merger of Ford and General Motors.
   b. Evidence of secret meetings by contractors to rig bids for highway construction projects.
   c. A proposed merger of a large shoe manufacturer and a chain of retail shoe stores.
   d. A proposed merger of a small life-insurance company and a regional candy manufacturer.

6. Suppose a proposed merger of firms would simultaneously lessen competition and reduce unit costs through economies of scale. Do you think such a merger should be allowed?

7. In the 1980s, PepsiCo Inc., which then had 28 percent of the soft-drink market, proposed to acquire the Seven-Up Company. Shortly thereafter the Coca-Cola Company, with 39 percent of the market, indicated it wanted to acquire the Dr. Pepper Company. Seven-Up and Dr. Pepper each controlled about 7 percent of the market. In your judgment, was the government's decision to block these mergers appropriate?

8. "The antitrust laws tend to penalize efficiently managed firms." Do you agree? Why or why not?

9. "The social desirability of any particular firm should be judged not on the basis of its market share but on the basis of its conduct and performance." Make a counterargument, referring to the monopoly model in your statement.

10. **Key Question** What types of industry, if any, should be subjected to industrial regulation? What specific problems does industrial regulation entail?

11. In view of the problems involved in regulating natural monopolies, compare socially optimal (marginal-cost) pricing and fair-return pricing by referring again to

Figure 11.9. Assuming that a government subsidy might be used to cover any loss resulting from marginal-cost pricing, which pricing policy would you favor? Why? What problems might such a subsidy entail?

12. **Key Question** How does social regulation differ from industrial regulation? What types of benefits and costs are associated with social regulation?

13. Use economic analysis to explain why the optimal amount of product safety may be less than the amount that would totally eliminate risks of accidents and deaths. Use automobiles as an example.

14. **(Last Word)** Under what law and on what basis did the Federal government find Microsoft guilty of violating the antitrust laws? What was the government's proposed remedy? In mid-2000 Microsoft appealed the district court decision to a higher court. Update the Microsoft story, using an Internet search engine. What is the current status of that appeal? Is it still pending? Did Microsoft win its appeal? Or was the district court's decision upheld?

15. **Web-Based Question:** *Enforcement of antitrust laws—who is responsible?* The U.S. antitrust laws are available at www.law.cornell.edu/uscode/15/ch1.html. Both the Federal Trade Commission's Bureau of Competition (www.ftc.gov/ftc/antitrust.htm) and the Antitrust Division of the Department of Justice (www.usdoj.gov/atr/index.html) enforce these laws. How do those agencies prevent duplication of effort? What are their current antitrust activities? Are any of those activities of major significance?

16. **Web-Based Question:** *The Consumer Product Safety Commission—what is it and what does it do?* What are the major functions of the Consumer Product Safety Commission (www.cpsc.gov)? What products are the subjects of the latest CPSC press release? Identify two product categories of interest to you from Recalls by Product. List three specific product recalls for each of your two product categories. What products are covered by other government agencies and not by the CPSC? List a relatively recent major product recall relating to the National Highway Traffic Safety Administration.

20

Agriculture
Economics and Policy

IF YOU EAT, you are part of agriculture! In the United States, agriculture is economically important for a number of reasons:

■ Agriculture is one of the nation's largest industries. Consumers spend about 14 percent of their personal consumption expenditures on food. Gross farm income was about $245 billion in 2000.

■ Agriculture is an industry that, in the absence of government farm programs, is a real-world example of the pure-competition model (Chapter 10). The industry consists of many price-taking firms selling virtually standardized products and can be understood by applying the supply and demand tools of competitive markets.

■ Agriculture provides evidence of the intended and unintended effects of government policies that interfere with the forces of supply and demand.

■ Farm policies are excellent illustrations of Chapter 31's special-interest effect and rent-seeking behavior.

■ Agriculture reflects the increasing globalization of markets. In recent decades the economic ups and downs of U.S. agriculture have been closely tied to American access to world markets. In 1999, U.S. farmers produced 46 percent of the world's soybeans, 40 percent of its corn, and 16 percent of its cotton.

These realities justify a full chapter on agriculture. Specifically, we want to examine the problems in agriculture that have resulted in government intervention, the types and outcomes of that intervention, and recent major changes in farm policy.

■ Economics of Agriculture

Over the years, U.S. farmers have faced severely fluctuating prices and periodically low incomes. Agriculture has always been a risky and difficult business. There are actually two separate problems: the **short-run farm problem** of year-to-year fluctuations of farm prices and incomes, and the **long-run farm problem** of the declining agricultural industry.

Short-Run Problem: Price and Income Instability

The short-run farm problem is the result of (1) an inelastic demand for agricultural products, combined with (2) fluctuations in farm output and (3) shifts of the demand curve for farm products.

Inelastic Demand for Agricultural Products

In industrially advanced economies, the price elasticity of demand for agricultural products is low. For farm products in the aggregate, the elasticity coefficient is between .20 and .25. These figures suggest that the prices of agricultural products would have to fall by 40 to 50 percent for consumers to increase their purchases by a mere 10 percent. Consumers apparently put a low value on additional farm output compared with the value they put on additional units of alternative goods.

Why is this so? Recall that the basic determinant of elasticity of demand is substitutability. When the price of one product falls, the consumer tends to substitute that product for other products whose prices have not fallen. But in relatively wealthy societies this "substitution effect" is very modest for food. Although people may eat more, they do not switch from three meals a day to, say, five or six meals a day in response to a decline in the relative prices of farm products. Real biological factors constrain an individual's capacity to substitute food for other products.

The inelasticity of agricultural demand is also related to diminishing marginal utility. In a high-income economy, the population is generally well fed and well clothed; it is relatively saturated with the food and fiber of agriculture. Consequently, additional farm products are subject to rapidly diminishing marginal utility. So it takes very large price cuts to induce small increases in food and fiber consumption.

Fluctuations in Output   Farm output tends to fluctuate from year to year, mainly because farmers have limited control over their output. Floods, droughts, unexpected frost, insect damage, and similar disasters can mean poor crops, while an excellent growing season means bumper crops. Such natural phenomena are beyond the control of farmers, yet those phenomena exert an important influence on output.

In addition to natural phenomena, the highly competitive nature of agriculture makes it difficult for farmers to form huge combinations to control production. If the thousands of widely scattered and independent producers happened to plant an unusually large or an abnormally small portion of their land one year, an extra-large or a very small farm output would result even if the growing season were normal.

Curve D in Figure 20.1 suggests the inelastic demand for agricultural products. Combining that inelastic demand with the instability of farm production, we can see why farm prices and incomes are unstable. Even if the market demand for agricultural products remains fixed at D, its price inelasticity will magnify small changes in output into relatively large changes in farm prices and income. For example, suppose that a "normal" crop of Q_n results in a "nor-

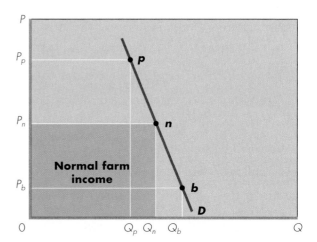

Figure 20.1

The effect of output changes on farm prices and income. Because of the inelasticity of demand for farm products, a relatively small change in output (from Q_n to Q_p or Q_b) will cause a relatively large change in farm prices (from P_n to P_p or P_b). Farm income will change from the taupe area to OP_ppQ_p or OP_bbQ_b.

mal" price of P_n and a "normal" farm income represented by the taupe rectangle. A bumper crop or a poor crop will cause large deviations from these normal prices and incomes because of the inelasticity of demand.

If a good growing season occurs, the resulting bumper crop of Q_b will reduce farm income to that of area $0P_bbQ_b$. When demand is inelastic, an increase in the quantity sold will be accompanied by a more-than-proportionate decline in price. The net result is that total revenue, that is, total farm income, will decline disproportionately.

Similarly, a poor crop caused by, say, drought will boost total farm income to that represented by area $0P_ppQ_p$. A decline in output will cause a more-than-proportionate increase in price and in income when demand is inelastic. Ironically, for farmers as a group, a poor crop may be a blessing, and a bumper crop a hardship. Conclusion: With a stable market demand for farm products, the inelasticity of that demand will turn relatively small changes in output into relatively larger changes in farm prices and income.

Fluctuations in Demand

The third factor in the short-run instability of farm income results from shifts in the demand curve for agricultural products. Suppose that somehow agricultural output is stabilized at the "normal" level of Q_n in Figure 20.2. Now, because of the inelasticity of the demand for farm products, short-run changes in the demand for those products will cause markedly different prices and incomes to be associated with this fixed level of output.

A slight drop in demand from D_1 to D_2 will reduce farm income from area $0P_1aQ_n$ to $0P_2bQ_n$. So a relatively small decline in demand gives farmers significantly less income for the same amount of farm output. Conversely, a slight increase in demand—as from D_2 to D_1—provides a sizable increase in farm income for the same volume of output. Again, large price and income changes occur because demand is inelastic.

It is tempting to argue that the sharp declines in farm prices that accompany a decrease in demand will cause many farmers to close down in the short run, reducing total output and alleviating the price and income declines. But farm production is relatively insensitive to price changes in the short run because farmers' fixed costs are high compared with their variable costs.

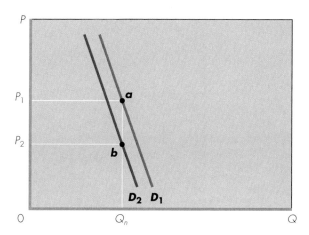

Figure 20.2

The effect of demand shifts on farm prices and income.   Because of the highly inelastic demand for agricultural products, a small shift in demand (from D_1 to D_2) will cause drastically different levels of farm prices (P_1 to P_2) and farm income (area $0P_1aQ_n$ to area $0P_2bQ_n$) to be associated with a fixed level of production Q_n.

Interest, rent, tax, and mortgage payments on land, buildings, and equipment are the major costs faced by the farmer. These are fixed charges. Furthermore, the labor supply of farmers and their families can also be regarded as a fixed cost. As long as they stay on their farms, farmers cannot reduce their costs by firing themselves. Their variable costs are the costs of the small amounts of extra help they may employ, as well as expenditures for seed, fertilizer, and fuel. As a result of their high proportion of fixed costs, farmers are usually better off working their land even when they are losing money, since they would lose much more by shutting down their operations for the year. Only in the long run will it make sense for them to exit the industry.

But why is agricultural demand unstable? The major source of demand volatility in U.S. agriculture springs from its dependence on world markets. As we show in Figure 20.3, that dependency has increased since 1950. The figure also reveals that, as a percentage of total U.S. farm output, farm exports are quite unstable.

The incomes of U.S. farmers are sensitive to changes in weather and crop production in other countries: Better crops abroad mean less foreign demand for U.S. farm products. Similarly, cyclical

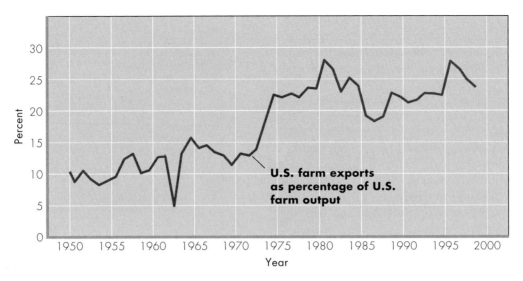

Figure 20.3

U.S. farm exports as a percentage of farm output, 1950–1999.   Exports of farm output have increased as a percentage of total farm output in the United States. This percentage, however, has been quite variable, contributing greatly to the instability of the demand for U.S. farm output.

Source: U.S. Department of Agriculture and Federal Reserve Bank of St. Louis.

fluctuations in incomes in Europe or Southeast Asia, for example, may shift the demand for U.S. farm products. Changes in foreign economic policies may also change demand. For instance, if the nations of western Europe decide to provide their farmers with greater protection from foreign competition, U.S. farmers will have less access to those markets and demand for U.S. farm exports will fall.

International politics also add to demand instability. Changing political relations between the United States and China and the United States and Russia have boosted exports to those countries in some periods and reduced them in others. Changes in the international value of the dollar may also be critical. Depreciation of the dollar increases the demand for U.S. farm products (which become cheaper to foreigners), whereas appreciation of the dollar diminishes foreign demand for U.S. farm products.

To summarize: The increasing importance of exports has amplified the short-run instability of the demand for U.S. farm products. Farm exports are affected not only by weather, income fluctuations, and economic policies abroad but also by international politics and changes in the international value of the dollar. (**Key Question 1**)

Figure 20.4 shows U.S. agricultural prices for cattle, hogs, corn, and wheat from 1950 to 1998.

The short-run problem of price volatility is clearly evident. So too is the long-run problem of generally declining farm prices.

Long-Run Problem: A Declining Industry

Two other characteristics of agricultural markets explain why agriculture has been a declining industry:

- Over time, the *supply* of farm products has increased rapidly because of technological progress.
- The *demand* for farm products has increased slowly, because it is inelastic with respect to income.

Let's examine each of these supply and demand forces.

Technology and Supply Increases   A rapid rate of technological advance has significantly increased the supply of agricultural products. This technological progress has many roots: the mechanization of farms, improved techniques of land management, soil conservation, irrigation, development of hybrid crops, availability of improved fertilizers and insecticides, polymer-coated seeds, and improvements in the breeding and care of livestock. The amount of capital used per farmworker

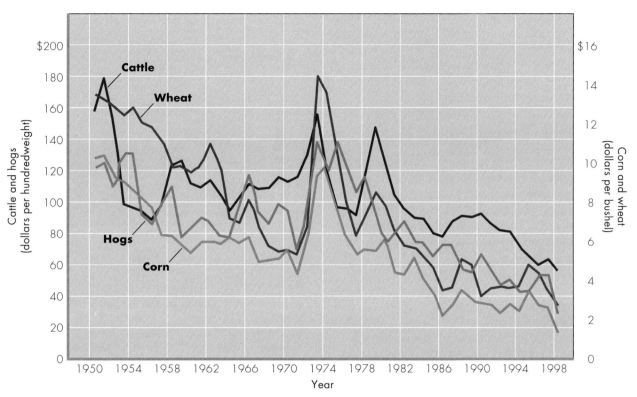

Figure 20.4

Inflation-adjusted U.S. agricultural prices, selected commodities, 1950–1998. Inflation-adjusted U.S. prices for cattle, hogs, corn, and wheat during the second half of the twentieth century reflect both volatility and general decline.

Source: Federal Reserve Bank of Minneapolis.

increased 15 times between 1930 and 1980, permitting a fivefold increase in the amount of land cultivated per farmer. The simplest measure of these advances is the increasing number of people a single farmer's output will support. In 1820 each farmworker produced enough food and fiber to support 4 people; by 1947, about 13. By 2000 each farmer produced enough to support 106 people. Unquestionably, the physical volume of farm output per unit of farm labor in agriculture has risen spectacularly. Over the last 50 years, this physical productivity in agriculture has advanced twice as fast as that in the nonfarm economy.

Most of the technological advances in agriculture have *not* been initiated by farmers but, rather, are the result of government-sponsored programs of research and education and the initiative of farm machinery producers. Land-grant colleges, experiment stations, county agents of the Agricultural Extension Service, educational pamphlets issued by

the USDA, and the research departments of farm machinery, pesticide, and fertilizer producers have been the primary sources of technological advance in U.S. agriculture.

Lagging Demand Increases in demand for agricultural products, however, have failed to keep pace with technologically created increases in the supply of the products. The reason lies in the two major determinants of agricultural demand: income and population.

Income-Inelastic Demand In developing countries, consumers must devote most of their meager incomes to agricultural products—food and clothing—to sustain themselves. But as income expands beyond subsistence and the problem of hunger diminishes, consumers increase their outlays on food at ever-declining rates. Once consumers' stomachs are filled, they turn to the amenities of life that manufacturing and services, not agriculture, provide. Economic growth in the United States has boosted average per capita income far beyond the level of subsistence. As a result, increases in the incomes of U.S. consumers now produce less-than-proportionate increases in spending on farm products.

The demand for farm products in the United States is *income-inelastic;* it is quite insensitive to increases in income. Estimates indicate that a 10 percent increase in real per capita after-tax income produces about a 2 percent increase in consumption of farm products. That means a coefficient of income elasticity of .2 (= .02/.10). So as the incomes of Americans rise, the demand for farm products increases far less rapidly than the demand for products in general.

Population Growth Once a certain income level has been reached, each consumer's intake of food and fiber becomes relatively fixed. Thus subsequent increases in demand depend directly on growth in the number of consumers. In most advanced nations, including the United States, the demand for farm products increases at a rate roughly equal to the rate of population growth. Because U.S. population growth has not been rapid, the increase in U.S. demand for farm products has not kept pace with the rapid growth of farm output.

Graphical Portrayal The combination of an inelastic and slowly increasing demand for agricultural products with a rapidly increasing supply puts strong downward pressure on farm prices and income. Figure 20.5 shows a large increase in agricultural supply accompanied by a very modest increase in demand. Because of the inelasticity of demand, those modest shifts result in a sharp decline in farm prices, accompanied by a relatively small increase in output. So farm income declines. On the graph, we see that farm income before the increases in demand and supply (measured by rectangle $0P_1aQ_1$) exceeds farm income after those increases ($0P_2bQ_2$). Because of an inelastic demand for farm products, an increase in supply of such products relative to demand creates persistent downward pressure on farm income.

Consequences The actual consequences over time have been those predicted by the pure-competition model. Because of the demand and supply conditions just outlined, many small, high-cost farms that cannot benefit from scale economies or productivity gains cannot operate profitably. In

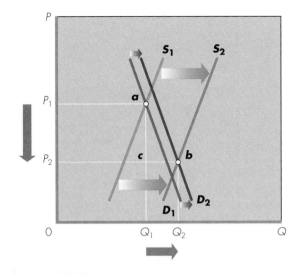

Figure 20.5

A graphical depiction of the long-run U.S. farm problem. In the long run, increases in the demand for U.S. farm products (from D_1 to D_2) have not kept pace with the increases in supply (from S_1 to S_2) that technological advances have permitted. Because agricultural demand is inelastic, these shifts have tended to depress farm prices (from P_1 to P_2) and reduce farm income (from $0P_1aQ_1$ to $0P_2bQ_2$) while increasing output only modestly (from Q_1 to Q_2).

the long run, financial losses in agriculture have triggered a massive exit of workers to other sectors of the economy, as shown by Table 20.1. They have also caused a major consolidation of smaller farms into larger ones. A person farming, say, 240 acres of

Table 20.1

U.S. Farm Employment and Number of Farms, 1950–1999

Year	Farm Employment*		Number of Farms, Thousands
	In Millions of People	As Percentage of Total Employment	
1950	9.9	17	5388
1960	7.1	11	3962
1970	4.5	6	2954
1980	3.7	4	2440
1990	2.9	2	2146
1999	3.0	2	2194

*Includes self-employed farmers, unpaid farmworkers, and hired farmworkers.
Sources: U.S. Department of Agriculture, Economic Research Service, www.usda.gov/nass, and U.S. Department of Commerce, Census Bureau, www.census.gov/.

corn three decades ago is today likely to be farming two or three times that number of acres. Huge corporate firms called **agribusinesses** have emerged in some areas of farming such as potatoes, beef, fruits, vegetables, and poultry.

Traditionally, the income of farm households was far below that of nonfarm households. But that has changed in the past decade. Outmigration and consolidation has boosted net farm income *per farm household*, as has the increasing number of members of farm households who are taking jobs in nearby towns and cities. As a result, the average income of farm households has increased relative to the income of nonfarm households. Presently, the average incomes of the two groups are very similar. (**Key Question 3**)

(As Global Perspective 20.1 shows, poor nations have much higher percentages of their labor forces in agriculture than do the United States and other industrialized nations.)

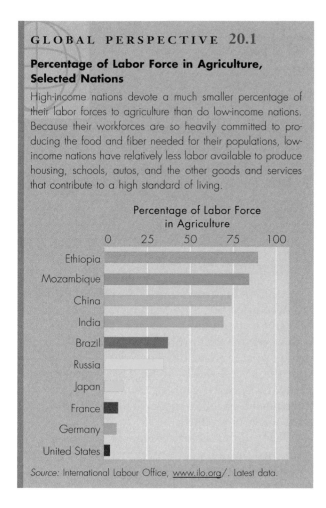

GLOBAL PERSPECTIVE 20.1

Percentage of Labor Force in Agriculture, Selected Nations

High-income nations devote a much smaller percentage of their labor forces to agriculture than do low-income nations. Because their workforces are so heavily committed to producing the food and fiber needed for their populations, low-income nations have relatively less labor available to produce housing, schools, autos, and the other goods and services that contribute to a high standard of living.

Percentage of Labor Force in Agriculture

Source: International Labour Office, www.ilo.org/. Latest data.

QUICK REVIEW 20.1

■ Agricultural prices and incomes are volatile in the short run because an inelastic demand converts small changes in farm output and demand into relatively larger changes in prices and income.

■ Technological progress has generated large increases in the supply of farm products over time.

■ Increases in demand for farm products have been modest in the United States, because demand is inelastic with respect to income and because population growth has been modest.

■ The combination of large increases in supply and small increases in demand has made U.S. agriculture a declining industry.

■ Economics of Farm Policy

The U.S. government has subsidized agriculture since the 1930s with a "farm program" that includes (1) support for farm prices, income, and output; (2) soil and water conservation; (3) agricultural research; (4) farm credit; (5) crop insurance; and (6) subsidized sale of farm products in world markets. However, the typical farmer and the average politician both have viewed the farm program as primarily a program to prop up prices and income, and it is this "price-support" aspect of farm policy that we will explore.

This topic is particularly timely, because in 1996 Congress abandoned 60 years of price supports for wheat, feed grains, cotton, and rice. (Price supports for peanuts, sugar, and tobacco remain, however). To understand the impact of that legislation, and its effects, we need to understand the purposes and outcomes of farm subsidies. Between 1990 and 1999, U.S. farmers received an average of $8 billion of subsidies each year. (As indicated in Global Perspective 20.2, farm subsidies are common in many nations.)

Rationale for Farm Subsidies

A variety of arguments have been made to justify farm subsidies over the decades:

■ Although farm products are necessities of life, many farmers have relatively low incomes, so they should receive higher prices and incomes through public help.

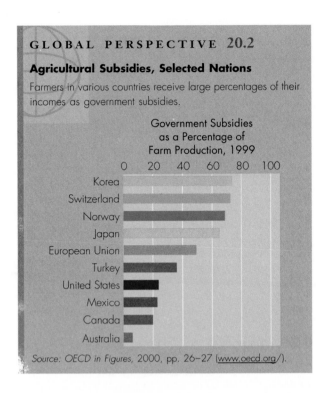

Source: OECD in Figures, 2000, pp. 26–27 (www.oecd.org/).

- The "family farm" is a fundamental U.S. institution and should be nurtured as a way of life.
- Farmers are subject to extraordinary hazards—floods, droughts, and insects—that most other industries do not face. Without government help, farmers cannot fully insure themselves against these disasters.
- While farmers face purely competitive markets for their outputs, they buy inputs of fertilizer, farm machinery, and gasoline from industries that have considerable market power. Whereas those industries are able to control their prices, farmers are at the "mercy of the market" in selling their output. The supporters of subsidies argue that agriculture warrants public aid in order to offset the disadvantageous terms of trade faced by farmers.

Background: The Parity Concept

The *Agricultural Adjustment Act of 1933* established the **parity concept** as a cornerstone of agricultural policy. The rationale of the parity concept can be stated in both real and nominal terms. In real terms, parity says that year after year for a fixed output of farm products, a farmer should be able to acquire a specific total amount of other goods and services. A particular real output should always result in the same real income: "If a farmer could take a bushel of corn to town in 1912 and sell it for enough money to buy a shirt, he should be able to sell a bushel of corn today and buy a shirt." In nominal terms, the parity concept suggests that the relationship between the prices received by farmers for their output and the prices they must pay for goods and services should remain constant. The parity concept implies that if the price of shirts tripled over some time period, then the price of corn should have tripled too. Such a situation is said to represent 100 percent of parity.

Figure 20.6 indicates why farmers would benefit from having the prices of their products based on 100 percent of parity. It shows the prices paid and received by farmers from 1910 to 1999 relative to prices in the 1910–1914 base period. By 1999 prices paid had increased 14-fold, while prices received had increased only 7 times compared with the base period.

The **parity ratio** graphed in Figure 20.6 is the ratio of prices received to prices paid, expressed as a percentage. That is:

$$\text{Parity ratio} = \frac{\text{prices received by farmers}}{\text{prices paid by farmers}}$$

In 1999 the parity ratio was 40 percent, indicating that prices received in 1999 could buy 40 percent as much as prices received in the 1910–1914 period. So farm policy calling for 100 percent of parity would require substantially higher prices for farm products.

Economics of Price Supports

The concept of parity provides the rationale for government price floors on farm products. In agriculture those minimum prices are called **price supports.** We have shown that, in the long run, the market prices received by farmers have not kept up with the prices paid by them. One way to achieve parity, or some percentage thereof, is to have the government establish above-equilibrium price supports for farm products.

Many different price-support programs have been tried, but they all tend to have similar effects, some of which are subtle and negative. Suppose in

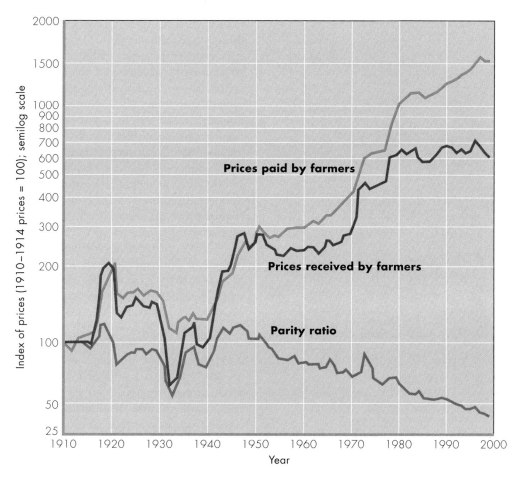

Figure 20.6

Prices paid and received by farmers, 1910–1999. Over the past five decades the prices paid by farmers have increased by more than prices received. As a result, the parity ratio—the ratio of prices received to prices paid—has substantially declined.

Source: U.S. Department of Agriculture, National Agricultural Statistics Service, www.usda.gov/nass.

Figure 20.7 that the equilibrium price is P_e and the price support is P_s. Then the major effects would be as follows:

Surplus Output

The most obvious result is a product surplus. Consumers are willing to purchase only Q_c units at the supported price, while farmers supply Q_s units. What about the Q_sQ_c surplus that results? The government must buy it to make the above-equilibrium price support effective. As you will see, this surplus farm output means that there is an overallocation of resources to agriculture.

Gain to Farmers

Farmers benefit from price supports. In Figure 20.7, gross farm revenue rises

from the free-market level represented by area $0P_ebQ_e$ to the larger, supported level shown by area $0P_saQ_s$.

Loss to Consumers

Consumers lose; they pay a higher price (P_s rather than P_e) and consume less (Q_c rather than Q_e) of the product. In some instances differences between the market price and the supported price are substantial. For example, the U.S.-supported price of a pound of sugar is about two times the world market price, and a quart of fluid milk is estimated to cost consumers twice as much as it would without government programs. Moreover, the burden of higher food prices falls disproportionately on the poor, because they spend a larger part of their incomes on food.

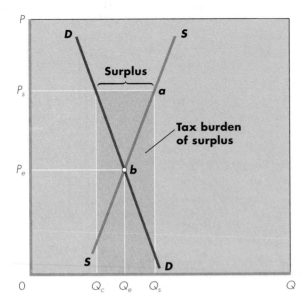

Figure 20.7
Effective price supports result in farm surpluses.
The market demand *D* and supply *S* of a farm product yield equilibrium price P_e and quantity Q_e. An above-equilibrium price support P_s results in consumption of quantity Q_c, production of quantity Q_s, and a surplus of quantity Q_sQ_c. The green rectangle represents a transfer of money from taxpayers to farmers.

Resource Overallocation   Society loses, because price supports create allocative inefficiency by encouraging an overallocation of resources to agriculture. A price floor (P_s) attracts more resources to the agricultural sector than would the free-market price (P_e). Viewed through the pure-competition model, the market supply curve in Figure 20.7 represents the marginal costs of all farmers producing this product at the various output levels. An efficient allocation of resources occurs at point *b*, where the market price P_e is equal to marginal cost. So the output Q_e reflects that efficient allocation of resources.

In contrast, the output Q_s associated with the price support P_s represents an overallocation of resources; for all units of output between Q_e and Q_s, marginal costs (measured on curve *S*) exceed the prices people are willing to pay for those units (measured on curve *D*). Simply stated, the marginal cost of the extra production exceeds its marginal benefit to society. Society incurs an *efficiency loss* from the price-support system.

Other Social Losses   Society at large loses in three other ways.

First, taxpayers pay higher taxes to finance the government's purchase of the surplus. This added tax burden is equal to the surplus output Q_sQ_c multiplied by its price P_s, as shown by the green area in Figure 20.7. Recall, too, that the mere collection of taxes imposes an efficiency loss (Figure 18.5). Also, the cost of storing surplus farm output adds to this tax burden.

Second, government's intervention in agriculture entails administrative costs. Thousands of government workers are needed to administer U.S. price supports and other farm programs.

Third, the *rent-seeking activity* involved—the pursuit of political support to maintain price supports—is costly and socially wasteful. Farm groups spend considerable sums to sustain political support for price floors and other programs that enhance farm incomes.

Environmental Costs   We know from Figure 20.7 that price supports encourage additional production. Although some of that extra output may come from the use of additional land, much of it comes from heavier use of fertilizer and pesticides. Those pesticides and fertilizers may pollute the environment (for example, groundwater) and create residues in food that pose health risks to farmworkers and consumers. Research shows a positive relationship between the level of price-support subsidies and the use of agrochemicals.

Moreover, farm policy may cause environmental problems in less obvious ways. First, farmers benefit from price supports only when they use their land consistently for a specific crop such as corn or wheat. That creates a disincentive to practice crop rotation, which is a nonchemical technique for controlling pests. Farm policy thus encourages the substitution of chemicals for other forms of pest control.

Second, we know from the concept of derived demand that an increase in the price of a product will increase the demand for relevant inputs. In particular, price supports for farm products increase the demand for land. And the land that farmers bring into farm production is often environmentally sensitive "marginal" land such as steeply sloped, highly erodable land or wetlands that provide wildlife habitat. Similarly, price supports result in the use of more water for irrigation, and the resulting runoff may contribute to soil erosion.

International Costs   Actually, the costs of farm price supports go beyond those indicated by Figure 20.7. Price supports generate economic distortions that cross national boundaries. For example, price supports make the U.S. agricultural market attractive to foreign producers. But inflows of foreign agricultural products would serve to increase supplies in the United States, aggravating the problem of U.S. surpluses. To prevent that from happening, the United States is likely to impose import barriers in the form of tariffs or quotas. Those barriers tend to restrict the output of more efficient foreign producers while encouraging more output from less efficient U.S. producers. The result is a less efficient use of world agricultural resources. This chapter's Last Word suggests that this is indeed the case for sugar.

Similarly, as the United States and other industrially advanced countries with similar agricultural programs dump surplus farm products on world markets, the prices of such products are depressed. Developing countries are often heavily dependent on world commodity markets for their incomes. So they are particularly hurt because their export earnings are reduced. Thus, U.S. subsidies for rice production have imposed significant costs on Thailand, a major rice exporter. Similarly, U.S. cotton programs have adversely affected Egypt, Mexico, and other cotton-exporting nations. (**Key Question 8**)

Reduction of Surpluses

Figure 20.7 suggests that programs designed to reduce market supply (shift S leftward) or increase market demand (shift D rightward) would help boost the market price toward the supported price P_s. Further, such programs would reduce or eliminate farm surpluses. The U.S. government has tried both supply and demand approaches to reduce or eliminate surpluses.

Restricting Supply   Until recently, public policy focused mainly on restricting farm output. In particular, **acreage allotments** accompanied price supports. In return for guaranteed prices for their crops, farmers had to agree to limit the number of acres they planted in that crop. The U.S. Department of Agriculture (USDA) first set the price support and then estimated the amount of the product consumers would buy at the supported price. It then translated that amount into the total number of planted acres

necessary to provide it. The total acreage was apportioned among states, counties, and ultimately individual farmers.

These supply-restricting programs were only partially successful. They did not eliminate surpluses, mainly because acreage reduction did not result in a proportionate decline in production. Some farmers retired their worst land and kept their best land in production. They also cultivated their tilled acres more intensively. Superior seed, more and better fertilizer and insecticides, and improved farm equipment were used to enhance output per acre. And nonparticipating farmers expanded their planted acreage in anticipation of overall higher prices. Nevertheless, the net effect of acreage allotment undoubtedly was a reduction of farm surpluses and their associated costs to taxpayers.

Bolstering Demand   Government has tried several ways to increase demand for U.S. agricultural products.

New Uses   Both government and private industry have spent large sums on research to create new uses for agricultural goods. The production of "gasohol," which is a blend of gasoline and alcohol made from grain, is one such attempt to increase the demand for farm output. A less significant example is the use of soybeans to replace wax in producing crayons. Most experts conclude that such endeavors have been only modestly successful in bolstering the demand for farm products.

Domestic and Foreign Demand   The government has also created a variety of programs to stimulate domestic consumption of farm products. For example, the objective of the food-stamp program is not only to reduce hunger but also to bolster the demand for food. Similarly, the Food for Peace program has enabled developing countries to buy U.S. surplus farm products with their own currencies, rather than having to use dollars. The Federal government spends millions of dollars each year to advertise and promote global sales of U.S. farm products. Furthermore, U.S. negotiators have pressed hard in international trade negotiations to persuade foreign nations to reduce trade barriers to the importing of farm products. The government's supply-restricting and demand-increasing efforts helped reduce the amount of surplus production, but they did not succeed in eliminating surpluses.

Criticism, Politics, and Reform

After 60 years of experience with government price-support programs, it became apparent that those programs were not working well. There was a growing feeling among economists and political leaders that the goals and techniques of farm policy needed to be reexamined and revised. In 1996, Congress ended the price-support programs for wheat, feed grains, cotton, and rice.

Criticisms

Before looking further at the 1996 reform, let's examine some of the key criticisms of the agricultural subsidies that led to it.

Symptoms, Not Causes

The subsidy strategy in agriculture was designed to treat the symptoms, not the causes, of the farm problem. The root cause of the problem was a misallocation of resources between agriculture and the rest of the economy. Historically, the problem has been one of too many farmers. The effect of that misallocation has been relatively low farm income. For the most part, public policy was oriented toward supporting farm prices and incomes rather than toward fixing the resource allocation problem itself.

Further, price and income supports have served to keep people in agriculture who otherwise would have moved to nonfarm occupations. That is, the price and income orientation of the farm program has slowed the reallocation of resources necessary to resolve the long-run farm problem.

Misguided Subsidies

Price supports and subsidy programs have traditionally benefited those farmers most who need them least. If the goal of farm policy is to raise low farm incomes, it follows that any program of Federal aid should be aimed at farmers with the lowest incomes. But the poor, low-output farmer does not produce and sell enough in the market to get much aid from price supports. Instead, the large corporate farm reaps the benefits by virtue of its sizable output.

In the year of the passage of the Freedom to Farm Act (1996), the 6 percent of all farms with sales of $250,000 or more received 46 percent of all direct government subsidies. The poorest 61 percent of all farmers—those who earned less than $20,000 from farming in that year—received about 4 percent of all direct-subsidy payments. If public policy is intended to supplement farm incomes, a strong case can be made for having its benefits vary inversely, rather than directly, with individual farm income.

Furthermore, an income-support program might better be geared to people than to products. Most economists say that, on equity grounds, direct income subsidies to struggling farmers are highly preferable to indirect price-support subsidies that go primarily to large, prosperous farmers. Better yet, say some economists, would be transition and retraining support for farmers willing to move out of farming into occupations and businesses in greater demand.

A related point concerns land values. The price and income benefits that farm programs provide tend to increase the value of farmland. By making crops more valuable, price supports make the land itself more valuable. Sometimes that tendency is helpful to farmers, but often it is not. Farmers rent about 50 percent of their farmland, mostly from well-to-do nonfarm landlords. Thus, price supports become a subsidy to people who are not actively engaged in farming.

Policy Contradictions

Because farm policy has many objectives, it often leads to contradictions. Whereas most subsidized research is aimed at *increasing* farm productivity and the supply of farm products, acreage-allotment programs require that farmers take land out of production in order to *reduce* supply. Price supports for crops mean increased feed costs for ranchers and high consumer prices for animal products. Tobacco farmers are subsidized at a time when serious health problems are associated with tobacco consumption. The U.S. sugar program raises sugar prices for domestic growers by imposing import quotas that conflict with free-trade policies. Conservation programs call for setting aside land for wildlife habitat, while price supports provide incentives to bring such acreage into production.

The Politics of Farm Policy

In view of these criticisms and inconsistencies, we might ask why the United States continued its price-support program for major crops for so many decades and still continues it for some farm products such as sugar, peanuts, and tobacco today. Why did it take so long for the government to restore free markets for at least some farm products?

Public Choice Theory Revisited
Public choice theory (Chapter 18) helps us answer these questions. Recall that rent-seeking behavior occurs when a group (a labor union, firms in a specific industry, or farmers producing a particular crop) uses political means to transfer income or wealth to itself at the expense of another group or of society as a whole. And recall that the special-interest effect involves a program or policy from which a small group receives large benefits at the expense of a much larger group whose members individually suffer small losses. Both rent-seeking behavior and the special-interest effect help explain the politics of farm subsidies.

Suppose a certain group of farmers, say, peanut or sugar growers, organize and establish a well-financed political action committee (PAC). The PAC's job is to promote government programs that will transfer income to the group (this is rent-seeking behavior). The PAC vigorously lobbies U.S. senators and representatives to enact or to continue price supports and import quotas for peanuts or sugar. The PAC does this in part by making political contributions to sympathetic legislators. Although peanut production is heavily concentrated in a few states such as Georgia, Alabama, and Texas, the peanut PAC will also make contributions to legislators from other states in order to gain support.

But how can a small interest group like peanut or sugar growers successfully lobby to increase its own income at the expense of society as a whole? Because, even though the total cost of the group's programs might be considerable, the cost imposed on each individual taxpayer is small (this is the special-interest effect). Taxpayers are likely to be uninformed about and indifferent to such programs,

since they have little at stake. Unless you grow sugar beets or peanuts, you probably have no idea how much these programs cost you as an individual tax-payer and consumer and therefore do not object when your legislator votes for, say, a sugar-support program. Thus, there is little or no lobbying to counter the PAC's efforts.

Political logrolling, the trading of votes on policies and programs, also works to perpetuate certain programs: Senator Foghorn agrees to vote for a program that benefits Senator Moribund's constituents, and Moribund returns the favor. Example: Many members of Congress who represent low-income urban areas vote in favor of farm subsidies. In return, representatives of agricultural areas support such programs as food stamps, which provide subsidized food for the poor. The result is a rural-urban coalition through which representatives from both areas provide benefits for their constituents and enhance their reelection chances. Such coalitions help explain why farm subsidies persist and why the food-stamp program was, until recently, regularly expanded over the years.

Large agribusinesses that supply inputs to agriculture also lend political support to farm subsidies because subsidies increase the amounts of agrochemicals and farm machinery that farmers are able to buy. And, needless to say, most of the thousands of government employees whose jobs depend on farm programs are highly supportive.

Public choice theory also tells us that politicians are likely to favor programs that have hidden costs. As we have seen, that is often true of farm programs. Our discussion of Figure 20.7 indicated that price supports involve not simply a transfer of money from taxpayer to farmer but costs that are hidden as higher food prices, storage costs for surplus output, costs of administering farm programs, and costs associated with both domestic and international misallocations of resources. Because those costs are largely indirect and hidden, farm programs are much more acceptable to politicians and the public than they would be if all costs were explicit.

Changing Politics
In spite of rent seeking, special interests, and logrolling, a combination of factors has led to a change in the politics of farm subsidies.

Declining Political Support
As the farm population has declined, agriculture's political power has weakened. The farm population was about 25

percent of the general population in the 1930s, when many U.S. farm programs were established; now it is less than 2 percent. Urban congressional representatives now constitute a 9-to-1 majority over their rural colleagues. An increasing number of legislators are critically examining farm programs for their effect on consumers' grocery bills as well as on farm incomes. Also, more farmers themselves are coming to resent the intrusion of the Federal government into their farming decisions. Many rural-state congressional members now support free-market agriculture.

World Trade Considerations   The United States has taken the lead to reduce barriers to world trade in agricultural products. That has also contributed to the more critical attitude toward farm subsidies, particularly price supports. The nations of the European Union (EU) and many other nations provide support for agricultural prices. And, to maintain their high domestic prices, they restrict imports of foreign farm products by imposing tariffs (excise taxes) and quotas (quantitative limits on imports of foreign goods). They then try to rid themselves of their domestic surpluses by subsidizing exports into world markets.

The effects on the United States are that (1) trade barriers hinder U.S. farmers from selling to EU nations and (2) subsidized exports from those nations depress world prices for agricultural products, making world markets less attractive to U.S. farmers.

Perhaps most importantly, farm programs such as those maintained by the EU and the United States distort both world agricultural trade and the international allocation of agricultural resources. Encouraged by artificially high prices, farmers in industrially advanced nations produce more food and fiber than they would otherwise. The resulting surpluses flow into world markets, where they depress prices. This means that farmers in countries with no farm programs—many of them developing countries—face artificially low prices for their exports, and that signals them to produce less. Overall, the result is a shift in production away from what would occur on the basis of comparative advantage. As an example, price supports cause U.S. agricultural resources to be used for sugar production, even though sugar can be produced at perhaps half the cost in the Caribbean countries and Australia.

Recognizing these distortions, in 1994 the world's trading nations agreed to reduce farm price-support programs by 20 percent by the year 2000 and to reduce tariffs and quotas on imported farm products by 15 percent. The United States made such a strong case against price supports in these discussions that its stance undoubtedly altered the domestic debate on whether supports should be continued within this country.

Recent Reform: Freedom to Farm

In 1996 Congress radically revamped 60 years of U.S. farm policy by passing the **Freedom to Farm Act.** This law immediately ended price supports and acreage allotments for wheat, corn, barley, oats, sorghum, rye, cotton, and rice. Farmers can now respond to changing crop prices by planting as much or as little of these crops as they choose. Moreover, they can freely switch to alternative crops. If the world demand for, say, cotton rises, U.S. farmers can now switch production from peanuts to cotton to take advantage of cotton's higher price. If the market price of corn falls, farmers can plant less corn and more sorghum. Markets, not government programs, are beginning to determine what products farmers grow, where they are grown, and what the total outputs will be.

Transition Payments and Expected Outcomes   To ease the transition away from farm subsidies, farmers are now guaranteed annual transition payments through 2002, although these payments are scheduled to decline as time passes. These payments, which will total nearly $37 billion, are not based on crop prices or farmers' incomes. Instead, they are based on the subsidies farmers formerly received as part of the price-support program. So a wheat farmer, for example, will receive declining annual cash payments for 7 years regardless of the price of wheat or the amount of wheat he or she grows. The purpose is to assist farmers during the transition, while freeing them to grow crops on the basis of market profitability, rather than on what qualifies for a Federal farm subsidy.

Over the long run, economists expect the Freedom to Farm Act to increase overall agricultural output in the United States. That may reduce farm prices and farm income further and hasten the exit of resources from agriculture. Economists also predict that the Freedom to Farm Act will increase the variability of agricultural prices and farm income from year to year. For example, when the price of corn is high, farmers who have planted corn will earn high incomes. But when others then plant corn, the increased output of corn at the end of the next growing season will increase its supply, lower its price, and reduce the income of all corn farmers. To protect themselves against the greater volatility of prices and income, farmers can be expected to use more tools to manage risk. For instance, they may diversify their plantings, sell crops for a set price per bushel in advance of their harvest, and consolidate into larger farms. Moreover, a sizable part of the Federal agricultural bureaucracy will no longer be needed, since paperwork will decline and the government will not have to monitor acreage allotments.

Emergency Aid The prices of several farm commodities severely declined in 1998 and 1999, due mainly to reduced export demand and strong crop production in the United States and worldwide. The lower farm revenues brought calls for repeal of the Freedom to Farm Act. So far, the Federal government has responded to the latest manifestation of the farm problem by substantially increasing direct subsidy payments to farmers. Examples: In 1998 it sped up the payment of the $5.5 billion of direct subsidies going to farmers under the Freedom to Farm Act. It also bought $250 million worth of wheat to donate to hungry countries. In 1999 it paid hog farmers $50 million to help them get through a period of extremely low pork prices that were driving hundreds of producers out of business. In late 1999 it provided farmers with an $8.7 billion emergency package of farm-income assistance and crop disaster relief. That brought the total government payments to farmers to a record $22 billion in 1999. This amount was 37 percent of the total $59 billion of cash farm income for 1999. A similar percentage was forecasted for 2000.

Clearly, the Federal government has not yet solved either the short-term farm problem or the long-term problem. Equally clear, the political clout of the farm lobby, although weaker than it was in the distant past, remains very strong. The policy debates will surely continue.

QUICK REVIEW 20.3

■ Farm policy in the United States has been heavily criticized for delaying the shift of resources away from farming, directing most subsidies to wealthier farmers, and being fraught with policy contradictions.

■ The persistence of price supports can largely be explained in terms of rent-seeking behavior, the special-interest effect, political logrolling, and other aspects of public choice theory.

■ Recently, the politics of farm subsidies has changed as a result of the declining political power of farmers and world trade considerations.

■ The Freedom to Farm Act of 1996 eliminated price supports and acreage allotments for many of the nation's crops, while continuing direct subsidies to farmers for 7 years. Due to declining U.S. agricultural revenues, the act has already come under considerable criticism.

The Sugar Program: A Sweet Deal

The Sugar Program Is a Sweet Deal for Domestic Sugar Producers, but It Imposes Heavy Costs on Domestic Consumers, Foreign Producers, and the American Economy.

The continuing U.S. sugar program uses price supports and import quotas to guarantee a minimum price of sugar for domestic sugar producers. The program has significant effects, both domestically and internationally.

Domestic Costs Price supports and import quotas have boosted the domestic price of sugar to twice the world price. The estimated aggregate cost to domestic consumers is about $1.9 billion per year. Furthermore, the effect of artificially high sugar prices is regressive, because low-income households spend a larger percentage of their incomes on food than do high-income households. On the other hand, each sugar grower receives from subsidies alone an amount estimated to be twice the nation's average family income. In one recent year, a single farm received an estimated $30 million in benefits. Many sugar producers obtain more than $1 million each year in benefits.

Import Quotas As a consequence of high U.S. domestic price supports, foreign sugar producers have a strong incentive to sell their output in the United States. But an influx of lower-priced foreign sugar into the U.S. domestic market would undermine U.S. price supports. The government therefore has imposed import quotas on foreign sugar. It decides how much sugar can be imported at a zero or very low tariff rate, and then it charges a prohibitively high tariff for any quantities above that amount. As the gap between U.S.-supported prices and world prices has widened, imports have declined as a percentage of sugar consumed in the United States. In 1975, about 30 percent of the sugar consumed in the United States was imported; currently about 16 percent comes from abroad. Domestic policy regarding the U.S. sugar industry largely dictates the nation's international trade policy with respect to sugar.

Developing Countries The loss of the U.S. market has had several harmful effects on developing sugar-exporting countries such as the Philippines, Brazil, and several Central American countries.

First, exclusion from the U.S. market has significantly reduced their export revenues—by an amount estimated to be many billions of dollars per year. That decline in export revenues is important, because many of the sugar-producing countries depend on such revenues to pay interest and principal on large debts owed to the United States and other industrially advanced nations.

Second, barred by quotas from sale in the U.S. market, the sugar produced by the developing countries has been added to world markets, where the increased supply has depressed the world price of sugar.

Third, domestic price supports have caused U.S. sugar production to expand to the extent that the United States may soon change from a sugar-importing to a sugar-exporting nation. That is, the U.S. sugar program may soon be a source of new competition for the sugar producers of the developing countries. Sugar price supports in the European Union have already turned that group of nations into sugar exporters.

U.S. Efficiency Loss The Government Accounting Office estimates that the sugar program benefits sugar producers by about $1 billion annually but costs U.S. consumers about $1.9 billion each year. The excess of losses over gains is therefore $900 million annually. This efficiency loss results from the overallocation of U.S. resources to growing and processing sugar beets and sugar cane.

Global Resource Misallocation Both domestically and globally, the sugar price-support programs of the United States and other industrially advanced economies have distorted the worldwide allocation of agricultural resources. Price supports have caused a shift of resources to sugar production by less efficient U.S. producers, and U.S. import quotas and consequent low world sugar prices have caused more efficient foreign producers to restrict their production. Thus high-cost producers are producing more sugar and low-cost producers are producing less, resulting in the inefficient use of the world's agricultural resources.

SUMMARY

1. In the short run, the highly inelastic demand for farm products transforms small changes in output and small shifts in demand into large changes in prices and income.

2. Over the long run, rapid technological advance, together with a highly inelastic and relatively slow-growing demand for agricultural output, has made agriculture a declining industry in the United States.

3. Historically, farm policy has been centered on price and based on the parity concept, which suggests that the relationship between prices received and paid by farmers should be constant over time.

4. The use of price floors or price supports has a number of economic effects: (a) It causes surplus production to occur; (b) it increases the incomes of farmers; (c) it causes consumers to pay higher prices for farm products; (d) it creates an overallocation of resources to agriculture; (e) it obliges society to pay higher taxes to finance the purchase and storage of surplus output; (f) it increases pollution because of the greater use of agrochemicals and vulnerable land; and (g) it forces other nations to bear the costs associated with import barriers and depressed world agricultural prices.

5. The Federal government has pursued with limited success programs to reduce agricultural supply and increase agricultural demand as a method of reducing the surpluses associated with price supports.

6. Economists have criticized U.S. farm policy for (a) confusing symptoms (low farm incomes) with causes

(excess capacity), (b) providing the largest subsidies to high-income farmers, and (c) creating contradictions among specific farm programs.

7. The persistence of agricultural subsidies can be explained in terms of public choice theory and, in particular, in terms of rent-seeking behavior, the special-interest effect, and political logrolling.

8. Political backing for price supports and acreage allotments has eroded for several reasons: (a) The number of U.S. farmers, and thus their political clout, has declined relative to the number of urban consumers of farm products; and (b) successful efforts by the United States to get other nations to reduce their farm subsidies have altered the domestic debate on the desirability of U.S. subsidies.

9. The Freedom to Farm Act of 1996 ended price supports and acreage allotments for wheat, corn, barley, oats, sorghum, rye, cotton, and rice. The government will pay farmers declining transition payments through the year 2002, but those payments will no longer depend on crop prices or the crop that is produced. The idea is to create a market-driven agricultural economy, rather than one managed by the Federal government.

10. Despite the Freedom to Farm Act, huge government subsidies to agriculture remain a fixture of U.S. agricultural policy. In 1999 they reached a record total of $22 billion. Both short-run and long-run farm problems remain unsolved.

TERMS AND CONCEPTS

short-run farm problem	agribusiness	parity ratio	acreage allotments
long-run farm problem	parity concept	price supports	Freedom to Farm Act

STUDY QUESTIONS

1. **Key Question** Carefully evaluate: "The supply and demand for agricultural products are such that small changes in agricultural supply result in drastic changes in prices. However, large changes in farm prices have modest effects on agricultural output." (Hint: A brief review of the distinction between supply and quantity supplied may be helpful.) Do exports increase or reduce the instability of demand for farm products? Explain.

2. What relationship, if any, can you detect between the fact that the farmer's fixed costs of production are large and the fact that the supply of most agricultural products is generally inelastic? Be specific in your answer.

3. **Key Question** Explain how each of the following contributes to the farm problem:
   a. The inelasticity of demand for farm products.
   b. The rapid technological progress in farming.
   c. The modest long-run growth in demand for farm commodities.
   d. The volatility of export demand.

4. The key to efficient resource allocation is shifting resources from low-productivity to high-productivity uses. In view of the high and expanding physical productivity of agricultural resources, explain why many economists want to divert additional resources from farming to achieve allocative efficiency.

5. Explain and evaluate: "Industry complains of the higher taxes it must pay to finance subsidies to agriculture. Yet the trend of agricultural prices has been downward while industrial prices have been moving upward, suggesting that on balance agriculture is actually subsidizing industry."

6. "Because consumers as a whole must ultimately pay the total income received by farmers, it makes no real difference whether the income is paid through free farm markets or through price supports supplemented by subsidies financed out of tax revenue." Do you agree?

7. If in a given year the indexes of prices received and paid by farmers were 120 and 165 respectively, what would the parity ratio be? Explain the meaning of that ratio.

8. **Key Question** Explain the economic effects of price supports. Explicitly include environmental and global impacts in your answer. On what grounds do economists contend that price supports cause a misallocation of resources?

9. Use supply and demand curves to depict equilibrium price and output in a competitive market for some farm product. Then show how an above-equilibrium price floor (price support) would cause a surplus in this market. Demonstrate in your graph how government could reduce the surplus through a policy that (*a*) changes supply or (*b*) changes demand. Identify each of the following actual government policies as primarily affecting the supply of or the demand for a particular farm product: acreage allotments; foodstamp program; Food for Peace program; a government buyout of dairy herds; export promotion.

10. Do you agree with each of the following statements? Explain why or why not.
    a. The problem with U.S. agriculture is that there are too many farmers. That is not the fault of farmers but the fault of government programs.
    b. The Federal government ought to buy up all U.S. farm surpluses and give them away to developing nations.

    c. All industries would like government price supports if they could get them; agriculture got price supports only because of its strong political clout.

11. What are the effects of farm subsidies such as those of the United States and the European Union on (*a*) domestic agricultural prices, (*b*) world agricultural prices, and (*c*) the international allocation of agricultural resources?

12. Use public choice theory to explain the persistence of farm subsidies in the face of major criticisms of those subsidies. If the special-interest effect is so strong, then what factors made it possible in 1996 for the government to end price supports and acreage allotments for several crops?

13. What is the major intent of the Freedom to Farm Act of 1996? Do you agree with that intent? Why or why not? Why have there been recent calls for repeal of the act?

14. **(Last Word)** Who benefits and who loses from the U.S. sugar subsidy program?

15. **Web-Based Question:** *Agriculture parity ratios— crop farmers and livestock farmers* The U.S. Department of Agriculture website, at www.usda.gov/ nass/aggraphs/agprices.htm, provides up-to-date color charts of current data for agricultural prices paid by farmers and received by farmers. On the basis of the most recent charts, how have crop farmers and livestock farmers been faring lately? Which group has fared the best in the last 2 years?

16. **Web-Based Question:** *Farm size and farm sales revenue* Check out the up-to-date color charts of current data relating to farm size and farm revenue at www.usda.gov/nass/aggraphs/landinfarms.htm. Which of these three states had the smallest and largest average farm sizes: California, Florida, or Texas? What was the average size of farms with sales revenue of less than $10,000 in the latest year? More than $100,000? What percentage of farms had $100,000 or more of sales? What percentage of land was in farms earning $100,000 or more?

21

Income Inequality and Poverty

EVIDENCE THAT SUGGESTS wide income disparity in the United States is easy to find. In 1999 movie producer George Lucas earned $400 million, television personality Oprah Winfrey earned $150 million, and author Tom Clancy made $66 million. In contrast, the salary of the president of the United States is $400,000, and the typical schoolteacher earns $45,000. A full-time minimum-wage worker at a fast-food restaurant makes about $10,000. Cash welfare payments to a mother with two children averages $5000. ■ In 1999 about 32.3 million Americans—or 11.8 percent of the population—lived in poverty. An estimated 500,000 people were homeless in that year. The richest fifth of the population received about 47 percent of total income, while the poorest fifth received only 4 percent. ■ What are the sources of income inequality? Is income inequality rising or falling? Is the United States making progress against poverty? What are the major income-maintenance programs in the United States? Has welfare reform succeeded? These are some of the questions that we will answer in this chapter.

■ Facts about Income Inequality

Average family income in the United States is among the highest in the world; in 1999, it was $62,636 per family. But that average tells us nothing about income inequality. To learn about that, we must examine how income is distributed around the average.

Distribution of Personal Income by Income Category

One way to measure **income inequality** is to look at the percentages of families in a series of income categories. Table 21.1 shows that about 11 percent

of all families had annual before-tax incomes of less than $15,000 in 1999, while another 15 percent had annual incomes of $100,000 or more. The data in the table suggest considerable inequality of family income in the United States.[1]

---

[1]The Census Bureau defines "families" as a group of two or more persons related by birth, marriage, or adoption and residing together. The bureau also gathers data for "households"—one or more persons occupying a housing unit. The distribution of personal income among households is slightly more unequal than the distribution among families.

Table 21.1

**The Distribution of U.S. Personal Income
by Families, 1999**

(1) Personal Income Category	(2) Percentage of All Families in This Category
Under $10,000	5.7
$10,000–$14,999	4.8
$15,000–$24,999	12.0
$25,000–$34,999	11.9
$35,000–$49,999	16.5
$50,000–$74,999	21.2
$75,000–$99,999	12.7
$100,000 and over	15.2
	100.0

Source: Bureau of the Census, www.census.gov/.

Table 21.2

**The Quintile Distribution of U.S. Personal Income
by Families, 1999**

(1) Quintile	(2) Percentage of Total Income	(3) Upper Income Limit
Lowest 20 percent	4.3	$22,826
Second 20 percent	9.9	39,600
Third 20 percent	15.6	59,400
Fourth 20 percent	23.0	88,082
Highest 20 percent	47.2	
Total	100.0	

Source: U.S. Bureau of the Census, www.census.gov/.

Distribution of Personal Income by Quintiles (Fifths)

A second way to measure income inequality is to divide the total number of income receivers into five numerically equal groups, or *quintiles*, and examine the percentage of total personal (before-tax) income received by each quintile. We do this in Table 21.2, where we also provide the upper income limit for each quintile. Any amount of income more than those listed in column 3 would place a family into the next-higher quintile.

The Lorenz Curve

We can display quintile distribution of personal income through a **Lorenz curve.** In Figure 21.1, we plot the cumulative percentage of families on the horizontal axis and the percentage of income they obtain on the vertical axis. The diagonal line 0*e* represents a *perfectly equal distribution of income* because each point along that line indicates that a particular percentage of families receive the same percentage of income. In other words, points representing 20 percent of all families receiving 20 percent of total income, 40 percent receiving 40 percent, 60 percent receiving 60 percent, and so on, all lie on the diagonal line.

By plotting the quintile data from Table 21.2, we obtain the Lorenz curve for 1999. Observe from point *a* that the bottom 20 percent of all families received 4.3 percent of the income; the bottom 40

percent received 14.2 percent (= 4.3 + 9.9), as shown by point *b*; and so forth. The gold area between the diagonal line and the Lorenz curve is determined by the extent that the Lorenz curve sags away from the diagonal and indicates the degree of income inequality. If the actual income distribution were perfectly equal, the Lorenz curve and the diagonal would coincide and the gold area would disappear.

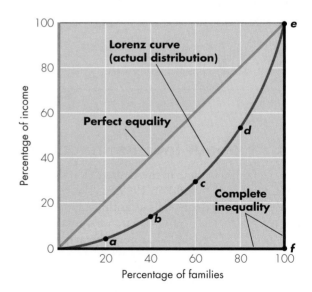

Figure 21.1

The Lorenz curve. The Lorenz curve is a graph of the percentage of total income obtained by cumulative percentages of families. It is a convenient means of displaying the degree of income inequality. Specifically, the area between the diagonal (the line of perfect equality) and the Lorenz curve represents the degree of inequality in the U.S. distribution of total income.

At the opposite extreme is a situation of complete inequality, where all families but one have zero income. In that case the Lorenz curve would coincide with the horizontal axis from 0 to point f (at 0 percent of income) and then would move immediately up from f to point e along the vertical axis (indicating that a single family has 100 percent of the total income). The entire area below the diagonal line (area $0ef$) would indicate this extreme degree of inequality. To generalize: The farther the Lorenz curve sags away from the diagonal, the greater is the degree of income inequality.

The Lorenz curve can also be plotted to contrast the income distributions of different ethnic and racial groups, of different age groups, and of different countries. **(Key Question 2)**

Income Mobility: The Time Dimension

The income data that we have been using so far have a major limitation: The income accounting period of 1 year is too short to be very meaningful. Because the Census Bureau data portray the distribution of income in only a single year, they may conceal a more equal distribution over a few years, a decade, or even a lifetime. If Brad earns $1000 in year 1 and $100,000 in year 2, while Jenny earns $100,000 in year 1 and only $1000 in year 2, do we have income inequality? The answer depends on the period of measurement. Annual data would reveal great income inequality, but there would be complete equality over the 2-year period.

This point is important because there is evidence to suggest considerable "churning around" in the distribution of income over time. In fact, for most income receivers, income starts at a relatively low level, reaches a peak during middle age, and then declines. A glance back at Figure 15.10 reveals this general pattern. It follows that if all people receive exactly the same stream of income over their lifetimes, considerable income inequality would still exist in any specific year because of age differences. In any single year, the young and the old would receive low incomes while the middle-aged receive high incomes.

If we change from a "snapshot" view of income distribution in a single year to a "time exposure" portraying incomes over much longer periods, we find considerable movement of income receivers among income classes. This correctly suggests that income is more equally distributed over a 5-, 10-, or 20-year period than in a single year. Such movement

of individuals or families from one income quintile to another over time is called **income mobility.**

A Federal Reserve Bank of Dallas study traced the movement of individuals from their quintile locations in 1975 to their quintile locations in 1991 and found that 95 percent of the people in the lowest income quintile in 1975 had moved to a higher quintile by 1991. Almost 30 percent of the lowest quintile had jumped to the richest quintile during that period. Undoubtedly this group included many people who were in college in 1975 but who graduated and became, say, high-income doctors, lawyers, and accountants by 1991. Nearly two-thirds of the people in the middle quintile changed to another quintile between 1975 and 1991. For the highest income quintile in 1975, about 37 percent had fallen to a lower quintile by 1991. Although the Federal Reserve Bank of Dallas has not updated this study, economists doubt that income mobility has appreciably changed over the past decade.

In short, there is significant individual and family income mobility over time; for many people, "low income" and "high income" are not permanent conditions. Also, the longer the time period considered, the more equal the distribution of income becomes.

Effect of Government Redistribution

The income data in Tables 21.1 and 21.2 include wages, salaries, dividends, and interest. They also include all cash transfer payments such as social security, unemployment compensation benefits, and welfare assistance to needy families. The data are before-tax data and therefore do not take into account the effects of personal income and payroll (social security) taxes that are levied directly on income receivers. Nor do they include in-kind or **noncash transfers,** which provide specific goods or services rather than cash. Noncash transfers include such things as Medicare, Medicaid, housing subsidies, subsidized school lunches, and food stamps. Such transfers are "incomelike," since they enable recipients to "purchase" goods and services.

One economic function of government is to redistribute income, if society so desires. Figure 21.2 and its table[2] reveal that government significantly

---

[2]The "before" data in this table differ from the data in Table 21.2 because the latter include cash transfers. Also, the data in Table 21.2 are for families, whereas the data in Figure 21.2 are for all households. Finally, the data in Figure 21.2 are based on a broader concept of income than are the data in Table 21.2.

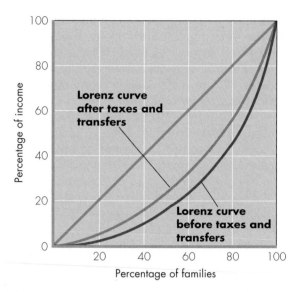

	Percentage of Total Income Received, 1999	
Quintile	(1) Before Taxes and Transfers	(2) After Taxes and Transfers
Lowest 20 percent	1.1	4.9
Second 20 percent	7.0	10.5
Third 20 percent	14.0	15.9
Fourth 20 percent	23.0	22.8
Highest 20 percent	54.8	46.0

Source: Bureau of the Census. The data include all money income from private sources, including realized capital gains and employer-provided health insurance. The "after taxes and transfers" data include the value of noncash transfers as well as cash transfers.

Figure 21.2

The impact of taxes and transfers on U.S. income inequality.   The distribution of personal income is significantly more equal after taxes and transfers are taken into account than before. Transfers account for most of the lessening of inequality and provide most of the income received by the lowest quintile of families.

redistributes income from higher- to lower-income households through taxes and transfers. This is shown by the fact that the U.S. distribution of household income before taxes and transfers are taken into account (dark green Lorenz curve) is substantially less equal than the distribution after taxes and transfers (light green Lorenz curve). Without government redistribution, the lowest 20 percent of households in 1999 would have received only 1.1 percent of total income. *With* redistribution, they received 4.9 percent, or more than four times as much.

Which contributes more to redistribution, government taxes or government transfers? The answer is transfers. Because the U.S. tax system is only modestly progressive, after-tax data would reveal only about 20 percent less inequality. Roughly 80 percent of the reduction in income inequality is attributable to transfer payments, which account for more than 75 percent of the income of the lowest quintile. Together with growth of job opportunities, transfer payments have been the most important means of alleviating poverty in the United States.

■ Causes of Income Inequality

There are several causes of income inequality in the United States. In general, the market system is an impersonal mechanism that embodies no conscience concerning what is an "equitable" or "just" distribu-

tion of income. It is permissive of a high degree of income inequality because it rewards individuals on the basis of the contribution that their resources make in producing society's output.

More specifically, the factors that contribute to income inequality are the following.

Ability

People have different mental, physical, and aesthetic talents. Some have inherited the exceptional mental qualities that are essential to such high-paying occupations as medicine, corporate leadership, and law. Others are blessed with the physical capacity and coordination to become highly paid professional athletes. A few have the talent to become great artists or musicians or have the beauty to become top fashion models. Others have very weak mental endowments and may work in low-paying occupations or may be incapable of earning any income at all. The intelligence and skills of most people fall somewhere in between.

Education and Training

Native ability alone rarely produces high income; people must develop and refine their capabilities through education and training. Individuals differ significantly in the amount of education and training they obtain and thus in their capacity to earn income. Such differences may be a matter of choice: Chin enters the labor force after graduating from high school, while Rodriguez takes a job only after earning a college degree. Other differences may be involuntary: Chin and her parents may simply be unable to finance a college education.

People also receive varying degrees of on-the-job training, which also contributes to income inequality. Some workers learn valuable new skills each year on the job and therefore experience significant income growth over time; others receive little or no on-the-job training and earn no more at age 50 they than they did at age 30. Moreover, firms tend to select for advanced on-the-job training the workers who have the most formal education. That added training magnifies the education-based income differences between less educated and better-educated individuals.

Discrimination

Discrimination in education, hiring, training, and promotion undoubtedly contributes to income inequality in the United States, although the degree is uncertain. If discrimination restricts racial and ethnic minorities (or women) to low-paying occupations, the supply of labor will be great relative to demand in those occupations. So wages and incomes will be low. Conversely, discrimination reduces the competition that whites (or men) face in the occupations in which they are predominant. Thus, labor supply is artificially limited relative to demand in those occupations, with the result that wages and incomes are high.

Preferences and Risks

Incomes also differ because of differences in preferences for market work relative to leisure, market work relative to work in the household, and types of market work. People who choose to stay home with children, work part-time, or retire early usually have less income than those who make the opposite choices. For example, the Heritage Foundation reports that people in the bottom 20 percent of the income distribution perform only about 6 percent of all hours worked in the economy. Those who are willing to take arduous, unpleasant jobs (for example, underground mining or heavy construction), to work long hours with great intensity, or to "moonlight" will tend to earn more.

Individuals also differ in their willingness to assume risk. We refer here not only to the race driver or the professional boxer but also to the entrepreneur. Although many entrepreneurs fail, many of those who develop successful new products or services realize very substantial incomes. That contributes to income inequality.

Unequal Distribution of Wealth

Income is a *flow;* it represents a stream of wage and salary earnings, along with rent, interest, and profits, as depicted in Chapter 2's circular flow diagram. In contrast, wealth is a *stock*, reflecting at a particular moment the financial and real assets an individual has accumulated over time. A retired person may have very little income and yet own a home, mutual fund shares, and a pension plan that add up to considerable wealth. A new college graduate may be earning a substantial income as an accountant, middle manager, or engineer but has yet to accumulate significant wealth.

As you will discover in this chapter's Last Word, the ownership of wealth in the United States is more unequal than the distribution of income. In 1998 the wealthiest 10 percent of all households owned 69 percent of total net worth (assets minus liabilities). The bottom 20 percent had no net assets at all; the bottom 40 percent had less than 2 percent of total net worth. This inequality of wealth leads to inequality in rent, interest, and dividends, which in turn contributes to income inequality. Those who own more machinery, real estate, farmland, stocks and bonds, and savings accounts obviously receive greater income from that ownership than people with less or no such wealth.

Market Power

The ability to "rig the market" on one's own behalf also contributes to income inequality. For example, in *resource* markets certain unions and professional groups have adopted policies that limit the supply of their services, thereby boosting the incomes of those "on the inside." Also, legislation that requires occupational licensing for, say, doctors, dentists, and lawyers can bestow market power that favors the licensed groups. In *product* markets, "rigging the market" means gaining or enhancing monopoly power, which results in greater profit and thus greater income to the firms' owners.

Luck, Connections, and Misfortune

Other forces also play a role in producing income inequality. Luck and "being in the right place at the right time" have helped individuals stumble into fortunes. Discovering oil on a ranch, owning land along a proposed freeway interchange, and hiring the right press agent have accounted for some high incomes. Personal contacts and political connections are other potential routes to attaining high income.

In contrast, economic misfortunes such as prolonged illness, serious accident, death of the family breadwinner, or unemployment may plunge a family into the low range of income. The burden of such misfortune is borne very unevenly by the population and thus contributes to income inequality. **(Key Question 4)**

QUICK REVIEW 21.1

▨ Data reveal considerable income inequality in the United States; in 1999 the richest fifth of all families received 47.2 percent of before-tax income, and the poorest fifth received 4.3 percent.

▨ The Lorenz curve depicts income inequality graphically by comparing percentages of total families and percentages of total income.

▨ The distribution of income is less unequal over longer time periods.

▨ Government taxes and transfers significantly reduce income inequality by redistributing income from higher-income groups to lower-income groups; the bulk of this redistribution results from transfer payments.

▨ Differences in ability, education and training, tastes for market work versus nonmarket activities, property ownership, and market power—along with discrimination and luck—help explain income inequality.

▮ Trends in Income Inequality

Over a period of years economic growth has raised incomes in the United States: In *absolute* dollar amounts, the entire distribution of income has been moving upward. But incomes may move up in *absolute* terms while leaving the *relative* distribution of income less equal, more equal, or unchanged. Table 21.3 shows the relative distribution of personal income over time. Recall that personal income is "before tax" and includes cash transfers but

not noncash transfers. Let's see how this income distribution in the United States has changed over three periods: 1929 to 1947, 1947 to 1969, and 1969 to 1999.

The 1929–1947 Period Comparison of the income distribution data for 1929 and 1947 suggests a significant reduction in income inequality over those years. The percentage of personal income going to the top quintile declined, and the percentages received by the other four quintiles increased. Many of the forces at work during the Second World War contributed to this decline in inequality. Wartime prosperity eliminated many of the low incomes caused by the severe unemployment of the 1930s, reduced wage and salary differentials, boosted depressed farm incomes through sharp increases in farm prices, temporarily diminished discrimination in employment, and was accompanied by a decline in property incomes as a share of the national income.

The 1947–1969 Period Many of the forces contributing to greater equality during the Second World War became less influential after the war. Between 1947 and 1969, the income distribution continued its trend toward less inequality, but at a far slower pace. The income share of the lowest income group rose by .6 of a percentage point between 1947 and 1969, while that of the wealthiest quintile fell by 2.4 percentage points.

The 1969–1999 Period The distribution of income by quintiles has become more unequal since 1969. In 1999 the lowest 20 percent of families received only 4.3 percent of total before-tax income, compared with 5.6 percent in 1969. Meanwhile, the income share received by the highest 20 percent rose from 40.6 to 47.2 percent. There are some signs, however, that the rising income inequality stalled in 1998, and perhaps peaked.

Global Perspective 21.1 compares income inequality in the United States (here by individuals, not by families) with that in several other nations. Income inequality tends to be highest in developing nations.

Causes of Growing Inequality

Economists suggest several major explanations for the growing U.S. income inequality of the past three decades.

Table 21.3

Percentage of Total Before Tax Income Received by Each One-Fifth, and by the Top 5 Percent, of Families, Selected Years

Quintile	1929	1935–1936	1947	1955	1969	1985	1999
Lowest 20 percent	} 12.5	4.1	5.0	4.8	5.6	4.8	4.3
Second 20 percent		9.2	11.8	12.2	12.4	10.9	9.9
Third 20 percent	13.8	14.1	17.0	17.7	17.7	16.9	15.6
Fourth 20 percent	19.3	20.9	23.1	23.7	23.7	24.3	23.0
Highest 20 percent	54.4	51.7	43.0	41.6	40.6	43.1	47.2
Total	100.0	100.0	100.0	100.0	100.0	100.0	100.0
Top 5 percent	30.0	25.6	17.2	16.8	15.6	16.1	20.3

Source: Bureau of the Census, www.census.gov/.

Greater Demand for Highly Skilled Workers Perhaps the most significant contributor to the growing income inequality has been an increasing demand by many firms for workers who are highly skilled and well-educated. Moreover, several industries requiring highly skilled workers have either recently emerged or expanded greatly, such as the computer software, business consulting, biotechnology, health care, and Internet industries. Because highly skilled workers remain relatively scarce, their wages have been bid up. Consequently, the wage differences between them and less skilled workers have increased.

Between 1980 and 1999 the wage difference between college graduates and high school graduates rose from 33 to 44 percent for women and from 29 to 51 percent for men. And the so-called *90-10 ratio*—earnings at the 90th percentile of the wage and salary distribution compared to earnings at the 10th percentile—rose from 3.6 in 1980 to 4.3 in 1999.

The rising demand for skill has also evidenced itself in rapidly rising pay for chief executive officers (CEOs), sizable increases in income from stock options, substantial increases in income for professional athletes and entertainers, and huge fortunes for successful entrepreneurs. This growth of "superstar" pay has also contributed to rising income inequality.

Demographic Changes The entrance of large numbers of less experienced and less skilled "baby boomers" into the labor force during the 1970s and 1980s may have contributed to greater income inequality in those two decades. Because younger workers tend to earn less income than older workers, their growing numbers contributed to income inequality. There has also been a growing tendency for men and women with high earnings potential to marry each other, thus increasing family income among the highest income quintiles. Finally, the number of families headed by single or divorced women has increased greatly. That trend has increased income inequality because such families lack a second major wage earner and also because the poverty rate for female-headed households is very high.

GLOBAL PERSPECTIVE 21.1

Percentage of Total Income Received by Top One-Fifth of Income Receivers, Selected Nations

The share of income going to the highest 20 percent of income receivers varies among nations. Frequently, income is less equally shared in poor nations than in rich ones.

Percentage of Total Income Earned by Top Fifth of Income Receivers

South Africa
Brazil
Guatemala
Mexico
United States
France
Italy
Norway

Source: World Development Report, 2000, pp. 238–239.

International Trade, Immigration, and Decline in Unionism Other factors are probably at work as well. Stronger international competition from imports has reduced the demand for and employment of less skilled (but highly paid) workers in such industries as the automobile and steel industries. The decline in such jobs has reduced the average wage for less skilled workers. It also has swelled the ranks of workers in already low-paying industries, placing further downward pressure on wages there. Similarly, the transfer of jobs to lower-wage workers in developing countries has exerted downward wage pressure on less skilled workers in the United States. Also, an upsurge in immigration of unskilled workers has increased the number of low-income families in the United States. Finally, the decline in unionism in the United States has undoubtedly contributed to wage inequality, since unions tend to equalize pay within firms and industries.

Two cautions: First, when we note growing income inequality, we are not saying that the "rich are getting richer and the poor are getting poorer" in terms of absolute income. Both the rich and the poor are experiencing rises in real income. Rather, what has happened is that, while incomes have risen in all quintiles, income growth has been fastest in the top quintile. Second, increased income inequality is not solely a U.S. phenomenon. The recent move toward greater inequality has also occurred in several other industrially advanced nations.

The Lorenz curve can be used to contrast the distribution of income at different points in time. If we also plotted Table 21.3's data for 1947 and 1969 as Lorenz curves in Figure 21.1, we would find that the curve shifted toward the diagonal between 1947 and 1969 and then shifted back away from the diagonal between 1969 and 1999.

▌Equality versus Efficiency

The main policy issue concerning income inequality is how much is necessary and justified. While there is no general agreement on the justifiable amount, we can gain insight by exploring the cases for and against greater equality.

The Case for Equality: Maximizing Total Utility

The basic argument for an equal distribution of income is that income equality maximizes the total consumer satisfaction (utility) from any particular level of output and income. The rationale for this argument is shown in Figure 21.3, in which we assume that the money incomes of two individuals, Anderson and Brooks, are subject to diminishing marginal utility. In any time period, income receivers spend the first dollars received on the products they value most—products whose marginal utility is high. As their most pressing wants become satisfied, consumers then spend additional dollars of income on less important, lower-marginal-utility goods. The identical diminishing-marginal-utility-from-income curves (MU_A and MU_B in the figure) reflect the assumption that Anderson and Brooks have the same capacity to derive utility from income.

Now suppose that there is $10,000 worth of income (output) to be distributed between Anderson and Brooks. According to proponents of income equality, the optimal distribution is an equal distribution, which causes the marginal utility of the last dollar spent to be the same for both persons. We can prove this by demonstrating that if the income distribution is initially unequal, then distributing income more equally can increase the combined utility of the two individuals.

Suppose that the $10,000 of income initially is distributed unequally, with Anderson getting $2500 and Brooks $7500. The marginal utility, a, from the last dollar received by Anderson is high, and the marginal utility, b, from Brooks' last dollar of income is low. If a single dollar of income is shifted from Brooks to Anderson—that is, toward greater equality—then Anderson's utility increases by a and Brooks' utility decreases by b. The combined utility then increases by a minus b (Anderson's large gain minus Brooks' small loss). The transfer of another dollar from Brooks to Anderson again increases their combined utility, this time by a slightly smaller amount. Continued transfer of dollars from Brooks to Anderson increases their combined utility until the income is evenly distributed and both receive $5000. At that time their marginal utilities from the last dollar of income are equal (at a' and b'), and any further income redistribution beyond the $2500 already transferred would begin to create inequality and decrease their combined utility.

The area under the MU curve and to the left of the individual's particular level of income represents the total utility of that income. Therefore, as a result of the transfer of the $2500, Anderson has gained utility represented by area G below curve MU_A, and Brooks has lost utility represented by

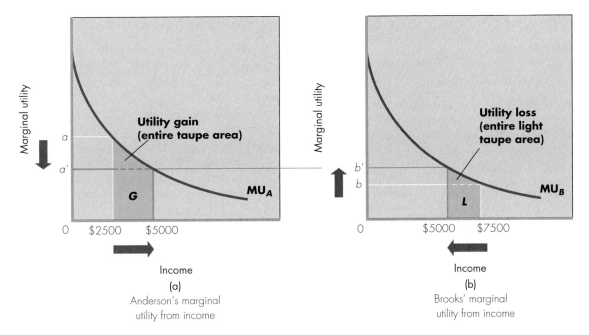

Figure 21.3

The utility-maximizing distribution of income. With identical marginal-utility-of-income curves MU$_A$ and MU$_B$, Anderson and Brooks will maximize their combined utility when any amount of income (say, $10,000) is equally distributed. If income is unequally distributed (say, $2500 to Anderson and $7500 to Brooks), the marginal utility derived from the last dollar will be greater for Anderson than for Brooks, and a redistribution toward equality will result in a net increase in total utility. The utility gained by equalizing income at $5000 each, shown by area G below curve MU$_A$ in panel (a), exceeds the utility lost, indicated by area L below curve MU$_B$ in (b).

area L below curve MU$_B$. Area G is obviously greater than area L, so income equality yields greater combined total utility than income inequality does.

The Case for Inequality: Incentives and Efficiency

Although the logic of the argument for equality is sound, critics attack its fundamental assumption that there is some fixed amount of output produced and therefore income to be distributed. Critics of income equality argue *that the way in which income is distributed is an important determinant of the amount of output or income that is produced and is available for distribution.*

Suppose once again in Figure 21.3 that Anderson earns $2500 and Brooks earns $7500. In moving toward equality, society (the government) must tax away some of Brooks' income and transfer it to Anderson. This tax and transfer process diminishes the income rewards of high-income Brooks and raises the income rewards of low-income Anderson; in so doing, it reduces the incentives of both to earn

high incomes. Why should high-income Brooks work hard, save and invest, or undertake entrepreneurial risks when the rewards from such activities will be reduced by taxation? And why should low-income Anderson be motivated to increase his income through market activities when the government stands ready to transfer income to him? Taxes are a reduction in the rewards from increased productive effort; redistribution through transfers is a reward for diminished effort.

In the extreme, imagine a situation in which the government levies a 100 percent tax on income and distributes the tax revenue equally to its citizenry. Why would anyone work hard? Why would anyone work at all? Why would anyone assume business risk? Or why would anyone save (forgo current consumption) in order to invest? The economic incentives to "get ahead" will have been removed, greatly reducing society's total production and income. In other words, the way the income pie is distributed affects the size of that pie. The basic argument for income inequality is that inequality is essential to maintain incentives to produce output and income—that is, to get the pie baked year after year.

The Equality-Efficiency Tradeoff

The essence of this income equality-inequality debate is that there is a fundamental **tradeoff between equality and efficiency:**

> The contrasts among American families in living standards and in material wealth reflect a system of rewards and penalties that is intended to encourage effort and channel it into socially productive activity. To the extent that the system succeeds, it generates an efficient economy. But that pursuit of efficiency necessarily creates inequalities. And hence society faces a tradeoff between equality and efficiency.[3]

The problem for a society that is inclined toward equality is to redistribute income in a way that minimizes the adverse effects on economic efficiency. Consider this leaky-bucket analogy: Assume that society agrees to shift income from the rich to the poor. But the money must be carried from affluent to indigent in a leaky bucket. The leak represents an efficiency loss—the loss of output and income—caused by the harmful effects of the redistribution on incentives to work, to save and invest, and to accept entrepreneurial risk. The leak also reflects the fact that resources must be diverted to the bureaucracies that administer the redistribution system.

How much leakage will society accept while continuing to agree to the redistribution? If cutting the income pie into more equal slices shrinks the pie, what amount of shrinkage will society tolerate? Is a loss of 1 cent on each redistributed dollar acceptable? 5 cents? 25 cents? 50 cents? This is the basic question in any debate over the ideal size of a nation's income-maintenance programs.

■ The Economics of Poverty

We now turn from the larger issue of income distribution to the more specific issue of very low income, or "poverty." A society with a high degree of income inequality can have either a high, moderate, or low amount of poverty. We need to learn about the extent of poverty in the United States, the characteristics of the poor, and the programs designed to reduce poverty.

Definition of Poverty

Poverty is a condition in which a person or a family does not have the means to satisfy basic needs for food, clothing, shelter, and transportation. The means include currently earned income, transfer payments, past savings, and property owned. The basic needs have many determinants, including family size and the health and age of its members.

The Federal government has established a minimum income level below which a person or a family is "in poverty." In 1999 an unattached individual receiving less than $8501 per year was said to be living in poverty. For a family of four, the poverty line was $17,029; for a family of six, it was $22,727. Applying these definitions to income data in the United States, we find for 1999 that 11.8 percent of the population—about 32.3 million people—lived in poverty.

Incidence of Poverty

Unfortunately for purposes of public policy, the poor are heterogeneous: They can be found in all parts of the nation; they are whites and nonwhites, rural and urban, young and old. But as Figure 21.4 indicates, poverty is far from randomly distributed. For example, the **poverty rate** (the percentage of the population living in poverty) for blacks is above the national average, as is the rate for Hispanics, while the rate for whites is below the average. In 1999, the poverty rates for blacks and Hispanics were 23.6 and 22.8 percent, respectively; the rate for whites was 9.8 percent.

Figure 21.5 shows that the incidence of poverty is extremely high among female-headed families, foreign-born people who are not citizens, and children under 18 years of age. Marriage is associated with a low poverty rate, and, thanks to the social security system, the incidence of poverty among the elderly is less than that for the population as a whole.

The high poverty rate for children is especially disturbing, because poverty tends to breed poverty. Poor children are at greater risk for a range of long-term problems, including poor health and inadequate education, crime, drug use, and teenage pregnancy. Many of today's impoverished children will reach adulthood unhealthy and illiterate and unable to earn above-poverty incomes.

Although in general there is considerable movement out of poverty, poverty is much more long-last-

---

[3]Arthur M. Okun, *Equality and Efficiency: The Big Tradeoff* (Washington, D.C.: Brookings Institution, 1975), p. 1.

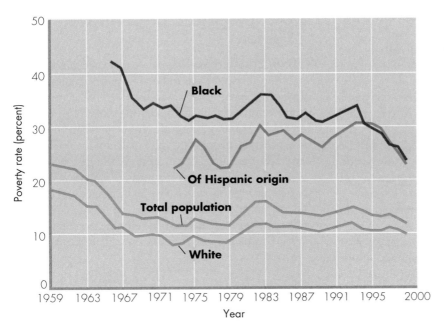

Figure 21.4

Poverty rates: for total population and by race and ethnicity, 1959–1999. Over the 1959–1999 period, poverty rates for blacks and Hispanics were much higher than the rate for the total population, while the rate for whites was below that for the total population. Although the national poverty rate declined sharply between 1959 and 1969, it stabilized in the 1970s only to increase significantly in the early 1980s. Recently, it has substantially declined.

ing among some groups than among others. In particular, black and Hispanic families, families headed by women, persons with little education and few labor market skills, and people who are dysfunctional because of drug use, alcoholism, or mental illness are more likely than others to remain in poverty.

Poverty Trends

As Figure 21.4 shows, the total poverty rate fell significantly between 1959 and 1969, stabilized at 11 to 13 percent over the next decade, and then rose in the early 1980s. In 1993 the rate was 15.1 percent, the highest since 1983. Since 1993 the rate has again turned downward, falling to 11.8 percent in 1999.

The "Invisible" Poor

The facts and figures on the extent and character of poverty may be difficult to accept. After all, the United States is an affluent society. The troubling statistics on poverty fit with our everyday assumptions of abundance mainly because much U.S. poverty is hidden; it is largely invisible.

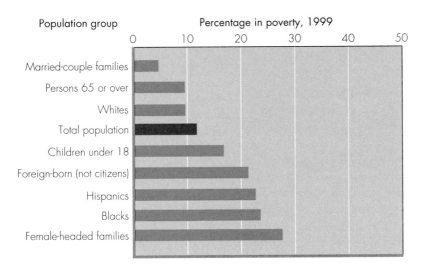

Figure 21.5

The distribution of poverty among selected population groups, 1999. Poverty is disproportionately borne by minorities, children, foreign-born residents who are not citizens, and families headed by women. People who are employed full-time, have a college degree, or are married tend to have low poverty rates.

There are three reasons for that invisibility. First, research has shown that as many as one-half of those in poverty are poor for only one or two years before climbing out of poverty. Many of those people are not visible as permanently downtrodden and needy. Second, the "permanently poor" are increasingly isolated geographically. Poverty persists in depressed areas of large cities and is not readily visible from the freeway. Similarly, rural poverty and the chronically depressed areas of Appalachia, the deep south, and the Indian reservations of the southwest are also off the beaten paths. Third, and perhaps most important, the poor are politically invisible. In general, they do not belong to advocacy organizations such as business groups (Chambers of Commerce), workers groups (unions and professional groups), or groups of senior citizens (such as the American Association of Retired People). They do not have newsletters and political lobbyists, and they do not propose legislation and endorse candidates. They have very little direct voice in U.S. politics and are therefore easy to ignore.

■ The Income-Maintenance System

The reduction of poverty is a widely accepted goal of public policy, and a number of income-maintenance programs have been devised to reduce it, the most important of which are listed in Table 21.4. Despite recent attempts to slow the upward trend in spending on such programs, they still involve enormous expenditures and large numbers of beneficiaries.

The U.S. income-maintenance system consists of two kinds of programs: (1) social insurance and (2) public assistance or "welfare." Both are known as **entitlement programs,** because all eligible persons are assured (entitled to) the benefits set forth in the programs.

Social Insurance Programs

Social insurance programs partially replace earnings that have been lost due to retirement, disability, or temporary unemployment; they also provide

Table 21.4

Characteristics of Major Income-Maintenance Programs

Program	Basis of Eligibility	Source of Funds	Form of Aid	Expenditures,* Billions	Beneficiaries, Millions
Social Insurance Programs					
Old Age, Survivors, and Disability Health Insurance (OASDHI)	Age, disability, or death of parent or spouse; individual earnings	Federal payroll taxes on employers and employees	Cash	$386	45
Medicare	Age or disability	Federal payroll tax on employers and employees	Subsidized health insurance	210	39
Unemployment compensation	Unemployment	State and Federal payroll taxes on employers	Cash	20	7
Public Assistance Programs					
Supplemental Security Income (SSI)	Age or disability; income	Federal revenues	Cash	29	7
Temporary Assistance for Needy Families (TANF)	Certain families with children; income	Federal-state-local revenues	Cash and services	23	7
Food stamps	Income	Federal revenues	Vouchers	20	18
Medicaid	Persons eligible for TANF or SSI and medically indigent	Federal-state-local revenues	Subsidized medical services	124	34
Earned-income tax credit (EITC)	Low-wage working families	Federal revenues	Refundable tax credit, cash	30	20

*Expenditures by Federal, state, and local governments; excludes administrative expenses.
Source: Statistical Abstract of the United States, 2000; other government sources. Latest data.

health insurance for the elderly. The main social insurance programs are "social security" (technically, Old Age, Survivors, and Disability Health Insurance, or OASDHI), unemployment compensation, and Medicare. Benefits are viewed as earned rights and do not carry the stigma of public charity. These programs are financed primarily out of Federal payroll taxes. In these programs the entire population shares the risk of an individual's losing income because of retirement, unemployment, disability, or illness. Workers (and employers) pay a part of wages into a government fund while they are working. The workers are then entitled to benefits when they retire or when a specified misfortune occurs.

OASDHI and Medicare

OASDHI is a gigantic social insurance program financed by compulsory payroll taxes levied on both employers and employees. Generically known as social security, the program replaces earnings lost because of a worker's retirement, disability, or death. Workers may retire at age 65 and receive full benefits or at age 62 with reduced benefits. When a worker dies, benefits accrue to his or her survivors. Special provisions provide benefits for disabled workers. Currently, social security covers over 90 percent of the workforce; some 45 million people receive OASDHI benefits averaging about $804 per month. Those benefits are financed with a payroll tax of 15.3 percent, with both the worker and the employer paying 7.65 percent on the first $76,200 of earnings (in 2000). The 7.65 percent tax is comprised of 6.2 percent for social security and 1.45 percent for Medicare. Self-employed workers pay a tax of 15.3 percent.

Medicare, which was added to OASDHI in 1965, provides hospital insurance for the elderly and disabled and is financed out of the payroll tax. This overall 2.9 percent tax is paid on all work income. Medicare also makes available a low-cost voluntary insurance program that helps pay doctor fees.

Unemployment Compensation

All 50 states sponsor unemployment insurance programs. **Unemployment compensation** is financed by a modest payroll tax, paid by employers, which varies by state and by the size of the firm's payroll. Any insured worker who becomes unemployed can, after a short waiting period (usually 1 week), become eligible for benefit payments. The program covers almost all wage and salary workers. The size of payments and the number of weeks they are made available vary considerably from state to state. Generally, benefits approximate 33 percent of a worker's wages up to a certain maximum

payment. Benefits averaged about $200 weekly in 1999. The number of beneficiaries and the level of total disbursements vary with economic conditions.

Public Assistance Programs

Public assistance programs (welfare) provide benefits for those who are unable to earn income because of permanent handicaps or have no or very low income and also have dependent children. These programs are financed out of general tax revenues and are regarded as public charity. They include "means tests" which require that individuals and families demonstrate low incomes in order to qualify for aid. The Federal government finances about two-thirds of the welfare program expenditures, and the rest is paid for by the states.

Many needy persons who do not qualify for social insurance programs are assisted through the Federal government's **Supplemental Security Income (SSI)** program. The purpose of SSI is to establish a uniform, nationwide minimum income for the aged, blind, and disabled who are unable to work and who do not qualify for OASDHI aid. Over half the states provide additional income supplements to the aged, blind, and disabled.

The **Temporary Assistance for Needy Families (TANF)** program is state-administered but is partly financed with Federal grants. The program provides cash assistance to families with children and also seeks to reduce welfare dependency by promoting job preparation and work. TANF's predecessor was the Aid for Families with Dependent Children (AFDC) program. But unlike that program, TANF has work requirements and limits on the length of time a family can receive welfare payments. In 1999 about 7 million people (including children) received TANF assistance.

The **food-stamp program** is designed to provide all low-income Americans with a "nutritionally adequate diet." Under the program, eligible households receive monthly allotments of coupons that are redeemable for food. The amount of food stamps received varies inversely with a family's earned income.

Medicaid helps finance the medical expenses of individuals participating in the SSI and the TANF programs.

The **earned-income tax credit (EITC)** is a tax credit for low-income working families, with or without children. The credit reduces the Federal income taxes such families owe or provides them with cash payment if the credit exceeds their tax liability. The purpose of the credit is to offset social security taxes paid by low-wage earners and thus keep the Federal government from "taxing families into poverty." In essence, EITC is a wage subsidy from the Federal government that works out to be as much as $2 per hour for the lowest-paid workers with families. Under the program many people owe no income tax and get direct checks from the Federal government once a year. Some 20 million recipients qualified for the EITC in 1999, and the total cost of the program was about $30 billion.

There are also several welfare programs that are not listed in Table 21.4. Most provide help in the form of noncash transfers. Head Start provides education, nutrition, and social services to economically disadvantaged 3- and 4-year-olds. Housing assistance in the form of rent subsidies and funds for construction is available to low-income families. Pell grants provide assistance to undergraduate students from low-income families.

QUICK REVIEW 21.2

☑   The basic argument for income equality is that it maximizes total utility by equalizing the marginal utility of the last dollar of income received by all people.

☑   The basic argument for income inequality is that it is necessary as an economic incentive for production.

☑   By government standards, 32.3 million people in the United States, or 11.8 percent of the population, lived in poverty in 1999.

☑   The U.S. income-maintenance system includes both social insurance programs and public assistance (welfare) programs.

■ Welfare: Goals and Conflicts

An ideal public assistance (welfare) program should achieve three goals. First, the program should be effective in getting individuals and families out of poverty. Second, it should provide adequate incentives for able-bodied, nonretired people to work. Third, its cost should be "reasonable." Unfortunately, these three goals conflict with one another, causing tradeoffs and necessitating compromises. To understand why, consider the three hypothetical welfare plans shown in Table 21.5.

Common Features

We first examine the two common elements in these three plans (and in real-world public assistance plans). First, there is a *minimum annual income* that the government will provide if the family has no earned income. Second, there is a *benefit-reduction rate*, which is the rate at which benefits are reduced or "lost" as a result of earned income.

Consider plan 1. The minimum annual income provided by the government is $8000, and the benefit-reduction rate is 50 percent. If a family earns no income, it will receive cash transfer payments totaling $8000. If it earns $4000, it will lose $2000 of transfer payments ($4000 of earnings × 50 percent benefit-reduction rate); its total income will then be $10,000 (= $4000 of earnings + $6000 of transfer payments). If it earns $8000, its transfer payments will fall to $4000, and so on. Note that at an income of $16,000, transfer payments are zero. The level of earned income at which the transfer payments disappear is called the *break-even income*.

Table 21.5

Tradeoffs among Goals: Three Public Assistance Plans

Plan 1 ($8000 Minimum Income and 50% Benefit-Reduction Rate)			Plan 2 ($8000 Minimum Income and 25% Benefit-Reduction Rate)			Plan 3 ($12,000 Minimum Income and 50% Benefit-Reduction Rate)		
Earned Income	Transfer Payment	Total Income	Earned Income	Transfer Payment	Total Income	Earned Income	Transfer Payment	Total Income
$ 0	$8000	$ 8,000	$ 0	$8000	$ 8,000	$ 0	$12,000	$12,000
4,000	6000	10,000	8,000	6000	14,000	8,000	8,000	16,000
8,000	4000	12,000	16,000	4000	20,000	16,000	4,000	20,000
12,000	2000	14,000	24,000	2000	26,000	24,000*	0	24,000
16,000*	0	16,000	32,000*	0	32,000			

*Indicates break-even income. Determined by dividing the minimum income by the benefit-reduction rate.

We might criticize plan 1 on the grounds that a 50 percent benefit-reduction rate is too high and therefore does not provide sufficient incentives to work. As earned income increases, the loss of transfer payments constitutes a "tax" on earnings. Some people may choose not to work when they lose 50 cents of each extra dollar earned. Thus in plan 2 the $8000 minimum income is retained, but the benefit-reduction rate is reduced to 25 percent. But note that the break-even level of income increases to $32,000, so many more families would now qualify for transfer payments. Furthermore, a family with any earned income under $32,000 will receive a larger total transfer payment. For both reasons, a reduction of the benefit-loss rate to enhance work incentives will raise the cost of the income-maintenance plan.

After examining plans 1 and 2, we might argue that the $8000 minimum annual income is too low—it does not get families out of poverty. Plan 3 raises the minimum income to $12,000 and retains the 50 percent benefit-reduction rate of plan 1. While plan 3 does a better job of raising the incomes of the poor, it too yields a higher break-even income than plan 1 and therefore will be more costly. Also, if the $12,000 income guarantee of plan 3 were coupled with plan 2's 25 percent benefit-reduction rate to strengthen work incentives, the break-even income level would shoot up to $48,000 and add even more to the costs of the public assistance program.

Conflicts among Goals

Clearly, then, the goals of eliminating poverty, maintaining work incentives, and holding down program costs are in conflict.

Plan 1, with a low minimum income and a high benefit-reduction rate, keeps cost down. But the low minimum income means that this plan is not very effective in eliminating poverty, and the high benefit-reduction rate weakens work incentives.

In comparison, plan 2 has a lower benefit-reduction rate and therefore stronger work incentives. But it is more costly, because it sets a higher break-even income and therefore pays benefits to more families.

Compared with plan 1, plan 3 has a higher minimum income and is more effective in eliminating poverty. While work incentives are the same as those in plan 1, the higher guaranteed income in plan 3 makes the plan more costly. **(Key Question 11)**

▮ Welfare Reform

The tradeoffs just mentioned shed light on the nation's relatively recent reform of the welfare system. The Personal Responsibility Act of 1996 resulted from a growing sense that welfare spending was not ending poverty. While the number of people receiving welfare benefits under the Aid to Families with Dependent Children (AFDC) program rose substantially in the 1980s and early 1990s, the number of people in poverty went up, instead of down. There was concern that the AFDC program was creating dependency on the government and thus robbing individuals and family members of motivation and dignity.

Temporary Assistance to Needy Families

The welfare reform of 1996 ended the Federal government's six-decade-old guarantee of cash assistance for poor families. Instead, the Federal government now pays each state a lump sum of Federal money each year to operate its own welfare and work programs. These lump-sum payments are called Temporary Assistance for Needy Families (TANF) funds. But the TANF reform did much more. It:
- Set a lifetime limit of 5 years on receiving TANF benefits and required able-bodied adults to work after receiving assistance for 2 years.
- Ended food-stamp eligibility for able-bodied persons age 18 to 50 (with no dependents) who are not working or engaged in job training programs.
- Tightened the definition of "disabled children" as it applies for eligibility of low-income families for Supplemental Security Income (SSI) assistance.
- Established a 5-year waiting period on public assistance for new legal immigrants who have not become citizens.

Assessment of TANF

Supporters of TANF believe that it already has played a key role in helping to end a "culture of welfare" in which dropping out of school, having a child, and going on welfare were allegedly becoming a normal way of life for part of the welfare population. They cite large declines in the welfare rolls as evidence of the law's effectiveness. In 1996 there were 12.6 million welfare recipients, including children, or 4.8 percent of the U.S. population. At the beginning of 2000 those totals had declined to 6.3 million and 2.3 percent. Experts attribute about half of the decline to welfare reform. The other half derives from the extraordinarily strong demand for labor and the low unemployment accompanying the economic expansion during that period.

Critics of the 1996 welfare reform say the approach places blame for poverty on its victims and not on the larger social and economic forces that actually cause it. They point out that nearly two-thirds of the people who receive TANF are children, not adults, and that the reform penalizes those children for their parents' inability or unwillingness to find and retain employment. Critics also say that the test

of TANF will come if the economy experiences recession and widespread unemployment. Those who have left welfare to take jobs in the recent strong labor market will surge back to welfare as they are laid off. To maintain their work requirements, states will have to expand their very expensive "public employment" programs. Critics say that such programs will prove to be far more costly to taxpayers than simply transferring income to those in need.

Such criticisms aside, it is fair to say that most economists judge the positive results of the 1996 welfare reform as strong confirmation of two economic principles: Economic growth is a powerful antipoverty force, and program incentives (and disincentives) matter.

Some Facts on U.S. Wealth and Its Distribution

In 2000 the Federal Reserve Reported Its Latest Findings on Household Wealth (Net Worth) in the United States. Between 1989 and 1998 Household Wealth Rose Rapidly and Became More Unequal.

The Federal Reserve conducts a *Survey of Consumer Finances* in the United States every 3 years through which it determines median household wealth, average household wealth, and the distribution of wealth. Median household wealth is the wealth received by the household at the midpoint of the distribution; average household wealth is simply total household wealth divided by the number of households. As shown in Table 1, median and average household wealth, adjusted for inflation, was considerably greater in 1998 than in 1989. That is, the value of household assets rose more rapidly than the value of liabilities, raising net worth—or wealth. Between 1995 and 1998, for example, median and average wealth rose by 18 percent and 26 percent, respectively. In general, American households are wealthier than they were before.

Table 2 looks at the distribution of American wealth for various percentile groups and reveals that the distribution of wealth is highly unequal. In 1998 the wealthiest 10 percent of households owned 68.7 percent of the total wealth and the top 1 percent owned 34 percent. The bottom 90 percent held only 31.3 percent of the total wealth. Not shown, the bottom 40 percent had negative net worth. They owed more than the value of their assets.

Moreover, the trend is toward greater inequality in the distribution of wealth. The lowest 90 percent of the population owned 33 percent of the wealth in 1992, but that percentage had fallen to 31.3 percent by 1998. The share of wealth owned by the wealthiest 1 percent increased from 30.2 percent in 1989 to 34 percent in 1998. The major source of the growing wealth for the top 10 and top 1 percent was a rise in the value of business assets and stock holdings. The bottom 90 percent of households own relatively few business assets. And, while the value of their stock holdings rose, stock holdings are a much smaller proportion of their total wealth than is the case for households in the top 10 percent of the wealth distribution.

So from a normative standpoint, Tables 1 and 2 present a "good news–bad news" combination. The good news is that median and average wealth in the United States rose substantially between 1989 and 1998. The bad news is that such wealth grew more rapidly for the top 10 percent of households than for the typical American household. In fact, between 1995 and 1998, the bottom 25 percent of households experienced average declines in wealth, when adjusted for inflation.

Tables 1 and 2 raise many unanswered questions: Will the growing inequality of wealth continue? If so, what are its implications for the character of the American society? Should government do more, or less, in the future to redistribute wealth? Would new government policies to redistribute wealth endanger or slow the creation of wealth and the growth of income for average Americans? Is this the time to eliminate the Federal estate tax, which is highly progressive?

Source: Arthur B. Kennickell, "An Examination of Changes in the Distribution of Wealth from 1989 to 1998: Evidence from the Survey of Consumer Finances," prepared for the Conference on Saving, Intergenerational Transfers, and the Distribution of Wealth, Jerome Levy Economics Institute, Bard College, June 2000.

Table 1

Median and Average Wealth, 1989, 1992, 1995, and 1998 (in 1998 dollars)

Year	Median	Average*
1989	$59,700	$236,900
1992	56,500	212,700
1995	60,900	224,800
1998	71,600	282,500

*The averages are so much higher than the medians because the billion-dollar wealth of a relatively few households greatly boosts the averages.

Table 2

Percentage of Total Wealth Held by Different Percentile Groups, 1989, 1992, 1995, 1998

Year	Percentile of Wealth Distribution		
	Bottom 90%	Top 10%	Top 1%
1989	32.7%	62.9%	30.2%
1992	33.0	67.0	30.1
1995	32.3	67.7	34.7
1998	31.3	68.7	34.0

SUMMARY

1. The distribution of income in the United States reflects considerable inequality. The richest 20 percent of families receive 47.2 percent of total income, while the poorest 20 percent receive only 4.3 percent.

2. The Lorenz curve shows the percentage of total income received by each percentage of families. The extent of the gap between the Lorenz curve and a line of total equality illustrates the degree of income inequality.

3. Recognizing that the positions of individual families in the distribution of income change over time and incorporating the effects of noncash transfers and taxes would reveal less income inequality than do standard census data. Government transfers (cash and noncash) greatly lessen the degree of income inequality; taxes also reduce inequality, but not nearly as much as transfers.

4. Causes of income inequality include differences in abilities, in education and training, and in job tastes, along with discrimination, inequality in the distribution of wealth, and an unequal distribution of market power.

5. Census data show that income inequality declined significantly between 1929 and the end of the Second World War but has increased since 1969. The major cause of the recent increases in income inequality is a rising demand for highly skilled workers, which has boosted their earnings significantly.

6. The basic argument for income equality is that it maximizes consumer satisfaction (total utility) from a particular level of total income. The main argument for income inequality is that it provides the incentives to work, invest, and assume risk and is necessary for the production of output, which, in turn, creates income that is then available for distribution.

7. Current statistics reveal that 11.8 percent of the U.S. population lives in poverty. Poverty rates are particularly high for female-headed families, young children, blacks, and Hispanics.

8. The present income-maintenance program in the United States consists of social insurance programs (OASDHI, Medicare, and unemployment compensation) and public assistance programs (SSI, TANF, food stamps, Medicaid, and earned-income tax credit).

9. Public assistance programs (welfare) are difficult to design because their goals of reducing poverty, maintaining work incentives, and holding down program costs are often in conflict with one another.

10. Before recent reforms, the Aid for Families with Dependent Children program was heavily criticized as administratively inefficient, detrimental to work incentives, and fostering dependence.

11. In 1996 Congress established the Temporary Assistance for Needy Families (TANF) program, which shifted responsibility for welfare from the Federal government to the states. Among its provisions are work requirements for adults receiving welfare and a 5-year lifelong limit on welfare benefits.

12. A strong economy and TANF reduced the U.S. welfare rolls by one-half between 1996 and 2000.

TERMS AND CONCEPTS

income inequality

Lorenz curve

income mobility

noncash transfers

tradeoff between equality and efficiency

poverty rate

entitlement programs

social insurance programs

OASDHI

Medicare

unemployment compensation

public assistance programs

Supplemental Security Income (SSI)

Temporary Assistance for Needy Families (TANF)

food-stamp program

Medicaid

earned-income tax credit (EITC)

STUDY QUESTIONS

1. Use quintiles to briefly summarize the degree of income inequality in the United States. What criticisms have been made of standard Census Bureau data on income inequality? How and to what extent does government contribute to income equality?

2. **Key Question** Assume that Al, Beth, Carol, David, and Ed receive incomes of $500, $250, $125, $75, and $50, respectively. Construct and interpret a Lorenz curve for this five-person economy. What percentage of total income is received by the richest quintile and by the poorest quintile?

3. Why is the lifetime distribution of income more equal than the distribution in any specific year?

4. **Key Question** Briefly discuss the major causes of income inequality. With respect to income inequality, is there any difference between inheriting property and inheriting a high IQ? Explain.

5. What factors have contributed to increased income inequality since 1969?

6. Use the "leaky-bucket analogy" to discuss the equality-efficiency tradeoff. Explain how welfare reform (TANF) has reduced the leak.

7. Should a nation's income be distributed to its members according to their contributions to the production of that total income or according to the members' needs? Should society attempt to equalize income or economic opportunities? Are the issues of equity and equality in the distribution of income synonymous? To what degree, if any, is income inequality equitable?

8. Analyze in detail: "There need be no tradeoff between equality and efficiency. An 'efficient' economy that yields an income distribution that many regard as unfair may cause those with meager incomes to become discouraged and stop trying. So efficiency may be undermined. A fairer distribution of rewards may generate a higher average productive effort on the part of the population, thereby enhancing efficiency. If people think they are playing a fair economic game and this belief causes them to try harder, an economy with an equitable income distribution may be efficient as well."[4]

9. Comment on or explain:
   a. Endowing everyone with equal income will make for very unequal enjoyment and satisfaction.
   b. Equality is a "superior good"; the richer we become, the more of it we can afford.
   c. The mob goes in search of bread, and the means it employs is generally to wreck the bakeries.
   d. Some freedoms may be more important in the long run than freedom from want on the part of every individual.
   e. Capitalism and democracy are really a most improbable mixture. Maybe that is why they need each other—to put some rationality into equality and some humanity into efficiency.
   f. The incentives created by the attempt to bring about a more equal distribution of income are in conflict with the incentives needed to generate increased income.

10. What are the essential differences between social insurance and public assistance programs? Why is Medicare a social insurance program whereas Medicaid is a public assistance program? Why is the earned-income tax credit considered to be a public assistance program?

11. **Key Question** The following table contains three hypothetical public assistance plans.

Plan 1		
Earned Income	Transfer Payment	Total Income
$ 0	$4000	$4000
2000	3000	5000
4000	2000	6000
6000	1000	7000

Plan 2		
Earned Income	Transfer Payment	Total Income
$ 0	$4000	$ 4,000
4,000	3000	7,000
8,000	2000	10,000
12,000	1000	13,000

Plan 3		
Earned Income	Transfer Payment	Total Income
$ 0	$8000	$ 8,000
4,000	6000	10,000
8,000	4000	12,000
12,000	2000	14,000

   a. Determine the minimum income, the benefit-reduction rate, and the break-even income for each plan.
   b. Which plan is the most costly? The least costly? Which plan is the most effective in reducing poverty? The least effective? Which plan contains the strongest disincentive to work? The weakest disincentive to work?
   c. Use your answers in part b to explain the following statement: "The dilemma of public assistance is that you cannot bring families up to the poverty level and simultaneously preserve work incentives (without work requirements) and minimize program costs."

12. What major criticisms of the U.S. welfare system led to its reform in 1996 (via the Personal Responsibility Act)? How did this reform try to address those criticisms? Do you agree with the general thrust of the reform and with its emphasis on work requirements and time limits on welfare benefits? Has the reform reduced U.S. welfare rolls or increased them?

13. **(Last Word)** Go to Table 1 in the Last Word and compute the ratio of average wealth to median wealth for each of the 4 years. What trend do you find? What is your explanation for the trend? The Federal estate tax redistributes wealth in two ways: by encouraging charitable giving, which reduces the taxable estate, and by heavily taxing extraordinarily large

---

[4]Paraphrased from Andrew Schotter, *Free Market Economics* (New York: St. Martin's Press, 1985), pp. 30–31.

estates and using the proceeds to fund government programs. Do you favor repealing the estate tax? Explain.

14. **Web-Based Question:** *How much family income does it take to be in the richest 5 percent?* The U.S. Census Bureau provides information on the historical distribution of family income at www.census.gov/hhes/www/income.html. What is the lower limit of family income for the richest 5 percent of families in the most recent year listed? Do the historical data in the table suggest that the poor are getting poorer and the rich are getting richer in absolute terms? Use the data at www.census.gov/hhes/histinc/f02.html to determine whether the relative income share of the richest 5 percent of families has increased in the past decade.

15. **Web-Based Question:** *Is poverty on the rise or on the decline?* The U.S. Census Bureau compiles information about poverty in the United States. Use the data at www.census.gov/hhes/www/poverty.html to answer the following questions:

   a. Is the number of people living below the official government poverty level higher or lower than it was in the preceding year? Than it was a decade earlier?

   b. Is the poverty rate (in percent) higher or lower than it was in the preceding year for the general population, children under 18, blacks, Asians, Pacific Islanders, and whites?

   c. How many states had increases in the poverty rate compared to the preceding year?

22

Labor Market Issues
Unionism, Discrimination, Immigration

IN THIS CHAPTER we examine three separate issues: unionism, discrimination, and immigration. All are significant facets of the U.S. labor market, but otherwise they are largely unrelated.

- In the first part of the chapter we look at labor unions. We see who belongs to unions, examine collective bargaining, and discuss the reasons for the recent decline of unionism. Then we assess the effect of unions on wages, efficiency, and productivity.

- We then turn to labor market discrimination and discuss the types and costs of discrimination, economic theories of discrimination, and current antidiscrimination policies.

- In the last part of the chapter we examine immigration: the inflow of people to the United States from abroad. Our focus is on the extent and effects of both legal and illegal immigration.

▌Unionism in America

In 2000 about 16 million U.S. workers—13.5 percent of employed wage and salary workers—belonged to unions. (Global Perspective 22.1 compares this percentage with those of several other nations.) Some 13 million of the 16 million U.S. union members belong to one of many unions that are loosely and voluntarily affiliated with the **American Federation of Labor and the Congress of Industrial Organizations (AFL-CIO).** Examples of AFL-CIO unions are the Teamsters, United Autoworkers, Communications Workers, and Carpenters. Another 3 million union members be-

long to **independent unions** that are not affiliated with the AFL-CIO. Among those unions are the National Education Association, the Nurses' Union, and the United Mine Workers.

Business Unionism

In the United States, unions generally have adhered to a philosophy of **business unionism:** unionism that is concerned with the short-run economic objectives of higher pay, better benefits, shorter hours, and improved working conditions. These unions have not pushed for long-run idealistic objectives aimed at significantly modifying or overthrowing

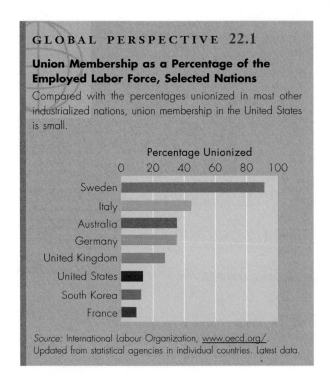

Union Membership

The likelihood that any particular worker will be a union member depends mainly on the industry in which the worker works and his or her occupation. Figure 22.1a shows that the rate of unionization (percentage of workers unionized) is high in government, transportation, construction, and manufacturing. The rate of unionization is very low in agriculture; finance, insurance, and real estate; retail trade; and services. Figure 22.1b shows that unionism also varies greatly by occupation. Protective service workers, transportation workers, craft workers, and machine operators have high rates of unionization; sales workers and managers have very low rates.

Because disproportionately more men than women work in the industries and occupations with high unionization rates, men are more likely to be union members than women. Specifically, 15 percent of male wage and salary workers belong to unions compared with 12 percent of women. For the same reason, blacks have higher unionization rates than whites: 17 percent compared with 13 percent. The unionization rate for Hispanics is 11 percent. Unionism in the United States is largely an urban phenomenon. Six heavily urbanized, heavily industrialized states (New York, California, Pennsylvania, Illinois, Ohio, and Michigan) account for approximately half of all union members.

the capitalistic system. Nor have union members organized into a distinct political party, such as the "labor parties" of several European nations. Unionism's political philosophy has been to reward its friends and punish its enemies at the polls, regardless of political party.

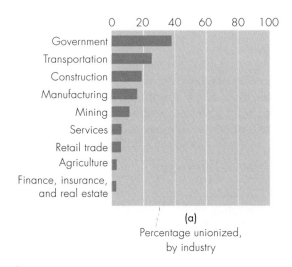

(a)
Percentage unionized, by industry

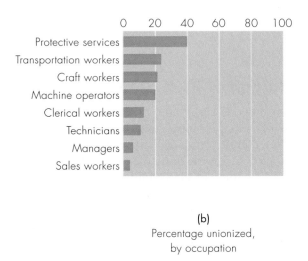

(b)
Percentage unionized, by occupation

Figure 22.1

Union membership as a percentage of employed wage and salary workers, selected industries and occupations, 2000.   In percentage terms, union membership varies greatly by (a) industry and (b) occupation.

Source: Bureau of Labor Statistics, www.bls.gov.

The Decline of Unionism

Since the mid-1950s, union membership has not kept pace with the growth of the labor force. While 25 percent of employed wage and salary workers belonged to unions in the mid-1950s, today only 13.5 percent are union members. Over recent years, even the absolute number of union members has declined significantly. More than 22 million workers were unionized in 1980 but only about 16 million in 2000.

What explains the decline in unionization, relatively and absolutely?

Structural Changes

According to the **structural-change hypothesis**, changes unfavorable to the expansion of union membership have occurred in both the economy and the labor force.

Employment has shifted away from traditionally unionized industries. For example, U.S. domestic employment has moved away from manufactured goods (where unions have been strong) and toward services (where unions have been weak). Also, consumer demand in some cases has shifted toward foreign manufactured goods and away from goods produced by union labor in the United States. Increased foreign competition in several highly unionized manufacturing industries such as automobile and steel has reduced unionized workforces and, therefore, union membership. And within manufacturing, production has shifted from highly unionized "old-economy" firms to software production, computer manufacturing, and other "high-tech" industries in which unionization is virtually nonexistent.

Another factor in the decline in unionism is that an unusually high proportion of the increase in employment in recent decades has been concentrated among women, youths, and part-time workers. These groups are allegedly difficult to organize into unions, because they are less strongly attached to the labor force. Furthermore, the long-term trend of industry to shift from the northeast and midwest, where unionism is "a way of life," to "hard-to-organize" areas of the south and southwest has reduced the growth of union membership.

An ironic possibility is that the relative decline of unionism may in part reflect the success that unions have achieved in gaining a sizable wage advantage over nonunion workers in the United States. Confronted with high union wages, employers may have substituted machinery for workers, subcontracted more work to nonunion suppliers, opened nonunion plants in less industrialized areas, or shifted production of components to low-wage nations. All these actions reduce the employment of union workers and thus the level of union membership.

The success of unions in raising wages may have also raised the prices of union-produced goods relative to the prices of goods produced by nonunion workers. If so, we would expect output and employment in lower-cost nonunion firms and industries to increase at the expense of output and employment in higher-cost union firms and industries.

Managerial Opposition

Another view of the decline of unionism is that intensified managerial opposition to unions has deterred union growth. According to this **managerial-opposition hypothesis,** the wage advantage that union workers enjoy causes union firms to be less profitable than nonunion firms. The managements of both nonunionized and unionized firms have therefore undertaken policies to oppose or dissuade unionization. One managerial strategy has been to employ labor-management consultants who specialize in mounting aggressive antiunion drives to dissuade workers from unionizing or, alternatively, to persuade union workers to decertify (officially vote out) their union. Also, confronted with strikes by union workers, management has increasingly hired permanent strikebreakers to take the place of striking workers, in the expectation that these nonunion workers will later vote to eliminate the union. A conciliatory strategy by management has been to improve working conditions and personnel policies. When management treats workers with dignity and respect, workers feel less need to join unions.

▌Collective Bargaining

Despite the decline of unionism, **collective bargaining** (the negotiation of labor contracts) remains an important feature of labor-management relations. The goal of collective bargaining is to establish a "work agreement" between the firm and the union.

The Work Agreement

Collective bargaining agreements (contracts) assume many forms. Some contracts are brief, taking up only 2 or 3 pages; others are lengthy and highly detailed, requiring 200 or 300 pages of print. Some agreements involve only a local union and a single plant; others set wages, hours, and working conditions for entire industries.

Typically, however, collective bargaining agreements cover several topics.

Union Status and Managerial Prerogatives

As for *union status,* the closed shop affords the union the greatest security. In a **closed shop,** a worker must be (or must become) a member of the union before being hired. Under Federal labor law, such shops are illegal in industries other than transportation and construction. In contrast, a **union shop** permits the employer to hire nonunion workers but provides that these workers must join the union within a specified period, say 30 days, or relinquish their jobs. An **agency shop** requires that nonunion workers pay union dues or donate an equivalent amount to charity. Union and agency shops are legal, except in the 20 states that expressly prohibit them through so-called **right-to-work laws.** In the **open shop,** an employer may hire either union or nonunion workers. Those who are nonunion are not obligated to join the union or to pay union dues; they may continue on their jobs indefinitely as nonunion workers. Nevertheless, the wages, hours, and working conditions set forth in the work agreement apply to the nonunion workers as well as to the union workers.

The management side of the union-status issue is *managerial prerogatives.* Most work agreements contain clauses outlining certain decisions that are reserved solely for management. These prerogatives usually cover such matters as the size and location of plants, the products to be manufactured, and the types of equipment and materials to be used in production and in production scheduling.

Wages and Hours

The focal point of any bargaining agreement is wages and hours. Both labor and management press for the advantage in wage bargaining. The arguments that unions use most frequently in demanding (and, by the firm, in resisting) wage boosts are (1) "what others are getting," (2) the employer's ability to pay, based on its profitability, (3) increases in the cost of living, and (4) increases in labor productivity. In some cases, unions achieve success in tying wages to the cost of living through **cost-of-living adjustment (COLA)** clauses.

Hours of work, voluntary versus mandatory overtime, holiday and vacation provisions, profit sharing, health plans, and pension benefits are other contract issues that must be addressed in the bargaining process.

Seniority and Job Protection

The uncertainty of employment in a market economy, along with the fear of antiunion discrimination on the part of employers, has made workers and their unions "job-conscious." The explicit and detailed provisions covering job opportunities that most agreements contain reflect this concern. Unions stress seniority (length of service) as the basis for worker promotion and for layoff and recall. They want the worker with the longest continuous service to have the first chance at relevant promotions, to be the last one laid off, and to be the first one recalled from layoff.

In recent years, unions have become increasingly sensitive to losing jobs to nonunion subcontractors and to overseas workers. Unions sometimes seek limits on the firm's ability to subcontract out work or to relocate production facilities overseas.

Grievance Procedures

Even the most detailed and comprehensive work agreement cannot spell out all the specific issues and problems that might occur during its life. For example, suppose that Nelson gets reassigned to a less pleasant job. Was this reassignment for legitimate business reasons or, as Nelson suspects, because of a personality conflict with a particular manager? Labor contracts contain *grievance procedures* to resolve such matters.

The Bargaining Process

The date for the beginning of collective bargaining on a new contract is usually specified in the existing contract and is typically 60 days before the current one expires. The union normally takes the initiative, presenting its *demands* in the form of specific wage, fringe-benefit, and other adjustments to the present union-management contract. The firm counters with an offer relating to these and other contract provisions. It is not unusual for the original union demand and the first offer by the firm to be far apart, not only because of the parties' conflicting interests but also because the parties know they are obligated by law to bargain in good faith. The initial "large-demand–low-offer situation" leaves plenty of room for compromise during the negotiations.

The negotiating then begins in earnest on items in dispute. Hanging over the negotiations is the *deadline,* which occurs the moment the present contract expires. At that time there is a possibility of a **strike**—a "work stoppage" by the union—if it thinks its demands are not being satisfactorily met. But there is also the possibility that at the deadline the firm may engage in a **lockout,** in which it forbids the workers to return to work until a new contract is signed. In this setting of uncertainty prior to the deadline, both parties feel pressure to find mutually acceptable terms.

Although bluster and bickering often occur in collective bargaining, labor and management display a remarkable capacity for compromise and agreement. Typically they reach a compromise solution that is written into a new contract. Nevertheless, strikes and lockouts occasionally do occur. When they happen, workers lose income and firms lose profit. To stem their losses, both parties usually look for and eventually find ways to settle the labor dispute and get the workers back to work.

Bargaining, strikes, and lockouts occur within a framework of Federal labor law, specifically the **National Labor Relations Act (NLRA)**. This act was first passed as the Wagner Act of 1935 and later amended by the Taft-Hartley Act of 1947 and the Landrum-Griffin Act of 1959. The act sets forth the dos and don'ts of union and management labor practices. For example, while union members can picket in front of a firm's business, they cannot block access to the business by customers, coworkers, or strikebreakers hired by the firm. Another example: Firms cannot refuse to meet and talk with the union's designated representatives.

Either unions or management can file charges of unfair labor practices under the labor law. The **National Labor Relations Board (NLRB)** has the authority to investigate such charges and to issue cease-and-desist orders in the event of violation. (The board also conducts worker elections to decide which specific union, if any, a group of workers might want to have represent them.) ▮ 22.1

> **QUICK REVIEW 22.1**
>
> ▪ About 13 million of the 16 million union workers in the United States are members of the AFL-CIO, with the rest belonging to independent unions. About 13.5 percent of U.S. wage and salary workers belong to unions.
>
> ▪ The rate of unionization varies greatly by industry and occupation (see Figure 22.1).
>
> ▪ The decline of unionism in recent decades has been attributed to (a) changes in the structures of the economy and the labor force and (b) growing managerial opposition to unions.
>
> ▪ Collective bargaining determines the terms of work agreements, which typically cover (a) union status and managerial prerogatives, (b) wages, hours, and working conditions, (c) control over job opportunities, and (d) grievance procedures.

▮ Economic Effects of Unions

What effects do unions have on the economy? Do unions raise wages? Do they increase or diminish economic efficiency?

The Union Wage Advantage

The three union models in Chapter 15 (see Figures 15.5, 15.6, and 15.7 and the accompanying discussions) all imply that unions are capable of raising wages. Has unionization really done so?

Empirical research overwhelmingly suggests that unions do raise the wages of their members relative to those of comparable nonunion workers, although the size of the union wage advantage varies according to occupation, industry, race, and gender. The consensus estimate is that the overall union wage advantage averages about 15 percent. On the other hand, unions have had little impact on the average level of real wages received by U.S. workers taken as a whole.

These two conclusions (higher union pay, no overall impact) may seem inconsistent, but they are not. The higher union wages apply to only a relatively small part of the labor force. Moreover, these wages may come at the expense of lower wages for some nonunion workers. As you will see (in Figure 22.2), higher wages in unionized labor markets may cause employers to hire fewer workers. The workers who are left unemployed may seek employment in nonunion labor markets. The resulting increase in the supply of labor in the nonunion labor markets reduces wage rates there. So the net result may be no change in the average level of wages.

The long-run relationship between productivity and the average level of real wages shown in Figure 15.1 suggests that unions have little power to raise the average real wage over long periods of time. But Figure 15.1 is an average relationship; it is therefore compatible with the idea that certain groups of (union) workers get higher relative wages while other (nonunion) workers simultaneously get lower real wages.

Efficiency and Productivity

Do labor unions increase or decrease efficiency and productivity? There is much disagreement on this question, but we can consider some of the ways in which unions might affect efficiency, both negatively and positively.

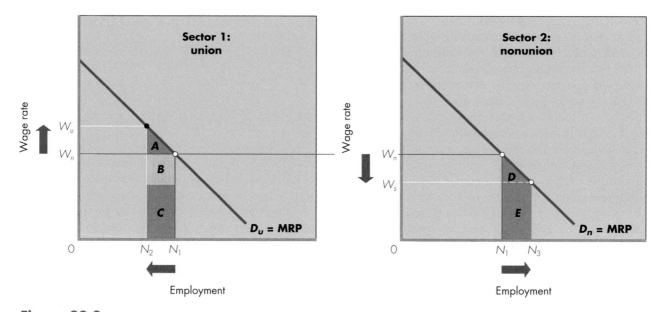

Figure 22.2

The effects of the union wage advantage on the allocation of labor. The higher wage W_u that the union receives in sector 1 causes the displacement of $N_1 N_2$ workers. The reemployment of these workers in sector 2 increases employment from N_1 to N_3 and reduces the wage rate there from W_n to W_s. The associated loss of output in the union sector is area $A + B + C$, while the gain in the nonunion sector is only $D + E$. The net loss of output is area B. This loss of output suggests that the union wage advantage has resulted in a misallocation of labor and a decline in economic efficiency.

Negative View

There are three ways in which unions might exert a negative impact on productivity and efficiency.

Losses via Featherbedding and Work Rules

Some unions undoubtedly have diminished efficiency by engaging in "make-work" or "featherbedding" practices and resisting the introduction of output-increasing machinery and equipment. These productivity-reducing practices often arise in periods of technological change. Historical examples: For many years the Brotherhood of Locomotive Firemen and Engineers insisted that a fireman be retained on train crews, even though his function had been eliminated by the shift from steam engines to diesel engines. Similarly, union painters resisted the use of spray guns and even limited the width of paintbrushes used on union jobs.

More generally, unions might reduce efficiency by establishing work rules and practices that impede putting the most productive workers in particular jobs. Under seniority rules, for example, workers may be promoted for their employment tenure rather than for their ability to perform the available job with the greatest efficiency. Also, unions might restrict the kinds of tasks workers may perform.

Contract provisions may prohibit sheet-metal workers or bricklayers from doing the simple carpentry work often associated with their jobs. Observance of such rules means, in this instance, that firms must hire unneeded and underused carpenters. Finally, critics of unions contend that union contracts often chip away at managerial prerogatives to establish work schedules, determine production targets, introduce new technology, and make other decisions contributing to productive efficiency.

Losses via Strikes

A second way unions may impair efficiency is through calling a strike. If union and management reach an impasse in their negotiations, a strike may result and the firm's production may cease for the strike's duration. If so, the firm will forgo sales and profit; workers will sacrifice income; and the economy could lose output.

Statistics on U.S. strike activity suggest that strikes are rare and the associated aggregate economic losses are less than might be expected. In 2000 only 39 strikes occurred that involved 1000 or more employees, up from 17 a year earlier. Furthermore, many strikes lasted only a few days. Between 1995 and 2000, the average amount of work time lost each year because of strikes was the equivalent of 4 hours per U.S. worker per year, which is less than 5 minutes per worker per week.

However, the economic costs associated with strikes may be greater or less than is suggested by the amount of work time lost. The costs may be greater if strikes disrupt production in nonstruck firms that either provide inputs to or buy goods and services from the struck firm. Example: An extended strike in the auto industry might reduce output and cause layoffs in firms producing, say, glass, tires, paints, and fabrics used in producing cars. It may also reduce sales and cause layoffs in auto dealerships.

On the other hand, the costs of strikes may be less than is implied by the work time lost by strikers if nonstruck firms increase their output to offset the loss of production by struck firms. While the output of General Motors declines when its workers strike, auto buyers may shift their demand to Ford, Honda, or Toyota, which will respond by increasing their employment and output. Thus, although GM and its employees are hurt by a strike, society as a whole may experience little or no decline in employment, real output, and income.

Losses via Labor Misallocation   A more subtle way in which unions might adversely affect efficiency is through the union wage advantage itself. Figure 22.2 shows (for simplicity) identical labor demand curves for a unionized sector and a nonunionized sector of the market for some particular kind of labor. We assume that there is pure competition in both the product market and all resource markets.

If there were no union in either sector initially, the wage rate that would result from the competitive hiring of labor would be W_n, while N_1 workers would be hired in each sector. Now suppose workers form a union in sector 1 and succeed in increasing the wage rate from W_n to W_u. As a consequence, N_1N_2 workers lose their jobs in the union sector. Assume that they all move to nonunion sector 2, where they are employed. This increase in labor supply (not shown) in the nonunion sector increases the quantity of labor supplied there from N_1 to N_3, reducing the wage rate from W_n to W_s.

Recall that the labor demand curves reflect the marginal revenue products (MRPs) of workers or, in other words, the contribution that each additional worker makes to domestic output. This means that area $A + B + C$ in the union sector represents the sum of the MRPs—the total contribution to domes-

tic output—of the workers displaced by the wage increase achieved by the union. The reemployment of these workers in nonunion sector 2 results in an increase in domestic output, indicated by area $D + E$. Because area $A + B + C$ exceeds area $D + E$, there is a net loss of domestic output. More precisely, because $A = D$ and $C = E$, the net loss attributable to the union wage advantage is represented by area B. Since the same amount of employed labor is now producing a smaller output, labor is being misallocated and inefficiently used.

From a slightly different perspective, after the shift of N_1N_2 workers from the union sector to the nonunion sector has occurred, workers will be paid a wage rate equal to their MRPs in both sectors. But the workers who shifted sectors will be working at lower-MRP jobs after the shift. An economy always obtains a larger domestic output when labor is reallocated from a low-MRP use to a high-MRP use. But here the opposite has occurred. And assuming the union can maintain the W_u wage rate in its sector, a reallocation of labor from sector 2 to sector 1 will never occur.

Attempts to estimate the output loss associated with union wage gains, however, suggest that the loss is small: perhaps .2 to .4 percent (or one-fifth of 1 percent to two-fifths of 1 percent) of U.S. GDP. In 2000 this cost would be about $20 to $40 billion, or $73 to $146 per person. **(Key Question 4)**

Positive View   Other economists take the position that, on balance, unions make a positive contribution to efficiency and productivity.

Longer-Run Positive Impacts: The Shock Effect
A wage increase won by a union may have a *shock effect* on affected firms, causing them in the long run to substitute capital for labor and in the very long run to implement productivity-increasing technologies. When faced with higher production costs due to the union wage increase, employers will be motivated to reduce costs by using more machinery and by seeking improved production techniques that use less of both labor and capital per unit of output. In fact, if the product market is reasonably competitive, a unionized firm with labor costs 10 to 15 percent higher than those of nonunionized competitors will not survive over long periods unless productivity can be raised. Hence, union wage pressure may generate managerial actions that increase worker productivity and justify the higher union wages. If so, the overall economy benefits.

Reduced Worker Turnover Unions may also contribute to raising productivity within firms through reduced worker turnover and improved worker security. A union functions as a *collective voice* for its members by taking their side in resolving disputes and improving working conditions.

If a group of workers are dissatisfied with their conditions of employment, they can respond in either of two ways: through the "exit mechanism" or through the "voice mechanism." With the **exit mechanism,** workers react to undesirable employers and working conditions by leaving their present jobs in search of better ones; they rely on the labor market. The use of this mechanism obviously increases worker turnover, the rate at which workers quit jobs and must be replaced.

With the **voice mechanism** workers communicate with the employer in an effort to improve working conditions and resolve worker grievances. It might be risky for individual workers to express their dissatisfaction to employers, because employers might retaliate by firing them as "troublemakers." But a union can provide workers with a collective voice to communicate problems and grievances to management and to press for satisfactory resolutions.

Unions may help reduce worker turnover in two ways:

■ Unions provide the voice mechanism as a substitute for the exit mechanism. They use communication to correct job dissatisfactions that otherwise would be "resolved" by workers through the exit mechanism of changing jobs.

■ The union wage advantage is a deterrent to job change. Higher wages make unionized firms more attractive places to work.

Compared with the rates at nonunion firms, the quit rate (resignation rate) for union workers is 31 to 65 percent lower, depending on the industry. A lower quit rate increases efficiency by giving a firm a more experienced, and thus a more productive, workforce. Also, having fewer resignations reduces the firm's recruitment, screening, and hiring costs. Finally, reduced turnover makes employers more willing to invest in the training (and therefore the productivity) of their workers. If a worker quits or "exits" at the end of, say, a year's training, the employer will get no return from providing that training. But lower turnover increases the likelihood that the employer will receive a return on the training it provides, thereby increasing its willingness to upgrade its workforce.

Increased Informal Training Much productivity-increasing training is transmitted informally. Workers who are more skilled may share their experience with less skilled workers on the job, during lunch, or during coffee breaks. However, a skilled senior worker may want to conceal his or her knowledge from less skilled junior workers, who might become competitors for the skilled worker's job. Because of union insistence on the use of seniority in such matters as promotion and layoff, worker security is enhanced and this problem is overcome. With that security, senior workers are more willing to pass on their job knowledge and skills to new or subordinate workers. Such informal training enhances the quality and productivity of the firm's workforce.

Mixed Research Findings Although many studies have tried to measure the effect of unionization on productivity, their results are inconclusive. For every study that finds that unions have a positive effect on productivity, another study using different methodology or data concludes that they have a negative effect. At present there simply is no generally accepted conclusion regarding the overall impact of unions on productivity.

> **QUICK REVIEW 22.2**
>
> ☐ Union wages average about 15 percent higher than comparable nonunion wages.
>
> ☐ Union work rules, strikes, and the misallocation of labor associated with the union wage advantage are ways by which unions may reduce efficiency.
>
> ☐ Unions may enhance productivity by causing a shock effect, by reducing worker turnover, and by providing the worker security that is a prerequisite to informal on-the-job training.

■ Labor Market Discrimination

Broadly defined, **labor market discrimination** occurs when equivalent labor resources are paid or treated differently even though their productive contributions are equal. Table 22.1 shows various economic disparities by race, ethnicity, and gender. These statistical differences result from a combination of nondiscriminatory and discriminatory factors. For example, studies indicate that about one-half the differences in earnings between men and women and whites and blacks can be explained by such

Table 22.1

Selected Economic Disparities by Gender, Race, and Ethnicity, 1999

Selected Measures	Blacks	Hispanics	Whites
Earnings and income			
Median weekly earnings:			
Men	$486	$406	$638
Women	$409	$348	$483
Median income of families	$31,778	$31,663	$51,224
Percent of families in poverty	23.6	22.8	9.8
Labor-force participation and employment			
Labor-force participation rate:			
Men	68.7	79.8	75.6
Women	63.5	55.9	59.6
Unemployment rate:			
Men	8.2	5.6	3.6
Women	7.8	7.6	3.8
Education			
Percent of population with at least 4 years of high school:*			
Men	76.1	57.7	86.8
Women	77.1	55.5	87.3
Percent of population with at least 4 years of college:			
Men	12.1	9.0	27.8
Women	14.3	9.6	23.4
Occupational distribution (percent of group's total employment)			
Managerial and professional occupations:			
Men and women	21.5	14.9	31.3
Service occupations:			
Men and women	21.8	19.8	12.2

*Population 18 years or older.

Source: Bureau of Labor Statistics, www.bls.gov/; Census Bureau, www.census.gov/.

nondiscriminatory factors as differences in education, age, training, industry and occupation, union membership, location, work experience, continuity of work, and health. (Of course, some of these factors may be influenced by discrimination.) The other half is an unexplained difference, the bulk of which economists attribute to discrimination.

In labor market discrimination, certain groups of people are accorded inferior treatment with respect to hiring, occupational access, education and training, promotion, wage rates, or working conditions even though they have the same abilities, education and training, and experience as the more preferred groups. People who practice discrimination are said to exhibit a prejudice or bias against the targets of their discrimination.

Types of Discrimination

Labor market discrimination may take several forms:

- **Wage discrimination** occurs when women or members of minorities are paid less than white males for doing the same work. This kind of discrimination is declining because of its explicitness and the fact that it clearly violates Federal law. But wage discrimination can be subtle and difficult to detect. For example, women and minorities sometimes find that their job classifications carry lower pay than job classifications held by white males, even though they are performing essentially the same tasks.

- **Employment discrimination** takes place when women or minority workers receive inferior treatment in hiring, promotions, assignments, temporary layoffs, and permanent discharges. This type of discrimination also encompasses sexual and racial harassment—demeaning treatment in the workplace by coworkers or administrators.

- **Occupational discrimination** occurs when women or minority workers are arbitrarily restricted or prohibited from entering the more desirable, higher-paying occupations. Businesswomen have found it difficult to break through the "glass ceiling" that prevents them from moving up to executive ranks. Blacks and Hispanics in executive and sales positions are relatively few. In addition, skilled and unionized work such as electrical work, bricklaying, and plumbing do not have high minority representation.
- **Human capital discrimination** occurs when women or members of minorities do not have the same access to productivity-enhancing investments in education and training as white males. Example: The lower average educational attainment (Table 22.1) of blacks and Hispanics has reduced their opportunities in the labor market.

Costs of Discrimination

Discrimination imposes costs on those who are discriminated against. The groups that discriminate get the good jobs and the better pay that are withheld from the targets of their discrimination. But discrimination does more than simply transfer benefits from women, blacks, and Hispanics to men and whites. Where it exists, discrimination actually diminishes the economy's output and income; like any other artificial barrier to free competition, it decreases economic efficiency and reduces production. By arbitrarily blocking certain qualified groups of people from high-productivity (and thus high-wage) jobs, discrimination prevents them from making their maximum contribution to the society's output, income, and well-being.

The effects of discrimination can be depicted as a point inside the economy's production possibilities curve, such as point D in Figure 22.3. At such a point, the economy obtains some combination of capital and consumption goods—here, $K_d + C_d$—which is less desirable than combinations represented by points such as X, Y, or Z on the curve. By preventing the economy from achieving productive efficiency, discrimination reduces the nation's real output and income. Very rough estimates suggest the U.S. economy would gain $325 billion per year

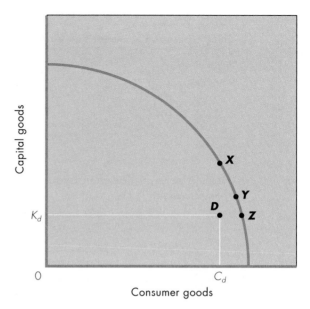

Figure 22.3
Discrimination and production possibilities.
Discrimination represents a failure to achieve productive efficiency. The cost of discrimination to society is the sacrificed output associated with a point such as D inside the nation's production possibilities curve, compared with points such as X, Y, and Z on the curve.

by eliminating racial and ethnic discrimination and $180 billion per year by ending gender discrimination.

▌Economic Analysis of Discrimination

Prejudice reflects complex, multifaceted, and deeply ingrained beliefs and attitudes. Thus, economics can contribute some insights into discrimination but no detailed explanations. With this caution in mind, let's look more deeply into the economics of discrimination.

Taste-for-Discrimination Model

The **taste-for-discrimination model** examines prejudice by using the emotion-free language of demand theory. It views discrimination as resulting from a preference or taste for which the discriminator is willing to pay. The model assumes that, for whatever reason, prejudiced people experience a subjective or psychic cost—a disutility—whenever they must interact with those they are biased against. Consequently, they are willing to pay a certain "price" to avoid interactions with the nonpreferred group. The size of this price depends directly on the degree of prejudice. 🔎 22.1

The taste-for-discrimination model is general, since it can be applied to race, gender, age, and religion. But our discussion focuses on employer discrimination, in which employers discriminate against nonpreferred workers. For concreteness, we will look at a white employer discriminating against black workers.

Discrimination Coefficient

A prejudiced white employer behaves as if employing black workers would add a cost. The amount of this cost—this disutility—is reflected in a **discrimination coefficient**, d, measured in monetary units. Because the employer is not prejudiced against whites, the cost of employing a white worker is the white wage rate, W_w. However, the employer's perceived "cost" of employing a black worker is the black worker's wage rate, W_b, *plus* the cost d involved in the employer's prejudice, or $W_b + d$.

The prejudiced white employer will have no preference between black and white workers when the total cost per worker is the same, that is, when $W_w = W_b + d$. Suppose the market wage rate for whites is $10 and the monetary value of the disutility the employer attaches to hiring blacks is $2 (that is, $d = 2). This employer will be indifferent between hiring blacks and whites only when the black wage rate is $8, since at this wage the perceived cost of hiring either a white or a black worker is $10:

$10 white wage = $8 black wage + $2 discrimination coefficient

It follows that our prejudiced white employer will hire blacks only if their wage rate is sufficiently below that of whites. By "sufficiently" we mean at least the amount of the discrimination coefficient.

The greater a white employer's taste for discrimination as reflected in the value of d, the larger the difference between white wages and the lower wages at which blacks will be hired. A "color-blind" employer whose d is $0 will hire equally productive blacks and whites impartially if their wages are the same. A blatantly prejudiced white employer whose d is infinity would refuse to hire blacks even if the black wage were zero.

Most prejudiced white employers will not refuse to hire blacks under all conditions. They will, in fact, *prefer* to hire blacks if the actual white-black wage difference in the market exceeds the value of d. In our example, if whites can be hired at $10 and equally productive blacks at only $7.50, the biased white employer will hire blacks. That employer is willing to pay a wage difference of up to $2 per hour for whites to satisfy his or her bias, but no more. At the $2.50 actual difference, the employer will hire blacks.

Conversely, if whites can be hired at $10 and blacks at $8.50, whites will be hired. Again, the biased employer is willing to pay a wage difference of up to $2 for whites; a $1.50 actual difference means that hiring whites is a "bargain" for this employer.

Prejudice and the Market Black-White Wage Ratio

For a particular supply of black workers, the actual black-white wage ratio—the ratio determined in the labor market—will depend on the collective prejudice of white employers. To see why, consider Figure 22.4, which shows a labor market for *black* workers. Initially, suppose the relevant labor demand curve is D_1, so the equilibrium *black* wage is $8 and the equilibrium level of black employment is 16 million. If we assume that the *white*

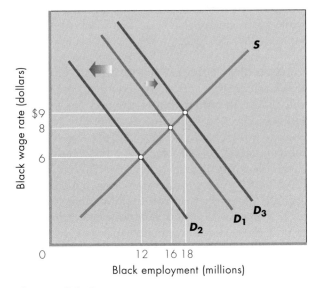

Figure 22.4

The black wage and employment level in the taste-for-discrimination model. An increase in prejudice by white employers as reflected in higher discrimination coefficients would decrease the demand for black workers, here from D_1 to D_2, and reduce the black wage rate and level of black employment. Not shown, this drop in the black wage rate would lower the black-white wage ratio. In contrast, if prejudice were reduced such that discrimination coefficients of employers declined, the demand for black labor would increase, as from D_1 to D_3, boosting the black wage rate and level of employment. The higher black wage rate would increase the black-white wage ratio.

wage (not shown) is $10, then the initial black-white wage ratio is .80 (= $8/$10).

Now assume that prejudice against black workers increases—that is, the collective *d* of white employers rises. An increase in *d* means an increase in the perceived cost of black labor at each black wage rate, and that reduces the demand for black labor, say, from D_1 to D_2. The black wage rate falls from $8 to $6 in the market, and the level of black employment declines from 16 million to 12 million. The increase in white employer prejudice reduces the black wage rate and thus the actual black-white wage ratio. If the white wage rate remains at $10, the new black-white ratio is .6 (= $6/$10).

Conversely, suppose social attitudes change such that white employers become less biased and their discrimination coefficient as a group declines. This decreases the perceived cost of black labor at each black wage rate, so the demand for black labor increases, as from D_1 to D_3. In this case, the black wage rate rises to $9, and employment of black workers increases to 18 million. The decrease in white employer prejudice increases the black wage rate and thus the actual black-white wage ratio. If the white wage remains at $10, the new black-white wage ratio is .9 (= $9/$10).

Competition and Discrimination

The taste-for-discrimination model suggests that competition will reduce discrimination in the very long run, as follows: The actual black-white wage difference for equally productive workers—say, $2—allows nondiscriminators to hire blacks for less than whites. Firms that hire black workers will therefore have lower actual wage costs per unit of output and lower average total costs than will the firms that discriminate. These lower costs will allow nondiscriminators to underprice discriminating competitors, eventually driving them out of the market.

But critics of this implication of the taste-for-discrimination model note that progress in eliminating racial discrimination has been modest. Discrimination based on race has persisted in the United States and other market economies decade after decade. To explain why, economists have proposed alternative models. **(Key Question 7)**

Statistical Discrimination

A second theory of discrimination centers on the concept of **statistical discrimination,** in which *people are judged on the basis of the average characteristics of the group to which they belong, rather than on their own personal characteristics or productivity.* The uniqueness of this theory is its suggestion that discriminatory outcomes are possible even where there is no prejudice.

Basic Idea   Suppose you are given a complex, but solvable, mathematical problem and told you will get $1 million in cash if you can identify a student on campus who is capable of solving it. The catch is that you have only 15 minutes, are restricted to the campus area, and must approach students one at a time. Who among the thousands of students—all strangers—would you approach first? Obviously, you would prefer to choose a mathematics, physics, or engineering major. Would you choose a man or a woman? A white, black, Hispanic, or Asian student? If gender or race plays any role in your choice, you are engaging in statistical discrimination.

Labor Market Example   How does statistical discrimination show itself in labor markets? Employers with job openings want to hire the most productive workers available. They have their personnel department collect information concerning each job applicant, including age, education, and prior work experience. They may supplement that information with preemployment tests, which they feel are helpful indicators of potential job performance. But it is very expensive to collect detailed information about job applicants, and it is difficult to predict job performance on the basis of limited data. Consequently, some employers looking for inexpensive information may consider the *average* characteristics of women and minorities in determining whom to hire. They are in fact practicing statistical discrimination when they do so. They are using gender, race, or ethnic background as a crude indicator of production-related attributes.

Example: Suppose an employer who plans to invest heavily in training a worker knows that on average women are less likely to be career-oriented than men, more likely to quit work in order to care for young children, and more likely to refuse geographic transfers. Thus, on average, the return on the employer's investment in training is likely to be less when choosing a woman than when choosing a man. All else equal, when choosing between two job applicants, one a woman and the other a man, this employer is likely to hire the man.

Note what is happening here. Average characteristics for a *group* are being applied to *individual* members of that group. The employer is falsely assuming that *each and every* woman worker has the same employment tendencies as the *average* woman. Such stereotyping means that numerous women who are career-oriented, who plan to work after having children, and who are flexible as to geographic transfers will be discriminated against.

Profitable, Undesirable, but Not Malicious

The firm that practices statistical discrimination is not being malicious in its hiring behavior (although it may be violating antidiscrimination laws). The decisions it makes will be rational and profitable, because *on average* its hiring decisions are likely to be correct. Nevertheless, many people suffer because of statistical discrimination, since it blocks the economic betterment of capable people. And since it is profitable, statistical discrimination tends to persist.

Occupational Segregation: The Crowding Model

The practice of **occupational segregation**—*the crowding of women, blacks, and certain ethnic groups into less desirable, lower-paying occupations*—is still apparent in the U.S. economy. Statistics indicate that women are disproportionately concentrated in a limited number of occupations such as teaching, nursing, and secretarial and clerical jobs. Blacks and Hispanics are crowded into low-paying jobs such as those of laundry workers, cleaners and household aides, hospital orderlies, agricultural workers, and other manual laborers.

Let's look at a model of occupational segregation, using women and men as an example.

The Model   The character and income consequences of occupational discrimination are revealed through a labor supply and demand model. We make the following assumptions:

- The labor force is equally divided between men and women workers. Let's say there are 6 million male and 6 million female workers.
- The economy comprises three occupations, X, Y, and Z, with identical labor demand curves, as shown in Figure 22.5.
- Men and women have the same labor-force characteristics; each of the three occupations could be filled equally well by men or by women.

Effects of Crowding   Suppose that, as a consequence of discrimination, the 6 million women are excluded from occupations X and Y and crowded into occupation Z, where they earn wage W. The men distribute themselves equally among occupations X and Y, meaning that 3 million male workers are in each occupation and have a common wage of M. (If we assume that there are no barriers to mobility between X and Y, any initially different distribution of males between X and Y would result in a wage differential between the two occupations. That would prompt labor shifts from the low- to the high-wage occupation until an equal distribution occurred.)

Because women are crowded into occupation Z, labor supply (not shown) is larger and their wage

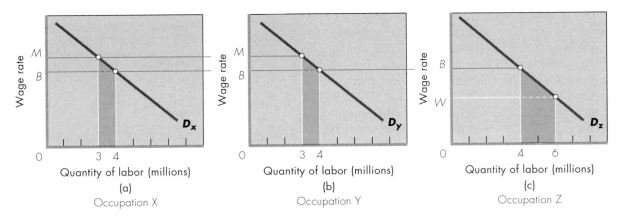

Figure 22.5

The economics of occupational segregation.   By crowding women into one occupation, men enjoy high wage rates of M in occupations X and Y, while women receive low wages of W in occupation Z. The elimination of discrimination will equalize wage rates at B and result in a net increase in the nation's output.

rate W is much lower than M. Because of the discrimination, this is an equilibrium situation that will persist as long as the crowding occurs. The occupational barrier means women cannot move into occupations X and Y in pursuit of a higher wage.

The result is a loss of output for society. To see why, recall again that labor demand reflects labor's marginal revenue product, which is labor's contribution to domestic output. Thus, the taupe areas for occupations X and Y in Figure 22.5 show the decrease in domestic output—the market value of the marginal output—caused by subtracting 1 million women from each of these occupations. Similarly, the light green area for occupation Z shows the increase in domestic output caused by moving 2 million women into occupation Z. Although society would gain the added output represented by the light green area in occupation Z, it would lose the output represented by the sum of the two taupe areas in occupations X and Y. That output loss exceeds the output gain, producing a net output loss for society.

Eliminating Occupational Segregation

Now assume that through legislation or sweeping changes in social attitudes, discrimination disappears. Women, attracted by higher wage rates, shift from occupation Z to X and Y; 1 million women move into X and another 1 million move into Y. Now there are 4 million workers in Z, and occupational segregation is eliminated. At that point there are 4 million workers in each occupation, and wage rates in all three occupations are equal, here at B. That wage equality eliminates the incentive for further reallocations of labor.

The new, nondiscriminatory equilibrium clearly benefits women, who now receive higher wages; it hurts men, who now receive lower wages. But women were initially harmed and men benefited through discrimination; removing discrimination corrects that situation.

Society also gains. The elimination of occupational segregation reverses the net output loss just discussed. Adding 1 million women to each of occupations X and Y in Figure 22.5 increases domestic output by the sum of the two taupe areas. The decrease in domestic output caused by losing 2 million women from occupation Z is shown by the light green area. The sum of the two increases in domestic output in X and Y exceeds the decrease in domestic output in Z. With the end of the discrimination, 2 million women workers have moved from occupa-

tion Z, where their contribution to domestic output (their MRP) is low, to higher-paying occupations X and Y, where their contribution to domestic output is high. Thus society gains a more efficient allocation of resources from the removal of occupational discrimination. (In terms of Figure 22.3, society moves from a point inside its production possibilities curve to a point closer to, or on, the curve.)

Example: The easing of occupational barriers has led to a surge of women gaining advanced degrees in some high-paying professions. In recent years, for instance, the percentage of law degrees and medical degrees awarded to women has exceeded 40 percent, compared with less than 10 percent in 1970. **(Key Question 9)**

QUICK REVIEW 22.3

■ Discrimination reduces domestic output and occurs when workers who have the same abilities, education, training, and experience as other workers receive inferior treatment with respect to hiring, occupational access, promotion, or wages.

■ Nondiscriminatory factors explain about one-half of the gender and racial earnings gaps; most of the remaining one-half is thought to reflect discrimination.

■ The taste-for-discrimination model sees discrimination as representing a preference or "taste" for which the discriminator is willing to pay.

■ The theory of statistical discrimination says that employers often wrongly judge individuals on the basis of average group characteristics rather than on personal characteristics, thus harming those discriminated against.

■ The crowding model of discrimination suggests that when women and minorities are systematically excluded from high-paying occupations and crowded into low-paying ones, their wages and society's domestic output are reduced.

■ Antidiscrimination Policies and Issues

The government has several ways of dealing with discrimination. One indirect policy is to promote a strong, growing economy. An expanding demand for products increases the demand for all workers. When the economy is at or near full employment, prejudiced employers must pay higher and higher wages to entice preferred workers away from other employers. Many, perhaps most, such employers are likely to decide that their taste for discrimination is not worth the cost. Tight labor markets also help overcome stereotyping. Once women and minorities obtain good jobs in tight labor markets, they have an opportunity to show they can do the work as well as white males.

A second indirect antidiscrimination policy is to improve the education and training opportunities of women and minorities. For example, upgrading the quantity and quality of schooling received by blacks and Hispanics will make them more competitive with whites for higher-paying positions.

The third way of reducing discrimination is through direct government intervention. As summarized in Table 22.2, the U.S. government has outlawed certain practices in hiring, promotion, and compensation and has required that government contractors take affirmative action to hire more women and minorities.

The Affirmative Action Controversy

Consider the last item in Table 22.2. **Affirmative action** consists of special efforts by employers to increase employment and promotion opportunities for groups that have suffered past discrimination and continue to experience discrimination. Saying that affirmative action has stirred controversy is an understatement. There are strong arguments for and against this approach to remedying discrimination.

In Support of Affirmative Action   Those who support affirmative action say that historically women and minorities have been forced to carry the extra burden of discrimination in their attempt to achieve economic success. Thus, they find themselves far behind white males, who have been preferred workers. Merely removing the discrimination burden does nothing to close the present socioeconomic gap. Aggressive action to hire women and minorities, not just equal opportunity, is necessary to counter the inherent bias in favor of white men if women and minorities are to catch up.

Supporters of affirmative action argue that job discrimination is so pervasive that it will persist for decades if society is content to accept only marginal antidiscriminatory changes in employment practices. Moreover, such changes are hampered by the fact that white males have achieved on-the-job seniority, which protects them from layoffs and places the burden of unemployment disproportionately on women and minorities. And women and minorities have been discriminated against in acquiring human capital: the education and job training needed to compete on equal terms with white males. Discrimination has supposedly become so highly institutionalized that extraordinary countermeasures are required.

Those who accept this line of reasoning endorse affirmative action and even preferential treatment as appropriate means for hastening the elimination of discrimination. In this view, affirmative action is not only a path toward social equity but also a good national strategy for enhancing efficiency and economic growth, since it brings formerly excluded groups directly into the productive economic mainstream.

Table 22.2
Major Antidiscrimination Laws and Policies in the United States

Equal Pay Act of 1963   Makes it illegal to pay men and women different wage rates if they "do equal work on jobs, the performance of which requires equal skill, effort, and responsibility, and which are performed under similar working conditions."

Title VII of the Civil Rights Act of 1964   Makes it unlawful for any employer "to refuse to hire or to discharge any individual, or otherwise to discriminate against any individual with respect to compensation, terms, conditions, or privileges of employment, because of such individual's race, color, religion, sex, or national origin."

Affirmative action requirement   Presidential executive orders issued in 1965 and 1968 outlaw discriminatory practices of businesses and other institutions holding government contracts. The 1968 order also states that the "contractor will take *affirmative action* to ensure that applicants are employed, and that employees are treated during employment, without regard to their race, color, religion, sex, or national origin." This affirmative action was to apply to employment, upgrading, demotion, and transfer; recruitment and recruitment advertising; layoff and termination; rates of pay and other forms of compensation; and selection for training, including apprenticeships.

Opposing View   Those who oppose affirmative action claim that it often goes beyond aggressive recruitment to become preferential treatment. In this view, affirmative action has sometimes prodded employers to hire less qualified women and minority workers. So economic efficiency is impaired. They also insist that preferential treatment is simply **reverse discrimination.** Preferential treatment and discrimination, they say, are simply two views of the same thing: To show preference for A is to discriminate against B.

Some opponents of affirmative action go further, contending that policies that give preferential treatment to disadvantaged groups have actually worked to the long-term detriment of those groups. Such policies, they say, have placed some persons in positions where their relative lack of skill becomes evident to their employers and coworkers. That has had two effects, both negative: First, majority workers who have themselves been passed over for jobs or promotions resent those who are given special treatment. Second, others may mistakenly stereotype the highly qualified women and minority members of the workforce, who have no need of preferential treatment, as "affirmative action hires." In this highly controversial view, continuing racial tension not only reflects the long legacy of discrimination but also the well-meant but ill-conceived affirmative action policy designed to end it.

Recent Developments

Affirmative action has recently come under harsh legal and political attack. A series of important Supreme Court decisions in 1986 and 1987 upheld the constitutionality of affirmative action programs, but subsequent decisions have undermined some of those programs. For example, in 1989 the Court declared illegal a program by the city of Richmond, Virginia, that was designed to provide a specified proportion of the city's construction work to minority-owned firms; the Court argued that the program constituted reverse discrimination. Another 1989 ruling permitted white firefighters in Birmingham, Alabama, to challenge an existing affirmative action program on grounds that the program denied them promotions in favor of less qualified blacks. That ruling triggered a number of reverse-discrimination lawsuits throughout the country. Other Court rulings have made it necessary for minorities to prove that job discrimination exists in a particular firm, not just in the overall industry or economy.

In mid-1995 the Court ruled that race-based preferences in Federal programs could be allowed only if the programs are "narrowly tailored" to remedy identifiable past discrimination in a particular firm or government entity. A Federal circuit court of appeals ruled later that year that public universities in Texas, Mississippi, and Louisiana may not justify affirmative action programs by citing the benefits of racial diversity. Later that year, the Supreme Court let this ruling stand.

On the political scene, in 1996 Congress debated legislation intended to restrict affirmative action, and the Clinton administration halted several Federal minority programs designed to give preference to minorities in Federal contracting. In 1996 Californians voted in favor of a state constitutional amendment ending all state programs that give gender or racial preferences in government hiring and contracting, as well as in public education. A year later, Washington State also passed a law that ended affirmative action in the public sector.

QUICK REVIEW 22.4

▪ The Equal Pay Act of 1963 and Title VII of the Civil Rights Act of 1964 outlaw wage and employment discrimination based on race, color, religion, gender, and national origin.

▪ Affirmative action programs are designed to overcome past and present discrimination through aggressive recruitment of women and minorities; they are highly controversial and recently have come under attack by those who feel they reflect reverse discrimination.

▪ Immigration

Immigration has long been a focus of controversy. Should more or fewer people be allowed to migrate to the United States? How should the problem of illegal entrants be handled?

Number of Immigrants

The annual flow of **legal immigrants** (who have permission to reside in the United States) was roughly 250,000 in the 1950s, 320,000 in the 1960s, and 500,000 to 600,000 during the 1970s and 1980s. In the 1990s, immigration averaged about 850,000 per year. About one-third of annual U.S. population growth in recent years has resulted from immigra-

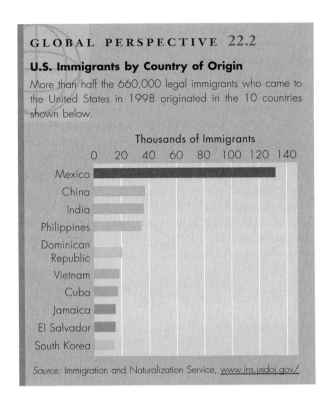

tion. (Global Perspective 22.2 shows the countries of origin of U.S. legal immigrants in a recent year.)

Such data are imperfect, however, because they do not include **illegal immigrants,** those who arrive without permission. The Census Bureau estimates that the net inflow of illegal immigrants (illegal aliens) is now about 100,000 per year, most coming from Mexico, the Caribbean, and Central America.

Economics of Immigration

Figure 22.6 provides some insight into the economic effects of immigration. In Figure 22.6a, D_u is the demand for labor in the United States; in Figure 22.6b, D_m is the demand for labor in Mexico. The demand for labor is greater in the United States, presumably because the nation has more capital and more advanced technologies that enhance the productivity of labor. (Recall from Chapter 14 that the labor demand curve is based on the marginal revenue productivity of labor.) Conversely, since machinery and equipment are presumably scarce in Mexico and technology less sophisticated, labor demand there is weak. We also assume that the before-migration labor forces of the United States and Mexico are c and C, respectively, and that both countries are at full employment.

Wage Rates and World Output
If we further assume that migration (1) has no cost, (2) occurs solely in response to wage differentials, and (3) is unimpeded by law in either country, then workers will migrate from Mexico to the United States until wage rates in the two countries are equal at W_e. At that level, CF (equals cf) workers will have migrated from Mexico to the United States. Although the U.S. wage level will fall from W_u to W_e, domestic output (the sum of the marginal revenue products of the entire workforce) will increase from $0abc$ to $0adf$. In Mexico, the wage rate will rise from W_m to W_e, but domestic output will decline there from $0ABC$ to $0ADF$. Because the gain in domestic output $cbdf$ in

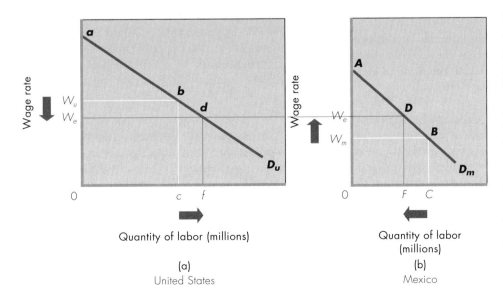

Figure 22.6

The simple economics of immigration. The migration of labor to high-income United States (a) from low-income Mexico (b) increases U.S. domestic output, reduces the average level of U.S. wages, and increases U.S. business income while having the opposite effects in Mexico. The U.S. domestic output gain of *cbdf* exceeds Mexico's domestic output loss of *FDBC*; thus the migration yields a net increase in world output.

(a)
United States

(b)
Mexico

the United States exceeds the output loss *FDBC* in Mexico, the world's output has increased.

We can conclude that the elimination of barriers to the international flow of labor tends to increase worldwide economic efficiency. The world gains because the freedom to migrate enables people to move to countries where they can make larger contributions to world production. Migration involves an efficiency gain. It enables the world to produce a larger real output with a given amount of resources.

Income Shares   Our model also suggests that the flow of immigrants will enhance business income (or capitalist income) in the United States and reduce it in Mexico. As just noted, before-immigration domestic output in the United States is represented by area 0*abc*. The total wage bill is 0W_u*bc*—the wage rate multiplied by the number of workers. The remaining triangular area W_u*ab* represents business income before immigration. The same reasoning applies to Mexico, where W_m*AB* is before-immigration business income.

Unimpeded immigration increases business income from W_u*ab* to W_e*ad* in the United States and reduces it from W_m*AB* to W_e*AD* in Mexico. U.S. businesses benefit from immigration; Mexican businesses are hurt by emigration. This is what we would expect intuitively; the United States is gaining "cheap" labor, and Mexico is losing "cheap" labor. This conclusion is consistent with the historical fact that U.S. employers have often actively recruited immigrants.

Complications and Modifications

Our model includes some simplifying assumptions and overlooks a relevant factor. We now relax some of the assumptions and introduce the omitted factor to see how our conclusions are affected.

Costs of Migration   We assumed that international movement of workers is without personal cost, but obviously it is not. There are both the explicit, out-of-pocket costs of physically moving a worker and his or her possessions and the implicit opportunity cost of lost income while the worker is moving and becoming established in the new country. Still more subtle costs are involved in adapting to a new culture, language, climate, and so forth. All such costs must be estimated by the potential immigrant and weighed against the expected bene-

fits of higher wages in the new country. A person who estimates that benefits exceed costs will migrate; a person who sees costs as exceeding benefits will stay put.

In terms of Figure 22.6, the existence of migration costs means that the flow of labor from Mexico to the United States will stop short of that needed to close the wage differential entirely. Wages will remain somewhat higher in the United States than in Mexico; the wage difference will not cause further migration and close up the wage gap because the marginal benefit of the higher wage will not cover the marginal cost of migration. Thus, the world production gain from migration will be reduced, since wages will not equalize.

Remittances and Backflows   Most migration is permanent; workers who acquire skills in the receiving country tend not to return home. However, some migrants view their moves as temporary. They move to a more highly developed country, accumulate some wealth or education through hard work and frugality, and return home to establish their own enterprises. During their time in the new country, migrants frequently make sizable remittances to their families at home. That causes a redistribution of the net gain from migration between the countries involved. In Figure 22.6, remittances by Mexican workers in the United States to their relatives in Mexico would cause the gain in U.S. domestic output to be less than shown and the loss to Mexican domestic output also to be less than shown.

Actual backflows—the return of migrants to their home country—might also alter gains and losses through time. For example, if some Mexican workers who migrated to the United States acquired substantial labor market or managerial skills and then returned home, their enhanced human capital might make a substantial contribution to economic development in Mexico.

Full Employment versus Unemployment
Our model assumes full employment in the sending and receiving countries. Mexican workers presumably leave low-paying jobs to take (more or less immediately) higher-paying jobs in the United States. However, in many cases the factor that "pushes" immigrants from their homelands is not low wages but chronic unemployment and underemployment. Many developing countries are overpopulated and have surplus labor; workers are either

unemployed or so grossly underemployed that their marginal revenue product is zero.

If we allow for this possibility, then Mexico actually gains (not loses) by having such workers emigrate. The unemployed workers are making no contribution to Mexico's domestic output and must be sustained by transfers from the rest of the labor force. The remaining Mexican labor force will be better off by the amount of the transfers after the unemployed workers have migrated to the United States. Conversely, if the Mexican immigrant workers are unable to find jobs in the United States and are sustained through transfers from employed U.S. workers, then the after-tax income of working Americans will decline.

Fiscal Impacts

What effects do immigrants have on tax revenues and government spending in the receiving country? Are immigrants contributors to output, or do they go on welfare and become a drain on the national treasury?

Prior to the 1970s, the immigrant population was less likely to receive public assistance than people born in the United States. Migrants were typically young, single men with significant education and job training. Thus they were readily employable and were net contributors. Illegal immigrants avoided the welfare system for fear of detection and deportation.

But since the 1970s the situation has reversed, and immigrants now use the welfare system proportionately more than natives. The main factor in the turnabout is the changing mix of immigrants, which today includes relatively fewer skilled workers and more unskilled workers. In fact, prior to its overhaul in 1996, critics of the U.S. welfare system claimed it was drawing unskilled (and often illegal) workers to the United States from some of the world's poorest nations. Indeed, immigrants made up more than 10 percent of Supplemental Security Income (SSI) rolls in 1998, compared with only 3.3 percent a decade earlier. As a result of this trend, the 1996 welfare reform (Personal Responsibility Act) denied welfare benefits to new immigrants for their first 5 years in the United States. **(Key Question 12)**

Immigration: Two Views

As we have noted, the traditional perception of immigration is that it consists of young, ambitious workers seeking opportunity in the United States. They are destined for success because of the courage and determination they exhibit in leaving their cultural roots to improve their lives. These energetic workers increase the supply of goods and services with their labor and simultaneously increase the demand for goods and services with their incomes and spending. In short, immigration is an engine of economic progress.

The counterview is that immigration is a socioeconomic drag on the receiving country. Immigrants compete with domestic workers for scarce jobs, pull down the average level of real wages, and burden the U.S. welfare system.

Both these views are far too simplistic. Immigration can either benefit or harm the receiving nation, depending on the number of immigrants; their education, skills, and work ethic; and the rate at which they can be absorbed into the economy without disruption. From a strictly economic perspective, nations seeking to maximize net benefits from immigration should expand immigration until its marginal benefits equal its marginal costs. The MB = MC conceptual framework explicitly recognizes that there can be too few immigrants, just as there can be too many. Moreover, it recognizes that from a strictly economic standpoint, not all immigrants are alike. The immigration of, say, a highly educated scientist has a different impact on the economy than does the immigration of a long-term welfare recipient.

QUICK REVIEW 22.5

■ All else equal, immigration reduces wages, increases domestic output, and increases business income in the receiving nation; it has the opposite effects in the sending nation.

■ Assessing the impacts of immigration is complicated by such factors as unemployment, backflows and remittances, and fiscal effects.

Orchestrating Impartiality

Have "Blind" Musical Auditions, in Which "Screens" are Used to Hide the Identity of Candidates, Affected the Success of Women in Obtaining Positions in Major Symphony Orchestras?

There have long been allegations of discrimination against women in the hiring process in some occupations. But such discrimination is usually difficult to demonstrate. Economists Claudia Goldin and Cecilia Rouse spotted a unique opportunity for testing such discrimination as it relates to major symphony orchestras. In the past, orchestras relied on their musical directors to extend invitations to candidates, audition them, and handpick new members. Concerned with the potential for hiring bias, in the 1970s and 1980s orchestras altered the process in two ways. First, orchestra members were included as judges, and, second, orchestras began open competitions using "blind" auditions with a physical "screen" (usually a room divider) to conceal the identity of the candidates. (These blind auditions, however, did not extend to the final competition in most orchestras.) Did the change in procedures increase the probability of women being hired?

To answer this question, Goldin and Rouse gained access to orchestral management files to examine auditions for eight major orchestras. These records contained the names of all candidates and identified those who advanced to the next round, including the ultimate winner of the competition. The researchers then looked for women in the sample who had "competed" in auditions both before and after the introduction of the blind screening.

There was a strong suspicion of bias against women in hiring musicians for the nation's finest orchestras. These positions are highly desirous, not only because they are prestigious but also because they offer high pay (often more than $75,000 annually). In 1970 only 5 percent of the members of the top five orchestras in the United States were women, and many music directors publicly suggested that women players, in general, have less musical talent.

The change to screens provided direct evidence of past discrimination. The screens increased by 50 percent the probability that a woman would be advanced from the preliminary rounds. The screens also greatly increased the likelihood that a woman would be selected in the final round. Without the screens about 10 percent of all hires were women, but with the screens about 35 percent were women. Today, about 25 percent of the members of top symphony orchestras are women, in contrast to 5 percent in 1970. The screens explain from 25 to 45 percent of the increases in the proportion of women in the orchestras studied.

Was the past discrimination in hiring an example of statistical discrimination based on, say, a presumption of greater turnover by women or more leaves for medical (including maternity) or other reasons? To answer that question, Goldin and Rouse examined information on turnover and leaves of orchestra members for the period 1960–1996. They found that neither differed by gender, so leaves and turnover should not have influenced hiring decisions.

Instead, the discrimination in hiring seemed to reflect a taste for discrimination by musical directors. Male musical directors apparently had a positive discrimination coefficient d. At the fixed (union-determined) wage, they simply preferred male musicians, at women's expense.

Source: Claudia Goldin and Cecilia Rouse, "Orchestrating Impartiality: The Impact of 'Blind' Auditions on Female Musicians," *American Economic Review*, September 2000, pp. 715–741.

SUMMARY

1. Currently there are about 16 million union workers in the United States, with most of them belonging to the loose federation called the AFL-CIO. Unionism has declined relatively in the United States since the mid-1950s. Some economists attribute this decline to changes in the composition of domestic output and in the demographic structure of the labor force. Others contend that employers, recognizing that unions reduce profitability, have more aggressively sought to dissuade workers from becoming union members.

2. Labor and management "live together" under the terms of collective bargaining agreements. Those agreements cover (a) union status and managerial prerogatives; (b) wages, hours, and working conditions; (c) seniority and job control; and (d) a grievance procedure.

3. There is disagreement about whether unions increase or decrease efficiency and productivity. The negative view cites (a) inefficiencies associated with featherbedding and union-imposed work rules, (b) loss of output through strikes, and (c) the misallocation of labor caused by the union wage advantage. The positive view holds that (a) through the shock effect, union wage pressure spurs technological advance and mechanization of the production process; (b) as collective-voice institutions, unions contribute to rising productivity by reducing labor turnover; and (c) the enhanced security of union workers increases their willingness to teach their skills to less experienced workers.

4. Discrimination relating to the labor market occurs when women or minorities having the same abilities, education, training, and experience as men or white workers are given inferior treatment with respect to hiring, occupational choice, education and training, promotion, and wage rates. Forms of discrimination include wage discrimination, employment discrimination, occupational discrimination, and human capital discrimination. Discrimination redistributes national income and, by creating inefficiencies, diminishes its size.

5. In the taste-for-discrimination model, some white employers have a preference for discrimination, measured by a discrimination coefficient *d*. Prejudiced white employers will hire black workers only if their wages are at least *d* dollars below those of whites. The model indicates that declines in the discrimination coefficients of white employers will increase the demand for black workers, raising the black wage rate and the ratio of black wages to white wages. It also suggests that competition may eliminate discrimination in the long run.

6. Statistical discrimination occurs when employers base employment decisions about *individuals* on the average characteristics of *groups* of workers. That can lead to discrimination against individuals even in the absence of prejudice.

7. The crowding model of occupational segregation indicates how white males gain higher earnings at the expense of women and minorities who are confined to a limited number of occupations. The model shows that discrimination also causes a net loss of domestic output.

8. Government antidiscrimination legislation and policies that involve direct government intervention include the Equal Pay Act of 1963, Title VII of the Civil Rights Act of 1964, and executive orders applicable to Federal contractors. The executive orders included requirements that these firms enact affirmative action programs to benefit women and certain minority groups.

9. Those who support affirmative action say it is needed to help women and minorities compensate for decades of discrimination. Opponents say affirmative action causes economic inefficiency and reverse discrimination. Recent Supreme Court decisions have limited the use of affirmative action programs to situations where past discrimination is clearly identifiable.

10. Supply and demand analysis suggests that the movement of migrants from a poor country to a rich country (a) increases domestic output in the rich country, (b) reduces the average wage in the rich country, and (c) increases business income in the rich country. The opposite effects occur in the poor country, but the world as a whole realizes a larger total output.

11. The outcomes of immigration predicted by simple supply and demand analysis become more complicated upon consideration of (a) the costs of moving, (b) the possibility of remittances and backflows, (c) the level of unemployment in each country, and (d) the fiscal impact on the taxpayers of each country.

TERMS AND CONCEPTS

American Federation of Labor and Congress of Industrial Organizations (AFL-CIO)

independent unions

business unionism

structural-change hypothesis

managerial-opposition hypothesis

collective bargaining

closed shop

union shop

agency shop

right-to-work laws

open shop

cost-of-living adjustment (COLA)

strike

lockout

National Labor Relations Act (NLRA)

National Labor Relations Board (NLRB)

exit mechanism

voice mechanism

labor market discrimination

wage discrimination

employment discrimination

occupational discrimination

human capital discrimination

taste-for-discrimination model

discrimination coefficient

statistical discrimination

occupational segregation

affirmative action

reverse discrimination

legal immigrants

illegal immigrants

STUDY QUESTIONS

1. Other things equal, who is more likely to be a union member: Stephen, who works as a salesperson at a furniture store, or Susan, who works as a machinist for an aircraft manufacturer? Explain.

2. Contrast the structural-change and managerial-opposition hypotheses as they relate to the decline in unionism. Which view do you think is more convincing?

3. Suppose that you are president of a newly established local union about to bargain with an employer for the first time. List the basic areas you want covered in the work agreement. Why might you begin with a larger wage demand than you actually are willing to accept?

4. **Key Question** What is the estimated size of the union wage advantage? How might this advantage diminish the efficiency with which labor resources are allocated?

5. Explain the logic of each of the following statements:
   a. By constraining the decisions of management, unions reduce efficiency and productivity growth.
   b. As collective-voice institutions, unions increase productivity by reducing worker turnover, inducing managerial efficiency, and enhancing worker security.

6. Explain how discrimination reduces domestic output and income. Demonstrate that loss using production possibilities analysis.

7. **Key Question** The labor demand and supply data in the following table relate to a single occupation. Use them to answer the questions that follow. Base your answers on the taste-for-discrimination model.
   a. Plot the labor demand and supply curves for Hispanic workers in this occupation.
   b. What are the equilibrium Hispanic wage rate and quantity of Hispanic employment?
   c. Suppose the white wage rate in this occupation

Quantity of Hispanic Labor Demanded, Thousands	Hispanic Wage Rate	Quantity of Hispanic Labor Supplied, Thousands
24	$16	52
30	14	44
35	12	35
42	10	28
48	8	20

   is $16. What is the Hispanic-to-white wage ratio?
   d. Suppose a particular employer has a discrimination coefficient d of $5 per hour. Will that employer hire Hispanic or white workers at the Hispanic-white wage ratio indicated in part c? Explain.
   e. Suppose employers as a group become less prejudiced against Hispanics and demand 14 more units of Hispanic labor at each Hispanic wage rate in the table. What are the new equilibrium Hispanic wage rate and level of Hispanic employment? Does the Hispanic-white wage ratio rise or fall? Explain.
   f. Suppose Hispanics as a group increase their labor services in that occupation, collectively offering 14 more units of labor at each Hispanic wage rate. Disregarding the changes indicated in part e, what are the new equilibrium Hispanic wage rate and level of Hispanic employment? Does the Hispanic-white wage ratio rise, or does it fall?

8. Males under the age of 25 must pay far higher auto insurance premiums than females in this age group. How does this fact relate to statistical discrimination?

Statistical discrimination implies that discrimination can persist indefinitely, while the taste-for-discrimination model suggests that competition might reduce discrimination in the long run. Explain the difference.

9. **Key Question** Use a demand and supply model to explain the impact of occupational segregation or "crowding" on the relative wage rates and earnings of men and women. Who gains and who loses from the elimination of occupational segregation? Is there a net gain or a net loss to society? Explain.

10. "Current affirmative action programs are based on the belief that to overcome discrimination, we must practice discrimination. That perverse logic has created a system that undermines the fundamental values it was intended to protect." Do you agree? Why or why not?

11. Suppose Ann and Becky are applicants to your university and that they have identical admission qualifications (SAT scores, high school GPA, etc.). Ann, who is black, grew up in a public housing development; Becky, who is white, grew up in a wealthy suburb. You can admit only one of the two. Which would you admit and why? Now suppose that Ann is white and Becky is black, all else equal. Does that change your selection? Why or why not?

12. **Key Question** Use graphical analysis to show the gains and losses resulting from the migration of population from a low-income country to a high-income country. Explain how your conclusions are affected by (*a*) unemployment, (*b*) remittances to the home country, (*c*) backflows of migrants to their home country, and (*d*) the personal characteristics of the migrants. If the migrants are highly skilled workers, is there any justification for the sending country to levy a "brain drain" tax on emigrants?

13. If a person favors the free movement of labor within the United States, is it then inconsistent to also favor restrictions on the international movement of labor? Why or why not?

14. Evaluate: "If the United States deported, say, 1 million illegal immigrants, the number of unemployed workers in the United States would decline by 1 million."

15. **(Last Word)** What two types of discrimination are represented by the discrimination evidenced in this chapter's Last Word?

16. **Web-Based Question:** *Union membership—falling or rising?* Go to the Bureau of Labor Statistics website, www.bls.gov, select Data and Frequently Requested Series for historical data on work stoppages (strikes). What has been the trend concerning the number of strikes involving more than 1000 workers over the past 20 years? Use the search feature at the BLS site to update the text's data on union membership. For the latest year, determine (*a*) the overall unionization rate for wage and salary workers, (*b*) the unionization rates for men and women wage and salary workers, and (*c*) the unionization rates for black, white, and Hispanic wage and salary workers. Have the unionization rates gone up, down, or stayed constant compared to the data reported in this chapter?

17. **Web-Based Question:** *The EEOC—what is it and what does it do?* Go to the website of the Equal Employment Opportunity Commission (EEOC), at www.eeoc.gov, to determine its role in enforcing the antidiscrimination laws. What specific laws does it enforce? List five of its most recent actions.

CHAPTER 23

The Economics of Health Care

RARELY CAN YOU read a newspaper or look at a television news program without encountering a story about the high costs of health care in the United States, seriously ill people who have no health insurance, or government health insurance programs that threaten to drain Federal and state budgets. Some news stories document disputes between employers and workers over sharing the cost of health insurance or cite instances of insurance companies dictating the medical care that doctors can provide. We even learn of companies that break their promises to provide health insurance to retirees and of lawsuits challenging such actions. Moreover, difficult ethical questions concerning "extreme care" for the acutely or terminally ill arise from time to time. ■ Health care accounts for 14 percent of U.S. GDP, making it worthy of specific study. Further, the tools of microeconomic analysis are particularly helpful in understanding the U.S. health care system, major health care issues, and actual and proposed reforms.

■ The Health Care Industry

Since the boundaries of the health care industry are not definite, it is difficult to define the industry. In general, it includes services provided in hospitals, nursing homes, laboratories, and physicians' and dentists' offices. It also includes prescription and nonprescription drugs, artificial limbs, and eyeglasses. Note, however, that many goods and services that may affect health are not included, for example, low-fat foods, vitamins, and health club services.

Health care is one of the largest U.S. industries, employing about 9 million people, including about 700,000 physicians, or 260 doctors per 100,000 of population. There are more than 6000 hospitals containing more than 1 million beds. Americans make more than 780 million visits to office-based physicians each year.

■ Twin Problems: Costs and Access

Two highly publicized problems are related to the U.S. health care system:

■ The cost of health care has risen rapidly in response to higher prices and an increase in the quantity of services provided. (Spending on health care involves both "prices" and "quantities" and is often loosely referred to as "health care costs.")

The price of medical care has increased faster than the overall price level, for example, rising by 2.9 percent in 1997, 3.2 percent in 1998, 3.3 percent in 1999, and 4 percent in 2000.

■ Forty-three million Americans do not have health insurance coverage, and many Americans have limited, or no, access to health care.

Efforts to reform health care have focused on controlling costs and making it accessible to everyone. Those two goals are related, since high and rising prices make health care services unaffordable to a significant portion of the U.S. population. In fact, a dual system of health care may be evolving in the United States. Those with insurance or other financial means receive the world's best medical treatment, but many people, because of their inability to pay, do not seek out even the most basic treatment.

■ High and Rising Health Care Costs

We now look at several aspects of health care spending and health care costs in the United States.

Health Care Spending

Health care spending in the United States is high and rising in both absolute terms and as a percentage of domestic output.

Total Spending on Health Care

Figure 23.1a gives an overview of the major types of U.S. health care spending. It shows that 33 cents of each health care dollar is spent on hospitals, while 20 cents goes to physicians and 26 cents for other health care services (dental, vision, and home care).

Figure 23.1b shows the sources of funds for health care spending. It reveals that about four-fifths of health care spending is financed by insurance. Public insurance (Medicaid, Medicare, and insurance for veterans, current military personnel, and government employees) is the source of 46 cents of each dollar spent. Private insurance accounts for 33 cents. So public and private insurance combined provide 79 cents of each dollar spent. The remaining 21 cents comes directly out of the health care consumer's pocket. It is paid mainly as insurance **deductibles** (that is, the insured pays the first $250 or $500 of each year's health care costs before the insurer begins paying) or **copayments** (that is, the insured pays, say, 20 percent of all health care costs and the insurance company pays 80 percent).

Recall that Medicare is a nationwide Federal health care program available to social security beneficiaries and persons with disabilities. One part of Medicare is a hospital insurance program that, after a deductible of $776 (in 2000), covers all reasonable costs for the first 60 days of inpatient care per "ben-

(a)
Health care expenditures

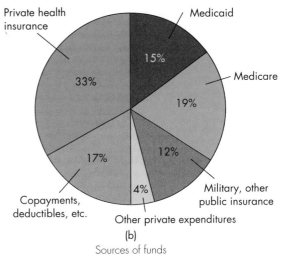

(b)
Sources of funds

Figure 23.1

Health care expenditures and finance. (a) Most health care expenditures are for hospitals and physicians' services. (b) Public and private insurance pays for roughly four-fifths of health care.

Source: Health Care Financing Administration, www.hcfa.gov/. Data are for 1998.

efit period" and lesser amounts (on a cost-sharing basis) for additional days. Coverage is also provided for posthospital nursing services, home health care, and hospice care for the terminally ill. The second part of Medicare, a medical insurance program (for physicians' services, laboratory and other diagnostic tests, and outpatient hospital services), is voluntary but is heavily subsidized by government. The $45.50 monthly premiums (in 2000) that participants pay cover about one-fourth of the cost of the benefits provided.

Medicaid provides payment for medical benefits to certain low-income people, including the elderly, the blind, persons with disabilities, children, and adults with dependent children. Those who qualify for Temporary Aid for Needy Families (TANF) and the Supplemental Security Income (SSI) program are automatically eligible for Medicaid. Nevertheless, Medicaid covers less than half of those living in poverty. The Federal government and the states share the cost of Medicaid. On average, the states fund 43 percent and the Federal government 57 percent of each Medicaid dollar spent.

Overall, about 21 percent of each dollar spent on health care is financed by direct out-of-pocket payments by individuals. The fact that most U.S. health care is paid for by private insurance companies or the government is an important contributor to rising health care costs.

Percentage of GDP

Figure 23.2 shows how U.S. health care spending has been increasing as a percentage of GDP. Health care spending absorbed 5.1 percent of GDP in 1960 but rose to 13.9 percent by 1999. The U.S. Health Care Financing Administration projects that national health care expenditures will reach 16.2 percent of GDP by 2008.

International Comparisons

Global Perspective 23.1 reveals that among the industrialized nations, health care spending as a percentage of GDP is highest in the United States. It is reasonable to assume that health care spending varies positively with output and incomes, but that doesn't account for the higher U.S. health expenditures as a percentage of GDP. For whatever reason, the United States is "in a league of its own" as to its proportion of output devoted to health care.

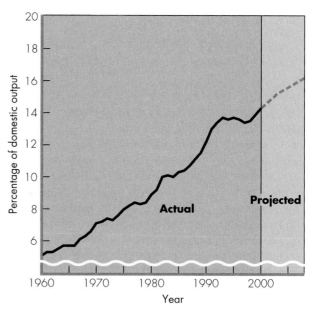

Figure 23.2

U.S. health care expenditures as a percentage of GDP. U.S. health care spending as a percentage of GDP has greatly increased since 1960 and is projected to rise still more.

Source: Health Care Financing Administration, www.hcfa.gov/.

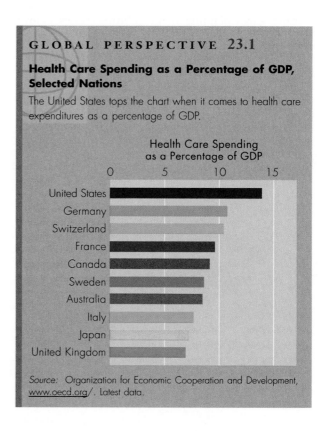

GLOBAL PERSPECTIVE 23.1

Health Care Spending as a Percentage of GDP, Selected Nations

The United States tops the chart when it comes to health care expenditures as a percentage of GDP.

Source: Organization for Economic Cooperation and Development, www.oecd.org/. Latest data.

Quality of Care: Are We Healthier?

It is difficult to compare the quality of health care from country to country. Yet there is general agreement that medical care (although not health and not "preventive treatment") in the United States is probably the best in the world. Average life expectancy in the United States has increased by 5 years since 1970, and U.S. physicians and hospitals employ the most advanced medical equipment and technologies. Furthermore, more than half the world's medical research funding is done in the United States. As a result, the incidence of disease has been declining and the quality of treatment has been improving. Polio has been virtually eliminated, ulcers are successfully treated without surgery, angioplasty and coronary bypass surgery greatly benefit those with heart disease, sophisticated body scanners are increasingly available diagnostic tools, and organ transplants and prosthetic joint replacements are more and more common.

That is the good news. But there is other news as well. Despite new screening and treatment technologies, the breast cancer mortality rate has shown little change. Tuberculosis, a virtually forgotten disease, has reappeared. The AIDS epidemic has claimed more than 430,000 American lives. More generally, some experts contend that high levels of health care spending do not result in significantly better health and well-being. U.S. health care expenditures are the highest in the world absolutely, as a proportion of GDP, and on a per capita basis. Yet many other nations rank higher than the United States in world life expectancy, maternal mortality, and in infant mortality. The U.S. Office of Technology Assessment has concluded that the United States ranks low internationally on many health indicators.

Economic Implications of Rising Costs

When the price of health care is rising, the cost of health insurance rises along with it. And, of course, increases in health care costs are the major reason for rising health care spending. But rising health care costs have other effects as well.

Reduced Access to Care   Because of rising health care costs, fewer employers offer health insurance to their workers. Consequently, the number of uninsured is large and growing. We will consider this issue in detail momentarily.

Labor Market Effects   Surging health care costs have two main effects on labor markets:

■ *Slower wage growth*   First, gains in workers' total compensation (wage plus fringe benefits, including health insurance paid for by employers) generally match gains in productivity. When health care costs (and thus insurance prices) rise more rapidly than productivity, firms that want to maintain the existing level of health care benefits for their workers must reduce the growth of the wage portion of the total compensation package. Thus, in the long run, workers bear the burden of rising health care costs in the form of slower-growing wages.

■ *Use of part-time and temporary workers*   The high cost of employer-provided health insurance has led some employers to restructure their workforces: Full-time workers with health insurance benefits are employed in smaller numbers, and uninsured part-time or temporary workers are employed in greater numbers. Similarly, a large, prosperous employer with a generous health care plan might reduce its health insurance expense by discharging its insured lower-wage workers—janitors, gardeners, and cafeteria staff—and replacing them with outside independent contractors who provide no health insurance to their employees.

Impact on Government Budgets   The budgets of Federal, state, and local governments are negatively affected by spiraling and sometimes unpredictable health care expenditures. In the past two decades, spending for health care through Medicare and Medicaid has been by far the fastest-growing segment of the Federal budget. To cover those rising expenditures, the government must either raise taxes or reduce the portion of the budget used for national defense, education, environmental programs, scientific research, and other spending categories.

The states are also finding it difficult to cover their share of the Medicaid bill. Most of them have been forced to raise their tax rates and search for new sources of revenue, and many of them have had to reduce spending on nonhealth programs such as infrastructure maintenance, welfare, and education. Local governments face similar budget strains in trying to finance public health services, hospitals, and clinics.

The Basic Problem

Increased spending on computers or houses would be a sign of prosperity, not a cause for alarm. What is different about increased spending on health care? The difference is that the peculiarities of the market for health care may result in inefficiently large increases in health care spending. We will see that this possibility arises from the way health care is financed, the asymmetry of information between consumers and providers, and the interaction of health care insurance with technological progress in the industry.

The production of health care requires scarce resources such as capital in the form of hospitals and diagnostic equipment and the highly skilled labor of physicians, technicians, and nurses. Some people suggest that the total production and consumption of health care in the United States are so large that health care, at the margin, is worth less than the alternative goods and services these resources could otherwise have produced. That is, the United States may be consuming health care beyond the MB = MC point that defines efficiency. If there is an overallocation of resources to health care, society incurs a real economic loss. Resources used excessively in health care could be used more productively to build new factories, support research and development, construct new bridges and roads, support education, improve the environment, or provide more consumer goods.

▮ Limited Access

The other health care problem is limited access. Even though there may be an overallocation of resources to health care, not all Americans can obtain the health care they need. In 1999 about 43 million Americans, or roughly 16 percent of the population, had no health insurance for the entire year. As health care costs (and therefore health care insurance premiums) continue to rise, the number of uninsured could grow.

Who are the medically uninsured? As incomes rise, so does the probability of being insured. So it is no surprise that the uninsured are concentrated among the poor. Medicaid is designed to provide health care for the poor who are on welfare. But many poor people work at low- or minimum-wage jobs without health care benefits, earning "too much" to qualify for Medicaid yet not enough to afford private health insurance. About 50 percent of the uninsured have a family head who works full-time. Many single-parent families, African-Americans, and Hispanics are uninsured simply because they are more likely to be poor.

Curiously, those with excellent health and those with the poorest health also tend to be uninsured. Many young people with excellent health simply choose not to buy health insurance. The chronically ill find it very difficult and too costly to obtain insurance because of the likelihood that they will incur substantial health care costs in the future. Because private health insurance is most frequently obtained through an employer, the unemployed are also likely to lack insurance.

Workers for smaller firms are also less likely to have health insurance. The main reason is that administrative expenses for a small firm may be 30 to 40 percent of insurance premiums, as opposed to only 10 percent for a large firm. Furthermore, corporations can deduct health insurance premiums from income for tax purposes, thereby realizing substantial tax savings. Small unincorporated businesses can deduct only part of their health insurance expenses.

Low-wage workers are also less likely to be insured. Earlier we noted that in the long run employers pass on the increasing expense of health care insurance to workers as lower wages. This option is not available to employers who are paying the minimum wage. Thus as health care insurance premiums rise, employers cut or eliminate this benefit from the compensation package for their minimum- and low-wage workers. As a result, these workers are typically uninsured.

Although many of the uninsured forgo health care, some do not. A few are able to pay for it out of pocket. Others may wait until their illness reaches a critical stage and then go to a hospital for admittance or to be treated in the emergency room. These methods of treatment are inappropriate and unnecessarily costly. It is estimated that hospitals provide more than $10 billion of uncompensated ("free") health care per year. The hospitals then try to shift these costs to those who have insurance or who can pay out of pocket. **(Key Question 2)**

▪ Why the Rapid Rise in Costs?

The rising prices, quantities, and costs of health care services are the result of the demand for health care increasing much more rapidly than supply. We will examine the reasons for this in some detail. But first it will be helpful to understand certain characteristics of the health care market.

Peculiarities of the Health Care Market

We know that purely competitive markets achieve both allocative and productive efficiency: The most desired products are produced in the least costly way. We also have found that many imperfectly competitive markets, perhaps aided by regulation or the threat of antitrust action, provide outcomes generally accepted as efficient. What, then, are the special features of the health care market that have contributed to rising prices and thus escalating costs to buyers?

▪ *Ethical and equity considerations* Ethical questions inevitably intervene in markets when decisions involve the quality of life, or literally life or death. Although we might not consider it immoral or unfair if a person cannot buy a Mercedes or a personal computer, society regards it as unjust for people to be denied access to basic health care. In general, society regards health care as an "entitlement" or a "right" and

is reluctant to ration it solely by price and income.

▪ *Asymmetric information* Health care buyers typically have little or no understanding of complex diagnostic and treatment procedures, while the physicians who are the health care sellers of those procedures possess detailed information. This creates the unusual situation in which the doctor (supplier) as the agent of the patient (consumer) tells the patient what health care services he or she should consume. We will say more about this shortly.

▪ *Spillover benefits* The medical care market often generates positive externalities (spillover benefits). For example, an immunization against polio, smallpox, or measles benefits the immediate purchaser, but it also benefits society because it reduces the risk that other members of society will be infected with a highly contagious disease. Similarly, a healthy labor force is more productive, contributing to the general prosperity and well-being of society.

▪ *Third-party payments: insurance* Because nearly four-fifths of all health care expenses are paid through public or private insurance, health care consumers pay much lower out-of-pocket "prices" than they would otherwise. Those lower prices are a distortion that results in "excess" consumption of health care services.

The Increasing Demand for Health Care

With these four features in mind, let's consider some factors that have increased the demand for health care over time.

Rising Incomes: The Role of Elasticities

Health care is a normal good, and therefore increases in domestic income have resulted in increases in the demand for health care. While there is some disagreement as to the exact income elasticity of demand for health care, several studies for industrially advanced countries suggest that the income elasticity coefficient is about 1. This means that per capita health care spending rises approximately in proportion to increases in per capita income. For example, a 3 percent increase in income will generate a 3 percent increase in health care expenditures. There is some evidence that income elasticity may be higher in the United States, perhaps as high as 1.5.

Estimates of the price elasticity of demand for health care imply that it is quite inelastic, with this coefficient being as low as .2. This means that the quantity of health care consumed declines relatively little as price increases. For example, a 10 percent increase in price would reduce quantity demanded by only 2 percent. An important consequence is that total health care spending will increase as the price of health care rises.

The relative insensitivity of health care spending to price changes results from four factors. First, people consider health care a necessity, not a luxury. There are few, if any, good substitutes for medical care in treating injuries and infections and alleviating various ailments. Second, medical treatment is often provided in an emergency situation in which price considerations are secondary or irrelevant. Third, most consumers prefer a long-term relationship with their doctors and therefore do not "shop around" when health care prices rise. Fourth, most patients have insurance and are therefore not directly affected by the price of health care. If insured patients pay, for example, only 20 percent of their health care expenses, they are less concerned with price increases or price differences between hospitals and between doctors than they would be if they paid 100 percent themselves. **(Key Question 7)**

An Aging Population   The U.S. population is aging. People 65 years of age and older constituted approximately 9 percent of the population in 1960 but almost 15 percent by 1999. Projections for the year 2030 indicate 20 percent of the population will be 65 or over.

This aging of the population affects the demand for health care because older people encounter more frequent and more prolonged spells of illness. Specifically, those 65 and older consume about three and one-half times as much health care as those between 19 and 64. In turn, people over 84 consume almost two and one-half times as much health care as those in the 65 to 69 age group. Health care expenditures are often extraordinarily high in the last year of one's life.

Looking ahead, in 2011 the 76 million people born between 1946 and 1964 will begin turning 65. We can expect that fact to create a substantial surge in the demand for health care.

Unhealthy Lifestyles   Substance abuse helps drive up health care costs. The abuse of alcohol, tobacco, and illicit drugs damages health and is therefore an important component of the demand for health care services. Alcohol is a major cause of injury-producing traffic accidents and liver disease. Tobacco use markedly increases the probability of cancer, heart disease, bronchitis, and emphysema. Illicit drugs are a major contributor to violent crime, health problems in infants, and the spread of AIDS. In addition, illicit-drug users make hundreds of thousands of costly visits to hospital emergency rooms each year. And eating high-fat diets contributes to heart disease and diabetes.

Other unhealthy behaviors also contribute to high health care costs. A 1996 Transportation Department study found that auto crash victims who did not buckle up incurred about $5000 more of health care expenses than buckled-up victims. Failure to wear seat belts contributed an additional $68 million of health care expense in just the seven states studied.

The Role of Doctors   Physicians may increase the demand for health care in several ways.

Supplier-Induced Demand   As we mentioned before, doctors, the suppliers of medical services, have much more information about those services than consumers, who are the demanders. While a patient might be well informed about food products or more complex products such as computers, he or she is not likely to be well informed about diagnostic tests such as magnetic resonance imaging or medical procedures such as joint replacements. Because of this asymmetric information (informational imbalance) the supplier, not the demander, decides what types and amounts of health care are to be consumed. This situation creates a possibility of "supplier-induced demand."

This possibility becomes especially relevant when doctors are paid on a **fee-for-service** basis, that is, paid separately for each service they perform. In light of the asymmetric information and fee-for-service arrangement, doctors have an opportunity and an incentive to suggest more health care services than are absolutely necessary (just as an auto repair shop has an opportunity and an incentive to recommend replacement of parts that are worn but still working).

More surgery is performed in the United States, where many doctors are paid a fee for each operation, than in foreign countries, where doctors are often paid annual salaries unrelated to the number of operations they perform. Furthermore, a relatively recent study concludes that doctors who own X-ray or ultrasound machines do four to four and one-half times as many tests as doctors who refer their patients to radiologists. More generally, studies suggest that up to one-third of common medical tests and procedures are either inappropriate or of questionable value.

The seller's control over consumption decisions has another result: It eliminates much of the power buyers might have in controlling the growth of health care prices and spending.

Defensive Medicine   "Become a doctor and support a lawyer," says a bumper sticker. The number of medical malpractice lawsuits admittedly is high. Today, every patient represents not only a need for medical care but also a possible malpractice suit. As a result, physicians tend to practice **defensive medicine.** That is, they recommend more tests and procedures than are warranted medically or economically in order to protect themselves against malpractice suits.

Medical Ethics   Medical ethics may drive up the demand for health care in two ways. First, doctors are ethically committed to use "best-practice" techniques in serving their patients. This often means the use of costly medical procedures that may be of only slight benefit to patients.

Second, public values seem to support the medical ethic that human life should be sustained as long as possible. This makes it difficult to confront the notion that health care is provided with scarce resources and therefore must be rationed like any other good. Can society afford to provide $5000-per-day intensive care to a comatose patient unlikely to be restored to reasonable health? Public priorities seem to indicate that such care should be provided, and those values again increase the demand for health care.

Role of Health Insurance

As we noted in Figure 23.1, 79 percent of health care spending is done not by health care consumers through direct out-of-pocket payments but by private health insurance companies or by the government through Medicare and Medicaid.

Individuals and families are faced with potentially devastating monetary losses from a variety of hazards. Your house may burn down; you may be in an auto accident; or you may suffer a serious illness. An insurance program is a means of protection against the huge monetary losses that can result from such hazards. A number of people agree to pay certain amounts (premiums) periodically in return for the guarantee that they will be compensated if they should incur a particular misfortune. Insurance is a means by which one pays a relatively small known cost for protection against an uncertain and much larger cost. While health insurance is in this way highly beneficial, it also contributes to rising costs and overconsumption of health care.

The Moral Hazard Problem   The moral hazard problem is the tendency of one party to an agreement to alter her or his behavior in a way that is costly to the other party. Health care insurance can change behavior in two ways. First, some insured people may be less careful about their health, taking fewer steps to prevent accident or illness. Second, insured individuals have greater incentives to use health care more intensively than they would if they did not have insurance. Let's consider both aspects of moral hazard.

Less Prevention   Health insurance may increase the demand for health care by encouraging behaviors that require more health care. Although most people with health care insurance are probably as careful about their health as are those without insurance, some may be more inclined to smoke, avoid exercise, and eat unhealthful foods, knowing they have insurance. Similarly, some individuals may take up ski jumping or rodeo bull riding if they have insurance covering the costs of orthopedic surgeons. And if their insurance covers rehabilitation programs, some people may be more inclined to experiment with alcohol or drugs.

Overconsumption   Insured people go to doctors more often and request more diagnostic tests and more complex treatments than they would if they were uninsured because, with health insurance, the price or opportunity cost of consuming health care is minimal. For example, many individuals with private insurance pay a fixed premium for coverage, and beyond that, aside from a modest deductible, their health care is "free." This situation differs from most markets, in which the price to the consumer reflects the full opportunity cost of each unit of the good or service. In all markets, price provides a direct economic incentive to restrict use of the product. The minimal direct price to the insured consumer of health care, in contrast, creates an incentive to overuse the health care system. Of course, the penalty for overuse will ultimately show up in higher insurance premiums, but all policyholders will share those premiums. The cost increase for the individual health consumer will be relatively small.

Also, the availability of insurance removes the consumer's budget constraint (spending limitation) when he or she decides to consume health care. Recall from Chapter 8 that budget constraints limit the purchases of most products. But insured patients face minimal or no out-of-pocket expenditures at the time they purchase health care. Because affordability is not the issue, health care is overconsumed.

Government Tax Subsidy

Federal tax policy toward employer-financed health insurance works as a **tax subsidy** that strengthens the demand for health care services. Specifically, employees do not pay Federal income or payroll tax (social security) on the value of the health insurance they receive as an employee benefit. Employees thus request and receive more of their total compensation as nontaxed health care benefits and less in taxed wages and salaries.

The government rationale for this tax treatment is that positive spillover benefits are associated with having a healthy, productive workforce. So it is appropriate to encourage health insurance for workers. The tax break does enable more of the population to have health insurance, but it also contributes to greater consumption of health care. Combined with

other factors, the tax break may result in an overconsumption of health care.

To illustrate: If the marginal tax rate is, say, 28 percent, $1 worth of health insurance is equivalent to 72 cents in after-tax pay. Because the worker can get more insurance for $1 than for 72 cents, the exclusion of health insurance from taxation increases purchases of health insurance, thus increasing the demand for health care. In essence, the 28-cent difference acts as a government subsidy to health care. One recent estimate suggests that this subsidy costs the Federal government $65 billion per year in forgone tax revenue and boosts private health insurance spending by about one-third. Actual health care spending may be 10 to 20 percent higher than otherwise because of the subsidy.

Graphical Portrayal

A simple demand and supply model illustrates the effect of health insurance on the health care market. Figure 23.3a depicts a competitive market for health care services; curve D shows the demand for health care services if all consumers are uninsured, and S represents the supply of health care. At market price P_u the equilibrium quantity of health care is Q_u.

Recall from our theory of competitive markets that output Q_u results in allocative efficiency, which means that there is no better alternative use for the resources allocated to producing that level of health care. To see what we mean by "no better use," we must realize that:

- As we move down along demand curve D, each succeeding point indicates, via the price it represents, the marginal benefit that consumers receive from that unit.
- The supply curve is the producers' marginal-cost curve. As we move up along the supply

(a)
Without health
insurance

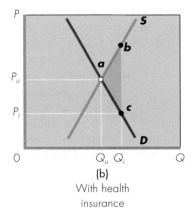

(b)
With health
insurance

Figure 23.3

Insurance and the overallocation of resources to health care. (a) Without health insurance, the optimal amount of health care consumed is Q_u, where the marginal benefit and marginal cost of health care are equal. (b) The availability of private and public insurance reduces the direct price of health care from P_u to P_i, resulting in its overconsumption (Q_i rather than Q_u) and an overallocation of resources to the health care industry. Area abc represents the efficiency loss from that overallocation.

curve, each succeeding point indicates the marginal cost of that unit of health care.

- For each unit produced up to the equilibrium quantity Q_u, marginal benefit exceeds marginal cost (because points on D are above those on S). At Q_u marginal benefit equals marginal cost, designating allocative efficiency. No matter what else those resources could have produced, the greatest net benefit to society is obtained by using those resources to produce Q_u units of health care.

But allocative efficiency occurs only when we pay in full for a product, as is assumed in Figure 23.3a. What happens when we introduce health insurance that covers, say, one-half of all health care costs? In Figure 23.3b, with health insurance paying half the price, the consumer in effect is confronted with price $P_i (= \frac{1}{2}P_u)$. The health care consumer reacts by purchasing Q_i units rather than just Q_u. This is economically inefficient because between Q_u and Q_i each unit's marginal cost to society (on curve S) exceeds its marginal benefit (on curve D). Each unit of health care between Q_u and Q_i reflects an overallocation of resources to health care. The total efficiency loss is represented by area *abc*. Because health insurance typically covers 80, not just 50, percent of health care costs, the efficiency loss in Figure 23.3b understates the actual efficiency loss to society. On the other hand, this loss may not be as large as the 80 percent figure would imply, because of the positive spillovers associated with health care.[1]

Figure 23.3b implies that there is a tradeoff between efficiency and equity. Standards of fairness or equity in the United States lead people to believe that all citizens should have access to basic health care, which is why government created social insurance in the form of Medicare and Medicaid. Also, it helps explain the Federal tax subsidy to private health insurance, which again makes health care more accessible. The problem, as Figure 23.3b shows, is that the greater the availability of insurance (and thus the more equitable society makes access to health care), the greater the overallocation of resources to the health care industry. This overallocation would be even greater if health care were provided completely "free" under a program of national health insurance. Consumers would purchase health care as long as

the marginal benefit to themselves as individuals was positive, regardless of the true cost to society. (**Key Question 10**)

Supply Factors in Rising Health Care Prices

Supply factors have also played a role in rising health care prices. Specifically, the supply of health care services has increased, but more slowly than demand. A combination of factors has produced this relatively slow growth of supply.

Supply of Physicians The supply of physicians in the United States has increased over the years; in 1975 there were 169 physicians per 100,000 people; by 1998 there were 260. But this increase in supply has not kept up with the increase in the demand for physicians' services. As a result, physicians' fees and incomes have increased more rapidly than average prices and incomes for the economy as a whole.

Conventional wisdom has been that physician groups, for example, the American Medical Association, have purposely kept admissions to medical schools, and therefore the supply of doctors, artificially low. But that is too simplistic. A rapidly rising cost of medical education seems to be the main cause of the relatively slow growth of doctor supply. Medical training requires 4 years of college, 4 years of medical school, an internship, and perhaps 3 or 4 years of training in a medical specialty. The opportunity cost of this education has increased, because the salaries of similarly capable people have soared in other professions. The direct expenses have also increased, largely due to the increasingly sophisticated levels of medical care and therefore of medical training.

High and rising education and training costs have necessitated high and rising doctors' fees to ensure an adequate return on this sort of investment in human capital. Physicians' incomes are indeed high, averaging about $200,000 in 1999, but so too are the costs of obtaining the skills necessary to become a physician. Data show that while doctors have high rates of return on their educational expenses, those returns are below the returns for lawyers and holders of masters of business administration degrees.

Slow Productivity Growth Productivity growth in an industry tends to reduce costs and increase supply. In the health care industry, such productivity growth has been modest. One reason is

---

[1]Technical footnote: There is no shortage at price P_i in Figure 23.3b. Insurance reduces the direct cost of health care to the insured, so in effect the supply curve shifts rightward (not shown) and intersects demand at point *c*.

that health care is a service, and it is generally more difficult to increase productivity for services than for goods. How, for example, would you significantly increase the productivity of nursing-home employees?

Also, competition for patients among many providers of health care has not been sufficiently brisk to force them to look for ways to reduce cost by increasing productivity. When buying most goods, customers typically shop around for the lowest price. This shopping requires that sellers keep their prices low and look to productivity increases to maintain or expand their profits. But patients rarely shop for the lowest prices when seeking medical care. In fact, a patient may feel uncomfortable about being operated on by a physician who charges the lowest price. Moreover, if insurance pays for the surgery, there is no reason to consider price at all. The point is that unusual features of the market for health care limit competitive pricing and thus reduce incentives to achieve cost saving via advances in productivity.

Changes in Medical Technology
Some technological advances in medicine have lowered costs. For example, the development of vaccines for polio, smallpox, and measles has greatly reduced health care expenditures for the treatment of those diseases. And reduced lengths of stays in hospitals have lowered the costs of medical care.

But many medical technologies developed since the Second World War have significantly increased the cost of medical care either by increasing prices or by extending procedures to a greater number of people. For example, because they give more accurate information, advanced body scanners costing up to $2000 per scan are often used in place of X rays that cost less than $100 for each scan. Desiring to offer the highest quality of service, hospitals want to use the very latest equipment and procedures. These newer, more expensive treatments are surely more effective than older ones. But doctors and hospital administrators both realize that the fixed high cost of such equipment means it must be used extensively to lower the cost per patient.

As another example, organ transplants are extremely costly. Before the development of this technology, a person with a serious liver malfunction died. Now a liver transplant can cost $200,000 or more, with subsequent medical attention costing $10,000 to $20,000 per year for the rest of the patient's life.

The historical willingness of private and public insurance to pay for new treatments without regard to price and number of patients has contributed to the incentive to develop and use new technologies. Insurers, in effect, have encouraged research into and development of health care technologies, regardless of their cost. Recently, when insurance companies resisted paying for new expensive treatments such as bone marrow transplants, public outcries led them to change their minds. So expanding insurance coverage leads to new, often more expensive medical technologies, which in turn lead to a demand for a wider definition of what should be covered by insurance. Example: After expensive magnetic resonance imaging (MRI) scans were developed, doctors and their patients demanded that such scans be covered under Medicare. After the government agreed to such coverage in 1985, sales of MRI machines rose dramatically.

Relative Importance
According to most analysts, the demand and supply factors we have discussed vary in their impact on escalating health care costs. As we noted, the income elasticity of demand for health care is estimated to be +1 to +1.5, meaning that increased income brings with it proportionate or more-than-proportionate increases in health care spending. But rising income does not alone explain the rocketing increase in health care spending as a percentage of total domestic output (income). Furthermore, government studies estimate that the aging population accounts for less than 10 percent of the current increase in per capita health care spending.

Most experts attribute the relative rise in health care spending to (1) advances in medical technology, combined with (2) the medical ethic of providing the best treatment available, (3) private and public health insurance, and (4) fee-for-service physicians' payments by health insurance firms. Through technological progress, great strides have been made in the diagnosis, treatment, and prevention of illness. But the third-party (insurance) payment system provides little incentive to limit the development or use of such technologies, because it has no mechanism to force an equating of marginal costs and marginal benefits. And the "best treatment available" ethic, together with the fee-for-service payment system, ensures that any new technology with a positive marginal benefit will get used and be billed for, regardless of the marginal cost to society.

Reform of the Health Care System

What, if anything, can be done to ensure access for more Americans to the health care system? And how might health care costs be contained? Reform of the health care system to achieve these two goals will be difficult. First, there is a tradeoff between the two objectives: Greater access to the system will mean rising costs. Second, health care reform is complex, because expectations (for example, access to the "best" medical care), tradition (the "right" to choose one's doctor), and the goals of self-interest groups (private insurers, health maintenance organizations, drug companies, physicians, and hospitals) all come into play.

This latter point is especially significant. The numerous affected interest groups will not passively accept rearrangement of costs and benefits in an industry that accounts for almost one-seventh of total U.S. spending. Physicians, hospitals, health insurers, health maintenance organizations, and drug companies seek to prevent price controls on their services and products. Older people—represented by AARP—want government to pay a larger portion of long-term (nursing-home) health care. Health insurance companies hope their business will not be curtailed by reforms. Labor unions advocate a generous basic-benefits package and oppose taxation of employer-financed health insurance. Drug companies want prescription drugs covered under

Medicare. Psychiatrists, physical therapists, acupuncturists, and chiropractors want their services included in any new proposal. Trial lawyers want existing malpractice laws left alone. Small businesses strongly oppose any law requiring all companies to provide health insurance for their employees. The beer, liquor and tobacco industries do not want additional "sin" taxes levied on them to help finance any reform proposal.

Universal Access

How can health care insurance, and thus health care, be made available to all U.S. citizens? Let's briefly consider three reform concepts.

"Play or Pay"   Because much of the nation's health insurance is paid by employers, one way is to expand that coverage using a **play-or-pay** approach. All employers would be required to either provide a basic health insurance program for their workers and their dependents ("play") or pay a special payroll tax to finance health insurance for uninsured workers ("pay"). Some form of publicly sponsored health care plan would cover people who are not in the labor force and thus uninsured.

Such plans, however, probably would lead to lower real wages. Also, unemployment might increase in firms currently paying wages at or near the minimum wage.

Tax Credits and Vouchers   Another approach, using tax credits and vouchers, would help the poor pay for health insurance. The Federal government would provide a tax credit, for example, of $1500 for a single person and $4000 for a family of four, to low-income individuals and families for use in purchasing health insurance. The size of the tax credit would diminish as the recipient's income rises. Those whose incomes are so low as to be exempt from the income tax would be issued a voucher for purchasing health insurance. This proposal is essentially a tax subsidy designed to make insurance more affordable to low-income people.

National Health Insurance   The most far-reaching and controversial reform concept is to establish a system of **national health insurance (NHI)** along the lines of the present Canadian system. The Federal government would provide a basic package of health care to every citizen at no direct charge or at a low cost-sharing level. The system would be financed out of tax revenues rather than out of insurance premiums.

NHI is not the same as socialized medicine. Under NHI the government would not own health care facilities such as hospitals, clinics, and nursing homes. Nor would health care practitioners such as doctors, nurses, and technicians be government employees. Under NHI the government would simply sponsor and finance basic health care for all citizens. Although the role of private health insurers would be reduced under NHI, they could provide health insurance for any medical procedures that were not covered in the basic NHI health care package.

Arguments for NHI
Proponents say that NHI is the simplest and most direct way of providing universal access to health care:

- It allows patients to choose their own physicians.
- It would reduce administrative costs. The present system, it is argued, is administratively chaotic and expensive because hundreds of private health care insurers are involved, each with its own procedures and claim forms. Administration costs in the Canadian system are less than 5 percent of total health care costs compared with almost 17 percent in the United States.
- It would separate health care availability from employment and therefore would eliminate the hiring of part-time and temporary workers as a way to avoid providing health care insurance.
- It would allow the government to use its single-insurer market power to contain costs. The government could apply its buying power to mandate fees for various medical procedures and thus control physician and hospital costs. Hospitals would operate on budgets set by the government.

Arguments Against NHI
Opponents of NHI provide weighty counterarguments:

- Government-determined price ceilings on physicians' services are not likely to control costs. Doctors can protect their incomes from fixed fees by manipulating the amount of care they provide a patient. Suppose the maximum fee for an office visit is $30. Doctors might spread a given number of diagnostic tests over three or four office visits, although all the tests could be done in one visit. Or a doctor might require an office visit to explain test results in-

stead of phoning the patient. Similar arguments apply to government regulation of hospital charges.

- In the Canadian system patients often have long waits for certain diagnostic procedures and surgeries. This is the result of the Canadian government's effort to control expenditures by restricting hospitals' capital spending. To illustrate, there are only one-fifth as many magnetic resonance imaging machines per million people in Canada as in the United States. This results in a waiting list for use of MRIs in Canada. NHI might strongly conflict with U.S. expectations of medical care "on demand."

- Doctors can mount "strikes" against low payments from the government, as they have done is several areas of Canada. Such disruptions in medical care rarely happen in the United States.

- The Federal government has a very poor record of containing costs. Despite its considerable buying power, the Department of Defense, for example, has a long history of cost overruns and mismanagement. And, as you have seen, spending has spiraled upward under the government's Medicare and Medicaid programs. Also recall (Figure 23.3b) that insurance is a critical factor in the overconsumption of health care. Under NHI a completely "free" basic health care package would prompt consumers to "purchase" health care as long as marginal benefits were positive, regardless of the true cost to society.

- Subtle and perhaps undesirable redistribution effects would result under NHI. Under private health insurance, a particular health care insurance package costs the same regardless of the insured's income. This makes the cost of insurance resemble a regressive tax, since low-income workers pay a larger percentage of their incomes for the insurance than do high-income insurees. If NHI were financed out of personal income tax revenues, this financing would be progressive. Under NHI those with low incomes would receive health insurance and pay little or none of the cost. While some might view this as desirable, others believe that income redistribution in the United States has been overdone and that further redistribution through NHI would be unfair. Depending on the type of tax and its size, employers and workers in industries such as automobile and steel might receive windfalls in the form of higher profits and wages when NHI replaced their health insurance programs. Employers and workers in small retail establishments and fast-food restaurants, where health insurance is typically absent, might not realize such gains.

Cost Containment: Altering Incentives

Can the United States control the growth of health care costs, prices, and spending by reducing incentives to overconsume health care?

Deductibles and Copayments Insurance companies have reacted to rising health care costs by imposing sizable deductibles and copayments on those they insure. Instead of covering all of an insuree's medical costs, a policy might now specify that the insuree pay the first $250 or $500 of each year's health care costs (the deductible) and 15 or 20 percent of all additional costs (the copayment). The deductible and copayment are intended to alleviate the overuse problem by creating a direct payment and therefore an opportunity cost to the health care consumer. The deductible has the added advantage of reducing the administrative costs of insurance companies in processing many small claims.

Managed Care Managed-care organizations (or systems) are those in which medical services are controlled or coordinated by insurance companies or health care organizations in order to reduce health care expenditures. In 1999 about 60 percent of all U.S. workers received health care through such "managed care." These organizations are of two main types:

- *Preferred provider organizations* Some insurance companies have set up **preferred provider organizations (PPOs),** which require that hospitals and physicians accept discounted prices for their services as a condition for being included in the insurance plan. The policyholder receives a list of participating hospitals and doctors and is given, say, 80 to 100 percent reimbursement of health care costs when treated by PPO physicians and hospitals. If a patient chooses a doctor or hospital outside the PPO, the insurance company reimburses only 60 to 70 percent. In return for being included as a PPO provider, doctors and hospitals agree to rates set by the insurance

company for each service. Because these fees are less than those usually charged, PPOs reduce health insurance premiums and health care expenditures.

- *Health maintenance organizations* Many Americans now receive their medical care from **health maintenance organizations (HMOs),** which provide health care services to a specific group of enrollees in exchange for a set annual fee per enrollee. HMOs employ their own physicians and contract for specialized services with outside providers and hospitals. They then contract with firms or government units to provide medical care for their workers, who thereby become HMO members. Because HMOs have fixed annual revenue, they may lose money if they provide "too much" care. So they have an incentive to hold down costs. They also have an incentive to provide preventive care in order to reduce the far larger expense of corrective care.

Both PPOs and HMOs are managed-care organizations because medical use and spending are "managed" by close monitoring of physicians' and hospitals' behavior; the purpose is to eliminate unnecessary diagnostic tests and remedial treatments. Doctors in managed-care organizations might not order an MRI scan or an ultrasound test or suggest surgery because their work is monitored and because they may have a fixed budget. In contrast, an independent fee-for-service physician may face little or no control and have a financial incentive to order the test or do the surgery. Doctors and hospitals in a managed-care organization often share in an "incentive pool" of funds when they meet their cost-control goals.

The advantages of managed-care plans are that they provide health care at lower prices than traditional insurance and emphasize preventive medicine. The disadvantages are that the patient usually is restricted to physicians employed by or under contract with the managed-care plan. Also, some say that the focus on reducing costs has gone too far, resulting in denial of highly expensive, but effective, treatment. In 2000 the U.S. Senate and House of Representatives passed different versions of a "patients' bill of rights" to regulate the practices of managed care-providers and establish a process for appealing HMO decisions. The idea of such a bill of rights has bipartisan political support, and therefore some compromise between the Senate and House versions is expected to become law.

Medicare and DRG   In 1983 the Federal government altered the way it makes payments for hospital services received by Medicare patients. Rather than automatically paying all costs related to a patient's treatment and length of hospital stay, Medicare submitted payments based on a **diagnosis-related-group (DRG) system.** Under DRG a hospital receives a fixed payment for treating each patient; that payment is an amount associated with the one of several hundred carefully detailed diagnostic categories that best characterize the patient's condition and needs.

DRG-system payments obviously give hospitals the incentive to restrict the amount of resources used in treating patients. It is no surprise that under DRG the length of hospital stays has fallen sharply and more patients are treated on an outpatient basis. Critics, however, argue that this is evidence of diminished quality of medical care.

Recent Laws and Proposals

Although Congress has rejected major reforms of the health care system, it has made some modest changes and is currently discussing further reforms:

- *Portability and accountability*   The Health Insurance Portability and Accountability Act of 1996 ensures that workers with a group health plan can continue to buy health insurance when they change their jobs or become self-employed, even if they have major health problems. It also prohibits group insurance plans from dropping coverage of a sick employee or of a business that has a sick employee.

- *Medical savings accounts*   The 1996 legislation also introduced, on a trial basis, medical saving accounts (MSAs) for small businesses, the self-employed, and the uninsured. Consumers can make tax-deductible contributions into these accounts, which include a catastrophic health insurance plan for large medical expenses.

Earnings on the funds in the account are tax-free, and the money in the account can be used to pay routine medical expenses. Unused funds continue to grow from year to year. Withdrawals for nonmedical purposes are permitted but are taxed as income.

MSAs are highly controversial. On the positive side, they encourage people to stay healthy and use funds in their medical account sparingly. That could decrease health care spending. But critics say that such accounts create an *adverse selection problem* (review Chapter 17) by pulling the healthiest and wealthiest people away from the general health insurance market, potentially raising premiums for others.

- *Prescription drug coverage*   Prescription drugs are not currently (2001) covered by Medicare, but such coverage is gaining much popularity in Congress. There are several reasons. First, prescription drugs have become a more significant part of health care costs and thus are claiming a larger percentage of the income of older Americans. Second, politicians are well aware of the growing number of Americans on Medicare who would welcome prescription-drug coverage. Finally, large Federal budget surpluses have reduced the political pressure to hold down Federal spending.

The debate over prescription-drug coverage centers on how best to provide it. Should all people on Medicare be covered, regardless of their incomes? If so, the Congressional Budget Office estimates that Medicare expenditures will rise from 2.3 percent of GDP in 2000 to 6.5 percent of GDP in 2030, rather than 4.4 percent. Or should government provide "free" or very low cost prescription-drug coverage *only* to lower-income Medicare recipients, while making similar coverage available for purchase (at cost) by higher-income seniors?

A Market for Human Organs?

A Market Might Eliminate the Present Shortage of Human Organs for Transplant. But There Are Many Serious Objections to Turning Human Body Parts into Commodities for Purchase and Sale.

Advances in medical technology make it possible for surgeons to replace some human body parts with donated "used parts," much like a backyard mechanic might replace a worn-out alternator in an automobile with one from a junked vehicle. It has become increasingly commonplace in medicine to transplant kidneys, lungs, livers, eye corneas, pancreases, and hearts from deceased individuals to those whose organs have failed or are failing. But surgeons and many of their patients face a growing problem: There are shortages of donated organs available for transplant. Not everyone who needs a transplant can get one. In 2000, there were 74,000 Americans on the waiting list for transplants. Indeed, an inadequate supply of donated organs causes an estimated 4000 deaths in the United States each year.

Why Shortages? Seldom, if ever, do we hear of shortages of used auto parts such as alternators, batteries, transmissions, or water pumps. What is different about organs for transplant? One difference is that there is a market for used auto parts but not for human organs. To understand this situation, observe the demand curve D_1 and supply curve S_1 in the accompanying figure. The downward slope of the demand curve tells us that if there were a market for human organs, the quantity of organs demanded would be greater at lower prices than at higher prices. Perfectly inelastic supply curve S_1 represents the fixed quantity of human organs now donated via consent before death. Because the price of these donated organs is in effect zero, quantity demanded Q_3 exceeds quantity supplied Q_1. The shortage of $Q_3 - Q_1$ is rationed through a waiting list of those in medical need of transplants. Many people die while still on the waiting list.

Use of a Market A market for human organs would increase the incentive to donate organs. Such a market might work like this: An individual might specify in a legal document that he or she is

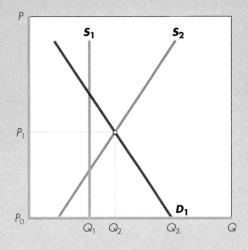

willing to sell one or more usable human organs upon death or near-death. The person could specify where the money from the sale would go, for example, to family, a church, an educational institution, or a charity. Firms would then emerge to purchase organs and resell them where needed for profit. Under such a system, the supply curve of usable organs would take on the normal upward slope of typical supply curves. The higher the expected price of an organ, the greater the number of people willing to have their organs sold at death. Suppose that the supply curve is S_2 in the figure. At the equilibrium price P_1, the number of organs made available for transplant (Q_2) would equal the number purchased for transplant (also Q_2). In this generalized case, the shortage of organs would be eliminated and, of particular importance, the number of organs available for transplanting would rise from Q_1 to Q_2. This means more lives would be saved and enhanced than is the case under the present donor system.

Objections In view of this positive outcome, why is there no such market for human organs? Critics of market-based solutions have two main objections. The first is a moral objection: Critics feel that turning human organs into commodities commercializes human beings and diminishes the special nature of human life. They say there is something unseemly about selling and buying body organs as if they were bushels of wheat or ounces of gold. (There is, however, a market for blood!) Moreover, critics note that the market would ration the available organs (as represented by Q_2 in the figure) to people who either can afford them (at P_1) or have health insurance for transplants.

Second, a health-cost objection suggests that a market for body organs would greatly increase the cost of health care. Rather than obtaining freely donated (although "too few") body organs, patients or their insurance companies would have to pay market prices for them, further increasing the cost of medical care. Moreover, as transplant procedures are further perfected, the demand for transplants is expected to increase significantly. Rapid increases in demand relative to supply would boost the prices of human organs and thus further contribute to the problem of escalating health care costs.

Supporters of market-based solutions to organ shortages point out that the laws against selling organs are simply driving the market underground. Worldwide, an estimated $1 billion–per-year illegal market in human organs has emerged. As in other illegal markets, the unscrupulous tend to thrive. Those who support legalization say that it would be greatly preferable to legalize and regulate the market for transplantable human organs.

SUMMARY

1. The U.S. health care industry comprises 9 million workers, including about 700,000 physicians and more than 6000 hospitals.

2. Health care spending has increased both absolutely and as a percentage of GDP.

3. Rising health care costs and prices have (a) reduced access to the health care system, (b) contributed to slower real wage growth and expanded the employment of part-time and temporary workers, and (c) caused governments to restrict spending on nonhealth programs and to raise taxes.

4. The core of the health care problem is an alleged overallocation of resources to the health care industry.

5. About 43 million Americans, or 16 percent of the population, do not have health insurance. The uninsured are concentrated among the poor, the chronically ill, the unemployed, the young, those employed by small firms, and low-wage workers.

6. Special characteristics of the health care market include (a) the belief that health care is a "right," (b) an imbalance of information between consumers and suppliers, (c) the presence of spillover benefits, and (d) the payment of most health care expenses by private or public insurance.

7. While rising incomes, an aging population, and substance abuse have all contributed to an increasing demand for health care, the role of doctors is also significant. Because of asymmetric information, physicians influence the demand for their own services. The fee-for-service payment system, combined with defensive medicine to protect against malpractice suits, also increases demand for health care.

8. The moral hazard problem arising from health insurance takes two forms: (a) People may be less careful of their health, and (b) there is an incentive to overconsume health care.

9. The exemption of employer-paid health insurance from the Federal income tax subsidizes health care.

10. Slow productivity growth in the health care industry and, more important, cost-increasing advances in health care technology have restricted the expansion of the supply of medical care and have boosted prices.

11. Reforms designed to increase access to the health care system include (a) "play-or-pay" proposals designed to increase employer-sponsored health insurance, (b) tax credits and vouchers to help low-income families afford health care, and (c) national health insurance.

12. Insurance companies have introduced deductibles and copayments in an attempt to contain health care prices and spending.

13. Managed-care organizations attempt to control their enrolled members' use of health care as a way of containing health care costs. In a preferred provider organization (PPO), a group of health providers agree to provide services to a defined group of patients at an agreed-upon rate for each service. In a health maintenance organization (HMO), groups of workers prepay for health services at an agreed-upon annual rate. The HMO then provides services to the group, using its own physicians or physicians and hospitals under contract.

14. Recent changes to the health care system include those associated with the Health Insurance Portability and Accountability Act of 1996, which (a) ensures paid access to continuing health insurance to workers who change jobs or become self-employed, even if they have medical problems; (b) prohibits insurance firms from dropping coverage of workers or businesses that have high medical bills; and (c) establishes, on a trial basis, medical savings accounts.

15. There is growing political consensus that prescription-drug coverage is needed under Medicare. Some think such coverage should be "free" (or highly subsidized) for everyone eligible for Medicare. Others would restrict the free coverage to lower-income people and have those with higher incomes share a substantial part of the insurance cost.

TERMS AND CONCEPTS

deductibles

copayments

fee for service

defensive medicine

tax subsidy

"play or pay"

national health insurance (NHI)

preferred provider organizations (PPOs)

health maintenance organizations (HMOs)

diagnosis-related-group (DRG) system

STUDY QUESTIONS

1. Why would increased spending as a percentage of GDP on, say, household appliances or personal computers in a particular economy be regarded as economically desirable? Why, then, is there so much concern about rising expenditures as a percentage of GDP on health care?

2. **Key Question** What are the "twin problems" of the health care industry as viewed by society? How are they related?

3. Briefly describe the main features of Medicare and Medicaid, indicating how each is financed.

4. What are the implications of rapidly rising health care prices and spending for (a) the growth of real wage rates and (b) government budgets? Explain.

5. Who are the main groups without health insurance?

6. List the special characteristics of the U.S. health care market and specify how each affects health care problems.

7. **Key Question** What are the estimated income and price elasticities of demand for health care? How does each relate to rising health care costs?

8. Briefly discuss the demand and supply factors that contribute to rising health costs. Specify how (a) asymmetric information, (b) fee-for-service payments, (c) defensive medicine, and (d) medical ethics might cause health care costs to rise.

9. "Health care expenditures have been rising principally because of the technological transformation of medical care." Do you agree? Explain.

10. **Key Question** Using the concepts in Chapter 21's discussion of consumer behavior, explain how health care insurance results in an overallocation of resources to the health care industry. Use a demand and supply diagram to specify the resulting efficiency loss.

11. How is the moral hazard problem relevant to the health care market?

12. What is the rationale for exempting a firm's contribution to its workers' health insurance from taxation as worker income? What is the impact of this exemption on allocative efficiency in the health care industry?

13. Comment on or explain:
    a. Providing health insurance to achieve equity goals creates a tradeoff with the efficient allocation of resources to the health care industry.

    b. Improved health habits are desirable but would not necessarily reduce health care costs. For example, the deaths of many smokers are caused by sudden and lethal heart attacks and are therefore medically inexpensive.

    c. If the government were to require employer-sponsored health insurance for all workers, the likely result would be an increase in the unemployment of low-wage workers.

14. Briefly describe (a) "play or pay," (b) tax credits and vouchers, and (c) national health insurance as means of increasing access to health care. What are the major criticisms of national health insurance?

15. What are (a) preferred provider organizations and (b) health maintenance organizations? In your answer, explain how each is designed to alleviate the overconsumption of health care.

16. Do you think prescription drugs should be covered under Medicare? Are you willing to pay a higher social security/Medicare tax to pay for this added benefit? Do you think the prescription-drug benefit should go to everyone covered by Medicare, including those who can easily afford to pay for prescription drugs out of pocket?

17. **(Last Word)** Do you favor the establishment of a market for "donated" human organs? Why or why not?

18. **Web-Based Question:** *Hospital charges—visit a hospital near you.* Visit the American Hospital Directory at www.ahd.com/ and search for two hospitals near you. Compare their average charges and average length of stay. Which type of treatment averages the most and which the least? Are the amounts for each hospital similar? Does this imply competition? Without insurance, could you afford an average heart operation at a hospital near you?

19. **Web-Based Question:** *AARP and health care— what is its opinion?* Visit the AARP home page, www.aarp.org/, and select Legislative Issues. Describe two such issues relating to *health care* or *long-term care* and summarize AARP's positions. Do you sense any particular bias in AARP's views? Who would pay for greater government benefits for older Americans?

6

International Economics
and the World Economy

24

International Trade

THE **WTO**, TRADE deficits, dumping. Exchange rates, the EU, the G-7 nations. The IMF, official reserves, currency interventions. Capital flight, special economic zones, the ruble. This is the language of international economics, the subject of Part 6. To understand the increasingly integrated world economy, we need to learn more about this language and the ideas that it conveys. ■ In this chapter we build on Chapter 6 by providing both a deeper analysis of the benefits of international trade and a fuller appraisal of the arguments for protectionism. Then in Chapter 25 we examine exchange rates and the balance of payments. A "bonus" Internet chapter at our website examines the transition economies of Russia and China.

■ Some Key Facts

In Chapter 6 we dealt with a number of facts about international trade. Let's briefly review them and add a few more:
- Exports of goods and services make up about 12 percent of total U.S. output. That percentage is much lower than the percentage in many other nations. Examples: Netherlands, 56 percent; Canada, 41 percent; New Zealand, 29 percent; the United Kingdom, 29 percent.
- The United States leads the world in the volume of exports and imports, as measured in dollars. Currently, the United States provides about one-eighth of the world's exports. Germany, Japan, Britain, and France follow in the list of the top five exporters by dollar volume.

- Since 1975, U.S. exports have doubled as a percentage of GDP.
- In 2000 the United States imported $450 billion more goods than it exported. But in that year U.S. exports of services exceeded imports of services by $81 billion. So the combined trade deficit of goods and services was $369 billion.
- The principal commodities among U.S. exports are semiconductors, computers, chemicals, consumer durables, and generating equipment. The principle imports are automobiles, computers, petroleum, and clothing.
- Like other advanced industrial nations, the United States imports some of the same categories of goods that it exports. Examples: automobiles, computers, chemicals, semiconductors, and telecommunications equipment.

- Most of U.S. export and import trade takes place with other industrially advanced nations, specifically Canada, nations of western Europe, and Japan.

- Although the United States, Japan, and western European nations dominate world trade (Global Perspective 24.1), several other nations have increased their roles significantly. Collectively, the southeast Asian economies of South Korea, Taiwan, Singapore, and Hong Kong (which is part of China), have expanded their share of world trade from 3 percent in 1972 to more than 10 percent today. Russia, the eastern European nations, and mainland China have also increased their international trade.

- International trade (and finance) link world economies (review Figure 6.1, page 94.) Through trade, changes in economic conditions in one place on the globe can quickly affect other places. Examples: In 1998 economic problems in the southeast Asian countries of South Korea, Indonesia, Malaysia, and the Philippines reduced demand for Japanese imports and negatively affected Japan's economy. In 2000, hikes in world oil prices threatened to slow economic growth in Europe and the United States.

- International trade and finance is often at the center of economic policy. Examples: The U.S.

Congress often grapples with international trade issues such as trade relations with China. The World Trade Organization (WTO) and the International Monetary Fund (IMF) regularly meet to establish rules relating to international trade and finance. Such meetings often attract protestors who oppose global capitalism.

With these facts in mind, we now look more closely at the economics of international trade.

▮ The Economic Basis for Trade

In Chapter 6 we found that international trade enables nations to specialize their production, enhance their resource productivity, and acquire more goods and services. Sovereign nations, like individuals and the regions of a nation, can gain by specializing in the products they can produce with greatest relative efficiency and by trading for the goods they cannot produce as efficiently. A more complete answer to the question "Why do nations trade?" hinges on three facts:

- The distribution of natural, human, and capital resources among nations is uneven; nations differ in their endowments of economic resources.

- Efficient production of various goods requires different technologies or combinations of resources.

- Products are differentiated as to quality and other nonprice attributes. A few or many people may prefer certain imported goods to similar goods made domestically.

To recognize the character and interaction of these three facts, think of Japan, for example, which has a large, well-educated labor force and abundant, and therefore inexpensive, skilled labor. As a result, Japan can produce efficiently (at low cost) a variety of **labor-intensive goods** such as cameras, portable CD players, video game players, and video recorders whose design and production require much skilled labor.

In contrast, Australia has vast amounts of land and can inexpensively produce such **land-intensive goods** as wheat, wool, and meat. Brazil has the soil, tropical climate, rainfall, and ready supply of unskilled labor that are needed for the efficient, low-cost production of coffee.

Industrially advanced economies with relatively large amounts of capital can inexpensively produce goods whose production requires much capital, including such **capital-intensive goods** as automobiles, agricultural equipment, machinery, and chemicals.

GLOBAL PERSPECTIVE 24.1

Shares of World Exports, Selected Nations

The United States has the largest share of world exports, followed closely by Germany and Japan. The seven largest export nations account for nearly 50 percent of world exports.

Percentage Share of World Exports, 1999

Nation	
United States	
Germany	
Japan	
France	
United Kingdom	
Canada	
Italy	

Source: World Trade Organization, www.wto.org.

All nations, regardless of their labor, land, or capital intensity, can find special niches for individual products that are in demand worldwide because of their special qualities. Examples: fashions from Italy, luxury automobiles from Germany, software from the United States, and watches from Switzerland.

The distribution of resources, technology, and product distinctiveness among nations, however, is not forever fixed. When that distribution changes, the relative efficiency and success with which nations produce and sell goods also changes. For example, in the past few decades South Korea has upgraded the quality of its labor force and has greatly expanded its stock of capital. Although South Korea was primarily an exporter of agricultural products and raw materials a half-century ago, it now exports large quantities of manufactured goods. Similarly, the new technologies that gave us synthetic fibers and synthetic rubber drastically altered the resource mix needed to produce these goods and changed the relative efficiency of nations in manufacturing them.

As national economies evolve, the size and quality of their labor forces may change, the volume and composition of their capital stocks may shift, new technologies may develop, and even the quality of land and the quantity of natural resources may be altered. As such changes occur, the relative efficiency with which a nation can produce specific goods will also change.

▌ Comparative Advantage: Graphical Analysis

Implicit in what we have been saying is the principle of comparative advantage, described through production possibilities tables in Chapter 6. We look again at that idea, now using graphical analysis. ↙ **24.1**

Two Isolated Nations

Suppose the world economy is composed of just two nations: the United States and Brazil. Each nation can produce both wheat and coffee, but at different levels of economic efficiency. Suppose the U.S. and Brazilian domestic production possibilities curves for coffee and wheat are as shown in Figure 24.1a and 24.1b. Note especially two characteristics of these production possibilities curves:

■ **Constant costs** The "curves" are drawn as straight lines, in contrast to the concave-to-the-origin production possibilities frontiers we examined in Chapter 2. This means that we have replaced the law of increasing opportunity costs with the assumption of constant costs. This substitution simplifies our discussion but does not impair the validity of our analysis and conclusions. Later we will consider the effects of increasing opportunity costs.

■ **Different costs** The production possibilities curves of the United States and Brazil reflect different resource mixes and differing levels of

(a)
United States

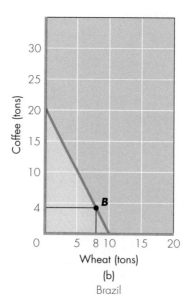

(b)
Brazil

Figure 24.1

Production possibilities for the United States and Brazil. The two production possibilities curves show the combinations of coffee and wheat that (a) the United States and (b) Brazil can produce domestically. The curves for both countries are straight lines because we are assuming constant opportunity costs. The different cost ratios, 1 coffee ≡ 1 wheat for the United States, and 2 coffee ≡ 1 wheat for Brazil, are reflected in the different slopes of the two lines.

technological progress. Specifically, they tell us that the opportunity costs of producing wheat and coffee differ between the two nations.

United States

In Figure 24.1a, with full employment, the United States will operate on its production possibilities curve. On that curve, it can increase its output of wheat from 0 tons to 30 tons by forgoing 30 tons of coffee output. This means that the slope of the production possibilities curve is -1 ($= -30$ coffee$/+30$ wheat), implying that 1 ton of coffee must be sacrificed for each extra ton of wheat. In the United States the domestic exchange ratio or **cost ratio** for the two products is 1 ton of coffee for 1 ton of wheat, or $1C \equiv 1W$. Said differently, the United States can "exchange" a ton of coffee for a ton of wheat. Our constant-cost assumption means that this exchange or opportunity-cost equation prevails for all possible moves from one point to another along the U.S. production possibilities curve.

Brazil

Brazil's production possibilities curve in Figure 24.1b represents a different full-employment opportunity-cost ratio. In Brazil, 20 tons of coffee must be given up to get 10 tons of wheat. The slope of the production possibilities curve is -2 ($= -20$ coffee$/+10$ wheat). This means that in Brazil the opportunity-cost ratio for the two goods is 2 tons of coffee for 1 ton of wheat, or $2C \equiv 1W$.

Self-Sufficiency Output Mix

If the United States and Brazil are isolated and are to be self-sufficient, then each country must choose some output mix on its production possibilities curve. It will choose the mix that provides the greatest total utility, or satisfaction. Assume that point A in Figure 24.1a is the optimal mix in the United States;

that is, society deems the combination of 18 tons of wheat and 12 tons of coffee preferable to any other combination of the goods available along the production possibilities curve. Suppose Brazil's optimal product mix is 8 tons of wheat and 4 tons of coffee, indicated by point B in Figure 24.1b. These choices are reflected in column 1 of Table 24.1.

Specializing Based on Comparative Advantage

We can determine the products in which the United States and Brazil should specialize as follows: The **principle of comparative advantage** says that total output will be greatest when each good is produced by the nation that has the lowest domestic opportunity cost for that good. In our two-nation illustration, the United States has the lower domestic opportunity cost for wheat; the United States need forgo only 1 ton of coffee to produce 1 ton of wheat, whereas Brazil must forgo 2 tons of coffee for 1 ton of wheat. The United States has a comparative (cost) advantage in wheat and should specialize in wheat production. The "world" (that is, the United States and Brazil) in our example would clearly not be economizing in the use of its resources if a high-cost producer (Brazil) produced a specific product (wheat) when a low-cost producer (the United States) could have produced it. Having Brazil produce wheat would mean that the world economy would have to give up more coffee than is necessary to obtain a ton of wheat.

Brazil has the lower domestic opportunity cost for coffee; it must sacrifice only $\frac{1}{2}$ ton of wheat in producing 1 ton of coffee, while the United States must forgo 1 ton of wheat in producing a ton of coffee. Brazil has a comparative advantage in coffee and should specialize in coffee production. Again, the world would not be employing its resources

Table 24.1

International Specialization According to Comparative Advantage and the Gains from Trade

Country	(1) Outputs before Specialization	(2) Outputs after Specialization	(3) Amounts Exported (−) and Imported (+)	(4) Outputs Available after Trade	(5) Gains from Specialization and Trade, (4) − (1)
United States	18 wheat 12 coffee	30 wheat 0 coffee	−10 wheat +15 coffee	20 wheat 15 coffee	2 wheat 3 coffee
Brazil	8 wheat 4 coffee	0 wheat 20 coffee	+10 wheat −15 coffee	10 wheat 5 coffee	2 wheat 1 coffee

economically if coffee were produced by a high-cost producer (the United States) rather than by a low-cost producer (Brazil). If the United States produced coffee, the world would be giving up more wheat than necessary to obtain each ton of coffee. Economizing requires that any particular good be produced by the nation having the lowest domestic opportunity cost, or the comparative advantage for that good. The United States should produce wheat, and Brazil should produce coffee.

In column 2 of Table 24.1 we verify that specialized production enables the world to get more output from its fixed amount of resources. By specializing completely in wheat, the United States can produce 30 tons of wheat and no coffee. Brazil, by specializing completely in coffee, can produce 20 tons of coffee and no wheat. The world ends up with 4 more tons of wheat (30 tons compared with 26) *and* 4 more tons of coffee (20 tons compared with 16) than it would if there were self-sufficiency or unspecialized production.

Terms of Trade

But consumers of each nation want both wheat *and* coffee. They can have both if the two nations trade the two products. But what will be the **terms of trade?** At what exchange ratio will the United States and Brazil trade wheat and coffee?

Because $1W \equiv 1C$ in the United States, the United States must get *more than* 1 ton of coffee for each ton of wheat exported; otherwise, it will not benefit from exporting wheat in exchange for Brazilian coffee. The United States must get a better "price" (more coffee) for its wheat in the world market than it can get domestically; otherwise, there is no gain from trade and it will not occur.

Similarly, because $1W \equiv 2C$ in Brazil, Brazil must get 1 ton of wheat by exporting some amount *less than* 2 tons of coffee. Brazil must be able to pay a lower "price" for wheat in the world market than it must pay domestically, or else it will not want to trade. The international exchange ratio or terms of trade must lie somewhere between

$1W \equiv 1C$ (United States' cost conditions)

and

$1W \equiv 2C$ (Brazil's cost conditions)

But where between these limits will the world exchange ratio fall? The United States will prefer a rate close to $1W \equiv 2C$, say, $1W \equiv 1\frac{3}{4}C$. The United

States wants to get as much coffee as possible for each ton of wheat it exports. Similarly, Brazil wants a rate near $1W \equiv 1C$, say, $1W \equiv 1\frac{1}{4}C$. Brazil wants to export as little coffee as possible for each ton of wheat it receives in exchange. The exchange ratio or terms of trade determine how the gains from international specialization and trade are divided between the two nations.

The actual exchange ratio depends on world supply and demand for the two products. If overall world demand for coffee is weak relative to its supply and if the demand for wheat is strong relative to its supply, the price of coffee will be lower and the price of wheat higher. The exchange ratio will settle nearer the $1W \equiv 2C$ figure the United States prefers. If overall world demand for coffee is great relative to its supply and if the demand for wheat is weak relative to its supply, the ratio will settle nearer the $1W \equiv 1C$ level favorable to Brazil. (We discuss equilibrium world prices later in this chapter.)

Gains from Trade

Suppose the international terms of trade are $1W \equiv 1\frac{1}{2}C$. The possibility of trading on these terms permits each nation to supplement its domestic production possibilities curve with a **trading possibilities line** (or curve), as shown in **Figure 24.2 (Key Graph).** Just as a production possibilities curve shows the amounts of these products a full-employment economy can obtain by shifting resources from one to the other, a trading possibilities line shows the amounts of two products a nation can obtain by specializing in one product and trading for the other. The trading possibilities lines in Figure 24.2 reflect the assumption that both nations specialize on the basis of comparative advantage: The United States specializes completely in wheat (at point W in Figure 24.2a), and Brazil specializes completely in coffee (at point c in Figure 24.2b).

Improved Options

Now the United States is not constrained by its domestic production possibilities line, which requires it to give up 1 ton of wheat for every ton of coffee it wants as it moves up its domestic production possibilities line from, say, point W. Instead, the United States, through trade with Brazil, can get $1\frac{1}{2}$ tons of coffee for every ton of wheat it exports to Brazil, as long as Brazil has coffee to export. Trading possibilities line WC' thus represents the $1W \equiv 1\frac{1}{2}C$ trading ratio.

KEY GRAPH

Figure 24.2
Trading possibility lines and the gains from trade.
As a result of specialization and trade, both the United States and Brazil can have higher levels of output than the levels attainable on their domestic production possibilities curves. (a) The United States can move from point *A* on its domestic production possibilities curve to, say, *A'* on its trading possibilities line. (b) Brazil can move from *B* to *B'*.

Quick Quiz 24.2

1. The production possiblities curves in graphs (a) and (b) imply:
   a. increasing domestic opportunity costs.
   b. decreasing domestic opportunity costs.
   c. constant domestic opportunity costs.
   d. first decreasing, then increasing, domestic opportunity costs.

2. Before specialization, the domestic opportunity cost of producing 1 unit of wheat is:
   a. 1 unit of coffee in both the United States and Brazil.
   b. 1 unit of coffee in the United States and 2 units of coffee in Brazil.
   c. 2 units of coffee in the United States and 1 unit of coffee in Brazil.
   d. 1 unit of coffee in the United States and $\frac{1}{2}$ unit of coffee in Brazil.

3. After specialization and international trade, the world output of wheat and coffee is:
   a. 20 tons of wheat and 20 tons of coffee.
   b. 45 tons of wheat and 15 tons of coffee.
   c. 30 tons of wheat and 20 tons of coffee.
   d. 10 tons of wheat and 30 tons of coffee.

4. After specialization and international trade:
   a. the United States can obtain units of coffee at less cost than it could before trade.
   b. Brazil can obtain more than 20 tons of coffee, if it so chooses.
   c. the United States no longer has a comparative advantage in producing wheat.
   d. Brazil can benefit by prohibiting coffee imports from the United States.

Answers: 1. c; 2. b; 3. c; 4. a

Similarly, Brazil, starting at, say, point *c*, no longer has to move down its domestic production possibilities curve, giving up 2 tons of coffee for each ton of wheat it wants. It can now export just $1\frac{1}{2}$ tons of coffee for each ton of wheat it wants by moving down its trading possibilities line *cw'*.

Specialization and trade create a new exchange ratio between wheat and coffee, reflected in each nation's trading possibilities line. This exchange ratio is superior for both nations to the unspecialized exchange ratio embodied in their production possibilities curves. By specializing in wheat and trading for

Brazil's coffee, the United States can obtain more than 1 ton of coffee for 1 ton of wheat. By specializing in coffee and trading for U.S. wheat, Brazil can get 1 ton of wheat for less than 2 tons of coffee. In both cases, self-sufficiency is undesirable.

Added Output

By specializing on the basis of comparative advantage and by trading for goods that are produced in the nation with greater domestic efficiency, the United States and Brazil can realize combinations of wheat and coffee beyond their production possibilities curves. *Specialization according to comparative advantage results in a more efficient allocation of world resources, and larger outputs of both products are therefore available to both nations.*

Suppose that at the $1W \equiv 1\frac{1}{2}C$ terms of trade, the United States exports 10 tons of wheat to Brazil and in return Brazil exports 15 tons of coffee to the United States. How do the new quantities of wheat and coffee available to the two nations compare with the optimal product mixes that existed before specialization and trade? Point A in Figure 24.2a reminds us that the United States chose 18 tons of wheat and 12 tons of coffee originally. But by producing 30 tons of wheat and no coffee and by trading 10 tons of wheat for 15 tons of coffee, the United States can obtain 20 tons of wheat and 15 tons of coffee. This new, superior combination of wheat and coffee is indicated by point A' in Figure 24.2a. Compared with the no-trade amounts of 18 tons of wheat and 12 tons of coffee, the United States' **gains from trade** are 2 tons of wheat and 3 tons of coffee.

Similarly, recall that Brazil's optimal product mix was 4 tons of coffee and 8 tons of wheat (point B) before specialization and trade. Now, after specializing in coffee and trading, Brazil can have 5 tons of coffee and 10 tons of wheat. It accomplishes that by producing 20 tons of coffee and no wheat and exporting 15 tons of its coffee in exchange for 10 tons of American wheat. This new position is indicated by point B' in Figure 24.2b. Brazil's gains from trade are 1 ton of coffee and 2 tons of wheat.

As a result of specialization and trade, both countries have more of both products. Table 24.1, which summarizes the transactions and outcomes, merits careful study.

The fact that points A' and B' are economic positions superior to A and B is enormously important. We know that a nation can expand its production possibilities boundary by (1) expanding the quantity and improving the quality of its resources or (2) re-

alizing technological progress. We have now established that international trade can enable a nation to circumvent the output constraint illustrated by its production possibilities curve. The outcome of international specialization and trade is equivalent to having more and better resources or discovering improved production techniques.

Trade with Increasing Costs

To explain the basic principles underlying international trade, we simplified our analysis in several ways. For example, we limited discussion to two products and two nations. But multiproduct and multinational analysis yields the same conclusions. We also assumed constant opportunity costs (linear production possibilities curves), which is a more substantive simplification. Let's consider the effect of allowing increasing opportunity costs (concave-to-the-origin production possibilities curves) to enter the picture.

Suppose that the United States and Brazil initially are at positions on their concave production possibilities curves where their domestic cost ratios are $1W \equiv 1C$ and $1W \equiv 2C$, as they were in our constant-cost analysis. As before, comparative advantage indicates that the United States should specialize in wheat and Brazil in coffee. But now, as the United States begins to expand wheat production, its cost of wheat will rise; it will have to sacrifice more than 1 ton of coffee to get 1 additional ton of wheat. Resources are no longer perfectly substitutable between alternative uses, as the constant-cost assumption implied. Resources less and less suitable to wheat production must be allocated to the U.S. wheat industry in expanding wheat output, and that means increasing costs—the sacrifice of larger and larger amounts of coffee for each additional ton of wheat.

Similarly, Brazil, starting from its $1W \equiv 2C$ cost ratio position, expands coffee production. But as it does, it will find that its $1W \equiv 2C$ cost ratio begins to rise. Sacrificing a ton of wheat will free resources that are capable of producing only something less than 2 tons of coffee, because those transferred resources are less suitable to coffee production.

As the U.S. cost ratio falls from $1W \equiv 1C$ and the Brazilian ratio rises from $1W \equiv 2C$, a point will be reached where the cost ratios are equal in the two nations, perhaps at $1W \equiv 1\frac{3}{4}C$. At this point the underlying basis for further specialization and trade—differing cost ratios—has disappeared, and further specialization is therefore uneconomical. And, most importantly, this point of equal cost ratios may be reached while the United States is still producing some coffee along with its wheat and Brazil is producing some wheat along with its coffee. The primary effect of increasing opportunity costs is less-than-complete specialization. For this reason we often find domestically produced products competing directly against identical or similar imported products within a particular economy. **(Key Question 4)**

The Case for Free Trade

The case for free trade reduces to one compelling argument: *Through free trade based on the principle of comparative advantage, the world economy can achieve a more efficient allocation of resources and a higher level of material well-being than it can without free trade.*

Since the resource mixes and technological knowledge of the world's nations are all somewhat different, each nation can produce particular commodities at different real costs. Each nation should produce goods for which its domestic opportunity costs are lower than the domestic opportunity costs of other nations and exchange those goods for products for which its domestic opportunity costs are high relative to those of other nations. If each nation does this, the world will realize the advantages of geographic and human specialization. The world and each free-trading nation can obtain a larger real income from the fixed supplies of resources available to it. Government trade barriers lessen or eliminate gains from specialization. If nations cannot trade freely, they must shift resources from efficient (low-cost) to inefficient (high-cost) uses in order to satisfy their diverse wants.

One side benefit of free trade is that it promotes competition and deters monopoly. The increased competition from foreign firms forces domestic firms to find and use the lowest-cost production techniques. It also compels them to be innovative with respect to both product quality and production methods, thereby contributing to economic growth. And free trade gives consumers a wider range of product choices. The reasons to favor free trade are the same as the reasons to endorse competition.

A second side benefit of free trade is that it links national interests and breaks down national animosities. Confronted with political disagreements, trading partners tend to negotiate rather than make war.

QUICK REVIEW 24.1

■ International trade is increasingly important to the United States and other nations of the world; the percentage of total output traded has increased since the Second World War.

■ International trade enables nations to specialize, increase productivity, and increase output available for consumption.

■ Comparative advantage means total world output will be greatest when each good is produced by the nation that has the lowest domestic opportunity cost.

■ Specialization is less than complete among nations because opportunity costs normally rise as any given nation produces more of a particular good.

■ Supply and Demand Analysis of Exports and Imports

Supply and demand analysis reveals how equilibrium prices and quantities of exports and imports are determined. The amount of a good or a service a nation will export or import depends on differences between the equilibrium world price and the equilibrium domestic price. The interaction of *world* supply and demand determines the equilibrium **world price**—the price that equates the quantities supplied and demanded globally. *Domestic* supply and demand determine the equilibrium **domestic price**—the price that would prevail in a closed economy that does not engage in international trade. The domestic price equates quantity supplied and quantity demanded domestically.

In the absence of trade, the domestic prices in a closed economy may or may not equal the world equilibrium prices. When economies are opened for international trade, differences between world and domestic prices encourage exports or imports. To see how, consider the international effects of such price differences in a simple two-nation world, consisting of the United States and Canada, that are both producing aluminum. We assume there are no trade barriers, such as tariffs and quotas, and no international transportation costs.

Supply and Demand in the United States

Figure 24.3a shows the domestic supply curve S_d and the domestic demand curve D_d for aluminum in the United States, which for now is a closed economy.

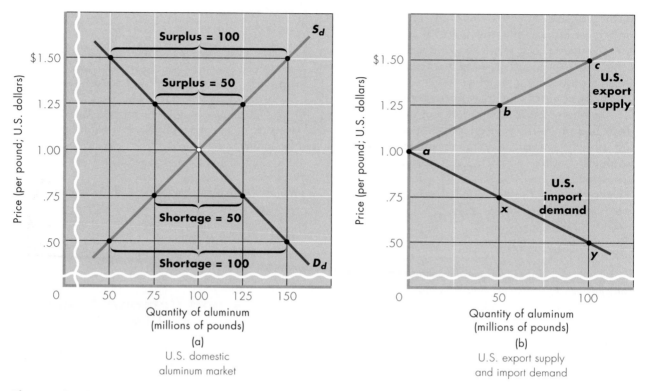

Figure 24.3

U.S. export supply and import demand. (a) Domestic supply S_d and demand D_d set the domestic equilibrium price of aluminum at $1 per pound. At world prices above $1 there are domestic surpluses of aluminum. At prices below $1 there are domestic shortages. (b) Surpluses are exported (top curve), and shortages are met by importing aluminum (lower curve). The export supply curve shows the direct relationship between world prices and U.S. exports; the import demand curve portrays the inverse relationship between world prices and U.S. imports.

The intersection of S_d and D_d determines the equilibrium domestic price of $1 per pound and the equilibrium domestic quantity of 100 million pounds. Domestic suppliers produce 100 million pounds and sell them all at $1 a pound. So there are no domestic surpluses or shortages of aluminum.

But what if the U.S. economy were opened to trade and the world price of aluminum were above or below this $1 domestic price?

U.S. Export Supply

If the aluminum price in the rest of the world (that is, Canada) exceeds $1, U.S. firms will produce more than 100 million pounds and will export the excess domestic output. First, consider a world price of $1.25. We see from the supply curve S_d that U.S. aluminum firms will produce 125 million pounds of aluminum at that price. The demand curve D_d tells us that the United States will purchase only 75 million pounds at $1.25. The outcome is a domestic surplus of 50 million

pounds of aluminum. U.S. producers will export those 50 million pounds at the $1.25 world price.

What if the world price were $1.50? The supply curve shows that U.S. firms will produce 150 million pounds of aluminum, while the demand curve tells us that U.S. consumers will buy only 50 million pounds. So U.S. producers will export the domestic surplus of 100 million pounds.

Toward the top of Figure 24.3b we plot the domestic surpluses—the U.S. exports—that occur at world prices above the $1 domestic equilibrium price. When the world and domestic prices are equal (= $1), the quantity of exports supplied is zero (point a). There is no surplus of domestic output to export. But when the world price is $1.25, U.S. firms export 50 million pounds of surplus aluminum (point b). At a $1.50 world price, the domestic surplus of 100 million pounds is exported (point c).

The U.S. **export supply curve,** found by connecting points a, b, and c, shows the amount of aluminum U.S. producers will export at each world price above $1. This curve *slopes upward*, indicating a direct or positive relationship between the world price and the amount of U.S. exports. *As world prices increase relative to domestic prices, U.S. exports rise.*

U.S. Import Demand

If the world price is below the domestic $1 price, the United States will import aluminum. Consider a $.75 world price. The supply curve in Figure 24.3a reveals that at that price U.S. firms produce only 75 million pounds of aluminum. But the demand curve shows that the United States wants to buy 125 million pounds at that price. The result is a domestic shortage of 50 million pounds. To satisfy that shortage, the United States will import 50 million pounds of aluminum.

At an even lower world price, $.50, U.S. producers will supply only 50 million pounds. Because U.S. consumers want to buy 150 million pounds at that price, there is a domestic shortage of 100 million pounds. Imports will flow to the United States to make up the difference. That is, at a $.50 world

price U.S. firms will supply 50 million pounds and 100 million pounds will be imported.

In Figure 24.3b we plot the U.S. **import demand curve** from these data. This *downsloping curve* shows the amounts of aluminum that will be imported at world prices below the $1 U.S. domestic price. The relationship between world prices and imported amounts is inverse or negative. At a world price of $1, domestic output will satisfy U.S. demand; imports will be zero (point *a*). But at $.75 the United States will import 50 million pounds of aluminum (point *x*); at $.50, the United States will import 100 million pounds (point *y*). Connecting points *a*, *x*, and *y* yields the *downsloping* U.S. import demand curve. *It reveals that as world prices fall relative to U.S. domestic prices, U.S. imports increase.*

Supply and Demand in Canada

We repeat our analysis in Figure 24.4, this time from the viewpoint Canada. (We have converted Canadian dollar prices to U.S. dollar prices via the exchange

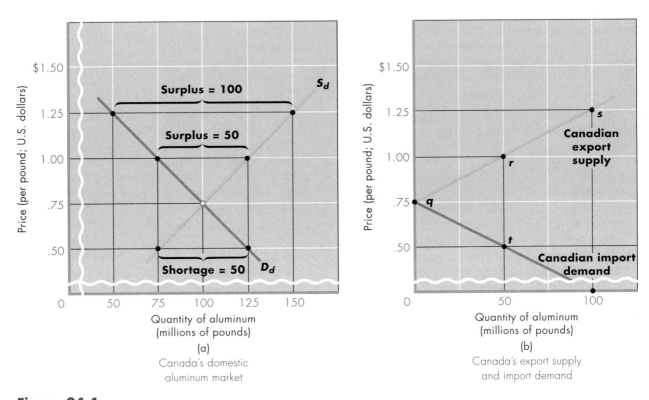

(a) Canada's domestic aluminum market

(b) Canada's export supply and import demand

Figure 24.4

Canadian export supply and import demand.   (a) At world prices above the $.75 domestic price, production in Canada exceeds domestic consumption. At world prices below $.75, domestic shortages occur. (b) Surpluses result in exports, and shortages result in imports. The Canadian export supply curve and import demand curve depict the relationships between world prices and exports or imports.

rate.) Note that the domestic supply curve S_d and the domestic demand curve D_d for aluminum in Canada yield a domestic price of $.75, which is $.25 lower than the $1 U.S. domestic price.

The analysis proceeds exactly as above except that the domestic price is now the Canadian price. If the world price is $.75, Canadians will neither export nor import aluminum (giving us point q in Figure 24.4b.) At world prices above $.75, Canadian firms will produce more aluminum than Canadian consumers will buy. Canadian firms will export the surplus. At a $1 world price, Figure 24.4a tells us that Canada will have and export a domestic surplus of 50 million pounds (yielding point r). At $1.25, it will have and will export a domestic surplus of 100 million pounds (point s). Connecting these points yields the upsloping Canadian export supply curve, which reflects the domestic surpluses (and hence the exports) that occur when the world price exceeds the $.75 Canadian domestic price.

At world prices below $.75, domestic shortages occur in Canada. At a $.50 world price, Figure 24.4a shows that Canadian consumers want to buy 125 million pounds of aluminum but Canadian firms will produce only 75 million pounds. The shortage will bring 50 million pounds of imports to Canada (point t in Figure 24.4b.) The Canadian import demand curve in that figure shows the Canadian imports that will occur at all world aluminum prices below the $.75 Canadian domestic price.

Equilibrium World Price, Exports, and Imports

We now have the tools for determining the **equilibrium world price** of aluminum and the equilibrium world levels of exports and imports when the world is opened to trade. Figure 24.5 combines the U.S. export supply curve and import demand curve in Figure 24.3b and the Canadian export supply curve and import demand curve in Figure 24.4b. The two U.S. curves proceed rightward from the $1 U.S. domestic price; the two Canadian curves proceed rightward from the $.75 Canadian domestic price.

International equilibrium occurs in this two-nation model where one nation's import demand curve intersects another nation's export supply curve. In this case the U.S. import demand curve intersects Canada's export supply curve at e. There, the world price of aluminum is $.88. The Canadian export supply curve indicates that Canada will export 25 million pounds of aluminum at this price. Also at this

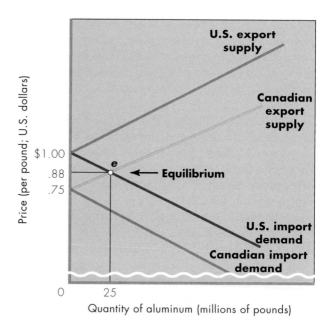

Figure 24.5

Equilibrium world price and quantity of exports and imports. In a two-nation world, the equilibrium world price (= $.88) is determined by the intersection of one nation's export supply curve and the other nation's import demand curve. This intersection also decides the equilibrium volume of exports and imports. Here, Canada exports 25 million pounds of aluminum to the United States.

price the United States will import 25 million pounds from Canada, indicated by the U.S. import demand curve. The $.88 world price equates the quantity of imports demanded and the quantity of exports supplied (25 million pounds). Thus there will be world trade of 25 million pounds of aluminum at $.88 per pound.

Note that after trade, the single $.88 world price will prevail in both Canada and the United States. Only one price for a standardized commodity can persist in a highly competitive world market. With trade, all consumers can buy a pound of aluminum for $.88, and all producers can sell it for that price. This world price means that Canadians will pay more for aluminum with trade ($.88) than without it ($.75). The increased Canadian output caused by trade raises Canadian per-unit production costs and therefore raises the price of aluminum in Canada. The United States, however, pays less for aluminum with trade ($.88) than without it ($1). The U.S. gain comes from Canada's comparative cost advantage in producing aluminum.

Why would Canada willingly send 25 million pounds of its aluminum output to the United States for U.S. consumption? After all, producing this output uses up scarce Canadian resources and drives up the price of aluminum for Canadians. Canadians are willing to export aluminum to the United States because Canadians gain the means—the U.S. dollars—to import other goods, say, computer software, from the United States. Canadian exports enable Canadians to acquire imports that have greater value to Canadians than the exported aluminum. Canadian exports to the United States finance Canadian imports from the United States. **(Key Question 6)**

▮ Trade Barriers

No matter how compelling the case for free trade, barriers to free trade *do* exist. Let's expand Chapter 6's discussion of trade barriers.

Excise taxes on imported goods are called **tariffs;** they may be imposed to obtain revenue or to protect domestic firms. A **revenue tariff** is usually applied to a product that is not being produced domestically, for example, tin, coffee, or bananas in the case of the United States. Rates on revenue tariffs are modest; their purpose is to provide the Federal government with revenue. A **protective tariff** is designed to shield domestic producers from foreign competition. Although protective tariffs are usually not high enough to stop the importation of foreign goods, they put foreign producers at a competitive disadvantage in selling in domestic markets.

An **import quota** specifies the maximum amount of a commodity that may be imported in any period. Import quotas can more effectively retard international commerce than tariffs. A product might be imported in large quantities despite high tariffs; low import quotas completely prohibit imports once quotas have been filled.

A **nontariff barrier (NTB)** is a licensing requirement that specifies unreasonable standards pertaining to product quality and safety, or unnecessary bureaucratic red tape that is used to restrict imports. Japan and the European countries frequently require that their domestic importers of foreign goods obtain licenses. By restricting the issuance of licenses, imports can be restricted. Great Britain uses this barrier to bar the importation of coal.

A **voluntary export restriction (VER)** is a trade barrier by which foreign firms "voluntarily" limit the amount of their exports to a particular country.

VERs, which have the effect of import quotas, are agreed to by exporters in the hope of avoiding more stringent trade barriers. Japanese auto manufacturers agreed to a VER on exports to the United States under the threat of higher U.S. tariffs or the imposition of low import quotas. Later in this chapter we will consider the arguments and appeals that are made to justify protection. 🔑 **24.1**

Economic Impact of Tariffs

Once again we turn to supply and demand analysis—now to examine the economic effects of protective tariffs. Curves D_d and S_d in Figure 24.6 show domestic demand and supply for a product in which a nation, say, the United States, has a comparative disadvantage—for example, video cassette recorders (VCRs). (Disregard curve $S_d + Q$ for now.) Without world trade, the domestic price and output would be P_d and q, respectively.

Assume now that the domestic economy is opened to world trade and that the Japanese, who

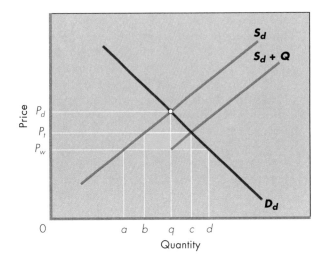

Figure 24.6

The economic effects of a protective tariff or an import quota. A tariff that increases the price of a good from P_w to P_t will reduce domestic consumption from d to c. Domestic producers will be able to sell more output (b rather than a) at a higher price (P_t rather than P_w). Foreign exporters are injured because they sell less output (bc rather than ad). The orange area indicates the amount of tariff paid by domestic consumers. An import quota of bc units has the same effect as the tariff, with one exception: The amount represented by the orange area will go to foreign producers rather than to the domestic government.

have a comparative advantage in VCRs, begin to sell their recorders in the United States. We assume that with free trade the domestic price cannot differ from the world price, which here is P_w. At P_w domestic consumption is d and domestic production is a. The horizontal distance between the domestic supply and demand curves at P_w represents imports of ad. Thus far, our analysis is similar to the analysis of world prices in Figure 24.3.

Direct Effects

Suppose now that the United States imposes a tariff on each imported VCR. The tariff, which raises the price of imported VCRs from P_w to P_t, has four effects:

- *Decline in consumption*   Consumption of video recorders in the United States declines from d to c as the higher price moves buyers up and to the left along their demand curve. The tariff prompts consumers to buy fewer recorders; they reallocate a portion of their expenditures to less desired substitute products. U.S. consumers are clearly injured by the tariff, since they pay $P_w P_t$ more for each of the c units they buy at price P_t.

- *Increased domestic production*   U.S. producers—who are not subject to the tariff—receive the higher price P_t per unit. Because this new price is higher than the pretariff world price P_w, the domestic VCR industry moves up and to the right along its supply curve S_d, increasing domestic output from a to b. Domestic producers thus enjoy both a higher price and expanded sales; this explains why domestic producers lobby for protective tariffs. But from a social point of view, the greater domestic production from a to b means that the tariff permits domestic producers of recorders to bid resources away from other, more efficient, U.S. industries.

- *Decline in imports*   Japanese producers are hurt. Although the sales price of each recorder is higher by $P_w P_t$, that amount accrues to the U.S. government, not to Japanese producers. The after-tariff world price, or the per-unit revenue to Japanese producers, remains at P_w, but the volume of U.S. imports (Japanese exports) falls from ad to bc.

- *Tariff revenue*   The orange rectangle represents the amount of revenue the tariff yields. Total revenue from the tariff is determined by multiplying the tariff, $P_w P_t$ per unit, by the number of recorders imported, bc. This tariff revenue is a transfer of income from consumers to government and does not represent any net change

in the nation's economic well-being. The result is that government gains this portion of what consumers lose by paying more for VCRs.

Indirect Effect

Tariffs have a subtle effect beyond what our supply and demand diagram can show. Because Japan sells fewer VCRs in the United States, it earns fewer dollars and so must buy fewer U.S. exports. U.S. export industries must then cut production and release resources. These are highly efficient industries, as we know from their comparative advantage and their ability to sell goods in world markets.

Tariffs directly promote the expansion of inefficient industries that do not have a comparative advantage; they also indirectly cause the contraction of relatively efficient industries that do have a comparative advantage. Put bluntly, tariffs cause resources to be shifted in the wrong direction—and that is not surprising. We know that specialization and world trade lead to more efficient use of world resources and greater world output. But protective tariffs reduce world trade. Therefore, tariffs also reduce efficiency and the world's real output.

Economic Impact of Quotas

We noted earlier that an import quota is a legal limit placed on the amount of some product that can be imported in a given year. Quotas have the same economic impact as a tariff, with one big difference: While tariffs generate revenue for the domestic government, a quota transfers that revenue to foreign producers.

Suppose in Figure 24.6 that, instead of imposing a tariff, the United States prohibits any imports of Japanese VCRs in excess of bc units. In other words, an import quota of bc recorders is imposed on Japan. We deliberately chose the size of this quota to be the same amount as imports would be under a $P_w P_t$ tariff so that we can compare "equivalent" situations. As a consequence of the quota, the supply of recorders is $S_d + Q$ in the United States. This supply consists of the domestic supply plus the fixed amount bc ($= Q$) that importers will provide at each domestic price. The supply curve $S_d + Q$ does not extend below price P_w, because Japanese producers would not export recorders to the United States at any price below P_w; instead, they would sell them to other countries at the world market price of P_w.

Most of the economic results are the same as those with a tariff. VCR prices are higher (P_t instead of P_w) because imports have been reduced from *ad* to *bc*. Domestic consumption of VCRs is down from *d* to *c*. U.S. producers enjoy both a higher price (P_t rather than P_w) and increased sales (*b* rather than *a*).

The difference is that the price increase of P_wP_t paid by U.S. consumers on imports of *bc*—the orange area—no longer goes to the U.S. Treasury as tariff (tax) revenue but flows to the Japanese firms that have acquired the rights to sell VCRs in the United States. For consumers in the United States, a tariff produces a better economic outcome than a quota, other things being the same. A tariff generates government revenue that can be used to cut other taxes or to finance public goods and services that benefit the United States. In contrast, the higher price created by quotas results in additional revenue for foreign producers. **(Key Question 7)**

Net Costs of Tariffs and Quotas

Figure 24.6 shows that tariffs and quotas impose costs on domestic consumers but provide gains to domestic producers and, in the case of tariffs, revenue to the Federal government. The consumer costs of trade restrictions are calculated by determining the effect the restrictions have on consumer prices. Protection raises the price of a product in three ways: (1) The price of the imported product goes up; (2) the higher price of imports causes some consumers to shift their purchases to higher-priced domestically produced goods; and (3) the prices of domestically produced goods rise because import competition has declined.

Study after study finds that the costs to consumers substantially exceed the gains to producers and government. A sizable net cost or efficiency loss to society arises from trade protection. Furthermore, industries employ large amounts of economic resources to influence Congress to pass and retain protectionist laws. Because these rent-seeking efforts divert resources away from more socially desirable purposes, trade restrictions impose that cost on society.

Conclusion: The gains that U.S. trade barriers create for protected industries and their workers come at the expense of much greater losses for the entire economy. The result is economic inefficiency.

Impact on Income Distribution

Tariffs and quotas affect low-income families proportionately more than high-income families. Because they act much like sales or excise taxes, these trade restrictions are highly regressive. That is, the "overcharge" associated with trade protection falls as a percentage of income as income increases. For example, a family with an annual income of $10,000 may pay an overcharge of $100 per year because of the trade restrictions on apparel, while a family with an income of $100,000 may pay a $500 overcharge. As a percentage of income, the lower-income family pays 1 percent (= $100 of overcharge/$10,000 of income); the higher-income family, only .5 percent (= $500/$100,000).

■ The Case for Protection: A Critical Review

Despite the logic of specialization and trade, there are still protectionists in some union halls, corporate boardrooms, and the halls of Congress. What arguments do protectionists make to justify trade barriers? How valid are those arguments?

Military Self-Sufficiency Argument

The argument here is not economic but political-military: Protective tariffs are needed to preserve or strengthen industries that produce the materials essential for national defense. In an uncertain world, the political-military objectives (self-sufficiency) sometimes must take precedence over economic goals (efficiency in the use of world resources).

Unfortunately, it is difficult to measure and compare the benefit of increased national security against the cost of economic inefficiency when protective tariffs are imposed. The economist can only point out that there are economic costs when a nation levies tariffs to increase military self-sufficiency.

All people in the United States would agree that it is not a good idea to import missile guidance systems from Iraq, yet the self-sufficiency argument is open to serious abuse. Nearly every industry can claim that it makes direct or indirect contributions to national security and hence deserves protection from imports.

Are there not better ways than tariffs to provide needed strength in strategic industries? When it is achieved through tariffs, this self-sufficiency increases the domestic prices of the products of the protected industry. Thus only those consumers who buy the industry's products shoulder the cost of greater military security. A direct subsidy to strategic industries, financed out of general tax revenues, would distribute those costs more equitably.

Increased Domestic Employment Argument

Arguing for a tariff to "save U.S. jobs" becomes fashionable as an economy encounters a recession. In an economy that engages in international trade, exports involve spending on domestic output and imports reflect spending to obtain part of another nation's output. So, in this argument, reducing imports will divert spending on another nation's output to spending on domestic output. Thus domestic output and employment will rise. But this argument has several shortcomings:

- *Job creation from imports*   While imports may eliminate some U.S. jobs, they create others. Imports may have eliminated the jobs of some U.S. steel and textile workers in recent years, but other workers have gained jobs unloading ships and selling imported cars and imported electronic equipment. Import restrictions alter the composition of employment, but they may have little or no effect on the volume of employment.

- *Fallacy of composition*   All nations cannot simultaneously succeed in restricting imports while maintaining their exports; what is true for one nation is not true for all nations. The exports of one nation must be the imports of another nation. To the extent that one country is able to expand its economy through an excess of exports over imports, the resulting excess of imports over exports worsens another economy's unemployment problem. It is no wonder that tariffs and import quotas meant to achieve domestic full employment are called "beggar my neighbor" policies: They achieve short-run domestic goals by making trading partners poorer.

- *Possibility of retaliation*   Nations adversely affected by tariffs and quotas are likely to retaliate, causing a "trade-barrier war" that will choke off trade and make all nations worse off. The Smoot-Hawley Tariff Act of 1930, which imposed the highest tariffs ever enacted in the United States, backfired miserably. Rather than increasing U.S. output, this tariff act only led to retaliatory restrictions by affected nations. That trade war caused a further contraction of international trade and lowered the income and employment levels of all nations. As stated by a U.S. international trade expert:

A trade war in which countries restrict each other's exports in pursuit of some illusory advantage is not much like a real war. On the one hand, nobody gets killed. On the other, unlike real wars, it is almost impossible for anyone to win, since the main losers when a country imposes barriers to trade are not foreign exporters but domestic residents. In effect, a trade war is a conflict in which each country uses most of its ammunition to shoot itself in the foot.[1]   **!** 24.1

- *Long-run feedbacks*   In the long run, forcing an excess of exports over imports cannot succeed in raising domestic employment. It is through U.S. imports that foreign nations earn dollars for buying U.S. exports. In the long run a nation must import in order to export. The long-run impact of tariffs is not an increase in domestic employment but, at best, a reallocation of workers away from export industries and to protected domestic industries. This shift implies a less efficient allocation of resources.

Diversification-for-Stability Argument

Highly specialized economies such as Saudi Arabia (based on oil) and Cuba (based on sugar) are dependent on international markets for their income. In these economies, wars, international political developments, recessions abroad, and random fluctuations in world supply and demand for one or two particular goods can cause deep declines in export revenues and therefore in domestic income. Tariff and quota protection are allegedly needed in such nations to enable greater industrial diversification. That way, these economies will not be so dependent on exporting one or two products to obtain the other goods they need. Such goods will be available domestically, thereby providing greater domestic stability.

There is some truth in this diversification-for-stability argument. There are also two serious shortcomings:

- The argument has little or no relevance to the United States and other advanced economies.

- The economic costs of diversification may be great; for example, one-crop economies may be highly inefficient at manufacturing.

---

[1]Paul Krugman, *Peddling Prosperity* (New York: Norton, 1994), p. 287.

Infant Industry Argument

The infant industry argument contends that protective tariffs are needed to allow new domestic industries to establish themselves. Temporarily shielding young domestic firms from the severe competition of more mature and more efficient foreign firms will give infant industries a chance to develop and become efficient producers.

This argument for protection rests on an alleged exception to the case for free trade. The exception is that young industries have not had, and if they face mature foreign competition will never have, the chance to make the long-run adjustments needed for larger scale and greater efficiency in production. In this view, tariff protection for such infant industries will correct a misallocation of world resources perpetuated by historically different levels of economic development between domestic and foreign industries.

Counterarguments There are some logical problems with the infant industry argument:

- In the developing nations it is difficult to determine which industries are the infants that are capable of achieving economic maturity and therefore deserving protection.
- Protective tariffs may persist even after industrial maturity has been realized.
- Most economists feel that if infant industries are to be subsidized, there are better means than tariffs for doing so. Direct subsidies, for example, have the advantage of making explicit which industries are being aided and to what degree.

Strategic Trade Policy In recent years the infant industry argument has taken a modified form in advanced economies. Now proponents contend that government should use trade barriers to reduce the risk of investing in product development by domestic firms, particularly where advanced technology is involved. Firms protected from foreign competition can grow more rapidly and achieve greater economies of scale than unprotected foreign competitors. The protected firms can eventually dominate world markets because of their lower costs. Supposedly, dominance of world markets will enable the domestic firms to return high profits to the home nation. These profits will exceed the domestic sacrifices caused by trade barriers. Also, advances in high-technology industries are deemed benefi-

cial, because the advances achieved in one domestic industry often can be transferred to other domestic industries.

Japan and South Korea, in particular, have been accused of using this form of **strategic trade policy.** The problem with this strategy and therefore with this argument for tariffs is that the nations put at a disadvantage by strategic trade policies tend to retaliate with tariffs of their own. The outcome may be higher tariffs worldwide, reduction of world trade, and the loss of potential gains from technological advances.

Protection-against-Dumping Argument

This argument contends that tariffs are needed to protect domestic firms from "dumping" by foreign producers. **Dumping** is the selling of excess goods in a foreign market at a price below cost. Economists cite two plausible reasons for this behavior. First, firms may use dumping abroad to drive out domestic competitors there, thus obtaining monopoly power and monopoly prices and profits for the importing firm. The long-term economic profits resulting from this strategy may more than offset the earlier losses that accompany the below-cost sales.

Second, dumping may be a form of price discrimination, which is charging different prices to different customers even though costs are the same. The foreign seller may find it can maximize its profit by charging a high price in its monopolized domestic market while unloading its surplus output at a lower price in the United States. The surplus output may be needed so that the firm can obtain the overall per-unit cost saving associated with large-scale production. The higher profit in the home market more than makes up for the losses incurred on sales abroad.

Because dumping is a legitimate concern, many nations prohibit it. For example, where dumping is shown to injure U.S. firms, the Federal government imposes tariffs called "antidumping duties" on the specific goods. But there are relatively few documented cases of dumping each year, and those few cases do not justify widespread, permanent tariffs.

In fact, foreign producers argue that the United States uses dumping allegations and antidumping duties to restrict legitimate trade. Some foreign firms clearly can produce certain goods at substantially less per-unit cost than U.S. competitors. So what may seem to be dumping actually is comparative advantage at work. If antidumping laws are abused, they might increase the price of imports and restrict competition in the U.S. market. Such reduced competition might enable U.S. firms to raise prices at consumers' expense. And even where true dumping does occur, U.S. consumers gain from the lower-priced product, at least in the short run, much as they gain from a price war among U.S. producers.

Cheap Foreign Labor Argument

The cheap foreign labor argument says that domestic firms and workers must be shielded from the ruinous competition of countries where wages are low. If protection is not provided, cheap imports will flood U.S. markets and the prices of U.S. goods—along with the wages of U.S. workers—will be pulled down. That is, the domestic living standards in the United States will be reduced.

This argument can be rebutted at several levels. The logic of the argument suggests that it is not mutually beneficial for rich and poor persons to trade with one another. However, that is not the case. A low-income farmworker may pick lettuce or tomatoes for a rich landowner, and both may benefit from the transaction. And U.S. consumers gain when they buy a Taiwanese-made pocket radio for $12 as opposed to a similar U.S.-made radio selling for $20.

Also, recall that gains from trade are based on comparative advantage, not on absolute advantage. Look back at Figure 24.1, and suppose that the United States and Brazil have labor forces of exactly the same size. Noting the positions of the production possibilities curves, observe that U.S. labor can produce more of either good. Thus, it is more productive. Because of this greater productivity, we can expect wages and living standards to be higher for U.S. labor. Brazil's less productive labor will receive lower wages.

The cheap foreign labor argument suggests that, to maintain our standard of living, the United States should not trade with low-wage Brazil. Suppose it does not. Will wages and living standards rise in the United States as a result? No. To obtain coffee, the United States will have to reallocate a portion of its labor from its efficient wheat industry to its inefficient coffee industry. As a re-

sult, the average productivity of U.S. labor will fall, as will real wages and living standards. The labor forces of both countries will have diminished standards of living because without specialization and trade they will have less output available to them. Compare column 4 with column 1 in Table 24.1 or points A' and B' with A and B in Figure 24.2 to confirm this point.

A Summing Up

The many arguments for protection are not weighty. Under proper conditions, the infant industry argument stands as a valid exception, justifiable on economic grounds. And on political-military grounds, the self-sufficiency argument can be used to validate some protection. But both arguments are open to severe overuse, and both neglect other ways of promoting industrial development and military self-sufficiency. Most of the other arguments are emotional appeals—half-truths and fallacies. They see only the immediate, direct consequences of protective tariffs, but ignore the fact that in the long run a nation must import in order to export.

There is also compelling historical evidence suggesting that free trade has led to prosperity and growth and that protectionism has had the opposite effects. Here are several examples:

- The U.S. Constitution forbids individual states from levying tariffs, and that makes the United States itself a huge free-trade area. Economic historians cite this as a positive factor in the economic development of the United States.
- The creation of the Common Market in Europe after the Second World War eliminated tariffs among member nations. Economists agree that the creation of this free-trade area, now the European Union, was a major ingredient in western European prosperity.
- The trend toward tariff reduction since the mid-1930s stimulated expansion of the world economy after the Second World War.
- The high tariffs imposed by the Smoot-Hawley Act of 1930 and the retaliation that it engendered worsened the Great Depression of the 1930s.
- In general, developing countries that have relied on import restrictions to protect their domestic industries have had slow growth compared to those that have pursued more open economic policies.

A nation will export a particular product if the world price exceeds the domestic price; it will import the product if the world price is less than the domestic price.

In a two-country world model, equilibrium world prices and equilibrium quantities of exports and imports occur where one nation's export supply curve intersects the other nation's import demand curve.

Trade barriers include tariffs, import quotas, nontariff barriers, and voluntary export restrictions.

A tariff on a product increases price, reduces consumption, increases domestic production, reduces imports, and generates tariff revenue for government; an import quota does the same, except a quota generates revenue for foreign producers rather than for the government imposing the quota.

Most arguments for trade protection are special-interest pleas that, if followed, would create gains for protected industries and their workers at the expense of greater losses for the economy.

∎ The World Trade Organization

As indicated in Chapter 6, the inefficiencies of trade protectionism have led nations to seek various ways to reduce tariffs and quotas. In 1994 more than 120 of the world's nations, which together constituted the **World Trade Organization (WTO),** agreed to several trade liberalizations to be fully implemented by 2005. These liberalizations include:

- Reductions in tariffs worldwide.
- New rules to promote trade in services.
- Reductions in agricultural subsidies that have distorted the global pattern of trade in agricultural goods.

- New protections for intellectual property (copyrights, patents, trademarks).
- The phasing out of quotas on textiles and apparel, replacing them with gradually declining tariffs.

When they are fully implemented in 2005, economists predict that these trade liberalizations will have boosted the world's GDP by $6 trillion, or 8 percent.

The 1994 agreement created the WTO to oversee the provisions of the agreement, resolve any disputes under the trade rules, and meet periodically to consider further trade liberalization. In 2001 some 140 nations belonged to the WTO. As a symbol of trade liberalization and global capitalism, the WTO has become a target of protest groups such as some labor unions (which fear loss of jobs and labor protections), environmental groups (which fear environmental degradation), socialists (who dislike capitalism and multinational corporations), and anarchists (who dislike government of any kind).

Economists agree that labor protections such as workplace safety, enforcement of child labor laws, and collective bargaining rights, as well as environmental concerns such as protection of forests and fisheries, are legitimate issues. But most economists believe these causes should not be used to slow or reverse trade liberalization. Trade liberalization increases world efficiency and world output. Rising standards of living enable developing and developed nations alike to "buy" more protections for labor and the environment. In this view, protestors should direct their political efforts toward changing the labor and environmental laws within the nations that they deem lacking in such protections. Trade liberalization is too important in its own right to be linked to a host of other, sometimes conflicting, political and economic causes.

Petition of the Candlemakers, 1845

French Economist Frédéric Bastiat (1801–1850) Devastated the Proponents of Protectionism by Satirically Extending Their Reasoning to Its Logical and Absurd Conclusions.

Petition of the Manufacturers of Candles, Waxlights, Lamps, Candlesticks, Street Lamps, Snuffers, Extinguishers, and of the Producers of Oil Tallow, Rosin, Alcohol, and, Generally, of Everything Connected with Lighting.

TO MESSIEURS THE MEMBERS OF THE CHAMBER OF DEPUTIES.

Gentlemen—You are on the right road. You reject abstract theories, and have little consideration for cheapness and plenty. Your chief care is the interest of the producer. You desire to emancipate him from external competition, and reserve the national market for national industry.

We are about to offer you an admirable opportunity of applying your—what shall we call it? your theory? No; nothing is more deceptive than theory; your doctrine? your system? your principle? but you dislike doctrines, you abhor systems, and as for principles, you deny that there are any in social economy: we shall say, then, your practice, your practice without theory and without principle.

We are suffering from the intolerable competition of a foreign rival, placed, it would seem, in a condition so far superior to ours for the production of light, that he absolutely inundates our national market with it at a price fabulously reduced. The moment he shows himself, our trade leaves us—all consumers apply to him; and a branch of native industry, having countless ramifications, is all at once rendered completely stagnant. This rival . . . is no other than the Sun.

What we pray for is, that it may please you to pass a law ordering the shutting up of all windows, skylights, dormer windows, outside and inside shutters, curtains, blinds, bull's-eyes; in a word, of all openings, holes, chinks, clefts, and fissures, by or through which the light of the sun has been in use to enter houses, to the prejudice of the meritorious manufacturers with which we flatter ourselves we have accommodated our country,—a country which, in gratitude, ought not to abandon us now to a strife so unequal.

If you shut up as much as possible all access to natural light, and create a demand for artificial light, which of our French manufacturers will not be encouraged by it?

If more tallow is consumed, then there must be more oxen and sheep; and, consequently, we shall behold the multiplication of artificial meadows, meat, wool, hides, and, above all, manure, which is the basis and foundation of all agricultural wealth.

The same remark applies to navigation. Thousands of vessels will proceed to the whale fishery; and, in a short time, we shall possess a navy capable of maintaining the honor of France, and gratifying the patriotic aspirations of your petitioners, the undersigned candlemakers and others.

Only have the goodness to reflect, Gentlemen, and you will be convinced that there is, perhaps, no Frenchman, from the wealthy coalmaster to the humblest vender of lucifer matches, whose lot will not be ameliorated by the success of this our petition.

Source: Frédéric Bastiat, Economic Sophisms (Edinburgh: Oliver and Boyd, Tweeddale Court, 1873), pp. 49–53, abridged.

SUMMARY

1. The United States leads the world in the volume of international trade. Since 1975 U.S. exports and imports have more than doubled as a percentage of GDP. Other major trading nations are Germany, Japan, the western European nations, and the southeast Asian economies of Hong Kong (part of China), South Korea, Taiwan, and Singapore.

2. World trade is based on three considerations: the uneven distribution of economic resources among nations, the fact that efficient production of various goods requires particular techniques or combinations of resources, and the differentiated products produced among nations.

3. Mutually advantageous specialization and trade are possible between any two nations if they have different domestic opportunity-cost ratios for any two products. By specializing on the basis of comparative advantage, nations can obtain larger real incomes with fixed amounts of resources. The terms of trade determine how this increase in world output is shared by the trading nations. Increasing (rather than constant) opportunity costs limit specialization and trade.

4. A nation's export supply curve shows the quantities of a product the nation will export at world prices that exceed the domestic price (the price in a closed, no-international-trade economy). A nation's import demand curve reveals the quantities of a product it will import at world prices below the domestic price. In a two-nation model, the equilibrium world price and the equilibrium quantities of exports and imports occur where one nation's export supply curve intersects the other nation's import demand curve.

5. Trade barriers take the form of protective tariffs, quotas, nontariff barriers, and "voluntary" export restrictions. Supply and demand analysis reveals that protective tariffs and quotas increase the prices and reduce the quantities demanded of the affected goods.

Sales by foreign exporters diminish; domestic producers, however, gain higher prices and enlarged sales. Consumer losses from trade restrictions greatly exceed producer and government gains, creating an efficiency loss to society.

6. The strongest arguments for protection are the infant industry and military self-sufficiency arguments. Most other arguments for protection are half-truths, emotional appeals, or fallacies that emphasize the immediate effects of trade barriers while ignoring long-run consequences. Numerous historical examples suggest that free trade promotes economic growth; protectionism does not.

7. In 2001 the World Trade Organization (WTO) consisted of 140 member nations. It oversees trade agreements among the nations, resolves disputes over the rules, and periodically meets to discuss and negotiate further trade liberalization. Recently, the WTO has become a focus of protests by labor groups, environmental groups, socialists, and anarchists. Most economists believe that trade liberalization is too important to be tied to other political and economic causes, which should be pursued independently of trade rules.

TERMS AND CONCEPTS

labor-intensive goods	trading possibilities line	tariffs	strategic trade policy
land-intensive goods	gains from trade	revenue tariff	dumping
capital-intensive goods	world price	protective tariff	World Trade Organization (WTO)
cost ratio	domestic price	import quota	
principle of comparative advantage	export supply curve	nontariff barrier (NTB)	
terms of trade	import demand curve	voluntary export restriction (VER)	
	equilibrium world price		

STUDY QUESTIONS

1. Quantitatively, how important is international trade to the United States relative to other nations?

2. Distinguish among land-, labor-, and capital-intensive commodities, citing one nontextbook example of each. What role do these distinctions play in explaining international trade? What role do distinctive products, unrelated to cost advantages, play in international trade?

3. Suppose nation A can produce 80 units of X by using all its resources to produce X or 60 units of Y by de-

voting all its resources to Y. Comparable figures for nation B are 60 units of X and 60 units of Y. Assuming constant costs, in which product should each nation specialize? Why? What are the limits of the terms of trade?

4. **Key Question** At the top of the next page are hypothetical production possibilities tables for New Zealand and Spain.

**New Zealand's Production Possibilities Table
(Millions of Bushels)**

Product	Production Alternatives			
	A	B	C	D
Apples	0	20	40	60
Plums	15	10	5	0

**Spain's Production Possibilities Table
(Millions of Bushels)**

Product	Production Alternatives			
	R	S	T	U
Apples	0	20	40	60
Plums	60	40	20	0

Plot the production possibilities data for each of the two countries separately. Referring to your graphs, answer the following:

   a. What is each country's cost ratio of producing plums and apples.

   b. Which nation should specialize in which product?

   c. Show the trading possibilities lines for each nation if the actual terms of trade are 1 plum for 2 apples. (Plot these lines on your graph.)

   d. Suppose the optimum product mixes before specialization and trade were alternative B in New Zealand and alternative S in Spain. What would be the gains from specialization and trade?

5. "The United States can produce X more efficiently than can Great Britain. Yet we import X from Great Britain." Explain.

6. **Key Question** Refer to Figure 3.5, page 51. Assume that the graph depicts the U.S. domestic market for corn. How many bushels of corn, if any, will the United States export or import at a world price of $1, $2, $3, $4, and $5? Use this information to construct the U.S. export supply curve and import demand curve for corn. Suppose the only other corn-producing nation is France, where the domestic price is $4. Which country will export corn; which will import it?

7. **Key Question** Draw a domestic supply and demand diagram for a product in which the United States does not have a comparative advantage. What impact do foreign imports have on domestic price and quantity? On your diagram show a protective tariff that eliminates approximately one-half of the assumed imports. What are the price-quantity effects of this tariff on (*a*) domestic consumers, (*b*) domestic produc-

ers, and (*c*) foreign exporters? How would the effects of a quota that creates the same amount of imports differ?

8. "The potentially valid arguments for tariff protection are also the most easily abused." What are those arguments? Why are they susceptible to abuse? Evaluate the use of artificial trade barriers, such as tariffs and import quotas, as a means of achieving and maintaining full employment.

9. Evaluate the following statements:

   a. Protective tariffs reduce both the imports and the exports of the nation that levies tariffs.

   b. The extensive application of protective tariffs destroys the ability of the international market system to allocate resources efficiently.

   c. Unemployment in some industries can often be reduced through tariff protection, but by the same token inefficiency typically increases.

   d. Foreign firms that "dump" their products onto the U.S. market are in effect providing bargains to the country's citizens.

   e. In view of the rapidity with which technological advance is dispersed around the world, free trade will inevitably yield structural maladjustments, unemployment, and balance-of-payments problems for industrially advanced nations.

   f. Free trade can improve the composition and efficiency of domestic output. Competition from Volkswagen, Toyota, and Honda forced Detroit to make a compact car, and foreign success with the oxygen process forced American steel firms to modernize.

   g. In the long run, foreign trade is neutral with respect to total employment.

10. Between 1981 and 1985 the Japanese agreed to a voluntary export restriction that reduced U.S. imports of Japanese automobiles by about 10 percent. What would you expect the short-run effects of that restriction to be on the U.S. and Japanese automobile industries? If this restriction were permanent, what would be its long-run effects in the two nations on (*a*) the allocation of resources, (*b*) the volume of employment, (*c*) the price level, and (*d*) the standard of living?

11. What is the WTO, and how does it relate to international trade? What problems, if any, arise when too many extraneous issues are tied to efforts to liberalize trade?

12. **(Last Word)** What point is Bastiat trying to make with his petition of the candlemakers?

13. **Web-Based Question:** *Trade liberalization—the WTO* Go to the website of the World Trade Organization (www.wto.org/) to retrieve the latest

news from the WTO. List and summarize three recent news items relating to the WTO. Search the sections Trade Topics and Resources to find information on both international trade and the environment and international trade and poverty. Summarize the WTO's major conclusions on these two topics.

14. **Web-Based Question:** *The U.S. International Trade Commission—what is it and what does it do?* Go to www.usitc.gov to determine the duties of the U.S. International Trade Commission (USITC). How does this organization differ from the World Trade Organization (question 13)? From the site map, find Sunset Reviews to determine what they are and how they relate to the Uruguay Round agreement of the WTO. Go to New Releases and identify and briefly describe three USITC rulings relating to charges of unfair international trade practices that harm U.S. producers.

25

Exchange Rates, the Balance of Payments, and Trade Deficits

I F Y O U T A K E a U.S. dollar to the bank and ask to exchange it for U.S. currency, you will get a puzzled look. If you persist, you may get a dollar's worth of change: One U.S. dollar can buy exactly one U.S. dollar. But on March 6, 2001, for example, 1 U.S. dollar could buy 885,000 Turkish lira, 1.93 Australian dollars, .68 British pounds, 1.54 Canadian dollars, 1.07 European euros, 118.88 Japanese yen, or 9.66 Mexican pesos. What explains this seemingly haphazard array of exchange rates? ■ In Chapter 24 we examined comparative advantage as the underlying economic basis of world trade and discussed the effects of barriers to free trade. Now we introduce the monetary or financial aspects of international trade: How are currencies of different nations exchanged when import and export transactions occur? What is meant by a "favorable" or an "unfavorable" balance of payments? What is the difference between flexible exchange rates and fixed exchange rates? What are the causes and consequences of the large U.S. trade deficits?

▮ Financing International Trade

One factor that makes international trade different from domestic trade is the involvement of different national currencies. When a U.S. firm exports goods to a Mexican firm, the U.S. exporter wants to be paid in dollars. But the Mexican importer possesses pesos. The importer must exchange pesos for dollars before the U.S. export transaction can occur.

This problem is resolved in foreign exchange markets, in which dollars can purchase Mexican pesos, European euros, South Korean won, British pounds, Japanese yen, or any other currency, and

vice versa. Sponsored by major banks in New York, London, Zurich, Tokyo, and elsewhere, foreign exchange markets facilitate exports and imports.

U.S. Export Transaction

Suppose a U.S. exporter agrees to sell $300,000 of computers to a British firm. Assume, for simplicity, that the rate of exchange—the rate at which pounds can be exchanged for, or converted into, dollars, and vice versa—is $2 for £1 (the actual exchange rate is about $1.50 = 1 pound). This means the British importer must pay the equivalent of £150,000 to the

U.S. exporter to obtain the $300,000 worth of computers. Also assume that all buyers of pounds and dollars are in the United States and Great Britain. Let's follow the steps in the transaction:

■ To pay for the computers, the British buyer draws a check for £150,000 on its checking account in a London bank and sends it to the U.S. exporter.

■ But the U.S. exporting firm must pay its bills in dollars, not pounds. So the exporter sells the £150,000 check on the London bank to its bank in, say, New York City, which is a dealer in foreign exchange. The bank adds $300,000 to the U.S. exporter's checking account for the £150,000 check.

■ The New York bank deposits the £150,000 in a correspondent London bank for future sale to some U.S. buyer who needs pounds.

Note this important point: *U.S. exports create a foreign demand for dollars, and the fulfillment of that demand increases the supply of foreign currencies (pounds, in this case) owned by U.S. banks and available to U.S. buyers.*

U.S. Import Transaction

Why would the New York bank be willing to buy pounds for dollars? As just indicated, the New York bank is a dealer in foreign exchange; it is in the business of buying (for a fee) and selling (also for a fee) one currency for another.

Let's now examine how the New York bank would sell pounds for dollars to finance a U.S. import (British export) transaction. Suppose a U.S. retail firm wants to import £150,000 of compact discs produced in Britain by a hot new musical group. Again, let's track the steps in the transaction:

■ The U.S. importer purchases £150,000 at the $2 = £1 exchange rate by writing a check for $300,000 on its New York bank. Because the British exporting firm wants to be paid in pounds rather than dollars, the U.S. importer must exchange dollars for pounds, which it does by going to the New York bank and purchasing £150,000 for $300,000. (Perhaps the U.S. importer purchases the same £150,000 that the New York bank acquired from the U.S. exporter.)

■ The U.S. importer sends its newly purchased check for £150,000 to the British firm, which deposits it in the London bank.

Here we see that *U.S. imports create a domestic demand for foreign currencies (pounds, in this case), and the fulfillment of that demand reduces the supplies of foreign currencies (again, pounds) held by U.S. banks and available to U.S. consumers.*

The combined export and import transactions bring one more point into focus. U.S. exports (the computers) make available, or "earn," a supply of foreign currencies for U.S. banks, and U.S. imports (the compact discs) create a demand for those currencies. In a broad sense, any nation's exports finance or "pay for" its imports. Exports provide the foreign currencies needed to pay for imports.

Postscript: Although our examples are confined to exporting and importing goods, demand for and supplies of pounds also arise from transactions involving services and the payment of interest and dividends on foreign investments. The United States demands pounds not only to buy imports but also to buy insurance and transportation services from the British, to vacation in London, to pay dividends and interest on British investments in the United States, and to make new financial and real investments in Britain. **(Key Question 2)**

■ The Balance of Payments

A nation's **balance of payments** is the sum of all the transactions that take place between its residents and the residents of all foreign nations. Those transactions include exports and imports of goods, exports and imports of services, tourist expenditures, interest and dividends received or paid abroad, and purchases and sales of financial or real assets abroad. The U.S. Commerce Department's Bureau of Economic Analysis compiles the balance-of-payments statement each year. *The statement shows all the payments a nation receives from foreign countries and all the payments it makes to them.*

Table 25.1 is a simplified balance-of-payments statement for the United States in 1999. Let's take a close look at this accounting statement to see what it reveals about U.S. international trade and finance. To help our explanation, we divide the single balance-of-payments account into three of its components: the *current account*, the *capital account*, and the *official reserves account*.

Current Account

The top portion of Table 25.1 summarizes U.S. trade in currently produced goods and services and is called the **current account.** Items 1 and 2 show U.S. exports and imports of goods (merchandise) in 1999. U.S. exports have a *plus* (+) sign because they

Table 25.1
The U.S. Balance of Payments, 1999 (in Billions)

Current account

(1) U.S. goods exports	$+ 684		
(2) U.S. goods imports	−1030		
(3) *Balance on goods*		$− 346	
(4) U.S. exports of services	+ 272		
(5) U.S. imports of services	− 191		
(6) *Balance on services*		+ 81	
(7) *Balance on goods and services*		− 265	
(8) Net investment income	− 18		
(9) Net transfers	− 48		
(10) **Balance on current account**		−331	

Capital account

(11) Foreign purchases of assets in the United States .	+ 760*		
(12) U.S. purchases of assets abroad	− 438*		
(13) **Balance on capital account**		+322	

Official reserves account

(14) **Official reserves**		+ 9	
		$ 0	

*Includes one-half of a $12 billion statistical discrepancy that is listed in the capital account.
Source: Survey of Current Business, October 2000 (www.bea.doc.gov).

are a *credit;* they earn and make available foreign exchange in the United States. As you saw in the preceding section, any export-type transaction that obligates foreigners to make "inpayments" to the United States generates supplies of foreign currencies in the U.S. banks.

U.S. imports have a *minus* (−) sign because they are a *debit;* they reduce the stock of foreign currencies in the United States. Our earlier discussion of trade financing indicated that U.S. imports obligate the United States to make "outpayments" to the rest of the world that reduce available supplies of foreign currencies held by U.S. banks.

Balance on Goods
Items 1 and 2 in Table 25.1 reveal that in 1999 U.S. goods exports of $684 billion did not earn enough foreign currencies to finance U.S. goods imports of $1030 billion. A country's *balance of trade on goods* is the difference between its exports and its imports of goods. If exports exceed imports, the result is a surplus on the balance of goods. If imports exceed exports, there is a trade deficit on the balance of goods. We note in item 3 that in 1999 the United States incurred a trade deficit on goods of $346 billion. (Global Perspective 25.1 shows U.S. trade deficits and surpluses relative to selected nations.)

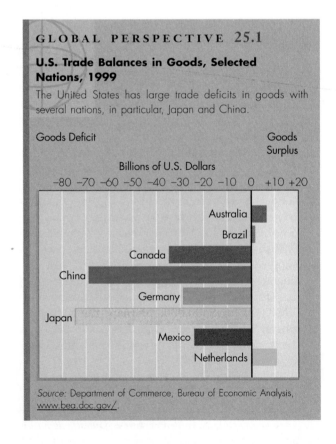

GLOBAL PERSPECTIVE 25.1

U.S. Trade Balances in Goods, Selected Nations, 1999

The United States has large trade deficits in goods with several nations, in particular, Japan and China.

Source: Department of Commerce, Bureau of Economic Analysis, www.bea.doc.gov/.

Balance on Services The United States exports not only goods, such as airplanes and computer software, but also services, such as insurance, consulting, travel, and brokerage services, to residents of foreign nations. Item 4 in Table 25.1 shows that these service "exports" totaled $272 billion in 1999 and are a credit (thus the + sign). Item 5 indicates that the United States "imports" similar services from foreigners; those service imports were $191 billion in 1999 and are a debit (thus the − sign). So the balance on services (item 6) in 1999 was $81 billion.

The **balance on goods and services** shown as item 7 is the difference between U.S. exports of goods and services (items 1 and 4) and U.S. imports of goods and services (items 2 and 5). In 1999, U.S. imports of goods and services exceeded U.S. exports of goods and services by $265 billion. So a **trade deficit** (or "unfavorable balance of trade") occurred. In contrast, a **trade surplus** (or "favorable balance of trade") occurs when exports of goods and services exceed imports of goods and services.

Balance on Current Account Item 8, *net investment income*, represents the difference between (1) the interest and dividend payments foreigners paid the United States for the use of exported U.S. capital and (2) the interest and dividends the United States paid for the use of foreign capital invested in the United States. Observe that in 1999 U.S. net investment income was a negative $18 billion worth of foreign currencies.

Item 9 shows net transfers, both public and private, between the United States and the rest of the world. Included here is foreign aid, pensions paid to U.S. citizens living abroad, and remittances by immigrants to relatives abroad. These $48 billion of transfers are net U.S. outpayments that decrease available supplies of foreign exchange. They are, in a sense, the exporting of goodwill and the importing of "thank-you notes."

By adding all transactions in the current account, we obtain the **balance on current account** shown in item 10. In 1999 the United States had a current account deficit of $331 billion. This means that the U.S. current account transactions (items 2, 5, 8, and 9) created outpayments of foreign currencies from the United States greater than the inpayments of foreign currencies to the United States.

Capital Account

The second account within the overall balance-of-trade account is the **capital account,** which summarizes the purchase or sale of real or financial assets and the corresponding flows of monetary payments that accompany them. For example, a foreign firm may buy a real asset, say, an office building in the United States, or a financial asset, for instance, a U.S. government security. Both kinds of transaction involve the "export" of the ownership of U.S. assets from the United States in return for inpayments of foreign currency. As indicated in line 11, these "exports" of ownership of assets are designated *foreign purchases of assets in the United States*. They have a + sign because, like exports of U.S. goods and services, they represent inpayments of foreign currencies.

Conversely, a U.S. firm may buy, say, a hotel chain (real asset) in a foreign country or some of the common stock (financial asset) of a foreign firm. Both transactions involve the "import" of the ownership of the real or financial assets to the United States and are paid for by outpayments of foreign currencies. These "imports" are designated *U.S. purchases of assets abroad* and, as shown in line 12, have a − sign; like U.S. imports of goods and services, they represent outpayments of foreign currencies from the United States.

Items 11 and 12 combined yield a **balance on capital account** of +$322 billion for 1999 (line 13). In 1999 the United States "exported" $760 billion of ownership of its real and financial assets and "imported" $438 billion. This capital account surplus brought in $322 billion of foreign currencies to the United States.

Official Reserves Account

The third account in the overall balance of payments is the official reserves account. The central banks of nations hold quantities of foreign currencies called **official reserves.** These reserves can be drawn on to make up any net deficit in the combined current and capital accounts (much as you would draw on your savings to pay for a special purchase). In 1999 the United States had a $9 billion deficit in the combined current and capital accounts (line 10 minus line 13). This balance in the U.S. international payments required that the U.S. government deplete its official reserves of foreign currencies by $9 billion (item 14). The + sign indicates that this drawing down and exporting of reserves is a credit—an inpayment from official reserves that was needed to balance the overall balance-of-payments account.

In some years, the current and capital accounts balances are positive, meaning that the United States earned more foreign currencies than it needed. The surplus would create outpayments, not to other countries, but to the stock of official reserves. As such, item 14 would have a − sign because it is a debit.

The three components of the balance of payments (the current account, the capital account, and the official reserves account) must together equal zero. Every unit of foreign exchange used (as reflected in a minus outpayment or debit transaction) must have a source (a plus inpayment or credit transaction).

Payments Deficits and Surpluses

Although the balance of payments must always sum to zero, economists and political officials speak of **balance-of-payments deficits and surpluses;** they are referring to imbalances between the current and capital accounts (line 10 minus line 13) that cause a drawing down or a building up of foreign currencies. A drawing down of official reserves (to create a positive official reserves entry in Table 25.1) measures a nation's balance-of-payments deficit; a building up of official reserves (which is shown as a negative official reserves entry) measures a nation's balance-of-payments surplus.

A balance-of-payments deficit is not necessarily bad, nor is a balance-of-payments surplus necessarily good. Both simply happen. However, any nation's official reserves are limited. Persistent payments deficits, which must be financed by drawing down those reserves, would ultimately deplete the reserves. That nation would have to adopt policies to correct its balance of payments. Such policies might require painful macroeconomic adjustments, trade barriers and similar restrictions, or a major depreciation of its currency. For this reason, nations seek to achieve payments balance, at least over several-year periods.

It is clear from Table 25.1 that in 1999 the United States had a large current account deficit, a large capital account surplus, and a relatively small payments deficit. Large current account deficits have been the norm for the United States in recent years. We need to examine the causes and consequences of trade deficits but will defer that discussion until later in this chapter. **(Key Question 3)**

QUICK REVIEW 25.1

▨ U.S. exports create a foreign demand for dollars, and fulfillment of that demand increases the domestic supply of foreign currencies; U.S. imports create a domestic demand for foreign currencies, and fulfillment of that demand reduces the supplies of foreign currency held by U.S. banks.

▨ The current account balance is a nation's exports of goods and services less its imports of goods and services plus its net investment income and net transfers.

▨ The capital account balance is a nation's sale of real and financial assets to people living abroad less its purchases of real and financial assets from foreigners.

▨ A balance-of-payments deficit occurs when the sum of the balances on current and capital accounts is negative; a balance-of-payments surplus arises when the sum of the balances on current and capital accounts is positive.

▮ Flexible Exchange Rates

Both the size and the persistence of a nation's balance-of-payments deficits and surpluses and the adjustments it must make to correct those imbalances depend on the system of exchange rates being used. There are two "pure" types of exchange-rate systems:

- **A flexible- or floating-exchange-rate system** through which demand and supply determine exchange rates and in which no government intervention occurs.
- **A fixed-exchange-rate system** through which governments determine exchange rates and make necessary adjustments in their economies to maintain those rates.

We begin by looking at flexible exchange rates. Let's examine the rate, or price, at which U.S. dollars might be exchanged for British pounds. In **Figure 25.1 (Key Graph)** we show demand D_1 and supply S_1 of pounds in the currency market. ◩ 25.1

The *demand-for-pounds curve* is downward-sloping because all British goods and services will be cheaper to the United States if pounds become less expensive to the United States. That is, at lower dollar prices for pounds, the United States can get more pounds and therefore more British goods and services per dollar. To buy those cheaper British goods, U.S. consumers will increase the quantity of pounds they demand.

K E Y   G R A P H

P

Dollar price of 1 pound

$3 — Dollar depreciates (pound appreciates)

Exchange rate: $2 = £1

S_1

2 — Dollar appreciates (pound depreciates)

1

D_1

0   Q_1 Q

Quantity of pounds

Figure 25.1

The market for foreign currency (pounds). The intersection of the demand-for-pounds curve D_1 and the supply-of-pounds curve S_1 determines the equilibrium dollar price of pounds, here, $2. That means that the exchange rate is $2 = £1. The upward green arrow is a reminder that a higher dollar price of pounds (say, $3 = £1, caused by a shift in either the demand or the supply curve) means that the dollar has depreciated (the pound has appreciated). The downward green arrow tells us that a lower dollar price of pounds (say, $1 = £1, again caused by a shift in either the demand or the supply curve) means that the dollar has appreciated (the pound has depreciated).

Quick Quiz 25.1

1. Which of the following statements is true?
   a. The quantity of pounds demanded falls when the dollar appreciates.
   b. The quantity of pounds supplied declines as the dollar price of the pound rises.
   c. At the equilibrium exchange rate, the pound price of $1 is $\frac{1}{2}$ pound.
   d. The dollar appreciates if the demand for pounds increases.

2. At the price of $2 for 1 pound in this figure:
   a. the dollar-pound exchange rate is unstable.
   b. the quantity of pounds supplied equals the quantity demanded.
   c. the dollar price of 1 pound equals the pound price of $1.
   d. U.S. goods exports to Britain must equal U.S. goods imports from Britain.

3. Other things equal, a leftward shift of the demand curve in this figure:

   a. would depreciate the dollar.
   b. would create a shortage of pounds at the previous price of $2 for 1 pound.
   c. might be caused by a major recession in the United States.
   d. might be caused by a significant rise of real interest rates in Britain.

4. Other things equal, a rightward shift of the supply curve in this figure would:
   a. depreciate the dollar and might be caused by a significant rise of real interest rates in Britain.
   b. depreciate the dollar and might be caused by a significant fall of real interest rates in Britain.
   c. appreciate the dollar and might be caused by a significant rise of real interest rates in the United States.
   d. appreciate the dollar and might be caused by a significant fall of interest rates in the United States.

The *supply-of-pounds* curve is upward-sloping because the British will purchase more U.S. goods when the dollar price of pounds rises (that is, as the pound price of dollars falls). When the British buy more U.S. goods, they supply a greater quantity of pounds to the foreign exchange market. In other words, they must exchange pounds for dollars to purchase U.S. goods. So, when the dollar price of pounds rises, the quantity of pounds supplied goes up.

The intersection of the supply curve and the demand curve will determine the dollar price of pounds. Here, that price (exchange rate) is $2 for £1.

Depreciation and Appreciation

An exchange rate determined by market forces can, and often does, change daily like stock and bond prices. When the dollar price of pounds *rises*, for example, from $2 = £1 to $3 = £1, the dollar has *depreciated* relative to the pound (and the pound has appreciated relative to the dollar). When a currency depreciates, more units of it (dollars) are needed to buy a single unit of some other currency (a pound).

When the dollar price of pounds *falls*, for example, from $2 = £1 to $1 = £1, the dollar has *appreciated* relative to the pound. When a currency appreciates, fewer units of it (dollars) are needed to buy a single unit of some other currency (pounds).

In our U.S.-Britain illustrations, depreciation of the dollar means an appreciation of the pound, and vice versa. When the dollar price of a pound jumps from $2 = £1 to $3 = £1, the pound has appreciated relative to the dollar because it takes fewer pounds to buy $1. At $2 = £1, it took £$\frac{1}{2}$ to buy $1; at $3 = £1, it takes only £$\frac{1}{3}$ to buy $1. Conversely, when the dollar appreciated relative to the pound, the pound depreciated relative to the dollar. More pounds were needed to buy a dollar.

Determinants of Exchange Rates

What factors would cause a nation's currency to appreciate or depreciate in the market for foreign exchange? Here are three generalizations:

- If the demand for a nation's currency increases (all else equal), that currency will appreciate; if the demand declines, that currency will depreciate.
- If the supply of a nation's currency increases, that currency will depreciate; if the supply decreases, that currency will appreciate.
- If a nation's currency appreciates, some foreign currency depreciates relative to it.

With these generalizations in mind, let's examine the determinants of exchange rates—the factors that shift the demand or supply curve for a certain currency.

Changes in Tastes
Any change in consumer tastes or preferences for the products of a foreign country may alter the demand for that nation's currency and change its exchange rate. If technological advances in U.S. wireless phones make them more attractive to British consumers and businesses, then the British will supply more pounds in the exchange market in order to purchase more U.S. wireless phones. The supply-of-pounds curve will shift to the right, causing the pound to depreciate and the dollar to appreciate.

In contrast, the U.S. demand-for-pounds curve will shift to the right if British woolen apparel becomes more fashionable in the United States. So the pound will appreciate and the dollar will depreciate.

Relative Income Changes
A nation's currency is likely to depreciate if its growth of national income is more rapid than that of other countries. Here's why: A country's imports vary directly with its income level. As total income rises in the United States, people there buy both more domestic goods and more foreign goods. If the U.S. economy is expanding rapidly and the British economy is stagnant, U.S. imports of British goods, and therefore U.S. demands for pounds, will increase. The dollar price of pounds will rise, so the dollar will depreciate.

Relative Price-Level Changes
Changes in the relative price levels of two nations may change the demand and supply of currencies and alter the exchange rate between the two nations' currencies.

The **purchasing-power-parity theory** holds that exchange rates equate the purchasing power of various currencies. That is, the exchange rates among national currencies adjust to match the ratios of the nations' price levels: If a certain market basket of goods costs $10,000 in the United States and £5,000 in Great Britain, according to this theory the exchange rate will be $2 = £1. That way, a dollar spent on goods sold in Britain, Japan, Turkey, and other nations will have equal purchasing power. ⚠ 25.1

In practice, however, exchange rates depart from purchasing power parity, even over long periods. Nevertheless, changes in relative price levels are a determinant of exchange rates. If, for example, the domestic price level rises rapidly in the United States and remains constant in Great Britain, U.S. consumers will seek out low-priced British goods, increasing the demand for pounds. The British will purchase fewer U.S. goods, reducing the supply of pounds. This combination of demand and supply changes will cause the pound to appreciate and the dollar to depreciate.

Relative Interest Rates
Changes in relative interest rates between two countries may alter their exchange rate. Suppose that real interest rates rise in the United States but stay constant in Great Britain. British citizens will then find the United States an attractive place in which to make financial investments. To undertake these investments, they will

have to supply pounds in the foreign exchange market to obtain dollars. The increase in the supply of pounds results in depreciation of the pound and appreciation of the dollar.

Speculation
Currency speculators are people who buy and sell currencies with an eye toward reselling or repurchasing them at a profit. Suppose speculators expect the U.S. economy to (1) grow more rapidly than the British economy and (2) experience a more rapid rise in its price level than will Britain. These expectations translate into an anticipation that the pound will appreciate and the dollar will depreciate. Speculators who are holding dollars will therefore try to convert them into pounds. This effort will increase the demand for pounds and cause the dollar price of pounds to rise (that is, cause the dollar to depreciate). A self-fulfilling prophecy occurs: The pound appreciates and the dollar depreciates because speculators act on the belief that these changes will in fact take place. In this way, speculation can cause changes in exchange rates. (We deal with currency speculation in more detail in this chapter's Last Word.)

Table 25.2 has more illustrations of the determinants of exchange rates; the table is worth careful study.

Flexible Rates and the Balance of Payments

Proponents of flexible exchange rates say they have an important feature: They automatically adjust and eventually eliminate balance-of-payments deficits or surpluses. We can explain this idea through Figure 25.2, in which S_1 and D_1 are the supply and demand curves for pounds from Figure 25.1. The equilibrium exchange rate of $2 = £1 means that there is no balance-of-payments deficit or surplus between the United States and Britain. At that exchange rate, the quantity of pounds demanded by U.S. consumers to import British goods, buy British transportation and insurance services, and pay interest and dividends on British investments in the United States equals the amount of pounds supplied by the British in buying U.S. exports, purchasing services from the United States, and making interest and dividend payments on U.S. investments in Britain. The United States would have no need to either draw down or build up its official reserves to balance its payments.

Suppose tastes change and U.S. consumers buy more British automobiles; the U.S. price level increases relative to Britain's; or interest rates fall in the United States compared to those in Britain. Any or all of these changes will increase the U.S. demand

Table 25.2

Determinants of Exchange Rates: Factors That Change the Demand for or the Supply of a Particular Currency and Thus Alter the Exchange Rate

Determinant	Examples
Change in tastes	Japanese autos decline in popularity in the United States (Japanese yen depreciates; U.S. dollar appreciates).
	European tourists flock to the United States (U.S. dollar appreciates; European euro depreciates).
Change in relative incomes	England encounters a recession, reducing its imports, while U.S. real output and real income surge, increasing U.S. imports (British pound appreciates; U.S. dollar depreciates).
Change in relative prices	Switzerland experiences a 3% inflation rate compared to Canada's 10% rate (Swiss franc appreciates; Canadian dollar depreciates).
Change in relative real interest rates	The Federal Reserve drives up interest rates in the United States, while the Bank of England takes no such action (U.S. dollar appreciates; British pound depreciates).
Speculation	Currency traders believe South Korea will have much greater inflation than Taiwan (South Korean won depreciates; Taiwan dollar appreciates).
	Currency traders think Finland's interest rates will plummet relative to Denmark's rates (Finland's markka depreciates; Denmark's krone appreciates).

Figure 25.2

Adjustments under flexible exchange rates and fixed exchange rates. Under flexible exchange rates, a shift in the demand for pounds from D_1 to D_2, other things equal, would cause a U.S. balance-of-payments deficit ab. That deficit would be corrected by a change in the exchange rate from $2 = £1$ to $3 = £1$. Under fixed exchange rates, the United States would cover the shortage of pounds ab by using international monetary reserves, restricting trade, implementing exchange controls, or enacting a contractionary stabilization policy.

for British pounds, for example, from D_1 to D_2 in Figure 25.2.

If the exchange rate remains at the initial $2 = £1$, a U.S. balance-of-payments deficit will occur in the amount of ab. At the $2 = £1$ rate, U.S. consumers will demand the quantity of pounds shown by point b but Britain will supply only the amount shown by a. There will be a shortage of pounds. But this shortage will not last because this is a competitive market. Instead, the dollar price of pounds will rise (the dollar will depreciate) until the balance-of-payments deficit is eliminated. That occurs at the new equilibrium exchange rate of $3 = £1$, where the quantities of pounds demanded and supplied are again equal.

To explain why this occurred, we reemphasize that the exchange rate links all domestic (U.S.) prices with all foreign (British) prices. The dollar price of a foreign good is found by multiplying the foreign price by the exchange rate (in dollars per unit of the foreign currency). At an exchange rate of $2 = £1$, a British automobile priced at £15,000 will cost a U.S. consumer $30,000 (= 15,000 × $2).

A change in the exchange rate alters the prices of all British goods to U.S. consumers and all U.S.

goods to British buyers. The shift in the exchange rate (here from $2 = £1$ to $3 = £1$) changes the relative attractiveness of U.S. imports and exports and restores equilibrium in the U.S. (and British) balance of payments. From the U.S. view, as the dollar price of pounds changes from $2 to $3, the British auto priced at £15,000, which formerly cost a U.S. consumer $30,000, now costs $45,000 (= 15,000 × $3). Other British goods will also cost U.S. consumers more, and U.S. imports of British goods will decline. A movement from point b toward point c in Figure 25.2 graphically illustrates this concept.

From Britain's standpoint, the exchange rate (the pound price of dollars) has fallen (from $£\frac{1}{2}$ to $£\frac{1}{3}$ for $1). The international value of the pound has appreciated. The British previously got only $2 for £1; now they get $3 for £1. U.S. goods are therefore cheaper to the British, and U.S. exports to Britain will rise. In Figure 25.2, this is shown by a movement from point a toward point c.

The two adjustments—a decrease in U.S. imports from Britain and an increase in U.S. exports to Britain—are just what are needed to correct the U.S. balance-of-payments deficit. These changes end when, at point c, the quantities of British pounds demanded and supplied are equal. **(Key Questions 6 and 9)**

Disadvantages of Flexible Exchange Rates

Even though flexible exchange rates automatically work to eliminate payment imbalances, they may cause several significant problems.

Uncertainty and Diminished Trade The risks and uncertainties associated with flexible exchange rates may discourage the flow of trade. Suppose a U.S. automobile dealer contracts to purchase 10 British cars for £150,000. At the current exchange rate of, say, $2 for £1, the U.S. importer expects to pay $300,000 for these automobiles. But if during the 3-month delivery period the rate of exchange shifts to $3 for £1, the £150,000 payment contracted by the U.S. importer will be $450,000.

That increase in the dollar price of pounds may thus turn the U.S. importer's anticipated profit into substantial loss. Aware of the possibility of an adverse change in the exchange rate, the U.S. importer may not be willing to assume the risks involved. The U.S. firm may confine its operations to domestic automobiles, so international trade in this product will not occur.

The same thing can happen with investments. Assume that when the exchange rate is $3 to £1, a U.S. firm invests $30,000 (or £10,000) in a British enterprise. It estimates a return of 10 percent; that is, it anticipates annual earnings of $3000 or £1000. Suppose these expectations prove correct in that the British firm earns £1000 in the first year on the £10,000 investment. But suppose that during the year, the value of the dollar appreciates to $2 = £1. The absolute return is now only $2000 (rather than $3000), and the rate of return falls from the anticipated 10 percent to only $6\frac{2}{3}$ percent (= $2000/$30,000). Investment is risky in any case. The added risk of changing exchange rates may persuade the U.S. investor not to venture overseas.[1]

Terms-of-Trade Changes   A decline in the international value of its currency will worsen a nation's terms of trade. For example, an increase in the dollar price of a pound will mean that the United States must export more goods and services to finance a specific level of imports from Britain.

Instability   Flexible exchange rates may destabilize the domestic economy, because wide fluctuations stimulate and then depress industries producing exported goods. If the U.S. economy is operating at full employment and its currency depreciates, as in our illustration, the results will be inflationary, for two reasons. (1) Foreign demand for U.S. goods may rise, increasing total spending and pulling up U.S. prices. Also, the prices of all U.S. imports will increase. (2) Conversely, appreciation of the dollar will lower U.S. exports and increase imports, possibly causing unemployment.

Flexible or floating exchange rates may also complicate the use of domestic stabilization policies in seeking full employment and price stability. This is especially true for nations whose exports and imports are large relative to their total domestic output.

∎ Fixed Exchange Rates

To circumvent the disadvantages of flexible exchange rates, at times nations have fixed or "pegged" their exchange rates. For our analysis of fixed exchange

rates, we assume that the United States and Britain agree to maintain a $2 = £1 exchange rate.

The problem is that such a government agreement cannot keep from changing the demand for and the supply of pounds. With the rate fixed, a shift in demand or supply will threaten the fixed-exchange-rate system, and government must intervene to ensure that the exchange rate is maintained.

In Figure 25.2, suppose the U.S. demand for pounds increases from D_1 to D_2 and a U.S. payment deficit ab arises. Now, the new equilibrium exchange rate ($3 = £1) is below the fixed exchange rate ($2 = £1). How can the United States prevent the shortage of pounds from driving the exchange rate up to the new equilibrium level? How can it maintain the fixed exchange rate? The answer is by altering market demand or market supply or both so that they will intersect at the $2 = £1 rate. There are several ways to do this.

Use of Reserves

One way to maintain a fixed exchange rate is to manipulate the market through the use of official reserves. Such manipulations are called **currency interventions.** By selling part of its reserves of pounds, the U.S. government could increase the supply of pounds, shifting supply curve S_1 to the right so that it intersects D_2 at b in Figure 25.2 and thereby maintains the exchange rate at $2 = £1.

How do official reserves originate? Perhaps a balance-of-payments surplus occurred in the past. The U.S. government would have purchased that surplus. That is, at some earlier time the U.S. government may have spent dollars to buy the surplus pounds that were threatening to reduce the exchange rate to below the $2 = £1 fixed rate. Those purchases would have bolstered the U.S. official reserves of pounds.

Nations have also used gold as "international money" to obtain official reserves. In our example, the U.S. government could sell some of its gold to Britain to obtain pounds. It could then sell pounds for dollars. That would shift the supply-of-pounds curve to the right, and the $2 = £1 exchange rate could be maintained.

It is critical that the amount of reserves and gold be enough to accomplish the required increase in the supply of pounds. There is no problem if deficits and surpluses occur more or less randomly and are of similar size. Then, last year's balance-of-payments surplus with Britain will increase the U.S. reserve of

---

[1]You will see in this chapter's Last Word, however, that a trader can circumvent part of the risk of unfavorable exchange-rate fluctuations by "hedging" in the "futures market" or "forward market" for foreign exchange.

pounds, and that reserve can be used to "finance" this year's deficit. But if the United States encounters persistent and sizable deficits for an extended period, it may exhaust its reserves, and thus be forced to abandon fixed exchange rates. Or, at the least, a nation whose reserves are inadequate must use less appealing options to maintain exchange rates. Let's consider some of those options.

Trade Policies

To maintain fixed exchange rates, a nation can try to control the flow of trade and finance directly. The United States could try to maintain the $2 = £1 exchange rate in the face of a shortage of pounds by discouraging imports (thereby reducing the demand for pounds) and encouraging exports (thus increasing the supply of pounds). Imports could be reduced by means of new tariffs or import quotas; special taxes could be levied on the interest and dividends U.S. financial investors receive from foreign investments. Also, the U.S. government could subsidize certain U.S. exports to increase the supply of pounds.

The fundamental problem is that these policies reduce the volume of world trade and change its makeup from what is economically desirable. When nations impose tariffs, quotas, and the like, they lose some of the economic benefits of a free flow of world trade. That loss should not be underestimated: Trade barriers by one nation lead to retaliatory responses from other nations, multiplying the loss.

Exchange Controls and Rationing

Another option is to adopt exchange controls and rationing. Under **exchange controls** the U.S. government could handle the problem of a pound shortage by requiring that all pounds obtained by U.S. exporters be sold to the Federal government. Then the government would allocate or ration this short supply of pounds (represented by *xa* in Figure 25.2) among various U.S. importers, who actually demand the quantity *xb*. In effect, this policy would restrict the value of U.S. imports to the amount of foreign exchange earned by U.S. exports. Assuming balance in the capital account, there would then be no balance-of-payments deficit. U.S. demand for British imports with the value *ab* would simply not be fulfilled.

There are major objections to exchange controls:

■ *Distorted trade* Like tariffs, quotas, and export subsidies (trade controls), exchange controls would distort the pattern of international trade away from the pattern suggested by comparative advantage.

■ *Favoritism* The process of rationing scarce foreign exchange might lead to government favoritism toward selected importers (big contributors to reelection campaigns, for example).

■ *Restricted choice* Controls would limit freedom of consumer choice. The U.S. consumers who prefer Volkswagens might have to buy Chevrolets. The business opportunities for some U.S. importers might be impaired if the government were to limit imports.

■ *Black markets* Enforcement problems are likely under exchange controls. U.S. importers might want foreign exchange badly enough to pay more than the $2 = £1 official rate, setting the stage for black-market dealings between importers and illegal sellers of foreign exchange.

Domestic Macroeconomic Adjustments

A final way to maintain a fixed exchange rate would be to use domestic stabilization policies (monetary policy and fiscal policy) to eliminate the shortage of foreign currency. Tax hikes, reductions in government spending, and a high-interest-rate policy would reduce total spending in the U.S. economy and, consequently, domestic income. Because the volume of imports varies directly with domestic income, demand for British goods, and therefore for pounds, would be restrained.

If these "contractionary" policies served to reduce the domestic price level relative to Britain's, U.S. buyers of consumer and capital goods would divert their demands from British goods to U.S. goods, reducing the demand for pounds. Moreover, the high-interest-rate policy would lift U.S. interest rates relative to those in Britain.

Lower prices on U.S. goods and higher U.S. interest rates would increase British imports of U.S. goods and would increase British financial investment in the United States. Both developments would increase the supply of pounds. The combination of a decrease in the demand for and an increase in the supply of pounds would reduce or eliminate the original U.S. balance-of-payments deficit. In Figure 25.2 the new supply and demand curves would intersect at some new equilibrium point on line *ab*, where the exchange rate remains at $2 = £1.

Maintaining fixed exchange rates by such means is hardly appealing. The "price" of exchange-rate stability for the United States would be a decline in output, employment, and price levels—in other words, a recession. Eliminating a balance-of-payments deficit and achieving domestic stability are both important national economic goals, but to sacrifice stability to balance payments would be to let the tail wag the dog.

QUICK REVIEW 25.2

■ In a system in which exchange rates are flexible (meaning that they are free to float), the rates are determined by the demand for and supply of individual national currencies in the foreign-exchange market.

■ Determinants of flexible exchange rates (factors that shift currency supply and demand curves) include changes in (a) tastes, (b) relative national incomes, (c) relative price levels, (d) real interest rates, and (e) speculation.

■ Under a system of fixed exchange rates, nations set their exchange rates and then maintain them by buying or selling reserves of currencies, establishing trade barriers, employing exchange controls, or incurring inflation or recession.

International Exchange-Rate Systems

In recent times the world's nations have used three different exchange-rate systems: a fixed-rate system, a modified fixed-rate system, and a modified flexible-rate system.

The Gold Standard: Fixed Exchange Rates

Between 1879 and 1934 the major nations of the world adhered to a fixed-rate system called the **gold standard.** Under this system, each nation must:

■ Define its currency in terms of a quantity of gold.

■ Maintain a fixed relationship between its stock of gold and its money supply.

■ Allow gold to be freely exported and imported.

If each nation defines its currency in terms of gold, the various national currencies will have fixed relationships to one another. For example, if the United States defines $1 as worth 25 grains of gold, and Britain defines £1 as worth 50 grains of gold, then a British pound is worth 2 × 25 grains, or $2. This exchange rate was fixed under the gold standard. The exchange rate did not change in response to changes in currency demand and supply.

Gold Flows   If we ignore the costs of packing, insuring, and shipping gold between countries, under the gold standard the rate of exchange would not vary from this $2 = £1 rate. No one in the United States would pay more than $2 = £1 because 50 grains of gold could always be bought for $2 in the United States and sold for £1 in Britain. Nor would the British pay more than £1 for $2. Why should they when they could buy 50 grains of gold in Britain for £1 and sell it in the United States for $2?

Under the gold standard, the potential free flow of gold between nations resulted in fixed exchange rates.

Domestic Macroeconomic Adjustments   When currency demand or supply changes, the gold standard requires domestic macroeconomic adjustments to maintain the fixed exchange rate. To see why, suppose that U.S. tastes change such that U.S. consumers want to buy more British goods. The resulting increase in the demand for pounds creates a shortage of pounds in the United States (recall Figure 25.2), implying a U.S. balance-of-payments deficit.

What will happen? Remember that the rules of the gold standard prohibit the exchange rate from moving from the fixed $2 = £1 rate. The rate cannot move to, say, a new equilibrium at $3 = £1 to correct the imbalance. Instead, gold will flow from the United States to Britain to correct the payments imbalance.

But recall that the gold standard requires that participants maintain a fixed relationship between their domestic money supplies and their quantities of gold. The flow of gold from the United States to Britain will require a reduction of the money supply in the United States. Other things equal, that will reduce total spending in the United States and lower U.S. real domestic output, employment, income, and, perhaps, prices. Also, the decline in the money supply will boost U.S. interest rates.

The opposite will occur in Britain. The inflow of gold will increase the money supply, and this will increase total spending in Britain. Domestic output, employment, income, and, perhaps, prices will rise. The British interest rate will fall.

Declining U.S. incomes and prices will reduce the U.S. demand for British goods and therefore reduce the U.S. demand for pounds. Lower interest rates in Britain will make it less attractive for U.S. investors to make financial investments there, also lessening the demand for pounds. For all these reasons, the demand for pounds in the United States will decline. In Britain, higher incomes, prices, and interest rates will make U.S. imports and U.S. financial investments more attractive. In buying these imports and making these financial investments, British citizens will supply more pounds in the exchange market.

In short, domestic macroeconomic adjustments in the United States and Britain, triggered by the international flow of gold, will produce new demand and supply conditions for pounds such that the $2 = £1 exchange rate is maintained. After all the adjustments are made, the United States will not have a payments deficit and Britain will not have a payments surplus.

So the gold standard has the advantage of maintaining stable exchange rates and correcting balance-of-payments deficits and surpluses automatically. However, its critical drawback is that nations must accept domestic adjustments in such distasteful forms as unemployment and falling incomes, on the one hand, or inflation, on the other hand. Under the gold standard, a nation's money supply is altered by changes in supply and demand in currency markets, and nations cannot establish their own monetary policy in their own national interest. If the United States, for example, were to experience declining output and income, the loss of gold under the gold standard would reduce the U.S. money supply. That would increase interest rates, retard borrowing and spending, and produce further declines in output and income.

Collapse of the Gold Standard

The gold standard collapsed under the weight of the worldwide Depression of the 1930s. As domestic output and employment fell worldwide, the restoration of prosperity became the primary goal of afflicted nations. They responded by enacting protectionist measures to reduce imports. The idea was to get their economies moving again by promoting consumption of domestically produced goods. To make their exports less expensive abroad, many nations redefined their currencies at lower levels in terms of gold. For example, a country that had previously defined the value of its currency at 1 unit = 25 ounces of gold might redefine it as 1 unit = 10 ounces of

gold. Such redefining is an example of **devaluation**— a deliberate action by government to reduce the international value of its currency. A series of such devaluations in the 1930s meant that exchange rates were no longer fixed. That violated a major tenet of the gold standard, and the system broke down.

The Bretton Woods System

The Great Depression and the Second World War left world trade and the world monetary system in shambles. To lay the groundwork for a new international monetary system, in 1944 major nations held an international conference at Bretton Woods, New Hampshire. The conference produced a commitment to a modified fixed-exchange-rate system called an *adjustable-peg system*, or, simply, the **Bretton Woods system.** The new system sought to capture the advantages of the old gold standard (fixed exchange rate) while avoiding its disadvantages (painful domestic macroeconomic adjustments).

Furthermore, the conference created the **International Monetary Fund (IMF)** to make the new exchange-rate system feasible and workable. The new international monetary system managed through the IMF prevailed with modifications until 1971. (The IMF still plays a basic role in international finance; in recent years it has performed a major role in providing loans to developing countries, nations experiencing financial crises, and nations making the transition from communism to capitalism.)

IMF and Pegged Exchange Rates   How did the adjustable-peg system of exchange rates work? First, as with the gold standard, each IMF member had to define its currency in terms of gold (or dollars), thus establishing rates of exchange between its currency and the currencies of all other members. In addition, each nation was obligated to keep its exchange rate stable with respect to every other currency. To do so, nations would have to use their official currency reserves to intervene in foreign exchange markets.

Assume again that the U.S. dollar and the British pound were "pegged" to each other at $2 = £1. And suppose again that the demand for pounds temporarily increases so that a shortage of pounds occurs in the United States (the United States has a balance-of-payments deficit). How can the United States keep its pledge to maintain a $2 = £1 exchange rate when the new equilibrium rate is, say, $3 = £1? As we noted previously, the United States can supply additional pounds to the exchange market, increasing the supply of pounds such that the equilibrium exchange rate falls back to $2 = £1.

Under the Bretton Woods system there were three main sources of the needed pounds:

- *Official reserves*   The United States might currently possess pounds in its official reserves as the result of past actions against a payments surplus.
- *Gold sales*   The U.S. government might sell some of its gold to Britain for pounds. The proceeds would then be offered in the exchange market to augment the supply of pounds.
- *IMF borrowing*   The needed pounds might be borrowed from the IMF. Nations participating in the Bretton Woods system were required to make contributions to the IMF based on the size of their national income, population, and volume of trade. If necessary, the United States could borrow pounds on a short-term basis from the IMF by supplying its own currency as collateral.

Fundamental Imbalances: Adjusting the Peg

The Bretton Woods system recognized that from time to time a nation may be confronted with persistent and sizable balance-of-payments problems that cannot be corrected through the means listed above. In such cases, the nation would eventually run out of official reserves and be unable to maintain its fixed-exchange-rate system. The Bretton Woods remedy was correction by devaluation, that is, by an "orderly" reduction of the nation's pegged exchange rate. Also, the IMF allowed each member nation to alter the value of its currency by 10 percent, on its own, to correct a so-called fundamental (persistent and continuing) balance-of-payments deficit. Larger exchange-rate changes required the permission of the Fund's board of directors.

By requiring approval of significant rate changes, the Fund guarded against arbitrary and competitive currency devaluations by nations seeking only to boost output in their own countries at the expense of other countries. In our example, devaluation of the dollar would increase U.S. exports and lower U.S. imports, correcting its persistent payments deficit.

Demise of the Bretton Woods System

Under this adjustable-peg system, nations came to accept gold and the dollar as international reserves. The acceptability of gold as an international medium of exchange derived from its earlier use under the gold standard. Other nations accepted the dollar as international money because the United States had accumulated large quantities of gold, and between 1934 and 1971 it maintained a policy of buying gold from, and selling gold to, foreign governments at a fixed price of $35 per ounce. The dollar was convertible into gold on demand, so the dollar came to be regarded as a substitute for gold, or "as good as gold." And since the discovery of new gold was limited, the growing volume of dollars helped provide a medium of exchange for the expanding world trade.

But a major problem arose. The United States had persistent payments deficits throughout the 1950s and 1960s. Those deficits were financed in part by U.S. gold reserves but mostly by payment of U.S. dollars. As the amount of dollars held by foreigners soared and the U.S. gold reserves dwindled, other nations began to question whether the dollar was really "as good as gold." The ability of the United States to continue to convert dollars into gold at $35 per ounce became increasingly doubtful, as did the role of dollars as international monetary reserves. Thus the dilemma was: To maintain the dollar as a reserve medium, the U.S. payments deficit had to be eliminated. But elimination of the payments deficit would remove the source of additional dollar reserves and thus limit the growth of international trade and finance.

The problem culminated in 1971 when the United States ended its 37-year-old policy of exchanging gold for dollars at $35 per ounce. It severed the link between gold and the international value of the dollar, thereby "floating" the dollar and letting market forces determine its value. The floating of the dollar withdrew U.S. support from the Bretton Woods system of fixed exchange rates and, in effect, ended the system.

The Current System: The Managed Float

The current international exchange-rate system (1971–present) is an "almost" flexible system called **managed floating exchange rates.** Exchange rates among major currencies are free to float to their equilibrium market levels, but nations occasionally use currency interventions in the foreign exchange market to stabilize or alter market exchange rates.

Normally, the major trading nations allow their exchange rates to float up or down to equilibrium levels based on supply and demand in the foreign exchange market. They recognize that changing economic conditions among nations require continuing changes in equilibrium exchange rates to avoid persistent payments deficits or surpluses. They rely on freely operating foreign exchange markets to accomplish the necessary adjustments. The result has been considerably more volatile exchange rates than those during the Bretton Woods era.

But nations also recognize that certain trends in the movement of equilibrium exchange rates may be at odds with national or international objectives. On occasion, nations therefore intervene in the foreign exchange market by buying or selling large amounts of specific currencies. This way, they can "manage" or stabilize exchange rates by influencing currency demand and supply.

For example, in 1987 the Group of Seven industrial nations (G-7 nations)—the United States, Germany, Japan, Britain, France, Italy, and Canada—agreed to stabilize the value of the dollar. During the previous 2 years the dollar had declined rapidly because of large U.S. trade deficits. Although the U.S. trade deficits remained sizable, the G-7 nations concluded that further dollar depreciation might disrupt economic growth in member nations (other than the United States). The G-7 nations therefore purchased large amounts of dollars to boost the dollar's value. Since 1987 the G-7 nations (now G-8 with the addition of Russia) have periodically intervened in foreign exchange markets to stabilize currency values.

In 2000, the United States and the European nations sold dollars and bought euros in an effort to stabilize the falling value of the euro relative to the dollar. In the previous year the euro (€) had depreciated from $1 = €1.17 to $1 = €.87.

The current exchange-rate system is thus an "almost" flexible exchange-rate system. The "almost" refers mainly to the periodic currency interventions by governments; it also refers to the fact that the actual system is more complicated than described. While the major currencies such as dollars, euros, pounds, and yen fluctuate in response to changing supply and demand, some developing nations peg their currencies to the dollar and allow their currencies to fluctuate with it against other currencies. Also, some nations peg the value of their currencies to a "basket" or group of other currencies.

How well has the managed float worked? It has both proponents and critics.

In Support of the Managed Float

Proponents of the managed-float system argue that is has functioned far better than many experts anticipated. Skeptics had predicted that fluctuating exchange rates would reduce world trade and finance. But in real terms world trade under the managed float has grown tremendously over the past several decades. Moreover, as supporters are quick to point out, currency crises such as those in Mexico and southeast Asia in the last half of the 1990s were not the result of the floating-exchange-rate system itself. Rather, the abrupt currency devaluations and depreciations resulted from internal problems in those nations, in conjunction with the nations' tendency to peg their currencies to the dollar or to a basket of currencies. In some cases, flexible exchange rates would have made these adjustments far more gradual.

Proponents also point out that the managed float has weathered severe economic turbulence that might have caused a fixed-rate system to break down. Such events as extraordinary oil price increases in 1973–1974 and again in 1981–1983, inflationary recessions in several nations in the mid-1970s, major national recessions in the early 1980s, and large U.S. budget deficits in the 1980s and the first half of the 1990s all caused substantial imbalances in international trade and finance. Flexible rates enabled the system to adjust to those events, whereas the same events would have put unbearable pressures on a fixed-rate system.

Concerns with the Managed Float

There is still much sentiment in favor of greater exchange-rate stability. Those favoring more stable exchange rates see problems with the current system. They argue that the excessive volatility of exchange rates under the managed float threatens the prosperity of economies that rely heavily on exports. Several financial crises in individual nations (for example, Mexico, South Korea, Indonesia, Thailand, Russia, and Brazil) have resulted from abrupt changes in exchange rates. These crises have led to massive "bailouts" of those economies via IMF loans. The IMF bailouts, in turn, may encourage nations to undertake risky and inappropriate economic policies since they know that, if need be, the IMF will come to the rescue. Moreover, some exchange-rate volatility has occurred even when underlying economic and financial conditions were relatively stable, suggesting that speculation plays too large a role in determining exchange rates.

Perhaps more importantly, assert the critics, the managed float has not eliminated trade imbalances, as flexible rates are supposed to do. Thus, the United States has run persistent trade deficits for many years, while Japan has run persistent surpluses. Changes in exchange rates between dollars and yen have not yet corrected these imbalances, as is supposed to be the case under flexible exchange rates.

Skeptics say the managed float is basically a "nonsystem"; the guidelines concerning what each nation may or may not do with its exchange rates are not specific enough to keep the system working in the long run. Nations inevitably will be tempted to intervene in the foreign exchange market, not merely to smooth out short-term fluctuations in exchange rates but to prop up their currency if it is chronically weak or to manipulate the exchange rate to achieve domestic stabilization goals.

So what are we to conclude? Flexible exchange rates have not worked perfectly, but they have not failed miserably. Thus far they have survived, and no doubt have eased, several major shocks to the international trading system. Meanwhile, the "managed" part of the float has given nations some sense of control over their collective economic destinies. On balance, most economists favor continuation of the present system of "almost" flexible exchange rates.

(a)
Balance of trade

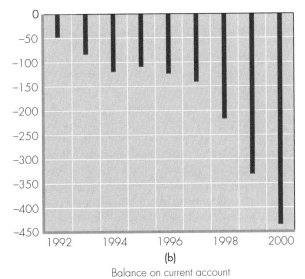

(b)
Balance on current account

> **QUICK REVIEW 25.3**
>
> ■ Under the gold standard (1879–1934), nations fixed exchange rates by valuing their currencies in terms of gold, by tying their stocks of money to gold, and by allowing gold to flow between nations when balance-of-payments deficits and surpluses occurred.
>
> ■ The Bretton Woods exchange-rate system (1944–1971) fixed or pegged exchange rates but permitted orderly adjustments of the pegs under special circumstances.
>
> ■ The managed floating system of exchange rates (1971–present) relies on foreign exchange markets to establish equilibrium exchange rates. The system permits nations to buy and sell foreign currency to stabilize short-term changes in exchange rates or to correct exchange-rate imbalances that are negatively affecting the world economy.

Figure 25.3
Recent U.S. trade deficits. U.S. trade deficits in (a) "goods" and "goods and services" and (b) the current account recently have been very large.
Source: U.S. Department of Commerce, Bureau of Economic Analysis, www.bea.doc.gov/.

▌ Recent U.S. Trade Deficits

Figure 25.3 reveals that U.S. trade and current account deficits over the past several years were large and persistent. For example, the trade deficit on goods for 2000 was $450 billion. That year, the trade deficit on goods and services was $369 billion, and the current account deficit was $435 billion.

Causes of the Trade Deficits

There are several reasons for these persistent trade deficits. First, since 1992 the U.S. economy has grown more rapidly than the economies of several major trading nations. This growth of income has boosted U.S. purchases of foreign goods (U.S. imports). In contrast, Japan, some European nations, and Canada have suffered either recession or slower income growth during this period. Thus, their purchases of U.S. goods (U.S. exports) have not kept pace with the rise of U.S. imports. Persistent U.S. trade imbalances with Japan are particularly noteworthy.

Second, a declining saving rate in the United States has contributed to U.S. trade deficits. The saving rate (saving/total income) in the United States has declined at the same time that the investment rate (investment/total income) has remained stable or even increased. The gap has been met through foreign purchases of U.S. real and financial assets, creating a large capital account surplus. Because foreigners are financing more of U.S. investment, U.S. citizens are able to save less and consume more, including consumption of imported goods. That is, the capital account surplus may partly cause the trade deficit, not simply result from it.

Implications of U.S. Trade Deficits

There is disagreement on whether the large trade deficits should concern the United States. Most economists see both benefits and costs to trade deficits.

Increased Current Consumption

At the time a trade deficit or a current account deficit is occurring, American consumers benefit. A trade deficit means that the United States is receiving more goods and services as imports from abroad than it is sending out as exports. Taken alone, a trade deficit allows the United States to consume outside its production possibilities curve. It augments the domestic standard of living. But there is a catch: The gain in present consumption may come at the expense of reduced future consumption.

Increased U.S. Indebtedness

A trade deficit is considered "unfavorable" because it must be financed by borrowing from the rest of the world, selling off assets, or dipping into foreign currency reserves. Recall that current account deficits are financed primarily by net inpayments of foreign currencies to the United States. When U.S. exports are insufficient to finance U.S. imports, the United States increases both its debt to people abroad and the value of foreign claims against assets in the United States. Financing of the U.S. trade deficit has resulted in a larger foreign accumulation of claims against U.S. financial and real assets than the U.S. claim against foreign assets. Today, the United States is the world's largest debtor nation. In 1999, foreigners owned $1.5 billion more of U.S. assets (corporations, land, stocks, bonds, loan notes) than the United States owned in foreign assets.

If the United States wants to regain ownership of these domestic assets, at some future time it will have to export more than it imports. At that time, domestic consumption will be lower because the United States will need to send more of its output abroad than it receives as imports. Therefore, the current consumption gains delivered by U.S. current account deficits may mean permanent debt, permanent foreign ownership, or large sacrifices of future consumption.

We say "may mean" above because the foreign lending to U.S. firms and foreign investment in the United States increases the U.S. capital stock. U.S. production capacity therefore might increase more rapidly than otherwise because of a large surplus on the capital account. Faster increases in production capacity and real GDP enhance the economy's ability to service foreign debt and buy back real capital, if that is desired.

In short, U.S. trade deficits are a mixed blessing. Their long-term impacts are largely unknown.

Speculation in Currency Markets

Are Speculators a Negative or a Positive Influence in Currency Markets and International Trade?

Most people buy foreign currency to facilitate the purchase of goods or services from another country. A U.S. importer buys Japanese yen to purchase Japanese autos. A Hong Kong financial investor purchases Australian dollars to invest in the Australian stock market. But there is another group of participants in the currency market—speculators—that buys and sells foreign currencies in the hope of reselling or rebuying them later at a profit.

Contributing to Exchange-Rate Fluctuations Speculators were much in the news in late 1997 and 1998 when they were widely accused of driving down the values of the South Korean won, Thailand baht, Ma-

laysian ringgit, and Indonesian rupiah. The value of these currencies fell by as much as 50 percent within 1 month, and speculators undoubtedly contributed to the swiftness of those declines. The expectation of currency depreciation (or appreciation) can be self-fulfilling. If speculators, for example, expect the Indonesian rupiah to be devalued or to depreciate, they quickly sell rupiah and buy currencies that they think will increase in relative value. The sharp increase in the supply of rupiah indeed reduces its value; this reduction then may trigger further selling of rupiah in expectation of further declines in its value.

But changed economic realities, not speculation, are normally the underlying causes of changes in currency values. That was largely the case with the southeast Asian countries in which actual and threatened bankruptcies in the financial and manufacturing sectors undermined confidence in the strength of the currencies. Anticipating the eventual declines in currency values, speculators simply hastened those declines. That is, the declines in value probably would have occurred with or without speculators.

Moreover, on a daily basis, speculation clearly has positive effects in foreign exchange markets.

Smoothing Out Short-Term Fluctuations in Currency Prices When temporarily weak demand or strong supply reduces a currency's value, speculators quickly buy the currency, adding to its demand and strengthening its value. When temporarily strong demand or weak supply increases a currency's value, speculators sell the currency. That selling increases the supply of the currency and

reduces its value. In this way speculators smooth out supply and demand, and thus exchange rates, over short time periods. This day-to-day exchange-rate stabilization aids international trade.

Absorbing Risk Speculators also absorb risk that others do not want to bear. Because of potential adverse changes in exchange rates, international transactions are riskier than domestic transactions. Suppose AnyTime, a hypothetical retailer, signs a contract with a Swiss manufacturer to buy 10,000 Swatch watches to be delivered in 3 months. The stipulated price is 75 Swiss francs per watch, which in dollars is $50 per watch at the present exchange rate of, say, $1 = 1.5 francs. AnyTime's total bill for the 10,000 watches will be $500,000 (= 750,000 francs).

But if the Swiss franc were to appreciate, say, to $1 = 1 franc, the dollar price per watch would rise from $50 to $75 and AnyTime would owe $750,000 for the watches (= 750,000 francs). AnyTime may reduce the risk of such an unfavorable exchange-rate fluctuation by hedging in the futures market. Hedging is an action by a buyer or a seller to protect against a change in future prices. The futures market is a market in which currencies are bought and sold at prices fixed now, for delivery at a specified date in the future.

AnyTime can purchase the needed 750,000 francs at the current $1 = 1.5 francs exchange rate, but with delivery in 3 months when the Swiss watches are delivered. And here is where speculators come in. For a price determined in the futures market, they agree to deliver the 750,000 francs to AnyTime in 3 months at the $1 = 1.5 francs exchange rate, regardless of the exchange rate then. The speculators need not own francs when the agreement is made. If the Swiss franc depreciates to, say, $1 = 2 francs in this period, the speculators profit. They can buy the 750,000 francs stipulated in the contract for $375,000, pocketing the difference between that amount and the $500,000 AnyTime has agreed to pay for the 750,000 francs. If the Swiss franc appreciates, the speculators, but not AnyTime, suffer a loss.

The amount AnyTime must pay for this "exchange-rate insurance" will depend on how the market views the likelihood of the franc depreciating, appreciating, or staying constant over the 3-month period. As in all competitive markets, supply and demand determine the price of the futures contract.

The futures market thus eliminates much of the exchange-rate risk associated with buying foreign goods for future delivery. Without it, AnyTime might have decided against importing Swiss watches. But the futures market and currency speculators greatly increase the likelihood that the transaction will occur. Operating through the futures market, speculation promotes international trade.

In short, although speculators in currency markets occasionally contribute to swings in exchange rates, on a day-to-day basis they play a positive role in currency markets.

SUMMARY

1. U.S. exports create a foreign demand for dollars and make a supply of foreign exchange available to the United States. Conversely, U.S. imports create a demand for foreign exchange and make a supply of dollars available to foreigners. Generally, a nation's exports earn the foreign currencies needed to pay for its imports.

2. The balance of payments records all international trade and financial transactions taking place between a given nation and the rest of the world. The balance on goods and services (the trade balance) compares exports and imports of both goods and services. The current account balance includes not only goods and services transactions but also net investment income and net transfers.

3. A deficit in the current account may be offset by a surplus in the capital account. Conversely, a surplus in the current account may be offset by a deficit in the capital account. A balance-of-payments deficit occurs when the sum of the current and capital accounts is negative. Such a deficit is financed with official reserves. A balance-of-payments surplus occurs when the sum of the current and capital accounts is positive. A payments surplus results in an increase in official reserves. The desirability of a balance-of-payments deficit or surplus depends on its size and its persistence.

4. Flexible or floating exchange rates between international currencies are determined by the demand for and supply of those currencies. Under flexible rates a currency will depreciate or appreciate as a result of changes in tastes, relative income changes, relative price changes, relative changes in real interest rates, and speculation.

5. The maintenance of fixed exchange rates requires adequate reserves to accommodate periodic payments deficits. If reserves are inadequate, nations must invoke protectionist trade policies, engage in exchange controls, or endure undesirable domestic macroeconomic adjustments.

6. The gold standard, a fixed-rate system, provided exchange-rate stability until its disintegration during the 1930s. Under this system, gold flows between nations precipitated sometimes painful changes in price, income, and employment levels in bringing about international equilibrium.

7. Under the Bretton Woods system, exchange rates were pegged to one another and were stable. Participating nations were obligated to maintain these rates by using stabilization funds, gold, or loans from the IMF. Persistent or "fundamental" payments deficits could be resolved by IMF-sanctioned currency devaluations.

8. Since 1971 the world's major nations have used a system of managed floating exchange rates. Market forces generally set rates, although governments intervene with varying frequency to alter their exchange rates.

9. Over the past several years the United States experienced large trade deficits. Causes include (a) faster growth of income in the United States than in some European nations, Canada, and Japan, resulting in expanding U.S. imports, and (b) a declining U.S. saving rate, which has produced a large capital account surplus and has freed U.S. income for spending on imports.

10. U.S. trade deficits have produced current increases in the living standards of U.S. consumers. The accompanying surpluses on the capital account have increased U.S. debt to the rest of the world and increased foreign ownership of assets in the United States. This greater foreign investment in the United States, however, has undoubtedly increased U.S. production possibilities.

TERMS AND CONCEPTS

balance of payments

current account

balance on goods and services

trade deficit

trade surplus

balance on current account

capital account

balance on capital account

official reserves

balance-of-payments deficits and surpluses

flexible- or floating-exchange-rate system

fixed exchange-rate system

purchasing-power-parity theory

currency interventions

exchange controls

gold standard

devaluation

Bretton Woods system

International Monetary Fund (IMF)

managed floating exchange rates

STUDY QUESTIONS

1. Explain how a U.S. automobile importer might finance a shipment of Toyotas from Japan. Trace the steps as to how a U.S. export of machinery to Italy might be financed. Explain: "U.S. exports earn supplies of foreign currencies that Americans can use to finance imports."

2. **Key Question** Indicate whether each of the following creates a demand for or a supply of European euros in foreign exchange markets:
   a. A U.S. airline firm purchases several Airbus planes assembled in France.
   b. A German automobile firm decides to build an assembly plant in South Carolina.
   c. A U.S. college student decides to spend a year studying at the Sorbonne in Paris.
   d. An Italian manufacturer ships machinery from one Italian port to another on a Liberian freighter.
   e. The U.S. economy grows faster than the French economy.
   f. A U.S. government bond held by a Spanish citizen matures, and the loan amount is paid back to that person.
   g. It is widely believed that the euro will depreciate in the near future.

3. **Key Question** Alpha's balance-of-payments data for 2001 are shown below. All figures are in billions of dollars. What are (a) the balance of trade, (b) the balance on goods and services, (c) the balance on current account, and (d) the balance on capital account? Does Alpha have a balance-of-payments deficit or surplus? Explain.

Goods exports	+ $40	Net transfers	+ $10
Goods imports	− 30	Foreign purchases	
Service exports	+ 15	of assets in the	
Service imports	− 10	United States	+ 10
Net investment income	− 5	U.S. purchases of	
		assets abroad	− 40
		Official reserves	+ 10

4. "A rise in the dollar price of yen necessarily means a fall in the yen price of dollars." Do you agree? Illustrate and elaborate: "The critical thing about exchange rates is that they provide a direct link between the prices of goods and services produced in all trading nations of the world." Explain the purchasing-power-parity theory of exchange rates.

5. Suppose that a Swiss watchmaker imports watch components from Sweden and exports watches to the United States. Also suppose the dollar depreciates,

and the Swedish krona appreciates, relative to the Swiss franc. Speculate as to how each would hurt the Swiss watchmaker.

6. **Key Question** Explain why the U.S. demand for Mexican pesos is downward-sloping and the supply of pesos to Americans is upward-sloping. Assuming a system of flexible exchange rates between Mexico and the United States, indicate whether each of the following would cause the Mexican peso to appreciate or depreciate:
   a. The United States unilaterally reduces tariffs on Mexican products.
   b. Mexico encounters severe inflation.
   c. Deteriorating political relations reduce American tourism in Mexico.
   d. The U.S. economy moves into a severe recession.
   e. The United States engages in a high-interest-rate monetary policy.
   f. Mexican products become more fashionable to U.S. consumers.
   g. The Mexican government encourages U.S. firms to invest in Mexican oil fields.
   h. The rate of productivity growth in the United States diminishes sharply.

7. Explain why you agree or disagree with the following statements:
   a. A country that grows faster than its major trading partners can expect the international value of its currency to depreciate.
   b. A nation whose interest rate is rising more rapidly than interest rates in other nations can expect the international value of its currency to appreciate.
   c. A country's currency will appreciate if its inflation rate is less than that of the rest of the world.

8. "Exports pay for imports. Yet in 2000 the nations of the world exported about $369 billion more worth of goods and services to the United States than they imported from the United States." Resolve the apparent inconsistency of these two statements.

9. **Key Question** Diagram a market in which the equilibrium dollar price of 1 unit of fictitious currency zee (Z) is $5 (the exchange rate is $5 = Z1). Then show on your diagram a decline in the demand for zee.
   a. Referring to your diagram, discuss the adjustment options the United States would have in maintaining the exchange rate at $5 = Z1 under a fixed-exchange-rate system.
   b. How would the U.S. balance-of-payments surplus that is created (by the decline in demand) get resolved under a system of flexible exchange rates?

10. Compare and contrast the Bretton Woods system of exchange rates with that of the gold standard. What caused the collapse of the gold standard? What caused the demise of the Bretton Woods system?

11. Describe what is meant by the term "managed float." Did the managed-float system precede or follow the adjustable-peg system? Explain.

12. What have been the major causes of the large U.S. trade deficits since 1992? What are the major benefits and costs associated with trade deficits? Explain: "A trade deficit means that a nation is receiving more goods and services from abroad than it is sending abroad." How can that be called "unfavorable"?

13. **(Last Word)** Suppose Winter Sports—a hypothetical French retailer of snowboards—wants to order 5000 snowboards made in the United States. The price per board is $200, the present exchange rate is 1 euro = $1, and payment is due in dollars when the boards are delivered in 3 months. Use a numerical example to explain why exchange-rate risk might make the French retailer hesitant to place the order. How might speculators absorb some of Winter Sports' risk?

14. **Web-Based Question:** *The U.S. balance on goods and services—what are the latest figures?* The U.S. Census Bureau reports the latest data on U.S. trade in goods and services at its website www.census.gov/indicator/www/ustrade.html. Over the past month, has the trade balance in goods and services improved (that is, yielded a smaller deficit or a larger surplus) or deteriorated? Is the relative trade strength of the United States compared to the rest of the world in goods or in services? Which product groups had the largest increases in exports? Which had the largest increases in imports?

15. **Web-Based Question:** *The yen-dollar exchange rate* The Federal Reserve Board of Governors provides exchange rates for various currencies for the last decade at www.federalreserve.gov/releases (Foreign Exchange Rates; Historical Data). Has the dollar appreciated, depreciated, or remained constant relative to the Canadian dollar, the European euro, the Japanese yen, the Swedish krona, and the Swiss franc over the past 5 years?

GLOSSARY

Note: Terms set in *italic* type are defined separately in this glossary.

ability-to-pay principle The idea that those who have greater *income* (or *wealth*) should pay a greater proportion of it as taxes than those who have less income (or wealth).

abstraction Elimination of irrelevant and noneconomic facts to obtain an *economic principle*.

acreage allotment program A pre-1996 government program that determined the total number of acres to be used in producing (reduced amounts of) various food and fiber products and allocated these acres among individual farmers. These farmers had to limit their plantings to the allotted number of acres to obtain *price supports* for their crops.

adjustable pegs The device used in the *Bretton Woods system* to alter *exchange rates* in an orderly way to eliminate persistent payments deficits and surpluses. Each nation defined its monetary unit in terms of (pegged it to) gold or the dollar, kept the *rate of exchange* for its money stable in the short run, and adjusted its rate in the long run when faced with international payments disequilibrium.

adverse selection problem A problem arising when information known to one party to a contract is not known to the other party, causing the latter to incur major costs. Example: Individuals who have the poorest health are most likely to buy health insurance.

advertising A seller's activities in communicating its message about its product to potential buyers.

affirmative action Policies and programs that establish targets of increased employment and promotion for women and minorities.

AFL-CIO An acronym for the American Federation of Labor–Congress of Industrial Organizations; the largest federation of *labor unions* in the United States.

agency shop A place of employment where the employer may hire either *labor union* members or nonmembers but where those who do not join the union must either pay union dues or donate an equivalent amount of money to a charity.

Alcoa case A 1945 case in which the courts ruled that the possession of monopoly power, no matter how reasonably that power had been used, was a violation of the antitrust laws; temporarily overturned the *rule of reason* applied in the *U.S. Steel case*.

allocative efficiency The apportionment of resources among firms and industries to obtain the production of the products most wanted by society (consumers); the output of each product at which its *marginal cost* and *price* or *marginal benefit* are equal.

antitrust laws Legislation (including the *Sherman Act* and *Clayton Act*) that prohibits anticompetitive business activities such as *price fixing*, bid rigging, monopolization, and *tying contracts*.

antitrust policy The use of the *antitrust laws* to promote *competition* and economic efficiency.

appreciation (of the dollar) An increase in the value of the dollar relative to the currency of another nation, so a dollar buys a larger amount of the foreign currency and thus of foreign goods.

asset Anything of monetary value owned by a firm or individual.

asymmetric information A situation where one party to a market transaction has much more information about a product or service than the other. The result may be an under- or overallocation of resources.

average fixed cost A firm's total *fixed cost* divided by output (the quantity of product produced).

average product The total output produced per unit of a resource employed (*total product* divided by the quantity of that employed resource).

average revenue Total revenue from the sale of a product divided by the quantity of the product sold (demanded); equal to the price at which the product is sold when all units of the product are sold at the same price.

average tax rate Total tax paid divided by total (taxable) income, as a percentage.

average total cost A firm's *total cost* divided by output (the quantity of product produced); equal to *average fixed cost* plus *average variable cost*.

average variable cost A firm's total *variable cost* divided by output (the quantity of product produced).

backflows The return of workers to the countries from which they originally migrated.

balance of payments (See *international balance of payments*.)

balance-of-payments deficit The amount by which the sum of the *balance on current account* and the *balance on capital account* is negative in a year.

balance-of-payments surplus   The amount by which the sum of the *balance on current account* and the *balance on capital account* is positive in a year.

balance on capital account   The foreign purchases of assets in the United States less American purchases of assets abroad in a year.

balance on current account   The exports of goods and services of a nation less its imports of goods and services plus its *net investment income* and *net transfers* in a year.

balance on goods and services   The exports of goods and services of a nation less its imports of goods and services in a year.

barrier to entry   Anything that artificially prevents the entry of firms into an industry.

barter   The exchange of one good or service for another good or service.

benefit-reduction rate   The percentage by which subsidy benefits in a *public assistance program* are reduced as earned income rises.

benefits-received principle   The idea that those who receive the benefits of goods and services provided by government should pay the taxes required to finance them.

bilateral monopoly   A market in which there is a single seller *(monopoly)* and a single buyer *(monopsony)*.

bond   A financial device through which a borrower (a firm or government) is obligated to pay the principal and interest on a loan at a specific date in the future.

brain drain   The emigration of highly educated, highly skilled workers from a country.

break-even income   The level of *disposable income* at which *households* plan to consume (spend) all their income and to save none of it; also, in an income transfer program, the level of earned income at which subsidy payments become zero.

break-even output   Any output at which a (competitive) firm's *total cost* and *total revenue* are equal; an output at which a firm has neither an *economic profit* nor a loss, at which it earns only a normal profit.

Bretton Woods system   The international monetary system developed after the Second World War in which *adjustable pegs* were employed, the *International Monetary Fund* helped stabilize foreign exchange rates, and gold and the dollar were used as *international monetary reserves.*

budget constraint   The limit that the size of a consumer's income (and the prices that must be paid for goods and services) imposes on the ability of that consumer to obtain goods and services.

budget line   A line that shows the different combinations of two products a consumer can purchase with a specific money income, given the products' prices.

business firm   (See *firm.*)

business unionism   Labor unionism that concerns itself with such practical and short-run objectives as higher wages, shorter hours, and improved working conditions.

capital   Human-made resources (buildings, machinery, and equipment) used to produce goods and services; goods that do not directly satisfy human wants; also called capital goods.

capital account   The section of a nation's *international balance-of-payments* statement that records the foreign purchases of assets in the United States (creating monetary inflows) and U.S. purchases of assets abroad (creating monetary outflows).

capital account deficit   A negative *balance on capital account.*

capital account surplus   A positive *balance on capital account.*

capital gain   The gain realized when securities or properties are sold for a price greater than the price paid for them.

capital goods   (See *capital.*)

capital-intensive commodity   A product that requires a relatively large amount of *capital* to be produced.

capitalism   An economic system in which property resources are privately owned and markets and prices are used to direct and coordinate economic activities.

capital stock   The total available *capital* in a nation.

cartel   A formal agreement among firms (or countries) in an industry to set the price of a product and establish the outputs of the individual firms (or countries) or to divide the market for the product geographically.

causation   A relationship in which the occurrence of one or more events brings about another event.

cease-and-desist order   An order from a court or government agency to a corporation or individual to stop engaging in a specified practice.

ceiling price   (See *price ceiling.*)

Celler-Kefauver Act   The Federal act of 1950 that amended the *Clayton Act* by prohibiting the acquisition of the assets of one firm by another when the effect would be less competition.

central economic planning   Government determination of the objectives of the economy and how resources will be directed to attain those goals.

ceteris paribus assumption   (See *other-things-equal assumption.*)

change in demand   A change in the *quantity demanded* of a good or service at every price; a shift of the *demand curve* to the left or right.

change in supply   A change in the *quantity supplied* of a good or service at every price; a shift of the *supply curve* to the left or right.

circular flow model The flow of resources from *households* to *firms* and of products from firms to households. These flows are accompanied by reverse flows of money from firms to households and from households to firms.

Civil Rights Act of 1964 Federal law that, in Title VII, outlaws *discrimination* based on race, color, religion, gender, or national origin in hiring, promoting, and compensating workers.

Clayton Act The Federal antitrust act of 1914 that strengthened the *Sherman Act* by making it illegal for firms to engage in certain specified practices.

closed economy An economy that neither exports nor imports goods and services.

closed shop A place of employment where only workers who are already members of a labor union may be hired.

Coase theorem The idea, first stated by economist Ronald Coase, that *spillover* problems may be resolved through private negotiations of the affected parties.

coincidence of wants A situation in which the good or service that one trader desires to obtain is the same as that which another trader desires to give up and an item that the second trader wishes to acquire is the same as that which the first trader desires to surrender.

COLA (See *cost-of-living adjustment*.)

collective bargaining The negotiation of labor contracts between *labor unions* and *firms* or government entities.

collective voice The function a *labor union* performs for its members as a group when it communicates their problems and grievances to management and presses management for a satisfactory resolution.

collusion A situation in which firms act together and in agreement (collude) to fix prices, divide a market, or otherwise restrict competition.

command system A method of organizing an economy in which property resources are publicly owned and government uses *central economic planning* to direct and coordinate economic activities; command economy.

communism (See *command system*.)

comparative advantage A lower relative or comparative cost than that of another producer.

compensating differences Differences in the *wages* received by workers in different jobs to compensate for nonmonetary differences in the jobs.

compensation to employees *Wages* and salaries plus *wage and salary supplements* paid by employers to workers.

competing goods (See *substitute goods*.)

competition The presence in a market of independent buyers and sellers competing with one another and the freedom of buyers and sellers to enter and leave the market.

competitive industry's short-run supply curve The horizontal summation of the short-run supply curves of the *firms* in a purely competitive industry (see *pure competition*); a curve that shows the total quantities offered for sale at various prices by the firms in an industry in the short run.

competitive labor market A resource market in which a large number of (noncolluding) firms demand a particular type of labor supplied by a large number of nonunion workers.

complementary goods Products and services that are used together. When the price of one falls, the demand for the other increases (and conversely).

concentration ratio The percentage of the total sales of an industry made by the four (or some other number) largest sellers in the industry.

conglomerate merger The merger of a *firm* in one *industry* with a firm in another industry (with a firm that is neither a supplier, customer, nor competitor).

conglomerates Firms that produce goods and services in two or more separate industries.

constant-cost industry An industry in which expansion by the entry of new firms has no effect on the prices firms in the industry must pay for resources and thus no effect on production costs.

consumer goods Products and services that satisfy human wants directly.

consumer sovereignty Determination by consumers of the types and quantities of goods and services that will be produced with the scarce resources of the economy; consumers' direction of production through their dollar votes.

consumer surplus The difference between what a consumer (or consumers) is willing to pay for an additional unit of a product or service and its market price; the triangular area below the demand curve and above the market price.

copayment The percentage of (say, health care) costs that an insured individual pays while the insurer pays the remainder.

copyright A legal protection provided to developers and publishers of books, computer software, videos, and musical compositions against the copying of their works by others.

corporate income tax A tax levied on the net income (profit) of corporations.

corporation A legal entity ("person") chartered by a state or the Federal government that is distinct and separate from the individuals who own it.

correlation A systematic and dependable association between two sets of data (two kinds of events); does not necessarily indicate causation.

cost-benefit analysis A comparison of the *marginal costs* of a government project or program with the *marginal benefits* to decide whether or not to employ resources in that project or program and to what extent.

cost-of-living adjustment (COLA) An automatic increase in the incomes (wages) of workers when inflation occurs; guaranteed by a collective bargaining contract between firms and workers.

cost ratio An equality showing the number of units of two products that can be produced with the same resources; the cost ratio 1 corn ≡ 3 olives shows that the resources required to produce 3 units of olives must be shifted to corn production to produce a unit of corn.

craft union A labor union that limits its membership to workers with a particular skill (craft).

creative destruction The hypothesis that the creation of new products and production methods simultaneously destroys the market power of existing monopolies.

credit An accounting item that increases the value of an asset (such as the foreign money owned by the residents of a nation).

cross elasticity of demand The ratio of the percentage change in *quantity demanded* of one good to the percentage change in the price of some other good. A positive coefficient indicates the two products are *substitute goods;* a negative coefficient indicates they are *complementary goods.*

crowding model of occupational discrimination A model of labor markets suggesting that *occupational discrimination* has kept many women and minorities out of high-paying occupations and forced them into a limited number of low-paying occupations.

currency appreciation (See *exchange-rate appreciation.*)

currency depreciation (See *exchange-rate depreciation.*)

currency intervention A government's buying and selling of its own currency or foreign currencies to alter international exchange rates.

current account The section in a nation's *international balance of payments* that records its exports and imports of goods and services, its *net investment income,* and its *net transfers.*

debit An accounting item that decreases the value of an asset (such as the foreign money owned by the residents of a nation).

declining industry An industry in which *economic profits* are negative (losses are incurred) and that will, therefore, decrease its output as firms leave it.

decreasing-cost industry An industry in which expansion through the entry of firms lowers the prices that firms in the industry must pay for resources and therefore decreases their production costs.

deductible The dollar sum of (for example, health care) costs that an insured individual must pay before the insurer begins to pay.

demand A schedule showing the amounts of a good or service that buyers (or a buyer) wish to purchase at various prices during some time period.

demand curve A curve illustrating *demand.*

dependent variable A variable that changes as a consequence of a change in some other (independent) variable; the "effect" or outcome.

depository institutions Firms that accept deposits of *money* from the public (businesses and persons); *commercial banks, savings and loan associations, mutual savings banks,* and *credit unions.*

depreciation (See *consumption of fixed capital.*)

depreciation (of the dollar) A decrease in the value of the dollar relative to another currency, so a dollar buys a smaller amount of the foreign currency and therefore of foreign goods.

derived demand The demand for a resource that depends on the demand for the products it helps to produce.

determinants of demand Factors other than price that determine the quantities demanded of a good or service.

determinants of supply Factors other than price that determine the quantities supplied of a good or service.

devaluation A decrease in the governmentally defined value of a currency.

developing countries (DVCs) Many countries of Africa, Asia, and Latin America that are characterized by lack of capital goods, use of nonadvanced technologies, low literacy rates, high unemployment, rapid population growth, and labor forces heavily committed to agriculture.

differentiated oligopoly An *oligopoly* in which the firms produce a *differentiated product.*

differentiated product A product that differs physically or in some other way from the similar products produced by other firms; a product such that buyers are not indifferent to the seller when the price charged by all sellers is the same.

diffusion The spread of an *innovation* through its widespread imitation.

dilemma of regulation The tradeoff faced by a *regulatory agency* in setting the maximum legal price a monopolist may charge: The *socially optimal price* is below *average total cost* (and either bankrupts the *firm* or requires that it be subsidized), while the higher, *fair-return price* does not produce *allocative efficiency.*

diminishing marginal returns (See *law of diminishing returns.*)

direct foreign investment   The building of new factories (or the purchase of existing capital) in a particular nation by corporations of other nations.

direct relationship   The relationship between two variables that change in the same direction, for example, product price and quantity supplied.

discrimination   The practice of according individuals or groups inferior treatment in hiring, occupational access, education and training, promotion, wage rates, or working conditions even though they have the same abilities, education and skills, and work experience as other workers.

discrimination coefficient   A measure of the cost or disutility of prejudice; the monetary amount an employer is willing to pay to hire a preferred worker rather than a nonpreferred worker.

diseconomies of scale   Increases in the *average total cost* of producing a product as the *firm* expands the size of its *plant* (its output) in the *long run*.

disposable income   *Personal income* less personal taxes; income available for *personal consumption expenditures* and *personal saving*.

dividends   Payments by a corporation of all or part of its profit to its stockholders (the corporate owners).

division of labor   The separation of the work required to produce a product into a number of different tasks that are performed by different workers; *specialization* of workers.

dollar votes   The "votes" that consumers and entrepreneurs cast for the production of consumer and capital goods, respectively, when they purchase those goods in product and resource markets.

domestic capital formation   The process of adding to a nation's stock of *capital* by saving and investing part of its own domestic output.

domestic price   The price of a good or service within a country, determined by domestic demand and supply.

double taxation   The taxation of both corporate net income (profits) and the *dividends* paid from this net income when they become the personal income of households.

dumping   The sale of products below cost in a foreign country or below the prices charged at home.

DuPont cellophane case   The antitrust case brought against DuPont in which the U.S. Supreme Court ruled (in 1956) that while DuPont had a monopoly in the narrowly defined market for cellophane, it did not monopolize the more broadly defined market for flexible packaging materials. It was thus not guilty of violating the *Sherman Act*.

durable good   A consumer good with an expected life (use) of 3 or more years.

earned-income tax credit   A refundable Federal tax credit for low-income working people designed to reduce poverty and encourage labor-force participation.

earnings   The money income received by a worker; equal to the *wage* (rate) multiplied by the amount of time worked.

economic analysis   The process of deriving *economic principles* from relevant economic facts.

economic concentration   A description or measure of the degree to which an industry is dominated by one or a handful of firms or is characterized by many firms. (See *concentration ratio*.)

economic cost   A payment that must be made to obtain and retain the services of a *resource*; the income a firm must provide to a resource supplier to attract the resource away from an alternative use; equal to the quantity of other products that cannot be produced when resources are instead used to make a particular product.

economic efficiency   The use of the minimum necessary resources to obtain the socially optimal amounts of goods and services; entails both *productive efficiency* and *allocative efficiency*.

economic growth   (1) An outward shift in the *production possibilities curve* that results from an increase in resource supplies or quality or an improvement in *technology*; (2) an increase of real output (*gross domestic product*) or real output per capita.

economic law   An *economic principle* that has been tested and retested and has stood the test of time.

economic model   A simplified picture of economic reality; an abstract generalization.

economic perspective   A viewpoint that envisions individuals and institutions making rational decisions by comparing the marginal benefits and marginal costs associated with their actions.

economic policy   A course of action intended to correct or avoid a problem.

economic principles   Widely accepted generalizations about the economic behavior of individuals and institutions.

economic profit   The *total revenue* of a firm less its *economic costs* (which include both *explicit costs* and *implicit costs*); also called "pure profit" and "above-normal profit."

economic regulation   (See *industrial regulation* and *social regulation*.)

economic rent   The price paid for the use of land and other natural resources, the supply of which is fixed (*perfectly inelastic*).

economic resources   The *land*, *labor*, *capital*, and *entrepreneurial ability* that are used in the production of goods and services; productive agents; factors of production.

economics   The social science dealing with the use of scarce resources to obtain the maximum satisfaction of society's virtually unlimited economic wants.

economic system   A particular set of institutional arrangements and a coordinating mechanism for solving the economizing problem; a method of organizing an economy, of which the *market system* and the *command system* are the two general types.

economic theory   A statement of a cause-effect relationship; when accepted by all economists, an *economic principle*.

economies of scale   Reductions in the *average total cost* of producing a product as the firm expands the size of plant (its output) in the *long run*; the economies of mass production.

economizing problem   The choices necessitated because society's economic wants for goods and services are unlimited but the *resources* available to satisfy these wants are limited (scarce).

efficiency loss of a tax   The loss of net benefits to society because a tax reduces the production and consumption of a taxed good below the level of allocative efficiency.

efficiency wage   A wage that minimizes wage costs per unit of output by encouraging greater effort or reducing turnover.

efficient allocation of resources   That allocation of an economy's resources among the production of different products that leads to the maximum satisfaction of consumers' wants, thus producing the socially optimal mix of output with society's scarce resources.

elastic demand   Product or resource demand whose *price elasticity* is greater than 1. This means the resulting change in *quantity demanded* is greater than the percentage change in *price*.

elasticity coefficient   The number obtained when the percentage change in *quantity demanded* (or supplied) is divided by the percentage change in the *price* of the commodity.

elasticity formula   (See *price elasticity of demand*.)

elastic supply   Product or resource supply whose price elasticity is greater than 1. This means the resulting change in quantity supplied is greater than the percentage change in price.

employment discrimination   Inferior treatment in hiring, promotions, work assignments, and such for a particular group of employees.

entitlement programs   Government programs such as *social insurance*, *food stamps*, *Medicare*, and *Medicaid* that guarantee particular levels of transfer payments or non-cash benefits to all who fit the programs' criteria.

entrepreneurial ability   The human resource that combines the other resources to produce a product, makes nonroutine decisions, innovates, and bears risks.

equality-versus-efficiency tradeoff   The decrease in *economic efficiency* that may accompany a decrease in *income inequality*; the presumption that some income inequality is required to achieve economic efficiency.

Equal Pay Act of 1963   Federal government legislation making it illegal to pay men and women different wage rates if they do equal work on jobs that require equal skill, effort, and responsibility and that are performed under similar working conditions.

equilibrium price   The *price* in a competitive market at which the *quantity demanded* and the *quantity supplied* are equal, there is neither a shortage nor a surplus, and there is no tendency for price to rise or fall.

equilibrium quantity   (1) The quantity demanded and supplied at the equilibrium price in a competitive market; (2) the profit-maximizing output of a firm.

euro   The common currency unit used by 12 European nations in the Euro Zone, which includes all nations of the *European Union* except Great Britain, Denmark, and Sweden.

European Union (EU)   An association of 15 European nations that has eliminated tariffs and import quotas among them, established common tariffs for goods imported from outside the member nations, allowed the free movement of labor and capital among them, and created other common economic policies. Includes Austria, Belgium, Denmark, Finland, France, Germany, Great Britain, Greece, Ireland, Italy, Luxembourg, the Netherlands, Portugal, Spain, and Sweden.

excess capacity   Plant resources that are underused when imperfectly competitive firms produce less output than that associated with achieving minimum average total cost.

exchange control   (See *foreign exchange control*.)

exchange rate   The *rate of exchange* of one nation's currency for another nation's currency.

exchange-rate appreciation   An increase in the value of a nation's currency in foreign exchange markets; an increase in the *rate of exchange* for foreign currencies.

exchange-rate depreciation   A decrease in the value of a nation's currency in foreign exchange markets; a decrease in the *rate of exchange* for foreign currencies.

exchange-rate determinant   Any factor other than the *rate of exchange* that determines a currency's demand and supply in the *foreign exchange market*.

excise tax   A tax levied on the production of a specific product or on the quantity of the product purchased.

exclusion principle   The ability to exclude those who do not pay for a product from receiving its benefits.

exclusive unionism The practice of a *labor union* of restricting the supply of skilled union labor to increase the wages received by union members; the policies typically employed by a *craft union*.

exhaustive expenditure An expenditure by government resulting directly in the employment of *economic resources* and in the absorption by government of the goods and services those resources produce; a *government purchase*.

exit mechanism The process of leaving a job and searching for another one as a means of improving one's working conditions.

expanding industry An industry whose firms earn *economic profits* and for which an increase in output occurs as new firms enter the industry.

expectations The anticipations of consumers, firms, and others about future economic conditions.

expected rate of return The increase in profit a firm anticipates it will obtain by purchasing capital (or engaging in research and development); expressed as a percentage of the total cost of the investment (or R&D) activity.

explicit cost The monetary payment a *firm* must make to an outsider to obtain a *resource*.

exports Goods and services produced in a nation and sold to buyers in other nations.

export subsidies Government payments to domestic producers to enable them to reduce the *price* of a good or service to foreign buyers.

export supply curve An upward-sloping curve that shows the amount of a product that domestic firms will export at each *world price* that is above the *domestic price*.

export transactions A sale of a good or service that increases the amount of foreign currency flowing to a nation's citizens, firms, and government.

external benefit (See *spillover benefit*.)

external cost (See *spillover cost*.)

external debt Private or public debt owed to foreign citizens, firms, and institutions.

externality (See *spillover*.)

factors of production *Economic resources: land, capital, labor,* and *entrepreneurial ability*.

fair-return price The price of a product that enables its producer to obtain a *normal profit* and that is equal to the *average total cost* of producing it.

fallacy of composition The false notion that what is true for the individual (or part) is necessarily true for the group (or whole).

fallacy of limited decisions The false notion that there are a limited number of economic decisions to be made

and thus, if government makes more decisions, there will be fewer private decisions to render.

farm problem The fact that technological advance, coupled with a price-inelastic and relatively constant demand, has made agriculture a *declining industry*; also, the tendency for farm income to fluctuate sharply from year to year.

Federal government The government of the United States, as distinct from the state and local governments.

Federal Trade Commission (FTC) The commission of five members established by the *Federal Trade Commission Act* of 1914 to investigate unfair competitive practices of firms, to hold hearings on the complaints of such practices, and to issue *cease-and-desist orders* when firms were found to engage in such practices.

Federal Trade Commission Act The Federal act of 1914 that established the *Federal Trade Commission*.

financial capital (See *money capital*.)

firm An organization that employs resources to produce a good or service for profit and owns and operates one or more *plants*.

fiscal federalism The system of transfers (grants) by which the Federal government shares its revenues with state and local governments.

fiscal policy Changes in government spending and tax collections designed to achieve a full-employment and noninflationary domestic output; also called *discretionary fiscal policy*.

fixed cost Any cost that in total does not change when the *firm* changes its output; the cost of *fixed resources*.

fixed exchange rate A *rate of exchange* that is set in some way and therefore prevented from rising or falling with changes in currency supply and demand.

fixed resource Any resource whose quantity cannot be changed by a firm in the *short run*.

flexible exchange rate A *rate of exchange* determined by the international demand for and supply of a nation's money; a rate free to rise or fall (to float).

floating exchange rate (See *flexible exchange rate*.)

food-stamp program A program permitting low-income persons to purchase for less than their retail value, or to obtain without cost, coupons that can be exchanged for food items at retail stores.

foreign competition (See *import competition*.)

foreign exchange control The control a government may exercise over the quantity of foreign currency demanded by its citizens and firms and over the *rates of exchange* in order to limit its *outpayments* to its *inpayments* (to eliminate a *payments deficit*).

foreign exchange market   A market in which the money (currency) of one nation can be used to purchase (can be exchanged for) the money of another nation.

foreign exchange rate   (See *rate of exchange*.)

Four Fundamental Questions (of economics)   The four questions that every economy must answer: what to produce, how to produce it, how to divide the total output, and how to ensure economic flexibility.

freedom of choice   The freedom of owners of property resources to employ or dispose of them as they see fit, of workers to enter any line of work for which they are qualified, and of consumers to spend their incomes in a manner that they think is appropriate.

freedom of enterprise   The freedom of *firms* to obtain economic resources, to use those resources to produce products of the firm's own choosing, and to sell their products in markets of their choice.

"Freedom to Farm" Act   A law passed in 1996 that revamped 60 years of U.S. farm policy by ending *price supports* and *acreage allotments* for wheat, corn, barley, oats, sorghum, rye, cotton, and rice.

free-rider problem   The inability of potential providers of an economically desirable but indivisible good or service to obtain payment from those who benefit, because the *exclusion principle* is not applicable.

free trade   The absence of artificial (government-imposed) barriers to trade among individuals and firms in different nations.

fringe benefits   The rewards other than *wages* that employees receive from their employers and that include pensions, medical and dental insurance, paid vacations, and sick leaves.

full employment   (1) The use of all available resources to produce want-satisfying goods and services; (2) the situation in which the *unemployment rate* is equal to the full-employment unemployment rate and there is frictional and structural but no cyclical unemployment (and the real output of the economy equals potential real output).

full production   Employment of available resources so that the maximum amount of (or total value of) goods and services is produced; occurs when both *productive efficiency* and *allocative efficiency* are realized.

functional distribution of income   The manner in which *national income* is divided among the functions performed to earn it (or the kinds of resources provided to earn it); the division of national income into wages and salaries, proprietors' income, corporate profits, interest, and rent.

gains from trade   The extra output that trading partners obtain through specialization of production and exchange of goods and services.

game theory   A means of analyzing the pricing behavior of oligopolists that uses the theory of strategy associated with games such as chess and bridge.

GDP   (See *gross domestic product*.)

General Agreement on Tariffs and Trade (GATT)   The international agreement reached in 1947 in which 23 nations agreed to give equal and nondiscriminatory treatment to one another, to reduce tariff rates by multinational negotiations, and to eliminate *import quotas*. It now includes most nations and has become the *World Trade Organization*.

generalization   Statement of the nature of the relationship between two or more sets of facts.

gold standard   A historical system of fixed exchange rates in which nations defined their currencies in terms of gold, maintained a fixed relationship between their stocks of gold and their money supplies, and allowed gold to be freely exported and imported.

government failure   Inefficiencies in resource allocation caused by problems in the operation of the public sector (government), specifically, rent-seeking pressure by special-interest groups, shortsighted political behavior, limited and bundled choices, and bureaucratic inefficiencies.

government purchases   Expenditures by government for goods and services that government consumes in providing public goods and for public (or social) capital that has a long lifetime; the expenditures of all governments in the economy for those final goods and services.

government transfer payment   The disbursement of money (or goods and services) by government for which government receives no currently produced good or service in return.

grievance procedure   The method used by a *labor union* and a *firm* to settle disputes that arise during the life of the collective bargaining agreement between them.

gross domestic product (GDP)   The total market value of all goods and services produced annually within the boundaries of the United States, whether by U.S. or foreign-supplied resources.

G-7 nations   A group of seven major industrial nations (the United States, Japan, Germany, United Kingdom, France, Italy, and Canada) whose leaders meet regularly to discuss common economic problems and try to coordinate economic policies (recently has also included Russia, making it unofficially the G-8).

guiding function of prices   The ability of price changes to bring about changes in the quantities of products and resources demanded and supplied.

health maintenance organizations (HMOs)   Health care providers that contract with employers, insurance companies, labor unions, or government units to provide health care for their workers or others who are insured.

Herfindahl index A measure of the concentration and competitiveness of an industry; calculated as the sum of the squared percentage market shares of the individual firms in the industry.

homogeneous oligopoly An *oligopoly* in which the firms produce a *standardized product.*

horizontal axis The "left-right" or "west-east" axis on a graph or grid.

horizontal merger The merger into a single *firm* of two firms producing the same product and selling it in the same geographic market.

household An economic unit (of one or more persons) that provides the economy with resources and uses the income received to purchase goods and services that satisfy economic wants.

human capital The accumulation of prior investments in education, training, health, and other factors that increase productivity.

human capital discrimination The denial of equal access to productivity-enhancing education and training to members of particular groups.

human capital investment Any expenditure undertaken to improve the education, skills, health, or mobility of workers, with an expectation of greater productivity and thus a positive return on the investment.

hypothesis A tentative explanation of cause and effect that requires testing.

illegal immigrant A person who enters a country unlawfully for the purpose of residing there.

IMF (See *International Monetary Fund.*)

immobility The inability or unwillingness of a worker to move from one geographic area or occupation to another or from a lower-paying job to a higher-paying job.

imperfect competition All market structures except *pure competition*; includes *monopoly, monopolistic competition,* and *oligopoly.*

implicit cost The monetary income a *firm* sacrifices when it uses a resource it owns rather than supplying the resource in the market; equal to what the resource could have earned in the best-paying alternative employment; includes a *normal profit.*

import competition The competition that domestic firms encounter from the products and services of foreign producers.

import demand curve A downsloping curve showing the amount of a product that an economy will import at each *world price* below the *domestic price.*

import quota A limit imposed by a nation on the quantity (or total value) of a good that may be imported during some period of time.

imports Spending by individuals, *firms,* and governments for goods and services produced in foreign nations.

import transaction The purchase of a good or service that decreases the amount of foreign money held by citizens, firms, and governments of a nation.

incentive function of price The inducement that an increase in the price of a commodity gives to sellers to make more of it available (and conversely for a decrease in price), and the inducement that an increase in price offers to buyers to purchase smaller quantities (and conversely for a decrease in price).

incentive pay plan A compensation structure that ties worker pay directly to performance. Such plans include piece rates, bonuses, *stock options,* commissions, and *profit sharing.*

inclusive unionism The practice of a labor union of including as members all workers employed in an industry.

income A flow of dollars (or purchasing power) per unit of time derived from the use of human or property resources.

income effect A change in the quantity demanded of a product that results from the change in *real income (purchasing power)* produced by a change in the product's price.

income elasticity of demand The ratio of the percentage change in the *quantity demanded* of a good to a percentage change in consumer income; measures the responsiveness of consumer purchases to income changes.

income inequality The unequal distribution of an economy's total income among households or families.

income-maintenance system A group of government programs designed to eliminate poverty and reduce inequality in the distribution of income.

increase in demand An increase in the *quantity demanded* of a good or service at every price; a shift of the *demand curve* to the right.

increase in supply An increase in the *quantity supplied* of a good or service at every price; a shift in the *supply curve* to the right.

increasing-cost industry An *industry* in which expansion through the entry of new firms raises the prices *firms* in the industry must pay for resources and therefore increases their production costs.

increasing marginal returns An increase in the *marginal product* of a resource as successive units of the resource are employed.

increasing returns An increase in a firm's output by a larger percentage than the percentage increase in its inputs.

independent goods   Products or services for which there is no relationship between the price of one and the demand for the other. When the price of one rises or falls, the demand for the other remains constant.

independent unions   U.S. unions that are not affiliated with the *AFL-CIO*.

independent variable   The variable causing a change in some other (dependent) variable.

indifference curve   A curve showing the different combinations of two products that yield the same satisfaction or *utility* to a consumer.

indifference map   A set of *indifference curves*, each representing a different level of *utility*, that together show the preferences of a consumer.

individual demand   The demand schedule or *demand curve* of a single buyer.

individual supply   The supply schedule or *supply curve* of a single seller.

industrially advanced countries (IACs)   High-income countries such as the United States, Canada, Japan, and the nations of western Europe that have highly developed *market economies* based on large stocks of technologically advanced capital goods and skilled labor forces.

industrial regulation   The older and more traditional type of regulation in which government is concerned with the prices charged and the services provided to the public in specific industries, in contrast to *social regulation*.

industrial union   A *labor union* that accepts as members all workers employed in a particular industry (or by a particular firm).

industry   A group of (one or more) *firms* that produce identical or similar products.

inelastic demand   Product or resource demand for which the *price elasticity coefficient* is less than 1. This means the resulting percentage change in *quantity demanded* is less than the percentage change in *price*.

inelastic supply   Product or resource supply for which the price elasticity coefficient is less than 1. The percentage change in *quantity supplied* is less than the percentage change in *price*.

inferior good   A good or service whose consumption declines as income rises (and conversely), price remaining constant.

inflation   A rise in the general level of prices in an economy.

information technology   New and more efficient methods of delivering and receiving information through use of computers, fax machines, wireless phones, and the Internet.

infrastructure   The capital goods usually provided by the *public sector* for the use of its citizens and firms (for example, highways, bridges, transit systems, wastewater treatment facilities, municipal water systems, and airports).

injunction   A court order directing a person or organization not to perform a certain act because the act would do irreparable damage to some other person or persons; a restraining order.

in-kind transfer   The distribution by government of goods and services to individuals for which the government receives no currently produced good or service in return; a *government transfer payment* made in goods or services rather than in money; also called a noncash transfer.

innovation   The first commercially successful introduction of a new product, the use of a new method of production, or the creation of a new form of business organization.

inpayments   The receipts of domestic or foreign money that individuals, firms, and governments of one nation obtain from the sale of goods and services abroad, as investment income and *remittances*, and from foreign purchases of its assets.

insurable risk   An event that would result in a loss but whose frequency of occurrence can be estimated with considerable accuracy. Insurance companies are willing to sell insurance against such losses.

interest   The payment made for the use of money (of borrowed funds).

interest income   Payments of income to those who supply the economy with *capital*.

interest rate   The annual rate at which interest is paid; a percentage of the borrowed amount.

interindustry competition   The competition for sales between the products of one industry and the products of another industry.

interlocking directorate   A situation where one or more members of the board of directors of a *corporation* are also on the board of directors of a competing corporation; illegal under the *Clayton Act*.

international balance of payments   A summary of all the transactions that took place between the individuals, firms, and government units of one nation and those of all other nations during a year.

international   balance-of-payments   deficit   (See *balance-of-payments deficit*.)

international   balance-of-payments   surplus   (See *balance-of-payments surplus*.)

international gold standard   (See *gold standard*.)

International Monetary Fund (IMF)   The international association of nations that was formed after World War II to make loans of foreign monies to nations with temporary *payments deficits* and, until the early 1970s, to administer the *adjustable pegs.* It now mainly makes loans to nations facing possible defaults on private and government loans.

international monetary reserves The foreign currencies and other assets such as gold that a nation can use to settle a *payments deficit.*

international value of the dollar The price that must be paid in foreign currency (money) to obtain one U.S. dollar.

invention The first discovery of a product or process through the use of imagination, ingenious thinking, and experimentation and the first proof that it will work.

inverse relationship The relationship between two variables that change in opposite directions, for example, product price and quantity demanded.

inverted-U theory A theory saying that, other things equal, *R&D* expenditures as a percentage of sales rise with industry concentration, reach a peak at a four-firm *concentration ratio* of about 50 percent, and then fall as concentration further increases.

investment Spending for the production and accumulation of *capital* and additions to inventories.

investment goods Same as *capital* or capital goods.

investment in human capital (See *human capital investment.*)

invisible hand The tendency of firms and resource suppliers that seek to further their own self-interests in competitive markets to also promote the interest of society.

kinked-demand curve The demand curve for a noncollusive oligopolist, which is based on the assumption that rivals will follow a price decrease and will ignore a price increase.

labor People's physical and mental talents and efforts that are used to help produce goods and services.

labor force Persons 16 years of age and older who are not in institutions and who are employed or are unemployed (and seeking work).

labor-force participation rate The percentage of the working-age population that is actually in the *labor force.*

labor-intensive commodity A product requiring a relatively large amount of *labor* to be produced.

labor productivity Total output divided by the quantity of labor employed to produce it; the *average product* of labor or output per hour of work.

labor theory of value (Web chapter) The Marxian idea that the economic value of any commodity is determined solely by the amount of labor that is required to produce it.

labor union A group of workers organized to advance the interests of the group (to increase wages, shorten the hours worked, improve working conditions, and so on).

laissez-faire capitalism (See *capitalism.*)

land Natural resources ("free gifts of nature") used to produce goods and services.

land-intensive commodity A product requiring a relatively large amount of land to be produced.

law of demand The principle that, other things equal, an increase in a product's price will reduce the quantity of it demanded, and conversely for a decrease in price.

law of diminishing marginal utility The principle that as a consumer increases the consumption of a good or service, the *marginal utility* obtained from each additional unit of the good or service decreases.

law of diminishing returns The principle that as successive increments of a *variable resource* are added to a *fixed resource,* the *marginal product* of the *variable resource* will eventually decrease.

law of increasing opportunity costs The principle that as the production of a good increases, the *opportunity cost* of producing an additional unit rises.

law of supply The principle that, other things equal, an increase in the price of a product will increase the quantity of it supplied, and conversely for a price decrease.

learning by doing Achieving greater *productivity* and lower *average total cost* through gains in knowledge and skill that accompany repetition of a task; a source of *economies of scale.*

least-cost combination of resources The quantity of each resource a firm must employ in order to produce a particular output at the lowest total cost; the combination at which the ratio of the *marginal product* of a resource to its *marginal resource cost* (to its *price* if the resource is employed in a competitive market) is the same for the last dollar spent on each of the resources employed.

legal cartel theory of regulation The hypothesis that some industries seek regulation or want to maintain regulation so that they may form or maintain a legal *cartel.*

legal immigrant A person who lawfully enters a country for the purpose of residing there.

liability A debt with a monetary value; an amount owed by a firm or an individual.

limited liability Restriction of the maximum loss to a predetermined amount for the owners (stockholders) of a *corporation.* The maximum loss is the amount they paid for their shares of stock.

limited-liability company An unincorporated business whose owners are protected by *limited liability.*

loanable funds *Money* available for lending and borrowing.

loanable funds theory of interest The concept that the supply of and demand for *loanable funds* determine the equilibrium rate of interest.

lockout An action by a firm that forbids workers to return to work until a new collective bargaining contract is signed; a means of imposing costs (lost wages) on union workers in a collective bargaining dispute.

logrolling The trading of votes by legislators to secure favorable outcomes on decisions concerning the provision of *public goods* and *quasi-public goods*.

long run (1) In *microeconomics*, a period of time long enough to enable producers of a product to change the quantities of all the resources they employ; period in which all resources and costs are variable and no resources or costs are fixed. (2) In *macroeconomics*, a period sufficiently long for nominal wages and other input prices to change in response to a change in the nation's price level.

long-run aggregate supply curve The *aggregate supply curve* associated with a time period in which input prices (especially *nominal wages*) are fully responsive to changes in the *price level*.

long-run competitive equilibrium The price at which firms in *pure competition* neither obtain *economic profit* nor suffer losses in the *long run* and the total quantity demanded and supplied are equal; a price equal to the minimum long-run *average total cost* of producing the product.

long-run farm problem The tendency for agriculture to be a declining industry as technological progress increases supply relative to an inelastic and slowly increasing demand.

long-run supply A schedule or curve showing the prices at which a *purely competitive industry* will make various quantities of the product available in the *long run*.

Lorenz curve A curve showing the distribution of income in an economy; the cumulated percentage of families (income receivers) is measured along the horizontal axis and cumulated percentage of income is measured along the vertical axis.

macroeconomics The part of economics concerned with the economy as a whole; with such major aggregates as the household, business, and government sectors; and with measures of the total economy.

managed floating exchange rate An *exchange rate* that is allowed to change (float) as a result of changes in currency supply and demand but at times is altered (managed) by governments via their buying and selling of particular currencies.

managerial-opposition hypothesis An explanation that attributes the relative decline of unionism in the United States to the increased and more aggressive opposition of management to unions.

managerial prerogatives The decisions that management of the firm has the sole right to make; often enumerated in the labor contract (work agreement) between a *labor union* and a *firm*.

marginal analysis The comparison of marginal ("extra" or "additional") benefits and marginal costs, usually for decision making.

marginal benefit The extra (additional) benefit of consuming 1 more unit of some good or service; the change in total benefit when 1 more unit is consumed.

marginal cost The extra (additional) cost of producing 1 more unit of output; equal to the change in *total cost* divided by the change in output (and, in the short run, to the change in total *variable cost* divided by the change in output).

marginal labor cost The amount total labor cost increases when a *firm* employs 1 additional unit of labor (the quantity of other resources employed remaining constant); equal to the change in the total cost of labor divided by the change in the quantity of labor employed.

marginal product The additional output produced when 1 additional unit of a resource is employed (the quantity of all other resources employed remaining constant); equal to the change in total product divided by the change in the quantity of a resource employed.

marginal productivity theory of income distribution The contention that the distribution of income is equitable when each unit of each resource receives a money payment equal to its marginal contribution to the firm's revenue (its *marginal revenue product*).

marginal rate of substitution The rate at which a consumer is prepared to substitute one good for another (from a given combination of goods) and remain equally satisfied (have the same *total utility*); equal to the slope of a consumer's *indifference curve* at each point on the curve.

marginal resource cost The amount the total cost of employing a *resource* increases when a firm employs 1 additional unit of the resource (the quantity of all other resources employed remaining constant); equal to the change in the *total cost* of the resource divided by the change in the quantity of the resource employed.

marginal revenue The change in *total revenue* that results from the sale of 1 additional unit of a firm's product; equal to the change in total revenue divided by the change in the quantity of the product sold.

marginal-revenue–marginal-cost approach A method of determining the total output where *economic profit* is a maximum (or losses a minimum) by comparing the *marginal revenue* and the *marginal cost* of each additional unit of output.

marginal revenue product The change in a firm's *total revenue* when it employs 1 additional unit of a resource (the quantity of all other resources employed remaining constant); equal to the change in total revenue divided by the change in the quantity of the resource employed.

marginal tax rate The tax rate paid on each additional dollar of income.

marginal utility   The extra *utility* a consumer obtains from the consumption of 1 additional unit of a good or service; equal to the change in total utility divided by the change in the quantity consumed.

market   Any institution or mechanism that brings together buyers (demanders) and sellers (suppliers) of a particular good or service.

market demand   (See *total demand*.)

market economy   An economy in which only the private decisions of consumers, resource suppliers, and firms determine how resources are allocated; the *market system*.

market failure   The inability of a market to bring about the allocation of resources that best satisfies the wants of society; in particular, the overallocation or underallocation of resources to the production of a particular good or service because of *spillovers* or informational problems or because markets do not provide desired *public goods*.

market for externality rights   A market in which firms can buy rights to discharge pollutants. The price of such rights is determined by the demand for the right to discharge pollutants and a *perfectly inelastic supply* of such rights (the latter determined by the quantity of discharges that the environment can assimilate).

market period   A period in which producers of a product are unable to change the quantity produced in response to a change in its price and in which there is a *perfectly inelastic supply*.

market system   All the product and resource markets of a *market economy* and the relationships among them; a method that allows the prices determined in those markets to allocate the economy's scarce resources and to communicate and coordinate the decisions made by consumers, firms, and resource suppliers.

median-voter model   The theory that under majority rule the median (middle) voter will be in the dominant position to determine the outcome of an election.

Medicaid   A Federal program that helps finance the medical expenses of individuals covered by the *Supplemental Security Income (SSI)* and *Temporary Assistance for Needy Families (TANF)* programs.

Medicare   A Federal program that is financed by *payroll taxes* and provides for (1) compulsory hospital insurance for senior citizens and (2) low-cost voluntary insurance to help older Americans pay physicians' fees.

medium of exchange   Any item sellers generally accept and buyers generally use to pay for a good or service; *money*; a convenient means of exchanging goods and services without engaging in *barter*.

merger   The combination of two (or more) firms into a single firm.

microeconomics   The part of economics concerned with such individual units as *industries*, *firms*, and *households* and

with individual markets, specific goods and services, and product and resource prices.

minimum efficient scale   The lowest level of output at which a firm can minimize long-run *average total cost*.

minimum wage   The lowest *wage* employers may legally pay for an hour of work.

monetary policy   A central bank's changing of the *money supply* to influence interest rates and assist the economy in achieving price stability, full employment, and economic growth.

money   Any item that is generally acceptable to sellers in exchange for goods and services.

money capital   Money available to purchase *capital*; simply *money*, as defined by economists.

money income   (See *nominal income*.)

monopolistic competition   A market structure in which many firms sell a *differentiated product*, into which entry is relatively easy, in which the firm has some control over its product price, and in which there is considerable *nonprice competition*.

monopoly   A market structure in which the number of sellers is so small that each seller is able to influence the total supply and the price of the good or service. (Also see *pure monopoly*.)

monopsony   A market structure in which there is only a single buyer of a good, service, or resource.

moral hazard problem   The possibility that individuals or institutions will change their behavior as the result of a contract or agreement. Example: A bank whose deposits are insured against loss may make riskier loans and investments.

most-favored-nation (MFN) status   An agreement by the United States to allow some other nation's *exports* into the United States at the lowest tariff level levied by the United States, then or at any later time.

MR = MC rule   The principle that a firm will maximize its profit (or minimize its losses) by producing the output at which *marginal revenue* and *marginal cost* are equal, provided product price is equal to or greater than *average variable cost*.

MRP = MRC rule   The principle that to maximize profit (or minimize losses), a firm should employ the quantity of a resource at which its *marginal revenue product* (MRP) is equal to its *marginal resource cost* (MRC), the latter being the wage rate in pure competition.

multinational corporations   Firms that own production facilities in two or more countries and produce and sell their products globally.

mutual interdependence   A situation in which a change in price strategy (or in some other strategy) by one firm will affect the sales and profits of another firm (or other firms). Any firm that makes such a change can expect the other rivals to react to the change.

mutually exclusive goals Two or more goals that conflict and cannot be achieved simultaneously.

national health insurance (NHI) A proposed program in which the Federal government would provide a basic package of health care to all citizens at no direct charge or at a low cost-sharing level. Financing would be out of general tax revenues.

National Labor Relations Act (Wagner Act of 1935) As amended, the basic labor-relations law in the United States; defines the legal rights of unions and management and identifies unfair union and management labor practices; established the *National Labor Relations Board*.

National Labor Relations Board (NLRB) The board established by the *National Labor Relations Act* of 1935 to investigate unfair labor practices, issue *cease-and-desist orders*, and conduct elections among employees to determine if they wish to be represented by a *labor union*.

natural monopoly An industry in which *economies of scale* are so great that a single firm can produce the product at a lower average total cost than would be possible if more than one firm produced the product.

negative relationship (See *inverse relationship*.)

net exports *Exports* minus *imports*.

net foreign factor income Payments by a nation of resource income to the rest of the world minus receipts of resource income from the rest of the world.

net investment income The interest and dividend income received by the residents of a nation from residents of other nations less the interest and dividend payments made by the residents of that nation to the residents of other nations.

net transfers The personal and government transfer payments made by one nation to residents of foreign nations less the personal and government transfer payments received from residents of foreign nations.

network effects Increases in the value of a product to each user, including existing users, as the total number of users rises.

net worth The total *assets* less the total *liabilities* of a firm or an individual; for a firm, the claims of the owners against the firm's total assets; for an individual, his or her wealth.

New Economy The label attached by some economists and the popular press to the U.S. economy since 1995. The main characteristics are substantially faster *productivity growth* and *economic growth*, caused by rapid technological advance and the emergence of the global economy.

NLRB (See *National Labor Relations Board*.)

nominal wage The amount of money received by a worker per unit of time (hour, day, etc.); money wage.

noncash transfer A *government transfer payment* in the form of goods and services rather than money, for example, food stamps, housing assistance, and job training; also called in-kind transfers.

noncollusive oligopoly An *oligopoly* in which the firms do not act together and in agreement to determine the price of the product and the output that each firm will produce.

noncompeting groups Collections of workers in the economy who do not compete with each other for employment because the skill and training of the workers in one group are substantially different from those of the workers in other groups.

nondurable good A *consumer good* with an expected life (use) of less than 3 years.

nonexhaustive expenditure An expenditure by government that does not result directly in the employment of economic resources or the production of goods and services; see *government transfer payment*.

nonprice competition Competition based on distinguishing one's product by means of *product differentiation* and then *advertising* the distinguished product to consumers.

nontariff barriers All barriers other than *protective tariffs* that nations erect to impede international trade, including *import quotas*, licensing requirements, unreasonable product-quality standards, unnecessary bureaucratic detail in customs procedures, and so on.

normal good A good or service whose consumption increases when income increases and falls when income decreases, price remaining constant.

normal profit The payment made by a firm to obtain and retain *entrepreneurial ability;* the minimum income entrepreneurial ability must receive to induce it to perform entrepreneurial functions for a firm.

normative economics The part of economics involving value judgments about what the economy should be like; focused on which economic goals and policies should be implemented; policy economics.

North American Free Trade Agreement (NAFTA) A 1993 agreement establishing, over a 15-year period, a free-trade zone composed of Canada, Mexico, and the United States.

OASDHI (See *Old Age, Survivors, and Disability Health Insurance*.)

occupational discrimination The arbitrary restriction of particular groups from entering the more desirable, higher-paying occupations.

occupational licensure The laws of state or local governments that require that a worker satisfy certain specified requirements and obtain a license from a licensing board before engaging in a particular occupation.

occupational segregation The crowding of women or minorities into less desirable, lower-paying occupations.

official reserves Foreign currencies owned by the central bank of a nation.

Old Age, Survivors, and Disability Health Insurance (OASDHI) The social program in the United States financed by Federal *payroll taxes* on employers and employees and designed to replace the *earnings* lost when workers retire, die, or become unable to work.

oligopoly A market structure in which a few firms sell either a *standardized* or *differentiated product*, into which entry is difficult, in which the firm has limited control over product price because of *mutual interdependence* (except when there is collusion among firms), and in which there is typically *nonprice competition.*

oligopsony A market in which there are only a few buyers.

OPEC (See *Organization of Petroleum Exporting Countries.*)

open economy An economy that exports and imports goods and services.

open-market operations The buying and selling of U.S. government securities by the *Federal Reserve Banks* for purposes of carrying out *monetary policy.*

open shop A place of employment in which the employer may hire nonunion workers and the workers need not become members of a *labor union.*

opportunity cost The amount of other products that must be forgone or sacrificed to produce a unit of a product.

Organization of Petroleum Exporting Countries (OPEC) A cartel of 11 oil-producing countries (Algeria, Indonesia, Iran, Iraq, Kuwait, Libya, Nigeria, Qatar, Saudi Arabia, Venezuela, and the UAE) that controls the quantity and price of crude oil exported by its members and that accounts for 60 percent of the world's export of oil.

other-things-equal assumption The assumption that factors other than those being considered are held constant.

outpayments The expenditures of domestic or foreign currency that the individuals, firms, and governments of one nation make to purchase goods and services, for *remittances*, to pay investment income, and for purchases of foreign assets.

output effect The situation in which an increase in the price of one input will increase a firm's production costs and reduce its level of output, thus reducing the demand for other inputs; conversely for a decrease in the price of the input.

paradox of voting A situation where paired-choice voting by majority rule fails to provide a consistent ranking of society's preferences for *public goods* or services.

parity concept The idea that year after year a specific output of a farm product should enable a farmer to acquire a constant amount of nonagricultural goods and services.

parity ratio The ratio of the price received by farmers from the sale of an agricultural commodity to the prices of other goods paid by them; usually expressed as a percentage; used as a rationale for *price supports.*

partnership An unincorporated firm owned and operated by two or more persons.

patent An exclusive right given to inventors to produce and sell a new product or machine for 20 years from the time of patent application.

payments deficit (See *balance-of-payments deficit.*)

payments surplus (See *balance-of-payments surplus.*)

payroll tax A tax levied on employers of labor equal to a percentage of all or part of the wages and salaries paid by them and on employees equal to a percentage of all or part of the wages and salaries received by them.

$P = MC$ rule The principle that a purely competitive firm will maximize its profit or minimize its loss by producing that output at which the *price* of the product is equal to *marginal cost*, provided that price is equal to or greater than *average variable cost* in the short run and equal to or greater than *average total cost* in the long run.

per capita GDP *Gross domestic product* (GDP) per person; the average GDP of a population.

per capita income A nation's total income per person; the average income of a population.

perfectly elastic demand Product or resource demand in which *quantity demanded* can be of any amount at a particular product *price*; graphs as a horizontal *demand curve.*

perfectly elastic supply Product or resource supply in which *quantity supplied* can be of any amount at a particular product or resource *price*; graphs as a horizontal *supply curve.*

perfectly inelastic demand Product or resource demand in which *price* can be of any amount at a particular quantity of the product or resource demanded; *quantity demanded* does not respond to a change in price; graphs as a vertical *demand curve.*

perfectly inelastic supply Product or resource supply in which *price* can be of any amount at a particular quantity of the product or resource demanded; *quantity supplied* does not respond to a change in price; graphs as a vertical *supply curve.*

per se violations Collusive actions, such as attempts by firms to fix prices or divide a market, that are violations of the *antitrust laws*, even if the actions themselves are unsuccessful.

personal consumption expenditures   The expenditures of *households* for *durable* and *nondurable consumer goods* and *services.*

personal distribution of income   The manner in which the economy's *personal* or *disposable income* is divided among different income classes or different households or families.

personal income   The earned and unearned income available to resource suppliers and others before the payment of *personal taxes.*

personal income tax   A tax levied on the *taxable income* of individuals, households, and unincorporated firms.

Personal Responsibility Act   A 1996 law that eliminated the Federal government's six-decade-long guarantee of cash assistance for poor families, whether adults in the family work or not; sets a limit of 5 years on receiving *Temporary Assistance for Needy Families (TANF)* benefits and requires that able-bodied adults work after 2 years to continue to receive public assistance.

personal saving   The *personal income* of households less *personal taxes* and *personal consumption expenditures; disposable income* not spent for *consumer goods.*

per-unit production cost   The average production cost of a particular level of output; total input cost divided by units of output.

plant   A physical establishment that performs one or more functions in the production, fabrication, and distribution of goods and services.

"play or pay"   A means of expanding health insurance coverage by requiring that employers either provide insurance for their workers or pay a special *payroll tax* to finance insurance for noncovered workers.

policy economics   The formulation of courses of action to bring about desired economic outcomes or to prevent undesired occurrences.

positive economics   The analysis of facts or data to establish scientific generalizations about economic behavior.

positive relationship   A direct relationship between two variables.

post hoc, ergo propter hoc fallacy   The false belief that when one event precedes another, the first event must have caused the second event.

potential competition   The new competitors that may be induced to enter an industry if firms now in that industry are receiving large *economic profits.*

poverty   A situation in which the basic needs of an individual or family exceed the means to satisfy them.

poverty rate   The percentage of the population with incomes below the official poverty income levels that are established by the Federal government.

preferred provider organization (PPO)   An arrangement in which doctors and hospitals agree to provide health care to insured individuals at rates negotiated with an insurer.

price   The amount of money needed to buy a particular good, service, or resource.

price ceiling   A legally established maximum price for a good or service.

price discrimination   The selling of a product to different buyers at different prices when the price differences are not justified by differences in cost.

price elasticity of demand   The ratio of the percentage change in *quantity demanded* of a product or resource to the percentage change in its *price;* a measure of the responsiveness of buyers to a change in the price of a product or resource.

price elasticity of supply   The ratio of the percentage change in *quantity supplied* of a product or resource to the percentage change in its *price;* the responsiveness of producers to a change in the price of a product or resource.

price fixing   The conspiring by two or more firms to set the price of their products; an illegal practice under the *Sherman Act.*

price floor   A legally determined price above the *equilibrium price.*

price leadership   An informal method that firms in an *oligopoly* may employ to set the price of their product: One firm (the leader) is the first to announce a change in price, and the other firms (the followers) soon announce identical or similar changes.

price-level stability   A steadiness of the price level from one period to the next; zero or low annual inflation; also called "price stability."

price maker   A seller (or buyer) of a product or resource that is able to affect the product or resource price by changing the amount it sells (or buys).

price support   A minimum price that government allows sellers to receive for a good or service; a legally established or maintained minimum price.

price taker   A seller (or buyer) of a product or resource that is unable to affect the price at which a product or resource sells by changing the amount it sells (or buys).

price war   Successive and continued decreases in the prices charged by firms in an oligopolistic industry. Each firm lowers its price below rivals' prices, hoping to increase its sales and revenues at its rivals' expense.

principal-agent problem   A conflict of interest that occurs when agents (workers or managers) pursue their own objectives to the detriment of the principals' (stockholders') goals.

private good   A good or service that is subject to the *exclusion principle* and is provided by privately owned firms to consumers who are willing to pay for it.

private property   The right of private persons and firms to obtain, own, control, employ, dispose of, and bequeath *land*, *capital*, and other property.

private sector   The *households* and business *firms* of the economy.

process innovation   The development and use of new or improved production or distribution methods.

product differentiation   A strategy in which one firm's product is distinguished from competing products by means of its design, related services, quality, location, or other attributes (except price).

product innovation   The development and sale of a new or improved product (or service).

production possibilities curve   A curve showing the different combinations of two goods or services that can be produced in a *full-employment, full-production* economy where the available supplies of resources and technology are fixed.

productive efficiency   The production of a good in the least costly way; occurs when production takes place at the output at which *average total cost* is a minimum and *marginal product* per dollar's worth of input is the same for all inputs.

productivity   A measure of average output or real output per unit of input. For example, the productivity of labor is determined by dividing real output by hours of work.

productivity growth   The percentage change in *productivity* from one period to another.

product market   A market in which products are sold by *firms* and bought by *households*.

profit   The return to the resource *entrepreneurial ability* (see *normal profit*); *total revenue* minus *total cost* (see *economic profit*).

profit-maximizing combination of resources   The quantity of each resource a firm must employ to maximize its profit or minimize its loss; the combination in which the *marginal revenue product* of each resource is equal to its *marginal resource cost* (to its *price* if the resource is employed in a competitive market).

profit-sharing plan   A compensation device through which workers receive part of their pay in the form of a share of their employer's profit (if any).

progressive tax   A tax whose *average tax rate* increases as the taxpayer's income increases and decreases as the taxpayer's income decreases.

property tax   A tax on the value of property (*capital, land, stocks* and *bonds*, and other *assets*) owned by *firms* and *households*.

proportional tax   A tax whose *average tax rate* remains constant as the taxpayer's income increases or decreases.

proprietor's income   The net income of the owners of unincorporated firms (proprietorships and partnerships).

protective tariff   A *tariff* designed to shield domestic producers of a good or service from the competition of foreign producers.

public assistance programs   Government programs that pay benefits to those who are unable to earn income (because of permanent disabilities or because they have very low income and dependent children); financed by general tax revenues and viewed as public charity (rather than earned rights).

public choice theory   The economic analysis of collective and government decision making, politics, and the democratic process.

public good   A good or service that is indivisible and to which the *exclusion principle* does not apply; a good or service with these characteristics provided by government.

public interest theory of regulation   The presumption that the purpose of the regulation of an *industry* is to protect the public (consumers) from abuse of the power possessed by *natural monopolies*.

public sector   The part of the economy that contains all government entities; government.

public utility   A firm that produces an essential good or service, has obtained from a government the right to be the sole supplier of the good or service in the area, and is regulated by that government to prevent the abuse of its monopoly power.

purchasing power   The amount of goods and services that a monetary unit of income can buy.

purchasing power parity   The idea that exchange rates between nations equate the purchasing power of various currencies. Exchange rates between any two nations adjust to reflect the price-level differences between the countries.

pure competition   A market structure in which a very large number of firms sells a *standardized product*, into which entry is very easy, in which the individual seller has no control over the product price, and in which there is no nonprice competition; a market characterized by a very large number of buyers and sellers.

pure monopoly   A market structure in which one firm sells a unique product, into which entry is blocked, in which the single firm has considerable control over product price, and in which *nonprice competition* may or may not be found.

pure profit   (See *economic profit.*)

pure rate of interest   An essentially risk-free, long-term interest rate that is free of the influence of market imperfections.

quantity demanded   The amount of a good or service that buyers (or a buyer) desire to purchase at a particular price during some period.

quantity supplied   The amount of a good or service that producers (or a producer) offer to sell at a particular price during some period.

quasi-public good   A good or service to which the *exclusion principle* could apply but that has such a large *spillover benefit* that government sponsors its production to prevent an underallocation of resources.

R&D   Research and development activities undertaken to bring about technological progress.

rate of exchange   The price paid in one's own money to acquire 1 unit of a foreign currency; the rate at which the money of one nation is exchanged for the money of another nation.

rate of return   The gain in net revenue divided by the cost of an investment or an *R&D* expenditure; expressed as a percentage.

rational behavior   Human behavior based on comparison of marginal costs and marginal benefits; behavior designed to maximize total utility.

rationing function of prices   The ability of market forces in competitive markets to equalize *quantity demanded* and *quantity supplied* and to eliminate shortages and surpluses via changes in prices.

real capital   (See *capital*.)

real GDP   (See *real gross domestic product*.)

real gross domestic product (GDP)   *Gross domestic product* adjusted for inflation; gross domestic product in a year divided by the GDP *price index* for that year, expressed as a decimal.

real income   The amount of goods and services that can be purchased with *nominal income* during some period of time; nominal income adjusted for inflation.

real interest rate   The interest rate expressed in dollars of constant value (adjusted for *inflation*) and equal to the *nominal interest rate* less the expected rate of inflation.

real wage   The amount of goods and services a worker can purchase with his or her *nominal wage;* the purchasing power of the nominal wage.

recession   A period of declining real GDP, accompanied by lower real income and higher unemployment.

Reciprocal Trade Agreements Act   A 1934 Federal law that authorized the president to negotiate up to 50 percent lower tariffs with foreign nations that agreed to reduce their tariffs on U.S. goods. (Such agreements incorporated the *most-favored-nation* clause.)

regressive tax   A tax whose *average tax rate* decreases as the taxpayer's income increases and increases as the taxpayer's income decreases.

regulatory agency   An agency, commission, or board established by the Federal government or a state govern-

ment to control the prices charged and the services offered by a *natural monopoly*.

rental income   The payments (income) received by those who supply *land* to the economy.

rent-seeking behavior   The actions by persons, firms, or unions to gain special benefits from government at the taxpayers' or someone else's expense.

resource   A natural, human, or manufactured item that helps produce goods and services; a productive agent or factor of production.

resource market   A market in which *households* sell and *firms* buy resources or the services of resources.

revaluation   An increase in the governmentally defined value of the nation's currency relative to other nations' currencies.

revenue tariff   A *tariff* designed to produce income for the Federal government.

reverse discrimination   The view that the preferential treatment associated with *affirmative action* efforts constitutes discrimination against other groups.

right-to-work law   A state law (in about 20 states) that makes it illegal to require that a worker join a *labor union* in order to retain his or her job; laws that make *union shops* and *agency shops* illegal.

roundabout production   The construction and use of *capital* to aid in the production of *consumer goods*.

rule of reason   The rule stated and applied in the *U.S. Steel case* that only combinations and contracts unreasonably restraining trade are subject to actions under the antitrust laws and that size and possession of monopoly power are not illegal.

rule of 70   A method for determining the number of years it will take for some measure to double, given its annual percentage increase. Example: To determine the number of years it will take for the price level to double, divide 70 by the annual rate of *inflation*.

sales tax   A tax levied on the cost (at retail) of a broad group of products.

saving   Disposable income not spent for consumer goods; equal to *disposable income* minus *personal consumption expenditures*.

scarce resources   The limited quantities of *land, capital, labor,* and *entrepreneurial ability* that are never sufficient to satisfy people's virtually unlimited economic wants.

scientific method   The procedure for the systematic pursuit of knowledge involving the observation of facts and the formulation and testing of hypotheses to obtain theories, principles, and laws.

seasonal variations   Increases and decreases in the level of economic activity within a single year, caused by a change in the season.

self-interest   That which each firm, property owner, worker, and consumer believes is best for itself and seeks to obtain.

seniority   The length of time a worker has been employed absolutely or relative to other workers; may be used to determine which workers will be laid off when there is insufficient work for them all and who will be rehired when more work becomes available.

separation of ownership and control   The fact that different groups of people own a *corporation* (the stockholders) and manage it (the directors and officers).

service   An (intangible) act or use for which a consumer, firm, or government is willing to pay.

Sherman Act   The Federal antitrust act of 1890 that made monopoly and conspiracies to restrain trade criminal offenses.

shirking   Workers' neglecting or evading work to increase their *utility* or well-being.

shortage   The amount by which the *quantity demanded* of a product exceeds the *quantity supplied* at a particular (below-equilibrium) price.

short run   (1) In microeconomics, a period of time in which producers are able to change the quantities of some but not all of the resources they employ; a period in which some resources (usually plant) are fixed and some are variable. (2) In macroeconomics, a period in which nominal wages and other input prices do not change in response to a change in the price level.

short-run competitive equilibrium   The price at which the total quantity of a product supplied in the *short run* in a purely competitive industry equals the total quantity of the product demanded and that is equal to or greater than *average variable cost*.

short-run farm problem   The sharp year-to-year changes in the prices of agricultural products and in the incomes of farmers.

short-run supply curve   A supply curve that shows the quantity of a product a firm in a purely competitive industry will offer to sell at various prices in the *short run;* the portion of the firm's short-run marginal cost curve that lies above its *average-variable-cost* curve.

shutdown case   The circumstance in which a firm would experience a loss greater than its total *fixed cost* if it were to produce any output greater than zero; alternatively, a situation in which a firm would cease to operate when the *price* at which it can sell its product is less than its *average variable cost*.

slope of a line   The ratio of the vertical change (the rise or fall) to the horizontal change (the run) between any two points on a line. The slope of an upward-sloping line is positive, reflecting a direct relationship between two variables; the slope of a downward-sloping line is negative, reflecting an inverse relationship between two variables.

Smoot-Hawley Tariff Act   Legislation passed in 1930 that established very high tariffs. Its objective was to reduce imports and stimulate the domestic economy, but it resulted only in retaliatory tariffs by other nations.

social insurance programs   Programs that replace the earnings lost when people retire or are temporarily unemployed, that are financed by payroll taxes, and that are viewed as earned rights (rather than charity).

socially optimal price   The price of a product that results in the most efficient allocation of an economy's resources and that is equal to the *marginal cost* of the product.

social regulation   Regulation in which government is concerned with the conditions under which goods and services are produced, their physical characteristics, and the impact of their production on society; in contrast to *industrial regulation*.

social security program   (See *Old Age, Survivors, and Disability Health Insurance*.)

social security trust fund   A Federal fund that saves excessive social security tax revenues received in one year to meet social security benefit obligations that exceed social security tax revenues in some subsequent year.

sole proprietorship   An unincorporated *firm* owned and operated by one person.

special economic zones   (Web chapter) Regions of China open to foreign investment, private ownership, and relatively free international trade.

special-interest effect   Any result of government promotion of the interests (goals) of a small group at the expense of a much larger group.

specialization   The use of the resources of an individual, a firm, a region, or a nation to concentrate production on one or a small number of goods and services.

speculation   The activity of buying or selling with the motive of later reselling or rebuying for profit.

spillover   A benefit or cost from production or consumption, accruing without compensation to nonbuyers and nonsellers of the product (see *spillover benefit* and *spillover cost*).

spillover benefit   A benefit obtained without compensation by third parties from the production or consumption of sellers or buyers. Example: A beekeeper benefits when a neighboring farmer plants clover.

spillover cost   A cost imposed without compensation on third parties by the production or consumption of sellers or buyers. Example: A manufacturer dumps toxic chemicals into a river, killing the fish sought by sport fishers.

SSI   (See *Supplemental Security Income*.)

standardized product   A product whose buyers are indifferent to the seller from whom they purchase it as long as the price charged by all sellers is the same; a product all units of which are identical and thus are perfect substitutes for each other.

startup (firm)   A new firm focused on creating and introducing a particular new product or employing a specific new production or distribution method.

state-owned enterprises   (Web chapter) Businesses that are owned by the government; the major types of enterprises in Russia and China before their transitions to the market system.

statistical discrimination   The practice of judging an individual on the basis of the average characteristic of the group to which he or she belongs rather than on his or her own personal characteristics.

stock (corporate)   An ownership share in a corporation.

stock options   Contracts that enable executives or other key employees to buy shares of their employers' stock at fixed, lower prices when the stock prices rise.

strategic trade policy   The use of trade barriers to reduce the risk inherent in product development by domestic firms, particularly that involving advanced technology.

strike   The withholding of labor services by an organized group of workers (a *labor union*).

structural-change hypothesis   The explanation that ascribes the decline of unionism in the United States to changes in the structure of the economy and of the labor force.

subsidy   A payment of funds (or goods and services) by a government, firm, or household for which it receives no good or service in return. When made by a government, it is a *government transfer payment*.

substitute goods   Products or services that can be used in place of each other. When the price of one falls, the demand for the other product falls; conversely, when the price of one product rises, the demand for the other product rises.

substitution effect   (1) A change in the quantity demanded of a *consumer good* that results from a change in its relative expensiveness produced by a change in the product's price; (2) the effect of a change in the price of a *resource* on the quantity of the resource employed by a firm, assuming no change in its output.

sunk cost   A cost that has been incurred and cannot be recovered.

superior good   (See *normal good*.)

Supplemental Security Income (SSI)   A federally financed and administered program that provides a uniform nationwide minimum income for the aged, blind, and disabled who do not qualify for benefits under the *Old Age,*

Survivors, and Disability Health Insurance or *unemployment insurance* program in the United States.

supply   A schedule showing the amounts of a good or service that sellers (or a seller) will offer at various prices during some period.

supply curve   A curve illustrating *supply*.

surplus   The amount by which the *quantity supplied* of a product exceeds the *quantity demanded* at a specific (above-equilibrium) price.

surplus payment   A payment to a resource that is not required to ensure its availability in the production process; for example, land rent.

surplus value   (Web chapter) The amount by which a worker's daily output in dollar terms exceeds his daily wage; the amount of the worker's output appropriated by capitalists as profit; a Marxian term.

tacit collusion   Any method used by an oligopolist to set prices and outputs that does not involve outright (or overt) *collusion*. *Price leadership* is a frequent example.

TANF   (See *Temporary Assistance for Needy Families*.)

tariff   A tax imposed by a nation on an imported good.

taste-for-discrimination model   A theory that views discrimination as a preference for which an employer is willing to pay.

tax   An involuntary payment of money (or goods and services) to a government by a *household* or *firm* for which the household or firm receives no good or service directly in return.

tax incidence   The person or group that ends up paying a tax.

tax subsidy   A grant in the form of reduced taxes through favorable tax treatment. For example, employer-paid health insurance is exempt from Federal income and payroll taxes.

technological advance   New and better goods and services and new and better ways of producing or distributing them.

technology   The body of knowledge and techniques that can be used to combine *economic resources* to produce goods and services.

Temporary Assistance for Needy Families (TANF)   A state-administered and partly federally funded program in the United States that provides financial aid to poor families; the basic welfare program for low-income families in the United States; contains time limits and work requirements.

terms of trade   The rate at which units of one product can be exchanged for units of another product; the price of a good or service; the amount of one good or service that must be given up to obtain 1 unit of another good or service.

theoretical economics The process of deriving and applying economic theories and principles.

theory of human capital The generalization that *wage differentials* are the result of differences in the amount of *human capital investment* and that the incomes of lower-paid workers are raised by increasing the amount of such investment.

total cost The sum of *fixed cost* and *variable cost.*

total demand The demand schedule or the *demand curve* of all buyers of a good or service; also called market demand.

total product The total output of a particular good or service produced by a firm (or a group of firms or the entire economy).

total revenue The total number of dollars received by a firm (or firms) from the sale of a product; equal to the total expenditures for the product produced by the firm (or firms); equal to the quantity sold (demanded) multiplied by the price at which it is sold.

total-revenue test A test to determine elasticity of *demand* between any two prices: Demand is elastic if *total revenue* moves in the opposite direction from price; it is inelastic when it moves in the same direction as price; and it is of unitary elasticity when it does not change when price changes.

total spending The total amount that buyers of goods and services spend or plan to spend; also called *aggregate expenditures.*

total supply The supply schedule or the *supply curve* of all sellers of a good or service; also called market supply.

total utility The total amount of satisfaction derived from the consumption of a single product or a combination of products.

township and village enterprises (Web chapter) Privately owned rural manufacturing firms in China.

trade balance The export of goods (or goods and services) of a nation less its imports of goods (or goods and services).

trade bloc A group of nations that lower or abolish trade barriers among members. Examples include the *European Union* and the nations of the *North American Free Trade Agreement.*

trade controls *Tariffs, export subsidies, import quotas,* and other means a nation may employ to reduce *imports* and expand *exports.*

trade deficit The amount by which a nation's *imports* of goods (or goods and services) exceed its *exports* of goods (or goods and services).

trademark A legal protection that gives the originators of a product an exclusive right to use the brand name.

tradeoff The sacrifice of some or all of one economic goal, good, or service to achieve some other goal, good, or service.

trade surplus The amount by which a nation's *exports* of goods (or goods and services) exceed its *imports* of goods (or goods and services).

trading possibilities line A line that shows the different combinations of two products that an economy is able to obtain (consume) when it specializes in the production of one product and trades (exports) it to obtain the other product.

transfer payment A payment of *money* (or goods and services) by a government to a *household* or *firm* for which the payer receives no good or service directly in return.

tying contract A promise made by a buyer when allowed to purchase a product from a seller that it will purchase certain other products from the same seller; a practice forbidden by the *Clayton Act.*

underemployment (1) The failure to produce the maximum amount of goods and services that can be produced from the resources employed; the failure to achieve *full production;* (2) a situation in which workers are employed in positions requiring less education and skill than they have.

undistributed corporate profits After-tax corporate profits not distributed as dividends to stockholders; corporate or business saving; also called retained earnings.

unemployment The failure to use all available *economic resources* to produce desired goods and services; the failure of the economy to fully employ its *labor force.*

unemployment compensation (See *unemployment insurance*).

unemployment insurance The social insurance program that in the United States is financed by state *payroll taxes* on employers and makes income available to workers who become unemployed and are unable to find jobs.

unemployment rate The percentage of the *labor force* unemployed at any time.

uninsurable risk An event that would result in a loss and whose occurrence is uncontrollable and unpredictable. Insurance companies are not willing to sell insurance against such a loss.

union shop A place of employment where the employer may hire either *labor union* members or nonmembers but where nonmembers must become members within a specified period of time or lose their jobs.

unit elasticity Demand or supply for which the *elasticity coefficient* is equal to 1; means that the percentage change in the quantity demanded or supplied is equal to the percentage change in price.

unit labor cost Labor cost per unit of output; total labor cost divided by total output; also equal to the *nominal wage* rate divided by the *average product* of labor.

unlimited liability Absence of any limits on the maximum amount that an individual (usually a business owner) may become legally required to pay.

unlimited wants The insatiable desire of consumers for goods and services that will give them satisfaction or *utility*.

urban collectives (Web chapter) Chinese enterprises jointly owned by their managers and their workforces and located in urban areas.

Uruguay Round The eighth and most recent round of trade negotiations under *GATT* (now the *World Trade Organization*).

U.S. Steel case The antitrust action brought by the Federal government against the U.S. Steel Corporation in which the courts ruled (in 1920) that only unreasonable restraints of trade were illegal and that size and the possession of monopoly power were not violations of the antitrust laws.

usury laws State laws that specify the maximum legal interest rate at which loans can be made.

utility The want-satisfying power of a good or service; the satisfaction or pleasure a consumer obtains from the consumption of a good or service (or from the consumption of a collection of goods and services).

utility-maximizing rule The principle that to obtain the greatest *utility* the consumer should allocate *money income* so that the last dollar spent on each good or service yields the same marginal utility.

value-added tax A tax imposed on the difference between the value of the product sold by a firm and the value of the goods purchased from other firms to produce the product; used in several European countries.

value judgment Opinion of what is desirable or undesirable; belief regarding what ought or ought not to be (regarding what is right or just and wrong or unjust).

variable cost A cost that in total increases when the firm increases its output and decreases when the firm reduces its output.

VAT (See *value-added tax*.)

vertical axis The "up-down" or "north-south" axis on a graph or grid.

vertical integration A group of *plants* engaged in different stages of the production of a final product and owned by a single *firm*.

vertical intercept The point at which a line meets the vertical axis of a graph.

vertical merger The merger of one or more *firms* engaged in different stages of the production of a final product.

very long run A period in which *technology* can change and in which *firms* can introduce new products.

voice mechanism Communication by workers through their union to resolve grievances with an employer.

voluntary export restrictions Voluntary limitations by countries or firms of their exports to a particular foreign nation to avoid enactment of formal trade barriers by that nation.

wage The price paid for the use or services of *labor* per unit of time (per hour, per day, and so on).

wage differential The difference between the *wage* received by one worker or group of workers and that received by another worker or group of workers.

wage discrimination The payment of a lower wage to members of a less preferred group than that paid to members of a more preferred group for the same work.

wage rate (See *wage*.)

wages The income of those who supply the economy with *labor*.

wealth Anything that has value because it produces income or could produce income. Wealth is a stock; income is a flow. Assets less liabilities; net worth.

welfare programs (See *public assistance programs*.)

Wheeler-Lea Act The Federal act of 1938 that amended the *Federal Trade Commission Act* by prohibiting and giving the commission power to investigate unfair and deceptive acts or practices of commerce (such as false and misleading advertising and the misrepresentation of products).

World Bank A bank that lends (and guarantees loans) to developing nations to assist them in increasing their *capital stock* and thus in achieving *economic growth;* formally, the International Bank for Reconstruction and Development.

world price The international market price of a good or service, determined by world demand and supply.

World Trade Organization (WTO) An organization established in 1994 to replace *GATT* to oversee the provisions of the *Uruguay Round* and resolve any disputes stemming from it.

WTO (See *World Trade Organization*.)

X-inefficiency The failure to produce any specific output at the lowest average (and total) cost possible.

Relevant economic statistics, selected years, 1980–2000

	1980	1981	1982	1983	1984	1985	1986	1987	1988
1 New business incorporations (thousands)	534	581	567	600	635	662	703	686	685
2 Business failures (thousands)	12	17	25	31	52	57	62	62	57
3 Sales by manufacturers (billions of dollars)*	1,913	2,145	2,039	2,144	2,335	2,331	2,221	2,378	2,596
4 Profits by manufacturers (billions of dollars)*	146	159	108	133	166	137	129	173	215
5 After-tax manufacturing profits per dollar of sales (cents)*	5	5	4	4	5	4	4	5	6
6 Index of business sector productivity (1992 = 100)	80.4	82.0	81.7	84.6	87.0	88.7	91.4	91.9	93.0
7 Annual change in business sector productivity (%)	−0.3	1.9	−0.4	3.6	2.8	2.0	3.0	0.5	1.2
8 Nonagricultural employees in goods-producing industries (millions)	26	25	24	23	25	25	25	25	25
9 Nonagricultural employees in service-producing industries (millions)	65	66	66	67	70	73	75	77	80
10 Compensation of employees (billions of dollars)	1,652	1,826	1,926	2,003	2,256	2,425	2,571	2,756	2,974
11 Average weekly hours in private nonagricultural industries	35.3	35.2	34.8	35.0	35.2	34.9	34.8	34.8	34.7
12 Average hourly earnings in private nonagricultural industries (dollars)	6.66	7.25	7.68	8.02	8.32	8.57	8.76	8.98	9.28
13 Average weekly earnings in private nonagricultural industries (dollars)	235	255	267	281	293	299	305	313	322
14 Prime interest rate (%)	15.27	18.87	14.86	10.79	12.04	9.93	8.33	8.21	9.32
15 Ten-year Treasury bond interest rate (%)	11.46	13.91	13.00	11.10	12.44	10.62	7.68	8.39	8.85
16 Net farm income (billions of dollars)	16.1	26.9	23.8	14.2	26.0	28.6	30.9	37.4	38.0
17 Index of prices received by farmers (1990–1992 = 100)	98	100	94	98	101	91	87	89	99
18 Index of prices paid by farmers (1990–1992 = 100)	75	82	86	86	89	86	85	87	91
19 Persons below poverty level (millions)	29.3	31.8	34.4	35.3	33.7	33.1	32.4	32.2	31.7
20 Poverty rate (% of population)	13.0	14.0	15.0	15.2	14.4	14.0	13.6	13.4	13.0
21 U.S. goods exports (billions of dollars)	224	237	211	202	220	216	224	250	320
22 U.S. goods imports (billions of dollars)	250	265	248	269	332	338	369	410	447
23 Trade balance on current account (billions of dollars)	2.3	5.0	−5.5	−38.7	−94.3	−118.2	−147.2	−160.7	−121.2
24 Industry R&D expenditures (billions of dollars)	31	40	41	45	52	58	61	63	68

*Series change in 1973
†Authors' estimate
Sources: *Economic Report of the President, 2001*; Bureau of Economic Analysis, Bureau of Labor Statistics, National Science Foundation, and Federal Reserve System.